OXFORD CLASSICAL MONOGRAPHS

Published under the supervision of a Committee of the Faculty of Classics in the University of Oxford

The aim of the Oxford Classical Monograph series (which replaces the Oxford Classical and Philosophical Monographs) is to publish books based on the best theses on Greek and Latin literature, ancient history, and ancient philosophy examined by the Faculty Board of Classics.

Sacred and Public Land in Ancient Athens

NIKOLAOS PAPAZARKADAS

OXFORD
UNIVERSITY PRESS

This book has been printed digitally and produced in a standard specification in order to ensure its continuing availability

OXFORD
UNIVERSITY PRESS

Great Clarendon Street, Oxford OX2 6DP
United Kingdom

Oxford University Press is a department of the University of Oxford. It furthers the University's objective of excellence in research, scholarship, and education by publishing worldwide.

Oxford is a registered trade mark of Oxford University Press in the UK and in certain other countries

Reprinted 2012

British Library Cataloguing in Publication Data
Data available

Library of Congress Cataloging in Publication Data
Data available

ISBN 978-0-19-969400-6

For S.P., K.P., A.P., E.M., L.J.

Preface

The title of this monograph, a study of non-private land in Athens, is deliberatly reminiscent of Finley's epoch-making *Land and Credit in Ancient Athens.* Yet, scope and approach are considerably different and my emulation is primarily a talismanic expression of admiration. The Oxford D.Phil. thesis on which this book is heavily based was submitted in 2004, but for various reasons I was unable to deal with most of the manuscript until 2008. I did, however, manage to work on the epigraphical appendix of my dissertation: that work, generously funded by the Andrew W. Mellon Foundation, has appeared in four separate articles that constitute much of the groundwork of the present volume. When in 2008 I resumed work with the aim of producing this monograph, upgrading the bibliography became a major preoccupation, and I hope to have carried out this task as adequately as possible. In general, I have included only a few items published after 2008, even fewer after 2009. Many crude ideas have hopefully been eliminated, but by and large this work reflects my intellectual concerns as they were in the opening years of the new millennium.

Detailed acknowledgements can be found in my thesis, which is deposited in the Bodleian Library. I would like, however, to single out two people. Angelos Matthaiou has been an inspiring teacher since I first met him almost twenty years ago. My training in 'hard epigraphy' is almost entirely his work. Most importantly, it was he who suggested the topic of this book. Robert Parker was for many years in Oxford an excellent teacher and friend, first as a supervisor and later as a mentor. Thanks to him I immersed myself in the study of religion, anthropology, and any topic imaginable, including, on one occasion, and rather briefly, the character of the Cultural Revolution. I emerged wiser from my viva, thanks to my examiners Charles Crowther and Peter J. Rhodes, who both helped me subsequently in a variety of ways. P. J. Rhodes, in particular, made important suggestions for improvement on a version of this book. Similarly, Robin Osborne, who had acted as my second adviser in my first graduate years at Oxford, twice read and commented on this book as my adviser for the Oxford Classical Monographs series. In recent years, and after moving to Berkeley, I have had the privilege of enjoying a stimulating and, most of all, friendly working environment, and of meeting some excellent students. Ryan Boehm and David Jacobson helped me substantially with the proof-reading of the manuscript. I am grateful to all my UCB colleagues, academic and administrative, but primarily to Ron Stroud, who not only warmly welcomed me at Berkeley along with his wife Connie, but who has already become one of the best friends and epigraphic colleagues I could imagine. His detailed comments have helped shape the final form of this book.

I am also indebted to the following for reasons each one of them knows very well: Polymnia Athanassiadi, Thomas Baldwin, Loukas Balomenos, Angelos Chaniotis, Christy Constantakopoulou, Dorothy Cowie, Matthew Haysom, Myrina Kalaitzi, Georgia Kokkorou-Alewras, Dimitris Kousouris, Barbara Kowalzig, Charalambos Kritzas, Anastasia Ladopoulou, Robin Lane Fox, Peter Liddel, Andronike Makres, Eleni Mantzourani, Maria Mili, Louise Miller, Graham Oliver, Dennis Saw, Eliza Sioumbara, Nikos Skoplakis, Bert Smith, Dimitirs Sourlas, Maria Stamatopoulou, Peter Thonemann, Sarah Thonemann, Rowan Tomlinson, Jenny Wallensten. Thanks are also due to Hilary O'Shea, Senior Editor for Classics and Ancient History at OUP, Tessa Eaton, Production Editor, and Taryn Campbell, Assistant Commissioning Editor, who all helped me substantially with the production of this book; and to Heather Watson, an extremely efficient copy-editor who saved me from innumerable mistakes.

For years I have enjoyed the facilities of the Bodleian Library and the Sackler Library (Oxford); the Libraries of the ASCSA, BSA, and EfA (Athens); the Doe & Moffitt Libraries and the Classics Library (Berkeley). Institutional assistance has come from New College (Oxford); St Hilda's College (Oxford); Faculty of Classics (Oxford); Trinity College (Dublin); the Epigraphical Museum (Athens). The thesis from which this book derived was awarded proxime accessit for the Conington prize (2004–6), and shared the Hellenic Foundation 2005 Annual Award for the best doctoral thesis in ancient/classical Greek studies in Great Britain. I am extremely grateful to the Alexander S. Onassis Public Benefit Foundation for generously funding the first three years of my graduate studies at Oxford, and the Faculty of Classics at Oxford for offering me a three-year scholarship. Writing a book is not only a matter of academic concentration but also of emotional support. This has long been given to me by my family and by Laura: to them I dedicate this book with love.

Contents

Abbreviations and Conventions

Most Greek names have been transliterated with the obvious exceptions of well-established Latinized forms. Translations of inscriptions are either my own or have been taken from standard collections of translated sources. Translations of literary texts are primarily those of the Loeb Classical Library, but in several cases I have made use of more up-to-date works. Abbreviations are the standard ones, as can be found in *OCD*[3], *L'Année philologique*, and in the *SEG* Consolidated Index for volumes XXXVI–XLV, pp. 677–88. The reader should also take heed of the following convention: inscriptions cited as T1, T2, T3 are taken from Appendix 1 of Lambert 1993; inscriptions cited as F1, F2, F3, etc., refer to epigraphical texts given in Lambert 1997*a*. For the convenience of the reader I am also providing the following basic list:

ADeltion	*Ἀρχαιολογικὸν Δελτίον*
Agora XIX	G. V. Lalonde, M. K. Langdon, and M. B. Walbank, *The Athenian Agora*, XIX: *Inscriptions: Horoi, Poletai Records, Leases of Public Lands* (Princeton, 1991)
APF	J. K. Davies, *Athenian Propertied Families: 600–300 B.C.* (Oxford, 1971)
CID	*Corpus des inscriptions de Delphes* (Paris, 1978–)
DTA	R. Wünsch, *Defixionum Tabellae Atticae Inscr. Gr.*, vol. 3, pt. 3 (Berlin, 1897)
FGrH	F. Jacoby, *Die Fragmente der griechischen Historiker* (Berlin, 1923–58)
I.Eleusis	K. Clinton, *Eleusis. The Inscriptions on Stone: Documents of the Sanctuary of the Two Goddesses and Public Documents of the Deme,* vol. IA: *Text*; vol. IB: *Plates* (Athens, 2005); vol. II: *Commentary* (Athens, 2008)
IG	*Inscriptiones Graecae* (Berlin, 1873–)
I.Oropos	V. Petrakos, *Οἱ ἐπιγραφὲς τοῦ Ὠρωποῦ* (Athens, 1997)
I.Rhamnous	V. Petrakos, *Ὁ δῆμος τοῦ Ραμνοῦντος* II: *οἱ ἐπιγραφές* (Athens, 1998)
LGPN II	M. J. Osborne and S. G. Byrne (eds.), *Lexicon of Greek Personal Names,* vol. II: *Attica* (Oxford, 1994)

ML	R. Meiggs and D. M. Lewis, *A Selection of Greek Historical Inscriptions to the End of the Fifth Century B.C.*, rev. edn. (Oxford, 1988)
NGSL	E. Lupu, *Greek Sacred Law: A Collection of New Documents* (Leiden and Boston, 2005)
OCD[3]	S. Hornblower and A. Spawforth (eds.), *The Oxford Classical Dictionary*, 3rd rev. edn. (Oxford, 2003)
PAA	J. S. Traill, *Persons of Ancient Athens* (Toronto, 1994–)
RO	P. J. Rhodes and R. Osborne, *Greek Historical Inscriptions, 404–323 BC* (Oxford, 2003)
SEG	*Supplementum Epigraphicum Graecum* (Amsterdam, 1923–)
Syll.[3]	W. Dittenberger, *Sylloge Inscriptionum Graecarum*, 3rd edn. (Leipzig, 1915–24)
ThesCRA	*Thesaurus cultus et rituum antiquorum*, vols. I–V (Los Angeles and Basel 2004–6)

1

Introduction

Sacred and Public Land: Modern Scholarly Responses

IT is an oft-repeated axiom that land constitutes the most precious asset of agricultural societies, and the same is by implication maintained with regard to the ancient Greek world. The Greeks' remarkable cultural achievements should not conceal the fact that their economic infrastructure was based mainly upon farming and, to a lesser extent, grazing.[1] As a result, all spheres of their activity were, in one way or another, propped up by their agricultural engagements. This is all well known and any further insistence on the significance of agriculture runs the risk of banality. Time and again scholars have dealt with a huge range of pertinent—sometimes imaginative—problems, from land tenure patterns to land productivity, to the extent that originality can no longer constitute a longed-for pursuit. Nevertheless, issues of sacred landed property in ancient Greece have not featured prominently in modern treatments. In contrast to other key features, sacred realty has long been considered a phenomenon deserving little, if any, attention, or at least this is the implication of the almost complete absence of germane specialized treatises. And yet, here and there one can find scholarly works that touch upon sacred realty. The piecemeal character of such works, however, usually results in more unanswered questions than solutions,

[1] See, for instance, Burford 1993; Chandezon 2003. A good synopsis of the significance of land in the wider framework of Classical economics can be found in Davies 2007. Without taking sides in the old debate between primitivists and modernists, I would only say that even the most unrepentant modernists would hardly negate the importance of landed wealth for ancient societies.

although this should not necessarily be deemed a flaw. When I first embarked on the present project, my declared intention was to analyse the tactics underlying the administration of sacred realty in Classical Athens, a polis that has provided an abundance of relevant, mainly epigraphical, material. In the process of my investigation I came to realize that other queries had to be answered in conjunction with my primary question: is one justified to talk about sacred lands as a separate category? To what extent did sacred and public lands overlap? Put in more general terms, how distinct were the spheres of sacred and secular in the ancient world? This last one is a rather old question. Accordingly, I have considered an exploration of the history of scholarship as necessary. My study of the germane modern literature has obviously been Athenocentric, but not exclusively so. Wherever I have considered it fruitful, I have not hesitated to cite works of broader aspirations.

Negligence of the issues has not always been the case. It was Böckh who first ventured, in his seminal *Die Staatshaushaltung der Athener*, to classify the various forms of non-private property. While distinguishing between holdings of the state or its subdivisions and of temples, he acknowledged at the same time that some of the sacred property was under the administration of secular executives. He should be credited with the recognition of the strong link between the income raised from the leasing of sacred lands with the funding of religious activity.[2] The late nineteenth century produced one of the few chapters devoted exclusively to sacred land. It can be found in the third book of Guiraud's grandiose work *La Propriété foncière en Grèce jusqu' à la conquête romaine.*[3] One encounters there all the merits and flaws of nineteenth-century historical positivism: an abundant use of literary and, more significantly, epigraphical sources—the importance of which had just started being appreciated—put in a diachronic and super-regional context that led to some far-fetched, unhistorical generalizations. As a source of information it still remains invaluable, in spite of the lack of interest with which it has been received by most recent scholars. Yet, its real value lies with the series of questions that Guiraud raised. He was the first to make the subtle distinction between divine ownership and human administration; the first to enumerate ways by which certain things were rendered sacred. He developed a classification of various categories of sacred property.

[2] Böckh 1886, 372–3.
[3] Guiraud 1893, 362–81.

He even attempted some rudimentary quantitative calculations drawing evidence from the work of preceding epigraphists. By far his most invaluable contribution was the placement of the relevant discussion within the frame of the basic political unit of ancient Greece, the polis. Almost a century prior to the better argued theories about what is known in academic jargon as polis religion, Guiraud grasped the significance of the articulation of religion within the polis structure and, in this light, he drew the inference that 'in effect, the property of the gods was an annex of public property'. However, another argument of his was more controversial: the claim that sacred property was not inalienable despite the fact that, by and large, its disposal was considered a sacrilegious crime. If sales of sacred lands did not occur often, this was not on the basis of some applicable legislation, rather it was the side effect of an unwritten perception of commiting impiety in doing so. On the contrary, inalienability of sacred lands and legal protection from potential transgressors were accepted by Andreades.[4] Although not explicitly stated, the articulation of his argument presupposes a segregation of sacred landholdings from public ones.[5]

Sacred tillable lands are all too often muddled up with shrines containing the altars of the honoured divinities, as can be seen in a series of important articles or other publications. This confusion permeates, for instance, Stengel's monograph on the Greek cults.[6] It can be traced in the work of as diligent a scholar as Burkert.[7] This misunderstanding might be accounted for by the ambiguity of the Greek word *temenos* (τέμενος), which can apply to both a sanctuary and an arable sacred estate.[8] The most recent victim of this ambiguity has been Malkin, author of the entry *temenos* in the third edition of the *Oxford Classical Dictionary*. Much earlier Latte had taken a far more scrupulous outlook by clarifying the aforementioned point.[9] By highlighting the administrative similarities between *Staatsländereien* and *temene* (τεμένη), he managed to capture the importance of the

[4] Andreades 1928, 238 with n. 1.
[5] Andreades 1928, 237–40, 337–8.
[6] Stengel 1920, 17–21.
[7] Burkert 1985, 86–7.
[8] The word τέμενος has been traditionally connected to the verb τέμνω (hence the idea that a piece of land is cut off for the gods), but see Frisk 1970, s.v. τέμενος; Windekens 1986, s.v. τέμενος. However, Beekes 2010, s.v. τέμενος, now finds the connection with τέμνω 'morphically and semantically satisfactory'.
[9] Latte 1934.

destination of the rent raised from land leases as a criterion for categorization.

In the meantime some more erudite attempts were made to approach the issue by focusing on well-documented areas. Not only arithmetical, but also topographical points were made by Kent in relation to the estates of Apollo Delios.[10] Although Kent did not concern himself with the theoretical ramifications of temple realty in relation to the political community that administered it, his work was a laborious monument of economic analysis. Jumping forward to 1994, we encounter an updated analysis of the economy of independent Delos, based on the vast amount of scholarly work produced in the interim. For our discussion, suffice it to say that Reger, though not primarily concerned with these conceptual problems, invariably refers to the Delian estates as 'the estates of Apollo', affirming a seamless link with the sanctuary's activities.[11] Chankowski's new monograph on the economy of Classical Delos continues in exemplary fashion the good work of her predecessors, and appears to reaffirm the meaningfulness of delineating a sacred sector of the economy. In her analysis of the sanctuary's wealth, Apollo's 'domaines fonciers' feature prominently as a substantial source of sacred income.[12]

Other scholars have deemed it more profitable to explore the legal aspects of sacred realty. A single statement in Finley's seminal *Land and Credit in Ancient Athens* has cast a long shadow on all subsequent discussions. Commenting upon demes as creditors, Finley claimed that 'the so-called temple funds were deme funds, of course, and the administrative technique, common in Athens and elsewhere, of handling such moneys through the temple had no special singificance, legally or otherwise'.[13] No mention of land is to be found here, but the implication is obvious: since no legal uniqueness can be attributed to sacred funds as opposed to secular ones, sacred lands should not be distinguished from public estates. Similar legal objections were raised by students of ancient Greek Law. Thus, for Harrison sacred property should not be taken as a separate legal category.

[10] Kent 1948.
[11] Reger 1994.
[12] Chankowski 2008, esp. 279–95.
[13] Finley 1952*a*.

Instead, emphasis should primarily be put on state ownership.[14] In another juristically orientated analysis, Behrend compiled a comprehensive catalogue of all Attic leases known up to his time.[15] He set under the same heading what he termed '*Tempel- und Staatsland*'. Interestingly, he dealt separately with landholdings belonging to various associations, a choice for which he deserves some credit. Yet nowhere did he pose the question of the possible dichotomy between public and sacred lands. On the contrary, his overall analysis indicates that he held words like *τεμένη* or *ἱερά* as merely descriptive terms of various categories of corporate landed property regardless of their exact status.[16] Starting from a more carefully couched principle, Todd emphasized the various leasing bodies involved in land transactions, namely the polis and other public or corporate bodies; to the latter he added the class of religious bodies.[17] However, at no point did he directly address the problem of sacred land. Although he chose to devote a subchapter to the legal dimensions of impiety—thus recognizing the uniqueness of religion—he did not deal with sacred lands in this context, save the peculiar case of the sacred olive trees (*μορίαι*).[18]

Returning to non-legal historians: Andreyev maintained that all sorts of non-privately held landholdings ought to be grouped together and be treated as a distinctive unit, which he termed 'public lands'.[19] Andreyev deserves further attention since his position in Classical scholarship has often been overlooked. As a member of Soviet academia he remained relatively isolated—not least because the bulk of his publications were in Russian—and his contribution would have remained minimal, were it not for an article published in English in 1974 in which he summarized his earlier work,[20] as well as for David Lewis's sharp eye which caught the importance of his Soviet colleague's production. Another interesting effort that has largely passed unnoticed is that of Hegyi in her article with the telling title '*Τεμένη*

[14] Harrison 1968, 235 n. 4; MacDowell 1978, 141–2, without elaborating on the issue, seems to endorse the public character of sacred lands by classifying them as state property.

[15] Behrend 1970.

[16] Behrend 1970, 106–7.

[17] Todd 1993, 247–9.

[18] Todd 1993, 306–7; following Lewis 1990, Todd 1993, 249 n. 19 recognized that 'agricultural land leased by the polis is characteristically described as "sacred" rather than as "public"', but he refrained from any further comment.

[19] Andreyev 1974, 25–6.

[20] Andreyev 1974.

ἱερὰ καὶ τεμένη δημόσια'.[21] Adducing an abundance of evidence, she argued strongly for the autonomy of sacred land. Nevertheless, her final conclusion that a differentiation between public and sacred *temene* could be sustained on whether their rent was put in the secular or the sacred treasury of a given city-state, was based on a misinterpretation of a corrupt passage from the Aristotelian corpus, and is consequently of little practical significance.[22]

Andreyev's model of interpretation was pushed to its limits by Osborne in a paper that sought to analyse the socioeconomic parameters of the leasing of land in ancient Greece.[23] By examining specific aspects of leasing, such as the officials involved, the scale of the let properties, and—much more difficult to grasp—the motives for leasing, Osborne drew various remarkable conclusions. For the purposes of our discussion, it suffices to say that he seemed confident in classifying sacred lands as, in effect, public property. Lewis himself can be classified among these scholars in view of his claim that 'the fact that Athens rarely retained public land for leasing ceases to be very meaningful when we consider that there was sacred land at Athens which was leased out by public officials on the instructions of the Assembly'.[24] 1991 saw the publication of volume no. XIX in the *Athenian Agora* series, which contained, among other material, inscriptions concerning leasing. The editor of the relevant section was, suitably, Michael Walbank, who had already published a series of articles on late Classical sacred leases in *Hesperia*.[25] The very title of his chapter in the nineteenth Agora volume ('Leases of Public Lands') is indicative of his perception of sacred lands: they were nothing but part of the state property. On the same issue, Faraguna's erudite, empirical approach to Athens' financial administration under Lykourgos has shown him to be much more cautious.[26] His basic distinction was between public lands, which were rendered profitable by being sold ('vedite di terre pubbliche'), and sacred estates, which were let to increase sacred revenues ('affiti di terre sacre'). His first assertion, however, begs the question, since Faraguna drew his main

[21] Hegyi 1976. In his recent methodical analysis, Migeotte 2006*a*, 189–90, has pointed out the deficiencies of Hegyi's appoach.

[22] Arist. [*Oec.*] 2.1346^b, 13–20.

[23] Osborne 1988.

[24] Lewis 1990, 251.

[25] Walbank 1983*a*; 1983*b*; 1983*c*; 1983*d*; 1984; 1985.

[26] Faraguna 1992.

evidence from the controversial *Rationes Centesimarum*, which will be discussed more extensively below. As for the category of sacred lands, the fact that Faraguna's phraseology was inconsistent inevitably produced some confusion and overlap between the terms sacred and public.[27]

All things considered, it appears that the end of the twentieth century saw a verdict in favour of the idea that sacred and public lands were one and the same. Not quite so. The general consensus was breached by Isager and Skydsgaard who questioned the new orthodoxy, with open reference to what they termed 'Finley's dogma'.[28] The Danish scholars argued that 'the Greeks themselves were fully aware when the question concerned land belonging to a god' and that 'this has turned out to be of great practical importance in agricultural contexts'. They provided a table of salient features of sacred lands, prominent among which stands their inalienability. However, they admitted that this concept could be challenged, if the *Rationes Centesimarum* proved to record sales of sacred estates, although they stayed attached to their interpretation of these transactions being leases rather than sales.[29] At the time of their publication they could not have been aware of Lambert's ongoing work on the inscriptions in question. The result of his study was a book entitled *Rationes Centesimarum*, which came out in 1997.[30] Even the subtitle of Lambert's monograph would suffice to pinpoint in advance the author's conclusions: the *Rationes Centesimarum* were sales of lands of public character accomplished during the administration of Lykourgos. Alhough Lambert did not directly address the problem of inalienability of sacred property, his contribution was the identification of a 'public-service' type of corporate landed property—that is, realty open for use by all members of any given political, territorial, or religious association.

To the best of my knowledge, over the last decade or so there have been five important scholarly pieces to address the problem of sacred land in one way or another. The overall tenor of Shipton's *Leasing and Lending* leaves no doubt about her understanding of sacred lands

[27] e.g. Faraguna 1992, 336: 'Questa impressione . . . viene confermata da un esame dei testi relativi all'affitto di terre pubbliche e sacre'.

[28] Isager and Skydsgaard 1992, 181–90. It is Isager, in fact, who has to be credited with the relevant observations, as seen in Isager 1992.

[29] Following Osborne 1985*a*, 56–9. The same idea was endorsed by Rosivach 1992.

[30] Lambert 1997*a*.

as a segment of Athens' public resources.[31] Dignas, working on the peculiar case of Hellenistic Mylasa, seems to adhere to the idea that, in general, temple lands were subject to special laws, their leasing aimed mainly at subsidizing cultic activity.[32] Ampolo put it in different terms: recognizing the necessity to differentiate between sacred and public lands in compliance with a theoretical distinction that the Greeks themselves held, he nonetheless declined to see any actual difference at the functional level.[33] And yet, as he had previously argued in the case of the economics of temples in Magna Graecia, the actual situation could have been so variable that even within the same polis a certain degree of oscillating responses is often observable.[34] Finally, Foxhall returned to the camp of Finley and his disciples, though, admittedly, via a more apt terminology. For her, one is entitled to speak of corporately owned and/or public land, although she went on to add the rather blurring modification that these are overlapping categories.[35] But the most important contribution to the topic has arguably been Horster's monograph on the landed property of the Archaic and Classical Greek sanctuaries.[36] Following the paradigm of Isager and Skydsgaard, Horster isolated and subsequently explored the category of sacred land in the wider context of cult economics. Interestingly, her supra-polis scope in a sense appears to anticipate a very recent historiographical trend,[37] although one feels that the focused polis perspective—Athens in our case—merits further consideration.

Most of the analyses presented above suffer, more or less, from the same problem: the bewilderment that one faces when one has to draw a line between the spheres of sacred and secular. This is not surprising. In contrast to other societies—like, for instance, the modern Greek one[38]—

[31] Shipton 2000, esp. 23–5. Even when citing Aristotle's *locus classicus* [*Ath. Pol.*] 47.4, she is consistent in her use of the term 'public lands'.

[32] Dignas 2000 and 2002.

[33] Ampolo 2000, 14–15.

[34] Ampolo 1992.

[35] Foxhall 2002, 216–17.

[36] Horster 2004. But as aptly observed by Signe Isager in her *BMCR* review of the book (Isager 2005), such statements as 'property dedicated to the sanctuary of x god' are inaccurate. The same criticism, I contend, applies to the title *Landbesitz griechischer Heiligtümer* etc.

[37] An extreme model is that advocated by Vlassopoulos 2007.

[38] In brief, the Orthodox Church in Greece is owner of huge swathes of landed property all over the country. Its influential role within Greek society and the

in ancient Greece the interweaving of the polis and religion was so close that one is tempted to treat them as one and the same thing.[39] The concept of polis religion has become very fashionable over the last couple of decades, in the wake of Sourvinou-Inwood's exposition of the relevant doctrinal framework.[40] To test some of the finer points of polis religion, students of Greek religion have attempted to explore the meaning of the duality *ἱερὰ καὶ ὅσια*, an idiomatic expression occuring often in texts of—mainly, but not exclusively—financial character. The linguistic argument may be indicative of a certain situation, but it cannot be conclusive. Burkert's exegesis of the antithetic scheme *ἱερός/ὅσιος* as applied to the economic realm was that whatever money was not consecrated to the gods could be disposed of: it was *ὅσιον* (*hosion*).[41] In a fundamental handling of the topic, Connor, while dismissing the simplistic Durkheimian thesis of a clear-cut division between the domains of sacred and secular, duly demonstrated some of the subtle nuances that underlay the Athenian mentality concerning these issues.[42] Far from being a mere formality, the collocation *ἱερὰ καὶ ὅσια* could reflect financial, social, and moral realities. Rather than being subject to political control, religion was embedded in the society, and yet at the same time it remained recognizable, a distinctive realm with its own connotations. In similar fashion, there were usually two distinctive treasuries, a secular/public and a sacred one. Nevertheless, even this accepted certainty was soon questioned by Samons, with straight reference to Connor, as well as to Parker's laconic statement that even the 'profane' is defined by direct reference to the sacred.[43] While denying the existence of a human sphere unrelated to the gods, Samons endorsed the existence of two parallel zones—a sacral and a non-sacral one—the latter understood as a realm

constitutional rights it enjoys have ensured that any efforts on the part of the political authorities to interfere with the administration of church property have met with total failure. In 1986 the socialist PM Andreas Papandreou sacked his high-profile Minister of Education and Creeds who had introduced a draft of the Bill 1700 stipulating the expropriation of monastic property, when a strong minority influenced by the clergy voiced its vehement opposition: see Koliopoulos and Veremis 2002, 150–1.

[39] e.g. Bruit Zaidman and Schmitt-Pantel 1992, a study overplaying the role of religion in the Greek polis.

[40] Sourvinou-Inwood 1990 and 2000. As was to be expected, some scholars have now started questioning the model of polis religion: see, for instance, Kindt 2009 (whose criticism, I feel, is less far-reaching than it purports to be).

[41] Burkert 1985, 269.

[42] Connor 1988.

[43] Parker 1996, 123–4 n. 9.

sanctioned by the gods, but not owned by them. Still, he dismissed the designation of this zone as profane on the pretext that such a definition is culturally biased and affected by modern Judaeo-Christian presuppositions.[44] His handling has some recognizable virtues, but his final conclusion seems slightly far-fetched, especially in the light of his own meticulous analysis of the Athenian funds. If the fusion between sacred and non-sacred that Samons envisages were true, then the Greek terminological distinction would become pointless. Clearly the treasury of Athena and/or the Other Gods was one thing, and that of the Athenian *demos*, τὸ δημόσιον, was another. Equally distinct were the respective administrative personel as well as the destination of the relevant funds. At any rate, Scullion's recent vigorous analysis of the Greeks' lexical and conceptual distinction between sacred and secular appears to have settled the issue for good.[45] It now remains to explore and lay out the implications of the distinction for our understanding of ancient economics.[46]

Advocates of the public character of sacred lands ought to provide an explicit definition of the term *public*. It is often overlooked that the way they apply the term in their approaches only marginally coincides, if at all, with the Greek word δημόσιος. In fact, 'public' usually refers to notions that go back to the principles of the German sociological School of the late nineteenth/early twentieth centuries, as expressed by Weber and his intellectual offspring.[47] Akin to this stands the question of the definition of state or civic cults. The late Sara Aleshire expressed grave concerns when she dealt with this question.[48] But if a definition of state-cult is, for the most part, elusive, it follows that a designation like *public temene* can be of mere theoretical value as a postulate. After all, an objection to all preceding discussion could be raised. It was implied above that some historians have overemphasized the involvement of state officials in the administration of sacred lands in order to designate the latter as public. This is methodologically inconsistent. To take a random

[44] Samons 2000, 21–2, 324–9; but cf. the pre-emptive criticism of this line of thought by Migeotte 1998.

[45] Scullion 2005, 111–19.

[46] See, for instance, the exploration of this topic in the framework of deme economics by Blok 2010.

[47] For a recent discussion of notions of 'public' in ancient Greece, see the French periodical *Ktema* 23 (1998), subtitled *Public et Privé en Grèce ancienne: Lieux, Conduites, Pratiques.*

[48] Aleshire 1994*b*.

example, one could claim that the publicly elected Athenian generals (στρατηγοί) were public officials, as indeed they were. It does not follow from this, however, that one cannot identify a distinctive military domain.[49] In other words, the fact that warfare was subject to public control does not necessitate that the internal military organization of the Athenian state could be seen merely through the spectrum of political structuring. There is definitely scope for subtler interpretative approaches, exactly as in the case of sacred lands. Different criteria can yield different answers. A composite set of criteria may result in a multitude of elucidations that would clarify the problem of sacred—and public—lands in all its aspects.

In general, the destination of the rent raised from sacred lands, itself part and parcel of sacred funds, should constitute a secure economic tool for checking the status of the estates of the gods. Yet its significance is often overlooked. More than three decades ago Linders struck a blow against the concept of secularization of sacred treasuries.[50] In addition to apprehending the connection between rent from temple land and sacred revenues (which will be central to our discussion), she proffered a thorough analysis of the interrelation between the gods and the state, which did not culminate in a categorical concurrence of the two sectors, the divine and the profane. More recently, a series of historians have strongly posited an effective dichotomy between sacred and secular/public funds.[51] But if this is so, then why should an analogous distinction between sacred and public estates not be tenable?

In fact the economic aspect of sacred lands would suffice to show that a further categorization is feasible, if not necessary. Revenue-bearing estates, alternatively known by their Greek technical term *temene* (τεμένη), comprised one class of sacred lands—the most important proportionately—but they were by no means unique. One can also find lands set aside for divinities and designated as uncultivable. The most illustrious examples are the Sacred Orgas on the frontier between Attica and the Megarid, and the plain of Krisa or Kirrha that belonged to the Delphian Apollo. In their case no analytical tools drawn from classical economics can be applied, for they would show an absurd condition of wasted natural resources that fits no modern mentality. One has to resort to the methods of

49 Cf. Fröhlich 1999.
50 Linders 1975.
51 e.g. Kallet-Marx 1989; Migeotte 1998 and 2006*a*.

anthropology in order to reconcile what at first sight appears to be an oxymoron. Wilamowitz, following an evolutionary religion model that is nowadays out of fashion, believed that sacred groves went back to very ancient times, and that, as a result, the classical Greeks refrained from putting them into cultivation.[52] Searching for an explanation of sacred untilled estates, Parker wondered whether the 'renunciation of one tract of . . . land [was] in exchange for the fructification of the rest', but it is obvious that he regarded this type of holy field as limited in extent.[53] Burkert called for caution in seeing some uncultivated sacred areas as a feature of the Mediterranean landscape, citing the Athenian Pelargikon as a model of exemplification.[54] More recently Horden and Purcell demonstrated how the sanctity of production is accomplished by *not* cultivating certain designated areas.[55] The phenomenon, of wide chronological distribution, is observable throughout the Mediterranean basin.

Of late, the author of a monograph on pastoralism put forward a more pragmatic explanation for this class of uncultivable sacred lands: Howe conceived of them as the response of political communities to disputes over frontiers.[56] That is, certain cities opted to use such marginal lands as pastures by consecrating them to divinities, thus indirectly affirming their own rights over the disputed areas. The idea, rather forcibly conveyed in the study in question, is not new in fact. It permeates, in a finer disguise, the studies of Sartre and Daverio-Rocchi, the former emphasizing the anthropological dimensions of marginal/border sacred territories.[57] Far more informative and erudite was a study by Chaniotis, who set his attention on a generally neglected area of Greece.[58] Chaniotis examined the prominent occurrence of the motif of sanctuary possession in Cretan interstate relationships during the Hellenistic period. Most importantly, he grasped the difference between ownership of a sanctuary and lands attached to it. For Chaniotis, polis territory and sacred lands cannot be identical, even though they may lie in a mutual superimposed relation. In fact, he even isolated a specific category

[52] Wilamowitz-Moellendorff 1929, 229, followed by Burkert 1996, 28–9 with n. 42.
[53] Parker 1983, 164.
[54] Burkert 1996, 29.
[55] Horden and Purcell 2000, 428.
[56] Howe 2008, 88–92.
[57] Sartre 1979; Daverio-Rocchi 1988.
[58] Chaniotis 1988.

of sacred land, namely 'Niemandsland'. Last but not least, he provided first-rank examples of 'heiliges, unbebautes Land' (sacred and uncultivable area) from a non-Athenian and rather unfamiliar context. Finally, one ought to mention the recent synoptic analysis by McInerney, who, building upon the work of his predecessors and combining anthropological theory with economic analysis, demonstrated how the consecration of borderland ('the quintessential liminal land') facilitated the taming of wilderness and the integration of pastoralism into the primarily agrarian economic systems of ancient Greece.[59]

So much for modern perceptions. Here is the place to address another almost insurmountable problem: the title of this book may be misleading in that, as will become obvious from the ensuing discussion, I have dealt not only with tillable lands or pasturage, but occasionally with other types of real property, such as buildings. This is hardly surprising, since the Greeks themselves did not draw clear-cut lines between these categories. Thus, for instance, most landholdings were furnished with some sort of agricultural shed. Conversely, an *οἰκία* (house) frequently came with the surrounding land which could be put to agricultural use.[60] The mines also constitute a peculiar case in the sense that their ownership status was not contingent on the status of the earth above them.[61] Temples, official premises, cemeteries, and streets have all been excluded from a lengthy treatment; to do otherwise would have required space and time not offered to the average monograph. In turn, these exclusions dissuaded me from using in the title the obvious alternative to the term 'land', i.e. 'real property'. Again, although Greek words or phrases such as *τὰ ἐνεργά* (productive property), *φανερὰ οὐσία* (visible property), or *ἔγγειος οὐσία* (landed property) come close to designating what students of modern common law would call real property, historians have recently highlighted the fluid socio-economic content of such terms, advocating their contextual investigation.[62] All in

[59] McInerney 2006.

[60] On the other hand, the occasional differentiation in *enktesis* formulas between ownership of a house (*οἰκίας*) and ownership of a house *and* land (*οἰκίας* and *γῆς*) suggests that the two were not always perceived as being identical: cf. Niku 2007, 131–3.

[61] See more recently Kakavoyiannis 2005.

[62] Todd 1993, 241–3 summarizing previous treatments by Harrison 1968, 228–235, and Gabrielsen 1986; see now Ferrucci 2005, who explores multiple interpretations of the ancient bipolar distinction *ἀφανής*/*φανερὰ οὐσία*. For modern legal definitions of the relevant terms see Lawson and Rudden 2002, 12–16, 22–6, and *passim*.

all, I have throughout this disquisition employed the terms 'land' and 'real property' (or 'realty') interchangeably, and I hope that readers will forgive my inconsistency upon the understanding that terminological and, therefore, conceptual concurrence is neither always feasible nor desired between two systems of thought as diverse as the ancient Greek and our modern western one can be.

The multitude of questions surrounding sacred and public property does not permit a wide-ranging and thorough treatment of absolutely everything. In this treatise I have taken the rather unfashionable approach of historical empiricism, but with a new historicism twist. Theoretical schemes can only be useful if applied to concrete evidence. Positive empiricism may be currently considered outmoded, but it constitutes the prerequisite for any decent theorization.[63] My aim has been to provide an exhaustive presentation of ancient testimonies of realty controlled by collectivities. I have focused on problems concerning land management, the personnel involved, and even the history of certain sacred areas. Particular emphasis has been put on the deployment of proceeds from leasing and sale of realty, as well as on their quantitative and qualitative significance for the economy of the controlling groups. In the following discussion I have divided my material on the basis of the human corporate groups that controlled such lands. The second chapter deals with sacred realty under the administration of the polis of Athens, whereas the third one covers such lands as managed by the two primary constituent parts of the Athenian polis, namely, the tribes and the demes. As will be shown, such landholdings lay more often than not under the nominal onwership of divinities. Yet certain properties—more often those of demes—appear to have been of secular character. In the fourth chapter I explore real property managed by other semi-public groups, namely phratries, *gene*, orgeones, and other, slightly more obscure, groups. These being in essence religious associations, their landholdings should a priori be of sacred character. Yet again, the actual situation turns out to be more complicated. In the fifth chapter I directly address the notorious problem of the alleged absence of public landholdings, that is secular property under the administration of Athens. In the appendices I can single out two topics of particular importance: the Sacred Orgas and the

[63] See the sensible thoughts of Ober 2006 on the need to theorize *and* respect the extant evidence.

administration of the *moriai*, the sacred olives of Athena. Both appendices should be seen as the logical continuation of the first chapter on sacred property controlled by the city-state of Athens. Other topics have a less direct connection to the issues at stake, but I considered that their treatment would substantially facilitate the examination of the overall picture. Also included in the appendices is a prosopographical database of lessees and guarantors of sacred property administered by the Athenian polis: the analysis of this roster helps to discount recent understatements about the socio-economic significance of corporate land.

2

The Athenian Polis as Administrator of Sacred Realty

1. A PRELIMINARY NOTE

In an era of historical analysis when the concept of *polis religion* is practically ubiquitous, the content of the present chapter, as suggested by its title, ought to be a straightforward affair. One anticipates here an analysis of real property attached to public—or, alternatively, state—cults. But as the late Sara Aleshire splendidly demonstrated more than a decade ago, coming up with an adequate definition of state-cult is an irksome task.[1] An array of diverse criteria ideally should be implemented to reach an unambiguous verdict, and yet the question is still likely to prove unanswerable.[2] One could dismiss the whole discussion as being of philological character. A public cult is one regulated by a polis, Athens in our case, regardless of the constitutional form. By regulation, one should understand financial administration, religious ordinance, and so on. No one would question that Athena Polias was the public cult par excellence in ancient Athens; literary evidence, epigraphical and numismatic material, and visual representations, all prove this point beyond any doubt. Or do they? If so, why was the priesthood of Athena Polias held by the *genos* Eteoboutadai, especially in view of the democratic priesthoods, that emphatically Athenian religious phenomenon?[3] I am only playing the devil's advocate here. Of course Athena Polias was the main Athenian

[1] Aleshire 1994*b*. [2] Cf. Cole 1995.

[3] Priesthoods: Feaver 1957; Aleshire 1994*a*; now Blok and Lambert 2009.

divinity,[4] and of course hers was a public cult. Furthermore, I do believe that administrative and financial criteria are fundamental in distinguishing such cults. When a public executive body—the Boule, the Assembly, a committee appointed by them—or even an Athenian magistrate, appears to regulate some aspect of a given cult, we are probably on the right track to identify such a cult as public. When such regulations appear twofold, or even manifold, the possibilities of successful identification rise substantially. To put it in more practical terms: decrees and laws, financial accounts, inventory lists, and *similia* are all good indications that one is dealing with cults controlled by the Athenian polis. In the influential article cited above, Aleshire identified as public the following cults: Athena and the Other Gods; the Eleusinian Goddesses; Asklepios. With the addition of Amphiaraos, this is a list I fully endorse and I have articulated the present chapter accordingly. I acknowledge, however, the difficulties inherent even in this classification. One of the most perplexing problems, for instance, concerns the cult of Apollo Zoster. He features amongst the Other Gods in the loans of 429/8. Yet other evidence would make us believe that his was a deme cult.[5] In improperly unscholarly fashion, I have to admit that the absence of any evidence for realty belonging to Apollo Zoster has spared me the trouble of seeking a satisfactory answer to this problem. What is clear, however, is that all questions of this type must be posed historically. Take the cult of Asklepios, for instance. It was indeed a public one, but only after 420 when it was introduced in Athens. Or consider that of Amphiaraos. Again, our evidence demonstrates the great concern of Athens to absorb and promote the cult of the Oropian god in the 330s–320s and probably earlier in the fourth century during the first Athenian occupation of Oropos. But nothing is known of the cult's treatment by the Athenians during the fifth century, when Oropia was firmly in Athenian hands.[6] In the ensuing discussion, such historical observations are made as clear as possible.

[4] Parker 2005, 395–7.
[5] Kourouniotes 1927–8; Feaver 1957, 153; Rhodes & Osborne 2003, 231–5.
[6] Thuc. 2.23.3 with Hornblower 1991, 279; Parker 1996, 148–9.

2. THE LANDED WEALTH OF ATHENA POLIAS AND THE OTHER GODS

For most of the fifth century the main treasury of Athens was that of Athena Polias. Being the poliadic goddess of Athens, Athena had by that time a huge accumulation of wealth of various types, not least real property.[7] We know indeed of a sacred house which was leased out for several years and its income used on the construction of the Propylaia.[8] Though the ownership of this house has been questioned, a *horos* found in the American excavations of the Agora proves that Athena did possess sacred buildings at roughly that time.[9] The same is true about the fourth century. The first six entries of the leasing records of 343/2 concern houses that presumably belonged to Athena, if we can apply a criterion of hierarchical significance in order to establish the divine proprietor.[10] As concerns the fifth century, a boundary stone from Marathon has often been thought to refer to the local shrine of Athena Hellotis, but in the absence of any specific epithet it might, in fact, have designated a sacred estate of Athena Polias.[11] Likewise, in view of a reference to the Acropolis, Athena is likely to have been the owner of the *temene* of the fragmentary *IG* I³ 419.[12] And on one interpretation favoured by D. M. Lewis, the

[7] The sacral treasury of Athens has recently been the subject of a very erudite treatment by Samons 2000, 28–50 and *passim* (building upon Samons 1993). Ferguson 1932 is still invaluable. See also Kallet-Marx 1989; Giovannini 1990. For inventories issued by the Treasurers of Athena see Harris 1995.

[8] *IG* I³ 462 l. 24; 463 l. 74; 466 l. 146; cf. Thompson 1970, 39; Walbank 1997, 39.

[9] *Agora* XIX H21 (=*IG* I³ 1050): [hό]ρ̣ος [οἰ|κ]ίας hιερ|ᾶς Ἀθηνᾶς | Πολιάδος (boundary of the sacred house of Athena Polias); see also the late 5th-cent. law *IG* I³ 237, esp. ll. 5–6: [μισ]|θόσεος γε͂ς καὶ οἰκιο͂ν (from? the leasing of land and houses), where, however, the ownership of the properties in question is unclear (cf. Behrend 1970, 99). Leasing of a house with the aim of funding sacrifices may underlie the fragmentary *IG* I³ 139 l. 4: τὲν δὲ οἰ[κίαν] (as for the house), where the presence of *hieropoioi* in l. 5 might allude to Athena Polias.

[10] *Agora* XIX L6 ll. 4–21. Much depends on the enigmatic line 4: [ἐ]ν Κυδαθηναίωι τῶν ΑΛ̣Ε̣[..]Λ̣[...⁵..] (at Kydathenaion, of the ALE[..]L[.....]), of which a satisfactory interpetation has yet to be provided (cf. Walbank 1983*a*, 111, 116 for various attempts).

[11] *IG* I³ 1082: hόρος | τεμένος | Ἀθενάας (boundary stone of the *temenos* of Athena); local shrine: Petrakos 1996, 65–6, but one would have expected hόρος hιερο͂ Ἀθενάας Ἑλότιδος, for the sake of clarity.

[12] Line 4 of *IG* I³ 419 should probably be restored as [Ἀθενάα]ς τεμέ[νε] (sacred estates of Athena).

opening lines of the lacunose decree *IG* I^3 59 refer to landed property belonging to Athena.[13] Finally, it is thanks to a judicial decision issued by the well-known proconsul Aemilius Juncus that we learn of a sacred threshing floor and other landed wealth that presumably belonged to Athena. This fragmentary inscription in in archaizing script, and it has been reasonably suggested that some older document extracted from a local archive was used in order to settle a dispute in the mid-second century AD.[14] If so, the archaizing pre-Euclidean script of *IG* II^2 3194 could push the existence of this property back to the fifth century BC.[15]

In the same period Athena's landed wealth expanded outside Attica's geographical limits. Even if the Euboean *temene* recorded in *IG* I^3 418 have now been dissociated from Athena, we still have Aelian's evidence that, following the island's conquest by the Athenians, part of the Lelantine Plain was consecrated to the tutelary goddess of Athens and subsequently leased out.[16] The exact date of

[13] *IG* I^3 59, ll. 2/3 with the restorations suggested in the *apparus criticus*: [- - - τὸς ταμίας τôν τês Ἀθεναίας μετὰ τô [βασιλέος? . . . .[13] . . . . . .| - - - τês Ἀ]θεναίας καὶ τὲν μ[ίσθοσιν?] (the treasurers of the monies of Athena along with the basileus . . . of Athena and the rental); also l. 7: [τ]ὸς μισθοτ[άς] (the lessees). As Lewis noted: 'Nisi fallimur, in vv. 1–11 de bonis deae locandis agitur'.

[14] *IG* II^2 3194, esp. ll. 8–9: [κ]αὶ τês hιε|ρ̣âς̣ ἅλο, and 13–14, τὲν ἅλο | τὲ[ν] hιεράν (threshing floor); ll. 9–10: πλέ|θρα, and 19 [προσχώ]ροις γύαις (cultivable land?); ll. 18–19: τοû τόπου | hύδορ ἔχοντ[ο]ς (water resources). The association with Athena is proposed here on the basis of the reference to 'the statue of Athena' (ll. 11–12: καὶ τὸ τês Ἀθενâς ἄγα[λμα]), but this may simply refer to a landmark, and in fact some other divinity might have been the nominal owner of this property (for an alternative, see Chapter 4, Section 4.2). On Aemilius Juncus, and the 'old archive' theory, see Oliver 1967, 52.

[15] But Aleshire 1999, has shown the artificial character of many archaizing documents of the Roman Imperial period. Hence, automatic chronological inferences may not be necessarily sound.

[16] Aelian, *VH* 6.1: Ἀθηναῖοι κρατήσαντες Χαλκιδέων κατεκληρούχησαν αὐτῶν τὴν γῆν ἐς δισχιλίους κλήρους, τὴν Ἱππόβοτον καλουμένην χώραν, τεμένη δὲ ἀνῆκαν τῇ Ἀθηνᾷ ἐν τῷ Ληλάντῳ ὀνομαζομένῳ τόπῳ, τὸ δὲ λοιπὸν ἐμίσθωσαν κατὰ τὰς στήλας τὰς πρὸς τῇ βασιλείῳ στοᾷ ἑστηκυίας, αἵπερ οὖν τὰ τῶν μισθώσεων ὑπομνήματα εἶχον. (After the Athenians had defeated the Chalkidians they divided their land, the so-called Hippobotos, two thousand parcels. They dedicated sacred estates to Athena in the area called Lelanton, and, subsequently, they leased them out according to the stelae recording the leases, which stood by the Royal Stoa). Aelian's manuscripts have τὴν δὲ λοιπήν (the remaining, i.e. country); τὸ δὲ λοιπόν is a commendable emendation suggested in *ATL* iii 296; cf. Meiggs 1972, 566–7. Smarczyk 1990, 99 is unaware of the philological difficulties of the passage. One of these *temene* is probably attested in *IG* I^3 1502, [τ]έμενος | [Ἀ]θηναίης (*temenos* of Athena); thus Smarczyk 1990, 92.

the operation remains in dispute, but here I am only concerned with the policy of consecration, rather than the historical event itself.[17] Such operations were probably carried out by specifically appointed committees, such as the *γεωνόμοι* attested in the decree for the foundation of Brea, though the latter admittedly refers to a colony and may reflect a slightly different situation.[18] Be that as it may, estates consecrated to the poliadic goddess of Athens are well attested all over the territory of the Delian League, including Aigina, Kos, and Samos.[19] Though most of the *horoi* under consideration mention *Ἀθεναία Ἀθενôν Μεδέοσα* (Athena who guards/rules over Athens), her identification with Athena Polias is nowadays taken for granted.[20] The interpretation of these documents (not only the ones referring to Athena, but also those relating to other Athenian divinities) has for years been controversial, not least because of some subtle epigraphical technicalities.[21] Current orthodoxy, however, holds that, far from

[17] The date of the event recounted by Aelian has been the subject of fierce controversy. *ATL* thought of the campaign of Tolmides; similarly Brunt 1966, 88; Gauthier 1966, 71 with n. 21; Vartsos 1972, 38–9; Meiggs 1972, 566; Smarczyk 1990, 93–8; Rosivach 1991, 437. Raubitschek 1943, 33 was the first to place the foundation of Athenian *temene* in Euboea in *c.*425, associating them with an expedition mentioned by Philochorus; thus also Mattingly 1961, 125 n. 8, 131–2 (cf. idem 2002).

[18] *IG* I^3 46 ll. 10-15: *γεονόμος δὲ* h*ελέσθ[αι δέκα | ἄνδρας], ἕνα ἐχ φυλε͂ς·* h*οῦτοι δὲ νεμάντ[ον τὲν | γε͂ν. Δεμ]οκλείδεν δὲ καταστε͂σαι τὲν ἀ[ποικί|αν αὐτο]κράτορα, καθότι ἂν δύνεται ἄ[ριστα. τ|ὰ δὲ τεμ]ένε τὰ ἐχσειρεμένα ἐᾶν καθά[περ ἐστ|ί, καὶ ἄλ]λα μὲ τεμενίζεν* (cf. Vartsos 1972, 100). Nevertheless, the two acts—the election of the *geonomoi* and the *temenismos*—appear to be separate events; for the various interpretative problems see Malkin 1984.

[19] Aigina: *IG* IV^2 .2 792-7 (*IG* I^3 1486-90): h*όρος | τεμένος | Ἀθεναίας* (boundary of the *temenos* of Athena), with minor orthographical variants, no further designation of Athena; cf. Barron 1983. See now Polinskaya 2009. Kos: *IG* I^3 1491 (and perhaps *IG* I^3 1491 bis); cf. Sherwin-White 1978, 36–8. Samos: *IG* XII (6) 238-44 (now superseding *IG* I^3 1492-95): variants of h*όρος | τεμένος | Ἀθεναίας | Ἀθενôν | μεδεόσες* (boundary of the *temenos* of Athena who rules over Athens); see Gallo 2005*a*, 250–1.

[20] See Anderson and Dix 1997; Ma 2009, 129, 143 n. 11. Incidentally, rentals from *temene* consecrated to Athena must be the reason for the occurrence of this epithet of Athena in lines 14–15 of the so-called Kolophon decree *IG* I^3 37 (contra Meiggs 1972, 295–6, who bases his arguments on a now obsolete analysis of religious sanctions in the framework of the Delian League; see below). The supplement *καὶ τô[ν μισθομάτον τε͂|ς Ἀθενᾶς τε͂ς] Ἀθενôν μεδεόσ[ες]* (. . . and of the leased properties of Athena who rules over Athens . . .) would provide an acceptable line-length.

[21] The old-fashioned approach was that established by Barron 1964 (cf. Shipley 1987, 114–17). The vexed epigraphical problem has always been the dating of the three-bar sigma (and, to a lesser extent, of the tailed rho) thought to disappear from Athenian public documents after 446. But this criterion has now collapsed after the work of Chambers, Galluci, and Spanos 1990, and Matthaiou 2004; see the overviews by Rhodes 2008, and Papazarkadas 2009*a*. Henry 2001, has remained alone in fighting

attesting the export of Athenian religion, such markers 'record the most abhorred of all imperial practices, appropriation of allied land for the benefit of absentee landlords, the gods and heroes of Athens'.[22] This view does justice to the fact that the findspots of the *horoi* in question coincide with places that at some point or another during the peak of the Athenian empire appear to have confronted Athens and, subsequently, to have been subjugated by her. Clear though the punitive facet of such land consecrations may seem, it should not be automatically presumed that it attests to the foundation of Athenian cleruchies. Of course, such sacred property was subject to the historical developments of the time and it may not have remained under Athenian possession after control of the islands had returned to the original inhabitants. We can firmly conclude that, after the end of the Peloponnesian War, Athena was deprived of her overseas landed assets.

Elsewhere we encounter a moat—situated near Diochares' Bath—that belonged to Athena. As revealed by a boundary-stone, the property was already consecrated to Athena in the early fourth century, but, amazingly, it is still attested in the Roman period.[23] The double tribal decree of Aiantis and Aigeis mentions the 'meadow of Athena', and it is just possible that this was a field consecrated to the patron-goddess of Athens on the occasion of Oropos' delineation by the *horistai*.[24] Still, the major expansion of Athena's landed assets in the fourth century is probably to be found in the Law on the Lesser

stubbornly for the three-bar *sigma* cause (but I note that Lougovaya-Ast 2006, 215–16, expresses her sympathy for the old criterion).

[22] Parker 1996, 144–5, synopsizing Smarczyk 1990, 58–153. See now Polinskaya 2009, who accepts the concept and carefully applies it to an overhaul of 18 horoi found at Aigina.

[23] See *Agora* XIX L10. ll. 40–2: *Ἀθηνᾶς τέλμα πρὸς ταῖς [πύλαις] | ταῖς παρὰ τὸ Διοχάρου[ς . . . ⁵..] | βαλανέον* (moat of Athena next to the [gates] by the Bath of Diochares), with Walbank 1983*b*, 197; 1983*d*, 212 n. 67. *SEG* XXI 651, *ὅρος τέλμα|τος Ἀθηνάας* (boundary stone of Athena's moat); cf. Faraguna 1992, 349; Mitchel 1970, 43 with n. 169 is wrong to assign the consecration to Lykourgos' programme of religious rejuvenation. The same property is probably recorded in the double decree for the restoration of Attic sanctuaries *SEG* XXVI 121 l. 48: *[τέμενος τὸ π]αρὰ τὰ μακρά τίχη Ἀθηνᾶς Πολιάδος* ([*temenos*] of Athena Polias by the Long Walls); cf. Judeich 1931, 425; Schlaifer 1940, 238–9 n. 6; Schmalz (2007–8) [2011]. If so, one had better restore *[τέλμα τὸ π]αρὰ τὰ μακρά τίχη Ἀθηνᾶς Πολιάδος* ([moat] of Athena Polias by the Long Walls).

[24] Agora XVI 84 l. 146 (with Papazarkadas 2009*b*): *[το]ῦ λειμῶνος τοῦ τῆς Ἀθη[ν]ᾶ̣ς̣.*

Panathenaia.[25] This legislation stipulated that the subsidy of the festival was to be carried out with funds from the *Νέα* (Nea). The source of funding should leave no doubt about the ownership of this area; it belonged to Athena.[26] Its location, however, has caused much controversy ever since the publication of the relevant part of the inscription. Lewis's interpretation of the term *νέα* as a variant of the word *νειά* (fallow) was rejected by Robert who associated the name *Νέα* with the newly acquired area of Oropos.[27] Other tentative topographical identifications have proved less convincing.[28] I would provisionally accept Robert's suggestion, with one modification. From a propagandistic point of view it would certainly be odd of the Athenians to call *Νέα* (New) an area on which they had had constant claims since the Archaic period. I would suggest, therefore, that the area was termed *Νέα* (New) in the sense of being an area newly consecrated to the goddess Athena.[29]

The other major group of divine landowners is the motley crew known as the Other Gods. Established by a legislative act attested in Kallias' Decree A,[30] their treasury experienced a history of numerous amalgamations with, and segregations from, the treasury of Athena throughout the Classical period.[31] This partial overlap between the two treasuries, witnessed, for instance, in a leasing context in a law cited by pseudo-Demosthenes,[32] requires that they are treated together here. Of primary significance is the series of mass leases attested from 343/2 onwards. Among the few *nomina sacra* preserved

[25] *SEG* XVIII 13 + *IG* II^2 334 (=RO 81); see Linders 1975, 38–57.

[26] Cf. Rosivach 1994, 54 with n. 113; 122–7 (the sacred character of the *Νέα* has been—wrongly in my view—denied by Langdon 1991, 64).

[27] Lewis 1959*b*; cf. Lewis 1968, 374 n. 18, contra Robert 1960 (followed by Rosivach 1991, 436–8). See now Rhodes & Osborne 2003, 400–1.

[28] Langdon 1987, 56–8 has suggested a volcanic islet off Lemnos, whereas O. Hansen 1989 opted for Halonnesos.

[29] Papazarkadas 2009*b*.

[30] Accepted by Rhodes 1993, 550; Blamire 2001, 104. The debate about the chronology of Kallias' decree has been fierce, the accumulated bibliography huge. The traditionally accepted date is that of 434/3 (see Ferguson 1932, 152–2; ML 52; Blamire 2000, 103 with n. 23). Samons 2000, 113–38 has proposed 432. Kallet-Marx 1993, 105–7 has opted for 431/0. Kennelly 2003 now urges for a distancing of the decree from 431.

[31] Linders 1975, 58–71.

[32] Dem. 43.58: *τοὺς δὲ μὴ ἀποδιδόντας τὰς μισθώσεις τῶν τεμενῶν τῶν τῆς θεοῦ καὶ τῶν ἄλλων θεῶν καὶ τῶν ἐπωνύμων ἀτίμους εἶναι* etc. (and those who do not pay their rentals for the sacred estates of the Goddess and the Other Gods and the Eponymous Heroes shall be *atimoi*).

on the stones, one encounters Athena Polias, Zeus Olympios, Artemis Agrotera, Herakles at Kynosarges, and Artemis Brauronia.[33] Athena Polias aside, the remaining deities are found grouped together in both the accounts of the Treasurers of the Other Gods of 429/8 and the records of loans from the sacred treasuries dating from 426/5 to 423/2.[34] It is a plausible guess that, if more divine names had been preserved in the late Classical leases, we would have found the same deities featuring as the ones attested in the fifth-century documents. Equally, it is not absurd to assume that part of the sums administered by the fifth-century treasurers included rentals from leased *temene*,[35] though to what extent such sacred landholdings would have overlapped with the fourth-century ones is impossible to know. Evidence for this hypothesis, though not abundant, does exist. The most famous fifth-century lease of sacred property is that of the *temenos* of Neleus and Basile from 418/7. Significantly, the Treasurers of the Other Gods are the final recipients of the relevant rental.[36] Theseus, Attic hero par excellence, whose property was also administered by the Treasurers of the Other Gods, had several *temene*, as we know from a Roman document which probably records properties going back to the Classical period.[37] More instructive is a lex sacra from the 430s laying down regulations for the protection of the river Ilissos near the *temenos* of Herakles at Kynosarges. Since the supervising magistrate appears to be the *basileus*, the *de jure* lessor of polis *temene*, there is a good chance that the area in question was partly or wholly the same as one of the leased *temene* of the fourth century.[38]

[33] Athena: *Agora* XIX L6 l. 3; L10 l. 40. Zeus Olympios: *Agora* XIX L6 ll. 77–8, 81. Artemis Agrotera: *Agora* XIX L6 ll. 90–1, 93–4, 97, 145. Herakles at Kynosarges: *Agora* XIX L6 l. 102. Artemis Brauronia: *Agora* XIX L6 ll. 164–5, 168–9 (cf. Walbank 1983*d*, 227).

[34] *IG* I^3 383; *IG* I^3 369 (=ML 72). In fact, Artemis Brauronia appears only in the latter inscription.

[35] So already Linders 1975, 66.

[36] Lease: *IG* I^3 84, with Linders 1975, 32–3; Faraguna 1992, 344; Blamire 2001, 116. Samons 2000, 53 rightly insists on the sanctity of such income.

[37] *SEG* XXVI 121 l. 48, τεμένη Θησέως, with Schmalz 2007–8 [2011], who rightly identifies these *temene* not as temples, but as 'income-bearing properties'.

[38] Lex sacra: *IG* I^3 257, esp. ll. 3–10: ἐπ[ιμ]ἐ̣λεσθαι δὲ | τὸμ βασιλέα· γράφσαι δ|ὲ ἐστέλει λιθίνει καὶ | στε̂σαι hεκατέροθι· με|δὲ δέρματα σέπεν ἐν το̂|ι hιλισο̂ι καθύπερθεν | το̂ τεμένος το̂ hερακλέ|[ο]ς (the *basileus* shall take care of these. Write these things on a stone *stele* and set them up on both sides. And do not wash skins in the Ilissos river above the *temenos* of Herakles); for the *basileus* as lessor of polis *temene* see

As in the case of Athena, the Other Gods also appear to have benefited from the expansion of Athenian hegemony. Concluding his account of the crushing of the Lesbian revolt by the Athenians in 427 Thucydides remarks: 'After that they did not assess the Lesbians for tribute. Instead they divided the land, apart from that of Methymna, into three thousand allotments, set aside three hundred as sacred to the gods, and to the remainder sent allotment-holders from the citizen body, chosen by lot.'[39] The plural form of the divine recipients of the expropriated properties makes it almost certain that the Other Gods are meant here.[40] *IG* I^3 418, a roster of *temene* at Chalkis and Eretria administered by the Athenian polis, has been deprived of a divine owner ever since it was realized that [*Ἀθενάα*]*ς τεμένε* (sacred estates of Athena) was an epigraphically untenable restoration.[41] A better supplement could be [*Ἴονο*]*ς τεμένε* (sacred estates of Ion). Not only does Ion feature as the divine owner of a *temenos* in a *horos* from Samos, he is also exactly the kind of divinity that could be used by the Athenians as propaganda against their disloyal Ionian allies, the Euboeans.[42] Nonetheless, whether he is to be identified with the puzzling Ion from Pleistieis in the accounts of the Treasurers of the Other Gods should, on current evidence, remain

Sections 3 and 5 below. We also know of a speech written by Isaeus entitled 'On the *temenos*' (Harp. s.v. *ἅμιπποι· Ἰσαῖος Τεμενικῷ*). The speech is lost, but the gloss *ἅμιπποι* points to the Athenian cavalry. Since we know that the Herakleion at Kynosarges was the training ground of the Athenian *hippeis* and given the expertise of Isaeus in cases regarding property, the speech might have been written for a dispute over the leasing of a *temenos* at Kynosarges.

[39] Thuc. 3.50.2: *ὕστερον δὲ φόρον μὲν οὐκ ἔταξαν Λεσβίοις, κλήρους δὲ ποιήσαντες τῆς γῆς πλὴν τῆς Μηθυμναίων τρισχιλίους τριακοσίους μὲν τοῖς θεοῖς ἱεροὺς ἐξεῖλον, ἐπὶ δὲ τοὺς ἄλλους σφῶν αὐτῶν κληρούχους τοὺς λαχόντας ἀπέπεμψαν*; cf. Brunt 1966, 81–2; Smarczyk 1990, 107–8; Parker 1994, 342 with n. 17.

[40] Gomme 1956, 327 and Samons 2000, 33 n. 32 believe that both Athena and the Other Gods are meant here.

[41] Raubitschek 1943, 30; Meiggs 1972, 567; Davies 1981, 58; Smarczyk 1990, 96. Morison 2003 now interprets *IG* I^3 420 in a similar fashion to *IG* I^3 418, but I am not entirely convinced that the former does not record properties in Athens, as usually assumed.

[42] *IG* XII (6) 245 (=*IG* I^3 1496) and *IG* XII (6) 246: h*όρος* | *τεμένος* | *Ἴονος* | *Ἀθένεθεν* (boundary of the *temenos* of Ion at Athens); see Tsakos 1977 [1982], 75–9 and especially Smarczyk 1990, 132–4, who stresses the importance of Ion as a vehicle for Athenian imperialistic propaganda against the Ionian Samians (cf. Parker 1996, 146–7). For Ionianism see Parker 1987*b*, 205–7 and Zacharia 2003, esp. 48–55 (with specific reference to *temene* at 52–3).

an open question.[43] But by far the most challenging case is that of the Aiginetan sacred estates of Apollo and Poseidon. The unprecedented pairing of the two deities, coupled with some historically biased readings of the relevant evidence, had long problematized the interpretation of the four *horoi* attesting to land belonging to Apollo and Poseidon.[44] It is now understood, however, that the most likely context for the erection of these *horoi* was the annexation of Aigina to Athens at the outbreak of the Peloponnesian War. If so, the identification of the two deities as Apollo Delios and Poseidon Erechtheus (?) respectively would appear to provide yet more evidence for a system of land accumulation profiting the major deities of the Athenian pantheon at the acme of Athenian power.[45]

These estates aside, most of the immovable property of the Other Gods lay in Attica. It was once thought that a landholding mentioned in a Teithrasian decree belonged to Datyl(l)os, a very obscure member of the Other Gods. Elsewhere, however, I have shown that Datyl(l)os is a ghost-name in the deme decree and such an association can no longer be sustained.[46] Equally fanciful is the interpretation of *IG* II[2] 2603 as a *horos* marking fields belonging to Artemis; the inscription is, in fact, a double dedication to Meter and Artemis.[47] An early fourth-century *horos* bearing the text [hó]ρο[ς | τε]μέν[ος | Δι]ὸς [Ὀλ|υμ]πί[ο] has sparked discussion about the continuity of the Peisistratid temple in the Classical period, or even about the existence of a ghost-Olympieion in some other location.[48] All these

[43] *IG* I[3] 383 ll. 147–9: Ἴονος | ἐκ Πλεισ|τιείον.

[44] For instance, Barron 1983, an otherwise very methodical study.

[45] *IG* IV[2].2 798–801: hόρος | τεμένος | Ἀπόλλωνος | Ποσειδῶνος (text variously disposed on the various stones), with Polinskaya 2009, 259–261, who also examines further possible identifications of the gods involved.

[46] 336 silver drachmas for Datyllos are recorded in *IG* I[3] 383 ll. 76–7: Δατύλλ̣[ο] | ἀργύρ[ιον]; Threiasian decree: *SEG* XXIV 151 ll. 11–12, καὶ τὸ χωριίο|[ν] ἥρ[ω]ο[ς Δα]τύλ[ο] (and the landholding of the her[o Da]tyl[o]s) as restored by Wilhelm 1935, 191, and accepted by Parker 2005, 65, but see Papazarkadas 2007*a*, no. D1a (καὶ τὸ χωρ̣ίο|[ν] ἥρ[ω]ο[ς . . . [5] . .]ας).

[47] Kirchner in *IG* II[2] 2603 printed h[ό]ρο[ς] | [χωρί]ων κα[ὶ ἱερô | Ἀρ]τέμιδος (boundary stone of the landholdings and the shrine of Artemis), based on misreadings by Tillyard 1904–5, 69 no. 15. But *IG* II[2] 2603 is actually a duplicate of *IG* II[2] 4670, which in turn is a duplicate of *IG* II[2] 5015 (cf. Dow 1938, 358). See now Papazarkadas 2004–9 [2010], 97–9, no. 3.

[48] *Agora* XIX H12; cf. H15: [ὅρος | τε]μένου[ς | Διό]ς *vacat* (boundary stone of the *temenos* of Zeus), but, as Lalonde ad loc. observes, the restorations are by no means certain.

speculations have to be dismissed. If anything, the *horos* points towards the existence of at least one estate consecrated to Zeus Olympios in the vicinity of the urban centre, unless we allow for a long-distance transportation of the stone.

Another candidate for inclusion in the roster of divine landowners is Athena Itonia. In Lykourgos' religious law of 335/4 the goddess's new *κόσμος*, i.e. her cultic equipment, was to be made 'from the first-fruits from her *temene*' (*ἐκ τῆς ἀπαρχῆς τῆς ἀπὸ τῶν τε[μενῶν]*).[49] Athena Itonia is an unusual divinity, somewhat un-Attic, more Boeotian or even Thessalian.[50] Still, she features in the inventories of the Other Gods of 429/8, she has recently emerged in the Athenian sacrificial calendar, and one of the earliest Attic boundary-stones might well have marked one of her *temene*.[51] An *ἀπαρχή* might be postulated in the case of another alien cult, that of the Thracian Bendis, which was officially recognized in 429 and whose income was also recorded in the inventory list *IG* I^3 383. For unfathomable reasons, she was paired with another somewhat obscure female deity, Adrasteia. Tantalizingly their income was specifically designated as deriving from the 'annual produce'.[52] Unless we postulate some otherwise unattested tax in kind, the entry probably refers to the produce from a newly consecrated landholding. This interpretation receives further corroboration from an Athenian decree, usually dated to 413/2, which regulated the cult of Bendis. Despite its

[49] *IG* II^2 333 ll. 18–9 (cf. Schwenk 1985, 123; Faraguna 1992, 352). Lambert 2005, 137–143 has now produced a new edition (= *SEG* LIV 143), in which he carefully investigates several important issues advocating a date *c.*335 for the text.

[50] See Parker 1996, 28 n. 64. Let it be briefly noted here that the nearest cultic centre of Athena Itonia outside Attica was at the Boeotian Koroneia. In the sacrificial calendar of the deme of Thorikos, an amendment records the offering of a sheep to the mysterious Heroines of the Koroneians (*SEG* XXXIII 147 l. 58: *[Ἡρ]ωΐνησιν Κορωνέων*). Daux 1983, 158–9 suggested a specific connection between the Boeotian polis and the deme of Thorikos (doubted by Lupu 2005, 149). I wonder if this association and the cult of—the presumably Koroneian—Athena Itonia should be seen in the same nexus.

[51] Accounts: *IG* I^3 383 ll. 151–2. Athenian *fasti*: Gawlinski 2007, face A, col. I, l. 12: *[Ἀθηναίαι Ἰτ]ωνίαι οἶ[s]*. *Horos*: *Agora* XIX H1, *[Ἀθ]εναίας | [Ἰτ]ονείας* (of [Ath]ena [It]oneia) from *c.*475–450 (Linders 1975, 16 was wrong to state that Athena Itonia does not feature in sources other than the accounts of *IG* I^3 383). The restoration has been doubted as impossible by Robertson 2005, 50 n. 15, without further explication.

[52] *IG* I^3 383 ll. 142–6: *Ἀδρα[στείας] | καὶ Βε[νδῖδος] | ἐγκυκλ[ίο] | καρπõ ἐκ̣ [τõν] | ἱερõν* (cf. *IG* I^3 369 ll. 67–8, *[Ἀδρασ]τείας* 𐅄ΔΔΔΠ⊢, *τ[όκος τούτο* ⊢· | *Βενδ]ῖδος* 𐅄ΔΔΔΠ⊢, *τόκος τού[το* ⊢], which suggests equal distribution of income between the two goddesses).

fragmentary condition, there are two unambiguous mentions of an ἐπαρχέ [*sic*], in a context which has been thought to imply the use of these first-fruits for subsidy of the goddess's cult. Here again, even if one rejects the association of the ἐπαρχέ with the ἐγκύλιος καρπός of *IG* I³ 383, one cannot see what the ἐπαρχέ might have been other than the first-fruits from Bendis' private estates.[53] And finally, the ἀπαρχέ of Apollo Pythios recorded in *IG* I³ 383 presupposes the existence of *temene* belonging to the god, such as those of Athena Itonia.[54]

Scholars often overlook or dismiss the sanctity of realty belonging to gods as a mere formality. Instead, they choose to emphasize the human agents, and consequently feel justified in designating such property as public.[55] The long-awaited, albeit partial, publication of

[53] *IG* I³ 136 ll. 20–3:

[..........*c*.28.............]ος καὶ ἐπα[ρχε...........*c*.26.........]
[..........*c*.26............. τ]ὲγ γενομέ[νεν...........*c*.27.........]
[..........*c*.24..........τὲ]ς ἐπαρχὲς ἐς [..............*c*.29.........]
[..........*c*.26...........]αν ὅσο δ' ἂν πρ[αθêι...........*c*.25.........]

See the restorations and the—overlooked—analysis of these lines by Pappadakis 1937, 812–13, who also suggested a connection with the accounts of the Treasurers of the Other Gods *IG* I³ 383 (see previous note). For a different view (ἐπαρχέ as a sacred levy) see Ferguson 1949, 142–4.

[54] *IG* I³ 383 ll. 236–8: [Ἀπό]λλονος Πυ|[θίο] ἐ ἀπαρχὲ ἀ|[ργυρ]ίο ἐμεδαπô (the *aparche* of Apollo Pythios reckoned in our own coinage). Schlaifer 1940, 235–6 with n. 1 identified this *aparche* with the tax levied on the Athenian military forces in *IG* I³ 138 for the upkeep of the shrine of Apollo. Jameson 1980, 224, however, has identified the latter as Apollo Lykeios, a view which renders Schlaifer's theory unsustainable (strangely, Schlaifer 1943*a*, 53–5 reached a conclusion similar to that endorsed here with regard to the ἀπαρχαί from the sacred grain collected by the *parasitoi* of Athena Pallenis, namely that they allude to the existence of a landholding owned by Athena; see Chapter 4, Section 4). At any rate, I think it is more prudent to take the word ἀπαρχέ of *IG* I³ 383 in its ordinary agricultural sense (cf. Stengel 1893). An entry in the Attic Stelae concerning the confiscated property of Pherekles of Themake may be relevant here. Lines 104–6 of ML 79 are usually restored as: ὀργά[δος] τὸ hέμισυ τêς ἐ[ντὸς τô] | Πυθ[ίο κ]αὶ διανόμο τô ἀπὸ [τô hιερô | τὸ δὲ ἄλλ]ο hέμισυ ἐγ Κυκάλει (half the *orgas* inside the Pythion and of the canal that runs from the shrine, the other half at Kykale). But it is inconceivable that a grove within a shrine would have been expropriated as private property; rather we should either endorse the old supplement by Meritt 1939, 76: τêς ἐ[πὶ τôι] | Πυθ[ίοι] (which is adjacent to Pythion), or restore ἐ[κτός] (outside), in which case the remaining part of the *orgas* might have indeed belonged to Apollo Pythios (cf. the famous *Sacred Orgas* of the Eleusinian Goddesses, and see L'Homme-Wéry 1996, 151–8).

[55] See Chapter 1. Anthropologists working in related fields have traditionally been much more cautious; cf. Trigger 2003, 326–7, who summarizing work carried out in non-Greek archaic societies, asserts that temple, i.e. cultic, land 'was regarded as constituting the estate of the presiding deity'.

the law from Brauron can now, significantly for our discussion, demonstrate the fragility of such arguments. The law—identified as such by virtue of the occurrence of the *νομοθέται*—promulgated extensive repairs within the shrine of Artemis Brauronia, one of the Other Gods. It is worth citing in full the opening clause, since the text is *terra incognita* to many historians:

> *ὅπως ἂν τὰ ἐν τῶι ἱ[ερῶι τῆς θεοῦ]*
> *[τ]ῆς Βραυρωνίας πάντα σᾶ εἶ καὶ ὑγιῆ καὶ ὁ νεώς, ὅ τε*
> *[ἀρχαῖος καὶ ὁ Πα]-*
> *ρθενών, στέγωσιν καὶ οἱ οἶκοι, τό τε ἀμφιπολεῖον ἐν ὧι [αἱ ἄρκτοι]*
> *διαιτῶνται καὶ τὰ ὑπερῶια τὰ ἐπὶ τοῦ ἀμφιπολείου καὶ [τὸ γυμν]-*
> *άσιον καὶ ἡ παλαίστρα καὶ οἱ ἱππῶνες καὶ τἆλλα πάντα [ὅσα ἡ]*
> *πόλις οἰκοδομήσασα ἀνέθηκεν τῆι θεῶι* etc.[56]

> In order that everything within the s[hrine of the goddess o]f Brauron be secure and in good shape, and the temples, both the [ancient one and the Pa]rthenon, be roofed, and also the premises and the *amphipoleion* in which [the *arktoi*] reside, and the storeys on the *amphipoleion*, and [the gymn]asium and the palaestra and the stables and anything else [that the] polis has built and dedicated to the goddess . . .

Two points are worth commenting on: (i) the divine ownership of the realty in question (the polis might have built the premises, but it automatically transferred ownership to the goddess through consecration), and (ii) the variety of the enumerated properties, namely two temples, houses, balconies, a gymnasium, a palaestra, and stables. Some of these premises undoubtedly served the shrine's cultic needs. Some others might have been leased out to raise cultic income. This might have been the case, for instance, with the stables—since we find stables being leased out in another sacred context[57]—or with the gymnasium and the palaestra. Indeed in *Agora* XIX L9 l. 28 one encounters a *παραδρομίς* (running corridor), an indispensable component of any gymnasium, featuring as a leased object. The

[56] *SEG* LII 104 ll. 2–7; text published by Themelis 2002, who repeatedly calls it a decree despite the clause *δεδόχθαι τοῖς νομοθέ|ταις* (resolved by the *nomothetai*) in ll. 8–9. Be that as it may, the inscription appears to be the last extant evidence of the Treasurers of the Other Gods (ll. 9–10). But see Stroud's sharp note on the 'oral history' of this text, in *SEG* LVI 172.

[57] *IG* I^3 395 ll. 1–2, [—] h*ιππόνον μί[σθοσις]*; see next section.

Athenians, we may assume, would occasionally lease out their gymnasia in order to generate income.[58]

At any rate, Artemis Brauronia owned at least one piece of realty in Philaidai, i.e. in the vicinity of her cultic centre.[59] Similarly, one of the *temene* of Zeus Olympios lay near a theatre—in all likelihood the Panathenaic stadium—and thus very close to the temple of the god.[60] It is tempting to apply such topographical considerations to identify divine owners. Thus, a block of properties in the area of Mounichia in Piraeus should belong to Artemis Mounichia,[61] and seaside properties in Phaleron to Apollo Delios.[62] Unfortunately, the topographical pattern is not so neat as to allow unequivocal inferences of this kind. One of the houses of Artemis Agrotera, for instance, was located in the deme Kollytos, rather removed from the goddess's cultic centre in Agrai.[63] It would be, therefore, more prudent merely to note the wide geographical distribution of properties belonging to Athena and/or the Other Gods.[64]

58 See Walbank 1983*b*, 181 with n. 6; Faraguna 1992, 352. The same type of property appears in *SEG* XXVI 121 l. 55, *πάσας καὶ παραδρ̣ο̣μίδας* (and cf. l. 54, where a palaestra is enumerated amongst sacred properties).

59 *Agora* XIX L6 ll. 164–5: [*Ἀρτέμιδος Βραυ*]|*ρωνίας ἐμ Φιλα*[*ϊδῶν*], with Walbank 1983*a*, 124.

60 *Agora* XIX L6 ll. 145-8: [*τέμ*]*ενος Διὸς 'Ολυμπίου π*|[. . . . .^{15} . . . .*σ*]*κηνὴ ἧι Εὔβουλο*|[*s* . . . .^{14} . . . .*στ*]*ά̣δ̣ιον τοῦ θεάτ*|[*ρου*] (*temenos* of Zeus Olympios [. . . s]tage where Euboulo[s . . .] stadium of the theatre); the latter might have been the Panathenaic stadium (cf. Dillery 2002, 464–6, and especially Matthaiou 2007), rather than the Dionysiac theatre (Walbank 1983*a*, 123–4). The shrine of *Agora* XIX L6 ll. 77–8: *Διὸς* | ['*Ολυμπίου ο*]*ἰκία παρὰ τὸ Διονύσιον* (house of Zeus Olympios next to the Dionysion), has been thought to be the Dionysion at Limnai, which was probably located near the Olympieion (Walbank 1983*a*, 118).

61 *Agora* XIX L9 ll. 64–89, esp. ll. 69–70: *ἕκτον κηπεῖον ἰόντι δ*[*εξιᾶς*^{vv}]| *χειρὸς Μουνι<χι>άζε* (a sixth small orchard on your ri[ght] hand side as you walk to Mounichia); ll. 86–7: [*ἔ*]*νατον κηπεῖον* [*δεξιᾶς χειρ*^{vv}]|*ὸς ἰόντι Μουνιχ*[*ιάζε*] (a ninth small orchard [on your right ha]nd side as you walk [to] Mounich[ia]); cf. Walbank 1983*b*, 185, who attempts, however, no identification of the divine owner.

62 *Agora* XIX L11, esp. l. 4: *παρὰ θάλα*[*τταν*] *vel παραθαλά*[*ττι*- - -] (perhaps even *παραθαλα*[*ττίδιον*], for which see Poll. *Onom.* 9.17), with Walbank 1983*c*, 201; l. 9: *Φαλ̣ηροῖ̣* (cf. *IG* I^3 383 ll. 153–4: [*Ἀ*]*πόλλονος Δ*|[*ε*]*λίο Φαλερô*(*ι*); for the cult of Apollo Delios see especially Matthaiou 2003). Walbank 1983*c*, 202 broaches various possibilities regarding the divine owner of the properties in question (including Apollo Delios), favouring, however, Artemis [Brauronia?].

63 *Agora* XIX L6 ll. 97–8: *Ἀρτέμι*[*δο*]*s Ἀ*[*γρο*]*τέρας οἰκίαν ἐ*|*ν Κολλυτῶι παρὰ τὸ* [*Ἰ*]*λ*[*ει*]*θυεῖ̣ο̣ν* (a house of Artemis Agrotera at Kollytos next to the shrine of Ilithyia); cf. Walbank 1983*a*, 118–19.

64 Walbank 1983*b*, 184–5, identifies the location of the properties listed in *Agora* XIX L9 ll. 23–60 as Northeastern Attica or Mesogaia; the former identification would

One last point is worth investigating. We have already more than once mentioned the series of sacred land leases that began in 343/2. This year falls in a period when the Athenian *fiscus* underwent a sequence of reforms with the aim of increasing both sacred and secular revenues,[65] and our leasing records have been justifiably thought to mark a reorganization of the relevant scheme.[66] Now, it was at some point in the 340s that the two boards of the Treasurers of Athena and of the Other Gods were again fused. The exact date of the merger has never been established on firm grounds, but the chronological proximity of this amalgamation with the leases of the estates of Athena and the Other Gods strongly suggests correlation.[67] In other words, the leasing record presupposes the fusion of the treasuries and, in fact, the two might have been components of the same legislative reform. If I am right, the latter would have been passed in 344/3 or early in 343/2. Building upon, but also modifying, a line of thought first introduced by Woodward,[68] I would suggest that such reforms might have been planned, at least to some extent, with the Great Panathenaia of 342/1 in mind, that is, the aim was to facilitate the celebration of the festival financially or otherwise.

3. THE SACRED PROPERTY OF THE ELEUSINIAN GODDESSES: ADMINISTRATIVE ASPECTS

For reasons beyond our comprehension, the Eleusinian sanctuary enjoyed a substantial degree of autonomy to the extent that a separate

gain credit, if one restored the divine owner in l. 1 as [Ἀπόλλωνος Ἀποτρο]παίου̣ (other restorations suggested by Walbank 1983*b*, 183–4 are contextually unconvincing), i.e. Apollo Apotropaios, who was of great importance in the Marathonian Tetrapolis (see now Lambert 2000*a*, 53–4; 2000*b*, 71–3).

65 Burke 1992, 203, 209; Lewis 1997, 212–21.

66 Cf. Leppin 1995, 566; Lambert 1997*a*, 287.

67 A point aptly noted by Lambert 1997*a*, 269 n. 204, who, nevertheless, did not pursue it further. Date of the amalgamation: 346/5 according to Woodward 1940, 404–6, followed by Linders 1975, 59–61, 101 n. 149; 342/1: Kirchner in the commentary of *IG* II^2 1455 (where he also took into consideration the archontic year 341/0); Ferguson 1932, 117 with n. 2 (but *Agora* XIX L6 should render such late dates out of the question).

68 Woodward 1940, 406: 'It is . . . likely . . . that such a change (i.e. the amalgamation) took place in a Panathenaic year'.

mechanism for its financial administration had to be invented by the Athenian polis. Already in the fifth century the Eleusinian Goddesses appear to have been the proprietors of substantial landed property which lay under the financial administration of the *epistatai*. This board, first created on the eve of the Peloponnesian War, pretty swiftly took over most of the responsibilities earlier held by the *hieropoioi*, including care of income and expenditure pertaining to the possessions, movable and immovable alike, of the Two Goddesses.[69] In financial accounts published around the time of the Peace of Nikias, the *epistatai* feature as collectors of rentals from land situated at Styra in Euboea.[70] Similarly, in 408/7 the same board received a substantial sum of 500 drachmas from the leasing of a *temenos* at Kythnos.[71] Now, since in the document from *c*.420 the *koinon* of the Kythnioi is attested as offering a contribution to the Eleusinian authorities, it is highly likely that the *temenos* at Kythnos is the latent source of funding in *IG* I^3 394.[72] At any rate, these two island estates do constitute a peculiar case, and it is certainly interesting that the other occasion when we find Styra and Kythnos coupled together is in the enumeration of the Greek fleet in the battle of Salamis, when Herodotus enigmatically notes that they were both Dryopian.[73] Be that as it may, as we have already seen, sacred estates

[69] See Busolt 1920, 501–2; Cavanaugh, 1996, 1–17; Samons II 2000, 166–7.

[70] *IG* I^3 394 l. 10: *[μίσθ]οσις Στυρόθ[εν]* (rental from Styra), and possibly *IG* I^3 392 l. 11: *τô κοινô μίσ[θοσις Στυρόθεν]* (from the *koinon* rental from Styra). If the connection between the two entries is sound, then the elusive *koinon* might be that of the Euboeans, for which see Larsen 1968, 97–103; Picard 1979, 205–51; Rhodes with Lewis 1997, 248–9). For the *temenos* at Styra see Smarczyk 1990, 130–2.

[71] *IG* I^3 386 l. 147 (with the new reading of Cavanaugh 1996, 102): 𐅅 *τε[μένος μίσ]θ̣οσιν ἐκ Κύθνο*: see Cavaignac 1908, 28–9; Kahrstedt 1934, 32; Raubitschek 1943, 35–6; Behrend 1970, 61; Davies 1981, 57; Garland 1984, 98; Smarczyk 1990, 129–30; Walbank 1991, 155; Faraguna 1992, 343. The identification of the sacred estate in question with a shrine of a female deity on the acropolis of Kythnos as suggested by Mazarakis-Ainian 1998, 371, is misconceived since it is based on an obsolete reading of the relevant line. Mitsopoulou 2005, 331–2 rightly observes that the location of the Kythnian *temenos* remains unknown. Clinton 2008, 60, follows Mazarakis-Ainian, but the *temenos* cannot be the same as the Kythnian shrine, even though the two were clearly administratively related.

[72] *IG* I^3 394 l. 7: *[παρὰ] Κυθνίο[ν τô κοινô]* ([from the koinon] of the Kythnians), with Lewis ad loc.; l. 8: *[παρὰ ?Κυθν]ίον τô κοινô*. If so, one should probably restore *IG* I^3 392 ll. 9–10, *[π|αρὰ Κυθ]νίον τô κο[ινô]*. Although Constantakopoulou 2007, 206–8, has now demonstrated that island *koina* were far from uncommon, this would still be our first testimony of a koinon of Kythnians.

[73] Hdt. 8.46: *Στυρέες δὲ τὰς αὐτὰς παρείχοντο νέας τάς καὶ ἐπ' Ἀρτεμισίῳ, Κύθνιοι δὲ μίαν καὶ πεντηκόντερον, ἐόντες συναμφότεροι οὗτοι Δρύοπες* (the Styrians provided

outside Attica supporting Athenian cults were not an uncommon phenomenon. At least with regard to the accounts of 408/7, the prominence of the rentals from the Kythnian *temenos* is easily explicable: after 413 the Peloponnesians had been plundering the Athenian countryside from their base at Dekeleia, and hence, somewhat ironically, it was easier for the Athenians to raise money from lands lying outside the Attic hinterland.[74] Interestingly, a recent survey of the acropolis of Kythnos has produced abundant ceramic evidence of Attic origin, and, what is more, evidence alluding to a sanctuary of Demeter Eleusinia. The cultic connection between Eleusis and Kythnos, as exemplified in the case of the Kythnian letting, seems to be deeply rooted.[75] Further realty generating income for the Eleusinian cult consists of the enigmatic stables (*ἱππῶνες*), which either nominally belonged to, or were rented out to, the Hero-Doctor,[76] as well as leased premises featuring in the same financial document.[77]

the same ships as at Artemision, the Kythnians one trireme and one penteconter: both these people are Dryopes); cf. Paus. 4.34.11: *εἰσὶ γὰρ καὶ οἱ Στυρεῖς Δρύοπες τὸ ἐξ ἀρχῆς . . . ἀλλὰ οἱ μὲν Στυρεῖς καλεῖσθαι Δρύοπες ὑπερφρονοῦσι* (The Styrians too are Dryopes in origin . . . yet they despise being called Dryopes), contra Thuc. 7.57.4: *καὶ τῶν μὲν ὑπηκόων καὶ φόρου ὑποτελῶν Ἐρετριῆς καὶ Χαλκιδῆς καὶ Στυρῆς καὶ Καρύστιοι ἀπ' Εὐβοίας ἦσαν . . . καὶ τὸ πλεῖστον Ἴωνες ὄντες οὗτοι πάντες καὶ ἀπ' Ἀθηναίων πλὴν Καρυστίων (οὗτοι δ' εἰσὶ Δρύοπες)*. The Herodotean connection was first noticed by Raubitschek 1943, 35, only to be dismissed as mere coincidence; thus also Smarczyk 1990, 131 n. 227.

74 On the contrary, Euboea had been lost to the Athenians already in 411 (Thuc. 8.95–6 with Gomme, Andrewes, and Dover 1981, 317–23, and Hornblower 2008, 1025–31) and, consequently, rentals from Styra would have ceased flowing into the Eleusinian purse.

75 See the study of Mitsopoulou 2005, especially 325–35.

76 *I.Eleusis* 23, ll. 1–2: - - - h*ιππόνον μί[σθοσις* | vacat]^{v} *τôι* h*έροι τôι ἰατ[ρôι]*. Walbank 1991, 154, and now Clinton 2008, 23, countenance the latter interpretation; cf. Spence 1993, 274 with n. 12. The connection between the two cults, though perplexing, seems to have been close, to judge from a similar entry in another fragment of Eleusinian accounts, i.e. *IG* I^3 393, ll. 3–4: *πα[ρὰ* . . . . . . 12 . . . . . .] *τô* h*έρο τô [ἰ]ατρô Φιλ[* - - -] | [.]*λο Ἐλευσιν[ίο καὶ συ]ναρχόντο[ν* etc.]. In my 2004 D.Phil. thesis I noted that the restoration *πα[ρὰ τôν ἐπιστατôν] τô* h*έρο τô [ἰ]ατρô Φιλ[ύ|λ]λο Ἐλευσιν[ίο καὶ συ]ναρχόντο[ν]* is very tempting by virtue of *IG* I^3 472 ll. 16–17, *παρὰ ταμιôν τôν ἄλλον θεô[ν]* | *[Φ]ιλύλλ[ο Ἐ]λευσ[ι]νίο* etc., where Philyllos appears to have been the chairman of the Treasurers of the Other Gods in 419/8. Clinton in *I.Eleusis* 37 has independently reached a similar albeit not identical conclusion proposing to read ll. 5–6 as *πα[ρὰ* . . . . . . 12 . . . . . .] *τ̣ô* h*έρο τô [ἰ]ατρô Φιλ[ύ|λ]λο Ἐλευσι̣[νίο* etc.]. Though it is difficult to see how the Eleusinian Goddesses would have been connected to the healing Hero, the involvement of Eleusinian authorities in the reception and establishent of the major healing-cult of Asklepios may suggest long-standing interaction between Demeter and Kore, on the one hand, and healing divinities, on the other; for the healing properties of Demeter in particular, see von Eickstedt 2001, 13–9 (but see Clinton 2008, 23, for further suggestions).

77 *IG* I^3 395 l. 5: [- - -] *οἰκεμάτον μίσθοσις*; it is not clear whether the preceding line (l. 4, *παρὰ κολακρετôν*) should be taken together with the entry

One specific piece of property deserves special treatment. The so-called Pelargikon constitutes one of the notorious enigmas of Athenian topography,[78] but its ownership status is no less enigmatic. Thucydides, for example, discusses the Pelargikon in the context of an oracle which ordained its uncultivability—a divine utterance overturned in, and by, the dire circumstances of the Peloponnesian War.[79] That the Pelargikon enjoyed a status of particular protection is known from the *Onomastikon* of Pollux, where the *paredroi* appear to impose a fine of three drachmas on transgressors upon the sacred precinct, and from Lampon's amendment to the decree of the first-fruits offered to the Eleusinian Goddesses, where the *basileus* was instructed to delineate the shrines within the Pelargikon and to forbid any quarrying activity within it.[80] It is widely held that the Pelargikon

under examination, that is whether the rentals from the houses had been handed down to the *epistatai* by the *kolakretai*. Strictly speaking, it is not impossible and, if so, on the basis of the identification of the *kolakretai* as the administrators of the *δημόσιον*, the public (i.e. secular) purse of Athens (so Samons 2000, 54–70; cf. Faraguna 1992, 178), the edifices in question might have been secular, not sacred property. Conversely, as Samons 2000, 57–8, acknowledges, our evidence suggests that the *kolakretai* might have been handling sacred funds as well (cf. Matthaiou 1989, 9; 13–16; 1990–1*b*, 184–9, who, on the basis of an exhaustive analysis of the relevant evidence, made a strong case for the *kolakretai* having originally held a religious office). Everything seems too uncertain to allow us unambiguous conclusions.

[78] Travlos 1971, 52–6, 91, 93, 127; Camp 1984.

[79] Thuc. 2.17.1: *τό τε Πελαργικὸν καλούμενον τὸ ὑπὸ τὴν ἀκρόπολιν, ὃ καὶ ἐπάρατόν τε ἦν μὴ οἰκεῖν καί τι καὶ Πυθικοῦ μαντείου ἀκροτελεύτιον τοιόνδε διεκώλυε, λέγον ὡς 'τὸ Πελαργικὸν ἀργὸν ἄμεινον,' ὅμως ὑπὸ τῆς παραχρῆμα ἀνάγκης ἐξῳκήθη* (And the area called Pelargikon, below the Acropolis, which was under a curse against occupation, and the final part of some oracle from Delphi likewise banned this by saying, 'The Pelargikon is better left unused', was occupied nevertheless under the pressure of the emergency; trans. by Lattimore 1998); see Gomme 1956, 63–5; Parker 1983, 164 with n. 115; Hornblower 1991, 269–70; Rubel 2000, 137–9.

[80] Poll. *Onom.* 8.101: *πάρεδροι οὗτοι . . . οὗτοι γὰρ παρεφύλαττον μή τις ἐντὸς τοῦ Πελασγικοῦ κείρει ἢ † καταπλέα ἢ ἐξορύττει, καὶ τῷ ἄρχοντι παρεδίδοσαν. τὸ δὲ τίμημα ἦν τρεῖς δραχμαὶ καὶ ἁπλοῦν τὸ βλάβος*, with Judeich 1931, 119 n. 1 and Gomme 1956, 63, who rightly argue that the triviality of the fine points towards the Archaic period; *IG* I^3 78 ll. 54–9: *τὸν δὲ βασ[ι]λέα* h*ορίσαι τὰ* h*ιερὰ τὰ ἐν τ[ô]|ι Πελαργικôι, καὶ τὸ λοιπὸν μὲ ἐν*h*ιδρύεσθαι βομὸς ἐν τôι Πελα|ργικôι ἄνευ τε̂ς βολε̂ς καὶ τô δέμο, μεδὲ τὸς λίθος τέμνεν ἐκ τô [Π]|ελαργικô, μεδὲ γε̂ν ἐχσάγεν μεδὲ λίθος. ἐὰν δέ τις παραβαίνει*^{v} | *τ⁝⁝οῦτον τι, ἀποτινέτο πεντακοσίας δραχμάς, ἐσαγγελλέτο δὲ* h|[o] *βασιλεὺς ἐς τὲν βολέν* (The *basileus* shall delimit the sanctuaries in the Pelargikon, and in the future altars shall not be erected in the Pelargikon without the consent of the Boule and the People, nor shall anyone cut stones out of the Pelargikon or

lay under the administration of the Eleusinian authorities for the following reasons: it was located near the urban Eleusinion; its protection was specifically regulated in the rider to the decree of the first-fruits referred to above; and it was probably the disputed area controlled by the Kerykes mentioned in Telemachos' foundation inscription of the Asklepieion.[81] However, the case for a link with Eleusis is only circumstantial. In other words, each testimony taken in isolation fails to provide a sound case for the Eleusinian ownership of the Pelargikon. At any rate, after the end of the fifth century the Pelargikon historically becomes a non-entity.

For most of the fourth century our knowlege of land administered by the Eleusinian officials is seriously defective, despite the fact that the cult seems to have flourished continuously. Early in the period Demeter and Kore owned sacred property located at Thorikos,[82] and towards the middle of the century the edges of the Sacred Orgas were consecrated to the Eleusinian duo. It is conceivable that the boundary stone *IG* II^2 2605 designated this area, but given that it was found in excavations at Eleusis it probably marked one of the sacred estates of Demeter (and Kore).[83] It is only with the famous Eleusinian accounts *IG* II^2 1672 (*I.Eleusis* 177) that we are allowed a more thorough glimpse of Eleusinian realty. As aptly noticed by Rhodes, the leasing of the *μισθώματα* in *IG* II^2 1672 was carried out by the *basileus* in cooperation with the *πάρεδροι*, the *ἐπιστάται Ἐλευσινόθεν*, and the *ἐπιμεληταὶ τῶν μυστηρίων*, a surprisingly extended board of lessors which certainly underscores the peculiarity of the transactions in

remove soil or stones. If anyone transgresses any of these regulations, he shall be fined five hundred drachmas and impeached by the *basileus* before the Boule; trans. by Fornara 1983, no. 140); cf. Keramopoullos 1934/5, 90–5; Travlos 1939/41, 60; Aleshire 1989, 8–9. Self-evidently, the *basileus* would have had jurisdiction over the Pelargikon in the Archaic period as well—if that is the era that Pollux' information derives from—since the *paredroi* were his assistants (themselves an archaic institution; cf. Rhodes 1993, 622).

[81] So Travlos 1971, 127; Fornara 1983, 163 suggests a mythological connection via Pelarge, daughter of Potneus.

[82] *IG* II^2 2600 (= *IG* I^3 869; cf. *SEG* XXXII 231): hόρος | τεμένους | τοῖν θεοῖν (boundary of the *temenos* of the Two Goddesses), if this is indeed an estate marker and not one of a shrine; cf. Dinsmoor 1982, 451–2.

[83] *IG* II^2 2605, now published as *I.Eleusis* 676 (ḥόρ̣ος | τεμένου[ς | Δ]ήμητρος) by Clinton, who tentatively suggests the date 375–350; idem 2008, 426, prudently notes that the stone marked not the shrine but sacred (landed) property, even suggesting the Rharian Field.

question.[84] Although the exact status of these *μισθώματα* remains textually ambiguous, they were probably rentals from *temene* and/or other types of realty owned by the Eleusinian Goddesses, just like those attested in the fifth century.[85] But for the time being it suffices to keep in mind that the income discussed here was to be spent on the celebration of the Great Mysteries.

That the *basileus* was one of the leasing agents could derive either from his overall responsibility for the *temene*, or from his special connection to the Eleusinian Mysteries.[86] In 352/1 he would have been in charge of letting out the *ἱερὰ ὀργάς* in the interest of Demeter and Kore, had the green light been given by the Delphic oracle.[87] The *paredroi* (*πάρεδροι*) of *IG* II² 1672 (*I.Eleusis* 177) must have been the two assistants of the *basileus* who, in curiously undemocratic fashion, were appointed by their own superior.[88] Since their functions could

[84] *I.Eleusis* 177 (*IG* II² 1672) ll. 370–6: [*εἰς μυστήρια*] | *τὰ μεγάλα ἔδωκαν ταμίαιν τοῖν θεοῖν οὐ μερισ[άν]των τῶ[ν ἀποδεκτῶν...... [12] ......μισθωμάτων]*, | *ἃ ἐμίσθωσεν ὁ βασιλεὺς καὶ οἱ πάρεδροι καὶ οἱ ἐ[πι]στάται οἱ [Ἐ]λε[υσινόθεν καὶ οἱ ἐπιμεληταὶ τῶν]* | *μυστηρίων, Εὐθυκράτης Δρακοντίδου Ἀφιδναῖ, Κ[α]λλικράτης Κ[α]λλι[κρατίδου Στειρι..*[c.3]*.· εἰς μυσ]*||*τήρια τὰ μεγάλα ἐπ Ἀριστοφάνους ἄρχοντος μισθ[ω]μάτων, ὧν ὁ βασιλε[ὺς καὶ οἱ πάρεδροι καὶ οἱ ἐπι]*|*στάται οἱ Ἐλευσινόθεν καὶ οἱ ἐπιμεληταὶ τῶν μυ[σ]τηρίων ἐμίσθωσαν [ἔδωκεν ταμίαιν τοῖν θεοῖν]* | *Αἰσχύλος Ἱππίσκου Παιονίδης ΗΗΔΔ οὐ μερισάντ[ω]ν τῶν ἀποδεκτῶν*, with Rhodes 1993, 556; cf. Faraguna 1992, 343.

[85] I note that Clinton 2008, 225, has now put forward a novel interpretation, according to which the *μισθώματα* were 'not rents...but salaries or the price of contracts for services at the Mysteries', and that Aischylos, Euthykrates, and Kallikrates were private donors. In view of the presence of the *basileus* in particular, I cling to my interpretation below. For relevant evidence see *I.Délos* 95 l. 9: [*μισθ*]*ώματα ἐκ τῶ[ν τεμενῶν τῶν ἐν Ῥηνείαι]*; *μίσθωμα* is the standard term for 'rent' in the Delian *ἱερὰ συγγραφή* (*I.Délos* 503), which was probably influenced by Athenian practices (see below, p. 60).

[86] *Basileus* and the Mysteries: [Lys.] 6.4: *φέρε γάρ, ἐὰν νυνὶ Ἀνδοκίδης ἀθῷος ἀπαλλαγῇ* <*δι’*> *ὑμᾶς ἐκ τοῦδε τοῦ ἀγῶνος καὶ ἔλθῃ κληρωσόμενος τῶν ἐννέα ἀρχόντων καὶ λάχῃ βασιλεύς, ἄλλο τι ἢ ὑπὲρ ὑμῶν καὶ θυσίας θύσει καὶ εὐχὰς εὔξεται κατὰ τὰ πάτρια, τὰ μὲν ἐν τῷ ἐνθάδε Ἐλευσινίῳ, τὰ δὲ ἐν τῷ Ἐλευσῖνι ἱερῷ, καὶ τῆς ἑορτῆς ἐπιμελήσεται μυστηρίοις, ὅπως ἂν μηδεὶς ἀδικῇ μηδὲ ἀσεβῇ περὶ τὰ ἱερά*; (Imagine that today, on account of yourselves, Andocides departs unscathed from this trial, and goes to draw lots as one of the Nine Archons, and is chosen as *basileus*: will he do anything else but conduct sacrifices and offer prayers according to ancestral custom, partly at the Eleusinion here, and partly at the sanctuary at Eleusis? and take charge of the festival of the Mysteries, responsible for ensuring that nobody commits a crime or acts impiously towards the sacred rites?); see Todd 2007, 415, 442–3.

[87] See Appendix I.

[88] Arist. [*Ath. Pol.*] 56.1. For a comprehensive treatment of the *πάρεδροι* see Kapparis 1998, 383–93. As Dow 1976, 80–1 and 84 has pointed out, their obligation to undergo audit (*εὔθυναι*) implies that they handled funds of some sort.

hardly have been restricted to the administration of the Eleusinion, there is a good chance that the *paredroi* helped the *basileus* with the leasing of other *temene* as well. Nevertheless, in the case of the Eleusinian *μισθώματα*, the involvement of the *paredroi* could well be the byproduct of their task of helping the *basileus* with the organization of the Mysteries. A late fourth-century decree of the genos of Kerykes bestows honours upon a certain Euthydemos, a *paredros* to the *basileus*, for having taken care of the Mysteries amongst other things, and it is legitimate to assume that the honorand's *ἐπιμέλεια περὶ τὰ μυστήρια* had something to do with the leasing of the *temene*.[89] As for the *ἐπιμεληταὶ τῶν μυστηρίων*, we know that they were four, two elected from the Assembly and two from the ranks of the Eumolpidai and the Kerykes respectively. According to our current state of knowledge, they seem to have been first established in a law concerning the Mysteries from just before the mid-fourth century, an invaluable, but sadly fragmentary, text which contained a clause prescribing general supervision of the Mysteries by the *ἐπιμεληταί*, followed by more specific instructions about the imposition of fines on misbehaving initiates.[90] The collaboration of the *ἐπιμεληταὶ τῶν μυστηρίων* with the other officials

[89] *IG* II² 1230. The inscription is now assigned by Tracy 1995, 139 to the Cutter of *IG* II² 1262, whose activity stretches from *c.*320 to *c.*296.

[90] *Agora* XVI no. 56 (*I.Eleusis* 138), esp. ll. 29–31: *κα[ὶ τὸς ἐπιμελητὰ]ς χρὴ ἐπιμελε̂σθαι τῆς ἑορτῆς τοῖν Θ̣[εο]ῖν [μετὰ τô βασιλέως καὶ διοικε̂|ν τ]ὰ Μυστήρια κατὰ τὰ πάτρια μετὰ το[ύτου καὶ Εὐμολ]πιδῶν καὶ Κηρύκων· προσαιρε̂σθα̣ι δὲ [τ]ὸ̣ν δ[ῆμον ἐπιμελητὰς δύο περὶ τὴ|ν] ἑ̣ο̣ρτὴν ἐξ Ἀθηναίων ἁπάντων ἐκ τῶν ὑ̣[πὲρ τριάκοντα] ἔτη γεγονότων καὶ Κηρύκων ἕνα καὶ [Εὐ]μολπιδ[ῶν ἕνα]* (And the *epimeletai* must supervise the festival of the Two Goddesses with the *basileus*, and must administer the Mysteries according to the ancient customs, with the *basileus* again and with the *Eumolpidai* and the *Kerykes*. And let the people elect in addition two *epimeletai* in charge of the festival from all the Athenians who are older than thirty years, and one *epimeletes* from the ranks of the Eumolpidai and another one from the ranks of the Kerykes), with Clinton 1980, 272, 280–2 (cf. Arist. [*Ath. Pol.*] 57.1: *[ὁ] δὲ βασιλεὺς πρῶτον μὲν μυστηρίων ἐπιμελεῖ[ται μετὰ τῶν ἐπιμελητῶν ὃ]ν ὁ δῆμ[ος χ]ειροτονεῖ, δύο μὲν ἐξ Ἀθηναίων ἁπάντων, ἕνα δ' [ἐξ Εὐμολπιδῶν, ἕνα] δ' ἐκ Κηρ[ύκω]ν* (The *basileus* is first responsible for the Mysteries, in conjunction with the overseers elected by the people—two from all Athenians, one from the *Eumolpidai*, one from the Kerykes), with Rhodes 1993, 636–7); see also Garland 1984, 116–17. The *terminus ante quem* for the introduction of the office is 347, as inferred from Dem. 21.171: *ὑμεῖς γάρ, ὦ ἄνδρες Ἀθηναῖοι, ἐχειροτονήσατε τοῦτον . . . καὶ μυστηρίων ἐπιμελητήν* (for it was you, men of Athens, who elected him . . . superintendent of the Mysteries); cf. MacDowell 1990, 389–90.

mentioned above in the leasing of the *temene* further emphasizes the central importance of the latter for the financing of the Eleusinian rites. Overall, it is a fair guess that the mid-fourth-century regulations of the Mysteries would have contained clauses concerning the *μισθώματα* of the Two Goddesses, but its fragmentary condition allows nothing but speculation.

Finally, the presence of the *epistatai* amongst the lessors of the Eleusinian temene suggests continuity, as far as the leasing aspect of Eleusinian finances is concerned. They issued the accounts of *IG* II^2 1672 (*I.Eleusis* 177) in conjunction with the Treasurers of the Two Goddesses, but strikingly it is only the *epistatai* who feature as lessors of the sacred landholdings, whereas the Treasurers stand merely at the receiving end of the transaction.[91] What differentiates the *epistatai* from the other magistrates involved in the leasing process is the former's overall supervision of the finances of the Eleusinian cult. Whereas the *ἐπιμεληταὶ τῶν μυστηρίων* were concerned with a very specific and chronologically confined aspect of the Eleusinian cult, as were the *basileus* and the *paredroi*, the *epistatai* were in fact the primary financial administrators of the Eleusinion, functioning for a continuous period of four years. It is worth noting that the *ἐπιστάται* provide the only trace of continuity between the fifth and fourth centuries as far as the land-leasing scheme is concerned. Thus, their collection of rentals from *temene* outside Attica should be seen against the background of their obligation to supervise the yearly income (*ἐπέτεια*) of the Two Goddesses, as stipulated in the so-called *epistatai*-decree; we can plausibly infer that the *ἐπέτεια* included sacred rentals as well.[92] At the lower chronological limit, the Eleusinian accounts of 329/8 are the last substantial piece of information we have about leasing of real property owned by the Two Goddesses. The partly, but plausibly, restored phrase *τὴν μίσθ[ωσιν]* of *IG* II^2 1551 (line 5) might indicate that the practice of leasing *temene* in the

[91] Cf. Busolt 1920, 501–2.

[92] *IG* I^3 32 ll. 20–2: *ἐπιμελêσθαι* (sc. *τòς ἐπιστάτας*) *δὲ καὶ τôν ἐπετε|ίον hà λαμβάνεται ṭοῖ[ν θ]εοῖν καὶ ἐάν τι* | *[ἀ]πολολòς πυνθάνονται [ἀ]νασόι[ζε]ν* (the *epistatai* shall take charge also of the annual income received by the Two Goddesses, and if they find out that anything is missing they shall recover it); cf. Kourouniotes 1932, 184. Clinton 2008, 54 also includes rentals amongst ordinary sources of yearly income of the Eleusinian cult, and ascribes their supervision to the *epistatai*.

context of the Eleusinian cult was still going on at the beginning of the third century.[93]

The handling of the *μισθώματα* in *IG* II² 1672 (*I.Eleusis* 177) constitutes a good example of allocation of funds for specific purposes, of the type encountered in the Law on the Lesser Panathenaia. The rentals were meant to cover outlay for the annually celebrated *Great Mysteries*. Now, an interesting point, and so far not commented on, is the clause *οὐ μερισάντων τῶν ἀποδεκτῶν*.[94] The normal practice was that of revenues ending up in the hands of the *apodektai* and thereafter allocated by them to designated officials, and, although *IG* II² 1672 (*I.Eleusis* 177) indicates that the rentals were paid directly to the Treasurers of the Two Goddesses, it is obvious that this is a peculiar case of divergence from the regular procedure, even more so because the payment under consideration was recorded under the entries of the tenth prytany, not of the ninth one in accordance with the regular procedure attested by pseudo-Aristotle.[95] Here, it has to be clarified that, contrary to the often repeated assertion of many modern scholars, the individuals attested as handing in rentals, namely Euthykrates, Kallikrates, and Aischylos, were not members of the Eleusinian personnel, but the actual payers of the elusive *μισθώματα*.[96] The most plausible interpretation seems to be that on the eve of the *Great Mysteries* an urgent need for cash arose that had to be met by curtailing the time-consuming involvement of the *apodektai* and, therefore, an agreement was reached that the lessees would disburse the rental directly to the Treasurers.

The accounts under consideration are a good reminder of the intricate realities underlying sacred finances and, more specifically, land administration. Thus, apart from the *μισθώματα* which, as demonstrated, concerned only a limited and very specific economic

[93] However, Clinton 2008, 165, has now suggested (contra Kirchner) that the fragment in question (*I.Eleusis* 164), as well as other similar, could not possibly postdate the end of the Classical period. Moreover, his interpretation of the inscription as a contract seems to militate against the view taken here.

[94] *IG* II² 1672 ll. 241–2, 246–7.

[95] Arist. [*Ath. Pol.*] 48.1–2, with Rhodes 1993, 559–60.

[96] The right interpretation is that of Kirchner in the commentary of *IG* (so also Davies in *APF*, pp. 7–8); see also Appendix VII: Catalogue, nos. 2; 27; 36. Clinton 2008, 225, aptly observes that 'parallel structure demands that Eythykrates and Kallikrates not be taken in apposition with *ἐπιμεληταὶ τῶν μυστηρίων*', though, as mentioned above, he considers them private donors.

aspect of the Eleusinian cult, we hear of the letting of the so-called ʻ*Ραρία* (Rharia) to none other than the famous Athenian orator Hypereides.[97] The Rharia, alternatively known as the ʻ*Ράριον πεδίον* (Rharian field), constitutes a most peculiar case.[98] Mythologically it was considered the first field on earth to have been sown with cereals and Pausanias transmits the information about sacrificial cakes being made from grain grown in the holy field of Triptolemos.[99] From a scholion on Pindar's *9th Olympian Ode* as well as from Aelius Aristeides we learn that the prize for the victors of the Eleusinian games was barley.[100] The missing link between these two titbits of information is to be traced in *IG* II^2 1672 (*I.Eleusis* 177); the prize was, in fact, a portion of the produce from the ʻ*Ραρία*.[101] It is noteworthy that the Eleusinia were thought to be the most ancient among the gymnastic contests,[102] which seems to confirm the belief that the ʻ*Ραρία* itself was of considerable antiquity, perhaps even the

[97] *I.Eleusis* 177 (*IG* II^2 1672), ll. 381–3: [*μισθω(τὴς)*] | ʻ*Ραρίας* ʻ*Υπερείδης Γλαυκίππου Κολλυ· παρὰ τούτου ἐλάβομεν μίσθωσιν μεδίμνω*[*ν κρι* 𐅅HΔΠIIII *ἐτῶν*] | *τεττάρων, γίγνονται μέδιμνοι ΧΧΗΗΗΗ*𐅄*ΔΔΠ*I; cf. Garland 1984, 96; Burford 1993, 22.

[98] Cf. Kern 1914.

[99] Chronicum Parium: *IG* XII (5) 444 ll. 24–5; *ἀφ' οὗ Τριπτό*[*λεμος πρῶτος* | *καρπὸν*] *ἔσπειρεν ἐν τῆι ʻΡαρίαι καλουμένηι Ἐλευσῖνι, ἔτη Χ*[*Η*]*ΔΔΔΔΠ*, *βασιλεύοντος Ἀθηνῶν* [*Ἐριχθέως*]; Paus. 1.38.6; *τὸ δὲ πεδίον τὸ ʻΡάριον σπαρῆναι πρῶτον λέγουσι καὶ πρῶτον αὐξῆσαι καρπούς, καὶ διὰ τοῦτο οὐλαῖς ἐξ αὐτοῦ χρῆσθαί σφισι καὶ ποιεῖσθαι πέμματα ἐς τὰς θυσίας καθέστηκεν* (They say that the plain called Rharion was the first to be sown and the first to grow crops, and for this reason it is the custom to use sacrificial barley and to make cakes for the sacrifices from its produce; trans. by Jones 1918); see Mylonas 1961, 14, 21; Brumfield 1981, 172.

[100] Schol. Pind. *Ol.* 9,150b: *ἄγεται δὲ αὐτόθι* (sc. *Ἐλευσῖνι*) *ἀγὼν Κόρης καὶ Δήμητρος, ὃς καλεῖται Ἐλευσίνια· οὗ ἔπαθλον κριθαί*; Aristid. *Or.* 22.4: *ἀγῶνά τε γυμνικὸν γενέσθαι πρῶτον Ἐλευσῖνι τῆς Ἀττικῆς καὶ τὸ ἆθλον εἶναι τοῦ καρποῦ τοῦ φανθέντος*; cf. Deubner 1932, 91–2; Simms 1975, 272–4; Brumfield 1981, 185.

[101] See the enumeration of the Eleusinian prizes in *I.Eleusis* 177 (*IG* II^2 1672), ll. 388–90: *εἰς τὴν πεντετηρίδα τ*[*ῶν Ἐλ*]*ε*[*υσινίων εἰς*] | *τὸν γυμνικὸν ἀγῶνα καὶ τῆς μουσικῆς καὶ τῆς ἱπποδρομία<ς> καὶ τοῦ πατρίου μέδιμνοι* [. . . . C.8 . . . .] | *εἰς τὴν ἱπποδρομίαν τὴν προστεθεῖσαν κατὰ ψήφισμα ἆθλα μέδιμνοι* 𐅄*ΔΔ*, which directly follows the clause concerning the offering of the rentals from the ʻ*Ραρία* (cf. Simms 1975, 269; Clinton 1979, 9–12). Foucart 1884, 200 duly observed the similarity between the sacred crop from the ʻ*Ραρία* and the oil from the sacred olive-trees (*μορίαι*) being offered as prizes to the victors of the festivals of Eleusinia and Panathenaia respectively.

[102] Arist. fr. 637 (Rose): *ἐνδοξόταται πάντων οἱ κατὰ τὴν ʻΕλλάδα ἀγῶνες· καὶ μὴν τούτων πρεσβύτατος ὁ τῶν Παναθηναίων, εἰ δὲ βούλει ὁ τῶν Ἐλευσινίων. ἡ τάξις τῶν ἀγώνων καθὰ Ἀριστοτέλης ἀναγράφεται· πρῶτα μὲν τὰ Ἐλευσίνια διὰ τὸν καρπὸν τῆς Δήμητρος*; see also Aristid. *Or.* 22.4 (supra, n. 100). For the Eleusinia in general, see Simms 1975 and Brumfield 1981, 182–95.

oldest among all sacred landholdings to be found in Attica. Its antiquity is also reflected in the primitivist financial strategy whereby the rental from the sacred field was paid in kind, rather than in cash.[103] At least its sacredness should be considered indisputable. Whereas the attempt to investigate the sacred status of landholdings leased out with the aim of subsidizing cultic activity sometimes runs the risk of circular conceptualization, the *῾Ραρία* provides a first-rate illustration of the point in question. On top of the unambiguous literary evidence for that, our Eleusinian accounts mention a remuneration made to two individuals, the first a metic who undertook to remove a corpse—a source of the most abhorrent pollution—from the *῾Ραρία*, and the second an unidentified person, but probably some sacred official, who subsequently purified the field by sacrificing a piglet.[104]

From the preceding discussion it will have become clear how important a proportion of income land administration provided to the Eleusinian shrines—a predictable inference regarding a primarily agricultural cult—and yet, this picture is severely distorted by an unfortunate happenstance, namely the non-preservation of the income-and-expenditure accounts of the ninth prytany of 329/8.[105] The significance of this loss is owing to the fact that rentals from polis *temene* were normally paid in the penultimate prytany of the civic year. However, one is forced to pose the question: did Eleusinian property receive the same administrative treatment as the *temene* mentioned by [Aristotle]? From this perspective, it is certainly

[103] However, payments in kind are found in the early Hellenistic *Tabulae Heracleenses*; cf. Ampolo 1992. And certain scholars (e.g. Walbank 1983*d*, 217–18) believe that the divine owners of the properties recorded in *Agora* XIX L10 had some share in the produce (*ὡραῖα*).

[104] *I.Eleusis* 177 (*IG* II^2 1672), ll. 181–2: *νέκυν ἀνελόντι ἐκ τῆς ῾Ραρίας μισθὸς Νίκωνι Ἐλευσῖνι οἰκοῦ* | [.· *τῶι κα*]*θήραντι τὴν ῾Ραρίαν, χοίρου τιμὴ* [:ΔΔ⊢]; (salary for Nikon who resides at Eleusis for picking up the corpse from the *Rharia*, and for purifying the Rharia, price of the piglet 21 drachmas), with Clinton 2005, 170, and idem 2008, 209; for death as a source of pollution see the thorough analysis by Parker 1983, 32–48, esp. 33 ('death within the temple is sacrilege'), who, strangely, misses our text. The most illustrious case of purification from death-related *miasma* is of course that of Delos (Thuc. 3.104.1–2); cf. the ban on burials within the sacred lands of Herakleia in *IG* XIV 645 l.137: *οὐδὲ τοφιῶνας ἐν τᾶι* h*ιαρᾶι γᾶι ποιήσει* (And he will not construct tombs within the sacred land). It is noteworthy that the removal of the cadaver from the *῾Ραρία* was carried out by a foreigner, presumably because no Athenians would be williing to expose themselves to pollution by touching the dead body.

[105] According to Kirchner in *IG*, we only have at our disposal the concluding—and very badly damaged—lines of the entry of that prytany, i.e. *IG* II^2 1672 ll. 214–15 (*I.Eleusis* 177 ll. 343–4).

remarkable that in the series of mass sacred leases from 343/2 onwards *temene* belonging to the two Goddesses are absent, an omission that the most recent editor of the texts felt inclined to discard as random.[106] But there is little plausibility in the theory that Eleusinian property would have been centrally administered along with that belonging to Athena and the Other Gods. With the exception of a *paradosis* of temple equipment by the Treasurers of the Other Gods to the Eleusinian *epistatai* in 363/2 (a transaction not devoid of interpretative riddles itself), we have virtually no other trace of concurrent jurisdiction of those two committees.[107] What is more, at least some of the temene mentioned in *IG* II^2 1672 (*I.Eleusis* 177) had been leased out in 331/0. But since the Agora sacred leases commenced in 343/2 and given that a decennial renewal is generally accepted to have applied to them, the Eleusinian leaseholds of 331/0 cannot be brought together with those of 343/2. The inference is inescapable: even if leasing of Eleusinian property was carried out by the *basileus* in a fashion similar to that described by [Aristotle], as our imperfect evidence indicates, the relevant scheme was separate from that concerning *temene* owned by other state-divinities, at a stage earlier than that of *merismos*, and actually as early as the leasing auction itself.

[106] Walbank 1983*d*, 229 acknowledges, however, some of the implications emanating from *I.Eleusis* 177 (*IG* II^2 1672); Faraguna 1992, 343 n. 28 observes that Walbank's hypothesis is 'alletantte, ma non solidamente fondata'.

[107] *I.Eleusis* 140 (*IG* II^2 1541), ll. 2–6: *τάδε παρέδωκε Λεπτίνης ἐκ Κοί τοῖς ταμίαις τῶν | ἄλλων θεῶν Χαιρεστράτωι Κολλυτεῖ καὶ συνά[ρ]|χουσι ἐπὶ Χαρικλείδου ἄρχοντος, οἱ δὲ ταμία[ι] | τοῖς ἐπιστάταις Ἀμφικτύονι Ἀφιδναίωι καὶ συνά|ρχουσι* (Leptines of Koile handed the following things over to the treasurers of the Other Gods, Chairestratos and his colleagues, and the treasurers handed them over to the superintendents, Amphiktyon of Aphidnai and his colleagues); see Linders 1975, 51, 60; Cavanaugh 1996, 9–11 (a major problem, of course, is to establish the constitutional role of Leptines, an otherwise well-known Athenian with a series of liturgies in his record; cf. Lehner 1890, 94; *APF* 9046). Note, however, that Clinton 1984, 58–60, has argued *e silentio* for a temporary abolition of the board of the *epistatai* between *c*.406 and 360, and a subsequent takeover of Eleusinian financial administration by the Treasurers of Athena and the Other Gods (contra Ferguson 1932, 94 n. 2, who argued, incorrectly, for shared jurisdiction pre-dating 408/7). Clinton 2008, 125–6, has now elaborated on this theory. The validity of Clinton's claim does not affect my argument concerning the state of affairs in 343/2, but it could explain the absence of evidence concerning Eleusinian realty before the Sacred Orgas affair in 352/1.

4. THE NEW POLIS-GODS AS PROPRIETORS OF REALTY

Despite the ostensible religious conservatism of Athens vis-à-vis imported gods, we now know that the Athenians were actually much more tolerant hosts of foreign cults than they professed themselves to be.[108] Some new divinities, however, came onto the scene too late to be brought into the administrative scheme which regulated the cults of the Other Gods. As a result their functions came under the effective administration of separate authorities. For the purposes of our discussion two such cults ought to be singled out, namely those of Asklepios and Amphiaraos.

At the beginning of the fourth century the Athenian assembly passed a decree instructing the *epimeletai* of the Asklepieion in the Piraeus to employ rental from the quarry of the god in order to provide for the preliminary sacrifices performed by the priest of Asklepios.[109] It is not obvious from the text when the quarry had come under the administration of the Asklepian officials, but there is scope to relate it to information deriving from a much later document. In *SEG* XXVI 121 (usually known, rather incongruously, as the decree for the restoration of Attic sanctuaries) one reads: *καὶ ψ̣ι̣λ̣ὰ̣ τὰ προσόντα τῶι Ἀσκληπιείωι τὰ ἀνεθέν|[τα - - - - - - - - τ]ῆς π̣όλ̣ε̣ω̣ς̣ [....8....] τ̣ο̣ῦ. ἄ̣[γο]ν̣τ̣ο̣ς̣ ἐ̣ν̣ τ̣ῶ̣ι̣ Π̣ε̣λ̣ο̣π̣ο̣ν̣νησιακῶι πολέμωι καὶ τὸ προσόν* (ll. 40–1). Now, the consistent topographical format of the decree makes it clear that we are dealing here with property situated at Piraeus, and, consequently, the Asklepieion meant is that of the port, not its urban counterpart.[110] It is also obvious that the properties at stake were consecrated at some point during the Peloponnesian

[108] See Garland 1992; Parker 1996, 152–87; Rubel 2000, 233–61.

[109] *IG* II^2 47 ll. 28–31: *ἐψηφίσθαι τῶι δήμωι τοὺς ἐπιστάτας τοῦ Ἀσκ|ληπιείο θύεν τὰ προθύματα ἃ ἐξηγεῖται [Εὐ]θύδη|μος ἀπὸ τοῦ ἀργυρίο τô ἐκ τô λιθοτομε̣[ί]ο̣ [τοῦ] θ̣|[ε]ô ἐξαιρομένο* (The People voted; the *epistatai* of the Asklepieion shall sacrifice the preliminary victims, which Euthydemos expounds, with money set aside from the God's quarry). The restoration of lines 29–30 is mine; *ἐκ τô λιθοτομε[ί]ο̣ [τô ν]ο[τ|ί]ο* (from the southern quarry) Wilamowitz at *IG*; *ἐκ τô λιθοτομε[ί]ο̣ [ἐκτ]|ὸ[ς τ]ô ἐξαιρομένο* (money from the quarry bar exempted money) Wilhelm 1942, 124–8). For the transaction here see Ampolo 1982, 252–5; Osborne 1985*a*, 104; Faraguna 1992, 342; von Eickstedt 2001, 23–7; Rhodes & Osborne 2003, 403.

[110] For the topographical format of *SEG* XXVI 121 see Culley 1977, 285–7; cf. Aleshire 1989, 35.

War,[111] and, although only ψ̣ι̣λ̣ά̣ (tillable lands) are explicitly mentioned, it is not inconceivable that the quarry of *IG* II^2 47 might also have been consecrated at the same time. The second piece of evidence concerning realty owned by Asklepios is the dedicatory inscription *IG* II^2 4969. According to this document, an unnamed god—in all likelihood Delphian Apollo—delivered an oracle whereby Demon of Paiania was to be appointed priest of Asklepios on the condition that he consecrated his house and the adjacent garden to the god. Here again the whole process had the official sanction of the Athenian assembly. The obvious inference is that Demon's consecrated properties were to be leased out to yield cultic income.[112] There are, however, some as yet unsolvable problems concerning the issue at stake. One is the date of the inscription, given that Asklepios' priesthoods have long been understood to operate in the official tribal order. Since the tribal cycles can be more or less determined the alternatives would be either 350/49 or 330/29.[113] The second, related, problem is the possible connection of our dedication to a cryptic mention of the *συνοικία* (tenement) of a certain Demon in Aeschines' *Against Timarchos*.[114] If that *συνοικία* could be identified with the *κῆπος* and *οἰκία* of the dedication, Aeschines' speech would provide a convenient *terminus ante quem* (346/5), but this theory presupposes that Demon is in both cases one and the same person, which is far from

[111] In fact Culley's restoration does not seem intelligible. I would tentatively supplement [*ἐπὶ . . .* ^{5}..] *τ̣ο̣υ̣ ἄ̣[ρχο]ν̣τ̣ο̣ς̣ ἐ̣ν̣ τ̣ῶ̣ι̣ Π̣ε̣λ̣ο̣π̣ο̣ν̣νησιακῶι πολέμωι* (when [. . . . ..]tos was archon at the time of the Peloponnesian War). Even the ending -*τ̣ο̣υ̣* for the archon's name is not certain; the termination might have been -*ι̣ο̣υ̣*, for instance, but Culley 1975 provides no *apparatus criticus* to indicate what traces of the letters read by him are preserved on the stone. If my suggestion is correct, one has to look for an archon between 420 (introduction of Asklepios' cult in Athens) and 404/3 (end of the Peloponnesian War).

[112] *IG* II^2 4969: [*ὁ*] *θεὸς ἔχρησεν τῶι δήμωι τῶι Ἀθην[αίων ἀναθεῖναι | τ]ὴν οἰκίαν τὴν Δήμωνος καὶ τὸν κῆ[πον τὸν προσόντα] | τῶι Ἀσκληπιῶι καὶ αὐτὸν Δήμωνα [ἱερέα εἶναι αὐτοῦ]* | *vacat* | *ἱερεύς Δήμων Δημομέλους Παιαν[ιεὺς ἀνέθηκε] | καὶ τὴν οἰκίαν καὶ τὸν κῆπον προσ[τάξαντος τοῦ θεοῦ] | καὶ τοῦ δήμου τοῦ Ἀθηναίων δόν[τος ἱερέα εἶναι] | τοῦ Ἀσκληπιοῦ κατὰ τὴν μαν[τείαν]* (the God ordained by oracle to the People of Athens that they dedicate the house of Demon and the adjacent orchard, and that Demon be his priest etc.); see Guiraud 1893, 364; Schlaifer 1943*b*; Aleshire 1989, 97–8, 163–4; Parker 1996, 179 with n. 92, 250; Purvis 2003, 94–5.

[113] Pritchett and Meritt 1940, 75, 80; Aleshire 1989, 163–4, 371.

[114] Aeschin. 1.125: *Πρῶτον μὲν γὰρ τὴν ἐν Κολωνῷ συνοικίαν τὴν Δήμωνος καλουμένην ψευδῆ φησι τὴν ἐπωνυμίαν ἔχειν· οὐ γὰρ εἶναι Δήμωνος* (First he says that the multiple-dwelling in Kolonos which is called Demon's house is wrongly named, because it is not Demon's; trans. by Fisher 2001).

certain. All in all, the question should remain open.[115] Finally, we do not know whether income from real property continued to benefit without interruption the cult of Asklepios down to the Roman Imperial period, date of *SEG* XXVI 121 (*IG* II^2 1035) with its explicit reference to the sacred landholdings of the Asklepieion. The theory that 'sacred revenues' of the god, attested in a first-century dedication by a priest, might have contained income from endowments such as that of Demon, can be no more than a plausible guess.[116]

With the Oropian Amphiaraos we stand on shakier ground. In his case, we do not merely deal with a straightforward, officially ratified introduction of a divinity, but with the appropriation of an alien cult that principally aimed at the political assimilation of neighbouring, non-Athenian territory. In this respect, one can detect certain similarities with the Athenian appropriation of lands belonging to dissident members of the Delian League and their consecration to state divinities. The geographical proximity of Oropos to Athens, however, provided scope for more ambitious and sinister plans. Following Alexander's restoration of Oropos to the Athenians,[117] the Amphiareion immediately became the laboratory in which Athens promoted her policy for the full incorporation of Oropos. A new, impressive fountain and a drainage system were constructed in the shrine. Public and private dedications started adorning the sanctuary. The major event, however, was the reorganization of the quadrennial festival of Amphiaraia (on the blueprint of the Great Panathenaia), which was first celebrated in the archonship of Kephisophon, in 329/8.[118] It has always been thought that the mastermind behind this ploy was none other than Lykourgos himself.[119] The truth is that the scheme for the glorification of the Amphiareion enjoyed the energetic support of the most prominent politicians of the time. These are, however, only

[115] Judeich 1931, 460; Schlaifer 1943*b*, 42–3. Davies in *APF* 3597 IV is hesitant, but Fisher 2001, 263–4 is now prone to accept the identification.

[116] See Aleshire 1989, 98 on *IG* II^2 4465 ll. 7–8, ἐκ τῶν τοῦ θε[οῦ] | προσόδω[ν].

[117] It has been traditionally accepted that Oropia was handed over by Philip II, as explicitly stated both by Paus. 1.34.1, and [Demad.] 9 (cf. Brun 2000, 58 with n. 11). However, Oropia is now thought to have been incorporated in the Athenian state only after 335. This new chronological orthodoxy, first cryptically uttered by Knoepfler 1985, 53 (cf. 1986, 73–4 with n. 9; 1993, 295) and endorsed by Petrakos in *I.Oropos* p. 497 and *passim*, has now been masterfully and exhaustively analysed by its main exponent Knoepfler 2001, 367–89. See also Rhodes and Osborne 2003, 372–3.

[118] Fountain: *I.Oropos* 295 (cf. *I.Oropos* 292; 293); dedications: *I.Oropos* 347-60.

[119] Mitchel 1970, 45–6; Humphreys 2004, 83–4.

the tangible effects of a financial preparation, part of which was the consecration of landed property to Amphiaraos. Our most important piece of information for this derives from Hypereides' speech *In Defence of Euxenippos*. It appears that the delimitation and consecration of the Oropian territory to Amphiaraos was carried out by fifty boundary commissioners (*ὁρισταί*).[120]

Far more conspicuous was the involvement of the renowned Atthidographer Phanodemos. Not only was he one of the ten *epimeletai* of the Amphiareia honoured by the Athenian assembly in 329/8,[121] he was also, in 332/1, the recipient of a golden crown in recognition of his succesful efforts—in his capacity as drafter of a law—for the pursuit of the interests of Amphiaraos and his sanctuary.[122] Another contemporary legislative edict, that of the funding of the Lesser Panathenaia, provides a clue for understanding the content of Phanodemos' legislation. The latter is revealed in the decree passed in Phanodemos' honour:

[120] Hyp. *Eux.* 16: *ταύτας τὰς φυλὰς ἔγραψας ἀποδοῦναι τὸ ὄρος τῷ Ἀμφιαράῳ καὶ τὴν τιμὴν ὧν ἀπέδοντο, ὡς πρότερον τοὺς ὁριστὰς τοὺς πεντήκοντα ἐξελόντας αὐτὸ τῷ θεῷ καὶ ἀφορίσαντας* (Your proposal was that these tribes give back the hill to Amphiaraos, with its sale price, on the ground that the fifty boundary commissioners had selected it beforehand and set it aside for the god); cf. ibid. 17: *εἰ δὲ μὴ προσηκόντως εἶχον αὐτό, ἀλλὰ τοῦ θεοῦ ὄν, διὰ τὶ τάς ἄλλας φυλὰς ἔγραφες αὐταῖς προσαποδιδόναι ἀργύριον; ἀγαπητὸν γὰρ ἦν αὐταῖς εἰ τὰ τοῦ θεοῦ ἀποδώσουσιν καὶ μὴ προσαποτείσουσιν ἀργύριον* (Conversely, if the hill was held by them improperly—because it was the god's—why were you proposing that the other tribes pay them money in exchange? They should have been happy to restore the god's property without also paying a fine!). Whitehead 2000, 209–11, whose translation I reproduce, understands the delimitation to have taken place after 335.

[121] *I.Oropos* 298 (note that the elected committee in question is one of the most remarkable agglomerations of celebrities in the history of Athens; cf. Humphreys 2004, 83–4).

[122] *I.Oropos* 297, esp. ll. 23-7: *ἐπαινέσαι Φανόδημον Διύλλ|ου Θυμαιτάδην φιλοτιμίας ἕνεκα τῆς | πρὸς τὸν θεὸν καὶ τὸ ἱερὸν τοῦ Ἀμφιαρ|άου καὶ στεφανῶσαι χρυσῶι στεφάνωι | ἀπὸ : Χ : δραχμῶν* (Praise Phanodemos, the son of Diyllos, of Thymaitadai on account of his good-will towards the God and the sanctuary of Amphiaraos, and crown him with a golden wreath worth 1000 drachmas). Schwenk 1985, 205 expressed her bewilderment at the fact that Phanodemos alone was honoured as single *nomothetes* 'for the fourth century... a board of 50 is the usual number'. Her whole approach lies in a misunderstanding of the procedure of *nomothesia* in 4th-cent. Athens. Phanodemos was not, strictly speaking, a *νομοθέτης*, merely the drafter of a law (for the procedure of *nomothesia* see Hansen 1985), just like *Ἀριστόνικος Ἀρισ[τοτέλους Μαραθώνιος]* with regard to the Law on the Lesser Panathenaia.

*ἐπειδὴ Φανόδημος Θυμαιτάδης κα-
λῶς καὶ φιλοτίμως νενομοθέτηκεν πε-
ρὶ τὸ ἱερὸν τοῦ Ἀμφιαράου ὅπως ἂν ἥ τε
πεντετηρὶς ὡς καλλίστη γίγνηται κα-
ὶ αἵ ἄλλαι θυσίαι τοῖς θεοῖς τοῖς ἐν τ-
ῶι ἱερῶι τοῦ Ἀμφιαράου καὶ πόρους πε-
πόρικεν εἰς ταῦτα ...*[123]

Phanodemos of Thymaitadai proposed a law in a fine and honourable way for the sanctuary of Amphiaraos, in order that the quadrennial festival and the other sacrifices for the gods who are co-worshipped in the sanctuary of Amphiaros may be as fine as possible, and he created revenues for these...

The phraseology is strikingly similar to that of the Law on the Lesser Panathenaia which stipulated the leasing of the *Νέα* in order that

*[... τῆι] Ἀθηνᾶι ἡ θυσία ὡς καλλίστ[η ἧι Πανα]-
[θηναίοις τοῖς μ]ικροῖς καὶ πρόσοδος ὡς πλεί[στη γέν]-
[ηται ἱεροποιο]ῖς*

...the sacrifice to Athena at the Little Panathenaia may be as fine as possible and the income for the *hieropoioi* be as great as possible...

The aim of the *nomos* is that a religious festival shall be performed as lavishly as possible.[124] It is equally clear from the honorific decree *I.Oropos* 297 that Phanodemos had successfully introduced legislation which ensured that the celebration of the quadrennial festival would be outstanding and that sacrifices to all divinities hosted in the Amphiaraeion would be duly performed. And it is also clear that he raised revenues to cover the relevant outlay as well as expenditure for constructions in the shrine. The connection between Phanodemos' law and that on the Lesser Panathenaia is not merely verbal; the two statutes are also connected chronologically and, on the assumption that the Nea was situated in Oropia, geographically. In view of all this, it seems highly likely that the revenues underlying Phanodemos' law were kindred to those employed for the celebration of the Lesser Panathenaia: they were rentals.[125] For what else could have been the

[123] *I.Oropos* 297 ll. 12–15; cf. Rhodes 1972, 98.

[124] RO 81 ll. 5–7; cf. Schwenk 1985, 90–2.

[125] Rosivach 1991, 438 and Faraguna 1992, 351–2 both came close to a similar conclusion, without stating their case clearly. In a brief but useful article, Sosin 2004, 5 briefly raised the possibility, which I have now articulated in a recent study (Papazarkadas 2009*b*). It has not escaped scholarly attention that the mass sacred

elusive source of sacred income, the *πόροι*, in the statute of Phanodemos? This theory also makes sense of the consecration of lands to Amphiaraos. Far from being a meaningless exercise, the marking-out by the fifty *horistai* of the sacred lands of the healing god was part and parcel of the Athenians' reorganization of the cult. In any case, our extant evidence suggests that the administration of the cult of Amphiaraos was eventually an autonomous affair, and Walbank's suggestion that Amphiaraos' estates might have featured in the leases of 343/2 onwards should be discounted.[126]

Two further points deserve attention. Phanodemos' honour did not come out of the blue. It was preceded by an unparalleled honouring of Amphiaraos, 'the only immortal to be voted a gold crown by the Athenian assembly'.[127] But this secular award to a divine figure is reminiscent of another unique bestowal of honours, namely the grant of citizenship to the deified Boreas by Thourioi. On that occasion (in essence, the introduction of Boreas' cult) the benevolent god, we are told, was allotted a house and a parcel of land.[128] It is in this light, I suggest, that one has to construe the grandiose treatment of Amphiaraos by the Athenians; the healing-god was recognized as a benefactor of Athens, being offered not only a golden crown,[129] but also landed property to satisfy his extramundane cultic needs. The second point concerns the date of the consecration. If the honours upon Phanodemos are indeed the palpable proof of the delimitation of sacred territory within Oropia, the process should be placed between 335/4 and 332/1 and more likely closer to the latter archontic year. After all, it may not be coincidental that the decree in honour of

leases discussed above started in 343/2, a year when Phanodemos was influential in the council (*IG* II^2 223, with Humphreys 1985, 232). Perhaps Phanodemos was a major proponent of leasing as a means of increasing sacred revenues.

126 Walbank 1983d, 227–8 n.122 (cf. Faraguna 1992, 337 n. 3); dismissed by Humphreys 1985, 232 n. 58 (now Humphreys 2004, 100 n. 58).

127 Parker 1996, 247 on *I.Oropos* 296 (332/1); see now Scafuro 2009.

128 Ael. *VH* 12.61, *ἐκ δὴ τούτων οἱ Θούριοι τῷ Βορρᾷ ἔθυσαν καὶ ἐψηφίσαντο εἶναι τὸν ἄνεμον πολίτην καὶ οἰκίαν αὐτῷ καὶ κλῆρον ἀπεκλήρωσαν καὶ καθ' ἕκαστον ἔτος ἐπετέλουν αὐτῷ* (as a result the Thurians offered sacrifices to Boreas, decreed rights of citizenship to the wind, allocated to him a house and a plot of land, and established an annual festival; trans. by Wilson 1997); see the good discussions by Jacquemin 1979, 191–3; Ampolo 1992, 26; 2000, 15. Scafuro's neat discussion of Amphiaraos would have benefited from examination of Aelian's extract.

129 Scafuro 2009 rightly contends that the template for the crowning of Amphiaraos was probably the same as that of honorific decrees for foreigners.

Phanodemos was passed in the ninth prytany of 332/1. It was the ninth prytany when payments of sacred rentals were normally made and, therefore, it would have been only in the same prytany of 332/1 that the Athenians would have appreciated the effectiveness of Phanodemos' financial legislation.[130] If so, the law and the subsequent delimitation should be dated in the preceding year, 333/2.

The story does not end here. As is now widely acknowledged, the sacred land of Amphiaraos is the territory termed *ἡ ἐπ' Ἀμφιαράου* in *IG* II^2 1672 (*I.Eleusis* 177) from the year 329/8.[131] Outside the sequence of the tribally divided territories, but along with Drymos and the Athenian cleruchies, the entry on Amphiaraos' land, concise though it is, provides us with two important titbits of information: Firstly, both wheat and barley were produced in the sacred area of Oropos. In fact, the ratio of barley to wheat production was one of the lowest among the *aparchai* recorded in the Eleusinian accounts. In turn, this high wheat production would suggest agricultural intensification. By means of elaborate arithmetical calculations, it is now held that something in the order of 17 per cent of the total area of Oropos belonged to the sanctuary.[132] Secondly, the agent of the offering was a certain Prokles, further designated as demarch. The latter term is generally taken to denote the demarch of Sounion,[133] but an objection can be raised: why should an individual in such a transaction be designated as holding an office, unless the latter had some relevance to the issue in question? In the preceding entries of the same inscription, the only magistrates recorded are generals, their presence being legally justifiable as agents of Athenian cleruchies. Granted our defective knowledge of Oropian nomenclature, we should not discount entirely the possibility that the office refers to the archon in charge of Oropos, although this by no means forces us

[130] For the importance of the ninth prytany see below, p. 61–2.

[131] *I.Eleusis* 177 (*IG* II^2 1672), ll. 401–3: *ἐκ τῆς ἐπ' | Ἀμφιαράου δήμαρχος Προκλῆς Σουνιεὺς κρι ΔΔ, πυρῶν Π μέδιμνοι ἐννέα ἡμιεκτεῖα, ὧν αὐτοὶ ἀπήν|εγκαν οὐδενὸς ἐγλέξαντος κρι ΔΠΙΙ, πυρῶν τρία ἡμέδιμνα* (From the land of Amphiaraos the demarch Prokles of Sounion 20 *medimnoi* of barley, five *medimnoi* and nine half-sixths of grain, of these they themselves conveyed 17 *medimnoi* of barley and three half-*medimnoi* of grain); cf. Langdon 1987, 56 n. 27; Cosmopoulos 2001, 75; Clinton 2008, 233 contra Whitehead 1982, 40–2.

[132] Jardé 1925, 38–41; Cosmopoulos 2001, 74–5.

[133] Whitehead 1982, 40–2, followed by Taylor 1997, 163.

to recognize Oropos as a constitutional Cleisthenic deme.[134] The explicatory clause *ὧν αὐτοὶ ἀπήν|εγκαν οὐδενὸς ἐγλέξαντος* appears to corroborate this assumption. If I understand it rightly, although Amphiaraos' property was not liable to taxation, a certain group (note *αὐτοί*) took the initiative in collecting and bringing in the first-fruits from the sacred land. It is doubtful that this would have been the venture of individuals who were not somehow linked to the administration of the area and, thus, one is tempted to interpret the demarchy of Prokles as relating to Oropos, not Sounion.

Presumably the Athenians managed to celebrate only two penteteric festivals, in 329/8 and in 325/4.[135] Their defeat by the Macedonians in 322 ended their occupation of Oropia. However, the administrative scheme developed regarding the consecrated lands of Amphiaraos outlived what might have been expected of it. In 80 or so, the Roman *publicani* tried to exact taxes from Oropia, but the Oropians refused to comply with the request on the grounds that the area of Oropos was sacred and therefore exempt from taxation. The *publicani* counter-attacked, claiming that the *Lex Censoria* did not apply to the case of Amphiaraos, since he was not, strictly speaking, a god, but a deified mortal, and, therefore, his real property did not fall under the category of sacred. The Oropians' response was to send delegates to Rome who presented themselves before a body of senators. Eventually, a verdict issued in 74 vindicated the Oropian side. According to the senatorial verdict the sacred officials of the Amphiareion were allowed to use revenue from the sacred land in order to subsidize sacrifices and athletic contests in honour of Amphiaraos and the deified Roman *Hegemony*, as previously ordered by Sulla himself.[136] This litigation bears such a strong resemblance to the

[134] For Athenian administration of Oropos during the Peloponnesian War, see [Lys.] 20.6: *οὗτος δὲ πρῶτον μὲν ἄρξας ἐν Ὠρωπῷ οὔτε προέδωκε* etc. (in the first place, when this man was a public official at Oropos, he did not betray the city etc.), with Apostolakes 2003, 140–2 (cf. Thuc. 2.23.3 with Hornblower 1991, 278–9). The closest parallel to the picture envisaged here would be the non-constitutional deme of Salamis, for which see Taylor 1997.

[135] See Petrakos' commentary in *I.Oropos* 520.

[136] *I.Oropos* 303, esp. ll. 45–9: *ὡσαύτως τῶι θεῷ Ἀμφιαράωι*^{vvv} | *καθιερωκέναι τῆς πόλεως καὶ τῆς χώρας λιμένων τε τῶν Ὠρωπίων*^{v} | *τὰς προσόδους ἁπάσας εἰς τοὺς ἀγῶνας καὶ τὰς θυσίας, ἃς Ὠρώπιοι*^{v} | *συντελοῦσιν θεῷ Ἀμφιαράωι, ὁμοίως δὲ καὶ ἃς ἂν μετὰ ταῦτα ὑπὲρ τῆς* | *νίκης καὶ τῆς ἡγεμονίας τοῦ δήμου τοῦ Ῥωμαίων συντελέσουσιν* (and similarly he consecrated to the god Amphiaraos all the income of the city and of the hinterland and of the harbours of the Oropians for the contests and the sacrifices

events that had taken place almost three centuries before that one cannot help recalling Karl Marx's well-known maxim about history repeating itself. Here again we get the same old tricks. The protagonists might have changed but the ingredients of the recipe remained the same: sacred rentals for sacred celebrations with an eye on political manipulation.

Finally, we have to move on chronologically, to the Roman Imperial period, to find evidence of another 'new' deity of Lykourgan Athens. In *SEG* XXVI 121, at least two sacred estates appear to be restored to Agathe Tyche: one was located in Piraeus, whereas the second *temenos* was located elsewhere, possibly but not certainly somewhere near the Long Walls.[137] The cult of Agathe Tyche, personification of that so-elusive 'Good Fortune', seems to have been introduced in the fourth century, possibly as early as the 360s, to judge from a trierarchic dedication.[138] It certainly became a state concern under Lykourgos. Hides from animals sacrificed to the goddess were sold by the *boonai*, as we know from *IG* II^2 1496.[139] More importantly, she is twice mentioned in the Lykourgan cultic law *SEG* LIV 143, in which we learn that she was served by *epistatai* and possibly treasurers.[140]

Whether provisions in this inscription for the preparation of her cultic equipment suggest a recent date of introduction is hard to tell. Her cultic officials almost certainly suggest an administrative scheme different from that of the Treasurers of the Other Gods. It may not be insignificant that the goddess features in close proximity to the other two new gods, Asklepios and Amphiaraos.[141] Perhaps Agathe Tyche was one of those divinities who in the 330s were endowed with landed property by Lykourgos' fellow citizens. Perhaps the *temene*

that the Oropians perform for the god Amphiaraos; likewise for the sacrifices they may subsequently perform for the victory and the hegemony of the Roman people).

[137] *SEG* XXVI 121 ll. 44, 48. Parker 1996, 231 n. 48, is agnostic about the location of the second *temenos*, but see Schmalz 2007–8 [2011].

[138] Tracy 1994, 242–3. The dedication of the trierarch Philippos, son of Iasidemos, is *IG* II^2 4564.

[139] Parker 1996, 231 notes that the 160 drachmas produced from the sale suggest small-scale sacrifices; cf. Parker 2005, 456.

[140] *SEG* LIV 143 ll. 19–20: *[π]οήσασθαι δὲ καὶ τῆι Ἀγαθῆι Τύχηι κ̣[όσμον τοὺ]ς̣ [ταμίας τῶν ἱερῶν χρημά]τ̣ων̣ τῆς Ἀγαθῆς Τύχης με||[τὰ τῶν ἐπι]στατῶν τοῦ ἱεροῦ τῆς Ἀγαθῆς Τύχης].*

[141] The two appear paired together in l. 21 of *SEG* LIV 143.

of the Augustan period were these same Lykourgan endowments.[142] The possibilities are numerous; the evidence is thin. Definitive conclusions ought to be withheld.

5. *ATHENAION POLITEIA* 47.4-5 AND THE LEASING OF SACRED LANDS IN CLASSICAL ATHENS

It will have become obvious from the preceding discussion that leasing constituted the canonical way of rendering sacred properties lucrative. Most of the evidence cited hitherto has been epigraphical, but its treatment has been rather uneven and unsystematic. In order to reconstruct the framework within which the Athenian sacred properties system operated, one should not err in overlooking literary sources. The Thucydidean report of Perikles' enumeration of the Athenian resources on the eve of the Peloponnesian War has been pivotal to most modern treatments of Athenian finances and, more broadly, of the city's history.[143] It is worth noting here that the scholiast to Thucydides considered the non-imperial revenue to include land-produce, by which one has to understand rentals.[144] However, outside Thucydides' oeuvre the most important fifth-century literary testimony of Athens' revenues is to be found not in Attic prose, but in comedy and more precisely in Aristophanes' *Wasps*. When an increasingly impatient Bdelykleon struggles to undermine his stubborn father's faith in the ruling classes' ostentatious accolade of the jurors, he embarks on an enumeration of the various sources of Athenian income.

[142] Mikalson 1998, 62–3, maintains that there is no evidence for the cult after the end of the 4th cent.: the era of Lykourgos seems to provide the best historical framework against which we can surmise the proliferation of the cult of Agathe Tyche.

[143] Thuc. 2.13.3–5; see Kallet-Marx 1993, 96–107.

[144] *τῆς εὐφορίας τῆς γῆς καὶ τῶν καταδικαζομένων καὶ τῶν λιμένων καὶ μετάλλων καὶ τῶν ἄλλων* (and from the produce of the earth, and from the convicts and the harbours and the mines and the rest); cf. Fornara 2003, 251 n. 1, 253 n. 16 (Kallet-Marx 1993, 100, 199, and Blamire 2001, 106 argue, wrongly I believe, that sacred rentals should be included in the imperial revenue, i.e. the 600 T, related by Thucydides).

καὶ πρῶτον μὲν λόγισαι φαύλως, μὴ ψήφοις ἀλλ' ἀπὸ χειρός,
τὸν φόρον ἡμῖν ἀπὸ τῶν πόλεων συλλήβδην τὸν προσιόντα,
κἄξω τούτου τὰ τέλη χωρὶς καὶ τὰς πολλὰς ἑκατοστάς,
πρυτανεῖα, μέταλλ', ἀγοράς, λιμένας, μισθώσεις, δημιόπρατα.

First of all reckon up roughly, not with counters but just on your hands, the amount of tribute that comes in to us altogether from the allied states, and apart from that the taxes, one by one, and the many one-per-cents, court fees, mines, markets, harbours, rentals, confiscations.[145]

For all the self-evident precautions against taking at face value information deriving from comedy, this seems like a more or less honest, albeit simplified, list. For the purposes of this treatment, it suffices to keep in mind that rentals from lands could rank as a respectable source of money for Athens in the 420s.[146] Apropos of polis-controlled sacred estates, the *locus classicus* is an extract from [Aristotle]'s *Athenaion Politeia.* In his account of the Boule's workings the author describes the involvement of the *basileus* in the leasing of the *temene*:

εἰσ[φ]έρει δὲ καὶ ὁ βασιλεὺς τὰς μισθώσεις τῶν τεμενῶν, ἀναγράψας ἐν γραμματείο[ις] λελε[υ]κωμένοις. ἔστι δὲ καὶ τούτων ἡ μὲν μίσθωσις εἰς ἔτη δέκα, καταβάλλεται δ' ἐπὶ τ[ῆς] θ' πρυτανείας· διὸ καὶ πλεῖστα χρήματα ἐπὶ ταύτης συλλέγεται τῆς πρυτανείας. εἰσφέρεται μὲν οὖν εἰς τὴν βουλὴν τὰ γραμματεῖα κατὰ τὰς καταβολὰς ἀναγεγραμμένα, τηρεῖ δ' ὁ δημόσιος· ὅταν δ' ᾖ χρημάτων [κ]αταβολή, παραδίδωσι τοῖς ἀποδέκταις αὐτὰ ταῦτα καθελὼν ἀπὸ [τῶν] ἐπιστυλίων, ὧν ἐν ταύτῃ τῇ ἡμέρᾳ δεῖ τὰ χρήματα καταβληθ[ῆ]ναι [καὶ] ἀπαλειφθῆναι· τὰ δ' ἄλλα ἀπόκειται χωρίς, ἵνα μὴ προεξαλει[φθ]ῇι.[147]

And the *basileus* introduces the leases of sacred lands, recording them on whitened tablets. These too are let for ten years, and the payment is made in the ninth prytany: so most of the money is collected in this prytany. The tablets, written out according to the times of payment, are brought in to the council and kept by the public slave. When there is a payment of money he hands these same tablets to the *apodektai* (receivers), taking down from the racks those relating to the men who have to pay money and have their records deleted on the day in question. The

[145] Ar. *Vesp.* 656–9 (trans. by Sommerstein 1996); cf. Olson 1996, 135; Kallet 1998, 45–6.
[146] Sommerstein 1996, 197; Samons 2000, 96 n. 59; Blamire 2001, 106.
[147] Arist. [*Ath. Pol.*] 47.4–5.

other tablets are kept separately so that they shall not be deleted prematurely.[148]

The passage, not devoid of a few textual problems as will be shown below, has undergone little thorough analysis, despite its importance for our comprehension of the leasing mechanism in Athens. Aristotle provides us with remarkable information, which, otherwise, would have been irretrievable, but he simultaneously raises a series of almost unanswerable questions. The office of the *basileus* was presumably one of the oldest magistracies in Attica. His principal duty was the handling of religious affairs at the polis level. As a result he was assigned the task of leasing out the landholdings of the main Athenian divinities.[149] This looks pretty straightforward. Problems arise when we take a closer look at the details. It is often maintained that the *basileus* acted along with the board of the ten *poletai* in the leasing of sacred properties. This idea has almost acquired axiomatic status, being lightly reiterated despite the scanty evidence in its favour.[150] One of the testimonia adduced in support of this view is the intact lease of the Neleion *IG* I[3] 84, but Langdon has persuasively demolished the view that in this particular transaction the *poletai* acted as leasing agents.[151] The second is the alleged participation of the *poletai* in the leasing of the land called Nea. But the advocates of the latter theory do not usually clarify whether they perceive Nea as a sacred estate, and, besides, they fail to point out that the *poletai* of the Law on the Lesser Panathenaia feature only in a restoration.[152] The third indication for the cooperation of the *poletai* with the *basileus* is a textual one. The extract under consideration directly follows Aristotle's account of the duties of the *poletai*. But the conjunction *καί* in

[148] Translation by Rhodes 1984.

[149] Busolt and Swoboda 1920–6, 1089–93; Carlier 1984, 324; Garland 1984, 111–12.

[150] Linders 1975, 32; Walbank 1991, 149–51, 166–7; Todd 1993, 248; Rosivach 1994, 122–4; Davies 1994, 209. Hansen 1999, 260; Rhodes and Osborne 2003, 176 (Faraguna 1992, 338 with n. 7 is sceptical).

[151] Langdon 1991, 64–5.

[152] RO 81 ll. 7–9: [*τὴν μὲν* | *Νέαν μισθούτω*]*σαν δέκα ἡμέραις πρότερον ν*[. . . .⁷ . . .] *οἱ πωληταὶ δέκ*|<*α*> *ἔτη* (let the *poletai* lease out the Nea ten days before the N . . . for ten years); cf. Schwenk 1985, 91–2. Langdon 1991, 64 accepts the restoration as convincing, but rejects the characterization of Nea as sacred land. In the same publication Walbank 1991, 150 draws the opposite conclusion by accepting the designation of Nea as a sacred estate! Faraguna 1992, 343 n. 25 is prudent at pointing out that much relies on a restoration.

the opening sentence of *Athenaion Politeia* 47.4 ought not to be adverbial in meaning and, therefore, need not be translated as 'in addition to'. If so, the grammatical analysis of the text does not offer any indications about the exact administrative links between the *basileus* and the *poletai.*[153] Here again, the only scholar who has refrained from misinterpreting the above passage is Langdon, who in his analysis of the role of the *poletai* reached the conclusion that the latter did *not* cooperate with the *basileus* in granting sacred leases.[154] There is some negative evidence in favour of this interpretation to be found in Pollux's *Onomastikon* where leasing of sacred lands is not enumerated among the tasks of the *poletai.*[155] Finally, *IG* II^2 295 and 310 seem to present the *basileus* acting on his own. In the former the *basileus* has been understood to either lease out or delimit sacred property and to be held subsequently accountable,[156] but its findspot away from the Agora is puzzling and it is not certain after all that the document is a lease.[157] *IG* II^2 310 is even harder to interpret, and Lambert has now prudently classified it as a *dubium*;[158] we simply cannot rely on this fragment too much.

The actual situation may not have been very clear-cut. As pointed out elsewhere, the leasing of the Eleusinian landholdings was carried out by the *basileus* in cooperation with the *πάρεδροι* (assistants), the *ἐπιστάται Ἐλευσινόθεν*, and the *ἐπιμεληταὶ τῶν μυστηρίων*. There I raised the possibility that the *paredroi*, in particular, might have

[153] The positioning of this task of the *basileus* in Aristotle's section on financial officials (see Rhodes 1993, 31–2) could be explained in various ways: Rhodes 1993, 556, accepts a link with the *poletai*, but the crucial factor may be the jurisdiction of the *Boule*, which is after all the wider thematic framework; cf. Arist. [*Ath. Pol.*] 50.1 (*τὰ μὲν οὖν ὑπὸ τῆς βουλῆς διοικούμενα ταῦτ' ἐστίν*), which rounds off the account of the *Boule*.

[154] Langdon 1991, 64–5. Strangely, earlier on Walbank 1983*d*, 226–7 was of the same opinion, but he has since changed his mind (see note 152).

[155] Poll. *Onom.* 8.99: *πωληταὶ τὰ τέλη πιπράσκουσι μετὰ τῶν ἐπὶ τὸ θεωρικὸν ᾑρημένων, καὶ τὰς τῶν ἐξ Ἀρείου πάγου μετὰ τὸν πρότερον λόγον φυγόντων οὐσίας, καὶ τὰ δεδημευμένα. πρυτανεύει δ' ἐξ αὐτῶν εἷς, ὃς τὰ πωλούμενα βεβαιοῖ. ἀπήγοντο δὲ πρὸς τούτους καὶ οἱ μετοίκιον μὴ τιθέντες.*

[156] Matthaiou apud Lambert 2005, 137 has suggested [*ἀπομισθωσά*]*τω* or [*ὁρισά*]*τω* in l. 9, and [*εὐθυνέ*]*σθω* in l. 11.

[157] The suburb of Ampelokipi, where the stone was found, might have been the location of the sacred land in question (thus tentatively Lambert 2005, 137); this would also speak against the involvement of the *poletai*, whose documents were erected in their headquarters (the *poleterion*) in the Agora (for its location see the brilliant new suggestion by Camp 2007, 658–9).

[158] Lambert 2005, 149 with nn. 79 and 80.

been assisting the *basileus* with his leasing duties in the case of other sacred properties as well. It is equally possible that, depending on the divine owner of the leased properties, the pertinent incumbents would have cooperated with the *basileus* as lessors. For what it is worth, evidence from the Roman period shows the *basileus* letting out sacred realty in conjunction with the *στρατηγὸς ἐπὶ τοὺς ὁπλίτας* (hoplite general) and the secretary of the *ἱερὰ διάταξις* (sacred foundation). Even if the involvement of the last two is a late invention, the *basileus*' function as lessor probably mirrors a genuinely old, venerable tradition.[159]

If there is some uncertainty about the magistrates involved in the sacred estates leasing scheme, Aristotle leaves us completely in the dark as regards the process proper. Until relatively recently, the *opinio communis* has been that land leases were conferred at public auctions, that is, in compliance with the practice followed in sales of confiscated property and leases of mining and tax-collecting concessions, and the extant evidence seems to sustain this conclusion.[160] However, in the early 1990s Hallof heretically suggested that the auctions conducted by the *poletai* might not have been as open as usually assumed and that in effect the succesful bidders were preselected individuals.[161] Though Hallof concerned himself with the *poletai* records and, as demonstrated above, there is no firm evidence to sustain the belief that the *poletai* were responsible for land leases, his observations may give rise to some scepticism, since whatever the specific issue at stake, Athens might have followed identical practices in different administrative matters. Regarding land leasing, deme and phratry leaseholds indicate that auctions constituted a normal practice and since the political sub-units of Athens tended to operate as microcosms of the polis itself, it is legitimate to surmise that in

[159] *SEG* XXVI 121 l. 16: [*ἀπομισθῶσαι δὲ αὐτὰ τὸν ἐπὶ τοὺς ὁπλίτας στρατηγὸν Μητρόδωρον μετὰ τοῦ βασι*]*λ̣έως καὶ τοῦ ταμίου* [*τῆς ἱ*]*ερᾶς διατ̣*[*άξε*]*ως* (let the hoplite general Metrodoros along with the *basileus* and the treasurer of the sacred *diataxis* lease out these *temene*); for the restorations cf. ibid. l. 12: *τ̣ὸν δ' ἐπὶ τοὺς ὁπλείτας στρατηγὸν Μητρόδωρον Ξένωνος μετὰ τοῦ βασιλέως Μαντίου* etc. By the Roman Imperial period, the hoplite general had acquired several religious functions, but he also carried out financial tasks, some of which were related to land administration: see Sarikakis 1951, 18–20, 71. Therefore, his role as a lessor and co-administrator of sacred property in the Augustan period should not come as a surprise.

[160] Walbank 1983*d*, 218, commenting on the evidence provided by the surviving rentals, opted for competitive bidding as the process followed; cf. Langdon 1994, 254–5.

[161] Hallof 1990.

organizing auctions they followed a procedure originally employed at the polis level.[162] This is an inference from probability, but it can receive some corroboration both from the Law on the Lesser Panathenaia, in which a mention of an auction can be plausibly restored and, more importantly, from the state decree *IG* I^3 84.[163] All the same, even if we were to accept the concept of auctioning, we would still be far from knowing all the subtle details of such procedures. For what are we to make of the stipulation to lease out the Nea *κατὰ δικληρίαν*? Should we think of two tenants or of multiple lessees of several double lots, as recently suggested?[164] Another interpeter has thought of competitive bidding starting at a minimum of 4000 drachmas and increased by established increments.[165] But the case of the Nea may not even be typical, and eventually we should simply acknowledge our ignorance.

Part and parcel of auctions, manipulated or not, was the provision of sureties, an aspect that has undeservedly drawn little scholarly attention and that is passed over in silence in the *Athenaion Politeia*.[166] Personal suretyship was a standard requirement for public contractors, as can be seen in the tract *de Vectigalibus*. While commenting upon the feasibility of hiring out public slaves to mine owners, Xenophon abruptly interrupts the cohesion of his narrative in order to add by way of supporting comparison the cases of leasing of realty and selling of taxes on behalf of the city. Subsequently, he talks about how the provision of guarantors could secure the city's property, namely the public slaves, in compliance with the practice

[162] *SEG* XXVIII 103 ll. 23–4; *IG* II^2 1241 ll. 52–3: *μισθωσάντωσαν Δυαλ|εῖς ὧι ἂν βούλωνται τοῦ πλείστου* (let the Dyaleis lease the plot out to whomever they want for the highest bid); *IG* II^2 2492 ll. 34–6: *ἑλέσθαι ἄνδρας οἵτινες | μετὰ τοῦ δημάρχο καὶ τῶν ταμιῶν καὶ τô μισθωτô ἀπ|οδώσονται τὰς ἐλάας τῶι τὸ πλεῖστον διδόντι* (let them select men, who are, with the demarch and the treasurers and the lessee, to sell the olive trees to the person offering the most) is erroneously adduced by Langdon 1994, 254 as evidence for the issue under consideration, since it pertains solely to the sale of the felled olive-trees, not to the lease of the landholding itself. For other evidence of competitive bidding see Wilson 2007, 125–9.

[163] RO 81 ll. 7–10: *[τὴν μὲν | Νέαν μισθούτω]σαν δέκα ἡμέραις πρότερον ν[. . . .^{7} . . . | οἱ πωληταὶ δέκ]<α> ἔτη κατὰ δικληρίαν τῶι τὸ π[λεῖστον | διδόντι]*; *IG* I^3 84 ll. 14–15: *ὁπ|[ό]σεν δ' ἂν ἄλφει μίσ[θ]οσιν τὸ τέμενος κατὰ τὸν ἐνιαυτὸν ἕκαστον* (and whatever money the *temenos* yields as its annual rent); l. 24, *ὁπόσο ἂν μισθόσεται*).

[164] Williams 2008.

[165] Sosin 2002, 123–5.

[166] The exception is of course Finley 1952*a*, a formidable treatment, but one mostly preoccupied with real security. Behrend 1970, 59 with n. 39; 124–7.

followed in the farming of the taxes.[167] He does not explicitly refer to guarantors in connection with *temene*, but this is probably a slip, for otherwise his mention of renting *temene*, shrines, and houses would look slightly out of place.[168]

That lessees were obliged to provide guarantors and not an *ἀποτίμημα* (pledge) is on its own a little striking, but not astonishing.[169] The idea behind furnishing sureties was that the polis could extract its money from the guarantors on the contractor's default. But if this was standard practice with regard to all kinds of contracts, the obligation to furnish two guarantors for sums of rent in excess of 600 drachmas points towards an elaborate fiscal system.[170] Walbank, the first to spot this pattern, did not pursue it further apart from pinpointing an alleged analogy, communicated to him by Lewis, in the leasing documents of Hellenistic, independent Delos. A good parallel can be drawn from the contract for the construction of an Ionic temple at Delos. Therein a contractor was expected to nominate one guarantor for every 1000 drachmas he bid for.[171] Close to this stands a clause from Agyrrhios' *Grain Tax Law*, in which each tax

[167] Xen. *Vect.* 4.19–20, *μισθοῦνται γοῦν καὶ τεμένη καὶ ἱερὰ καὶ οἰκίας καὶ τέλη ὠνοῦνται παρὰ τῆς πόλεως. ὅπως γε μὴν τὰ ὠνηθέντα σῴζηται, τῷ δημοσίῳ ἔστι λαμβάνειν ἐγγύους παρὰ τῶν μισθουμένων, ὥσπερ καὶ παρὰ τῶν ὠνουμένων τὰ τέλη* (with Gauthier 1976, 147–9). (For they rent *temene* and shrines and houses and they also buy from the city the right to farm taxes (my translation). The treasury can insure the slaves purchased by requiring some of the lessees to provide guarantors, as it does in the case of tax-farmers; trans. by Marchant in Marchant and Bowersock 1968).

[168] The reason behind Xenophon's presumed omission is, I think, purely philological. If he had mentioned guarantors with regard to the leasing of *temene*, he would have been obliged to form an awkward phrase, namely *ὅπως γε μὴν τὰ ὠνηθέντα σῴζηται, τῷ δημοσίῳ ἔστι λαμβάνειν ἐγγύους παρὰ τῶν μισθουμένων, ὥσπερ καὶ παρὰ τῶν μισθουμένων etc.* In order to avoid this faltering repetition, Xenophon opted to mention only the tax farmers instead, who, after all, represented a financially, and therefore rhetorically, more congenial case. The explanation by Gauthier 1976, 148–9 seems to me circular and, therefore, unsatisfactory.

[169] Finley 1952*a*, 92–7.

[170] Walbank 1983*a*, 135 n. 159; 1983*d*, 208 n.15; 1991, 163. It is the proportional system that perplexes and not the provision for multiple guarantors for which see Partsch 1909, 254–7.

[171] *IG* II^2 1678A (=*I.Délos* 104–4), ll. 17–18: *τοὺ[ς δ' ἐγγυη]|τὰς καθιστάναι κατὰ : X : ἀξιοχρέως* (let them provide guarantors, one for every 1000 drachmas). The document belongs to the period of Amphictionic administration, probably in the years before 360. Chankoswki 2005, has strongly argued that Delos was used as a quasi-laboratory of financial experimentations by the Athenians. If so, *I.Délos* 104-4 reflects Athenian managerial habits.

purchaser had to provide two solvent guarantors per portion.[172] In brief, *ἀξιόχρεως* seems to be the key phrase, referring to the contractor's obligation to provide sureties adequate to cover the price of the contract in question (see also Appendix on *IG* II^2 1593).[173] Whether the guarantors had to belong to the same census class as the lessee is unknown and, though such a provision is archaic in tone, it is clearly attested in the bouleutic oath.[174]

A lessee's obligation to furnish personal suretyship was already legislated for in the mid-fifth century, to judge from the occurrence of some form of the word *ἐγγυητής* in *IG* I^3 252 (l. 8)—an inscription generally assumed to be a lease of land—but it is impossible to say whether the proportional surety system was being implemented at the time. In *IG* I^3 84 more than one guarantor is implied, although only one lessee was expected to bid for the Neleion.[175] Since that was a property of considerable size and the successful bidder would be granted a great number of perks (e.g. unlimited use of rain water),[176] the rent was presumably quite high, maybe higher than

[172] *SEG* XLVIII 96 ll. 29–31: *ἐγγυητ<ὰ>ς καταστήσ[ε]|ι ὁ πριάμενος δύο κατὰ τὴν μερίδα ἀξι[ό]|χρεως, οὓς ἂν ἡ βουλὴ δοκιμάσηι* (the buyer of the tax will provide per portion two solvent guarantors, whomever the Council has approved) with Stroud 1998, 64–5.

[173] See Ar. *Eccl.* 1064–5: *ἀλλ' ἐγγυητάς σοι καταστήσω δύο | ἀξιόχρεως* (but I will provide for you two solvent guarantors), which imitates legal language (Ussher 1973, 222). The use of the term *ἀξιόχρεως* clearly puts emphasis on the financial adequacy of the guarantor; contrast the clause *[ἐγγ|υ]ητὰς παρέξει δύο ἀρεστοὺς Κ[λυτίδαι|ς]* (he will provide two guarantors acceptable to the Klytidai) from the famous leasing document of the Chian association of Klytidai (*SEG* XXII 508 B1 ll. 11–13), which points towards a more arbitrary selection, definitely one not exclusively based on economic considerations (cf. Behrend 1990, esp. 243–4).

[174] Dem. 24.144: *οὐδὲ δήσω Ἀθηναίων οὐδένα, ὃς ἂν ἐγγυητὰς τρεῖς καθιστῇ τὸ αὐτὸ τέλος τελοῦντας* (Nor will I imprison any Athenian who offers three sureties taxed in the same class as himself; trans. by Vince 1935); in Dem. 24.148 the oath is called Solonian (cf. Rhodes 1972, 194); see also Arist. [*Ath. Pol.*] 4.2 (cf. Rhodes 1993, 114–15).

[175] For *IG* I^3 252 see also Chapter 3, Section 1.1 below. Neleion: *IG* I^3 84 ll. 24–6, *τὸν δὲ μισθοσάμενον τὸ τέμ|ενος καὶ ὁπόσο ἂν μισθόσεται ἀντενγραφσάτο ὁ βασιλεὺς ἐς τὸν τ|οῖχον καὶ τὸς ἐγγυετὰς κατὰ τὸν νόμον ὅσπερ κεῖται τôν τεμενôν* (the *basileus* shall write on the wall the name of the lessee of the *temenos* and the rental and the names of the guarantors according to the law for the *temene*). The implications of the plural form of the noun were long ago noticed by Partsch 1909, 255 n. 2.

[176] Note, for instance, that in the orgeonic sacred law *IG* II^2 1361 water resources were envisaged as a distinct object of sale (ll. 8–10: *ὅπως δ' ἂν ἡ οἰκία καὶ | τὸ ἱερὸν ἐπισκε[υ]άζηται, τὸ ἐν[οίκιον τῆ]ς οἰ[κίας] καὶ τὸ ὕδωρ ὅσου ἂμ πραθῆι, ε|[ἰς τὴν ἐ]πισκευὴν τοῦ ἱεροῦ [καὶ τῆς] οἰκίας, εἰς ἄλλο δὲ μηδὲν ἀναλίσκειν*) (So that the house and the sanctuary be repaired, the orgeones shall invest the rental from the house and

600 drachmas, a fact that would account for the provision of multiple guarantors, but further corroborative evidence for such a hypothesis is not available. We do not know when a proportional suretyship system was introduced in the process of purchasing the right to collect taxes, but the story related by Plutarch in his *Life of Alcibiades*, if genuine, would indicate that this was not yet the case in the late fifth century and that this device was first established in relation to leasing of sacred domains.[177]

The other titbit of information we get from the *Athenaion Politeia* concerns the duration of the leases: they were all fixed for a period of ten years. Here *IG* I^3 84, a lease granted for a period of twenty years, indicates that, if anything, the system had undergone some alterations since the late fifth century.[178] If one looks at other Attic examples, one will find practically no direct proof of [Aristotle]'s assertion. *IG* I^3 252, a document usually described as a ten-year lease, is generally considered to have been issued by a tribe.[179] The *temene* of Nemesis at Rhamnous or the *temene* in the Piraeus did not fall under the jurisdiction of the Athenian polis, and the ten-year lease pattern can only be seen as administrative mimicry.[180] The same can be said about the early Hellenistic leases of the orgeonic sanctuary of Egretes and the phratric land of the Dyaleis respectively.[181] The lease of Nea, again, is thought to have been for ten years on the basis of a restoration about which even its proposer felt uneasy.[182] Outside Attica, however, we do find decennial leases, the most characteristic example being the letting of the sacred estates of Apollo at Delos and Rheneia.[183] The Delian

whatever income is fetched from the sale of the water in repairs of the sanctuary and the house, and in nothing else).

[177] See Plut. *Alc.* 5, in which Alcibiades stands as the only guarantor for his metic protégé, even when the stakes get high. Russell 1995, 195 is keen to accept the veracity of the episode, as does Stroud 1998, 30–1 n. 51.

[178] *IG* I^3 84 ll. 37–8, μισθôν δὲ κατὰ | εἴκοσι ἐτôν (the lease will be for twenty years).

[179] Osborne 1988, 282; see Chapter 3, Section 1 below.

[180] *I.Rhamnous* 180 ll. 8–9, with Jameson 1982; *IG* II^2 2498 ll. 17–21, but note the peculiarity of Piraeus where the demarch was, uniquely, appointed by lot by the State and not by the deme (Arist. [*Ath. Pol.*] 54.8, with Rhodes 1993, 611).

[181] *IG* II^2 2499 ll. 1–3, and *IG* II^2 1241 ll. 4–9, 42–53 (with Lambert 1993, 302; 306–7, contra Behrend 1970, 93).

[182] Lewis 1959*b*, 243.

[183] Fifth-cent. Amphictionic accounts mentioning decennial leases: *IG* I^3 402 (=ML 62) ll. 16 (restored); 20–1; 25. From the 4th cent. no information concerning the duration of the Amphictionic leases survives (unless *IG* II^2 1641b l. 7: [- - -] της δεκαετίας Θέολλ[ος] (of the ten-year period, Theolos . . .) is relevant, but this seems

system has long been overlooked by students of Athenian economics, unjustifiably in my view, for it was the Athenians who had control of the Delian sanctuary for most of the fifth and fourth centuries and their accumulated experience might have influenced their internal administrative schemes.[184] Tréheux believed that the *ἱερὰ συγγραφή* of independent Delos, that is the administrative scheme for sacred properties, was in fact an Athenian invention adopted by the Delians after 314, and, if so, ten-year leases, a universal feature of the Delian leasing mechanism, must have been part and parcel of the respective Athenian apparatus.[185]

Other length patterns have long been known: five-, twenty-, or forty-year leases and occasionally the odd ones 'in perpetuity'.[186] At the polis level, one should pay due attention to the *'Ράριον πεδίον* ('Rharian field', or 'Rharia'), which has been traditionally considered to have been let out for four years.[187] Nevertheless, one can object that it is the nature of the epigraphical evidence, the accounts of a board whose tenure of office lasted four years, that distorts our picture. Thus, the chronological formula [*ἐτῶν*] | *τεττάρων* (four years) may not correspond to the duration of the lease of Rharia, but rather reflect the quadrennial accountability of the *ἐπιστάται Ἐλευσινόθεν*.[188] Alternatively, and given that the produce from Rharia was destined to be used as prize for the victors of the quadrennial

unlikely), and Kent 1948, 259–60 urges agnosticism as to whether ten-year leases were the norm or the exception, although Tréheux 1949, 1009 thinks that was the formal pattern. Another non-Attic example is the infamous lease of the confiscated Plataian lands (Thuc. 3.68.4: *τὴν δὲ γῆν δημοσιώσαντες ἀπεμίσθωσαν ἐπὶ δέκα ἔτη* (and after confiscating the land they let it out on ten-year leases), with Bruce 1968, 196–7; Hornblower 1991, 463–4).

184 Kent 1948, esp. 258–62, is still good for the Amphictionic period, but see now Chankowski 2008, a work that formidably addresses the concerns expressed above. For the political history of Delos under the Second Athenian Confederacy, see Dreher 1995, 198–234.

185 Tréheux 1944–5, 293; cf. Brunet 2002, 252–3. It is true, however, that from 314 to 300—the year favoured as the date of *ἱερὰ συγγραφή* of independent Delos by Reger 1994, 281–3—letting periods were irregular and, therefore, continuity, if any, was not uninterrupted (cf. Reger 1994, 192). For Athenian influence on the temple economy of Delos see Chankowski 2001 and 2008.

186 Behrend 1970, 116; Osborne 1987, 42–3, table 2 provides, amongst other things, a good codified panorama of lease lengths; cf. Osborne 1988, 283 and Walbank 1983*d*, 216 n. 71.

187 Thus Jardé 1925, 96 n. 2 and Davies in *APF* no. 13912, both based on *IG* II^2 1672 ll. 253–7, which covers the quadrennium 332/1-329/8.

188 *IG* II^2 1672 ll. 253–4 = *I.Eleusis* 177 ll. 382–3.

Eleusinia, there would be a certain degree of pragmatism in leasing out the sacred field for a period of four years.[189] By and large, there seems to have been no particular reason for ten-year agreements other than conventional practicality, in conformity to the decennial numerical system. In the Roman period the Athenians seem to have reconsidered the effectiveness of their ten-year leases, for they turned to four-year ones.[190] Religiously, there could be no justification for such an option, since no Athenian festival or other sacred ritual ever operated in a ten-year cycle. Administratively, there were no magistracies functioning over a period of ten years or any period of time precisely divisible by ten, except, of course, from the annual offices. In practical terms, this means that any sacred estate let for ten years would have raised income to be dispensed by three different quadrennial boards of sacred treasurers. This brings up the issue of the recipients of income from leasing of *temene*.

In the *Athenaion Politeia* the *apodektai*, who were in charge of receiving revenues from various sources, rentals included, are attested as disbursing the various proceeds to the appropriate authorities.[191] Lamentably, [Aristotle]'s narrative is condensed and indiscriminate, and the author does not explicitly mention the various recipients of the allocations of the *apokektai*, no doubt because he was merely interested in expounding the role of the latter.[192] Full treatment of the subject will be reserved for the next section. For the time being it is worth noting that rentals were eventually paid to the *apodektai* in the

[189] But the triennial Lesser Eleusinia were also subsidized from the produce of the *'Ραρία*; for the festival's periodicity see Rhodes 1993, 608–9, and now Parker 2005, 468–9, who concludes that 'the periodicity of the festival is problematic'.

[190] *SEG* XXVI 121 l. 16: [*ἀπομισθῶσαι δὲ αὐτὰ τὸν ἐπὶ τοὺς ὁπλίτας στρατηγὸν Μητρόδωρον μετὰ τοῦ βασι*]*λ̣έως καὶ τοῦ ταμίου* [*τῆς ἱ*]*ερᾶς διατ̣*[*άξε*]*ως εἰς τετραετίαν* (see n. 159 above).

[191] Arist. [*Ath. Pol.*] 48.2: *τῇ μὲν οὖν προτεραίᾳ δέχονται τὰς* [*πάσα*]*ς καὶ μερίζουσι ταῖς ἀρχαῖς, τῇ δ' ὑστεραίᾳ τόν τε μερισμὸν εἰσ*[*φέρου*]*σι γράψαντες ἐν σανίδι καὶ καταλέγουσιν ἐν τῷ βουλευτηρίῳ* (On the first day the *apodektai* receive all the payments and allocate them to the officials. On the next day they introduce the allocation: they write it on a tablet and read it out in the council-house), with Rhodes 1993, 557–60; Arist. *Pol.* 1321^{b}.31–3: *ἄλλη δ' ἀρχὴ πρὸς ἣν αἱ πρόσοδοι τῶν κοινῶν ἀναφέρονται, παρ' ὧν φυλαττόντων μερίζονται πρὸς ἑκάστην διοίκησιν· καλοῦσι δ' ἀποδέκτας τούτους καὶ ταμίας* (Another office is that to which the revenues of the common funds are paid in, the officials who guard them and by whom they are divided out to the several administrative departments; these magistrates are called *apodektai* and treasurers).

[192] Cf. Bertelli 1993, 75–7.

ninth prytany of the political year. Epigraphically, this calendrical arrangement is known from *IG* I^3 84, but contemporary evidence is missing.[193] Still, [Aristotle]'s assertion can be backed by an epigraphic piece of evidence that has long perplexed scholars. The bulk leases of *temene* from 343/2 onwards contain an irregular rubric, which dictates that the gathering or the conveyance of the *ὡραῖα*, the fruits in season, should coincide with the payment of the rentals.[194] As far as grain is concerned, the most common crop in Mediterranean agriculture, harvesting took place between May and June, a period which roughly coincides with the ninth prytany of the Athenian civic calendar.[195] Faraguna, one of the few scholars to ponder this passage, objected to this interpretation that other products had a different harvesting time.[196] Nevertheless, olives and grapes could be turned into olive oil and wine respectively, whereas figs could easily be dried—in fact, they regularly were—and, therefore, be offered as *ὡραῖα* out of their harvesting times.[197] Last but not least, the sacrificial calendar of the Marathonian Tetrapolis which contains an offer of *ὡραῖα* to the obscure hero Hyttenios early in the month Skirophorion (mid-June) shows that the term *ὡραῖα* was notionally closely connected to that period of the year, and this should put Faraguna's grievances at rest.[198]

[193] See Behrend 1970, 117 n. 81. The way the relevant clause in *IG* I^3 84 is phrased suggests that it had not been regular up to this point (418/7) to pay rentals in the ninth prytany, but a later law might have regularized what had beforehand been merely a customary practice; cf. Mattingly 1968, 471.

[194] *Agora* XIX L10 ll. 35–9: *[τ]ά[δ]ε ὕστερον ἐμισθώ[θη ὁ | α]ὐτὸς αὐτοῖς χρόνος [ἐστὶν] | τῆς καταθέσεως τῆς μ[ισθώ]|σεως καὶ τῶν ὡραίων | τῆς κομιδῆς* (The following were leased out subsequently. For these the time of the payment of the rental will coincide with the gathering of the crops in season). In recent years most scholars have interpreted *κομιδή* as 'conveyance' (e.g. Walbank 1983*d* 217), but Biraschi 2004, has now argued in favour of the old translation 'harvesting'. I find the former contextually better, but less so textually. Yet, I think the distinction is less important than usually assumed. For *ὡραῖα* in a leasing context see *IG* II^2 2492 ll. 7–9: *ἐὰν δὲ μὴ ἀποδιδῶσιν εἶναι ἐνεχυρασίαν Αἰ|ξωνεῦσιν καὶ ἐκ τῶν ὡραίων τῶν ἐκ τοῦ χωρίου καὶ | ἐκ τῶν ἄλλων ἁπάντων τοῦ μὴ ἀποδιδόντος* (If they do not pay, there will be securing of the rent for the Aixoneis out of the seasonal crops from the estate and out of all the other property of him who has not paid).

[195] Osborne 1987, 13–15 with table 3; Isager and Skydsgaard 1992, 21–6.

[196] Faraguna 1992, 339–40.

[197] Isager and Skydsgaard 1992, 26–43.

[198] *SEG* L 168, face A, col. II, ll. 30–1: *Σκιροφοριῶνος*^{v} *πρὸ Σκίρων Ὑττηνίωι τὰ ὡρα[ῖ]|α* (cf. Richardson 1895, 222).

Be that as it may, the collection of rentals from the *apodektai* was the final stage of a long procedure which largely lay under the control of the *demosios*, the public slave attached to the Boule. He had to keep financial contracts—not only leases of sacred property, but such other transactions as mine concessions—written on whitened boards. Literate public slaves routinely carried out much of the bureaucratic burden inherent in the Athenian administration. It is, therefore, not surprising to find here a *demosios* entrusted with the keeping of sensitive financial records.[199] Yet the Athenian secretariat is a notoriously complicated topic and, given what [Aristotle] tells us in 54.3 in conjunction with independent evidence, it is not impossible that this function of the *demosios* in relation to sacred leases only reflects a practice current at the time of the composition of the *Athenaion Politeia*. In any case, the *demosios*' presence in this capacity underscores the fact that the leasing scheme operated under the auspices of the Boule.[200] The council's authority over finances is well documented throughout the Classical period and one should not overstress the religious dimension of the councillors' involvement.[201] Rather the Boule retained the supervision of sacred finance, exercising public control. It has been suggested that its role consisted in ratifying the lease-contracts auctioned by the *basileus*, probably by virtue of approving the suggested guarantors.[202] This may not be wrong, but the Boule's involvement might have been multifaceted. Thus, extended bouleutic cognizance is evident in the probouleumatic decree *IG* I^3 84. The νομοθεσία, the procedure whereby Athens rendered profitable such sacred lands as the Νέα and the territory of Amphiaraos in the 330s, was similarly commenced by the Boule. Finally, the λελευκωμένα γραμματεῖα had to be deposited in the Bouleuterion, which was the venue of the payments to the *apodektai*, as confirmed by a law evoked by the speaker of Demosthenes' 24th oration,

[199] According to a law from 374/3 (RO 25), the approvers of the silver coinage (δοκιμασταί) were such public slaves. A public slave called Eukles was ordered in *IG* II^2 120 to carry out, along with the prytaneis, an inspection of the objects stored in the *Chalkotheke*; cf. Rhodes 1993, 601; Pébarthe 2006, 166–7; Hunter 2006.

[200] As implied by the fact that the *basileus* had to bring in the μισθώσεις to the Boule (Rhodes 1993, 556).

[201] Boule and finance: Rhodes 1972, 88–113.

[202] Thus Langdon 1991, 63 with n. 33.

presumably the law regulating the centralized financial allocation known as *μερισμός*.[203]

During his account concerning the *apodektai*, [Aristotle] briefly touches upon the problem of state defaulters, a category which certainly included those who failed to pay their rentals on time.[204] In case of default they were obliged to pay double the initial amount and, if they failed again, the Boule maintained the right to order their imprisonment. The passage presents similar difficulties to the ones highlighted above, namely no differentiation is made between different categories of defaulters. As it happens, most of the relevant literature has evolved around debtors who were previously involved in transactions concerning taxes, mines-concessions, building contracts, or *similia*.[205] In a speech in the Demosthenic corpus, however, an explicit mention of those defaulters who had leased sacred estates is made:

> *Τοὺς δὲ μὴ ἀποδιδόντας τὰς μισθώσεις τῶν τεμενῶν τῶν τῆς θεοῦ καὶ τῶν ἄλλων θεῶν καὶ τῶν ἐπωνύμων ἀτίμους εἶναι καὶ αὐτοὺς καὶ γένος καὶ κληρονόμους τοὺς τούτων, ἕως ἂν ἀποδῶσιν.*[206]
>
> And those who do not pay their rentals for the sacred estates of the Goddess and the Other Gods and the Eponymous Heroes shall be *atimoi*, themselves and their family and their heirs, until they pay the rentals.

The penalty for unpaid rentals was, therefore, *atimia*, disenfranchisement, loss of citizen rights. However, *atimia* was a rather flexible term to the extent that modern scholars have been able to single out two different forms of it, a severe type with total forfeiture of civic rights and a mild one of temporary, revocable consequences.[207] The law quoted in the oration *Against Macartatus* specifies a rather strict form

[203] Dem. 24.96: *Ἔτι τοίνυν, ὦ ἄνδρες Ἀθηναῖοι, τὴν διοίκησιν ἀναιρεῖ, τήν θ' ἱερὰν καὶ τὴν ὁσίαν. ὡς δέ, ἐγὼ φράσω. ἔστιν ὑμῖν κύριος νόμος, καλῶς εἴπερ τις καὶ ἄλλος κείμενος, τοὺς ἔχοντας τά θ' ἱερὰ καὶ τὰ ὅσια χρήματα καταβάλλειν εἰς τὸ βουλευτήριον*; cf. Arist. [*Ath. Pol.*] 48.1 (for which see next section). For the budgetary system of *μερισμός* see Rhodes 1972, 99–103; Faraguna 1992, 179–94.

[204] Arist. [*Ath. Pol.*] 48.1: *κἄν τις ἐλλίπῃ καταβολήν, ἐνταῦθ' ἐγγέγραπται, καὶ διπλά[σιον ἀ]νάγκη τὸ [ἐλλ]ειφθὲν καταβάλλειν ἢ δεδέσθαι, καὶ ταῦτα εἰσπράτ[τειν ἡ βο]υλὴ καὶ δῆσαι [κυ]ρία κατὰ τοὺς νόμους ἐστίν* (If anyone misses his payment, he is recorded there, and is obliged to pay double the missing sum or go to prison: the council has full power to exact these sums and to imprison in accordance with the laws; trans. by Rhodes 1984) cf. Rhodes 1972, 148–51; 1993, 557–9.

[205] Rhodes 1972, 148–51.

[206] Dem. 43.58 (cf. Andreyev 1974, 43).

[207] Hansen 1976, esp. 75–90 remains the ultimate treatment of *atimia*.

of *atimia*, for the penalty could fall on the whole family and the heirs of the defaulters. On the other hand, discharge of the debt would result in removal of the penalty, so, strictly speaking, the punishment was not as severe as, for instance, in the case of traitors.[208]

A problem arises in that *atimia* was meaningful only with regard to citizens.[209] Epigraphic evidence, however, suggests that metics could also be lessees of sacred property.[210] Notwithstanding the *ἰσοτελής* lessee named Apemon, who might have enjoyed the legal status of a citizen, though this remains a controversial topic, there is a discrepancy here since metics were the *ἄτιμοι* par excellence.[211] This paradox can be remedied in two ways.[212] Firstly, one can postulate the existence of a separate statute which covered instances of metics falling behind with their payment obligations. Alternatively, one can envisage a legislative change which is not recorded in our sources. Recently, the speech *Against Macartatus*, generally assumed to be spurious, has been tentatively re-established as genuine by Usher.[213] Even more crucial is its date: *c.*345.[214] The inscribed leases we possess and in which metics appear to have rented *temene* date from 343/2 onwards, and Walbank, their most recent editor, has argued for some Euboulean administrative revision as the instigation behind their publication.[215] If so, this novelty might have included a provision which, for the first time, entitled metics to rent sacred property. It is not without its importance that, approximately a decade before, Xenophon had published his pamphlet *Poroi* in which he acknowledged the metics' contribution to the economics of Athens and urged his fellow Athenians to invent ways and means of securing more permanent residence of metics in their polis.[216]

208 Todd 1993, 142–3.

209 Hansen 1976, 55–6 with n. 8; MacDowell 1978, 73–5; Todd 1993, 142.

210 See Appendix VII: Catalogue, nos. 5; 6; 23; 87.

211 Giglioni 1970, lxii–lxiii.

212 For the the legal status of an *ἰσοτελής* see Whitehead 1977, 11–13, who observes that there is no clear-cut attestation of foreigners acquiring the right to own land upon being granted isotelic status.

213 Usher 1999, 244; 266–7 with n. 78. The authenticity of the speech has now been asserted by MacDowell 2009, 87.

214 Thompson 1976, 63; MacDowell 2009, 87 thinks of the late 340s.

215 Walbank 1983*d*, 227–8.

216 Xen. *Vect.* 2.6: *εἶτα ἐπειδὴ καὶ πολλὰ οἰκιῶν ἔρημά ἐστιν ἐντὸς τῶν τειχῶν καὶ οἰκόπεδα, εἰ ἡ πόλις διδοίη οἰκοδομησομένοις ἐγκεκτῆσθαι οἳ ἂν αἰτούμενοι ἄξιοι δοκῶσιν εἶναι, πολὺ ἂν οἴομαι καὶ διὰ ταῦτα πλείους τε καὶ βελτίους ὀρέγεσθαι τῆς Ἀθήνησιν οἰκήσεως* (Then again, since there are many vacant sites for houses within

Although there is a striking overlap between the treatment of those in arrears of their rentals and other categories of defaulters, it is clear that the same law did not apply to all these categories. Rather, for the sake of administrative convenience identical procedures were followed in all cases. Indeed, Aristotle in [*Athenaion Politeia*] 48.1 speaks of the treatment of state defaulters as being regulated by the laws (*κατὰ τοὺς νόμους*). From Demosthenes' speech *Against Timokrates*, it seems that these were the *νόμοι τελωνικοί* (laws concerning tax farming).[217] This partial overlap generated confusion already in antiquity, and even today presents the modern scholar with unfathomable complexities. The law moved by Timokrates in the 350s, for which the plaintiff of Demosthenes' 24th oration brought a *graphe paranomon* against the proposer, laid down a very lenient handling of those who had incurred fines.[218] In his lengthy and painstaking scrutiny of the illegalities of the law in question, the accuser claimed that Athens' damage would consist in losing the otherwise double fine of defaulters on secular liabilities and the decuple fine of those owing sacred money.[219] But Timokrates' statute did not affect lessees of *temene*, if this is how one should understand the phrase *τῶν τὰ μισθώσιμα μισθουμένων*, who were to carry on operating under the

the walls, if the state allowed approved applicants to erect houses on these and granted them the freehold of the land, I think that we should find a larger and better class of persons desiring to live at Athens; trans. by Marchant in Marchant and Bowersock 1968) is the most relevant by virtue of its referring to acquisition of real property; see Gauthier 1976, 56–74, 223–5. Whitehead 1977, 125–9, was more reluctant to reach the conclusion that Xenophon's advice affected actual Athenian policy and has been rightly criticized by Lambert 1997*a*, 281 with n. 247, for this. Dillery 1993, 1–2, contains a useful review of the relevant bibliography, though he misreads Lewis 1990, 259, who *does not* explicitly connect Xenophon's *Poroi* with the attestation of metics as lessees in the mass leases of the 340s and 330s; cf. also Burke 1992, 208–10; Vannier 1993.

217 Dem. 24.96 with the scholia ad loc. (cf. Rhodes 1972, 149–50).

218 Dem. 24.39–40.

219 Dem. 24.82: *ἐνταυθὶ πάλιν τῶν ἱερῶν μὲν χρημάτων τὴν δεκαπλασίαν ὑφήρηται, τῶν δ' ὁσίων, ὁπόσων ἐν τῷ νόμῳ διπλασιάζεται, τὸ ἥμισυ* (Here again he has stolen away the right of the sacred funds to a tenfold payment, and one half of the claim of the secular treasury, in cases where double payment in required by law); Dem. 24.83: *εἰ μὲν ἔγραψε καθιστάναι τοὺς ἐγγυητὰς ἢ μὴν ἐκτείσειν τὸ τίμημα τὸ γιγνόμενον, προσπεριειλήφει τοὺς νόμους ἂν καθ' οὓς τὰ μὲν διπλâ, τὰ δὲ καὶ δεκαπλâ γίγνεται τῶν ὀφλημάτων* (If he had proposed that sureties should be appointed to guarantee the payment of the accruing penalty, he would have embraced in his enactment the statutes under which certain debts are doubled, and others multiplied by ten; trans. by Vince 1935).

previously established laws.[220] Given that rentals of *temene* fell in effect under the category of sacred money, is there here ground to assume that those in arrears of sacred rentals had to pay ten times the initial renting fee? It seems very unlikely. Firstly, it would be a counter-incentive for citizens willing to embark on sacred leases to know that, in case of personal financial mischance, they would have to pay ten times the agreed rental. Moreover, one has valid reason to distrust Demosthenes' claims. In a *poletai*-record from the late 340s the property of Nikodemos, son of Aristomenes, of Oinoe was confiscated for a debt he owed to the hero Aias in his capacity as superintendent (*ἐπιμελητής*) of the Aiantis tribe, and yet his debt was merely doubled in the archonship of Archias (346/5), even though the relevant money was recognized as sacred (*ἱερόν*).[221] It results from this that either Demosthenes had deliberately been disingenuous in relation to sacred debts or that the multiplication of the latter by a factor of ten had fallen into disuse by that time. For lack of better evidence, we can assume that defaulters on payments of sacred rentals would be liable to a fine double the amount of the outstanding instalment/s and that [Aristotle] was accurate in his statement.

A last point is worth investigating. The law stipulating the condemnation of debtors with regard to *temene* seems to have already been in existence in the late fifth century. The decree of Patrokleides (quoted by Andocides in *On the Mysteries*) for the emergency restoration to full civic rights of disenfranchised Athenians after the

[220] Dem. 24.40: *περὶ δὲ τῶν ὠνουμένων τὰ τέλη καὶ τῶν ἐγγυωμένων καὶ ἐκλεγόντων, καὶ τῶν τὰ μισθώσιμα μισθουμένων καὶ ἐγγυωμένων, τὰς πράξεις εἶναι τῇ πόλει κατὰ τοὺς νόμους τοὺς κειμένους* (But in the case of the tax-farmers, their sureties, and their collectors, and of the lessees of leasable properties and their sureties, the polis may exact payment according to the established laws); Dem. 24.59: *ἄνευ δὲ τούτων αὐτὸς ὡμολόγησεν μὴ ἐπὶ πᾶσι τὸν αὐτὸν τεθηκέναι, πλὴν περὶ τῶν τελωνῶν καὶ τῶν μισθουμένων καὶ τῶν τούτων ἐγγυητῶν χρῆσθαι προσγράψας τῷ νόμῳ* (But, leaving those names out of the question, we have his own admission that his law is not of universal application, for he added a clause excepting from its operation tax-farmers, lessees, and their sureties; trans. by Vince 1935). Already back in the 19th cent. Dindorf 1849, 981 had understood the *μισθώσιμα* as entailing *agri publici* (by which he presumably meant *temene*). The choice of the term *μισθώσιμα* is odd, and maybe it should be replaced by *μισθώματα*, a variant transmitted in codices SFY.

[221] *Agora* XIX P26 ll. 506-11: *ὅτι ἐπιμελητὴς γενόμε|νος τῆς Αἰαντίδος φυλῆς καὶ ἐγλέξας τὸ ἱερ|ὸν ἀργύριον τῆς φυλῆς οὐκ ἀποδέδωκεν καὶ ἐ|κγεγραμμένο : ἐν ἀκροπόλει τῶι Αἴαντι καὶ ὀ|φείλοντος : 𐅆Η𐅄ΔΠ⊢ΙΙΙΙ: καὶ τούτο τοῦ ἀργυρίο | δεδιπλωμένο αὐτῶι ἐπὶ Ἀρχίου ἄρχοντος*; see Meritt 1936, 413; Finley 1952*a*, 94–5; Hallof 1990, 414 (none of them providing satisfactory interpretations).

disaster at Aigos Potamoi and in anticipation of a major Spartan assault, enumerated, amongst other categories, those defaulters registered with the *praktores*, the Treasurers of Athena and the Other Gods, as well as the *basileus*.[222] Dalmeyda was probably right to suggest that the most likely explanation for the *basileus*' involvement in cases of debtors would be his responsibility as lessor of *temene*.[223] The juxtaposition of three different orders of officials in the decree of Patrokleides must correspond to three different sectors of jurisdiction and if so, Rhodes's assertion that extraction of all debts on behalf of the Boule was the responsibility of the board of *praktores* falls short of proof, at least as concerns *temene*.[224] Indeed, in the Attic law on the protection of olive trees, the *praktores* featured as extractors of fines due to the *demosion*, whereas sacred debts had to be registered with the Treasurers of Athena, a clear-cut example of distinct cognizance in separate economic realms.[225] On the other hand, we know of one instance when the *basileus* was instructed to employ a *praktor*—but not the whole collegium—and the Secretary (presumably of the Boule) to register the fines he imposed on pilgrims who were guilty of misconduct during the Eleusinian Mysteries.[226] In conclusion, the

[222] Andoc. 1.77: *Περὶ δὲ τῶν ἐγγεγραμμένων εἰς τοὺς πράκτορας ἢ τοὺς ταμίας τῆς θεοῦ καὶ τῶν ἄλλων θεῶν ἢ τὸν βασιλέα, (ἢ εἴ τις μὴ ἐξεγράφη) μέχρι τῆς ἐξελθούσης βουλῆς ἐφ' ἧς Καλλίας ἦρχεν, ὅσοι ἄτιμοι ἦσαν [ἢ] ὀφείλοντες* etc. For the decree see in general Boegehold 1990.

[223] Dalmeyda 1930, 41 n. 1 citing Hauvette-Besnault, *De Archonte Rege*, 58 ff. (*non vidi*); cf. MacDowell 1962, 115. Böckh 1886, vol. I 190, writing before the discovery of the manuscript of the *Athenaion Politeia*, had pretty much reached the same conclusion when he wrote that the *basileus* had to collect 'die an die Stammheroen fallenden Bussen' (cf. Stahl 1891, 257 n. 1), based, in all likelihood, on the afore-cited Dem. 43.58 (see above, n. 32). He presumably thought that the Treasurers of Athena and the Other Gods had cognizance of the leases of the respective *temene*. But the amalgamated board of these Treasurers (Ferguson 1932, 104–9) should not be thought of as participating in leasing out *temene*, to judge from the conjunctive formula *ἢ . . . ἢ*; rather the implied debts comprised unpaid fines or shares from sales of confiscated properties.

[224] Rhodes 1993, 559.

[225] Dem. 43.71: *ὅτου δ' ἂν καταγνωσθῇ, ἐγγραφόντων οἱ ἄρχοντες, πρὸς οὓς ἂν ᾖ ἡ δίκη, τοῖς πράκτορσιν ὃ τῷ δημοσίῳ γίγνεται· <ὃ δὲ τῇ θεῷ γίγνεται>, τοῖς ταμίαις τῶν τῆς θεοῦ* (And when a person shall have been convicted, the archon before whom the case was brought shall make a report to the collectors of the amounts due to the public treasury, and of the amount due to the goddess, to the Treasurers of the Goddess; trans. by Murray 1939).

[226] *I.Eleusis* 138 ll. 33–5: *[εἶναι δὲ τῶι βασ|ι]λ̣εῖ τῶμ πρακτόρων ἕνα καὶ τὸγ γραμματ̣[έα ἀπὸ νομη]ν̣ίας ἀρξάμενον μέχρι ὃ ἂν μύσται λυθ̣ῶσιν, καὶ γράψ̣[αι τούτους τὰς ζημ|ία]ς ἃς ἂν ὁ βασιλεὺς ἐπιβάλῃι ἢ τῶ[ν] ἡιρ[ημένων μετὰ β]ασιλέως ἐπιμελεῖσθαι*, with Clinton 1980, 283, and idem 2008, 121.

question of who had to extract rentals due for *temene*, obscured by our ignorance of the exact powers of the ten *praktores*, should remain open owing to lack of evidence.[227]

Scholars have only occasionally questioned why, if leases were registered, as Aristotle states, on whitened boards (which, of course, have not been preserved owing to their perishable material), archaeological excavations have brought to light leases inscribed on stone.[228] At first glance, this is reminiscent of the question of why some decrees or laws were published on stone, whereas some others were not. There is a fundamental difference, however. *Athenaion Politeia* 47.4–5 per se would imply that there was only one type of written land lease record. However, in conjunction with the preceding account of the contracts leased out by the *poletai*, it has been plausibly suggested that there were, in reality, two different sets of records: one which contained the contracts themselves, and another one listing the names of the purchasers according to payment days.[229] Subsequently it was only the latter series of documents that was erased.[230] Although this suggestion has been made on the presumption that the *poletai* cooperated with the *basileus* in granting *temene* contracts, it can stand even if one takes the opposite view. In other words, the nominal issuing authority of the *γραμματεῖα* concerning the *temene* was the *basileus*—the effective issuer being the public slave—but the system was identical to the one followed in the case of the *γραμματεῖα* issued by the *poletai*.

This does not solve the enigma of the existence of bulk land records on stone. Stone inscriptions, slow to be manufactured and considered of permanent value, did have a special significance, according to a universally accepted doctrine. But if a strong case can be made for the

[227] On *praktores* see Hansen 1980–1, 160, who has conveniently collected all the relevant testimonies. As for defaulters on rentals from *temene*, no specific case is attested, either epigraphically or in literature (Dem. 57.63 refers to deme-owned *temene*, and even his account is dishearteningly vague). Note that in the extensive *poletai* records (*Agora* XIX, P) there is not a single instance of unpaid rentals resulting in confiscation.

[228] Only Langdon 1991, 61, Walbank 1991, 167 with n. 137, and Faraguna 1992, 340–1, have attempted to solve this riddle, even though inconclusively.

[229] Thomas 1989, 53–4 with n. 128; Sickinger 1999, 68–70, 127–9. Rhodes 2001*a*, 33–4; 41 n. 7, and 2001*b*, 138; 148 n. 18 is more sceptical. For *λελευκωμένα γραμματεῖα/λευκώματα* in general see Wilhelm 1909*a*, 246–9; Pritchett 1996, 27–8.

[230] Thus Sickinger 1999, 68–70.

democratic necessity of having decrees or laws inscribed on stone, the same argument cannot be sustained easily in the case of land leases. One can claim that the silence of [Aristotle] is a strong indication, if not a proof, that sacred lettings were not required by law to be recorded on stone.[231] This misses the point in that the lists of sacred estates we possess do not, in fact, correspond to the γραμματεῖα mentioned by [Aristotle].[232] Whereas the latter were individual archival reminders of who owed what to the Athenian polis, the former had a different layout: sacred properties described in sundry terms were accompanied by a rather vague designation of their location, the name of the lessee, the rental, and the name/s of the guarantor/s, and, more significantly, they were arranged in columns under headings bearing *sacra nomina*.[233] This classification clearly puts emphasis on the divine proprietors and their total possessions. There is a striking and long-acknowledged similarity between these rosters and the *poletai* records, and, to a lesser extent, between them and the so-called *Rationes Centesimarum*, but they should not be seen as a direct product of fourth-century epigraphic mimesis.[234] As it happens, *temene* located at Euboea and administered by Athens had already been recorded in an almost identical fashion in the fifth century (*IG* I^3 418), and the same might have been true of (sacred?) property situated at Chersonesos (*IG* I^3 417) and at some undesignated place, probably in Attica (*IG* I^3 420), though the condition of the last two inscriptions is too fragmentary to allow any trustworthy conclusions.[235] Moreover, we have at our disposal the lower part of a list of leased estates from Salamis, dating to shortly before the mid-fourth century. Here again, the layout is similar: property name, lessee, guarantor, and rental.[236] The list format allowed any interested individual, either magistrate or private citizen, to spot the exact tenure status of a landholding that belonged to a specific deity. Conversely, detecting an individual's interests invested in a sacred landholding

[231] Thus Faraguna 1992, 341.

[232] A wider truth perfectly understood by Davies 1994, 205–6.

[233] Walbank 1983*a*, 101.

[234] Thus Langdon 1991, 61 with n. 27 and Walbank 1991, 167. *Rationes Centesimarum* in relation to land leases: Lambert 1997*a*, 272 n. 217.

[235] Euboean *temene*: Raubitschek 1943, 28–33. Morison 2003, would now see *IG* I^3 420 as a property record for an Athenian colony or cleruchy, but I am not convinced by his interpretation.

[236] *IG* II^2 1590a; see Chapter 4, Section 4.

would be a physically and mentally painful, time-consuming endeavour. These lists were in effect not designed to fulfil such purposes. Even if one took pains to use them in order to find out who rented which *temenos*, what would remain irretrievable was whether certain individuals had fulfilled their obligations, that is, whether they had paid the due rentals or they had been declared defaulters. This aim could only be accomplished by consulting the relevant whitened boards, or, to put it more subtly, by cross-examining them with the inscribed leases. On similar grounds, and for the further reason that no magistrates are actually mentioned by name on the stones, it seems unlikely that lapidary leases could have served per se as the vehicle of magistrates' obligation to undergo audit and examination (εὔθυναι).[237]

In sum, Walbank's suggestion—on which, however, he did not elaborate—that there might have been a religious significance in these inscribed records may have some truth in it. Inscriptions regulating religious finances were frequently publicized; the accounts and the inventories of the Treasurers of Athena and the Other Gods, of the Supervisors of Eleusis, of Artemis Brauronia, of the Delian Amphictions, and the Tribute Lists, all fall within this category. Administrative functionality, democratic ideology, and religious symbolism have been variously suggested as motives for epigraphic registration.[238] At the risk of being branded overly reconciliatory, I would tentatively propose that a combination of all of the above accounted for the lease records, but I would cast my vote of preference for the third factor. The aforementioned *IG* I^3 418 bears the invocation θεοί as its heading, a feature shared with other sacred accounts from the same period.[239] This divine ratification might have disappeared by the fourth century, but its attestation in the earliest

[237] Thus Langdon 1991, 61, lukewarmly doubted by Walbank 1991, 167. Public acccountability in its firm sense, i.e. an obligation arising from the need to avoid maladministration, is examined and finally rejected as a motive for inscribing 'accounts', leases included, by Davies 1994, esp. 209–11 (the fact that he regards sacred lands to have been let out by the *poletai* does not affect his argument). Lambert 1997*a*, 272–6 thinks that the *Rationes Centesimarum* should be seen in the light of the Athenian culture of accountability, but these, unlike our leases, did entail the names of the public officials who had acted as selling agents. Similarly, Harris 1995, 20–2 sees accountability as the background for inscribing inventories of sacred possessions.

[238] Lewis 1986, 71–2.

[239] e.g. *IG* I^3 292; 325; 365; 370; 386; 387.

document of this series is revealing of a certain mentality which emphasizes the element of sacredness.[240]

Of course, the whole question is related to the problem of the exact publication place of these inscriptions. Walbank has argued for the Royal Stoa (*βασίλειος στοά*) as the location where these records were erected,[241] but as none has been found in situ, this should remain only an assumption, though a plausible one, especially in the light of a passage from Aelian's *Varia Historia*. In that passage the Roman historian recounts how, after the subjugation of Chalkis by the Athenians, the area called *Λήλαντος τόπος* (the Lelantine Field) was consecrated to Athena and rented out 'according to the stelae set up by the Royal Stoa, which held the records of the leases'.[242] The aforementioned *IG* I^3 418 has been traditionally put in the historical context offered by Aelian, and given its similarity to our fourth-century lease records there are grounds for deducing their erection near the *Basileios Stoa*.[243] After all, the Royal Stoa, as the seat of the *basileus*, was laden with religious connotations and was also the place where the revised sacrificial calendar of Nikomachos was inscribed after the fall of the Thirty and the restoration of the democracy.[244] Rather predictably, *IG* I^3 84 may be of some help here: in that the *basileus* was instructed 'to copy on the wall the [name of the] lessee, the fetched rent and the [names of the] guarantors according to the law about the temene'.[245] The locative adjunct *εἰς τὸν τοῖχον* with the definite article is clearly emphatic. Now, the board of the *nomothetai*, who were assigned the task of codifying the Draconian and Solonian laws after the fall of the Thirty, inscribed the revised laws in the Royal Stoa. We happen to know this because of Andocides' testimony.[246]

240 Pounder 1984.

241 Walbank 1991, 167 suggested the *Basileios Stoa* by virtue of the *basileus* issuing the documents in question.

242 Aelian, *VH* 6.1 (see n. 16 above).

243 Walbank 1991, 154 with n. 24.

244 Nikomachos' sacrificial calendar: Parker 1996, 218–20, and now Lambert 2002*c*.

245 *IG* I^3 84 ll. 23–5 (see n. 175 above).

246 Andoc. 1.82: *καὶ ἐψηφίσασθε, δοκιμάσαντες πάντας τοὺς νόμους, εἶτ' ἀναγράψαι ἐν τῇ στοᾷ τούτους τῶν νόμων οἳ ἂν <ἀεὶ> δοκιμασθῶσι*; 1.85: *ἐδοκιμάσθησαν μὲν οὖν οἱ νόμοι, ὦ ἄνδρες, κατὰ τὸ ψήφισμα τουτί, τοὺς δὲ κυρωθέντας ἀνέγραψαν εἰς τὴν στοάν* (There was a revision of the laws, gentlemen, in obedience to this decree, and such as were approved were inscribed in the Stoa; trans. by Maidment 1941). To be fair, Andocides does not explicitly mention the *Basileios Stoa*, but this identification

Otherwise, the enacting decree of Teisamenos, which Andocides cites verbatim, makes no mention of the stoa at all, but only of 'the Wall' (εἰς τὸν τοῖχον), the implication being that to the Athenians of the late fifth century 'the Wall' (ὁ τοῖχος) was a location easily recognizable without the need for further specification.[247] Walbank considered the wall (τοῖχος) of *IG* I³ 84 to refer to the wall of the *temenos* of Kodros, but Lewis and Thompson argued that it was none other than the rear wall of the Royal Stoa and, in view of Andocides' evidence, their judgement should be preferred.[248] Overall, it appears that leasing documents were indeed inscribed in, or near, the Royal Stoa. Walbank also allowed for the possibility that there were some duplicate copies of leases erected on the Acropolis, but this seems less likely.[249]

A final technical problem in our passage is the interpretation of the enigmatic *epistylia* (ἐπιστύλια) and their exact location. Traditionally they have been interpreted as pigeon-holes, and they are so taken in the relevant entry in the authoritative LSJ.[250] This explanation, however, is exclusively based on the passage under consideration and finds no independent confirmation. It would be linguistically and conceptually more economical to assume that the *epistylia* were exactly what we know them to have been from other sources, namely architectural elements, usually wooden or stone beams, standing on top of columns and comprising the superstructure of ancient buildings.[251] If the building implied as the repository for these records was the Metroon—known also as the Old Bouleuterion in modern jargon—the main public archive of Classical Athens, then the γραμματεῖα would have presumably been attached to the upper

has generally been endorsed by most scholars (e.g. Ostwald 1986, 513 with n. 60; Rhodes 1991, 90–1; contra Robertson 1990, 43–52).

[247] Andoc. 1.84: τοὺς δὲ κυρουμένους τῶν νόμων ἀναγράφειν εἰς τὸν τοῖχον, ἵνα περ πρότερον ἀνεγράφησαν, σκοπεῖν τῷ βουλομένῳ (those laws which are approved shall be inscribed upon the wall, where they were inscribed aforetime, for anyone who wishes to see; trans. by Maidment 1941).

[248] Lewis on *IG* I³ 84; Thompson's view reported *per epistulam* to Walbank 1991, 154 n. 26. Pébarthe 2006, 237 speaks of 'un mur', clearly not thinking of the Royal Stoa.

[249] Walbank 1983*d*, 226 n. 119.

[250] First suggested by Sandys 1893, 174, and recently endorsed by Rhodes 1993, 557. For the slightly different view that the ἐπιστύλια were horizontal wooden shelves see Wilhelm 1909*a*, 248; Valavanis 2002, 249. Pébarthe 2006, 159, thinks of 'étagères'.

[251] Orlandos and Travlos 1986, s.v. ἐπιστύλια; Hellmann 1992, 136.

part of it, either by nails or some similar means.[252] Unfortunately the remains of the edifice traditionally recognized as the Metroon are too scanty to allow anything but the most speculative restorations.[253]

To recapitulate: Aristotle's account of the leasing of sacred estates in Classical Athens seems to draw material from a law and possibly a series of legislative amendments concerning *temene*. Already in operation in the fifth century, the 'law about the *temene*' (*νόμος περὶ τῶν τεμενῶν*) might have undergone some minor changes, or even a considerable revision in the interim between 418/7 (date of the first explicit mention of such a law), and the time of the composition of the *Athenaion Politeia*. Thus, it is highly unlikely that the law was not surveyed, re-edited, or otherwise fiddled with in the two terms of the *anagrapheis*' work of revising the Athenian code of laws, both after the oligarchic coup of 411/0 and the end of the Thirty's reign of terror in 403.[254] The same law, one suspects, is implied in the decree on the Sacred Orgas.[255] As argued elsewhere, the authorization of the general *ἐπὶ τὴν χώραν* to safeguard the Attic sanctuaries alludes to a further modification of the law on the *temene*. Clauses originating in this law and contained in the *Athenaion Politeia* can be tentatively codified as following:

(i) The *basileus* leased out the *temene*.
(ii) The lease length was stipulated as ten years.
(iii) Payments had to be made yearly, in the ninth prytany.
(iv) Rentals had to be paid in to the *apodektai*.

Clauses inferred from epigraphic or other sources are:

(v) In the process of bidding, each lessee had to provide a solvent citizen guarantor for every leased *temenos*. For *temene* fetching a price

[252] Metroon as the building to be understood in Arist. [*Ath. Pol.*] 47–8: Sickinger 1999, 127–9. Pébarthe 2006, 158 is non-committal.

[253] Archaeological report of the classical Metroon/Old Bouleuterion: Thompson 1937, 127–35; for the recent debate on its exact layout see Miller 1995 contra Shear Jr. 1995. For similar problems concerning the Hellenistic Metroon see the splendid analysis by Valavanis 2002.

[254] Ostwald 1986, 497–524; Rhodes 1991.

[255] RO 58 ll. 16–18: *[ἐπι]μελεῖσθαι [δ]ὲ τῆς ἱερᾶς ὀργάδος καὶ τῶν ἄλλω|[ν ἱερῶν ἁπάν]ṭων τῶν Ἀθήνησιν ἀπὸ τῆσδε τῆς ἡμέρας εἰς τὸν | [ἀεὶ χρόνον οὓ]ς τε ὁ νόμος κελεύει περὶ ἑκάστου αὐτῶν*, but reading with Lambert 2005, 132 *[τεμε]ṇῶν* and thus translating: 'From this day onwards those specifically so commanded by the law are to look after the Sacred Orgas and all the other sacred *temene* at Athens'; see Appendix I.ii.

higher than 600 drachmas two suretyships had to be offered and so on.

(vi) The *apodektai* had to disburse the rentals from the *temene* to the appropriate sacred officials.

(vii) The latter had to use the rentals to defray whatever sacred expenditure occurred, mainly sacrifices.

Some clauses like iv to vii might have been repeated in, or derived from, other laws, like the 'tax-farming laws' (*νόμοι τελωνικοί*), the 'law about the merismos' (*μερισμός*), and so on. As already suggested, this overlap would have occasionally created considerable confusion, and since it is an impossible task to put those various statutes in a chronological sequence, let alone to discover their original content, it is equally hopeless to reconstruct the exact phrasing of the *law about the temene* beyond the vaguest of terms.

6. INVESTING SACRED RENTALS

The fusion of religion within ancient Greek society, as summarized in the concept of 'polis religion', has often resulted in utterly confusing abstractions. Such is, for instance, the affirmation of many scholars that the separation between the sacred and secular realms is a modern, biased misconception. But as far as Athenian economics is concerned, such a position falters when juxtaposed to a long-acknowledged terminological *topos*, the distinction between *ἱερά* and *ὅσια* money.[256] Thus, for most of the fifth century the main

[256] Ferguson 1932, 3; Maffi 1982; Connor 1988; Faraguna 1992, 177–9. Demosthenes' *Against Timokrates* abounds with such references, e.g. Dem. 24.82 (n. 219 above); 112: *ὑφείλοντο χρήματα πολλὰ τὰ μὲν ἱερά, τὰ δ' ὅσια* (they had embezzled large sums of money, in part *hiera*, in part *hosia*); 137: *καὶ δόξαντας ἔχειν ἱερὰ χρήματα καὶ ὅσια* (and those who are declared to be detaining *hiera* and *hosia* money; trans. by Vince 1935). See also Pl. *Leg.* IX 857b: *Πῶς δὴ λέγομεν, ὦ ξένε, μηδὲν διαφέρειν τῷ κλέπτοντι μέγα ἢ σμικρὸν ὑφελομένῳ, καὶ ἐξ ἱερῶν ἢ ὁσίων, καὶ ὅσα ἄλλα ἐστὶν περὶ κλοπὴν πᾶσαν ἀνομοιότητα ἔχοντα;* (How comes it, stranger, that we are ruling that it makes no difference to the thief whether the thing he steals be great or small, and whether it come from the *hiera* or the *hosia*, etc.; trans. by Bury 1926); Pl. *Resp.* 344a: *ἔστιν δὲ τοῦτο τυρρανίς, ἣ οὐ κατὰ σμικρὸν τἀλλότρια καὶ λάθρᾳ καὶ βίᾳ ἀφαιρεῖται, καὶ ἱερὰ καὶ ὅσια καὶ ἴδια καὶ δημόσια, ἀλλὰ συλλήβδην*; Arist. [*Ath. Pol.*] 30.2: *καὶ ταμίας τῶν ἱερῶν χρημάτων τῇ θε[ῷ] καὶ τοῖς ἄλλοις θεοῖς δέκα καὶ ἑλληνοταμίας καὶ τῶν ἄλλων ὁσίων χρημάτων ἁπάντων εἴκοσιν οἳ διαχειριοῦσιν*

treasury of Athens was that of Athena Polias with, second in importance and financial capacity, that of the Other Gods. The third treasury of Athens, τὸ δημόσιον, is generally believed to have been of lesser significance at the time.[257] But the existence of a public purse and, therefore, the parallel keeping of separate chests, was surely generated by certain practical and/or ideological attitudes, such as those embodied in the ἱερόν/ὅσιον dichotomy. Yet it would be at least uncritical to say that this distinction was always clear-cut. On the contrary, it frequently became blurred. No doubt, this confusion arose from the administrative strategem whereby the polis handled both budgets in an increasingly diffuse way,[258] the last development of which was the creation of the office of ὁ ἐπὶ τῇ διοικήσει.[259] Nonetheless, I can state in advance my conviction that administratively secular and sacred economics never ended up coinciding. It is in this context that I intend to investigate the employment of sacred rentals by the Athenians in the Classical period.

> ἀπὸ μισθωμάτων. Δίδυμός φησιν ὁ γραμματικὸς ἀντὶ τοῦ ἐκ τεμενικῶν προσόδων. ἑκάστῳ γὰρ θεῷ πλέθρα γῆς ἀπένεμον, ἐξ ὧν μισθουμένων αἱ εἰς τὰς θυσίας ἐγίνοντα δαπάναι.
>
> From rentals. Didymos the grammarian says, in the sense of 'from income from *temene*'; for they dedicated tracts of land to each god, which they leased out in order to cover the expenditure for the sacrifices.[260]

This well-known lemma from Harpocratio's *Lexicon* gives a succinct, but illuminating, glimpse of an important financial device employed by Athens—and, no doubt, other Greek city-states—for the efficient performance of religious rituals.[261] More widespread

(. . . ten treasurers of the sacred funds of the Goddess and the Other Gods, twenty *hellenotamiai* to administer their own treasury and all other secular funds), with Rhodes 1993, 391–2; Harp. s.v. ὅσιον. As has aptly been observed recently by Samons 2000, 325–9, the term ὅσιος should not be rendered as 'secular', but, in opposition to ἱερός, as 'non-sacral', denoting what did not belong to gods and yet was sanctioned by them.

257 A fact that has often led to totally unfounded claims, e.g. Bruit Zaidman and Schmitt-Pantel 1992, 94: '[s]trictly speaking, the state of Athens had no public finances'.

258 Cf. Blok 2010, 80–2.

259 For this office, see Lewis 1997, and now Rhodes 2007, 349–55.

260 Harp. S.V. ἀπὸ μισθωμάτων; cf. Hegyi 1976, 84; Faraguna 1992, 341–2 with n. 20; Dignas 2002, 97.

261 Thus already Guiraud 1893, 362–81.

than sometimes thought, the principle of setting aside lands for the supply of customary offerings to gods is already a *topos* in theoreticians' treatises, such as Hippodamos' oeuvre as epitomized by Aristotle, Plato's *Laws*, and pseudo-Aristotle's *Rhetorica ad Alexandrum*.[262] At a more practical level, two examples are worth citing, since they reflect Athenian mentality: Nikias' consecration of a land-holding to Delian Apollo for the subsidy of sacrificial banquets, and Xenophon's similar offering of the tithe from a consecrated estate at Skillous for the performance of sacrifices to Artemis Ephesia.[263]

To say that sacred economics have been met with scholarly indifference would be wide of the mark. We know quite a lot about the so-called temple inventories as well as the system of public sacrifices in Classical Athens, but details remain by and large elusive. Here is the place to pose the double question: to what extent does independent evidence confirm the statement of Didymus and what were the exact means of exploitation of rentals from sacred properties administered by Athens? In his learned monograph on the Athenian system of public sacrifices Rosivach argued for the need to distinguish the *patrioi thysiai* (*πάτριοι θυσίαι*, i.e. ancestral sacrifices) from the relatively newer *epithetoi heortai* (*ἐπίθετοι ἑορταί*, i.e. additional

[262] Arist. *Pol.* 1267^b30–5, *διῄρει* (sc. *Ἱππόδαμος*) *δ' εἰς τρία μέρη τὴν χώραν, τὴν μὲν ἱερὰν τὴν δὲ δημοσίαν τὴν δ' ἰδίαν· ὅθεν μὲν τὰ νομιζόμενα ποιήσουσι πρὸς τοὺς θεούς, ἱεράν* etc. (The territory also he proposed to divide into three parts, a sacred, a public and a private; that from which the customary worship of the gods could be maintained would be sacred...; trans. by Rackham 1944). Pl. *Leg.* 738d-e: *ἐν δὲ τῇ τῆς γῆς διανομῇ πρώτοις ἐξαίρετα τεμένη τε καὶ πάντα τὰ προσήκοντα ἀποδοτέον, ὅπως ἂν σύλλογοι ἑκάστων τῶν μερῶν κατὰ χρόνους γιγνόμενοι τοὺς προσταχθέντας εἴς τε τὰς χρείας ἑκάστας εὐμάρειαν παρασκευάζωσι καὶ φιλοφρονῶνταί τε ἀλλήλους μετὰ θυσιῶν καὶ οἰκειῶνται καὶ γνωρίζωσιν* (And in the distribution of the land he should assign first to these divinities choice domains with all that pertains to them, so that, when assemblies of each of the sections take place at the appointed times, they may probvide an ample supply of things requisite, and the people may fraternize with one another at the sacrifices and gain knowledge and intimacy), with Isager and Skydsgaard 1992, 184; ibid. 759e: *ταμίας δὲ δὴ τῶν τε ἱερῶν χρημάτων ἑκάστοις τοῖς ἱεροῖς καὶ τεμενῶν καὶ καρπῶν τούτων καὶ μισθώσεων κυρίους αἱρεῖσθαι* etc. (and we must choose treasurers to control the sacred funds in each of the sanctuaries, and the sacred estates, with their produce and their rents; trans. by Bury 1926) [Arist.] *Rhet. ad Alex.* 1425^b: *πρῶτον μὲν οὖν σκεπτέον εἴ τι τῶν τῆς πόλεως κτημάτων ἠμελημένον ἐστὶ καὶ μήτε πρόσοδον ποιεῖ μήτε τοῖς θεοῖς ἐξαίρετόν ἐστιν.*

[263] Plut. *Vit. Nic.* 3.6: *καὶ χωρίον μυρίων δραχμῶν πριάμενος καθιέρωσεν, οὗ τὰς προσόδους ἔδει Δηλίους καταθύοντας ἑστιᾶσθαι, πολλὰ καὶ ἀγαθὰ Νικίᾳ παρὰ τῶν θεῶν αἰτουμένους*, with Guarducci 1974, 246–7; Isager and Skydsgaard 1992, 183. Xen. *Anab.* 5.3.4–11, with Purvis 2003, 65–120.

feasts).[264] The former were presumably subsidized from revenue raised through leasing of sacred lands as part of a 'self-supporting' scheme.[265] Rosivach's main position, though basically correct, needs modification at certain points. As it happens, his belief in the intimate linkage between rentals from sacred properties and financing of ancestral sacrifices was based on the following excerpt from Isocrates' *Areopagitikos*:

> *οὐδὲ τὰς μὲν ἐπιθέτους ἑορτάς, αἷς ἑστίασίς τις προσείη, μεγαλοπρεπῶς ἦγον, ἐν δὲ τοῖς ἁγιωτάτοις τῶν ἱερῶν ἀπὸ μισθωμάτων ἔθυον.* (Isoc. *Areop*. 29)
>
> They did not sumptuously conduct the additional festivals at which there was feasting, while making the sacrifices for the holiest of rites using rentals. (Translation by Mirhady and Too 2000).

Isocrates' attitude to the leasing practice may seem disparaging, but his account probably reflects a practice current in his day and should, therefore, be taken at face value.[266] A similar pattern appears in an often overlooked late fifth-century passage; in his scornful account of democratic Athens' proclivity for massive sacred feasts, the *Old Oligarch* relates:

> *Θυσίας δὲ καὶ ἱερὰ καὶ ἑορτὰς καὶ τεμένη γνοὺς ὁ δῆμος ὅτι οὐχ οἷόν τέ ἐστιν ἑκάστῳ τῶν πενήτων θύειν καὶ εὐωχεῖσθαι καὶ ἵστασθαι ἱερὰ καὶ πόλιν οἰκεῖν καλὴν καὶ μεγάλην, ἐξηῦρεν ὅτῳ τρόπῳ ἔσται ταῦτα. θύουσιν οὖν δημοσίᾳ μὲν ἡ πόλις ἱερεῖα πολλά· ἔστι δὲ ὁ δῆμος ὁ εὐωχούμενος καὶ διαλαγχάνων τὰ ἱερεῖα.* (Xen. [*Ath. Pol.*] 2.9).
>
> As for sacrifices and shrines and feasts and *temene*, the *demos* realise that each individual of the poor does not have the ability to sacrifice and provide a feast and set up sanctuaries and create a beautiful and great city to live in, and so they have found a way by which all these things can be acquired. Hence it is the state which at public expense sacrifices many victims, but it is the *demos* who enjoy the feasts, and to whom the victims are allocated.

[264] Rosivach 1994, 54–5, 115, 146–7; see also Parker 1996, 7–8 n. 25, 152 n. 3.

[265] Faraguna 1992, 342 with n. 20; Rosivach, 1994, 121–7.

[266] Mikalson 1983, 95–7; Garland 1929, 23–4; especially Faraguna 1992, 341–2 with n. 20 who rightly reprimands Norlin 1929, 123 and Mathieu 1942, 70 n. 2. Regardless of the exact year of the Areopagitikos (see Wallace 1986 for the various dates before, during, or after the Social War), the financial crisis that Athens experienced in the 350s would hardly have left the leasing sector unscathed.

I have underlined the four nouns above in order to bring out the obvious connection of this excerpt with Isocrates' aphorism via Harpocratio. Contrary to what Rosivach would have us believe,[267] pseudo-Xenophon alludes to the practice of leasing out *temene* in order to raise money for performance of sacrifices. More tacit are such allusions as can be found in Lykourgos' *Contra Leocratem*. Thus, in the preface of his speech, the Athenian *überpatriot* evokes the assistance of the gods for the successful prosecution of Leokrates 'who has betrayed the temples, shrines, and estates of the gods as well as the honours granted by the laws and the sacrificial rites handed down by your ancestors'.[268] Here again, Lykourgos' line of argument—by his desertion Leokrates had endangered the sacred precincts and, by default, the traditional sacrifices subsidized from them—is brought out by the seamless link between sacred rentals and cultic activity.[269]

Returning to the theme of the *πάτριοι θυσίαι*, we may note that the magistrate in charge of their performance was the *basileus*, who would occasionally receive assistance from the polemarch, though the latter's role is not quite clear to us.[270] The *basileus*' involvement in

[267] Rosivach 1994, 121; cf. Parker 1996, 128–9. Commentators of this paragraph have been undeviatingly perplexed. Frisch 1942, 255, e.g., translates *τεμένη* as 'temples', and analyses accordingly. Similarly, Brock and Heath 1995, 564–5, understand the *τεμένη* to be 'sanctuaries'. Gray 2007, 200, vaguely speaks of the loose connection of the four accusatives of respect to the ensuing infinitives. Marr and Rhodes 2008 cautiously translate 'precincts', but do not elaborate.

[268] Lycurg. *Leoc.* 1: {*τὸν*} *προδόντ' αὐτῶν καὶ τοὺς νεὼς καὶ τὰ ἕδη καὶ τὰ τεμένη καὶ τὰς ἐν τοῖς νόμοις τιμὰς καὶ θυσίας τὰς ὑπὸ τῶν ὑμετέρων προγόνων παραδεδομένας*; cf. ibid. 143: *οὐχ ὧν τοὺς νεὼς καὶ τὰ ἕδη καὶ τὰ τεμένη προὔδωκε*; (Has he not, then, betrayed the temples and the altars and the sacred estates?)

[269] That *temene* here should be understood not as the generic term for shrines, but in its narrower sense of profit-generating tillable lands, can be seen not only in the juxtaposition of the term to the word *νεώς* (temples), but also in section 147 of the same speech (*ἀσεβείας δ' ὅτι τοῦ τὰ τεμένη τέμνεσθαι καὶ τοὺς νεὼς κατασκάπτεσθαι τὸ καθ' ἑαυτὸν γέγονεν αἴτιος*), where the language used is that of devastation of agricultural land; cf. Hanson 1998, 190–4, with ample documentation of the verb *τέμνω* meaning 'to cut/ravage' cultivated plants. Revealingly, *τέμνω* does not occur amongst the multitude of infinitives assembled by Pollux to describe the act of destroying a temple (Poll. *Onom.* 1.12, with Theodoridis 2003, 76).

[270] Arist. [*Ath. Pol.*] 57.1: *ὡς δ' ἔπος εἰπεῖν καὶ τὰς πατρίους θυσίας διοικεῖ οὗτος* (sc. *ὁ βασιλεύς*) *πάσας* (And one might say, that he administers all the traditional sacrifices), with Rhodes 1993, 639; Pl. *Plt.* 290e: *τῷ γὰρ λαχόντι βασιλεῖ φασι τῇδε τὰ σεμνότατα καὶ μάλιστα πάτρια τῶν ἀρχαίων θυσιῶν ἀποδεδόσθαι* (For they say the holiest and the ancestral *par excellence* of the ancient sacrifices are performed by the man who has been allotted as the *basileus*). For the co-operation of the polemarch

the *patrioi thysiai* and his duty as leasing agent of the polis-*temene* provide the best, albeit indirect, hint in support of the hypothesis that, in effect, sacred rentals were meant to subsidize the patrimonial Athenian cults. Indeed, one of the festivals that the *basileus* is explicitly attested as having under his supervision was the Eleusinian Mysteries and, revealingly, he was also the administrative lessor of estates, the rentals from which subsidized the festival.[271] Clear as this may seem, there is an acknowledged difficulty in defining what the ancestral sacrifices exactly were. Despite their title, not all of them were necessarily old. Take the sacrifices to Artemis Agrotera, for instance. First established after the victorious battle of Marathon in 490, their performance was the duty of the polemarch;[272] and yet for Rosivach the late establishment of the cult would necessitate its classification as an *additional feast*. However, by virtue of its absence from the Dermatikon Account, Rosivach had to acknowledge that Artemis Agrotera was puzzlingly omitted.[273] I think the presence of the polemarch points in the opposite direction. Even more important is the fact that Artemis features amongst the landowning divinities in the leases from 343/2 onwards.

So the investigation of the ancestral sacrifices on the basis of chronological considerations proves fruitless. A further point raised by Rosivach was that Nikomachos' sacrificial calendar consisted exclusively of the ancestral sacrifices that were to be subsidized from sacred rentals.[274] Yet the recently re-edited Athenian sacrificial

see Arist. [*Ath. Pol.*] 3.3: *σημεῖον καὶ [τὸ] μηδὲν τῶν πατρίων τὸν ἄρχ[ο]ντα διοικεῖν, ὥσπερ ὁ βασιλεὺς καὶ ὁ πολέμαρχος, ἀλλ' ἁπλῶ[ς] τὰ ἐπίθετα* (That the office of the *archon* was the last of these is confirmed by the fact that the *archon* is not responsible for any of the traditional festivals, as the *basileus* and *polemarch* are, but only for the newer creations; trans. by Rhodes 1984), with Rhodes 1993, 101–2; cf. Garland 1992, 24–5.

[271] *I.Eleusis* 177 (*IG* II[2] 1672), ll. 370–6, for which see above, Section 3; Poll. *Onom.* 8.90: *ὁ δὲ βασιλεὺς μυστηρίων προέστηκε μετὰ τῶν ἐπιμελητῶν καὶ Ληναίων καὶ ἀγώνων τῶν ἐπὶ λαμπάδι, καὶ τὰ περὶ τὰς πατρίους θυσίας διοικεῖ* (The *basileus* presides over the Mysteries, along with the supervisors, and over the Lenaia and the torch-contests, and administers affairs relating to the ancestral sacrifices).

[272] Arist. [*Ath. Pol.*] 58.1: *ὁ δὲ πολέμαρχος θύει μὲν θυσίας τῇ τε Ἀρτέμιδι τῇ Ἀγροτέρᾳ καὶ τῷ Ἐνυαλίῳ* (the polemarch performs the sacrifices to Artemis Agrotera and to Enyalios), with Rhodes 1993, 650; see also Garland 1992, 24, and Parker 2005, 398, 461–2.

[273] *Dermatikon* Accounts (*IG* II[2] 1496): Rosivach 1994, 48–67, and esp. 57–8 with regard to Artemis Agrotera; cf. Mikalson 1998, 36–9.

[274] Rosivach 1994, 47.

calendar contains various entries which disprove this assumption, not least the entry about the celebration of the Epidauria, which cannot have begun in Athens before the arrival of the cult of Asklepios in 420, and that of the Eleusinia, which features in the Dermatikon account, and should, according to Rosivach's argument, have been deemed an *epithetos heorte* rather than a *patrios thysia*.[275] But the most unequivocal evidence against the view that the revised sacrificial calendar contained only ancestral sacrifices is the famous 30th Lysianic speech delivered against Nikomachos, an *anagrapheus* of the appointed commission. It was the latter's insertion of innovative rites in the code that ostensibly incited the prosecutor's fury against the defendant.[276] We now have good modern accounts of the trial, which demonstrate that Nikomachos was not on the wrong side, as the plaintiff would have had us believe.[277] But, after all, what were the *patrioi thysiai*? Was the whole 'patrios debate' not part of the wider 'ancestral constitution' discourse so fashionable after the oligarchical coup of 411? The problem of the *patrios politeia* is itself immense and here only passing references can be made to the debate. In what is arguably the most substantial treatment of the topic, Ostwald aptly observed that following the misfortunes of the Sicilian expedition and the turmoil of 411 the Athenians became obsessed with 'the patrios politeia (ancestral constitution), the patrioi nomoi (ancestral laws), and all the other patria that they believed had once guaranteed the political stability and greatness of Athens'.[278] Thus, sacrifices like the ones performed by the pre-Cleisthenic Ionian tribes were presumably archaic and therefore 'ancestral', and I have argued elsewhere that an early fourth-century inscription concerns the leasing of lands on behalf of the pre-Cleisthenic trittys of the Epakreis.[279]

[275] Athenian sacrificial calendar: Lambert 2002*c* (*SEG* LII 48). Epidauria: *SEG* LII 48, face B, fr. 4, col. II (with Lambert 2002*c*, 387–8); Eleusinia: *SEG* LII 48, face A, fr. 3, col. III, ll. 60–78 (with Lambert 2002*c*, 377-80). For a further demolition of Rosivach's theory see Lambert 2002*a*, 79 with n. 15.

[276] Rhodes 1991, 87–9; Parker 1996, 45 n. 6; Todd 1996, 104. Rosivach 1994, 160–1 tried, unsuccesfully in my view, to explain away some of the contradictions of his theory, although some of his points, such as the repercussions of the Peloponnesian War, are worth considering.

[277] Dow 1960, 274–5, 291–2; Connor 1991, 52–3; Parker 1996, 218–20; Todd 1996; Edwards 1999, 154–62.

[278] Ostwald 1986, 343.

[279] Papazarkadas 2007*b* on *IG* II^2 2490.

In sum, any effort to apply a universal criterion for the classification of certain sacrifices in the revised sacrificial calendar as ancestral is doomed to fail. We simply do not know, and I doubt whether the Athenians themselves would have had a unanimous comprehension of what, in effect, constituted an ancestral sacrifice.[280] Nothing in the preserved pieces of the official Athenian *fasti* proves beyond doubt that sacred rentals were a source of funds for the polis sacrifices, apart from a plausible supplement in an otherwise problematic fragment.[281] Perhaps sacred rentals are implied in another heavily restored rubric, namely *ἐκ τῶν σ[υγγραφῶν]*.[282] Although most scholars tend to identify the *συγγραφαί* of Lysias' speech with the draft of the decree which enacted the recodification of Athens' *fasti*, I am inclined to agree with Robertson's interpretation that the *συγγραφαί* were the draft sacred regulations that had to be collected from various stelae by Nikomachos and his colleagues.[283] If so, we may recall the draft which regulated the lease of the *temenos* of Kodros—a piece of evidence missed by Robertson—and we may further suggest that rentals could indeed have funded the Athenian *fasti*.[284] Interestingly, the new fragment of the *fasti* contains inter alia a provision for a sheep to be offered to Athena Itonia, whom we have already encountered as owner of sacred property.[285] At any rate, the theory that the Peloponnesian War had disrupted the leasing system has surely some validity, but the extant evidence does not allow a

[280] Cf. Finley 1975, 34–40 and Walters 1976, 133–4 about the elasticity of the term *patrios* in Classical Athens.

[281] *SEG* LII 48, face B, fr. 12, l. 2: [- - -]*ομάτον ΛΙΕ*[- - -], traditionally restored [*ἀναλ*]*ομάτον*, i.e. expenses, but Lambert 2002*c*, 390 would also consider [*μισθ*]*ομάτον*, i.e. rentals.

[282] Thus Robertson 1990, 70–1; Lambert now prints l. 77 of *SEG* LII 48, face A, fr. 3 as *ἐκ τῶν στ̣[ηλῶν]* (from the *stelae*), but acknowledges that the dotted letter might be an *ypsilon* (cf. *SEG* LII 48, face B, fr. 12, l. 4: [*κατὰ*? *τ*]*ὰς χσυγγραφά*[*s*]).

[283] Lys. 30.17: *χρὴ θύειν τὰς θυσίας τὰς ἐκ τῶν κύρβεων καὶ τῶν στηλῶν κατὰ τὰς συγγραφάς* (we should perform the sacrifices from the *kyrbeis* and the stelae according to the *syngraphai*); 21: *ὅταν μὲν κατὰ τὰς συγγραφὰς ποιῶμεν, ἅπαντα τὰ πάτρια θύεται* (when we act according to the *syngraphai*, the traditional sacrifices are performed in full); cf. Rhodes 1991, 95; Parker 1996, 45 n. 6; Lambert 2002*c*, 377–8, 391; contra Robertson 1990, 68–71.

[284] *IG* I^3 84 ll. 6–7: *τὸ δὲ τέμενος ὁ βασιλεὺς ἀπομισθοσάτο* [*κ*]|*ατὰ τὰς χσυνγραφάς*. Similar is the terminology in another 5th-cent. document of Athenian origin: *I.Délos* 89 (*IG* I^3 402), ll. 18–19: *ὥστε ἀποδιδόναι τὴμ μίσθωσ*[*ιν ἁπάντων τότων τὸς με*|*μ*]*ισθωμένος κατὰ τὰς συγγραφάς* (that the lessees shall pay in the rental of all these according to the *syngraphai*).

[285] Gawlinski 2007, face A, l. 12: [*Ἀθηναίαι Ἰτ*]*ωνίαι οἶ*[*s*].

definitive answer to the questions posed.[286] In fact, the leasing scheme has to be investigated within the wider financial framework of the Athenian state. Now, the speaker of the oration *Against Nikomachos* brings out an interesting point. He accuses Nikomachos of having put further financial constraint on the polis at a time when a series of disbursements, such as war compensation to the Spartans and the Boeotians, were pending and the city was incapable of spending money on the reconstruction of the walls and the naval sheds.[287] By this, he makes it sound as if sources of sacred funding and secular expenditure were complementary. Although one has to be careful with the biased information disseminated by the cunning speaker of the Lysianic oration—for it was in his interest to let his audience believe that Nikomachos was culpable of wreaking havoc on Athenian economics—his account seems to echo the technicalities of the financial allocation known as *μερισμός* (*merismos*).

This observation offers the opportunity to resume the investigation of the role of the *apodektai*, a topic only briefly broached in the course of the analysis of [Aristotle]'s passage on polis *temene*. Ten in number, representing the ten Athenian tribes, the *apodektai* were the magistrates charged with the task of collecting an array of revenues, which inevitably included rentals from *temene*, and then distributing

[286] Effect of the Peloponnesian War: Rosivach 1994, 160.

[287] Lys. 30.21–2: *ὃς ἐν δυοῖν μὲν ἐτοῖν πλείω ἤδη τοῦ δέοντος δώδεκα ταλάντοις ἀνήλωσε, παρ' ἕκαστον δὲ τὸν ἐνιαυτὸν ἐπεχείρησεν ἓξ ταλάντοις τὴν πόλιν ζημιῶσαι, καὶ ταῦτα ὁρῶν αὐτὴν ἀποροῦσαν χρημάτων καὶ Λακεδαιμονίους μὲν ἀπειλοῦντας, ὅταν μὴ ἀποπέμψωμεν αὐτοῖς τὰ χρήματα, Βοιωτοὺς δὲ σύλας ποιουμένους, ὅτι οὐ δυνάμεθα δύο τάλαντα ἀποδοῦναι, τοὺς δὲ νεωσοίκους <καὶ> τὰ τείχη περικαταρρέοντα* etc. (But he is a man who in two years has already spent twelve talents more than necessary, and has tried to defraud the city of six talents per year, even though he could see that the city needed money, that the Spartans were making threats whenever we did not send them payments, that the Boeotians were resorting to raids because we were unable to repay two talents, and that the shipsheds and the city walls were in ruins; trans. by Todd 2000). Let me briefly note here the importance of the last point raised by the prosecutor. The reconstruction of the Athenian walls after their demolition by the Spartans is traditionally assigned to Konon, following his success against the Spartan fleet in the battle of Knidos in August 394. However, our speech shows that already in 399 the Athenians broached the possibility of repairing the walls. Indeed, independent epigraphical evidence indicates that work on the walls was already under way before Knidos (see *IG* II^2 1656–7 with Rhodes and Osborne 2003, 46–9, who provide all the post-Knidos testimonia). At a completely different level, these observations would strongly support the theory that Polykrates' speech on the trial of Socrates was actually delivered in 399 and it was not a later fabrication as generally assumed on the basis of a reference to the reconstruction of the Athenian circuit wall (see Hansen 1995*b*, 8). The whole topic deserves a thorough re-examination.

them as part of the financial scheme of *merismos*.[288] In spite of its clear importance for Athenian economics, the *merismos* has strangely received little attention from scholars. Two exceptions have been Rhodes—who has described it as a more professional pattern of financial administration, whereby 'various *ἀρχαί* were given an annual allowance for their ordinary expenses', whereas previously certain portions of public money were earmarked for particular outlay—and Faraguna.[289] It is worth investigating the validity of this claim and, more broadly, the nature of this financial procedure, since it is so obviously relevant to the problem of the usage of sacred rentals. In this light, it is important that the *apodektai* (thought already in antiquity to have been created by Cleisthenes in order to supersede the *kolakretai*) are first attested in *IG* I^3 84 from 418/7. This inscribed lease of the Neleion reveals a situation similar to the one described by Aristotle, but goes further in presenting the board of the Treasurers of the Other Gods as the final recipients of the relevant proceeds from the *apodektai*.[290] Though it is often assumed that the *merismos* was a fourth-century innovation,[291] one wonders whether the operation of the *apodektai* in this context should not be perceived as either the first extant testimony of the system, or as a primeval version of it, a kind of

[288] Arist. [*Ath. Pol.*] 48.1–2: [*Εἰσὶ*] *δ' ἀποδέκται δέκα κεκληρωμένοι κατὰ φυλάς· οὗτοι δὲ παραλαβόντες τὰ [γρα]μματεῖα, ἀπαλείφουσι τὰ καταβαλλόμενα χρήματα ἐναντίον τ[ῆς βουλῆς] ἐν τῷ βουλευτηρίῳ, καὶ πάλιν ἀποδιδόασιν τὰ γραμματεῖα τ[ῷ δη]μοσίῳ... τῇ μὲν οὖν προτεραίᾳ δέχονται τὰς [πάσα]ς καὶ μερίζουσι ταῖς ἀρχαῖς, τῇ δ' ὑστεραίᾳ τόν τε μερισμὸν εἰσ[φέρου]σι γράψαντες ἐν σανίδι καὶ καταλέγουσιν ἐν τῷ βουλευτηρίῳ* (There are ten *apodektai*, appointed tribally by lot: they take over the tablets and delete the sums paid, in the presence of the council in the council house, and give back the tablets to the public slave again etc.; trans. by Rhodes 1984), with Rhodes 1993, 557–60; Arist. *Pol.* 1321^b.31–3: *ἄλλη δ' ἀρχὴ πρὸς ἣν αἱ πρόσοδοι τῶν κοινῶν ἀναφέρονται, παρ' ὧν φυλαττόντων μερίζονται πρὸς ἑκάστην διοίκησιν· καλοῦσι δ' ἀποδέκτας τούτους καὶ ταμίας*; cf. Poll. *Onom.* 9.97.

[289] Rhodes 1972, 99–103; Faraguna 1992, 179–85; 191–4 (Sakellariou 1999, 266–70 is useful, but somewhat inaccessible).

[290] *IG* I^3 84 ll. 15–18: *κ|αταβαλλέτο τὸ ἀργύριον ἐπὶ τῆς ἐνάτες πρυτανείας τοῖς ἀποδέκ|ται[s], οἱ δὲ ἀποδέκται τοῖς ταμίαισι τôν ἄλλον θεôν παραδιδόντον | [κ]ατὰ τὸν νόμον* (He shall pay down the money to the *apodektai* in the ninth prytany, and the *apodektai* will hand it over to the Treasurers of the Other Gods, in accordance with the law); cf. Rhodes 1972, 99 with n. 3; Linders 1975, 32–6; 91–2; Faraguna 1992, 179, 344.

[291] *IG* II^2 29 ll. 18–22: *μερίσαι δὲ τ|ὸ ἀργύριον τὸ εἰρημένον τὸς ἀποδέ|κτας ἐκ τῶν καταβαλλομένων χρημά||[τ]ων, ἐπειδὰν τὰ ἐκ τῶν νόμων μερ[ίσω|σι]* (The *apodektai* will allocate the aforesaid money from the money deposited after they will have allocated what the laws ordain) is often considered the first attestation of the *μερισμός* (date: 386/5); see Rhodes and Osborne 2003, 82–3.

proto-*merismos*. But if so, the system must have been much subtler than usually portrayed, for the *apodektai* in *IG* I³ 84 are instructed to allocate not some unspecifed monetary sum, but the very income realized from the leasing of the Neleion. In this sense, it would be very illuminating if we managed to identify the baffling law regulating the transaction (*IG* I³ 84 l. 18, [κ]ατὰ τὸν νόμον). This has variously been interpreted as the law [*sic*] which established the board of the Treasurers of the Other Gods (i.e. ML 58),[292] or even the law about the *temene*,[293] but it may be in fact the law about the *merismos*, the last two explanations not being mutually exclusive. Even outside the narrow scope of rentals, one can detect similar indications regarding the *merismos*. Thus, in the famous Athenian law on silver coinage the *apodektai* were instructed to reimburse the salary of the newly appointed approver in the Piraeus 'from the same source as for the mint-workers'.[294] Here again, the allocation seems to concern not only the destination of the funds controlled by the *apodektai*, but also, and more significantly, the sources of revenues.

At any rate, if the *merismos* was already in operation at the time of the Peace of Nikias, then my suggestion above that it also underlay the discourse about the calendar of Nikomachos might receive further corroboration. We have to return to a careful examination of the various *testimonia* to clarify the picture. Rentals of *temene* should theoretically end up under the control of sacred officials and, by deduction, the Treasurers of Athena must have received income from leases of Athena's *temene*. In *IG* II² 334 (RO 81B) the income raised from the lease of the Nea was to be used for the funding of the Lesser Panathenaia; in that case it was the *hieropoioi* who were commanded to use the rent to buy sacrificial victims along with the *boonai*, but it is not certain whether they had received the money directly from the *apodektai* or through the Treasurers of Athena.[295]

[292] Thus Lewis 1960, 193 n. 13; Rhodes 1972, 99 n. 3; Faraguna 1992, 344; but this seems wrong, for Kallias' first document is a decree, not a law.

[293] Behrend 1970, 59; Linders 1975, 92 n. 85; Faraguna 1992, 344.

[294] RO 25 (*SEG* XXVI 72), ll. 52–5: *μεριζόντων οἱ <ἀ>ποδέκται ὅσομπερ τ̣[ῶι] | ἐν ἄστει δοκιμαστῆι, ἐς δὲ τὸν λοιπὸγ χρόν[ον ἕνα]||ι αὐτῶι τὴμ μισθοφορίαν ὅθεμπερ τοῖς ἀργυ̣[ροκό]||ποις*; cf. Stroud 1974*a*, 184.

[295] RO 81B (*IG* II² 334), ll. 16-20: *[ἀ]πὸ δὲ τῶν τε[τταρ]άκοντα μνῶν καὶ τῆς μι||[ᾶς τῶν ἐκ τῆς μ]ισθώσεως τῆς Νέας βοωνήσαντες οἱ ἱερ||[οποιοὶ μετὰ τ]ῶν βοώνων πέμψαντες τὴν πομπὴν τῆι θε||[ῶι θυόντων τα]ύτας τὰς βοῦς ἁπάσας ἐπὶ τῶι βωμῶι τῆς | [Ἀθηνᾶς τῶι με]γάλωι*. Lewis 1959*b*, 245 restored lines 19–21 of the law preceding

Similarly, it is clear that in the Eleusinian accounts *IG* II^2 1672 (*I.Eleusis* 177), although rentals (*μισθώματα*) end up in the fund of the Treasurers of the Two Goddesses without the mediation of the *apodektai*, we have a digression from the normal procedure, and that money being disbursed through the *apodektai*, i.e. by means of the *merismos*, was the normal practice.[296]

Maybe we should not press our evidence too hard. I have already mentioned the rental from the quarry of Asklepios that subsidized the preliminary sacrifices offered by the *epistatai* of the Piraean shrine. The *apodektai* appear to have had no involvement at all and the whole transaction probably took place outside the framework of *merismos*, if the system was in operation by that time, which is far from certain. The date of the lease in question should help us discount a commonly held, but ultimately mistaken, notion, namely that setting aside certain funds for specific purposes is a characteristic of the Lykourgan administration. Such a mechanism of endowments is often thought to mark a professionalization of Athenian economics that can only be assigned to the era of Lykourgos.[297] This holds true for Nea in relation to the Lesser Panathenaia, the Rharian Field in relation to the Eleusinia, and the Eleusinian precincts as source of income for the Mysteries. Yet we can now see that Lykourgos only built upon pre-existing schemes. Such endowments aside, it is not compulsory to assume that sacred rentals of any given deity would have exclusively funded that deity's festivities. Phanodemos' law on Amphiaraos' cult, for instance, demonstrates that more than one deity would have been the recipient of sacrifices offered in the sanctuary, even though the only nominal owner of the relevant revenues—mainly sacred rentals as I have argued above—was

the decree (*SEG* XVIII 13 = RO 81A) as [*οἱ δὲ ἀ|ποδέκται με*]*ρ̣ιζόντων αὐτὸ εἰς ταῦ*[*τα τοῖς ἱεροποιο|ῖς*], but while the participation of the *ἀποδέκται* is almost certain in the light of the verb [*με*]*ρ̣ιζόντων* (cf. Faraguna 1992, 181 with n. 34), the rest is very conjectural, as Lewis himself admitted. Indeed, in *IG* I^3 375 (410/9 BC) the *ἱεροποιοὶ κατ' ἐνιαυτόν* received a considerable sum of money from the Treasurers of Athena for the Panathenaic hekatomb, a fact that could reinforce the assumption that the rent from Nea ended up in the hands of the *hieropoioi* through the Treasurers of Athena (cf. Rosivach 1994, 113). For a new approach to the financial provisions of the Law on the Lesser Panathenaia see now Sosin 2002, 123–5, although his restoration *τ*[*ῶν ἐνεστηκότων ἀ|ποδεκτῶν με*]*ρ̣ιζόντων* of ll. 19–20 (=*SEG* LII 92) lacks Attic parallels; cf. Lambert 2005, 144–5 n. 69.

296 *I.Eleusis* 177 (*IG* II^2 1672), ll. 370–6, for which see Section 3 above.

297 Lewis 1959*b*, 246; Sosin 2002.

Amphiaraos.[298] Given the intricate cultic interconnections evident in the case of *σύνναοι θεοί* (gods worshipped in the same temple), this is hardly surprising. Yet a similar financial mechanism is attested in various deme documents, e.g. in *I.Rhamnous* 180, where the income from a *temenos* owned by Nemesis appears to subsidize other local cults as well.[299] The extended cognizance of financial committees such as that of the Treasurers of the Other Gods makes it almost certain that such would have been the case with the investment of sacred rentals controlled by the polis of Athens. This remark could explain a striking financial feature of the Athenian sacrificial calendar. A long time ago Dow argued that an entry of the total sacrificial cost for a whole month in the *fasti* disproved the interpretation of the various rubrics as sources of funding and instead suggested that they should be understood as sources of authority. Scholars have unanimously embraced Dow's interpretation.[300] Yet the analysis offered above should suffice to prove that this reckoning system is not incompatible with the idea of sacred rentals funding whole sets of sacrifices, as opposed to offerings to individuals deities.

Despite what the quotes of Harpocratio, Isocrates, and pseudo-Xenophon might suggest, rentals were not exclusively siphoned to subsidy of sacrifices. Another significant set of expenses covered by rentals was construction or repairs of cultic and cult-related buildings. It has now been demonstrated that, contrary to a misconception that goes back to antiquity, the bulk of the expenditure for the vast building programme on the Acropolis in the mid-fifth century was covered by Athena's sacred purse, which certainly consisted, to some extent at least, of rentals.[301] Regarding fifth-century fiscal policy, one

[298] *I.Oropos* 297, esp. ll. 13–15: *κα|ὶ αἱ ἄλλαι θυσίαι τοῖς θεοῖς τοῖς ἐν τ|ωῖ ἱερῶι τοῦ Ἀμφιαράου* (...and the other sacrifices to the gods worshipped in the shrine of Amphiaraos).

[299] See Chapter 3, Section 2.v below. The same principle applied to Delos; cf. Isager and Skydsgaard 1992, 187.

[300] *SEG* LII 48, face A, fr. 3, col. I, ll. 16–17: [*κεφάλ*]*ạιον* | [- - -] ⊢II (capital).

[301] The issue was first raised by Connor 1988, 167 with n. 22 (Does it follow that sacred buidlings were normally paid from funds called *hiera* and public buildings from those called *hosia*?), only to be left unresolved. A sound positive answer was given by Kallet-Marx 1989 (cf. Kallet 1998, 48–52), who demonstrated that, contrary to general misconception, the Parthenon was mainly funded from Athena's treasury, not from the imperial reserve (as most famously claimed by Plut. *Per.* 12–4). Thus also, independently, Giovannini 1990, esp. 137–9. For similar, albeit less pronounced, inferences, see Thompson 1970; cf. Price 1999, 64–5 (contra Blamire 2001, 100–1).

should mention the fragmentary *IG* I^3 44. If this document is indeed an enacting lease—and it should be, given the terms *μίσθοσιν* (l. 4), *γε̂ς* (l. 7), and *χορ[ί]ο* (l. 10)—then the only conceivable involvement of the commission designated as *τοι̂ς ἐμ πόλ̣[ει]* (l. 9) is as investors of rentals in constructions on the Acropolis.[302] More unequivocal is the statement in *IG* I^3 84 that revenue from the *temenos* of Neleus and Basile was to subsidize the fencing of the shrine.[303] The link between rentals and building activity is emphasized even more in documents concerning the Eleusinian cult. *IG* I^3 395, a record of income to be spent on constructions in Eleusis, contains at least two entries of rentals deriving from leased facilities.[304] In 352/1 the Athenians contemplated—even though, for reasons explained elsewhere, they did not achieve it—financing repairs in the Eleusinian sanctuary with rentals from the Sacred Orgas. Earlier on in the fourth century they seem to have used rentals from the quarry of Asklepios in order to subsidize the construction of the sanctuary, if this is the right reading of the relevant decree.[305] But overall, pertinent documents tend to be cryptic concerning the exact provenance of money employed for building activities, merely stating either the financing authorities or the sacred nature of the employed budgets. Thus, according to the first-fruits decree, the three granaries in Eleusis were to be built with money from the sacred treasury of the Two Goddesses.[306] Let us also briefly mention here the law from Brauron which promulgated the

[302] Cf. Meritt 1945, 85–6; Behrend 1970, 55; Walbank in *Agora* XIX L1 (the board of the *νομε̂[ς]* in l. 11—otherwise unattested in Attica—is reminiscent of the Orchomenian *νομω̂ναι*, collectors of pasture tax, for whom see Hodkinson 1988, 48, and Chandezon 2003, 43–4; this remark would corroborate the identification of the document as a lease). If my suggestion is sound, then the document should postdate 447, the year when the Periclean building programme on the Acropolis began.

[303] *IG* I^3 84 ll. 8–9: *τὸ δὲ ἀργύριον ἐς τὲν ἐ̂ρχ|σιν ἀπὸ τô τεμένος εἶναι* (the money for the fencing-in [of the shrine] shall come from the leasing of the *temenos*).

[304] *IG* I^3 395 l. 1: h*ιππόνον μί[σθοσις]*; l. 5: *οἰκεμάτον μίσθοσις*, followed by expenditures (l. 6: *ἀναλόματα τάδε*) concerning purchase and transport of building materials, wages to builders, and *similia* (ll. 8–20).

[305] *IG* II^2 47 ll. 31–2: *τὸ δὲ ἄλλο ἀργύριον [κα]τα[βά]λλ|[ε]ν ἐς τὴν οἰκοδομίαν τοῦ ἱερô*. This clause follows immediately after the one instructing the *epimeletai* to employ income from the quarry to fund sacrifices. Although one would expect *τὸ δὲ λοιπὸν ἀργύριον*, it is difficult to see what the *ἀργύριον* for the shrine would have been, if not the surplus from the rentals. See also Osborne 1985*a*, 104; Faraguna 1992, 342; von Eickstedt 2001, 23–7.

[306] *IG* I^3 78 (ML 73), ll. 10–12: *οἰκοδομε̂σαι δὲ σιρὸς τρε̂ς Ἐλευσι̂ν | ι κατὰ τὰ πάτρια* h*όπο ἂν δοκε̂ι τοι̂ς* h*ιεροποιοι̂ς καὶ τôι ἀρ[χ]ιτ|έκτονι ἐπιτέδειον ἐ̂ναι ἀπὸ τô ἀργυρίο τô τοι̂ν θεοι̂ν* (They shall construct three storage-pits at Eleusis in accordance with the

refurbishment of buildings within the shrine from Artemis' personal revenues.[307] In this case at least it is fair to assume that rentals contributed to Artemis' revenues (*πρόσοδοι*), since the goddess features as one of the divine owners of polis *temene* in our inscribed documents.

Another noteworthy feature of the law from Brauron is the mention of the *apodektai* as the actual distributors of Artemis' sacred money, and with this remark we can return to the examination of the *merismos*. The other known instance of sacred officials receiving an allowance from the *apodektai* is that of the *ἱερῶν ἐπισκευασταί*.[308] Epigraphically the 'repairers of the sanctuaries' are only known from a document dating to the period of the first Athenian occupation of Oropos in the fourth century, where they were allocated an amount of money from the purse of Amphiaraos in order to disburse it to an individual commisioned with the repair of the fountain and the spring houses of the sanctuary.[309] The *θησαυρός* of Amphiaraos certainly received contributions from pilgrims as well as fines, at least in the period of the Theban occupation.[310] However, in the

ancestral custom, at whatever place seems to the *hieropoioi* and the architect to be suitable, out of the funds of the Two Goddesses; trans. by Fornara 1983, no. 140).

[307] *SEG* LII 104 ll. 20–2: *τοὺς δὲ ἀποδέ||[κτ]ας μερίζειν τοῖς μισθωταῖς τῶν ἔργων τὸ ἀργύριον ἐκ τῶν πρ[ο|σόδ]ων τῆς Ἀρτέμιδος* (The *apodektai* shall allocate to the contractors of the works the money from the revenue of Artemis).

[308] Arist. [*Ath. Pol.*] 50.1, *κληροῦνται δὲ καὶ ἱερῶν ἐπισκευασταὶ δέκα ἄνδρες, οἳ λαμβάνοντες τριάκοντα μνᾶς παρὰ τῶν ἀποδεκτῶν ἐπισκευάζουσιν τὰ μάλιστα δεόμενα τῶν ἱερῶν* (There are appointed by lot repairers of the temples, a board of ten men, who are given thirty minas by the *apodektai* and repair the temples which are most in need of attention; trans. by Rhodes 1984), with Rhodes 1993, 572–3, 780 (cf. Faraguna 1992, 182).

[309] *I.Oropos* 290 ll. 22–5: *παραδôναι τὸ ἄλλο τοῖς τῶν ἱε|ρῶν ἐπισκευαστạῖς, τὸς δὲ τῶν | ἱερῶν {ι} ἐπισκευαστὰς παραδôν τῶι| μισθωτεῖ τô ἔργο* (They shall hand the remaining money over to the repairers of the temples, and the repairers of the temples will deliver it to the contractor of the works), with Knoepfler 1986.

[310] RO 27 = *I.Oropos* 277 ll. 9–13, *ἂν δέ τις ἀδικεῖ ἐν τοῖ ἱεροῖ ἢ ξένος ἢ δημότ|ης, ζημιούτω ὁ ἱερεὺς μέχρι πέντε δραχμέων | κυρίως καὶ ἐνέχυρα λαμβανέτω τοῦ ἐζημιωμ|ένου, ἂν δ' ἐκτίνει τὸ ἀργύριον, παρεόντος τô | ἱερέος ἐμβαλέτω εἰς τὸν θησαυρόν* (If anyone commits an offence in the sanctuary, either a foreigner or a member of the community, let the priest have power to inflict punishment of up to five drachmas and let him take guarantees from the man who is punished, and if he pays the money let him deposit it into the treasury when the priest is present); ll. 20–3 *ἐπαρ|χὴν δὲ διδοῦν τὸμ μέλλοντα θεραπεύεσθαι ὑ|πὸ τοῦ θεοῦ μὴ ἔλ<α>ττον ἐννέ' ὀβολοὺς δοκίμου ἀργ|υρίου καὶ ἐμβάλλειν εἰς τὸν θησαυρὸν* (Whoever comes to be cured by the god is to pay a fee of not less than nine obols of good silver and deposit them in the treasury).

second period of Athenian control of Oropos the god is known to have been owner of landed assets and it is not inconceivable that some income from the leasing of those *temene* flowed into the same θησαυρός.[311]

There is one last type of outlay for which sacred rentals might have been used, namely war-related expenditure. The amply documented Athenian habit of funding military campaigns with money from the sacred purse of Athena has often proved a slight embarassment to modern historians.[312] At least some of them feel uneasy about the fact that sacral funds were eventually directed to secular enterprises. Two points could neutralize such concerns. The first is the fact that although the Athenians regularly took loans from the sacred treasuries, they insisted on paying interest.[313] This stratagem is particularly well known from the accounts of the *logistai* of 426–422 (ML 72). This in turn reveals a mentality whereby sacral funds were not merely a liability. It is true that at the end the Athenians were unable to pay back their debts, but this is the accidental consequence of their eventual defeat in the Peloponnesian War. At any rate, there is no indisputable evidence for the Athenians investing sacral rentals in war operations, although I would leave open the possibility that any surpluses remaining after sacred rentals had been invested in subsidy of cultic activity and/or other sacred expenditure might end up in the form of loans for war operations. Still, this interpretation mainly applies to Attic *temene*. Nevethleless, there is one particular set of sacred precincts of which much has already been said and which might have come into existence in the first place as a result of the war-funding situation under examination, namely Athenian *temene* outside Attica.

[311] The sacrificial regulation *I.Oropos* 278 appears to contain one entry referring to rentals (l. 11, μισθωμ[- - -]; for the possible meaning see Chaniotis in *SEG* XLVII 488 (sale of priesthood), and Lupu 2003, 331, who favours the meaning 'rentals'. Note that the Koan *thesauros* of Asklepios received income from leases, according to a plausible restoration (*LSCG* 155A ll. 9–13).

[312] *IG* I^3 363 (ML 55): expenses for the Samian War covered with Athena's sacred funds, 441/0; cf. Kallet-Marx 1989, 259–60. *IG* I^3 369 (ML 72): sacred loans from 426/5 to 423/2 with retrospective references to the interest owed for the years 433/2–427/6; cf. Samons 2000, 209–10.

[313] A significant point, the importance of which was already realized by Guiraud 1893, 375; cf. Lewis 1990, 259; Blamire 2001, 108–9.

As shown above, such *temene* were located in areas of the Delian League that at one point or another had revolted against Athens and, subsequently, had been subjugated by her.[314] It has always been a problem to establish the motives behind the foundation of such *temene*, a problem ultimately related to the question of the exact status of Athenian overseas settlements, especially cleruchies.[315] One theory would have it that they were consecrated in order to support the religious life of the newly settled Athenian population. Although this is not intrinsically impossible, such *temene* would probably produce income much bigger than strictly required. Take, for instance, the 300 sacred lots founded in Lesbos. Scholars are usually preoccupied with the 2700 lots assigned to Athenian settlers, losing sight of the fact that the sacred landholdings would have yielded, on the basis of the figures provided by Thucydides, an awesome annual sum of 10 talents.[316] In my view, a more plausible suggestion is that rentals from those *temene* would have been paid back to the divine funders of the Athenian military campaigns, Athena and the Other Gods. A great number of *horoi* marking Athenian sacred estates have been found in Samos, for example, and, significantly, the military expedition against Samos seems to have been subsidized mainly, if not exclusively, with funds from Athena's purse. As late as 410/9 the treasury of Athena is seen to receive money from Samos and Eretria respectively, in what has been rightly considered a fictional transaction.[317] Meiggs and Lewis argued that the designation ἐχσάμο reflects the island's importance as the main operation base of the Athenian fleet and does not refer to the

[314] See now Polinskaya 2009, especially 250–4.

[315] For which see more recently Cargill 1995; Salomon 1997; Zelnick-Abramovitz 2004; Moreno 2009.

[316] Thuc 3.50.1–2 (cf. Andreades 1928, 398–9; Kallet-Marx 1993, 145). In an otherwise brilliant discussion, Gauthier 1966, 77–88, does not make the distinction between sacred lands and cleruchic ones.

[317] *IG* I^3 375 ll. 16–18: *hενδεκάτει τε̂ς πρυτανείας hε|λλενοταμίαις παρεδόθε Προχσένοι Ἀφιδναίοι καὶ συνάρχοσιν στρατεγο̂ι ἐχς Ἐρετρίας ⁝ Εὐκλείδει ἀνομολόγ|εμα ΧΧΧ𐅅ΗΗΔΔΔΔΙ*; ll. 20–1, *τριακοστε̂ι τε̂ς πρυτανείας τὰ ἐχσάμο ἀνομολογέθε ⁝ hελλενοταμίαι ⁝ Ἀναιτίοι Σφεττίοι καὶ παρέδροι [Π]|ολυαράτοι Χολαργει̂ 𐅄ΤΤΧ*; ll. 34–6, *ἕκτει καὶ τριακοστε̂ι τε̂ς πρυτανείας τὰ ἐχσάμο ἀνομολογέσα[ντο hοι σύ]μμαχ[οι | το]ι̂ς στρατεγοι̂ς ἐς Σάμοι Δεχσικράτει Αἰγιλιει̂ 𐅉𐅉ΤΧ ⁝ Πασιφο̂ντι Φρεαρρίοι ⁝ 𐅈Τ ⁝ Ἀριστοκρά[τει . . . .⁸ . . . .]ι ⁝ 𐅈 ⁝ Ε[. . .]| [. . .] Εὐονυμει̂ ⁝ 𐅈ΧΧΧ𐅅ΗΗΗ𐅄ΔΔΔΔΠ𐅂 ⁝ Νικεράτοι Κυδαντίδει τριεράρχοι ⁝ ΧΧΧ Ἀριστοφάνει Ἀνα[φλυστίοι τριε]ράρ[χοι]*, with ML 84 ad loc. Samons 2000, 269–74 has now provided a meticulous analysis of the passage; cf. Flament 2006, 170–1.

source of revenue. At first glance their interpretation seems cogent, but it fails to explain the revenue deriving from Eretria. What connects Samos and Eretria, however, is the existence of Athenian sacred estates as attested by the series of Samian *horoi* and by the list of leased *temene IG* I^3 418.[318] As it happens, a payment similarly designated ἐχσ[άμο] had been made in the ninth prytany of 418/7, that is at this time of the political year when rentals were normally paid.[319] It is in this light, I suggest, that Athenian *temene* outside Attica should primarily be viewed. They were simultaneously the product of booty, the symbolic image of Athens' hegemony, and a stable source of revenue for the increment of the sacred treasuries that kept funding Athenian imperialism throughout the fifth century.[320] For these very reasons the same *temene* simply disappeared with the collapse of the Athenian empire.

7. THE ECONOMIC SIGNIFICANCE OF SACRED RENTALS

Thus, it appears that sacred realty constituted a significant element of Athenian finances, especially of that aspect of the budget concerning religion. It was significant because, through leasing, such property could provide a stable source of income. In order to broach this rather subjective evaluation, one should ideally have a full set of data of sources of cultic income, such as private donations, liturgies, fines, and taxes.[321] Unfortunately, this is not the case and it is doubtful that

[318] *IG* I^3 418 l. 9, [ἐν Ἐρε]τ̣ρ̣ία̣ι Αἰγαλ̣[. . . ^{5}..]; l. 14, ἐν Ἐρε[τρίαι - - -] (Knoepfler 1997, 425 n. 142 has suggested [ἐν Ἐρε]τ̣ρ̣ία̣ι Αἰγάλ̣[ησι] for l. 9). Of course only some of the vouchers in *IG* I^3 375 would have recorded rentals. For a similar conclusion see Smarczyk 1990, 85.

[319] *IG* I^3 370 ll. 18-19: ἐπὶ τ[ε̂ς Πανδιονίδος ἐνά]τες πρυτανευόσες τ[ρίτει καὶ δεκάτει hεμέραι τε̂ς π]ρυτανείας παρέδομεν τô ἐχσ|άμο ἀργ[υρίο κατὰ τὸν ἐνιαυτὸν ἐπ]ελθόντος hελλενοτ[αμίαις etc. (When Pandionis held the ninth prytany, on the thirteenth day of the prytany, we transferred to the *hellenotiamiai* the annual revenue from Samos). ML 77 repeat the assertion of the authors of *ATL* that this rubric proves that Samos was still paying war indemnities. I can only say that their suggestion is just as plausible as mine (annual sacred rentals).

[320] Not unreasonably, Polinskaya 2009, 253–4, 262–3, sees such *temene* primarily as a manifestation of Athenian piety (coupled with notions concerning Athenian identity), without entirely dismissing the financial explanation advocated here.

[321] See the good pages of Horster 2004, 192–213.

it ever will be, unless some future find revolutionizes our knowledge. Other methods of investigation are, therefore, called for. Now, the best preserved record of sacred leases, *Agora* XIX L6, has been thought to have contained annual revenues in the order of four to six (4–6) talents.[322] The year of the record is 343/2 when Euboulos was still in the driving seat of the Athenian economy and Lykourgos had not yet entered the stage, at least not in any detectable way. When he did in 336/5 or so, we learn from Plutarch's *Vita Lycourgi*, he managed to raise the city's revenues from 600 talents up to 1200 talents per year.[323] Earlier on, at the end of the Social War, the city's revenue did not add up to more than 130 talents,[324] but by 346 it was already 400 talents; that is, it was increasing at a rate of almost 30 talents per year.[325] We can then plausibly assume that in 343/2 the annual Athenian revenue, sacred and secular income combined, would have roughly been in the order of 500 talents.[326] Six talents, 1.2 per cent of that amount, may not appear very impressive at first sight, though it is by no means negligible. Yet we have to allow for sacred rentals coming into the Athenian coffers from other sources, such as the property of the Eleusinian Goddesses and that of Asklepios.[327]

When Lykourgos took over the Athenian fiscal policy, he undertook to further increase sacred revenues, rentals included. The so-called Dermatikon account is the best example of the pains taken by the Lykourgan administration in that respect. The consecration of the Oropian territory to Amphiaraos would have been a welcome, albeit unexpected, step in this direction. But if the acquisition of Oropos was a windfall, the continuation of the leasing policy introduced by Euboulos was deliberate throughout. Four fragmentary records of sacred leases, all dated to the Lykourgan era on epigraphical grounds, are preserved.[328] Although generally thought to represent a decennial

322 Walbank 1983*d*, 213; Osborne 1988, 285 took the average of 5 talents per year.
323 Humphreys 1985, 204 (now Humphreys 2004, 84); Burke 1992, 202–3.
324 Dem. 10.97: *ἦν ποτ' οὐ πάλαι παρ' ὑμῖν, ὅτ' οὐ προσῄει τῇ πόλει τάλαντα ὑπὲρ τριάκοντα καὶ ἑκατόν*, with Cawkwell 1963, 61–2 n. 85; Humphreys 1985, 204.
325 *FGrH* 115 F166: *τριακοσίας δὲ τριήρεις κεκτημένοι καὶ σχεδὸν τετρακοσίων ταλάντων προσόδους λαμβάνοντες.*
326 I disagree here with the assertion of Burke 1992, 215 that 'during the Eubulan era, total annual income to the state . . . never exceeded 400 talents'.
327 See above, p. 41.
328 *Agora* XIX L9; L10; L11; L12.

revision of the leases first conferred in 343/2, there is no indisputable proof of overlap between them and *Agora* XIX L6.[329] Consequently, I am forced to abandon this interpretation and see the Lykourgan records as evidence for the expansion of a pre-existing leasing system, probably by rendering profitable properties that had been lying idle. On the basis of Walbank's calculations, *Agora* XIX L9–L12 contained in total yearly revenues of 9.5 talents and, thus, sacred rentals flowing into the Athenian budget during the Lykourgan epoch would have amounted to almost 15.5 talents. As seen above, at the peak of Lykourgos' activity the annual income of Athens was raised to 1200 talents; still 15.5 talents would have represented 1.29 per cent of this sum, which is only slightly higher than the 1.2 per cent estimated for the Euboulean epoch. In other words, in the Lykourgan period there was a homologous interrelation between the increase of sacred rentals and the overall increase of Athenian revenues. Yet again, it ought to be emphasized that the calculations above include neither rentals from Oropia nor from the Eleusinian sanctuary, nor from the two Asklepeia. Thus, the addition of 41 mnas from the leasing of the Nea and of 220 drachmas as one of the Eleusinian *μισθώματα* would increase the estimated percentage to 1.35 per cent. Hypereides' rent in kind amounted to 2732 *medimnoi* of barley in four years: an annual 683 *medimnoi* of barley. If we convert this quantity of grain into monetary value, assuming a price of three drachmas per *medimnos* of barley, we reach an annual rental of 2049 drachmas.[330] Incorporating this number in our calculations, the percentage of sacred rentals in the annual income of Athens would rise up to 1.38 per cent. Nonetheless, even on the basis of wildly optimistic estimates, I do not think that sacred rentals would have amounted to anything more than 2 per cent of the annual state income at the time and, in all likelihood, a figure near 1.5 per cent is closer to reality.

Here is the place to delve into a passage from the *Athenaion Politeia* that I have deliberately not yet examined. In an unusually judgemental statement [Aristotle] explains that the ninth prytany

[329] Walbank 1983*d*, 214–15, who, however, acknowledges the absence of any evidence corroborating his hypothesis; cf. Osborne 1988, 289.

[330] *I.Eleusis* 177 (*IG* II^2 1672), ll. 381–4. The price of 3 drachmas per *medimnos* is that attested in the same accounts ll. 411–12: *πρα|θεισῶν ἐκ τριῶν δραχμῶν τὸν μέδιμνον ἕκαστον ὡς ὁ δῆμος ἔταξεν*; cf. Stroud 1998, 32–3, and Clinton 2008, 228–32.

experienced a flow of cash (πλεῖστα χρήματα).[331] But what sort of cash is implied, and how is one to understand his remark? The salient sentence directly follows Aristotle's statement that sacred rentals were paid in the ninth prytany and, as it stands, the obvious implication would be that leases of *temene* contributed substantially to Athenian finances. This is of course at odds with the picture drawn above. Conversely, Aristotle might have been referring to the accumulative pecuniary effect of revenues from sundry sources, i.e. taxes, fines, sales of confiscated properties and sacred land leases, flowing into the Athenian budget simultaneously.[332] Self-evidently, expropriated properties could hardly have been considered a regular source of income, despite various speeches suggesting that confiscations did occur with some frequency.[333] Moreover, not all taxes were paid in the ninth prytany, for some had to be paid monthly and some others three times a year.[334] But all in all, it seems that most payments were indeed made in the ninth prytany and that sacred rentals constituted a considerable part of them.

Whatever the truth, the percentage can be deemed as substantial or insignificant depending on one's point of view. We can undertake another line of investigation, that of contextualization of the data available. The median price of an ox, as calculated on the basis of *IG* I^3 375, was 51.14 drachmas, and the six talents of *Agora* XIX L6 would have purchased almost 704 oxen. This is a very low average; however, if we make the calculations on the basis of 100 drachmas per ox (price attested in the Panathenaic prizes), the rentals of 343/2 would have subsidized the purchase of 360 oxen.[335] Again the estimated minimum of 15.5 talents for the Lykourgan period would have funded the acquisition of 1818 oxen, on the basis of the low price, or 930 oxen at the higher one. This is all very sketchy. As shown above, rentals might

[331] Arist. [*Ath. Pol.*] 47.4: διὸ καὶ πλεῖστα χρήματα ἐπὶ ταύτης συλλέγεται τῆς πρυτανείας.

[332] Faraguna 1992, 180 incorrectly connects only μισθώσεις to the payments made in the ninth prytany.

[333] Langdon 1991, 58–9 is concise, but fundamental.

[334] Arist. [*Ath. Pol.*] 47.3: ἀναγράφουσιν δὲ χωρὶς μὲν οὓς δεῖ κατὰ π[ρυ]τανείαν ἑκάστην καταβάλλειν, εἰς δέκα γραμματεῖα, χωρὶς δὲ οὓς τρὶς τοῦ [ἐ]νιαυτοῦ, γραμματεῖον κατὰ τὴν καταβολὴν ἑκάστην ποιήσαντες, χωρὶς δ' οὓς [ἐπ]ὶ τῆς ἐνάτης πρυτανείας. Rhodes 1972, 150 deftly observed that 'this concentration on the ninth prytany is an oversimplification'.

[335] For prices of oxen see Rosivach 1994, 71 n. 11.

have been invested in construction of cultic premises, rather than in actual sacrifices,[336] and of course not all sacrificial victims would have been oxen. Moreover, the way I have conducted the statistical analysis above may be totally misleading in hinting at a budgeting mentality alien to the ancient Greeks. Inflation phenomena apart, the prices of the sacrificial victims might have been conditioned by the availability of funds.[337] However, the overall impression is that sacred rentals in the 340s–320s would have, more or less, sufficed to cover expenditure for the lavish public sacrifices in which Athens indulged her citizens.

We could attempt another quantitative approach to the topic of sacred estates. Andreyev once maintained that such property represented almost 10 per cent of the entire Athenian territory.[338] His estimation, however, was methodologically flawed in that his calculations included sacred lands administered by all kinds of public or semi-public bodies.[339] Here I will confine my discussion to polis *temene* only. According to Polybius the aggregate *τίμημα* (assessed wealth) in Attica in the year 378/7 fell short of 6000 talents by 250, but in 354 Demosthenes could maintain that it did amount to 6000 talents.[340] Students of Athenian economics are familiar with the notorious problems surrounding these as well as other kindred passages. Starting with Böckh, numerous special treatments have been published with often incompatible results and disagreement over the exact meaning of the *τίμημα* (*timema*). It has been interpreted as the whole capital value of Athenian properties or as a mere taxable fraction of it. Even on the former interpretation there has been no agreement as to whether it only included the immovable properties or the annual produce as well, or even whether it solely entailed

336 See, for instance, the 30 mnas (=1/2 talent) received annually by the *ἐπισκευασταὶ τῶν ἱερῶν* (Arist. [*Ath. Pol.*] 50.1).

337 For inflation phenomena see Loomis 1998, 240–50; for the amateurism of ancient Greek—and undoubtedly Athenian—budgeting see Austin and Vidal-Naquet 1977, 118–28.

338 Andreyev 1974, 43; followed by Lewis 1973*a*, 199, and Jameson 1977, 125.

339 Andreyev 1974, 25–6.

340 Pol. 2.62.7: *τὰς εἰς τὸν πόλεμον εἰσφορὰς ἐτιμήσαντο τήν τε χώραν τὴν Ἀττικὴν ἅπασαν καὶ τὰς οἰκίας, ὁμοίως δὲ καὶ τὴν λοιπὴν οὐσίαν· ἀλλ' ὅμως τὸ σύμπαν τίμημα τῆς ἀξίας ἐνέλιπε τῶν ἑξακισχιλίων διακοσίοις καὶ πεντήκοντα ταλάντοις*, with Walbank 1957, 268–9; Dem. 14.19: *κελεύω, ἐπειδὴ τὸ τίμημ' ἐστὶ τῆς χώρας ἑξάκισχιλίων ταλάντων* etc.

private properties.[341] However, independent evidence suggests that cult-related lands controlled by demes and phratries were subject to *eisphora*.[342] On the basis of annual rent calculated at a rate of 12 per cent, Walbank estimated that the leases in *Agora* XIX L6 represented land worth between 33 and 50 talents.[343] The higher figure would represent just 0.83 per cent of the total value of Athenian real property. Nevertheless, Walbank's estimated 12 per cent is unacceptably high, and one should endorse Osborne's 8 per cent rate as a more possible figure.[344] This would produce a considerably higher 75 talents as the capital value of polis *temene*, i.e. 1.25 per cent of the 6000 talents τίμημα. If we include in our calculations the properties attested in *Agora* XIX L9–L12, the total value of polis *temene* in the 330s–320s would have amounted to 193.75 talents, that is 3.23 per cent of the 6000 talents *timema*. But in the 390s the levying of the *eisphora* was calculated on a *timema* which included the values of slaves,[345] and if we substract this value from the whole *timema*, the percentage that polis *temene* would have represented would rise considerably, albeit indeterminably. Once more, it must be emphasized that the properties of the Eleusinian twosome and of Asklepios were probably not included in the Agora records. The alleged 17 per cent of the Oropian territory consecrated to Amphiaraos is not included here either. Still, my guess is that, even if we press our calculations to their most extreme limits, the polis *temene* would have hardly constituted a fraction bigger than 4 per cent of the total Athenian arable territory.

It is unfeasible to do any better with the available data. The calculations I have provided above should be used with extreme caution to provide a very rough idea of what was going on in the late Classical period. Diachronic investigation of the economic significance of sacred rentals is impossible. Thus, the estimated annual

[341] de Ste. Croix 1953 and Thomsen 1964 remain the main modern accounts (containing full bibliography). See more recently Christ 2007.

[342] See Chapter 3, Section 2.ii (demes); also Gabrielsen 1987.

[343] Walbank 1983*d*, 215.

[344] Osborne 1988, 285 (cf. Stroud 1998, 32). Andreyev 1974, 39 would lower further the rate of sacred lands (thus, raising their estimated value) on the basis of their 'non-entrepreneurial' nature, but this begs the question.

[345] Isoc. 17.49, with Davies 1981, 146. I note, however, that Christ 2007 has now suggested that the *eisphora* before 378/7 was not assessed proportionally to the size of the property of individual citizens. In other words, he rejects the existence of a *timema* system in the early 4th cent.

yield of 6 talents of *Agora* XIX L6 appears trivial in comparison to the annual income of 10 talents flowing into the Athenian sacred treasuries in 427 from the *temene* of Lesbos alone. But, as highlighted above, Athenian *temene* abroad constituted a historical anomaly brought out by the extreme conditions of the Peloponnesian War. In relative terms sacred rentals would have constituted 1–2 per cent of the gross annual income. In absolute terms tillable lands lying under the administration of the polis of Athens would have comprised roughly 4 per cent of the total landed property in Attica. Athens, of course, also controlled the silver mines, which were potentially much more profitable. Moreover, a certain amount of realty lay under the sway of other public or semi-public organizations, but any effort at quantification is destined to fail. The general impression is that the majority of lands in Attica were in private ownership and this should be taken into account when analysing the character of the Athenian economy.

3

The Constitutional Subunits of Athens as Administrators of Realty

1. THE LANDED ASSETS OF THE ATTIC TRIBES

i. The early phase

To say that the creation of the ten tribes (*phylai*; Greek *φυλαί*) was by far the most artificial aspect of the Cleisthenic reforms would hardly be an overstatement. Whereas the demes were founded on the basis of pre-existing nucleated settlements, the tribes were created with the explicit aim of having the citizens of the newly born democracy distributed over wide geographical zones as a means of pre-empting local coalitions of the kind that had caused so much political turmoil during the Archaic period.[1] To begin with, one could argue that each tribe possessed, or rather administered, at least one piece of realty, namely the shrine of the eponymous hero after whom it was named and with whom it was, in a sense, bound. But this claim is complicated by the theory that the priesthoods of certain tribes were under the control of specific *gene*.[2] If true, such an administrative intermingling could possibly, though not necessarily, indicate that those tribal cultic centres were under the effective possession of the relevant *gene*.

[1] Lewis 1963; Ostwald 1988, 316–19; Rhodes 1993, 250–4; Jones 1999, 155–6; Ober 2008, 140–2. Anderson 2003, 34–42 and *passim*, contends that it was primarily Cleisthenes' reforms (including the creation of the ten tribes) that created Attica as a unified political space.

[2] Gentilician priesthood of the cults of the heroes of Akamantis, Kekropis, and Hippothontis: Schlaifer 1940, 251–7 accepted by Kearns 1985, 193–4; 1989, 85, and now raised to status of almost certainty by Parker 1996, 118, 285–6, 292–3 n. 21 (cf. now Blok and Lambert 2009, 111).

Nevertheless, the venues of the phyletic cults will not occupy me in the course of the present discussion.[3]

It is sometimes thought that *IG* I^3 252, a very fragmentary stele dating to the mid-fifth century, provides the earliest attestation of a lease conferred by a *phyle*.[4] The find-spot of the stone, the slopes of the Acropolis, does not preclude such an attribution.[5] Despite its defective preservation, the inscription seems to record a ten-year lease encompassing agricultural provisions, including one for the planting of legumes, which in turn may indicate fallowing.[6] Somehow a board of *epimeletai* (*ἐπιμεληταί*) appears involved, perhaps acting as lessors or as rent-collectors, the two tasks not being mutually exclusive. In terms of direct evidence about land administered by tribes, *IG* I^3 252 is almost a unicum, at least for the early Classical period.

At first glance, however, it appears that relevant, albeit indirect, evidence does exist, even though it is of the most unexpected provenance. A series of boundary stones, discovered in Samos and dated to the second half of the fifth century, in a period when the island lay under Athenian sway, records sacred estates under the nominal ownership of the Athenian eponymous heroes.[7] They have often been

[3] In fact not all *phylai* are attested as owning shrines of their eponymous heroes; Oineis, for instance, is not, but this may be the result of faulty documentation (*Agora* XIX H 70, the supposed marker of the tomb of the eponymous hero, *ὅρος σήμ[ατος]|Οἰνέως*, probably refers to a homonymous mortal, since the name is attested in the Attic prosopography (cf. *LGPN* II s.v. *Οἰνεύς*), a point missed by Parker 2000, 58). Again, and more characteristically, the Erechtheis *phyle* worshipped its hero in the Erechtheion which could hardly have been property of the *phyle*. For all this see the relevant chapters in Kron 1976 (conveniently synopsized by Parker 1996, 119). For an up-to-date summary with the bibliography after Kron's study, see Jones 1999, 156–61.

[4] A tribe has been envisaged as the source of authority behind this text because of the half-restored *ἐκ τε̂ς φυ[λε̂ς]* in conjunction with the word *Ἀρχεγε̂τ[ι]* (for the connection of the ten Attic *phylai* with an Archegetes, 'Founder', cf. Lévêque and Vidal-Naquet 1966, 48); cf. Osborne 1988, 282. Note that Walbank 1974, 164 n. 10 claimed the ll. 7–19 of the decree, in Ionic alphabet, date to the 4th cent. (but cf. Walbank 1991, 156 for a more tentative chronology in the late 5th or early 4th cent.). I refrain from speculating on the possible implications of lowering the date of the second part of the decree, especially in view of the attribution of a new fragment to *IG* I^3 252 by Mrs Peppa-Delmousou (personal communication).

[5] The cultic centres of at least 3 tribes are tentatively or safely located on the Acropolis; cf. n. 3 above.

[6] Cf. Jameson 1977, 130; Moreno 2007, 327–8.

[7] *IG* XII (6) 247-51 (the *horoi* read h*όρος|τεμένος|ἐπονύμον|Ἀθένηθεν* in varying Attic orthography). The idea put forward by Barron 1964, 38–41 that these heroes

associated with a law quoted in the Demosthenic speech *Against Macartatus*, which attests leasing of sacred landholdings belonging to the *eponymoi*, as well as with other literary sources which represent the *eponymoi* in a financial capacity.[8] By and large, the crux of the problem is whether a cult of the *eponymoi* as a group was ever practised in Athens, as a dedication of ten kylikes to them on behalf of the Boule seems to imply.[9] Perhaps it is more logical to assume that such a common cult, if it ever existed, would not have been under the jurisdiction of the ten tribes individually, but rather under state control. On the other hand, our epigraphical records of leases of *temene* conferred by the polis of Athens do not make any mention of the *eponymoi* as divine proprietors. Moreover, those parts of Athenian legislation referring to the eponymous heroes probably do so in their role as tribal representatives.[10] Or, to look at the issue from another angle, a landholding of the hero Aigeus, which has, of late, been resuscitated in a re-edition of a long-known Teithrasian decree, was almost certainly property administered by the tribe Aigeis.[11]

But if the discussion of the Samian *termini sacri* turns out to be inconclusive, we do have evidence at our disposal of tribal landholdings outside Attica. In 303/2 Antiochis honoured a certain Euthydemos, of no further civic identification,[12] for having acted as an advocate on behalf of the *phyle* along with the tribal priest in a case

were the sons of Ion and, therefore, represented the four old Ionian tribes has not met with general acceptance. It was first rejected by Tsakos 1977 [1982], 74–9, and anew by Parker 1996, 145 with n. 94 (cf. Smarczyk 1990, 138–41).

[8] [Dem.] 43.58: *τοὺς δὲ μὴ ἀποδιδόντας τὰς μισθώσεις τῶν τεμενῶν τῶν τῆς θεοῦ καὶ τῶν ἄλλων θεῶν καὶ τῶν ἐπωνύμων ἀτίμους εἶναι*; cf. Dem. 24.8: *ἰδὼν δ' ἠδικηκότα κοινῇ πᾶσαν τὴν πόλιν καὶ περὶ τὴν εἴσπραξιν τῶν εἰσφορῶν καὶ περὶ τὴν ποίησιν τῶν πομπείων, καὶ χρήματα πολλὰ τῆς θεοῦ καὶ τῶν ἐπωνύμων καὶ τῆς πόλεως ἔχοντα καὶ οὐκ ἀποδιδόντα, ἦλθον ἐπ' αὐτὸν μετ' Εὐκτήμονος*; [Dem.] 58.14: *ἕτερον δὲ τρίτον, ὃς ὁμοίως κελεύει κατά τε τῶν ὀφειλόντων τῷ δημοσίῳ τὰς ἐνδείξεις τὸν βουλόμενον ποιεῖσθαι τῶν πολιτῶν, καὶ ἐάν τις ὀφείλῃ τῇ Ἀθηνᾷ ἢ τῶν ἄλλων θεῶν ἢ τῶν ἐπωνύμων τῳ.*

[9] Rotroff 1978; cf. Lewis 1979 and Kearns 1985, 198. Both Kearns 1989, 83 and Parker 1996, 119–20 n. 63 consider a collective cult of the *eponymoi* as uncertain.

[10] Smarczyk 1990, 141–2; see also the evidence cited in n. 33 below.

[11] Papazarkadas 2007*a*, 157, reading *τὸ χωρ̣ί̣ο̣ν̣ τὸ Αἰ[γ]έως̣* in *SEG* XXIV 151, l. 10.

[12] The identification of the honorand with the homonymous councillor of Acharnai (tribe Oineis) of 303/2 (*LGPN* II, s.v. *Εὐθύδημος* (17)), as tentatively suggested by Jordan and Rotroff 1999, 152 (in the course of their analysis of a lead curse tablet), is sheer imagination; the lack of a demotic for our Euthydemos is certainly owing to the fact that he was a member of the honouring tribe, i.e. Antiochis.

concerning a *temenos* at Lemnos.[13] This sacred estate appears to have been assigned previously to Antiochis, but later on its status was contested. The over-technical term *ἀφορισθέν* ('marked-off') is reminiscent of a formula found in a state decree concerning the Athenian cleruchy of Lemnos (*[τ]ὰ ὄρη καὶ τὰ ἀφορίσματα*), and this coincidence probably implies a certain proximity of content between the two documents, the nature of which cannot be established.[14] Active though the ten tribes might have been outside Attica, it is mainly in Oropos that their presence is most noticeable, as will be shown below.

ii. The Athenian reacquisition of Oropos and the tribal land allotment

Following their reacquisition of Oropos in 335, the Athenians set in motion a major scheme which aimed at the effective administration of the new area.[15] The historical specifics derive mainly from Hypereides' speech *In Defence of Euxenippos* and, though already briefly recounted, it is worth restating those aspects of the episode touching upon the ten tribes, especially since serious misinterpretations keep being reiterated.[16] Upon a decision of the Athenian assembly, the hills of Oropos were broken up into five roughly equal lots. Subsequently these regions were allotted to the five pairs into which the ten Athenian tribes had been randomly divided. Before that, however, an appointed board of fifty boundary-commissioners (*ὁρισταί*) had set aside part of Oropia for the god Amphiaraos. Here it is imperative to emphasize that, contrary to common belief, the two allocations took place on different occasions. Not only is this explicitly stated by Hypereides, but, as we later learn, it was soon discovered that the tribal pair Akamantis and Hippothoontis had mistakenly been allocated land belonging to Amphiaraos. It is hardly credible that the

13 *ISE* 8, ll. 6–13: *καὶ ἐπὶ Λε|πτίνου ἱερέως σύνδικος γενό|μενος ὑπὲρ τοῦ τεμένους τοῦ ἐ|ν Λήμνωι τοῦ ἀφορισθέντος πρ|ὸς τοὺς ἀμφισβητήσαντας εἰσ|έπραξε τὸ ἀφορισθὲν χωρίον τ|ῆι φυλῆι μετὰ τοῦ ἱερέως Λεπ|τίνου*; for the term *σύνδικος* as applied to representatives of civic associations (such as tribes) in court see Rubinstein 2000, 43–4, who, however, fails to cite this example.

14 *Agora* XIX L3, l. 18 (387/6); cf. Karouzos 1923, 87; Stroud 1971, 172 ('the *ἀφορίσματα* . . . may be sacred properties or *temene*'); Smarczyk 1990, 103–4.

15 See Chapter 2, Section 4 above, and Papazarkadas 2009*b*.

16 The superb analysis of the Hypereidean speech by Whitehead 2000, 153–262 is a sine qua non of what follows; see also Parker 2005, 107–8.

horistai would have made such a major blunder as to assign the same piece of land to both Amphiaraos and the two tribes on the same occasion: the two allocations were chronologically unconnected.[17] At any rate, the politician Euxenippos was ordered by the Athenian assembly to perform incubation in the shrine of the god in order to reach a verdict. His decision presumably vindicated the tribes, since Polyeuktos of Kydantidai brought a charge against Euxenippos, after he himself had unsuccessfully proposed a decree whereby the two tribes were ordered to return to the god both his land and the income that had been generated from its exploitation.[18]

The follow-up to the story is not known in its entirety, but by virtue of a much-worn decree issued by the tribes Aigeis and Aiantis, we know that by 330 or thereabouts serious problems had arisen. It now emerges that in practice the tribal land allotment had experienced severe difficulties and a re-evaluation of the landed assets of the tribes was deemed imperative. It is likely that unscrupulous individuals had trespassed upon tribal land, and that the two tribes set up a committee to review the situation and to delimit again the lands concerned.[19] The joint tribal decree does not stand alone in highlighting complications regarding tribal possessions in Oropos. In the Hellenistic decree of Antiochis mentioned above, Euthydemos was honoured, inter alia, for looking after the tribe's landholdings in Oropos after having been elected by his fellow tribesmen.[20] In view of the explicit mention of Oropos in conjunction with the occurrence of the rare word *ἔφυλος* ('wooded'), there can be little doubt that the honorific decree refers to the same wide territory mentioned by both Hypereides and the decree of Aigeis and Aiantis. What remains questionable is whether, given

[17] Hyp. *Eux.* 16: *αἱ φυλαὶ σύνδυο γενόμεναι τὰ ὄρη τὰ ἐν Ὠρωπῷ διείλοντο, τοῦ δήμου αὐταῖς δόντος . . . ταύτας τὰς φυλὰς ἔγραψας ἀποδοῦναι τὸ ὄρος τῷ Ἀμφιαράῳ καὶ τὴν τιμὴν ὧν ἀπέδοντο, ὡς πρότερον τοὺς ὁριστὰς τοὺς πεντήκοντα ἐξελόντας αὐτὸ τῷ θεῷ καὶ ἀφορίσαντας*; for the meaning of *τὰ ὄρη* (literally 'the hills') see Gschnitzer 1958, 84 n. 5; Whitehead 2000, 207–8.

[18] For a good synopsis of the story see Isager and Skydsgaard 1992, 186.

[19] Decree enacted by Aigeis and Aiantis: *Agora* XVI 84 (ed. pr. by Langdon 1987; for a fresh approach see Papazarkadas 2009*b*).

[20] *ISE* 8 (=*SEG* III 117), ll. 13–21: *καὶ πάλιν αἱρεθεὶς ὑπὸ τ|[ῶν] φυλετῶν ἐπὶ τὰ ἐν Ὠρωπῶι ἐπ̣|[ὶ γῆν] ἔφυλον νεμηθεῖσαν ταῖς | [φυλαῖ]ς ἐπεμελήθη ὑπὲρ τῆς Ἀν|[τιοχίδος] φυλῆς, ὅπως ἂν μηθὲν | [βλαβερὸν γένητ]αι τοῖς φυ[λ]έ[τ|αις, καὶ αἴτιος ἐγ]ένετο λαβεῖ|[ν . . . δραχμὰς ἀργ]υρίου Ἀντιο|[χίδαις]* (ll. 14–15 are restored as *ἐπ[ὶ | τὴν] ἔφυλον* by Keramopoullos *apud* Karouzos 1923, 88 n. 2; *ἐγ[γ|ύην] ἔφυλον* by Oikonomides 1958, 77.

the date of the inscription (303/2), Euthydemos' beneficence pertains to a second division of the Oropian territory in the late fourth century or to the old one of the 330s, though most scholars would rather opt for the first interpretation.[21] Be that as it may, Euthydemos' official role with regard to Oropos must have been that of *ἐπιμελητής* (*epimeletes*), if the verb *ἐπεμελήθη* ('he looked after') is indicative of the office.

To this testimony one can compare *IG* II[2] 1165, an early third-century (?) decree of Erechtheis, by which the tribe bestowed posthumous honours upon Antisthenes, son of Nikandros, of Lamptrai.[22] Now Antisthenes seems to have been an efficient holder of financial tribal offices during his lifetime, but the best preserved part of the inscription reveals another reason for his tribesmen's readiness to recognize his contribution. He had proposed a decree whereby the *epimeletai* of the tribe were to inspect biannually the properties of the *phylai* in order to ensure that the landholdings were cultivated in compliance with the official contracts and that no boundary-stones had been tampered with.[23] A case has been made that Antisthenes was, in fact, one of the *epimeletai* envisaged in his own decree.[24] If so, his role would be comparable to that of Euthydemos of *ISE* 8. Taking this assumption one step further, it is tempting to see here an echo of

[21] Karouzos 1923, the first editor of the text, thought that the recounted events should be dated prior to 312 (on which point he is confused, the date should be 319; see Papazarkadas 2009*b*, 178). De Sanctis, 1926 argued for a new bestowal of Oropos to Athens by Demetrios the Besieger in 304 or thereabouts, a view endorsed by Robert 1960, 200–2; Moretti in *ISE* 8; Habicht 1997, 77 with n. 38. If so, this new redistribution of Oropian lands would have certainly been different from the previous one because of the earlier creation of the two new tribes, i.e. Antigonis and Demetrias (a point missed by Petrakos 1968, 31).

[22] Kirchner gives the date of *IG* II[2] 1165 as '*a. 300-250*'. It is very likely that Antisthenes' father was Nikandros, Treasurer of the Sacred Monies of Athena in 343/2 (*IG* II[2] 1443, l. 6; cf. *LGPN* II, s.v. *Νίκανδρος* (31); *PAA* 10688; Jones 1999, 176). If so, Antisthenes would have been active already in the late 4th cent. Having examined a squeeze of *IG* II[2] 1165 in the Centre for the Study of Ancient Documents at Oxford, I would contend that an earlier date—towards the end of the 4th cent.—for the decree is perfectly tenable.

[23] *IG* II[2] 1165 ll. 17–22: *ὅπως ἂν [Ἐρεχ]θεῖ|δαι εἰδῶ[σιν ἅπ]αντες τὰ ἑαυτῶν κτήματα καὶ οἱ ἐπιμεληταὶ | οἱ αἰεὶ καθιστάμενοι κατ' ἐνιαυτὸν βαδίζοντες ἐπὶ τὰ κτήμ|ατα δὶς τοῦ ἐνιαυτοῦ ἐπισκοπῶνται τά τε χωρία εἰ γεωργεῖτ|αι κατὰ τὰς συνθήκας, καὶ τοὺς ὅρους εἰ ἐφεστήκασιν κατὰ τ|ὰ αὐτά*; Lipsius 1905–15, 697 n. 74, wrongly identified these *horoi* as hypothecation stones, an error for which he was reproached by Finley 1952*a*, 213 n. 49; unrepentantly Jones 1999, 177 reiterated the same mistake.

[24] Jones 1999, 175–6.

the perplexities arising from the land allotment of the 330s, just as in the decree of Antiochis. Although the decree of Antisthenes makes no explicit mention of Oropos, it is certainly noticeable that the bulk of our data concerning tribal landed property dates to the late fourth century; that is, it postdates the division of Oropos amongst the tribes. It is worth noting that, apart from evidence already adduced, the tribal lease *IG* II^2 1168 has been tentatively placed in the third century independently from any preconceptions regarding the possible historical context.[25]

In any event, towards the end of the Classical period the Attic tribes ended up possessing areas as extensive as they ever had. However, a crucial question remains: how is one to explain the strong involvement of the ten tribes in the administration of the territory of Oropos? Oropos had always been a desideratum for the Athenians and as soon as that quasi-Boeotian territory came under the control of Athens, the Athenians hastened to incorporate it. The deep concern of Lykourgos and his circle about the administration of the Amphiaraeion is the religious facet of this policy. The radical restructuring of the military institution of the *ephebeia* is the other side of the same coin, as the new chronology for the recovery of Oropos incontrovertibly demonstrates.[26] The Athenian state, I contend, used the *phylai* for a dual military and political-administrative absorption of the newly acquired territory of Oropos. It can be no coincidence that the tribal document *Agora* XVI 84 features officials (or tax-collectors?) called ὑλῶναι ('timber-buyers') cooperating with representatives of Aigeis and Aiantis, arguably for the financial exploitation of the forested wealth of Oropos.[27] Arboriculture, apiculture, pastoralism, and even hunting were also likely means by which the polis of Athens would have rendered Oropos a lucrative area—always via the tribes.[28] All in all, the tribes represented, by their very nature, a

[25] Andreyev 1974, 38 considered the creation of *phyle* lands as a rather late phenomenon.

[26] The theory of the existence of the ephebate as early as 361 (so Reinmuth 1971, 2; 123–4) has been demolished by Lewis 1973*b*; Mitchel 1975; De Marcellus 1994. But what is important is the realization that the terminus post quem for the introduction of the institution is not 336/5, as traditionally believed, but 335/4: see Knoepfler 2001, 381–2.

[27] See now Papazarkadas 2009*b*, 174–80. I cannot rule out the possibility that the *hylonai* were actually tribally appointed officials representing the central government.

[28] Humphreys 2004, 112–3; Papazarkadas 2009*b*, 176–7.

far preferable choice to the demes, for instance, which due to their more marked territorial features could not respond to the new circumstances of managing the conquered territories as effectively as the Attic tribes.

iii. Administration of *phyle*-properties and tribal economics

It is certainly a sad fact that the only substantial piece of epigraphical evidence regarding leasing of tribal property is a long-lost document of an unidentified *phyle*, *IG* II^2 1168. For what it is worth, this text reveals a situation similar to that encountered at other levels of Athenian administration: provision of guarantors on behalf of the lessees, rentals paid in instalments, designation of the actual collectors of rentals, and punishment clauses for those lessees falling behind in their obligations. To be sure, the first point cannot be considered typical, since, outside of state-conferred leases, placement of sureties was the exception rather than the rule amongst the Athenian political subunits. Interestingly, a guarantor is also envisaged in *IG* I^3 252 (l. 8), a fact that raises the possibility that provision of guarantors was part and parcel of tribal leasing procedures. It is not difficult to see why this would have been so. In contrast to lesser components of the Athenian political structure, the tribes were of substantial size and had a very loose territorial character. Consequently, the system of selection that seems to have been favoured by smaller public or semi-public bodies with regard to the appointment of lessees would have proved less adequate in the case of tribal leases. The inherent impersonal character of such transactions necessitated the demand for the placement of sureties. There is also a clause on seizure in case of default of payment that can only be matched by similar provisions in the lease of Aixoneis (*IG* II^2 2492) and that of the phratry of Dyaleis (*IG* II^2 1241).[29] The stipulation for the tripartite payment of the rental is also idiosyncratic, and I would provisionally ascribe it to the

[29] *IG* II^2 1168 ll. 10–16: *ἐὰν [δ]ὲ [μὴ ἀ]|ποδιδῶσιν κατὰ τὰ[s] γενομένα[s συγγραφάς, ἐ]|νεχυρασίαν εἶναι αὐ[τ]ῷ[ν καὶ] τῶι̣ [ταμί]|α̣ι καὶ τοῖs ἐπιμεληταῖs· τὰ̣s δὲ̣ [ἐνεχυρ]|ασίας ἐκ τῶν τοῦ μι[σ]θωσαμένου [εἶναι κα]|ὶ τοῦ ἐγγυητοῦ αὐτοῦ τρό[π]ω[ι ὁπο]ί[ωι] | ἂν βούλωνται*; restorations by Wilhelm 1935, 205; cf. Harrison 1971, 244–7.

presence of the three *epimeletai*.[30] Incidentally, *IG* II^2 1168 is the only extant lease wherein payment of part of the rental was arranged for the beginning of the year with no calendrical specification, the implication being that money was demanded by the *phyle* for the coverage of ensuing, albeit unspecified, expenditure. The anonymity of the issuing *phyle* does not allow any speculation on the possible cultic or other significance behind the choice of Gamelion and Thargelion as dates for the payment of the remaining rental. At any rate, what is merely a plausible guess in other tribal documents appears in full clarity here: the *epimeletai* have expanded jurisdiction over land issues, although, uniquely, a treasurer also features.

This persistent occurrence of *epimeletai* with regard to land administration is remarkable. Either directly or indirectly, the terminology employed seems to imply that the Attic *phylai* constantly assigned the task of managing the tribal landed assets to boards of *epimeletai*.[31] Working on a larger dossier of documents and without drawing dividing lines between different sectors of tribal activity Jones recently reached a similar conclusion with regard to the overall internal organization of the *phylai*. We can safely conclude that the *epimeletai*, probably three in number, were the primary tribal magistrates.[32] Just like the demarch in relation to deme property, the tribal *epimeletai* were expected, rather than constitutionally obliged, to manage the realty of their *phylai*. Other tribal personnel engaged in land administration include the treasurer, the *syndikoi*, and the *horistai*. The last of these officials were obviously of some importance, to judge from their presence not only in the double tribal decree, but also in the dedication *IG* II^2 2824, if theirs is indeed the elusive tribal office in line 1.[33] Another aspect of land administration involving

[30] *IG* II^2 1168 ll. 4–8: *καὶ [καταβάλλειν τὸ] | μὲν πρῶτον μέρος τῆς μι[σθώσεως ἀρχομέν]||ου τοῦ ἐνιαυτοῦ, τὸ δὲ δεύτε[ρον μέ]||ρος τοῦ Γαμηλιῶνος μηνός, [τὸ δὲ τ]||ελευταῖον τοῦ Θαργηλιῶν[ος μηνός]*. The only comparable financial mechanism would be the four-month office of the treasurers of the non-constitutional deme of Salamis, as attested in Wilhelm 1909*b*, 135 (not in any epigraphic corpus), ll. 4–5: *[τὸ δὲ γενόμενον ἀνάλωμα δοῦναι τὸ]ν ταμία[ν τὸν τὴν δ]ευ[τέραν] | τετράμηνον ταμιεύοντα* etc. (cf. Taylor 1997, 247).

[31] *Epimeletai* appear in *IG* I^3 252, *IG* II^2 1165, *IG* II^2 1168, and are alluded to in *ISE* 8.

[32] Jones 1999, 174–8; cf. Traill 1986, 79–90.

[33] *IG* II^2 2824 ll. 1–2: *[ὁριστ]αὶ καὶ ταμίας οἱ ἐπὶ Θεοφράστου ἄρχοντος | [στεφανωθέ]ντες ὑπὸ τῶν φυλετῶν*; Whitehead 2000, 210 n. 180; cf. Jones 1999, 180–1; *[λογιστ]αί*, Pittakys, *Ephemeris* 1860, 1877; *[ἐπιμελητ]αί*, Koehler in *IG* II

tribes should be mentioned briefly, although it is generally thought not to be strictly related to land owned by tribes. The (in)famous *IG* II^2 1672 contains a full list of the first-fruits offered in 329/8 to the Eleusinian Goddesses arranged by tribes, and the relevant entry has often been used to estimate the average grain production of Attica.[34] However, the determined scholars engaging in this painstaking task have usually been so preoccupied with arithmetic that they have not dealt with the administrative aspects of the problem. For instance, in contrast to the *aparche* from the cleruchies, which was brought in by generals, we are unaware of the officials undertaking the same task on behalf of the tribes. Were they tribal officials such as the *epimeletai*? If so, would they have made use of their experience as administrators of their own tribes' realty? Moreover, was agricultural produce from tribal lands included in the first-fruits recorded in *IG* II^2 1672? I raise these points in order to demonstrate the extent of our ignorance, although I suspect that one has to give an affirmative answer to the third question.

Other questions are more worth asking, beyond technical minutiae, even though answers may not always be available. What was, for instance, the nominal and legal status of tribal properties? What was their contribution to tribal budgets? And following from these queries, what can tribal land administration tell us about the notional perception of the tribes proper? A considerable problem faced by the modern student of the institution of tribes is that of conceptualizing the exact status of the economics of the *phylai* perceived as internally organized associations. More patently than in the case of demes, each *phyle* was under the titular divine protection of its eponymous hero—a trait that has produced comments such as 'the phylai were first and foremost religious associations'.[35] Indeed, this peculiarity seems to have generated such collective terms as *Κεκροπίδαι*, *Αἰγηίδαι*, *Ἀντιοχίδαι*, and so on, literally the descendants of Kekrops, Aigeus, and Antiochos respectively.[36] The same notion is sometimes reflected in the financial

1209 (refuted by Traill 1986, 90–2). For the date (313/2 rather than 340/39) see Wilhelm 1942, 146.

[34] *IG* II2 1672 ll. 262–71; cf. Jardé 1925, 47–53; Garnsey 1985; 1988, 99–105; Sallares 1991, 79–80.

[35] Thus Jones 1987, 60; cf. Parker 1996, 103–4.

[36] See Hedrick 1991, 242; Parker 1996, 120–1.

realm.[37] The inventory lists of some of the heroes surely designate such properties as being sacred rather than secular.

Just as in the case of other Attic associations, the expenses of the ten tribes must have fallen under one or another of the following categories: (i) costs for publication of tribal documents, (ii) bestowal of honours, usually crownings, upon real or imaginary benefactors,[38] and (iii) performance of cultic activity, mainly sacrifices.[39] Unlike the demes, the tribes appear to have lacked a substantial source of income, mainly direct levies, though I raised in n. 37 the possibility that the debt of the *epimeletes* of Aiantis, Nikodemos, might have resulted from his collecting an unidentified sacred tax.[40] Lending was a most obvious means of raising income, but in Attica proper only one such transaction involving a *phyle* is known.[41] On the other hand, the recent publication of a horos from Lemnos featuring the tribe Akamantis as creditor on land security is a good reminder that we should always be ready to re-evaluate any provisional inferences.[42] Moreover, a decree of Pandionis from the Athenian cleruchy of Samos shows that the tribe relied heavily on interest from loans for the subsidy of its cultic activity.[43] However, ever since the publication

[37] e.g. *Agora* XIX P26 ll. 505–10; *καὶ ἐκγεγραμμένου ἐν ἀκροπόλει|ἐπιβολὴν ὀφλόντος ὅτι ἐπιμελητὴς γενόμε|νος τῆς Αἰαντίδος φυλῆς καὶ ἐγλέξας τὸ ἱερ|ὸν ἀργύριον τῆς φυλῆς οὐκ ἀποδέδωκεν καὶ ἐ|κγεγραμμένο: ἐν ἀκροπόλει τῶι Αἴαντι καὶ ὀ|φείλοντος:* 𐅅*Η*𐅄*ΔΠΠΙΙΙΙ*; ll. 521-4: *οὐκ ἀ|ποδόντος τοῦτο τὸ ἀργύριον τῆι Αἰαντίδι φ|υλεῖ ἐπιμελητοῦ γενομένο Νικοδήμου καὶ ἐ|γλέξαντος τὸ ἱερὸν ἀργύριον τοῦ Αἴαντος* (the verb *ἐγλέγω* might imply tax collection); Dem. 58.14: *ὃ φανήσεται οὗτος, ὀφείλων καὶ οὐκ ἐκτετεικὼς ἑπτακοσίας δραχμάς, ἃς ὤφλεν ἐν ταῖς εὐθύναις τῷ ἐπωνύμῳ τῆς αὑτοῦ φυλῆς*; maybe also *SEG* XXIII 78 ll. 7–8: [*ἀποτινέτω χ*]*ιλίας δραχμὰς ἱ*|[*ερὰς τῶι Ἀκάμαντι*] (cf. Mitsos 1965).

[38] See Jones 1999, 166–7 (with collection of all the available data), 169; in this class of expenditure I include the peculiar case of Erechtheis undertaking to bring up Antisthenes' orphaned daughter as an *ἐπίκληρος* (*IG* II^2 1165).

[39] Jones 1987, 60.

[40] Note that the *ateleia* occasionally awarded by tribes (*IG* II^2 1140; 1147; *SEG* XXIII 78b, with Mitsos 1965, 132) does not pertain to tribal taxation, but to exemption from liturgies, which were not an item of tribal budgets.

[41] *IG* II^2 2670: *ὅρος χωρίο προικὸς* | *Ἱπποκλείαι Δημοχά*|[*ρ*]*ος Λευκονοιῶς Τ·* | [*ὅσ*]*ωι πλείονος ἄξι*|[*ον*], *Κεκροπίδαις* | [*ὑπό*]*κειται καὶ Λυκ*|[*ομί*]*δαις καὶ Φλυεῦ*|[*σι*]; but this appears to be a solidarity transaction, not one aiming at profit.

[42] Culasso Gastaldi 2006, 516–19, no. 4: *ὅρος χω*[*ρίο πε*]|*πραμέν*[*ο ἐπὶ*]|*λύσει Ἀ*[*καμα*]|*ντίδαις* (cf. Cargill 1995, 245–6).

[43] *IG* XII (6) 255, esp. ll. 2–5: *ἐπειδὴ οἱ δ*[*α*|*νεισάμενοι παρὰ τοῦ ἥρωος*] *χρήματα οὐ καταβάλλουσ*[*ιν* | *τοὺς τόκους, ἀφ' ὧν νόμος θ*]*ύεσθαι τῶι Πανδίονι καὶ τοῖς* [*ἄλ*|*λοις θεοῖς*] etc. (cf. Klaffenbach 1926, 36–8; Schlaifer 1940, 252 n. 1; Cargill 1995, 182–3).

of the catalogue of councillors and archons of the same cleruchy one has to be extremely cautious: the document in question has demonstrated that at least at Samos—and, no doubt, in other cleruchies as well—the administrative apparatus was based on the blueprint of, but was different from, that of Athens.[44] Is the issuing body of the financial document *IG* XII (6) 255 the tribe Pandionis in toto, or just the cleruchic branch of the tribe? If the latter is true, what is the exact financial interaction between the two bodies, if any? I simply pose these questions without claiming to know the answers, though, it has to be said, the *temenos* of Antiochis at Lemnos may allude to interconnection.[45] In general, tribal finances appear to have been low, not in terms of sheer volume—one of the *epimeletai* of Aigeis, for instance, managed 666 drachmas 4 obols in the early 340s[46]—but in proportion to the size of the *phylai*. All things considered, it appears that exploitation of land resources and, more infrequently, buildings,[47] was crucial for the subsidy of tribal activities. Though only plausibly envisaged in the case of a decree of Erechtheis concerning sacrifices, rentals must have provided a steady flow of cash for the coverage of tribal cultic needs.[48] Yet, before the Oropian affair, tribal landed assets cannot have been vast. That this was so can be seen in the *Rationes Centesimarum*, where, amongst all Athenian public or semi-public associations, *phylai* are the only ones not to feature as land-vendors. If this *argumentum e silentio* is worth anything, it

[44] The list is now published as *IG* XII (6) 262; cf. the observations made by Hallof and Habicht 1995, esp. 301–3.

[45] Shipley 1987, 161 and Jones 1987, 196 think of local tribes; Parker 1994, 343 n. 19 of a 'branch-tribe'.

[46] *Agora* XIX P26 ll. 498–530. It is often thought that tribal economics were divided into three equal shares administered by each *epimeletes* individually (cf. Ferguson 1938, 13–14 n. 2, followed by Schlaifer 1940, 252 n. 1 and Parker 1996, 104 n. 7). If so, Aigeis' income in that particular year would have been 666 drachmas 4 obols $\times$ 3 = 2000 drachmas.

[47] As implied by the fragmentary honorific decree *IG* II^2 1164 l. 9: *καὶ τῶν οἰκι[ῶν]*, in a context which might have been under the jurisdiction of the *epimeletai* (cf. Jones 1987, 60).

[48] *LSCG* 30 (*SEG* XXV 140), ll. 8–9: *ἀναλίσκειν δ' ὅ τι | γίγνεται ἐκ τ[ῶν μισθωμάτων]*. The defective prescript of the decree of Aigeis and Aiantis calls for offering of sacrifices which *might* have been subsidized with income from their Oropian property (*Agora* XVI 84 ll. 3–4: *[δε|δ]όχθαι ταῖς [φ]ṿλαῖς θ̣ῦσ[αι]*, with Papazarkadas 2009*b*, 177).

probably means that the tribes simply did not have any land surplus to alienate.[49]

It cannot be determined how clear-cut a distinction was made between sacred tribal money and secular funds. The impression one gets is that at an earlier period the sacred character of tribal economics was more prominent than later.[50] That this notional modification corresponds to an actual reorientation of the financial infrastructure of the tribes is no more than a plausible hypothesis. I have already implied that this phenomenon might be attributable to the grant of the Oropian hills to the tribes. In turn, the land assignment might have been connected with a renewed emphasis on the military importance of the tribes. In the third century documents related to the tribes are increasingly of a military character, mainly decrees honouring tribal military officers, such as phylarchs, hipparchs, and so on.[51] In the meantime the addition of the two Macedonian tribes and the simultaneous rearrangement of the demes within the enlarged tribal system must have affected tribal economics as well, albeit in a way that has left no discernible traces.

2. THE REAL PROPERTY OF THE ATTIC DEMES

i. Prolegomenon

In the 57th Demosthenic speech the defendant Euxitheos reminded his jurors of the hatred he aroused in many of his fellow demesmen when he tried, acting in his capacity as demarch of Halimous, to put an end to the encroachments and the inconsistency of many

[49] A possibility not broached by Lambert 1997*a*, 220. The fact that the sales were apparently arranged in the official tribal order (Lewis 1973*a*, 190–1; Lambert 1997*a*, 5–7) is irrelevant.

[50] Sacred money administered by tribes: *IG* I^3 252 (mid-5th cent.); *IG* I^3 377, ll. 21–2, with Meritt 1974, 262–3 and Traill 1986, 79–80, who consider the case as a loan of sacred tribal money to the state-*logistai* (406/5); *Agora* XIX P26 (347/6); *IG* XII (6) 255 (*c.*330). Tribal funds of no tangible religious connotations: *Agora* XVI 84, with Papazarkadas 2009*b*, 177–8 (late 330s–early 320s); *IG* II^2 1165, esp. l. 11: *ἐκ τῶν κοινῶν προσόδων* (*c.*300). But Pl. *Leg.* 884, *εἰς μέγιστα δέ, ὅταν εἰς ἱερὰ γίγνωνται, καὶ διαφερόντως αὖ μεγάλα, ὅταν εἰς δημόσια καὶ ἅγια ἢ κατὰ μέρη κοινὰ φυλετῶν ἤ τινων ἄλλων τοιούτων κεκοινωνηκότων*, aptly demonstrates the overlap between the public/secular and sacred spheres in a tribal context; on this point see Saunders 1972, 90.

[51] Bugh 1988, 186–91; 1998, 83–9; Kralli 2006, 551–5.

Halimousians who refused to fulfil their financial obligations towards their deme. Prominent among Euxitheos' actions stood his endeavour to collect money due to the deme from lessees of *temene*.[52] This passage, in its rueful isolation, perfectly summarizes the main theme of the present Section, namely administration of realty at the deme level.

As every student of Athenian political history knows, the demes were, in essence, a microcosm of the polis itself at a multitude of levels: religion and politics, economics, and social structure alike.[53] This reckoning is not meant to dismiss the existence of huge dissimilarities between individual demes. For instance, there was little in common between the urban and, dare one say, multicultural Piraeus and peripheral, agricultural Atene, to take the two opposite extremes.[54] It seems, however, that even tiny demes were possessors of real property, mainly agricultural land and pasturage, but also quarries and edifices like houses, workshops, and theatres.[55] The presence of deme-controlled realty should suffice to demonstrate the existence of the controversial and long-disputed territoriality of the Attic demes. The treatment of this topic will be postponed until the penultimate subsection of this chapter. First, an attempt will be made at a detailed treatment of the modes of exploitation of realty on behalf of demes and the interaction between deme economics and deme landed assets.

ii. The mechanism of leasing

Leasing constituted the obvious way of rendering a property lucrative, and demes did not constitute an exception in that respect.[56] This

[52] Dem. 57.63: *Εἰ δὲ δεῖ τὴν δημαρχίαν λέγειν, δι' ἣν ὠργίζοντό μοί τινες, ἐν ᾗ διάφορος ἐγενόμην εἰσπράττων ὀφείλοντας πολλοὺς αὐτῶν μισθώσεις τεμενῶν καὶ ἕτερ' ἃ τῶν κοινῶν διηρπάκεσαν, ἐγὼ μὲν ἂν βουλοίμην ὑμᾶς ἀκούειν, ἀλλ' ἴσως ἔξω τοῦ πράγματος ὑπολήψεσθε ταῦτ' εἶναι* (cf. Osborne 1988, 282; Isager and Skydsgaard 1992, 189–90).

[53] Kearns 1985, 200–1; Whitehead 1986, *passim*; Jones 1999, 51–150.

[54] For these two demes see the monographs by Garland 1987 and Lohmann 1993 respectively.

[55] Andreyev 1974, 38; Nemes 1980; Osborne 1985*a*, 186.

[56] Nemes 1980, 6; Whitehead 1986, 152–8. For leasing in Attica, beyond the fundamental treatments of Behrend 1970 and Walbank in *Agora* XIX, pp. 149–69, see MacDowell 1978, 140–2; Osborne 1988 (of wider geographical scope).

practice is attested as early as the fifth century, in the famous decree of Plotheia, and we would certainly be able to trace it back to the time of the foundation of demes by Cleisthenes, were it not for lack of evidence.[57] Indeed, there is reason to believe that the *naukrariai*, the alleged predecessors of the Cleisthenic demes, had been involved in leasing out property already in Archaic times, if we are to give credence to the lexicographers.[58] We also know of a fifth-century deme decree containing the terms of the lease of two *temene*, one consecrated to Dionysos and the other to Herakles. The stone itself is lost, and the inscription remains unpublished, but David Lewis, the doyen of Attic epigraphy who had seen photographs of the text, dated it to the mid-fifth century and ascribed it to the deme Thorikos.[59] Chronologically the vast bulk of evidence comes from the fourth century and, more precisely, the second half of it.[60] In stark contrast to the centralized mechanism that regulated the management of *temene* controlled by the polis, demes lacked a unified administrative system. Instead, they tended to work along predefined lines, making use of the acquired experience of their own officials. This flexible response to problems surrounding deme-land administration accounts for a rather diverse and complicated picture which will be analysed below, before further, more elaborate, questions are asked.

The onus of leasing out lands presumably lay with the demarch, the paramount deme magistrate, but, if so, it is frustrating that demarchs are explicitly attested as leasing agents only in a handful of cases.[61] Apart from the Demosthenic passage cited above, the most revealing document is the decree of Teithras from the mid-fourth century, in which the demarch was instructed to write down the names of the lessees of deme properties, to extract the rentals and, assisted by three

[57] Plotheia: *IG* I^3 258 (= *IG* II^2 1172), with Haussoulier 1884, 64; Whitehead 1986, 166–8 contra Behrend 1970, 73–4. To this one could hesitantly add the even older *lex sacra IG* I^3 243 (*Agora* XIX LA1, esp. ll. 97–100), part of which may contain a lease carried out by the urban deme of Melite (cf. Walbank 1991, 153), but the epigraphical remarks by Lalonde 1999, 13–16 render this hypothesis highly unlikely.

[58] Phot. s.v. *ναύκραροι· τὸ παλαιὸν Ἀθήνησιν οἱ νῦν δήμαρχοι καὶ οἱ ἐκμισθοῦντες τὰ δημόσια*; Ammonios s.v. *ναύκραροι· οἱ εἰσπρασσόμενοι τὰ δημόσια κτήματα καὶ ναυκράρια οἱ τόποι ἐν οἷς ἐνέκειτο τὰ κτήματα* (see Chapter 4 below).

[59] For the convoluted story of this inscription see Matthaiou 2009, 206.

[60] Osborne 1985*a*, 54–6.

[61] Coumanoudis and Gofas 1978, 299 dismiss the demarch's role as merely 'auxiliaire', but this does not do justice to the complexities of his task.

demesmen, to erase the names of previous lessees.[62] Likewise, in 332/1 the demarch of Eleusis was commanded by a decree to lease out the quarry of Herakles ἐν Ἄκριδι in an assembly of the demesmen.[63] Yet demarchs feature as selling agents in the *Rationes Centesimarum*, which we have reason to believe replicated in a more elaborate form the fiscal realities underlying leasing transactions, and this role probably reflects the demarchs' functions as lessors.[64] Indirectly, a demarch's cognizance in realty administration can be seen in the decree concerning the Sacred Orgas *I.Eleusis* 144 (*IG* II² 204), where demarchs are envisaged as legitimate participants in the protection of the Attic sacred precincts, and in the Eleusinian accounts *I.Eleusis* 177 (*IG* II² 1672), where a demarch is attested as having collected and handed over to the Eleusinian officials grain harvested at the sacred land of Amphiaraos at Oropos.[65] In the same text, the man collecting the tithe from Salamis is usually identified as the archon of the island, who according to Aristotle was the equivalent of the demarch of Piraeus.[66] In most cases, however, it is the demesmen as a whole who appear to carry out leasing transactions.[67] The inference is ineluctable: though not legally obliged, a demarch was the obvious candidate to lease out a property on behalf of his deme due to his expertise in financial affairs.[68]

[62] Papazarkadas 2007*a*, D1a (= *SEG* XXIV 151), ll. 4–5, *ἀναγρά[ψαι τὸ]ν δήμαρχο|[ν] ὁπ[όσ]οι κατάπαξ μεμίσθωνται τῶν κοινῶν*; 32–3: *τ[ὰ|ς δὲ μισθώσεις ἀπο]διδόν̣αι τῶι δημάρχωι*; cf. Faraguna 1997, 22–3.

[63] *SEG* XXVIII 103 l. 23: *μ[ισ]θοῦν τὸν δήμαρχον ἐν τῆι ἀγορᾶι τῶν δημοτῶν*; the masterly *editio princeps* of this double document was produced by Coumanoudis and Gofas 1978. See now the editions by Clinton (*I.Eleusis* 85), Lupu (*NGSL* 2), and Alipheri 2009.

[64] Beyond some plausible, but unprovable, restorations, two cases are unquestionable in the *Rationes Centesimarum*: the demarch of Oinoe *Μνησαρχίδη[s]* (F7 l. 27), and that of Halaieis *Φι[λήριφος?] | Ạἰσχέου* (F9A ll. 17–18); cf. Whitehead 1986, 132 with n. 68; Lambert 1997*a*, 250.

[65] *I.Eleusis* 144 ll. 16–23; *I.Eleusis* 177 ll. 401–2: *ἐκ τῆς ἐπ' | Ἀμφιαράου δήμαρχος Προκλῆς Σουνιεὺς κρι ΔΔ, πυρῶν Π μέδιμνοι ἐννέα ἡμιεκτεῖα*, with Whitehead 1982, 40–2 (Prokles understood to be the demarch of Sounion), and Clinton 2008, 233 (Prokles acting as demarch of Oropos).

[66] *I.Eleusis* 177 ll. 403–4: *ἐξαλαμῖνος Τιμόθεος Ἀλωπε κρι ΔΔΔΔ | δέκα ἡμιεκτεῖα δύο χοίνικες*, with Taylor 1997, 162–4 (who, however, maintains that the archon of Salamis could never have been called a demarch); cf. Arist. [*Ath. Pol.*] 54.8.

[67] On this and the problem of the legal standing of corporate groupings see the concise, but very illuminating, note by Cohen 1992, 63 n. 6; see also Ustinova 2005 on the concept of the juristic person of cult associations.

[68] Whitehead 1986, 121–39 presents the full range of a demarch's duties.

In two instances, however, an alternative to this system is attested, with small boards of demesmen, under the nominal leadership of certain individuals, undertaking the task of letting out properties.[69] These ad hoc committees called *merē* (μέρη) are almost unprecedented as an institution.[70] The incentive behind their creation is difficult to establish. Convenience was certainly one reason, with the *meritai* (μερῖται) releasing the demarch from some of his many burdens. Benefaction might have been another motive, and their function has actually been described as a quasi-liturgy. Indeed, this hypothesis is corroborated by prosopographical analysis of the eight Kytherian μερῖται, which shows two important elements: (*a*) two family branches are discernible, and (*b*) at least one of these families can be classified as upper-class. This picture is reminiscent of elite family politics dominating deme life as seen in other contexts, like *IG* II^2 2820, an inscribed offering to Aphrodite by a group of Halaieis who had been assigned the task of erecting a statue of the goddess by their fellow demesmen.[71] In addition, in the case of the Rhamnousian μερῖται, local idiosyncrasy may be accounted for. As Osborne has demonstrated, thanks to an abundance of epigraphical documents, Rhamnous was replete with ad hoc boards of military, civic, or other nature, partly due to its location as a trading post, partly due to its defensive character as a frontier fort, and, to some extent, because of the prominent shrine of Nemesis.[72]

As far as the leasing process goes, some sort of public auction can be envisaged. Indeed, in an Eleusinian decree moved by Philokomos, son of Phalanthides, the lease of quarry rights was stipulated to be conferred on whoever offered the largest amount of money.[73] Nonetheless, no such information can be extracted from other deme

[69] Kytheros: *IG* II^2 2496 ll. 2–8: *κατὰ τάδε ἐμίσθωσαν Ἀντί|μαχος Ἀμφιμάχου, Φειδόστρατος | Μνησιχάρου, Δημάρετος Λεωσθένο|υ, Κτησίας Κτησιφῶντος, Κτήσιππος | Κτησιφῶντος, Κτησιχάρης Κτησιφ|ῶντος, Κτησίας Τιμοκράτου, Χαιρέα|ς Μνησιχάρου Κυθηρίων οἱ μερῖται*; Rhamnous: *I.Rhamnous* 180 ll. 3–4: *[κ]ατὰ τάδε μισθοῦσιν οἱ δημόται [ο]ἱ̣ [ἐ]κ τοῦ Ἀ[ρ]|χίππου μέρους καὶ Στησίου*; ll. 36–7: *[κατὰ τάδε μισθοῦσι]ν οἱ δημόται οἱ ἐκ [το]ῦ Ἀρ̣χ[ί|ππου μέρους καὶ Στη]σίου.*

[70] The best analysis of the *μέρη* remains that of Jameson 1982, 72–3.

[71] That some of these demesmen were influential beyond the local level can be seen in their inclusion in *IG* II^2 1593, a list of tax-farmers, as I argue elsewhere; cf. Whitehead 1986, 239–41.

[72] Osborne 1990, 277–85.

[73] *SEG* XXVIII 103 ll. 23–4: *μ[ισ]θοῦν τὸν δήμαρχον ἐν τῆι ἀγορᾶι τῶν δημοτῶν τῶ|ι τὸ πλεῖ[σ]τον διδόντι* (improved readings by Alipheri 2009).

documents. The sale of timber by the Aixoneis can be used only as a paradigm of comparison in this respect.[74] Though mistakenly adduced as evidence for concession of leases at public auctions,[75] the axed olive trees that were to be sold to the highest bidder constitute a case related to, but distinct from, the lease of the landholding called Phelleis. We should not forget here that Andreyev once objected to the notion of competitive bidding on the grounds that half the preserved rentals are round sums, and his observation should not be lightly dismissed.[76]

Another characteristic of deme leases distinguishing them from leases held at the polis-level is the lack of any universal pattern concerning the letting periods. Once more, in the double Eleusinian decree of 332/1, the decision is left to the demesmen, a prime manifestation of the flexibility that demes demonstrated.[77] As for other demes, the mere fact that the few surviving decrees concerning leases contain clauses about the lease length demonstrates that this was always an open issue in need of specific arrangement, not something regulated a priori by any pre-existing statutes. Only Piraeus and Rhamnous seem to have followed the usual decennial leasing practice, but, so far as the former deme is concerned, the fact that the demarch was exceptionally appointed by the Athenian assembly and not by the demesmen of Piraeus might have played a role.[78]

Similarly diverse were the payment methods or, more precisely, the number of rent instalments. Whitehead considered the reasons behind this diversity unfathomable, but some guesses can be ventured.[79] When the Eleusinians stipulated that the rent from the quarry of Herakles had to be paid in the month of Metageitnion, during the assembly of the demesmen at the urban Theseion, there should be no doubt that they did so with an eye to some sort of public scrutiny.[80] The same mentality seems to underlie the lease of the *temenos* of

[74] *IG* II^2 2492 ll. 35–6: *ἀπ|οδώσονται τὰς ἐλάας τῶι τὸ πλεῖστον διδόντι.*

[75] Thus Langdon 1994, 254.

[76] Andreyev 1974, 43–4.

[77] *SEG* XXVIII 103 ll. 33–6: *διαχẹιροτονῆσạι δὲ αὐτί̣κα μάλα τοὺς δη|μότ̣ạς ẹ̓ά̣ν τε εἰ̣ς ἐ̣νιạυτὸν δοκεῖ μισθοῦṿ, ẹ̓άν τε εἰς πλ|έω χρόνον, ὁπότερα δ̣᾿ ἂν δοκεῖ, ṭαῦτạ κύρια εἶναι καὶ μι|σθ̣ọῦṿ π̣ρὸς ταῦτα τὸν δήμạρχοṿ.*

[78] Arist. [*Ath. Pol.*] 54.8, *κληροῦσι δὲ καὶ εἰς Σαλαμῖνα ἄρχοντα, καὶ εἰς Πει[ραι]έα δήμ̣αρ[χ]ον.*

[79] Whitehead 1986, 155.

[80] *SEG* XXVIII 103 (text by Alipheri 2009), ll. 24–8: *τὸν δὲ <μ>ισθωσάμενον ἀποδιδόν|αι τὴν μίσθωσιν τὴν μὲν ἐπὶ Νικήτου ἄρχοντος ἐν ὧι ἂν | χρό<u>νωι</u> τοὺς δημότας*

Nemesis at Rhamnous, wherein the payment of the rental was preplanned for the deme assembly in the month Poseideon.[81] But this is not the end of the story. In Eleusis the aforementioned arrangement was stipulated to start from the year following the archonship of Niketes (332/1). As for the latter year, the lessee had to pay the rent at a time proposed by him and approved by the Eleusinians, but *before* the sacrifice to Herakles.[82] It is exactly this specification that constitutes the key to our comprehending rent payment procedures. Since the rent had been earmarked for a specific purpose, its prompt payment was crucial for the timely fulfilment of this plan. Public control was desirable, but not the only motive of the Eleusinian lessees. Priority was given to financial considerations. It is against this background that one has to review the various items of evidence. Demes chose to have rents paid to them in advance of anticipated expenditure and at some date convenient for public supervision of the transactions. My guess is that when a specific month was designated as the payment period of some rent, the same month, or the following one at the very most, was in all likelihood the time when that money was destined to be spent. This hypothesis can be cross-checked to and confirmed by non-deme evidence. When the orgeones of Egretes leased out the shrine of the hero, they stipulated that the rent should be paid in two equal shares, one on the first day of Boedromion and the other on the first day of Elaphebolion.[83] No explicit justification for this arrangement is given, but an ensuing clause indirectly provides the answer. In Boedromion, the lessee had to make the building

πείθει, πρὸ τῆς θυσίας, μετὰ δὲ Νι|κήτην ἄρχοντα εἰς τὸν Μεταγειτνιῶνα μῆνα ταῖς ἀρχα[v]*|ιρεσίαις, ὅταν οἱ δημόται ἀγοράζωσιν ἐν τῶι Θησείωι* (this clause renders Metageitnion month, July–August, of 332 a terminus post quem for the decrees). For the *ἀρχαιρεσίαι* as referring to a deme assembly see Coumanoudis and Gofas 1978, 298 and Parker 1993, 26–7, contra Whitehead 1986, 89–90, who thinks of a tribal assembly.

[81] *I.Rhamnous* 180 ll. 13–15 with *SEG* LIV 239: *τὴμ μίσθωσιν καταθήσε||[ι] πρὸς τὸν σ̣[ύλλογ]ον τοῦ Ποσ[ι]δεῶνος μηνὸς τ|αῖς ἀγοραῖ̣[s]* (cf. Coumanoudis and Gofas 1978, 304). For the supplement *σ[ύλλογ]ον* see Papazarkadas 2004, 69: the actual recipient of the rentals would arguably be the assembly of the demesmen of Rhamnous.

[82] *SEG* XXVIII 103 ll. 24-8 (see n. 80 above).

[83] *IG* II^{2} 2499 ll. 18–24: *τὴν δὲ μίσθωσιν | ἀποδώσει Διόγνητος τῶι ἀεὶ ταμιε|ύοντι τῶν ὀργεώνων ἑκάστου τοῦ ἐν|ιαυτοῦ τὴμ μὲν ἡμίσεαν τὰς : Η : δραχμὰ[s] | τοῦ Βοηδρομιῶνος τῆι νουμηνίαι,*[v] *| τὴν δὲ λοιπὴν τὰς : Η : δραχμὰς τοῦ Ἐλα|φηβολιῶνος τῆι νουμ<η>νίαι.*

in the shrine available to the orgeones for the sacrifice to the hero.[84] We may conclude that, having half the rent paid to them on the first day of Boedromion, the orgeones ensured they had adequate funds at their disposal for the performance of their sacrifice.[85] Likewise, the Teithrasians picked out the month Elaphebolion as the time of payment of rentals owed to them, though they could well have chosen Metageitnion when they too would have gathered at the Theseion for the *ἀρχαιρεσίαι*.[86] Moreover, as the accusative temporal form [*εἰς*] *τὸν Ἐλαφηβολιῶνα μῆνα* implies, they did not condense payments for a particular occasion such as a deme assembly, but they distributed them over a wider span of roughly thirty days. Unfortunately the preserved fragment of the Teithrasian sacrificial calendar contains only expenditure incurred in the month Boedromion, and thus my hypothesis above cannot be cross-examined and consequently verified or disproved.[87]

A similar consideration may be envisaged with regard to the lease of the Aixonian land called Phelleis to Autokles and his son Auteas. The rental had to be deposited in the month Hekatombaion.[88] By having the money paid to them at the beginning of the political and religious year, the Aixoneis presumably sought to ensure that whatever fiscal needs might arise in the course of the year would not catch them by surprise. As for payments divided in two or three instalments, various factors should be allowed for. Thus the Prasieis asked the lessee Kirrias and his descendants to pay their rent in two parts, one in the month Metageitnion and the other in a now-lost month, but either Mounychion or Thargelion.[89] It is tempting to see here the choice of Metageitnion as being generated by considerations similar

[84] *IG* II[2] 2499, ll. 24–8: *ὅταν δὲ |θύωσιν οἱ ὀργεῶνες τῶι ἥρωι τοῦ Βο|ηδρομιῶνος, παρέχειν Διόγνητον τ|ὴν οἰκίαν, οὗ τὸ ἱερόν ἐστιν, ἀνεωιγ|μένην.*

[85] See Osborne 1988, 287–8; Walbank 1991, 160; Parker 1996, 110 (who also reaches the conclusion that the rent was used 'no doubt to finance the feast').

[86] Papazarkadas 2007a: D1a (*SEG* XXIV 151) ll. 32–4, *τ[ὰ|ς δὲ μισθώσεις ἀπο]|διδό̣ν̱αι τῶι δημάρχωι τῶ[ι | ἀεὶ δημαρχο̂ντι εἰς] τὸν Ἐλαφηβολιῶνα μῆνα*; cf. Behrend 1970, 79, and Whitehead 1986, 155 n. 41.

[87] *Fasti* of Teithras: Pollitt 1961, 293–7 (= *SEG* XXI 542); cf. Whitehead 1986, 186–7.

[88] *IG* II[2] 2492, ll. 5–7: *τὴν δ|ὲ μίσθωσιν ἀποδιδόναι τοῦ Ἑκατομβαιῶνος μη|νός.*

[89] *IG* II[2] 2497 (with *SEG* XXI 645), ll. 9–14: *[ἀποδ]ιδόναι δὲ τὴμ μίσθωσ|[ιν Κιρρίαν] καὶ τοὺς ἐκγόνους α|[ὐτοῦ Πρασιε]ῦσιν τὴμ μὲν ἡμίσε|[αν ἐν τῶι Μεταγ]ειτνιῶνι μηνὶ ἕ|[κτηι ἱσταμένου?, τ]ὴν δὲ ἡμίσεαν | [ἐν τῶι Μουνιχιῶν vel Θαργηλιῶν]ι μηνί; ἕ[κτηι φθίνοντος]* (l. 12) is also tenable.

to those found in the Eleusinian document, namely the gathering of the demesmen in Athens for the election of magistrates, especially if we accept a reference to a precise chronological point within the month in the broken line 12. This interpretation now finds welcome corroboration from the very recent publication of the third extant Prasian lease. In the new text it is stated explicitly that the first instalment had to be paid in Metageitnion during the election of the magistrates.[90] On the other hand, the distribution of the rent into two instalments may conceal some specific pecuniary need, such as two separate sets of expenditure, of which we are completely unaware.

A question worth addressing is how demes secured their interests in lease transactions. Demes seem to have employed an array of different tactics, and once more their response to the relevant problems proves far from unanimous. Sometimes they demanded sureties. This is the case in *SEG* XXVIII 103, where the lessee was expected to provide two guarantors regardless of the amount of the rental.[91] Such a loose provision differentiates deme practices from the systemized surety methods favoured by the polis, wherein the number of guarantors provided was dependent upon the amount of the rent. As in Eleusis, personal surety backed the lease commissioned by the deme of Kytheros,[92] and a guarantor is mentioned in a Hellenistic lease which might or might not have been undertaken by a deme.[93] Strangely enough, other leasing documents contain no apparent provisions of either security or surety. For two of them, *IG* II^2 2491, probably a lease from Acharnai, and the lease from Prasiai *IG* II^2 2497, the lack of such clauses may be ascribed to their fragmentary condition. At least in the fully preserved lease *IG* II^2 2492, the Aixoneis maintained the right to expropriate part of the lessees' property in case they failed to pay the due rent, a procedure

[90] *SEG* LI 153 (Matthaiou 2000–3), ll. 5–9: *ἀποδι|δ]όναι δὲ τ̣ὴ[ν μίσθωσιν τὴν μὲν ἡμίσ|ε]αν ἐν τῶι Μετ[αγειτνιῶνι ταῖς ἀρχ$^{\nu}$|αι]ρεσί<α>ις, τὴν δ' [ἡμίσεαν τοῦ . . .^{6}. . . |..]ιῶνος μηνός.*

[91] But the guarantors had to be 'solvent/trustworthy', according to the important new reading *ἀξιοχρέους* by Alipheri 2009, instead of [*ὀμουμέν*]*ους*, as in the ed. pr. and in *I.Eleusis* 85; *SEG* XXVII 103 ll. 29–31: *ἐγγυητά{τα]}ς <τε> καταστησάτω ὁ μισθωσάμενος δύο ἄνδρας | ἀξιοχρέους, ἦ μὴν ἀποδώσειν τὴν μίσθωσιν πᾶσαν ἐν τῶ|ι χρό[νω]ι τῶι εἰρημένωι.*

[92] *IG* II^2 2496 ll. 20–2: *ἐνγυητὴς τοῦ ποιήσειν τὰ γεγρα|μμένα Ἐξηκίας Ἀφιδναῖος ἐν τῶι χρόνωι τῶι γεγρα|μμένωι.* The guarantor is the father of the lessee *Εὐκράτης*.

[93] *IG* II^2 2503 l. 11.

technically called *ἐνεχυρασία*.[94] But while some scholars would like to see here a third safeguard system operating along side those of surety and security, the fact is that *ἐνεχυρασία* was part and parcel of the security procedure. Indeed, the way the relevant clause is articulated in the Aixonian document reveals that it was taken for granted that the lessees Autokles and Auteas had considerable personal property to prop up their transaction. Close to *IG* II^2 2492 stands another document traditionally assigned to Aixone: the elliptical inscription *IG* II^2 1196. This text brings out an elaborate situation in which defaulters on rentals of grazing fields could refer their case to the deme assembly in its capacity as a court, the verdict of which was final. What has not received proper attention is that the lessees, pending arbitration, had to provide *ἐνέχυρα* (pledges) in order to affirm that they would respect the final decision. Here again *ἐνεχυρασία* was a possible outcome.[95]

A unique apparatus was employed by the deme of Prasiai, for there the defaulting lessee was expected to pay a 1000-drachma fine, which was considerably more than his due rental.[96] The main document deserves further consideration. The name of the lessee Polys(s)thenes (*sic*) appears to have been erased from the stone already in antiquity, presumably because of some breach of contract.[97] If the Prasieis had wanted to annul the contract entirely, they could theoretically have destroyed the stone instead of just effacing the name of the lessee. The

[94] *IG* II^2 2492 ll. 7–9: *ἐὰν δὲ μὴ ἀποδιδῶσιν εἶναι ἐνεχυρασίαν Αἰ|ξωνεῦσιν καὶ ἐκ τῶν ὡραίων τῶν ἐκ τοῦ χωρίου καὶ | ἐκ τῶν ἄλλων ἁπάντων τοῦ μὴ ἀποδιδόντος* (cf. Finley 1952*a*, 222–3 n. 6; Harrison 1971, 244–7; Whitehead 1986, 125).

[95] *IG* II^2 1196a ll. 13–15: *ὅσοι̱ | δὲ ἂν αὐτῶν μήτε ἐμμένωσιν μ]ήτε ἀποδιδῶσιν ἃ ὀ[φ]είλουσιν μήτε τὰ ἐνέχ||[υρα τὰ πρότερα ἀπολαβόντες ἄλλα ἐν]ẹ́χυρα ἀνέπ[α]φα ἀνθυποτιθῶσιν* etc. (new readings by Papazarkadas 2007*a*, 160–6, who also deals with the provenance, chronology, and legalistic aspects of this inscription).

[96] *SEG* XXI 644 ll. 7–11: *κ|[αὶ ἀπο]τεισάτω Πολ[υσ]σθ̣ένη[ς] ἢ ο|ἱ ἔκγονοι αὐτοῦ οἱ μὴ ποιοῦντε|ς τὰ γεγραμμένα : X : δραχμὰς τῶι δ|ήμωι τῶι Πρασιέων*. The amount of the rental is not preserved on the stone. However, the stoichedon style of the inscription in conjunction with the fairly secure restoration of ll. 2–3, [*ἀποδιδόναι μὲν τὴν*] *μίσθωσ|[ιν . .*³ *. ἑκάστου τοῦ ἐν]ιαυτοῦ*, imply a three-digit figure for the rent. Since the fine could hardly have been less than the rental, the highest, epigraphically acceptable, rent worth less than 1000 drachmas would have been 𐅅HH, i.e. 700 drachmas. Self-evidently, numerous supplements are feasible below this figure, e.g. 𐅅HΔ (610 drachmas), *HHH* (300 drachmas), and so on.

[97] Vanderpool, McCredie, and Steinberg 1962, 56. A new Prasian lease (*SEG* LI 153) displays the same feature, i.e. erasure of the lessee's name without reinscription of a new one (Matthaiou 2000–3, 75). The significance of the occurrence of this pattern in two different, but contemporary, documents issued by the same deme eludes us.

implication is that they probably intended to reactivate the contract with a new lessee, but quite possibly they did not. The rest is simply irretrievable.[98]

In Piraeus, on the other hand, one encounters a completely different system. For rentals up to 10 drachmas the lessees had to nominate a guarantor, but for higher amounts they were expected to provide security.[99] The relevant clause has been interpreted as imposing restrictions on metics in renting landed property, since they did not own real property.[100] It is true that the 10 drachmas sum sounds 'ridiculously low' and 'infinitesimal', to borrow two phrases from Moses Finley.[101] Nevertheless, it should not be seen as an artificial quota, but rather as a dividing line between two distinct types of property. Whitehead rightly argued that the figure in question is a proof that such low-valued properties did exist in demes.[102] This can be nicely seen in the *Rationes Centesimarum* where a series of plots of land were sold at the price of 50 drachmas, which on the basis of the (in)famous 8 percent rate correspond to properties fetching an annual rent of much less than 10 drachmas.[103] The explanation for such puny prices lies within the leasing document of Piraeus itself with its clear distinction between pasturage (*ἐννόμια*) and arable land.[104]

[98] In the badly preserved *IG* II^{2} 598 one can see the opposite pattern. The numeral preceding the word *δραχμῶ|[ν]* (ll. 3–4) was erased (so Kirchner in the *apparatus criticus* of *IG*), perhaps in anticipation of some readjustment of the initial rental, which, again for reasons that lie beyond our comprehension, never materialized.

[99] *IG* II^{2} 2498 ll. 3–6: *τοὺς μισθω|[σ]αμένους ὑπὲρ : Δ : δραχμὰς καθιστάναι ἀποτίμημα τῆς μ|[ι]σθώσεως ἀξιόχρεων, τοὺς δὲ ἐντὸς Δ δραχμ<ῶ>ν ἐγγυ<η>τὴ|[ν] ἀποδιδόμενον τὰ ἑαυτοῦ τῆς μισθώσεως*, for which see Finley 1952*a*, 283–4 n. 38 and Whitehead 1986, 157. Note that, at deme level, the mixed suretyship/pledge system is also found in the decree of the Plotheians in relation to loans offered to individuals (*IG* I^{3} 258 ll. 20–2: *ὃς ἂν [πεί|θ]ηι τὸς δανείζοντας ἄρχοντα[ς τιμ]|ήματι ἢ ἐγγυητῆι*), a parallel, though a distant one; cf. Harris 1993, 78, 86.

[100] So Isager 1983, 32–3 (the translation of which I owe to Dr Wallensten) followed by Whitehead 1986, 157; Osborne 1988, 289 n. 28; Isager and Skydsgaard 1992, 189–90.

[101] Finley 1952*a*, 96, 284.

[102] Whitehead 1986, 155 with n. 39, though his view that the figure 134 drachmas and 2 ½ obols presupposes a rent worth 2 ½ obols seems to me flawed; rather the latter represents a fraction of a bigger rent.

[103] 4 drachmas, in fact; for the prices of the properties of the *Rationes Centesimarum* see Lambert 1997*a*, 229 n. 56; for the 8% rate see Andreyev 1974, 16; Lambert 1997*a*, 257–63 (cf. also the rental of 1.5 drachmas in *I.Eleusis* 177 (*IG* II^{2} 1672), l. 428: *ἐνοίκιον* ⊢, to the best of my knowledge the lowest attested figure in Attic sources!).

[104] *IG* II^{2} 2498 ll. 12–22, with Hodkinson 1988, 48–9. Note the evident suitability of littoral areas for pastoralism due to the existence of salt, a highly nutritional

Lessees of the former, which include the properties called *Θεσμοφόριον* and *τὸ τοῦ Σχοινοῦντος*, were only instructed to pay their rentals in due time, whereas lessees of tillable land were offered further instructions about the work they were allowed to undertake within the *temene*. It is self-evident that pasturage was considered a cheaper option than the much more demanding agricultural lands, and it is this category that may correspond to properties evaluated for less than 10 drachmas. Far from totally debarring metics from renting land, the clause in lines 7–9 of *IG* II^2 2498 drew a distinction between pasturage which could be leased out to metics and agricultural land to which only citizens could have had access by means of placing personal security. Seen in a historical perspective *IG* II^2 2498 may be subject to another as yet unsuspected approach. By 322 Athens had lost her ancestral constitution as a result of her defeat by the Macedonians, and a considerable number of citizens had been disenfranchised.[105] Traditionally the Piraeus had been a hub of the lower strata of Athenian society and one can imagine how in 321/0, year of the decree under consideration,[106] a huge crowd of impoverished ex-citizens would have striven to earn their living in the area of the port, no longer enjoying the benefits of the abolished democracy. Given this, the stipulated 10 drachmas ceiling would have enabled the landless amongst them to bid for pasturage and thus enhance their petty means.[107]

Sometimes, regulations were laid down regarding the settlement between the deme and the tenants in case war action resulted in the destruction of the leased parcel and/or the crops. Here again it is not quite clear whether such provisions were meant to protect the lessor or the renter, or to distribute fairly the burden of the recovery

ingredient for sheep and goats. This feature is emphasized by some of the toponyms of the leased areas such as *Σχοινοῦς*, 'rushy area', *Παραλία*, 'coast', and *Ἁλμυρίς*, 'salt land' (cf. Conwell 1993, 54–6), though, admittedly, only the first is classified as pasturage. For another occurrence of *ἐννόμια* in a deme context see *IG* II^2 1196, with Papazarkadas 2007*a*, 165 (for a different interpretation, see Chandezon 2003, 22–4).

[105] Only 9000 citizens out of an initial 21,000 met the 2000 drachmas property qualification and, accordingly, kept their civic rights (Ferguson 1911, 22–3; Habicht 1997, 40; Baynham 2003).

[106] Or 318/7, since, as Cook 1987, 31 aptly observes, Archippos (*IG* II^2 2498 l. 1: *ἐπὶ Ἀρχίππου ἄρχοντος*) was the name of the eponymous archons of both 321/0 and 318/7. Obviously, due to the proximity of the two dates, my argument is not affected.

[107] Cf. Andreyev 1974, 44.

between the two parties.[108] In the four best preserved cases, the lessee and the leasing deme were expected to share the remaining crops.[109] But since not all contracts contained similar provisions, it remains a mystery why some demes were more concerned with potential ravaging by enemies than others. This might be accounted for by the geographical factor. Prasiai and Aixone were both coastal demes and, therefore, by definition more susceptible to enemy invasions, and Teithras, though an inland deme, was fairly close to the coast.[110] Ironically, one of the stones bearing a Prasian pact was found in the excavation of a Ptolemaic camp from the Chremonidean War; that is, it indirectly fell victim to the very danger that the leasing agent tried to pre-empt![111] This raises the question of the precise source of worries regarding enemy activities. There is a possibility that the invasions of the fifth century, especially the permanent presence of raiding Peloponnesian troops during the Dekeleian War, had remained vivid in popular collective memory.[112] Alternatively, the increasing power of Macedonia after the mid-fourth century might have brought about an intensified state of alert. The latter hypothesis may receive some corroboration from the fact that the Aixonian lease dates to 346/5 and the Teithrasian one can be placed, on orthographical grounds, at approximately that time, but the issue remains unresolved.[113]

[108] Whitehead 1986, 156 seems to believe that such provisions constituted safeguards for the tenant; he may be right if Behrend 1970, 121 with n. 103 correctly contends that the norm in the Greek world was that war could not be accepted as an alibi for not fulfilling one's rent obligations.

[109] Aixone: *IG* II^2 2492 ll. 12–14: *ἐὰν δὲ πολέμιοι ἐξείργωσι ἢ διαφθείρ|ωσί τι, εἶναι Αἰξωνεῦσιν τῶν γενομένων ἐν τῶι χ|ωρίωι τὰ ἡμίσεα*; Teithras: *SEG* XXIV 151 (Papazarkadas 2007*a*, D1a), ll. 17–19: *ἐὰν δὲ πολέ[μ|ιοι φθείρω] σι τῶι ἔχοντι τὸ χωρίον τὰ ἡμίσε[α ἀπ]οδι[δό]ν[α]ι Τειθρασίοις ὧν ἂν λάβει ἐκ τô χω|ρίο]*; Prasiai: *SEG* XXI 644 ll. 11–16: *ἐὰν δὲ πολέμ|ιοι ἐμβάλωσι στρατόπεδον εἰς|τὴν Ἀττικὴν κ[αὶ δι]αφθείρωσι τ|ὸν καρπόν, τὰ ἡμ[ίσε]α τῶν λειφθέ|ντων εἶναι ⟦Πολ[υσσθέν]ους⟧, τὰ δὲ | ἡμίσεα Πρασιέων*; *SEG* LI 153 (Matthaiou 2000–3), ll. 9–12: *ἐὰ[ν δέ τι πολέμιοι*^{vv}*|βλ]άψωσιν, ἀποδιδό[ναι . . . . .*^{10}*. . . . . Π|ρα]σιεῦσιν ὁποτέρ[αν τῶν ἡμισεῶν ἢ τὰ ἡ]μίσεα τῶν ἐν τῶι χ[ωρίωι]* (incidentally *ὁπότερ[ον τῶν ἡμισέων]* seems a better supplement). The relevant clause in *IG* II^2 1211, l. 5 (*καὶ ἐν πολέμ[ωι]*) is too fragmentary to be of any help; cf. Papazarkadas 2007*a*, 170–1.

[110] Location of Prasiai: Traill 1975, 42 and 1986, 129; Matthaiou 2000–3, 75–6. Location of Aixone: Traill 1975, 50 and 1986, 136. Location of Teithras: Traill 1975, 41; Steinhauer 2001*b*, 86.

[111] Habicht 1997, 144–5.

[112] Hanson 1998, 153–73.

[113] Cf. De Souza 1999, 30–42.

Also flexible was the demes' stance towards taxation of leased properties. Internal evidence reveals that two types of taxation were applicable to deme properties: (*a*) taxes imposed by the demes themselves, and (*b*) *eisphorai*, which were levied by the polis.[114] The first category merits further consideration, because its existence is counterfactual; that is, it can be inferred from clauses that proclaim the leasing demes' willingness to refrain from collecting such taxes.[115] This protectionist policy severely undermines Finley's dogma that deme property was, in effect, identical to private property, for few, if any, private lessors could have afforded to pay a tax imposed by a deme in the renters' stead. In actual terms, this means that demes had the flexibility to render their assets more desirable in the leasing market by providing tax exemptions.

The real question, nevertheless, and one that has not yet been posed, regards the precise nature of the taxes that demes were entitled to impose. One can automatically think of the *ἐγκτητικόν*, the tax exacted by demes from non-demesmen proprietors.[116] The problem is that this tax might not have been as universal as usually assumed.[117] I wish to bring to the fore an epigraphical document that, for reasons to be highlighted below, can be employed as a case-study. As it happens, *IG* II[2] 2496, a lease of the Kytherioi, is the only extant text of this kind where the rented property is located outside the territory of the issuing authority, and more precisely in the Piraeus. This is a fortunate coincidence, since Piraeus is the only deme which we firmly know to have levied the *ἐγκτητικόν*.[118] Even more happily, the tenant of the property—a workshop, a house, and a small dwelling—was an Acharnian, therefore an outsider both to Kytheros and to Piraeus. There are two clauses pertaining to taxation in this document: first it is promulgated that the leased property will be exempt from all taxes (l. 13, *ἀτελὲς ἁπάντων*), and second, and in contradiction to the

114 Behrend 1970, 119–20.

115 *IG* II[2] 2496 l. 13: *ἀτελὲς ἁπάντων*; *IG* II[2] 2497 ll. 4–5: *ἀτ|[ελὲς κ]αὶ ἀνεπιτίμητον εἰσφορ[ᾶς καὶ] τῶν ἄλλων ἁπάντων*; *IG* II[2] 2498 ll. 6–7: *ἐπὶ τοῖσδε μ|[ι]σθοῦσιν ἀνεπιτίμητα καὶ ἀτελῆ*; cf. *SEG* LI 153 l. 5, *ἀνε[πιτίμητον ἁπάντων]*. See also Gallo 2005*b*, 180–1.

116 Jones 1999, 64–5.

117 Whitehead 1986, 76 with n. 38; 150.

118 *IG* II[2] 1214 ll. 25–8: *τελεῖν δὲ αὐτὸμ τὰ αὐτὰ τέλη ἐν | τῶι δήμωι ἅπερ ἀγ καὶ Πειραιεῖς καὶ μὴ ἐ|γλέγειμ παρ' αὐτοῦ τὸν δήμαρχον τὸ ἐγκ|τητικόν* (cf. Whitehead 1986, 150; Garland 1987, 76; 195).

previous one, that if any *eisphora* or any other fee is to be levied by any means, the tenant Eukrates will have to pay on the basis of the assessed value of 7 mnas (ll. 25–8, ἐὰ|ν δέ [τι]ς εἰσφορὰ γίγνηται ἢ ἄλλο τι ἀπ[ότ]εισμα τρό|πωι ὁτ<ω>ιοῦν, εἰσφέρειν Εὐκράτην κατὰ τὸ τίμημα κα|θ' ἑπτὰ μνᾶς)![119] The absence of any explicit reference to the ἐγκτητικόν is striking here. The only tax envisaged is the (emergency) *eisphora*, quite a different kind of levy, followed by a vague mention of an ἀπότεισμα (payment). The latter is phrased in such a matter-of-fact way that it is almost impossible to accept that it pertains to a regular tax like the ἐγκτητικόν. Various interpretations are available here. There is a possibility that an ἐγκτητικὸν τέλος had not been introduced by the time of *IG* II^2 2496, i.e. the late Classical period, for our other piece of information concerning this tax, *IG* II^2 1214, dates to the first half of the third century. If it had been introduced, however, the Piraeans presumably could not extract it from the tenant, that is they did not have the authority to do so. In fact, an ἐγκτητικόν could only underlie the provision ἀτελὲς ἁπάντων. The indirect inference would be that the taxing authority was none other than the deme of Kytheros.

With regard to the *eisphora*, Whitehead, following Finley, observed that in the five epigraphically attested cases pertaining to demes, the burden of paying this state tax is borne three times by the deme and twice by the tenants.[120] The length of the lease seems to be irrelevant to this point, a reminder that perpetual leases did not equate to transfer of ownership.[121] Nor is the chronological parameter pertinent.[122] The difference between an *eisphora* and a tax imposed by a deme is easy to detect. The former was levied by the polis and a deme

[119] For this clause see Thomsen 1964, 48; 53.

[120] Whitehead 1986, 155–6 following Finley 1952*a*, 281 n. 26. *Eisphora*: paid by the deme: *IG* II^2 2492, ll. 24–6; *IG* II^2 2497, ll. 5–6; *IG* II^2 2498, ll. 7–9; paid by the lessee: *IG* II^2 2496, ll. 25–8; *SEG* XXIV 151(=Papazarkadas 2007*a*, D1a), ll. 30–2.

[121] Inexplicably Finley 1952*a*, 281 n. 26, Thomsen 1964, 63–4 n. 124, and Brun 1983, 5 n. 6 have all argued for the opposite. True, the two cases where the tenant pays the *eisphora* are perpetual leases, but so is *IG* II^2 2497, where the lessee is released of this burden. Thus, even if the length of the tenancy was understandably taken into consideration with regard to the *eisphora*, the connection was not regulated by a postulate.

[122] Note that in *IG* II^2 2492, collection of *eisphora* is mentioned as a potentiality, though we know that a law passed in 347/6 rendered *eisphora* a regular tax for as long as until 323/3 (Thomsen 1964, 237–42; Brun 1983, 49–54). Similarly the relevant clause in *IG* II^2 2498 could be nothing else but an automatic response of the issuing body, for in 321/0 (or 318/7), date of the decree, there would have been no realistic

had no right to refuse payment of it.[123] However, demes could take advantage of their constitutional involvement in the collection of the *eisphora* and adjust its handling as they wished.[124] By doing so they could render their properties more sought after in the leasing market, just as in the case of the treatment of their own taxes. Here again, demes were clearly better positioned than private individuals.

iii. Other forms of deme property administration

Making profit out of landed properties was usually the end of an intricate process, a preliminary stage of which was maintenance. Though scarce, there is evidence about the pains taken by demes to prevent damage to their realty. Louis Robert has illuminated one such document, the only extant decree from Kephisia, which dealt with the protection of the deme's palaestra from trespassing herds of animals,[125] a recurring theme in the ancient Greek world, but one surprisingly underrepresented in Athens.[126] Protection of vegetation from greedy individuals evidently underlay the minute provisions

expectation for defeated Athens to impose a military tax, such as the *eisphora* (Thomsen 1964, 238 with n. 245).

[123] Cf. Isager 1992, 121–2; Davies 1981, 133–50, esp. 137–8, for sanctuaries liable to proeisphora.

[124] Deme jurisdiction in collecting *eisphora*: Davies 1981, 143–50; Whitehead 1986, 132–3. Christ 2007, 59–60 simply calls this interpretation plausible.

[125] *SEG* XXXII 147 (Vanderpool 1969), with *BE* (1971) no. 286, ll. 7–8: *[καὶ τ]ὴν κρήνην ἔφραξεν ὥ[στε τὰ πρόβατα μὴ εἰσι]έναι εἰς αὐτὴν καὶ τἄλλα φι[λότιμός ἐστι πρὸς] | τὸν δῆμον τῶν Κ[ηφισιέων]*. Morison 2000 (*SEG* L 159) proposes to read *καὶ τἄλλα φι[λοτίμως ἔπραξε]*. Incidentally, the palaestra falls within the category of sacred property, since all gymnasia were attached to sanctuaries (usually, but not always, to shrines of Hermes and Herakles; cf. Delorme 1960, 444–57); see also Morrison 2000, 97–8.

[126] Burford 1993, 19–21. The only other adducible Attic examples are the sacred regulation *IG* II^2 310 (see my brief treatment in Papazarkadas 2004–9 [2010], 102–3, no. 6), and the Eleusinian lease of tenements (*συνοικίαι*) *I.Eleusis* 176 (*IG* II^2 2500), l. 12: (*[μήτε κτῆνο]ς μηθὲν ἀνατ[ρέφειν]*). For examples outside Attica, see RO 59 ll. 35–7: *πρόβατα δ[ὲ | μὴ] ἐξέστω ἐμβιβάσκεν εἰς τὸ τέμενος μηδενί· εἰὰν δ' [ἐμ|βιβά]σκηι, ἔστω [τὰ] πρόβατα ἱερὰ τοῦ Διὸς τοῦ Τεμενίτου* (Amorgos); *SEG* XLVIII 1037B ll. 2–6: *ἢ ὗς ἢ βοσκήματα ἐντὸς τῶν [περιρ]|ραντηρίων ὅσα μὴ εἵνεκεν θυσίας εἰσ|ῆκται, ἐνόχους μὲν εἶναι καὶ ταῖς ἀραῖς, | ζημιοῦσθαι δὲ αὐτοὺς καὶ ὑπὸ τῶν ἱερο|ποιῶν* etc. (Delos); detailed discussion of this and other evidence in Chandezon 2003, 293–306.

against removing flora from the precinct of Apollo Erithaseos.[127] Since the executor of the predefined penalties was a demarch, the cult in question was one administered by a deme, the identity of which remains an unsolvable mystery. We are on firmer ground with regard to similar provisions encountered in *IG* II^2 1177. There, the issuing authority was the deme of Piraeus represented by its archon, who once more was to bring charges against law-breaking pilgrims. Specific instructions were given that the gathering of wood in the shrines—presumably those of Piraeus—had to be regulated by the relevant ancient laws.[128] This stipulation should not be seen as a wholesale ban against such timber gathering, for a law cited by [Demosthenes] concerning the exploitation of olive-trees demonstrates that cutting wood could, to some extent, be conceded for cultic purposes.[129] The reasons behind such a protectionist policy can only be guessed. Apart from occasionally using wood for their cultic needs, deme authorities might have opted for the exploitation of timber for their demes' financial benefit. Alternatively, they were simply responding to the nuisance caused by timber collectors operating in sacred precincts.

Of course the major indicators of demes' preoccupation with protecting their properties are the elaborate agricultural clauses of the leasing contracts. These provisions were passed not only with the aim of intensifying agricultural production, but also with an eye on the preservation of natural resources. Demes such as Aixone, Piraeus, Rhamnous tried, to varying degrees and by different means, to combine their financial interests with the demands of the properties they controlled and their technical knowledge. Fallowing, planting, digging of trenches and *similia* can all be found in the relevant documents and they reveal a complex understanding of the difficulties inherent in ancient agriculture.[130] Here is the place to remember the case of the Aixonian land call *Φελλείς*. Linguistic considerations and

[127] *IG* II^2 1362 ll. 5-7: *μὴ κόπτειν τὸ ἱερὸν τοῦ Ἀπόλλωνος μηδὲ [φ]|έρει<ν> ξύλα μηδὲ κοῦρον μηδ[ὲ] φρύγανα μηδὲ | φυλλό[β]ολα ἐκ τοῦ ἱεροῦ* (one should not fell trees in the shrine of Apollo, nor should one carry timber or loppings or dry sticks or fallen leaves out of the shrine), with Dillon 1997, 115–16.

[128] *IG* II^2 1177 ll. 17–21: *περὶ δ|ὲ τῆς ὑλασίας τ[ῶ]ν ἱερῶν εἰάν τις | ὑλάζηται, κυρίους εἶναι τοὺς ἀρ|χαίους νόμους οἳ κεῖ<ν>ται περὶ το|ύτων* (concerning the gathering of wood in the shrines, should someone fetch wood, let the ancient laws which have been set for these matters be valid), with Dillon 1997, 116.

[129] [Dem.] 43.71.

[130] For agricultural clauses in inscriptions—an enormous topic—see Osborne 1987, 39–46; Isager and Skydsgaard 1992; Burford 1993, 110–24; Brunet, Rougemont, and Rousset 1998; Jones 2004, 27–34.

archaeological contextualization have now made it clear that the diverse agricultural strategies employed in the well-known document of the mid-fourth century can only be seen as the final stage of a long procedure of land improvement. The rocky ground of the Archaic period had become by 346/5 a most productive landholding encompassing the Mediterranean triad.[131]

The Piraean document *IG* II^2 1177 briefly examined above is important in highlighting another aspect of deme activity concerning realty, that of delimitation. The concluding paragraph of the decree orders the demarch to set up the stele bearing the community's resolution in cooperation with a board of *horistai*.[132] No doubt the erection of the decree by the *horistai* comes as a consequence of some earlier function of theirs in the now missing opening lines of the decree, in all likelihood the delimitation of the Piraean shrines.[133] There is a good possibility that one of the demarcated properties was the sacred precinct Thesmophorion (*Θεσμοφόριον*) of the leasing document *IG* II^2 2498, since in *IG* II^2 1177 the demarch, along with the priestess in charge, had to supervise the conduct of pilgrims during the local Thesmophoria, and the relevant resolution had to be recorded on a stele 'near the ascent leading to the Thesmophorion'.[134] It is, in any case, interesting to notice the total overlap between the operation of the *horistai* in *IG* II^2 1177 and that of the Aixonian treasurers in *IG* II^2 2492, who were assigned the task of setting up two copies of the leasing contract as well as of placing boundary stones around the landholding itself.[135] But if he duties are identical, the rationale is different; in contrast to the Piraean *horistai*, the delimiting competence of the Aixonian treasurers emanated from

[131] Moreno 2007, 51–3, 64–5; Krasilnikoff 2008, 42–5.

[132] *IG* II^2 1177 ll. 21–3: *ἀναγρ[ά]ψαι δὲ τόδε τὸ ψήφισ|μα τοὺς ὁριστὰς μετὰ τοῦ δημάρ|χου καὶ στῆσαι* etc.

[133] Whitehead 1986, 141 pleads ignorance about the reasons behind the appearance of *horistai* in *IG* II^2 1177; but another remark he makes, namely that in other Piraean inscriptions the *horistai* are *not* attested as inscribing and erecting stelae (Whitehead 1986, 141 n. 120), should suffice to show that in our case this task of the *horistai* is the by-product of some other duty of theirs.

[134] *IG* II^2 1177 ll. 1–3 (*[ἐπιμελεῖσθαι - - - τὸν δήμαρχον | μετὰ] τῆς ἱερείας τὸν [ἀεὶ δημαρχ|οῦ]ντα τοῦ Θεσμοφορίου*), 8 (*ὅταν ἡ ἑορτὴ τῶν Θεσμοφορίων*), 23–4 (*καὶ στῆσαι πρὸς τῆι ἀναβάσει | τοῦ Θεσμοφορίου*); see Parker 2005, 75.

[135] *IG* II^2 2492 ll. 20–4: *τὴν δὲ μίσθωσιν ἀναγράψαντας ε|ἰστήλας λιθίνας τοὺς ταμίας τοὺς ἐπὶ Δημοσθένου|ς δημάρχου {s} στῆσαι τὴν μὲν ἐν τῶι ἱερῶι τῆς Ἥβης ἔν|δον, τὴν δ' ἐν τεῖ λέσχει, καὶ ὅρους ἐπὶ τῶι χωρίωι μὴ ἔ|λαττον ἢ τρίποδας ἑκατέρωθεν δύο.*

their fiscal tasks. These two boards find their counterpart in a well-known decree from Sounion, where an elected commission of three men had to coordinate efforts with Leukios, the donor of a landholding to be turned into an agora, for the spatial organization of that agora on precise guidelines put forward by the deme assembly.[136] Similarly, two identical *horoi* marking the sacred courtyard of Hero Archegetes in Rhamnous were probably posted by the deme authorities.[137] These examples constitute our only uncontested epigraphical evidence for the demarcation of properties on behalf of demes, unless we also count the symbolic representation of delimitation as alluded to in a sacrifice offered by the Erchians to Zeus Horios.[138] In general, the picture we get is more that of automatic response to short-lived exigencies, rather than that of an orchestrated apparatus dealing with marking off properties. This picture, it has to be said, matches the amateurism of the polis in that respect.[139]

Exploitation of real property at the deme level was not exclusively confined to leasing. Other financial transactions can be shown to have been indirectly linked to realty. Loans out on interest were a rather frequent financial activity of demes,[140] but few scholars have posed

[136] *IG* II^2 1180 ll. 6–12: *ἐλ|έσθαι αὐτίκα μάλα τρε|ῖς ἄνδρας, οἵτινες ὁριο|ῦσιν τὴν ἀγορὰν μετὰ | Λευκίο μὴ ἐλάττω τῆ|ι μὲν δυοῖν πλέθροιν, | τῆι δὲ πλέθρου*. The absence of the term *horistai* is insignificant, since the verb *ὁριοῦσιν* renders unambiguous what is at stake here.

[137] *I.Rhamnous* 79–80: *[ὅ]ρος αὐλῆς | ἱερᾶς Ἥρωος | Ἀρχηγέτου*, with the commentary of Petrakos ad loc., who justifiably points out spatial restrictions.

[138] *SEG* XXI 541 IV ll. 29–31: *Διὶ Ὁρίωι, Ἐ|ρχιᾶσι, χοῖ|ρος*, with Jameson's ingenious suggestion that the divine recipient oversaw disputes 'between demes over winter grazing in the lowlands' (Jameson 1988, 117 n. 24). Note also the tenuous evidence of *Agora* XIX L15 l. 2: *καὶ ὅρους ὅσο[υς]*, which might be a deme-lease, according to Walbank ad loc.

[139] That is, the polis lacked a centralized mechanism in delimiting properties. This task is undertaken by the *basileus* in the case of the Pelargikon (*IG* I^3 78 ll. 55–6: *τὸν δὲ βασιλέα* h*ορίσαι τὰ* h*ιερὰ τὰ ἐν τ[ô]|ι Πελαργικôι*), by an unknown number of *horistai* in the case of the Neleion (*IG* I^3 84 l. 7: *καὶ τὸς ὁριστὰς ἐπιπέμφσαι ὁρίσαι τὰ* h*ιερὰ ταῦτα*), by a board of 50 *horistai* in the case of the Oropian territory (Hyp. Eux. 16: *ὡς πρότερον τοὺς ὁριστὰς τοὺς πεντήκοντα ἐξελόντας αὐτὸ τῷ θεῷ καὶ ἀφορίσαντας*, with Whitehead 2000, 210). Morison 2003, 111–12 has seen individuals setting boundaries for a bath in *IG* I^3 420, l. 12 (*[τὸ] βαλαν[ε̂ον* h*ορ]ίοσι*), but his restoration is either a solecism (present tense would have been h*ορίζοσι*) or presupposes a future (i.e. [h*ορ]ιôσι*, but Morison translates it as a present), which is out of place in a text of this type.

[140] Though not that frequent according to Millett 1991, 172–8 attacking Andreyev 1974, 22. Millett's tendency to donwplay the importance of lending in the framework of demes, as well as other corporate groups, on the basis of some shaky statistics seems to me somewhat frivolous. In particular his assertion that 4 deme-texts recording credit

the question where the initial capital that sustained lending might have come from. The only firm piece of evidence on this point is the clause concerning the sale of timber in the lease from Aixone. The price fetched was stipulated to be converted into a loan offered at a rate of 1 percent per month.[141] This fourth-century practice can only offer a hint, but evidence that goes back to the fifth century implies that some demes already had a well-established fund to draw upon. It is certainly not without interest that all such lending activities were performed through sacred establishments controlled by demes. Some modern historians have even suggested, not totally unreasonably, that the Attic demes can be seen as small laboratories, where economic experiments were first conducted before being applied elsewhere.[142] In any case, there is good reason to assume that part of the initial capital available for loans emanated from leased landed properties.

If the notion of lands standing at the inception of lending activities is necessarily slightly conjectural, their presence at the other end of such transactions can be established on firmer ground. We should start with a surprising, and therefore somewhat controversial, piece of evidence, the Plotheian decree *IG* I^3 258. Amongst the intricate fiscal procedures attested in this document, none has been more enigmatic than that of ll. 22–5. The Greek is difficult, perhaps even ungrammatical in a fashion all too familiar from other deme ordinances: *ἀπὸ δὲ τô τόκο [τε κ]|αὶ τῶμ μισθώσεων ἀντὶ ὅτο ἂν τ[ῶν κε]|φαλαίων ὠνήματα ἧι μί[σ]θωσιν φ[έρο]|ṿτα, θύειν τὰ ἱερά*. In other words, the Plotheians were to make their sacrifices 'from the interest and the rents, in place of whatever of the totals there may be purchases bearing rent', according to Davies's literal translation,[143] which must

in comparison to the total number of the Attic demes (139) is paltry (Millett 1991, 173) does not account for the fact that our total sample of deme documents is itself tiny; Whitehead 1986, appendix 3 contains 140 deme documents, that is almost 1 document per deme, with some demes having no representation at all (Jones 1999, 100–1 n. 54 provides addenda). In the totality of deme documents recording deliberate financial activity, the four documents cited by Millett represent a much higher proportion.

[141] *IG* II^2 2492 ll. 36–8: *τοῦ δὲ | εὑρόντος ἀργυρίου λογισάμενοι ἐπὶ δραχμεῖ τὸν τό|κον τὸν ἥμυσυν ἀφελεῖν ἀπὸ τῆς μισθώσεως* (reckoning the interest on the money which is raised at one drachma, they are to reduce the rent by half the amount; translation by Burford 1993); cf. Millett 1991, 105, 176, 233, who repeatedly, and erroneously, refers to the inscription as a document of Halai Aixonides.

[142] Chankowski 2005, esp. 77–8.

[143] Davies 2001, 124; similar is the force of the German translation by Behrend 1970, 'aus den Pachtzinsen für das, etwas mit den Kapitalien als pachtzinsbringendes

render the gist of the extract, even though it does not automatically facilitate interpretation. One possibility is that the Plotheians simply used part of their capital reserve to buy landed property. Alternatively, they decided to use interest from loans in order to purchase landed property which they could subsequenly let out to generate cultic income in the form of rentals. Both scenarios are intriguing, but the latter in particular would be an extremely complicated version of what Davies has already called a non-straightforward matter, 'procuring resources from which a reliable income of indefinite duration could be derived, in the forms of produce or rent or interest'. It would then be an unparalleled case, although we should not too readily dismiss the likelihood of small communities developing fairly intricate financial strategies.

Regardless of this minor point, the same decree unproblematically attests to a theme that most historians are familiar with: the connection between land and credit through the property guarantee required from borrowers of deme loans (and from lessees of deme lands, as we shall see immediately).[144] With regard to the former, there exists a small series of *hypothecation* horoi recording properties pledged to demes.[145] The same principle is explicitly stated not only in the Plotheian financial document, but also in a decree from Hagnous where the priests of the local deities are given instructions to lend money on security in the form of plots of land, houses, or tenements.[146] The transfer of privately held property to a deme could theoretically occur on default of a debtor, either borrower or lessee, but even that situation is far from clear.[147] Only one such case seems to emerge in the literary sources, the prosecution brought by a young

Object gekauft wird', which is quoted verbatim by the editors of *IG*, no doubt because of the difficulty of the excerpt in question.

[144] Plotheia: *IG* I^3 258 ll. 20–3: *δανείζοντας ὅ[στι]|ς ἂν πλεῖστον τόκον διδῶι, ὃς ἂν [πεί|θ]ηι τὸς δανείζοντας ἄρχοντα[ς τιμ]|ήματι ἢ ἐγγυητῆι* ('...lending money to whoever may give the greatest interest, he who may persuade the lending officials by valuation or guarantor'; trans. Davies 2001, 124); cf. Whitehead 1986, 158–9, 166).

[145] *IG* II^2 2670 (Phlya); *IG* II^2 2761b (Halai Aixonides); *Agora* XIX H93 (Kerameis); *Agora* XIX H99 (Phegous), all cited by Whitehead 1986, 159.

[146] RO 63 ll. 27–30: *ἐὰν <δ>έ τ[ινι δέ]|ει ἀργύριον, δανείζειν τοὺς ἱερέα[ς] ἀξιοχρείωι ἐπ[ὶ χωρίω]|ι ἢ οἰκίαι ἢ | συνοικίαι καὶ ὅρον ἐ<φ>[ισ]τάναι, οὗ ἂν εἶ [θεοῦ πα]|ραγράφοντα ὅ⟦υ⟧του ἂν εἶ τὸ ἀργύριο[ν]*, who following Traill 1986, 132, identify the deme as Hagnous, rather than Myrrhinous. For both texts see also Millett 1991, 173–5.

[147] Andreyev 1974, 44.

Sphettian against his fellow demesmen for a landholding offered as a pledge and subsequently seized.[148] In real life, demes might quite often have received cash instead of realty in case of debtors' default. This seems very probable in the case of *hypothecation* horoi recording multiple creditors. Thus, in the case of the dowry *apotimema* offered by the tribe Kekropis, the *genos* Lykomidai and the deme Phlya, the mortgaged landholding would be more probably sold to cover the pledge in case the debtor failed to repay the one talent amount.[149] At any rate, there are no known instances of property held jointly by more than one group with the exception of the idiosyncratic case of the Oropian tribal allotments.[150] All things considered, demes would certainly from time to time end up acquiring real property that previously belonged to individuals. This would suffice to explain the existence of deme property outside the strict limits of a deme's periphery, a notion that has annoyed scholars much too often. Nowadays it is acknowledged that this is part of the explanation behind the phenomenon of demes alienating property which lay within other demes' territory, as attested in the *Rationes Centesimarum*. The latter can be conveniently used as a bridge to pass onto the third main axis of deme realty administration; namely, property sales.

iv. Sales of lands controlled by demes

The recent authoritative re-edition of the *Rationes Centesimarum* gives evidence for a unique scheme of sales of lands that took place in the second half of the fourth century under the auspices of the central administration.[151] As far as demes are concerned, they feature

[148] Dion. Hal. *Isae.* 10: *ὁ δὲ Ἰσαῖος ἐν ἀμφισβητήσει χωρίου τοῦ ὑπὸ τῶν δημοτῶν κατεσχημένου, οἷς τὸ χωρίον ὑπέκειτο* etc.; Harp. s.v. *Σφηττός· Ἰσαῖος ἐν τῷ Πρὸς δημότας περὶ χωρίου* etc. (cf. Whitehead 1986, 130; Millett 1991, 172–3; Lambert 1997*a*, 187).

[149] *IG* II^2 2670: *ὅρος χωρίο προικὸς | Ἱπποκλείαι Δημοχά||[ρ]ος Λευκονοιῶς Τ· | [ὅσ]ωι πλείονος ἄξι||[ον], Κεκροπίδαις ||[ὑπό]κειται καὶ Λυκ||[ομί]δαις καὶ Φλυεῦ||[σι].*

[150] Hyp. *Eux.* 16, with the good note by Whitehead 2000, 206–7, who emphasizes the singular form *ἔλαχεν* as indicative of joint ownership. The same peculiar land pattern almost certainly generated the double tribal decree *Agora* XVI 84, for which see now Papazarkadas 2009*b*.

[151] *Rationes Centesimarum* (alternatively known as the *hekatoste*-inscriptions): Lambert 1997*a*.

as sellers, arranged in the official tribal order, in the first two opisthographic stelae. Sales on behalf of demes are conducted in a way identical to that of leases, either through the agency of demarchs or through boards of officials reminiscent of the leasing μερῖται.[152] However, the most surprising trait of the *Rationes Centesimarum* is the operation of *komai* as selling groups amongst the demes.[153] If they were indeed hereditary groups with local features, *komai* presumably kept operating along the lines of demes in a way that has left only vestigial traces.[154] Their presence in the *Rationes Centesimarum* reveals an administrative function with regard to realty that severely undermines our comprehension of demes.[155] The problem is that from the one example of an association of *komai* we know more about, the *Tetrakomoi*, it cannot be shown that *komai* were merely subdivisions of demes or even that they corresponded precisely to their homonymous demes.[156] Several *komai* of the Classical era seem to have turned into demes in the Roman period, some of them maybe as early as Hellenistic times.[157] It is only natural to infer from this that at least these specific *komai* were recognizable local units which grew in importance over time and were finally promoted into the status of semi-constitutional demes. Even the very presence of *komai* in the first two stelae of the *Rationes Centesimarum* would seem to confirm their territorial dimensions, although the argument is somewhat circular.

In all the best-attested cases of *komai* in the *Rationes Centesimarum* the selling agent is a κώμαρχος (or κώμης ἄρχων), a magistracy neatly fitting that of δήμαρχος.[158] If the selling agents in F8B, 49 are rightly restored as [ἐπιμελη]ταί, we may have an instance of a

[152] Multiple selling agents: F2, ll. 27–33.

[153] Andreyev 1974, 39.

[154] For Attic *komai* the most up-to-date discussion is Lambert 1997*a*, 220–1; cf. Hansen 1995*a*, 69 n. 98.

[155] In that respect, *komai* function here as 'municipalities'; thus Hansen 1995*a*, 71–3 (cf. Whitehead 1986, 27 n. 98; Millett 1991, 147). Humphreys 2008, 16 thinks of hamlets.

[156] Tetrakomoi: Parker 1996, 328–9; Lambert 1997*a*, 190–2.

[157] For instance Petalidai and Hyporeia, which both feature in the catalogue of demes of *c*.200 *IG* II^2 2362 (=*SEG* XXXVI 230), ll. 59, 61 (see Traill 1975, 87–8, 90; 1986, 55; Lambert 1997*a*, 193–4; cf. Lewis 1973*a*, 192–3). Humphreys 2008, 16 n. 16 justifiably maintains that the distribution of *komai* might not have been even throughout Attica.

[158] Lambert 1997*a*, 250–1 with n. 137 (the relevant passages are: F7 B l. 3: [Ὑπωρείων κώμαρχο]ς Νίκανδρος; l. 20: [Πεταλι]δ̣ῶ̣ν κ̣ώμαρχος; F9 B l. 9: [. . . . $^{c.6–10}$ . . . . .]ν κώμης

kome being represented not by a *komarchos* or a *komes archon*, but by a board of *epimeletai*, an office which is attested at least once in conjunction with a *kome*.[159] The recipient of the income from the relevant sales might have been the *kome* per se, but might well have been the deme on whose behalf the *kome* acted. Since *komai* seem to have had an independent financial agenda, the former explanation should be preferred.[160] If so, such money would have been used for cultic activity or other recurrent expenditure such as the performance of the dramatic contests of the *Tetrakomoi*.

The other remarkable feature of the *hekatoste*-inscriptions is the surprisingly high percentage of properties designated as 'outlying estates' (*ἐσχατιαί*).[161] This term has been analysed to the point of exhaustion, so suffice it to say that it applies to marginal tracts of land, usually, but not necessarily, hilly, with a slight potential for agriculture and a greater one for grazing.[162] This is important, for we have reason to believe that demes were the public body primarily involved in pasturage. Indeed, the pastures of Piraeus and Aixone directly, and the *κοπρών* of the Kytherioi indirectly, point to the existence of livestock in deme-controlled lands.[163] Percentagewise, however, the vast majority of the alienated landholdings bore the generic designation *χωρίον* with the odd occurrence of other descriptive terms, such

ἄρχοντες κώμης; l. 18, [.....$^{c.7-11}$.....] *κώμης ἄρχων*). For the problem of the number of such magistrates per *kome* see Parker 1996, 329.

[159] *IG* II^2 2830 l. 1; the possibility is not considered by Lambert 1997*a*, 195. However, one could supplement [*μερῖ*]*ται*, in which case the selling group would have been a deme.

[160] See *IG* II^2 1213, where a financial transaction in the context of some cultic performance is at stake. Note, however, the presence of a deme in the same context (cf. Lambert 2000*b*, 78).

[161] 21 certain cases in a total of 80 properties = 26.2% (Lambert 1997*a*, 225–9).

[162] *Ἐσχατιαί*: Lewis 1973*a*, 210–12; Lambert 1997*a*, 225–9; Jameson 2002; Krasilnikoff 2008, 45–8.

[163] *IG* II^2 2498 ll. 12–13: <*τ*>|*ἆλλα ἐννόμια* (with Chandezon 2003, 19–21); Papazarkadas 2007*a*, D2a (*IG* II^2 1196), l. 7: *τοῦ ἐννο*[*μ*]*ίου τὴν τιμήν*; *IG* II^2 2496 l. 11: *τὸ οἰκημάτιον τὸ ἐπὶ τοῦ κοπρῶνος* (for such dung-heaps see Hodkinson 1988, 49–50, though Ault 1999, 550–9 has now argued that *koprones* need not refer strictly to animal dung, but should be seen as waste disposal pits). Note also the Aixonian *Φελλεῖς* (*IG* II^2 2492) and the Teithrasian *φελλεύς* (*SEG* XXIV 152, l. 2), both of which might imply grazing (Osborne 1985*a*, 20–1; Papazarkadas 2007*a*, 160; Krasilnikoff 2008). Finally, the one shrine of Pan, the god traditionally associated with pastoralism, whose status we know of was under the control of the deme Phyle: Men. *Dysc.* 3, with Parker 2005, 69–70.

as οἰκία (house) and κῆπος (orchard).[164] Certainly, there is a very characteristic dearth of property terms in the *Rationes Centesimarum* in comparison to the other important set of land transactions, the leases of sacred properties controlled by the polis of Athens.[165] In particular, the absence of the term τέμενος or *similia* induced Lambert to conclude that sacred properties were not included in the sales of properties on behalf of the demes, and this appears right in principle.[166] Lambert also claimed that the landholdings sold would not have been revenue-generating properties. I cannot fully endorse this interpretation, for analysis of deme economics shows that in fact demes possessed lands of non-sacred character that could become cash-yielding through leasing. Nothing suggests that demes, or their subdivisions, the *komai*, regularly disposed of their landed assets. Quite the reverse, the *Rationes Centesimarum* were a one-off, a privatization project which, once accomplished, was never repeated.[167]

v. Rentals, deme economics, and religion

In his outstanding analysis of the financial systems of the Attic demes, Whitehead identified three main sources of income: (i) taxes and liturgies (jointly classified), (ii) rents, and (iii) interest on loans.[168] To these he elsewhere added fines, though these obviously could not have constituted a regular source of money because of their random and unpredictable character.[169] Despite Whitehead's perspicacious remarks, there is still scope for probing into the topic of rentals as a vital element of deme economics. A good starting point is another valid remark made by the same scholar, namely that the largest proportion of a deme's expenditure fell in the realm of religion.[170]

That religion was an omnipresent factor in ancient Greek society is such a commonplace that scholars often speak of 'embedded religion',

[164] Lambert 1997*a*, 238.
[165] Walbank 1983*a*; 1983*b*; 1983*c*; 1984.
[166] Lambert 1997*a*, 237, 239–40.
[167] Lambert 1997*a*, 280–91.
[168] Whitehead 1986, 149–60. This tabulation had first been formed by Finley 1952*a*, 96–7. See also Nemes 1980, 5.
[169] Whitehead 1986, 169.
[170] Whitehead 1986, 163–4.

and no modern study is considered comprehensive without at least one reference to the concept of polis-religion.[171] There is no reason why this religious ubiquity should not make its appearance in the agenda of the Attic demes and, in fact, much relevant information concerns the sacred domain in one way or another. Financial documents, sacrificial calendars, honorific decrees praising pious individuals, a whole series of documents show in effect that the diffusion of religion into deme life was so widespread that one is entitled to speak of 'deme-religion'.[172] In the financial sector one can identify a pattern similar to the one encountered at the polis level, namely a distinction between sacred and secular money.[173] As early as the mid-fifth century the deme of Ikarion published its financial accounts, in which there featured separate entries for money designated as *ὅσιον* and money designated as belonging to Dionysos and the eponymous hero Ikaros.[174] Similarly, in the roughly contemporary accounts issued by the Rhamnousian demarchs, the purse in question was designated as belonging to Nemesis.[175] So what do deme leases reveal

171 Polis-religion: Sourvinou-Inwood 1990; 2000.

172 Mikalson 1977; Osborne 1985*a*, 178–82; Whitehead 1986, 176–222; Parker 1987*a*; Cole 1995, 294; Verbanck-Piérard 1998. The term *deme-religion* is coined here in analogy to the concept of *polis-religion*. Most scholars speak of *deme-cults*. Ch. 3 in Parker 2005, 'Places of Cult: Athens and the Demes', is nothing less than an exciting, comprehensive treatment of *deme-religion*.

173 The collocation of *ἱερὰ καὶ ὅσια* has been elegantly analysed by Connor 1988. We now have a very fresh analysis by Blok 2010. See also Introduction.

174 *IG* I^3 253, a much-overlooked text (but see Connor 1988, 165, Kearns 1989, 98, and the new epigraphic edition by Makres 2004, 129–31 = *SEG* LIV 57; one should now add Blok 2010, 65-9). Let us here briefly note a certain paradox. The secular fund (*ὅσιον*) of Ikarion appears to have been considerably bigger than either of the two sacred treasuries and this at a time when Athenian economics was still predominantly sacred (on this point see more recently Samons II 2000, 28–83 and *passim*). Two possible explanations can be put forward. Either the low deposits of the two sacred purses reflect some outstanding expenditure, such as constructions of cultic buildings (cf. the similar interpretation of the absence of Nemesis from the accounts of the Treasurers of the Other Gods suggested by Petrakos in the commentary of *I.Rhamnous* 182, responding to ML 53), but note that Travlos 1988, 85 highlighted the absence of 5th-cent. buildings in Ikarion. Or part of the sacred funds of Ikarion, especially those of Dionysos (for Ikarios this seems unlikely), had been transferred to the treasury of the Other Gods after its foundation (cf. the entry for Dionysos—but which one?—in *IG* I^3 369 (=ML 72), l. 81). The latter hypothesis can stand, if we accept the lower chronology for the Ikarian accounts, i.e. early 420s. For a different set of considerations, see Blok 2010, 65–9.

175 *I.Rhamnous* 182 (*IG* I^3 248), ll. 3–4: *τô τε̂ς Νεμέσ|εος ἀργυρίο*; ll. 9–12: *τô δὲ ἄ|λλο ἀργυρίο : τ|ô τε̂ς Νεμέσεο|ς*; also defined simply as the *sacred money* in ll. 17–18: *τô ἱε|ρô ἀργυρίο* and ll. 21–2: *τô ἱ|ερô ἀργυρίο*.

with regard to deme-religion and, more specifically, how are they connected to deme economics?

It should have become clear by now that some of the landed assets controlled by demes fell within the category of sacred property. This is the case with the *temene* leased out by the deme of Halimous and the two *temene* of Nemesis at Rhamnous, with the Herakleion and the Dionysion at Thorikos, presumably with the rented properties of the Plotheians, and definitely with the quarries of Herakles at Akris in Eleusis.[176] The landholding leased by the Teithrasians was surrounded by sacred establishments,[177] and the property of the Kytherians in the Piraeus was probably adjacent to the sanctuary where the inscribed contract was to be set up.[178] Finally, an unknown shrine seems to have been the object of a lease that has been reinterpreted recently as a deme document.[179] Now, it has to be understood that these sacred properties were linked administratively to cults which were operating within the framework of demes, not to ones controlled

[176] Halimous: Dem. 57. 63 (the divine owner or owners of these *temene* are unknown; however, it is a fair assumption that Dionysos was one of them: the decree of the Halimousians *SEG* II 7 in honour of Harisandros for the sacrifices he performed on behalf of the deme had to be set up in the local Dionysion); Rhamnous: *I.Rhamnous* 180; Thorikos (unpublished material): Matthaiou 2009, 206; Plotheia: *IG* I^3 258 (but Blok 2010, 73 n. 30, hesitantly suggests that the land was not sacred); Eleusis: *SEG* XXVIII 103, esp. ll. 21–3, where the sacred ownership of the quarries is, bizarrely, overemphasized, as the new reading by Alipheri 2009 unmistakably shows: *τὰς λιθοτομίας τὰς Ἐλευσῖνι ἐ|ν Ἄκṛιḍịι, ἐπειδή εἰσιν ἱεραὶ τοῦ Ἡρακλέως τοῦ ἐν Ἄκρι|δι, μι[σ]θοῦν τὸν δήμαρχον*. Alipheri herself thinks that the quarries are restored to the god after a spell of neglect.

[177] Papazarkadas 2007*a*, D1a (*SEG* XXIV 151), ll. 9–12: *τὸ [χ]ωρίον τὸ Τείθραντι ὧι γε[ί]των [β]ọ|[ρᾶ]θε[ν τὸ] χωṛίọṿ τὸ Αἰ[γ]έωṣ καὶ τὸ ἡṛῶιον τὸ Ἐπ̣|[ιγ]ό[νου?], νοτ[ό]θεν δὲ τὸ Ἡ̣ράκλεịον καὶ τὸ χωρίọ|[ν] ἥρ[ω]ο[ς . . .⁵. .]ας καὶ τὸ τ̣ô Δ̣ιὸς τέμενος* (cf. Osborne 1988, 283 n. 12, and my comments ad loc.). Note that at the bottom of the same stele, a decree (*SEG* XXIV 153) was inscribed honouring a certain Euthippos for his contribution to the construction of a statue (probably that of Kore; cf. Möbius 1924, 6): the stele retains an aura of sacredness.

[178] *IG* II^2 2496. The leased workshop was located in Piraeus (l. 9: *τὸ ἐργαστήριον τὸ ἐν Πειραεῖ*) and the inscribed contract was to be set up *[παρὰ τ]ὸν ἥρω* (l. 25; no further geographical designation). Since *IG* II^2 2496 was discovered in Piraeus, far from the conjectured site of Kytheros, it is a fair conclusion that the shrine of the Hero was situated in Piraeus and, thus, probably near the leased properties. Note also that the document bears a chronological formula based on the name of the priest of the Hero (ll. 1–2: *ἐπὶ Φιλιππίδου ἱερέ|ως*), a fact which would underpin the presumption that the properties in question were cult-related.

[179] *IG* II^2 598, especially ll. 1–3: *[Κ]τησίας εἶπεν· μι|[σθῶσαι - - - τ]ὸ ἱερὸν Ἀρχεστρ|[άτωι]*; Walbank 1997, 39–40 has offered some good reasons for it to be a document issued by a deme or a tribe.

by the polis of Athens via centrally and democratically allotted officials.[180] Evidence pertaining to this type of sacred realty can be found in texts other than leases, such as the decree of the Piraeans *IG* II^2 1177, where the demarch and the priestess of the local Thesmophorion had to implement the decisions of the demesmen concerning pilgrims' behaviour within the shrine, and *IG* II^2 1362, an edict of the priest of Apollo Erithaseos in which the sacred magistrate and the demarch of an unnamed deme had to protect the flora of the god's sanctuary.[181] And it is evidence from Piraeus again (admittedly not a typical deme but a deme nevertheless) that has shown that more than one god (or hero) could own landed property that made up what we could call the sacred landscape of the Attic deme. For in *IG* II^2 2498, a document that we have already analysed for its financial ramifications, we can identify a series of divine proprietors: self-evidently Theseus as owner of the *temenos* called Theseion, and Demeter (of the Thesmophorion), and perhaps even Paralos of the property called Paralia. A boundary stone found long ago in Keratea may designate an estate belonging to the local divinity Aphrodite of Kephale, though the ambiguity of the term *temenos*, especially when taken out of context, does not allow us to establish whether in this case it applies to a landholding or to a sanctuary.[182] Last, we have the intriguing evidence of the *diadikasia*-document *IG* II^2 1932, where, on one interpretation, Meneleos, Herakles, and the Dioskouroi, appear as owners of landed (?) property administered by the deme of Phegaia.[183]

More explicit, even though little known, are two examples also attested on boundary stones. Recent excavations in the area of Thorikos brought to light a slab with the laconic text h*όρος*|*ὑπερπεδίο*. Inspired by the apparent rarity of the second word, the excavator pondered various interpretations,[184] but, as Robert Parker readily detected,[185] the decipherment of the crucial word is offered by a

[180] For the distinction see Linders 1975, 12–16, 80–2.

[181] See above, p. 127.

[182] *IG* II^2 2604: h*όρος* | *τεμένους*| *Ἀφροδίτης* | *Κεφαλῆθεν* (4th cent.).

[183] *IG* II^2 1932, ll. 12–15: *Φηγαιῆς* | *Μενέλεως ἀρχηγέτης ἀντ[ί - - -]* | *Ἡρακλῆς ἀρχηγέτης ἀντί [- - -]* | *Διοσκόρω ἀντὶ Νικοστρά[το - - -]*. Various interpretations have been put forward regarding this and other aspects of the *diadikasia*-documents, but at least Davies 1981, 137–8, Rhodes 1982, 12–13, and even Gabrielsen 1987, 40-1, 47-8, seem to agree that the divinities appear here as property-owners.

[184] Ed. pr.: Salliora-Oikonomakou 2001 [2003] (=*SEG* LI 158).

[185] As reported in *SEG* LII 157.

famous text traditionally associated with this specific area, the so-called lex sacra from Thorikos. Therein a hero called Ὑπερπέδιος and his female aides-de-camp are offered a sheep and a sacrificial table.[186] Thus, the new *horos* probably marked the precinct of Hyperpedios (thus hόρος|Ὑπερπεδίο). But since the hero's name has unmistakable territorial connotations, it is possible that the *horos* also marked the high plateau that had christened Hyperpedios in the first place. Perhaps, then, the precinct-plateau was where the aforementioned sacrifices were offered every Thargelion, and it is also likely, but by no means certain, that the precinct provided revenue for the expenses incurred. The second example is a much older find: a boundary stone discovered in the 1930s by members of the German Archaeological Institute. The horos—virtually unknown in modern scholarship—designated a 'sacred landholding of the hero Angelos'.[187] On the basis of the lettering of the stoichedon text, Kirchner and Dow dated the horos to the beginning of the fourth century. Here, in this humble stone, we see the harmonious marriage of the religious and the economic: a minor divinity (Angelos) giving his name to a minor rural deme (Angele, bouleutic quota: 2) and in turn granted land by the grateful demesmen. There can be no doubt that other demes had similarly endowed their eponymous heroes or their legendary founding fathers with landed property.[188]

In theory, income raised from such properties should have been used by deme authorities for their cultic needs—what is coined in ancient sources δημοτικά as opposed to δημοτελῆ—and the polis itself would have had no jurisdiction over it.[189] But is this premise

[186] *NGSL* 1, ll. 48–9: *Ὑπερπεδίωι οἶν, Ἡρωΐνησι̣[ν Ὑπερ]|πεδίο τράπεζαν.*; cf. Parker 2005, 72.

[187] Kirchner and Dow 1937, 9: *ὅρος χ|ωρίο ἱ|εροῦ ἥ|ρω Ἀγγ|έλου*. The text has not been included in *SEG*, and can be found neither in Kearns's important monograph on Attic heroes nor in Parker's books on Athenian religion.

[188] The Aixonian lex sacra *SEG* LIV 214 now shows that the Archegetes of the deme had his own priest (and a well-treated one at that!). And we have already seen (n. 137 above) property belonging to the Archegetes of Rhamnous. See also Parker 2005, 70–2 on the importance of such 'deme-holding' (*δημοῦχοι*) gods and heroes.

[189] Harp. s.v. *δημοτελῆ καὶ δημοτικὰ ἱερά· διέφερον ἀλλήλων καὶ τῶν ὀργεωνικῶν καὶ τῶν γενικῶν, ὡς Δείναρχος δηλοῖ ἐν τῷ κατὰ Στεφάνου* (repeated almost verbatim by Phot. s.v. *δημοτελῆ καὶ δημοτικὰ ἱερά*); Hsch. s.v. *δημοτελῆ ἱερά· καὶ δημοτελῆ μέν, εἰς ἃ θύματα διδῷ ἡ πόλις· δημοτικὰ δέ, εἰς ἃ οἱ δῆμοι*; Dem. 43.71: *ἐάν τις ἐλάαν Ἀθήνησιν ἐξορύττῃ, ἐὰν μὴ εἰς ἱερὸν Ἀθηναίων δημόσιον ἢ δημοτικόν* etc. (with Faraguna 1998, 175); cf. Whitehead 1986, 178 n. 8; Parker 1996, 7 with n. 22; Sourvinou-Inwood 2000, 43; Pirenne-Delforge 2005, 58.

confirmed by the evidence? Furthermore, how meaningful is the distinction between sacred and secular landholdings in the context of demes? For Finley this last question would have caused no concern, since he once famously claimed that the 'so-called temple funds were deme funds and the administrative technique common in Athens and elsewhere of handling such moneys through the temple had no special significance, legally or otherwise'.[190] On the contrary, there was indeed a special, although non-legal, significance, as will be argued below.

To begin with, it has long been observed that the *fasti sacri* of demes, precious sources of information for us if we are to understand deme-religion at work, were principally financial documents, well-planned efforts on behalf of demes to keep a valid account of their sacrificial expenses, the most expensive item in their annual budgets.[191] To defray such costs, demes had to secure a steady flow of money into their funds by various means, and leasing out their landed assets constituted a mostly reliable option.[192] Despite a surprising scholarly neglect of the topic, the close bond between leasing and religious performance should not come as a surprise. The mechanism is well known at all levels of Athenian administration, from the level of the central government, as in the case of the Oropian Nea, through that of the *gene* (e.g. the decree of the Salaminioi), down to the realm of the orgeones.[193] With regard to demes, the most unambiguous attestation of this financial strategy is the double decree from Eleusis for the lease of the quarry of Herakles, in which the relevant income was earmarked for the performance of sacrifices to Herakles himself and strict penalties were envisaged for anyone who tried to modify the decision of the Eleusinians thereon.[194] Equally explicit is the

[190] Finley 1952*a*, 95, justifiably criticized by Isager 1992, 119.

[191] Dow 1968, 177–85.

[192] Rosivach 1993, 53.

[193] Nea and the Lesser Panathenaia: *Agora* XIX L7. Rentals funding sacrifices of the Salaminioi: *Agora* XIX L4a. Rental subsidizing the sacrifice to the orgeonic hero *Egretes*: *IG* II^2 2499 ll. 18–26; cf. Migeotte 1998.

[194] *SEG* XXVIII 103 ll. 3–6: *ἐπειδὴ Φιλόκωμος εἰσηγήσατο τοῖς δημότα|ις π[ερὶ τ]ῆς Ἄκριδος ἀποδόσθαι τῶι θεῶι τὴν | λιθ[οτομ]ίαν, ὅπως ἂν ἡ θυσία γίγνηται ὡς καλ|λίστη*; ll. 19–20: *ὅπως ἂν τῶι Ἡρακλεῖ τῶι ἐν Ἄκριδι πρόσ|οδος ἦι ὡς πλείστη καὶ ἡ θυσία θύηται ὡς καλλίστη*; ll. 31–3: *τὸν δὲ δήμαρχον λαβόντα τοῦτ|ο τὸ ἀργύριον παρέχειν εἰς τὴν ἑορτὴν τοῦ Ἡρακλέως τ|ο[ῦ ἐν Ἄκ]ριδι*; ll. 36–9: *μὴ ἐξέστω δὲ εἰπεῖν μη|θένα τοῦτο τὸ ἀργύριον ὡς δεῖ ἄλλοθί που τρέψαι ἢ εἰς | τὴν θυσίαν τοῦ Ἡρακλέως, μηδὲ τοῖς ἱερομνήμοσιν ἐπι|ψηφίσαι, μηδὲ τῶι δημάρχωι* (i.e. an entrenchment clause),

statement in the fifth-century Plotheian decree that a certain category of sacrifices had to be funded from rentals, though admittedly the latter constituted only a fraction of such expenditure, the most substantial source of money being interest on loans.[195]

The same reality is reflected in our two surviving deme leases of theatres, that of Acharnai (*IG* II^2 1206), the rental from which was to be funnelled partly to an annual sacrifice, and that of the Piraeus (*Agora* XIX L13), the leasing of which was carried out with the aim of repairing the theatre itself through a self-investment scheme.[196] It has to be noted here that theatres were perceived as sacral, not secular, buildings, since they were attached to shrines of Dionysos and primarily used as venues for the performance of dramatic competitions, which were, in effect, religious events.[197] The case of the theatre at Mounychia is important in illuminating a further point: sacred expenditure was not exclusively restricted to sacrifices. The Plotheian document, for instance, lists expenses for a Herakleion amongst festival expenditure and this has been taken to refer to repairs in a shrine of Herakles.[198] Numerous decrees have been preserved conferring honours upon individuals who had personally financed construction or repairs of shrines.[199] They all make it clear that this kind

with Coumanoudis and Gofas 1978, 302–3. See also Ampolo 1982, 254–5; Whitehead 1986, 124; Faraguna 1992, 346; Alipheri 2009, 187–91.

[195] *IG* I^3 258 ll. 22–6 (with the discussion at p. 130 above); cf. Faraguna 1992, 345–6, and now Blok 2010, 72–3.

[196] See Papazarkadas 2007*a*, 167–9; Csapo 2007, 90–6. Piraeus: see now Carusi 2006, 20–1.

[197] This is explicitly stated by Demosthenes in his speech *Against Meidias*, where he accuses the defendant of having committed impiety by maltreating him in the precinct of the god (Dem. 21.55: *τὸν οὖν εἴς τινα τούτων τῶν χορευτῶν ἢ τῶν χορηγῶν ὑβρίζοντ᾽ ἐπ᾽ ἔχθρᾳ, καὶ ταῦτ᾽ ἐν αὐτῷ τῷ ἀγῶνι καὶ ἐν τῷ τοῦ θεοῦ ἱερῷ, τοῦτον ἄλλο τι πλὴν ἀσεβεῖν φήσομεν*; 74: *ἐγὼ δ᾽ ὑπ᾽ ἐχθροῦ . . . ἐναντίον πολλῶν καὶ ξένων καὶ πολιτῶν ὑβριζόμην, καὶ ταῦτ᾽ ἐν ἱερῷ*). Of course the crime had been committed in the theatre, so the identification of the two (theatre = shrine of the god) is inescapable (cf. MacDowell 1990, 275). Archaeologically the connection can be seen in the theatre of Thorikos next to which stood a small temple of Dionysos (Mussche 1998, 31, 58–9). For a full treatment of related issues see Sinn 2005. In her recent innovative study, Paga 2010 has tried to emphasize the function of deme theatres as civic centres, downplaying, I feel, too much their sacred features.

[198] *IG* I^3 258 l. 4: [ἐ]ς *τὸ Ἡρακλεῖον* 𐅇*XX*, for which see Haussoullier 1884, 64. Blok 2010, 73–4, now entertains the possibility that the Herakleion was a treasury, but inexplicably does not include the amount of 7000 drachmas in her interesting set of calculations.

[199] e.g. *IG* II^2 1215 (deme unknown).

of benefaction was an expression of pious behaviour. Yet again deme practice matches that of the central administration, with construction and reconstruction of sacred buildings falling within the category of religious expenditure.[200]

In a previous section the suggestion was made that different payment patterns might occasionally reflect localized cultic needs and some evidence was adduced in support of this theory, which in turn bolsters the idea of rentals eventually funding religious projects. Yet the link between deme rentals and cultic activity can be seen clearly in the important double lease from Rhamnous, in which the detailed clauses on the agricultural operations that have to be undertaken by the lessees are followed by what has been described as a 'short sacrificial calendar'.[201] Unfortunately, these *fasti* are very elliptical. There are at least three, maybe four, divine recipients of offerings identifiable in the crucial lines: Zeus Herkeios, Apollo Lykeios, [Arte]mis or [The]mis, and an unknown divinity of whose name (in the dative) only the final *iota* is preserved. There is also a second reference to Apollo (l. 86, [*Ἀπόλ*]*λωνο*[*ς*]), but since the form is obviously in the genitive, the god cannot have featured as a recipient of offerings. Maybe something along the lines of [*ὁ ἱερεὺς τοῦ Ἀπόλ*]*λωνο*[*ς*] could be considered here, with the priest of Apollo being commanded to perform a sacrifice or receiving his share of perks.[202] Both Zeus Herkeios and Apollo Lykeios are otherwise unattested in Rhamnous. The former occurs in the sacrificial calendar from Thorikos receiving two sacrifices, whereas the latter receives two offerings according to the Erchian *fasti*, one at Athens and one in the deme.[203] There is some indirect evidence, however, that at least Apollo Lykeios enjoyed a high status in Rhamnous, namely the frequent occurrence of the otherwise rather uncommon personal name *Λυκέας* amongst

[200] See the neat remarks by Parker 2005, 65; on polis building see Chapter 2, Section 6.

[201] '[*Β*]*ραχὺ ἡμερολόγιο θυσιῶν*'; so Petrakos in his notes on *I.Rhamnous* 180 ll. 82–90; cf. Petrakos 1999, 329.

[202] Alternatively, and given the nature of the text, it is very tempting to restore the name of a month: thus, [*Ἐλαφηβο*]*λ*(*ι*)*ῶνος*, [*Θαργη*]*λ*(*ι*)*ῶνος* or [*Γαμη*]*λ*(*ι*)*ῶνος*. Only further inspection of the stone could confirm or disprove my assumption.

[203] *SEG* XXI 541, col. I, ll. 1–5: *Μεταγειτνιῶ|νος δωδεκάτε|ι, Ἀπόλλωνι* ᵛ *Λ|υκείωι, ἐν ἄστ|ει, οἶς, οὐ φο*; col. V, ll. 31–6: *Γαμηλιῶνος|ἑβδόμηι ἱσ|ταμένο, Ἀπό|λλωνι Λυκε|ίωι, Ἐρχιᾶσ|ι, οἶς* (on Apollo Lykeios in Athens, see Jameson 1980).

Rhamnousians.[204] As for the female deity [Arte]mis or [The]mis, preference should be given to the second option, since Themis played a conspicuous role in the religious life of Rhamnous receiving at least one sacrifice described as 'ancestral'.[205]

What matters for the purposes of our discussion is that in *I.Rhamnous* 180 the *sacra nomina* of the sacrificial calendar are preceded by two very fragmentary lines which have been interpreted as a regulation for the use of the rentals by the *hieromnemones* for the subsidy of the prescribed, presumably annual, sacrifices.[206] Unfortunately, the title *hieromnemones* is not fully preserved, so this interpretation, though plausible, should remain hypothetical. The main difficulty is that the office of the *hieromnemones* is otherwise unattested in Rhamnous, the closest parallel being that of the *hieropoioi*, a board with patent financial responsibilities.[207] On the other hand, the Eleusinian lease *SEG* XXVIII 103 implies that the local *hieromnemones* were involved in the handling of deme rentals and this offers a good parallel for the alleged Rhamnousian board.[208] Finally, it should be noted that elsewhere in the Greek world the analogous office of the

[204] See *LGPN* II s.v. *Λυκέας* (all Athenians called Lykeas whose demotic affiliation is known are Rhamnousians); cf. the prosopographical index in *I.Rhamnous*, p. 236. For nomenclature generated by cult titles see Parker 2000, 55.

[205] Thus in the honorific decree of 222/1 *I.Rhamnous* 32 ll. 10–11: *ἔθυσεν δὲ καὶ τεῖ Θέμιδι καὶ τεῖ Νεμέσει καὶ τοῖς ἄλλοις | θεοῖς οἷς πάτριον ἦν*; of course one cannot entirely dismiss the possibility that the goddess honoured in the sacrificial calendar is Apollo's sister, Artemis.

[206] Petrakos provides this interpretation in his brief commentary on the inscription, but not any restorations. Maybe lines 82–3 could be partly restored as [*θύειν τοὺς ἱερομνή*]*μονας ἐκ τῶν* [*μισ|θώσεων τῶν τεμενῶν*]. Kirchner in *IG* II^2 2494 l. 20 (=*I.Rhamnous* 180 l. 83) has [*κατ' ἐνιαυτὸ*]*ν ἕκαστον*; [*εἰς τὸν ἐνιαυτὸ*]*ν ἕκαστον* can stand as well. The restoration seems pretty plausible, even though it not included by Petrakos in his corpus.

[207] See *I.Rhamnous* 181 (*IG* I^3 247 bis, p. 957), a lead receipt of money transferred from the *epistatai* to the *hieropoioi*. The latter are also attested disbursing money for the erection of decrees. For the administration of the Rhamnousian Nemesion see Petrakos 1999, 275–6. A very interesting new analysis of *I.Rhamnous* 181, has now been offered by Blok 2010, 77–9, who concludes that [*δε*]*μόσιον* (l. 10) refers to the non-sacred budget of the deme. This use of [*δε*]*μόσιον* to refer to an Attic deme rather than the Athenian polis would be unprecedented. I would rather see here Rhamnous interacting with the central administration in a way that, on present evidence, cannot be fully understood.

[208] See *SEG* XXVIII 103 ll. 38–9, where the *hieromnemones* are denied jurisdiction over the destination of the rental in a way which suggests that, under normal circumstances, they did have such empowerment. It is perhaps in this light that one has to understand the presence of *hieromnemones* in a document of the Cholargeis for the financial organization of the local Thesmophoria (*IG* II^2 1184 ll. 1–2), for which

mnemones (*μνῆμονες*) appears to have been closely linked to issues of land administration: perhaps, after all, their Attic counterparts had similar responsibilities, which are simply not well attested in our record.[209]

Be that as it may, the connection between rents and sacrifices seems inescapable. This leads to a very interesting, if puzzling, observation. The two leased *temene* of *I.Rhamnous* 180 nominally belonged to the goddess Nemesis, and yet income raised from them was destined to fund sacrifices performed in honour of other deities. And even if we allow for the possibility that the goddess of line 88 is Themis, who at Rhamnous forms a cultic pair with Nemesis,[210] the other two recognizable gods, Apollo Lykeios and Zeus Herkeios, cannot be shown to have any specific affiliation to Nemesis. It is difficult to generalize from this piece of information as concerns land administration in all 139 Attic demes. In other words, it is hard to figure out whether sacred lands controlled by demes could raise income for religious purposes regardless of the nominal ownership of the *temene*. The decree of the Plotheians arguably points in this direction.[211] In its heading with the itemized list of *κεφάλαια*, 'capitals', available to Plotheia the rubric *μισθώσεων*, 'rentals', is not associated with any particular items of cultic expenditure and, moreover, a clause in the main body of the decree makes it clear that rentals were to subsidize three different categories of sacrifices: local ones, sacrifices at state festivals and quadrennial ones.[212] Another long-neglected document which can be brought into the discussion is the fragmentary opisthographic stele *IG* II² 1211. As I have argued elsewhere, this text provides further evidence for subsidy of cultic activity from rentals of lands administered by the unknown issuing

see Jones 1999, 124–5. If line 8 in side B of *IG* II² 1216 can be restored as [*ἱερομν*]*ήμονα*[*s*], then we may have a further example of this board in a deme context.

209 On *mnemones* as land experts, see more recently Faraguna 2000, 110–12.

210 Stafford 1997, 160–1; Petrakos 1999, 190.

211 The point was not missed by Davies 2001, 124: 'The money was to be kept safe "for Plotheieis" rather than for any particular deity'.

212 Arangio-Ruiz 1936, 450–1 with n. 14 has demonstrated that the rubric in question does not refer to expenditure incurred by the deme acting as lessee, but income from leases to be invested in cultic activity. Thus also Behrend 1970, 74, and Osborne 1988, 282, who considers the underlying leased properties as sacred. For the tripartite categorization of sacrifices (*IG* I³ 258 ll. 25–8: *θύεν τὰ ἱερὰ τά ἐς Πλωθει*[*ᾶς κ*]|*οινὰ καὶ τὰ ἐς Ἀθηναίος ὑπὲρ Πλ*[*ωθέ*|*ω*]*ν τô κοινô καὶ τὰ ἐς τὰς πεντετ*[*ηρ*|*ίδ*]*ας*) see Mikalson 1977, 426; Osborne 1985*a*, 180–1; Whitehead 1986, 166.

deme authority. As in the Rhamnousian text, the cultic framework does not seem to be confined to one particular divinity, but rather entails a set of diverse and unconnected offerings, one of which may be referring to the state festival of Anthesteria.[213] Of course, the Rhamnousian enigma may be due to the nature of the divine owner of the properties. Nemesis, the most revered Rhamnousian deity, was in effect the patron goddess of the deme,[214] and by a stroke of abstractive symbolism her personal budget might have equated to that of the deme.[215] Her cultic significance had of course a very tangible effect, namely an immense fund assigned to the goddess. These two factors taken together would suffice to explain how part of the goddess's income could be channelled to the cult of divinities of secondary status within the framework of Rhamnous. By contrast, Herakles was not so crucial a god in the framework of Eleusis, where, if one were to identify a deity as tutelary, that would be Dionysos.[216]

The foregoing examination has further implications. Students of Greek religion will be familiar with Dow's analysis of the intact sacrificial calendar from Erchia: its layout with the five numbered columns of roughly equally distributed expenses corresponds to the contribution of five different liturgists or groups of liturgists.[217] The vast majority of scholars have endorsed this interpretation and yet

[213] Thus Hamilton 1992, 32; 60–1. A new edition of *IG* II^2 1211 along with detailed discussion of the various sacrifices and offerings attested in the text can be found in Papazarkadas 2007*a*, 169–171.

[214] Cole 1995 offers an invaluable discussion on tutelary divinities; cf. Lévêque and Vidal-Naquet 1996, 48.

[215] For the cult of Nemesis at Rhamnous see Petrakos 1999, 188–90. Whitehead 1986, 160–1 n. 77 raises the possibility that Rhamnous might have had other funds besides the one of Nemesis. Note, however, that in the only genuine deme decree from Rhamnous where a formula concerning the erection of the stele is preserved, the expenditure is disbursed by the *hieropoioi* (*I.Rhamnous* 15 ll. 7–9: ἀναγράψαι δὲ^{v}|[ἐν στ]ήλῃ λιθίνῃ καὶ στῆσαι τοὺς ἱεροποιοὺς ἐν τῶι ἱερῶ|[ι τῆ]ς Νεμέσεως; cf. Papazarkadas 2004). We now know of a fund called κοινόν ('common') operating during the Hellenistic period (*I.Rhamnous* 22 ll. 16–17: τὸ δὲ γε|[νόμενον ἀν]ᾀλωμα μερίσαι τὸν ταμίαν ἐκ τοῦ κοινοῦ; *I.Rhamnous* 26 ll. 31–2: [τ]ὸ δ̣ὲ γ̣[ε][ν]όμενον ἀνάλωμα μερίσαι ἐκ τοῦ κο[ι]ν̣οῦ̣ [ταμ]εί[ου]), but that was employed for decrees passed by the koinon of the soldiers (στρατιῶται).

[216] See for example the punitive clause in the decree published by Threpsiades 1939, 178 ll. 18–21 (=*IG* II^2 1194 ll. 14–17): κα[ὶ] καλείτω αὐτὸν [ὁ δήμαρχος ὁ ἀε]|ὶ δημ̣αρχῶν εἰς τὴν [προεδρίαν ἢ ὀφε]|ιλέτω ^{v}Η^{v} δραχμὰς [ἱερὰς τῶι Διον]|ύσωι.

[217] Dow 1965, 193–5, and 1968, 183–4, refining a suggestion made by Daux 1963, 616.

one is forced to ask:[218] is it necessarily so? Another feasible conjecture would be, for instance, that each set of sacrifices was to be funded from a different leased parcel of land in accordance with the well-known practice. Part of Dow's thesis was based on the now outdated notion that prior to demes the aristocratic gene had the monopoly of sacrifices, but demes assumed responsibility as part of a general move from the private to the public sphere. Much as we know from the six, partly or wholly, preserved deme *fasti*, the truth is that our ignorance of religious finances is still enormous. With the exception of the calendar of the Marathonian Tetrapolis, which contained a list of private contributions on its obverse face, all other such documents remain totally cryptic about the provenance of the finances they contain.[219]

In sum, the investigation above seems to conform with the pattern delineated at the polis level whereby rentals from sacred properties flowed into sacred treasuries. Of course, leasing operated along with, and sometimes in interrelation with, other systems, namely funding from loans and private contributors.[220] In the domain of demes, sacred rentals ended mainly, but not exclusively, in financing local cultic activity. By this one has to understand purchases of sacrificial victims, perks to sacred officials, organization of processions, acquisition of cultic equipment, and construction or refurbishment of shrines. Given the variety of the involved expenditure one should expect that more than one magistracy was involved in the actual administration of these rentals but, as it happens, we know more about the technicalities of the leasing procedure than about the handling of the relevant income once raised. Clearly the role of the demarchs was crucial: not only did they lease out lands,[221] as the *archon basileus* did at the polis level, they often collected the generated income in a way reminiscent of the *apodektai*. The role of

[218] So Jameson 1982, 73; Lambert 2000*a*, 67–8.

[219] Marathonian Tetrapolis: *IG* II^2 1358; see now the revised text *SEG* L 168, with Lambert 2000*a*, 62–7 for the private financiers.

[220] For private contributions see, apart from the Marathonian *fasti* (previous n.), the decree of the deme of Kollytos where loans from private individuals to the deme are envisaged as a means of raising money for sacrifices (to Agathe Tyche, according to Walbank 1994, 238, but this is now rejected by Matthaiou 2008, who has republished the inscription after attaching to it a new fragment).

[221] One can also adduce as evidence, albeit hypothetical, the presumed role of the demarchs in collecting rentals on behalf of cultic groups, such as the trittys of the Epakreis, for which see Papazarkadas 2007*b*.

the *hieromnemones* in relation to handling of deme rentals was discussed above in the context of *I.Rhamnous* 180. Although the diversity of deme nomenclature might indicate that other officials would have been involved in sacred land administration, this should remain hypothetical.[222]

vi. Non-sacral deme property

We are still left with the question: what about deme leases that simply lack any reference to the final destination of the anticipated income? In this category one can include the Aixonian *Φελλεῖς* (*IG* II^2 2492), the two Prasian plots (*IG* II^2 2497 and *SEG* XXI 644), and two very fragmentary leases from Acharnai which seem to confer to the lessee the right to exploit water resources (*IG* II^2 2491 with *SEG* XXI 642 and *IG* II^2 2502), all of which are characterized by the absence of any religious connotations.[223] Elsewhere I have shown that contrary to the prevailing scholarly consensus it is not a proven fact that the Aixonian pastures (*ἐννόμια*) of *IG* II^2 1196 were sacred.[224] Nor can any religious aspect be detected in the fragmentary lease of a tenement-house by the Eleusinians.[225] This may not be coincidental. Admittedly the ambiguous nature of some of these texts might, to some extent, be due to their poor state of preservation, but it might well reflect the elaborate fiscal realities of certain demes which, as highlighted above, had both a sacral and a non-sacral budget. The nature of the latter cannot be established with precision. What was the origin of the Ikarian *ὅσιον* money, for instance, which at one point could sustain an income increase of 400 drachmas within an accounting period (which may or may not have been one year long)? And

[222] See, for instance, *IG* I^3 258.3: [*τα*]*μίαιν ἐς τὰ δι' ἔτος ἱερὰ* 𐅅.

[223] Duly observed by Osborne 1988, 283. Equally unclear is the status of the landholdings in the early 3rd-cent. decree of Piraeus *Agora* XVI 160 (l. 4 *δήμωι κτημάτων*). Finally the *χωρίον* in the military decree *I.Eleusis* 191 (ll. 16–17: *κατεσκεύακεν δὲ* [*καὶ πρὸς τὴν ἀσφά*]|*λειαν τοῦ χωρίου*) is now taken by Clinton 2008, 250 to refer not to agricultural land, but to the whole district of Eleusis.

[224] Papazarkadas 2007*a*, 164–5.

[225] *I.Eleusis* 176 (previously *IG* II^2 2500), a tantalizing document because of its poor state of preservation. Contra earlier interpretations (cf. Kirchner in *IG*), Clinton 2008, 184, now quite reasonably suggests that the document does not attest to any sort of transaction between the Eleusinians and the Thriasians.

how are we to understand deme budgets designated as *κοινά*?[226] These questions will be dealt with jointly, for their treatment has some bearing on our understanding of deme rentals.

The distinction between *ἱερά* and *ὅσια* money as attested at the polis level has already been discussed. Conceptually the *ἱερά* belonged to the gods, whereas the *ὅσια* to the polis. We can now add: *ὅσια* could also be perceived as pertaining to individual demes.[227] Apparently not all demes followed the same pattern, and any relevant discussion runs the risk of falling into the trap of oversimplification. At any rate, with regard to the *ὅσιον* budgets, we can plausibly infer, on the model of the sacred reserves, that they contained non-sacred fines, taxes, private contributions, and, more significantly for our discussion, revenue from non-sacred lands, such as those confiscated by demes, or simply landholdings that had always been under the control of demes without having been set aside to any deities. As shown elsewhere, it is exactly this category of properties that feature in the *Rationes Centesimarum* and here is the moment to delve into this topic.

Modern scholarship holds that the reforms of Cleisthenes modified rather than completely altered a pre-existing administrative scheme, and the same presumably applies to the demes. Clearly, there is no way to retrieve the exact administrative scope of those proto-demes, let alone their land-tenure mechanism. But at least in the fourth century it was genuinely believed that demes had evolved from the pre-existing *naukrariai*.[228] Now, *naukrariai* are a notoriously opaque institution.[229] Nevertheless, the extant evidence, though meagre, indicates that the *naukraroi*, the representatives of the *naukrariai*, had

[226] e.g. *SEG* XXIV 151 ll. 2–4: *ὅπως ἂν σᾶ ἧι τ|οῖς δημόταις τὰ κοινὰ καὶ εἰδῶσι Τειθράσιοι τὰ ὑπάρχ|ο[ντα] καὶ τὰ προσιόντα*; *I.Eleusis* 70 (*IG* II² 1186), ll. 35–6: *δοῦναι δὲ εἰς θυσ||[ί]αν Δαμασίαι Η δραχμὰς ἀπὸ τοῦ κοινοῦ*; cf. *IG* II² 1206 ll. 12–14 (partly restored), with Papazarkadas 2007*a*, 169.

[227] At the deme level see, apart from *IG* I³ 243, the decree *IG* II² 1215 ll. 6–9: *κ|αὶ διατελεῖ λέγων καὶ πράττων τὰ β|έλτιστα ὑπὲρ τε τῶν ἱερῶν καὶ τῶν ὁ|σίων* (deme unknown).

[228] Arist. [*Ath. Pol.*] 21.5: *κατέστησε δὲ καὶ δημάρχους, τὴν αὐτὴν ἔχοντας ἐπιμέλειαν τοῖς πρότερον ναυκράροις*, in conjunction with Arist. [*Ath. Pol.*] 8.3 (cf. Rhodes 1993, 151–3, 257). See Whitehead 1986, 33; Lambert 1993, 252–3 n. 35.

[229] The most up-to-date treatment, but not necessarily the best (despite its favourable reception by Stroud 2002, 122), with almost, but not entirely, all the pertinent evidence, is that of Wallinga 2000.

cognizance over financial matters, including land management.[230] In the light of such information, it seems quite conceivable that the administration of the naukraric lands of the Archaic period would have passed under deme control upon Cleisthenes' reforms. Since no religious jurisdiction can be recognized in the case of the *naukraroi*,[231] there is no reason to posit any sacred aspect for their landed assets. I suggest, therefore, that the erstwhile naukraric lands would have been converted into those secular deme landholdings that make their appearance in our sources. As it happens, the notion of non-sacral landed assets is the only conceivable way to interpret the extensive *ὅσιον* reserve in Ikarion at a time when the equivalent polis-fund was insubstantial. This, I contend, was the byproduct of the Attic synoecism.[232] When Attica achieved its political unification, corporate lands presumably passed under the jurisdiction of whatever local entities had already managed them, an inference propped up by Thucydides' renowned digression on the synoecism.[233] The result was that the polis of Athens never came to own public arable lands, only sacred ones, whereas demes did maintain landholdings of considerable size.

There is one example where the connection between non-sacral lands and a non-sacral budget can be hypothesized with a certain degree of plausibility, namely Aixone, which did possess a non-sacred fund; thus it is a fair guess that the rental from the Phelleis flowed into this purse.[234] The same may be assumed in the case of Prasiai, which,

[230] Langdon 1991, 68 with n. 57.

[231] Unless we accept a doubtful etymology which would make them 'guardians of the temples' (so Billigmeier and Dusing 1981, contra Lambert 1993, 254 n. 42, and Wallinga 2000, 134 with n. 2).

[232] Snodgrass 1982, 668–9, 676–7; Whitehead 1986, 8–9; Parker 1996, 10–17.

[233] Thuc. 2.15.2: *καὶ καταλύσας τῶν ἄλλων πόλεων τά τε βουλευτήρια καὶ τὰς ἀρχὰς ἐς τὴν νῦν πόλιν οὖσαν, ἓν βουλευτήριον ἀποδείξας καὶ πρυτανεῖον, ξυνώκισε πάντας, καὶ νεμομένους τὰ αὑτῶν ἑκάστους ἅπερ καὶ πρὸ τοῦ ἠνάγκασε μιᾷ πόλει ταύτῃ χρῆσθαι*, with Hornblower 1991, 262–4, who translates 'they continued to live on their own lands'. This is not entirely wrong, but I suspect that the notion of locally based corporate land administration rather than mere private ownership underlies *νεμομένους* (a notoriously difficult word; cf. Guizzi 1997, 50–2). See also Frost 1994, 173; Parker 1996, 10–15. Cf. Thuc. 2.16.2 with Skydsgaard 2000; Whitehead 2001.

[234] Non-sacral fund at Aixone: *IG* II^2 1198 ll. 13–18: *δοῦ|ναι δὲ αὐτοῖς καὶ εἰς θυ|[σ]ίαν τὸν δήμαρχον Δωρό|[θε]ον καὶ τοὺς ταμίας : Δ | [δ]ραχμὰς ἀπὸ τῆς προσόδ|ου τῶν δημοτῶν*. This budget should be contrasted to the one consecrated to Hebe.

apart from the lease of the Theodoreion and of two other unnamed non-sacral estates, seems to have sold a series of secular landholdings.[235] To probe into the problem of the demotic non-sacral budgets, we should ideally be in the position of investigating the issue at the other end, that of the destination of the relevant income. A most revealing testimony is again the supply of 10 drachmas from the demesmen's budget (*πρόσοδος τῶν δημοτῶν*) of Aixone to a pair of *choregoi* for the performance of a sacrifice commemorating the honours bestowed upon them. This piece of evidence reveals that non-sacral reserves and cultic expenditure were not mutually exclusive. What marks out the sacrifice of the Aixonian document as exceptional, however, is that, far from being a regular item in the annual religious agenda of Aixone, it comprised an ad hoc liability. Put in other words, whereas income belonging to divinities would normally be earmarked for the offering of regular sacrifices, non-sacral money would be spent for covering financial exigencies, religious ones included.[236] Other items of expenditure to be funded from non-sacral funds would comprise the making of honorific wreaths, erection of decrees, and construction or maintenance of public works such as military installations, streets, and so on.[237] But this has already taken us way beyond the strict scope of this monograph.

vii. Lessees and purchasers of deme properties

So far, the focus of the present treatment has primarily been on financial considerations with the occasional glance at other fields when deemed necessary. But an economic phenomenon within a society that was not self-evidently preoccupied with profit as such cannot be adequately dealt with only from a financial perspective.

[235] Prasian lettings: *IG* II^2 2497; *SEG* XXI 644; Matthaiou 2000–3 (*SEG* LI 153); cf. Lambert 1997*a*, 185.

[236] To that effect one can adduce the evidence of *I.Eleusis* 70 (*IG* II^2 1186), an Eleusinian decree honouring the Theban benefactor Damasias, esp. ll. 35–6: *δοῦναι δὲ εἰς θυσ|[ί]αν Δαμασίαι Η δραχμὰς ἀπὸ τοῦ κοινô*. Here *τὸ κοινόν* is probably the non-sacral fund of the deme, for, if it had been the sacred treasury of Dionysos, the Eleusinians would hardly have failed to designate it as such (cf. *I.Eleusis* 101, ll. 19–21: *[ἢ ὀφε]|ιλέτω* ^{V} *Η* ^{V} *δραχμὰς [ἱερὰς τῶι Διον]|ύσωι*).

[237] Whitehead 1986, 161–3.

There still remains much to be said on other aspects of land administration, aspects which impact upon ideology and social behaviour.

It has long been observed that certain characteristics of deme leases imply a quasi-liturgical facet and, consequently, their social ramifications might have been as important as the financial ones, if not more so.[238] Take, for example, the lease of the quarry of Herakles at Akris. The enacting decree per se is quite straightforward, but, seen in a wider context, it unfolds a complicated reality. It is preceded by an honorific decree in praise of Philokomos, the proposer of the leasing enactment.[239] But along with Philokomos, the impetus behind the financial transaction that boosted Herakles' income, the Eleusinians honoured the lessee Moirokles for his bid.[240] Clearly, the Eleusinians viewed Moirokles not simply as an entrepreneur, but as a pious fellow demesman who offered service to the god and, by implication, to his associates. Still, the rationale of the whole affair remains elusive. On what grounds was the lessee Moirokles obliged to cover the cost of 100 drachmas for the golden crown bestowed on Philokomos?[241] Whatever the exact truth is, the double decree from Eleusis is nicely paralleled by the lease of the Piraean theatre, which is also accompanied by an amendment in honour of Theaios and the four lessees/purchasers of the theatre.[242] If Theaios can be assumed, by analogy to the Eleusinian example, to have been the proposer of the leasing scheme,[243] the four individuals praised did nothing but bid for what should normally have been normal business, but apparently counted for more than that to the Piraeans. Last but not least, Xanthippos was offered a lease in perpetuity by the Teithrasians in recognition of his competent administration of their *κοινά*.[244] This last point has not

[238] Andreyev 1974, 43; Whitehead 1986, 157; Liddel 2007, 279.

[239] Self-evidently, the two decrees were inscribed in the opposite order to that in which they were passed; cf. Coumanoudis and Gofas 1978, 293.

[240] *SEG* XXVIII 103 ll. 14–17: *ἐπαινέσαι δ|ὲ Μοιροκλέα Εὐθυδήμου, ὅτι τοῖς δημόταις ἐ|πιμελεῖται, ὅπως ἂν ἧι πρόσοδος ὡς πλείστη, | καὶ στεφανῶσαι θαλλοῦ στεφάνωι.*

[241] *SEG* XXVIII 103 ll. 12–14: *εἰς δὲ τὸν στέφανον τὸ ἀργ̣|ύριον δοῦναι Φιλοκώμωι ἐναντίον τῶν δημ[ο]|τῶν ἑκατὸν δραχμὰς Μοιροκλέα.* Interestingly, Alipheri 2009, 188, now believes that the offer of 100 drachmas for the crowning of Philokles was part of Moirokles' original bid for the quarries.

[242] *Agora* XIX L13 ll. 32–40.

[243] Cf. Whitehead 1986, 249 n. 121.

[244] *SEG* XXIV 151 ll. 6–9 (with the improved readings by Papazarkadas 2007*a*, 155–6): *ἐπε[ι]δὴ Ξ|ά̣ν̣θιπ̣π̣ός ἐστι ἀνὴρ ἀγαθὸς περ[ὶ] τὰ κοινὰ τὰ Τε|[ιθρασ]ίω[ν], ἐ[ψ]ηφίσθαι Τειθ[ρ]ασίοις μι<σ>θῶσαι Ξ̣|α̣νθί̣[ππω]ι τὸ [χ]ωρίον τὸ Τείθραντι.*

been fully appreciated by scholars.[245] The document in question opens with a requirement to keep a record of the lessees of the κοινά, the communal landholdings, as a means of safeguarding the deme's corporate property (again τὰ κοινά). The persistent occurrence of this term demonstrates that Xanthippos had held some financial office. Consequently, by renting out property to Xanthippos the Teithrasians did honour their adroit administrator, but they probably did so with an eye to the effective management of their landed assets. In fact, some have even suggested that the lease itself was a concealed liturgy.[246] No doubt, the case of Xanthippos is a good manifestation of the fusion of the social and financial spheres to the point that 'corporate lessor and lessee are seen as mutually beneficent'.[247]

Another pattern concerning deme leasing is the very high percentage (76.5 percent) of lessees who were members of the leasing demes.[248] The *Rationes Centesimarum* seem now to confirm this picture at a slightly different level, that of purchases of deme properties, with 68 percent of the buyers being members of the demes whose property they purchased.[249] It is valid to maintain that these statistics reflect the lessees' and purchasers' spirit of beneficence towards their groups, as highlighted above, but some prosopographical observations might help to produce a more nuanced analysis. Amongst the identifiable lessees, Kirrias son of Poseidippos, the tenant of the Θεοδώρειον, stakes out the best claims for prominence by virtue of his trierarchic family.[250] Perhaps a similar background can be seen in the case of Moirokles, the lessee of the Eleusinian quarry: dedicator of

[245] With the exception of Osborne 1988, 288–9, whose translation highlights well the point in question.

[246] Walbank 1991, 156–7; Jones 2004, 119. Rosivach 1994, 140–1, who holds similar views, contends, in addition, that Xanthippos' case indirectly proves that leasing was economically advantageous for the renters.

[247] Osborne 1988, 289.

[248] Andreyev 1974, 43–4; Whitehead 1986, 157–8; Rosivach 1994, 138–140; Cohen 2000, 127 (Osborne 1988, 290 inaccurately asserts that only the lease of the Piraean theatre features lessees from demes other than those which authorize the transactions). My calculations allow for at least one Halimousian renting property from his own deme, though there were obviously many more (cf. Dem. 57.63, ὀφείλοντας πολλοὺς αὐτῶν μισθώσεις τεμενῶν; 'since many of them owed rentals from *temene*').

[249] Lambert 1997*a*, 248–9 with n. 128.

[250] Stemma of the family: *APF* 12132. See also Appendix VII: Catalogue, no. 31.

an offering to Dionysos,[251] arbitrator in 330/29,[252] proposer of honours to the famous financial administrator Xenokles,[253] Moirokles was definitely a busy individual.[254] Whether he is the same as the energetic homonymous politician of the fourth century is contestable, but, if he is, he stands in a category on his own as a first-rate statesman actively participating in his deme's life. A certain trait of his family's activity deserves further probing. His father, Euthydemos, priest of Asklepios,[255] had been involved in the lease of a quarry carried out by the *epimeletai* of the Piraean Asklepieion.[256] It is tempting to read here a dual mentality going through the family's history, namely an expertise concerning quarrying activities combined with a willingness to act as cult patrons. On the other hand, Autokles and Auteas, the father-and-son lessees of the *Φελλεύς* in *IG* II^2 2492, were certainly prominent figures in the affairs of their deme, to judge from the honours bestowed upon the latter for a demotic *choregia*, but no more than that; outside Aixone they were upstarts.[257] If the above individuals can be thought of as having undertaken leases with the aim of rendering service to their local communities, in other cases the benevolence might have been addressed to specific cults. The tenant of the temenos of Nemesis at Hermes, i.e. Hierokles, was almost certainly a member of a distinguished Rhamnousian family with demonstrable interest in the local cults.[258] And Aristophanes, one of the four lessees of the Piraean theatre, features in an inscription from Piraeus, heading a list of contributors to the construction of a

[251] *IG* II^2 2845, l. 1.

[252] So Koumanoudes and Matthaiou 1987, 17–18, 21–2 on *SEG* XXXVII 124 ll. 13–14, but see Aleshire 1991, 245–6.

[253] *IG* II^2 1191 ll. 5–6, with Papagiannopoulos-Palaios 1929, 238.

[254] *LGPN* II, *Μοιροκλῆς* (1); full bibliography in Alipheri 2009, 188 n. 5.

[255] *LGPN* II, *Εὐθύδημος* (26); cf. Aleshire 1991, 244.

[256] *IG* II^2 47 with Coumanoudis and Gofas 1978, 295; Osborne 1985*a*, 104.

[257] Honorific decree: Kyparissis and Peek 1941, 218–19. Its date (*Θεόφραστος ἄρχων*: 340/39 or 313/2), is disputed. *LGPN* II and *PAA* have the early chronology. Kyparissis and Peek 1941, 219; Pickard-Cambridge 1968, 49 with n. 3; Whitehead 1986, 376 all prefer the late one. Note that even as late as 313/2 Auteas would have been the tenant of the Phelleis, unless devoid of it on breach of contract.

[258] He is identified by Petrakos in the prosopographical index of *I.Rhamnous* as the dedicator of a pedestal to the god Aristomachos-Amphiaraos (*I.Rhamnous* 171). A possible agnate of his—Hierokles, son of Hieropoios—dedicated to Nemesis the statue of his mother Aristonoe, who had served as a priestess of the goddess (*I.Rhamnous* 133). For the family tomb of these prominent Rhamnousians see Petrakos 1999, 387–99 and the funerary inscriptions *I.Rhamnous* nos. 270–83.

statue and the repair of a shrine.[259] His recorded activity is, therefore, cult-orientated and restricted to his deme.

But what about lessees of deme properties who were outsiders to the leasing demes? The problem is that they comprise such a small statistical sample that estimations about their motives can hardly be more than guesses. Eukrates of Aphidnai, the lessee of the Kytherian property in *IG* II^2 2496, is completely unknown, as is his father Exekias, the guarantor of the deal. The same is true about Melesias of Lamptrai, one of the two non-Piraean lessees of the Dionysian theatre, as well as about Pythylos of Oa, the only non-demesmen in the list of lessees of Teithrasian landholdings *SEG* XXIV 152. However, it is noteworthy that the latter appears to have leased a property along with a member of Teithras, the only instance of joint tenancy in the Teithrasian record.[260] It is tempting to postulate here that some family interrelationship underlies this transaction, with Pythylos breaking the deme barrier by means of his acquaintance to Antias. Family bonds seem to have played a major role in land transactions, as can be seen in the aforementioned case of Autokles and Auteas. A rather conjectural case can be made about the other non-Piraean individual of *Agora* XIX L13, Arethousios, son of Aristoleos, of Pelex. The extreme rareness of his name makes it possible that he is the same Arethousios as the defendant of the 53rd Demosthenic speech,[261] but this is rather irrelevant here. I argued above, and I have also argued elsewhere, that in the dedication *IG* II^2 2329 there are at least two father-and-son pairs, one of which is Aristophanes, a lessee of the theatre at Mounychia, and his father Smikythos. The latter's name is followed by a certain Aristoleos and,

[259] *IG* II^2 2329 l. 4. Smikythos (l. 10) may be Aristophanes' father (but this cannot be the case if I am right about the demotic of this man, as *per* Papazarkadas 2004–9 [2010], 104); cf. *LGPN* II, *Σμίκυθος* (55). The cult is unidentifiable, but one wonders whether the divinity honoured was Dionysos, in which case Aristophanes' two attested contributions would have had a very specific target. At any rate, as I argue elsewhere, the historical context of *IG* II^2 2329 might have been Lykourgan (Papazarkadas 2004–9 [2010], 104–5, no. 8).

[260] Pythylos of Oa renting property with Antias of Teithras: *SEG* XXIV 152 ll. 2–4, with Papazarkadas 2007*a*, 155-60, where I raise the alternative possibility that their cooperation might have been triggered by the necessities of animal transhumance. Jones 2004, 119–20, twice seems bemused by the origin of the lessee from Oe (but our deme is Oa, not Oe; the mistake is repeated by Krasilnikoff 2008, 38).

[261] So Traill in *PAA* 160750, 160755.

though his demotic is lost, I consider it very likely that he can be identified with the father of Arethousios.[262] If so, then we would have a case of two generations of families participating jointly in two different projects. Cultic motivations might have inspired purchasers of lands owned by demes others than theirs. The buyer of a Sphettian landholding, Demokedes of Aphidnai (F6B, 37–9), is known from a dedication to Hermes at Sphettos (*IG* II^2 4628) and this can hardly be a coincidence.[263] Of course such considerations would apply to both parties of the transactions, sellers and purchasers alike. In other words, Demokedes might have sought to strengthen his pre-existing relationship with the locality in question by acquiring land in it, but in return the Sphettians would have preferred a purchaser with demonstrable interest in their community to any random outsider.

All in all, *philotimia*, either towards demes or towards cults, or both, seems to have been an important factor underlying land transactions both as concerns lessees and purchasers.[264] With regard to the latter, Lambert has now offered an extensive prosopographical analysis which provides more than a hint about their liturgical ethos and their financial and social prominence.[265] I would single out one specific individual, Euthykrates, son of Drakontides, buyer of an eschatia at Aphidna (F7B, 8), a prominent figure in Athenian politics during the 330s and 320s, but, more significantly, a lessee of a landholding belonging to the Eleusinian goddesses in 331/0.[266] In his case how is one to distinguish a beneficial attitude from profiteering investment on landed interests? But with this remark we are once more back to the realm of economy. Pursuit of profit was not incongruous with the idea of rendering service to one's political or religious association, in fact these were the two sides of a ceaselessly oscillating equation.

262 The name is extremely rare in Attic prosopography so as to render the identification very likely. *LGPN* II has three entries.

263 Lambert 1997*a*, 155.

264 For the concept of *philotimia* in the context of demes see Whitehead 1983; 1986, 241–52; Rosivach 1994, 129–131, 141; Jones 2004, 55–59. See also the good discussion by Wilson 2000, 144–97, on *philotimia* in relation to the institution of choregia.

265 Lambert 1997*a*, 243–50 drawing on his prosopographical observations at pp. 149–82.

266 See Appendix VII: Catalogue, no. 27.

viii. The territorial aspect of the Attic demes

No longer can one postpone addressing the delicate topic of the constitutional versus the territorial deme. The debate can be roughly summarized as follows. In 1963 David Lewis published a short, but influential, article where he questioned contemporary scholarly orthodoxy that Cleisthenes perceived the division of the Attic territory into 139 or so demes as a geographical venture.[267] Shortly afterwards Thompson published an even more polemical piece in which he underplayed the importance of the 'geographical deme', though, it has to be said, he did not entirely dismiss it.[268] Nowadays, no one genuinely believes that demes lacked territoriality.[269] I do not intend to enter this debate in depth, which in its entirety lies beyond the scope of this monograph, but merely to probe into the palpable aspects of demes' territoriality. One problem has to be highlighted in advance: The way the relevant discussion has been conducted so far has been undermined by scholars' unconscious tendency to treat the institution of demes synchronically, as if demes did not evolve over time, and, moreover, by their inclination to fuse two different topics, the process by which Cleisthenes set up demes and the patent territorial aspect of demes in the fourth century from which most of our evidence comes. For all these reasons the concept of deme territoriality needs some clarification.

The work of the Copenhagen Polis Centre during the last decade or so has done much to increase our understanding of the concept of the ancient polis. Their results can be briefly, and necessarily elliptically, summarized as follows. For a community to be classified as a polis three criteria must be met: (1) the people, (2) the territory (*χώρα*), and (3) the administration.[270] Now if the universal belief that demes imitated in effect the organization of the polis (Athens in our case) is true, we would expect Attic demes to have had a recognizable territory, a *chora*. Can this idea stand the scrutiny of the extant evidence? There is one inscription which has been used—and dare one say, abused—as evidence in support of this, namely *IG* II^2 2623, which has been supplemented as *ὅρος Π*[*ει*]|*ραέων* [*χώ*|*ρ*]*ας*

[267] Lewis 1963.
[268] Thompson 1971.
[269] For a recent review of the relevant scholarship see Jones 1999, 56–7.
[270] Hansen 1998, 51–4.

(boundary stone of the territory of the Piraeans).[271] Notwithstanding that this would be, at any rate, a *unicum*, Lambert has now plausibly argued that one could equally well supplement ὅρος Π̣|ε̣ιραέων | [οἰκί]ας, which by virtue of extant parallels should be preferred.[272] So, other evidence should be adduced in the pursuit of the elusive notion.

Prominent amongst alleged 'indubitable' proofs of the demes' territoriality stand the numerous boundary stones and especially the so-called rupestral *horoi* which are found in increasing numbers all over Attica.[273] I have put the characterization 'indubitable' into inverted commas, for a fierce debate has been raging since the first discoveries of rock-cut *horoi* as to their exact nature. Demarcation of private properties and delineation of trittyes-territories have been suggested as reasons behind the engraving of rupestral *horoi*, but the general consensus is now that they marked the precise boundaries of individual demes.[274] A lot of them, it has been observed, mark conspicuous geographical elements such as ridges, valleys, hills,[275] in brief the kind of topographical features that tend to serve as boundary markers between localities even today, as anyone acquainted with the realities of modern Greek villages knows. Despite the protestation of Jones, that there is contradictory overlap of functions here, this is, indeed, a good indicator that rupestral *horoi* marked deme boundaries. A few efforts have been made to link the carving of some of these *horoi* to the administrative reorganization of the Attic demes with the introduction of the two Macedonian tribes by Demetrios the

[271] Cf. Whitehead 1986, 28–9. Jones 1999, 59 proposed ὅρος Π[ει]ραέων | χ̣ᾶς, but this Doric form has surely no place in Attica, and has to be rejected.

[272] Lambert 2004 (see *SEG* LIV 240), dismissing his earlier suggestion (Lambert 1997a, 192 n. 1) that the inscription should be read as ὅρος Π[ει]|ραέων [ἀγ|ορ]ᾶς.

[273] For rupestral *horoi* ('Felsinschriften' in German) see Goette 1994, 120–30. It is common knowledge in academic circles that Langdon has found dozens of rupestral inscriptions (most of them not *horoi*), but his discoveries still await full publication. For some teasers see Langdon 2005 (reported in *SEG* LV 83-5), where he points out that the said inscriptions are to be found in what appears to be grazing land.

[274] So Langdon 1985*a*, 9–10; Stanton 1994*a*, 222; Lohmann 1994, 282–90; Stanton 1996, 353–5; Langdon 1999, 494; Salliora-Oikonomakou 2001 [2003], 161–3. Note here, that, as already observed, many anonymous *horoi* cached in various archaeological storerooms all over Attica with no indication of provenance might have marked deme boundaries.

[275] See for instance, the notorious rupestral *horoi* discovered at the hill of Zagani in Mesogaia (Steinhauer 2001*a*, 33–4, with *SEG* LI 154).

Besieger in 307/6 and the subsequent legal complexities.[276] However, those scholars who contend that no single occasion can be adduced for the inception of rupestral *horoi* seem to be correct. Their opinion needs some modification, however. In a concise theoretical analysis, Ober rightly emphasized the uncertainty of interpreting succinct documents like *horoi* when they lack explicit denotations.[277] It is true that most of the *horoi* under consideration date to the fourth century at the earliest, but instead of opting for one *terminus*, one had better scan the wider circumstantial frame and, within that, seek various occasions that might have given rise to the need for defining deme boundaries. In that respect, a wide range of possibilities for the ascription of rupestral *horoi* within historical termini can arise. The *Rationes Centesimarum*, for instance, with the Athenian polis inducing, if not coercing, the demes to alienate some of their landed assets, might represent such a case. The sporadic acquisition of landed properties by demes outside their territories in the course of the fourth century as the side-effect of a peculiar security system can constitute another such case. One could add the increasing preoccupation of Athens with the taxation system of *eisphora*, which was levied, at least down to 378, via the demes.[278]

Some markers, however, go back to the fifth century, perhaps even to the time of Cleisthenes. Thus inscriptions found in the recent excavations of Acharnai and the adjacent demes might be ascribed to technical works, such as the extensive water system.[279] And one of the earliest rupestral *horoi*, long thought to designate a shrine of Zeus, has now been convincingly shown to delimit property belonging to the deme Melite. In the same thesis, Lalonde gave a boost to the theorem of deme territoriality by demonstrating that not only the demes of the Attic countryside, but also the big urban municipalities, such as Melite and Kollytos, had very specific dimensions. Deme

[276] This is the ingenious interpretation by Traill 1982, 162–8 of six *horoi* reading ὅρ(ο)ς *Π*(*αραλίας καὶ*) *Μ*(*εσογαίας*) presumably separating the two homonymous demes of two different trittyes (contra Stanton 1994*a*, 221).

[277] Ober 1995; cf. Ober 2006.

[278] Davies 1981, 143–50.

[279] See Platonos-Yiota 2004, 427 (=*SEG* LIV 81), and especially *SEG* L 88, with Platonos-Yiota 2004, 91, 292 (cf. *SEG* LIV 80, where following the excavator's interpretation I tentatively suggested a reference to the Acharnian ἐνναία, 'fountain' or 'spring').

boundaries occasionally gave rise to confusion, but also generated deme pride and evertually fostered a distinct deme identity.[280]

Other evidence for deme territoriality can be briefly mentioned here. The metic formula 'οἰκῶν ἐν + deme name', and the demarchs' obligation to bury unwanted corpses lying within the confines of their demes have both been adduced by Lalonde.[281] Many inscriptions, especially the *poletai* records, contain references to properties specified by virtue of the demes where they were situated.[282] This argument is most compelling. A related issue is the nomenclature of some demes with its striking territorial connotations.[283] But by far the most assertive and hitherto undetected evidence in favour of demes' territoriality can be found in a series of third-century Rhamnousian inscriptions which bestow honours upon various individuals, mainly military personnel, for having competently protected the territory of the deme (χώρα).[284] One last point may reinforce the remarks made above. It has already been noted more than once that *eschatiai* feature heavily in the extant deme record. Now *eschatiai* are often described by lexicographers as being near frontiers, a fact that has perplexed modern scholars, since outlying estates are frequently found in inland demes, far away from the actual frontier of Attica. We should not criticize the lexicographers too lightly: given the frequently hilly location of *eschatiai* as well as the position held here, namely that hills often marked the territorial limits of individuals demes, the

[280] Lalonde 2006*b*.

[281] Lalonde 2006*a*, 96–7; for the metic formulas see also Niku 2007, 22–3.

[282] Langdon 1985*a*, 7–8; Lohmann 1994, 287; Jones 1999, 64.

[283] Cf. Arist. [*Ath. Pol.*] 21.5: *προσηγόρευε δὲ τῶν δήμων τοὺς μὲν ἀπὸ τῶν τόπων, τοὺς δὲ ἀπὸ τῶν κτισάντων*, with Rhodes 1993, 257–8.

[284] The examples are abundant (one can trace them using the index in *I.Rhamnous*, s.v. χώρα), but the decree in honour of Epichares, general during the Chremonidean war, who protected the cultivation, and secured the harvesting, of the crops by the Rhamnousian farmers, can be singled out (*I.Rhamnous* 3, ll. 8–12: *καὶ τὸν σῖτ[ον καὶ τ]οὺς ξυλίνους καρποὺς μέχρι τριάκοντα σταδίων συνεκόμισεν | τοῦ [στ]ρατο[πέδου ὄν]τος [ἐν τῆι] χώραι, καταστησάμενος κρυπτοὺς ἐπὶ τὰς σκο*ᵛ|*[πὰς, παρ]ε̣[φε]δρεύων αὐτὸς μετὰ τῶν στρατιωτῶν, ὅπως ἀσφαλῶς γένηται ἡ*ᵛ | *[συγκομιδὴ τῶν κ]αρπῶν τοῖς γεωργοῖς· τέτμηκεν δὲ καὶ τὰς ἀμπέλους ἐφ' ὅσον | [κυριεύω]ν ἦν τῆς χώρας*, with the new readings by Steinhauer 2009). Some scholars believe that Epichares was *στρατηγὸς ἐπὶ τὴν χώραν* (Kralli 2006) but in the extract above *χώρα* clearly refers to the hinterland of Rhamnous; cf. Oliver 2007, 138–9, 152–3. In his comprehensive study Couvenhes 1999, rightly points out that the Hellenistic era saw a preoccupation with the defence of the 'territoires' (plural) of Attica.

eschatiai could indeed be liminal in the sense of coinciding with the borderline of demes.

ix. Epilogue

Simply stating that individual demes had recognizable territories does not take us far in relation to deme landed assets. More subtly put, it is one thing to acknowledge that private landholdings lay within the territory of one deme, with whatever consequences this might have had in terms of administration, taxation, or *similia*, and another thing to claim that a deme owned and managed real property. Undoubtedly a deme's *chora* contained both types of property. Private landholdings are not going to preoccupy us here. Deme-property is, however, an intricate problem. From the preceding discussion it will have become obvious that two subcategories of real property controlled by demes can be roughly discerned: realty nominally belonging to divinities worshipped in the framework of demes and 'secular' property with no religious connotations whatsoever. It is the latter class that arguably features in the *Rationes Centesimarum*, since for the demes to dispose of their *temene* would mean depriving their sanctuaries of a rudimentary source of funding. The most recent editor of the *hekatoste*-inscriptions claimed that the properties there recorded did not include revenue-yielding lands, that is lands that could otherwise have been leased out, but marginal, unowned properties or even commonly held ones. In the light of the high proportion of outlying estates (ἐσχατιαί), this inference seems basically right. It is secondarily sustained by other internal evidence like the landholdings and outlying estates designated as *demosiai* (δημόσιαι). Lambert has contended that, despite deme-officials acting here as agents of realty sales and the etymological relationship between the adjective δημόσιος and the noun δῆμος, the former cannot refer to deme properties: the δημόσιαι at Poros were not owned by the deme.[285] My conviction is that we can arrive at a compromise of the conflicting views: the *Rationes Centesimarum* included both commonly held

[285] F7 A ll. 9–18: *ẹ̓σχατιὰ ἐν Πόρωι̣ τὸ δ[ημόσια?] | καλούμενον vac. | [ὠ]ṿη Χ̣αιρέδημος Χάρητο[ς - -] | ἕτερον χωρίον ἐν Π[όρωι τὸ δημό]|σια καλούμενον vac. | ὠνη Πιστίας Πιστίου Π[- -] | ἑτέρα ἐσχατιὰ ἐν Βή[σαι] | ὠνη Κλεομέδων Λέοντος Α/ [- -] | ἑτέρα ἐσχατιὰ ἐν Πόρω̣[ι τὸ δη]|μόσιαι ἅλωι καλούμε[νον]*, with Lambert 1997*a*, 208–9.

properties of the type identified by Lambert *and* secular tillable lands belonging to demes. One could add to these categories properties that would have been confiscated from individuals by the deme authorities in charge. Thus, a *poletai* record contains a reference to an οἰκόπεδον belonging to Melite, a property which might have come under the administration of the deme as a result of forfeiture.[286]

The analysis above appears to assert the notion of deme territoriality, but there still remains an array of interrelated problems. One deserves to be singled out, albeit briefly: how could a deme have kept track of its own landholdings? The concept of land cadastres has been variably ignored or repudiated, but the discussion has been obscured by a certain misunderstanding, namely that those engaged in it tend to think in terms of a centralized land archive. Classical Athens almost certainly did not possess such an administrative tool, but Faraguna has recently made a strong case in support of the existence of deme land-records.[287] Even if such records did not exist at the time of the foundation of the demes, the acquisition and subsequent accumulation of new deme lands, especially those lying outside a deme's territory, would have made cadastres a desirable, if not indispensable, tool.

At any rate, in the early Hellenistic period deme documents start becoming increasingly rare up to the point of almost total disappearance towards the end of the third century.[288] This tendency applies to those texts dealing with land administration too. That a crisis underlies this pattern can now be shown by archaeological land surveys. Whereas the fifth and fourth centuries are marked by a boom in the number of inhabited sites all over the Attic countryside, the third century sees a drastic and dramatic decline—in most cases a complete disappearance—of previously residential findspots, not to be resettled till the Roman era.[289] The pattern is easily observable at all levels of the Athenian polis, although it is not uniform. The vast plain of Mesogaia continued to be cultivated, for instance, but marginal lands, the primary indicator of agricultural intensification in the

[286] *Agora* XIX P17 l. 16: *καὶ οἰκόπεδον Μελιτέων.*

[287] Faraguna 1997 (cf. Faraguna 2000).

[288] Whitehead 1986, 41; Jones 1999, 143–50.

[289] Lohmann 1993, *passim*, esp. 248; Lohmann 1995, esp. 530–3; Cosmopoulos 2001, 74–9.

fourth century, were almost totally abandoned. A deteriorating situation of almost constant war undoubtedly played a critical role,[290] but there were probably further aggravating factors that will be investigated in the concluding chapter of this book.

[290] For all these see now Oliver 2007, esp. 100–10.

4

The Non-Constitutional Associations of Athens as Administrators of Realty

1. THE REAL PROPERTY OF THE ATTIC PHRATRIES

i. Types of phratric realty

The phratries, hereditary groups of a restricted, yet recognizable, territorial nature, which for the better part of the Classical period controlled access to citizenship, have recently resurfaced in studies of Athenian political organization after years of serious neglect, mainly thanks to the efforts of the 'anglophone' historical school.[1] The more specific theme of phratric property has also received its fair share of attention,[2] but for the sake of completeness a résumé of the relevant scholarship will be offered here. There is one category of realty owned by phratries of which we have abundant evidence, namely phratric sanctuaries. Four markers designating such sacred establishments have been found,[3] and I think there are good reasons for adding a fifth one to this list.[4] They all give testimony to the dual ownership of

[1] Hedrick 1990; Lambert 1993; Parker 1996, 104–8; Jones 1999, 195–220.

[2] Lambert 1993, 191–203 is the fundamental treatment.

[3] Lambert 1993, T2 = *IG* II[2] 4974 (Apollo Hebdomeios of the Achniadai); T6 = *Agora* XIX H9 (Kephisos of the phratry Gleontis); T11 = *IG* II[2] 4973 (Apollo Patroos of the Therrikleidai); T13 = *IG* I[3] 1057 (Zeus Xenios of the phratry Thymaitis); cf. Lambert 1993, 192 (NB these numbers, taken from Lambert 1993, and his classification of the phratric documents, will be used throughout this chapter).

[4] Namely the enigmatic T1 (*IG* II[2] 2621), a marker of property of 'uncertain nature' according to Lambert, which comes from the same findspot as T2 and which pertains to property owned by the same phratry, i.e. Achniadai. Now, T1 has an erasure in lines 4–6, from which one can read only *H*⟦. . .⟧*O* (l. 4). It would be tempting to restore h⟦εβδ⟧ο|⟦μείο⟧ (the specific epithet of Apollo occurring in T2) using the Attic

the shrines in question: they belonged to specific divinities, but they were administered by the human agents that phratries *qua* collective subjects were. On the other hand, markers that only refer to the two most prominent divinities worshipped by phratries, namely Zeus Phratrios and Athena Phratria (especially when they lack any further designations), probably record property administered by the central government and not by individual phratries and, therefore, should not occupy us in the course of this study.[5]

Two boundary stones are of a slightly different kind, in that they delineate what appears to be secular property, namely houses (*οἰκίαι*).[6] These edifices have been interpreted as meeting venues for the phratries that owned them,[7] or even, on the obvious parallel of the house (*οἶκος*) of the Chian phratry of the Klytidai, as quasi-shrines.[8] Another *οἰκία*—probably an agricultural shed, rather than a proper residence—lay in the estate of the phratry Dyaleis and was expected to be repaired and properly maintained by the lessee of the

alphabet. As T1 dates to the early 4th cent., it can be plausibly inferred that the erased text had initially been written in pre-Euclidean Attic script. Still, one cannot see the reasons for the erasure. Lambert 1993, 281 tentatively suggested that the property in question had come into the possession of the Achniadai as a result of default on a debt, and that, subsequently, a new text was inscribed to declare the new owner unequivocally. This is not compelling, since the examples cited by him are all mortgage *horoi* (later reused as such), not common boundary stones.

[5] Thus Jones 1999, 200–11, contra Hedrick 1988, 193–4, and 1991, 241–8, who is prone to see most of the phratric documents discovered in the area of the Agora as evidence of activity of individual phratries. Incidentally, T25 (*IG* II^2 4975), *ἱερὰ Διὸς | Φρατρίο | καὶ Ἀθηνᾶ[ς]*, should be excluded from the list of boundary stones (contra Hedrick 1988, 193 and Lambert 1993, 359); the inscription was incised on a marble tile, but nothing suggests that this was done on a second use. The word *ἱερά* should probably be construed as a feminine nominative singular form, not a plural neuter, modifying an assumed *κεραμίς* (which can refer to marble tiles as well; cf. LSJ^9 s.v. *κεραμίς*, citing *IG* II^2 1622 B 21–2 and 25–6). For such sacred tiles see Wace 1905–6, 348–9 and 1906–7, 38–9 (Sparta, but citing examples from other areas); Thompson and Wycherley 1972, 76 n. 217, a cover tile inscribed *IEP*[*A*] found in the South Stoa I.

[6] T22 (*IG* II^2 2622): *ὅρο[ς] | οἰκία[ς] | φρατέρ[ων]*; *SEG* XLVI 229: *ὅρο[ς] | οἰκία[ς]|φρα[τρία]|ς Ἰω[νιδῶν]*, with Lambert 1996, 79–81.

[7] So Guarducci 1937, 53; Hedrick 1991, 255–6; Lambert 1996, 80; Jones 1999, 203.

[8] House of the Klytidai: *LSCG* no. 118 (*Syll.*^{3} 987), esp. ll. 2–4: *[ἐν τῶ]ι τεμένει [τῶν Κ|λ]υτιδῶν [ο]ἶκον τεμένιον ἱερὸν οἰ[κ|ο]δομήσασθαι*, which shows that this *oikos* was a sacred building. I think that, despite the different cases that Athens and Chios present, the two Athenian phratric *oikiai* have a good chance of being similar to that of the Chian Klytidai. Note, furthermore, the phratric sub-group (or phratry) called House of Dekeleieis; cf. Hedrick 1990, 48; Lambert 1993, 104–5.

land.[9] There is a chance that those premises might have been leased out by the phratric owners with the aim of raising income, though independent confirmation of this hypothesis is lacking.[10] Two recently published inscriptions from Rhamnous suggest another way by which phratries might have acquired possession of houses. In the hypothecation *horoi* in question, a phratry, or a phratric sub-group, appears to lend money on security in the form of a house, and it is a fair inference that upon the debtor's default the ownership of the buildings would have been transferred to the phratry.[11] Such a way of acquiring property was always a possibility, and indeed documents recording phratries as crediting organizations are not unusual,[12] although it has recently been questioned whether the actual lenders were the phratries proper or some unofficial subdivisions of them.[13] Finally, one has to mention the enigmatic boundary stone of a property belonging to the phratry Medontidai, either an agora or,

[9] T5 (*IG* II[2] 1241), ll. 17–18: *ἐπ[ι]σκευάζειν δ|ὲ τὴν οἰκίαν Διόδωρον* (Let Diodoros repair the house); ll. 32–3: *μηδὲ τὴν οἰκίαν καθ̣[ε]|λεῖν* (. . . nor shall he be permitted to demolish the house), with Lambert 1993, 305.

[10] For an interpretation of *oikiai* in agricultural leases as farmstead residences see Jones 2000 contra Osborne 1985*c*, 122–7 (agricultural amenities).

[11] *I.Rhamnous* 187 ll. 2–4: *ὅρος οἰκίας πεπραμέ|νης ἐπὶ λύσει φράτερ|σι τοῖς μετὰ Ἀντιφίλο*; *SEG* LI 164 ll. 1–3: *ὅρος οἰκίας|πεπρ[α]μένης ἐπὶ λύσει φράτερσι τοῖς με|τ̣ὰ̣ [Ἀντι]φίλου*. Both texts translate as 'Boundary stone of a house sold subject to redemption to the phrateres with Antiphilos'.

[12] See RO 36 (*Agora* XIX P5), ll. 16–25: *Κιχωνί|δης Διογείτονος Γαργήτ καὶ κοινὸν φρατέρων Με|δοντιδῶν ἐνεπησκήψατο ἐνοφείλεσθαι ἑαυτῶι κ|αὶ τοῖς φράτερσι ἐν τῆι οἰκίαι τῆι Ἀλωπεκῆσι Η δ|ραχμάς, ἣν ἀπέγραψεν Θεόμνηστος Ἰωνί Θεοσέβος | εἶναι Ξυπετα ᾗι γείτων βορρᾶ ἡ ὁδὸς ἡ ἐς τὸ Δαιδά|λε<ι>ον φέρουσα καὶ τὸ Δαιδάλειον, νοτόθεν Φίλιππ|ος Ἀγρυλῆ, ἀποδομένο ἐμο<ὶ> καὶ τοῖς φράτερσιν τὴ|ν οἰκίαν ταύτην Θεοφίλου Ξυπε : τô πατρὸς τοῦ Θεο|σέβος· ἔδοξεν ἐνοφείλεσθαι* (Kichonides son of Diogeiton of Gargettos and the group of the phrateres of the Medontidai put in a prior claim that there was a debt of 100 drachmas to himself and the members of the phratry on the house of Alopeke which Theomnestos of Ionidai registered as public property, on the grounds that it was the property of Theosebes of Xypete of which the neighbours were, on the north, the road leading to the sanctuary of Daedalus and the sanctuary of Daedalus, and, on the south, Philippos of Agryle, Theophilos of Xypete the father of Theosebes having sold this house to me and to the members of the phratry), with Finley 1952*b*, 479–80; *IG* II[2] 2723 (T21): *ὅρος χωρίου | πεπραμένου | ἐπὶ λύσει Κηφι|σοδώρωι Λευκον | Χ𐅅 καὶ φράτερ|σι τοῖς μετὰ Ἐρα|τοστράτο Ἀνα|φλυ ΗΗ καὶ Γλ[α]|υκίδαις 𐅅Η κ[αὶ] | Ἐπικλείδαις | Η𐅄 καὶ φράτερ|σι τοῖς μετὰ Νί[κ]|ωνος Ἀναφλ Η*, with Premerstein 1910, 108–16; Andrewes 1961, 11; Lambert 1993, 349–50; *I.Rhamnous* 186 ll. 2–4: *ὅρος χωρίου πεπραμένου | ἐπὶ λύσηι φράτερσι τοῖς μετ᾽ Ἀντι|φίλο ΗΗ*; *I.Rhamnous* 187 and *SEG* LI 164 (for which see previous note).

[13] Lambert 1993, 78–9.

more vaguely, an area controlled by the association.[14] It seems that, on the parallel of the agora of the *genos* Salaminioi, the first interpretation should be preferred, although, even then, it is unclear whether that would have been a venue for phratric gatherings or merely a commercial market. Such then is the evidence about realty owned by phratries: shrines, houses, and other facilities, to which categories one can add landholdings such as those recorded in *IG* II^2 1241 and in the *Rationes Centesimarum*.[15] It remains now to investigate the exact modes of the exploitation of such properties.

ii. Exploitation of phratric realty

Despite the ample amount of evidence regarding property owned by phratries, it is striking that, contrary to the case of other corporate groups, only one inscribed lease issued by a phratry has survived, namely *IG* II^2 1241.[16] The document has received erudite scrutiny from generations of historians, so here only a synopsis is offered with

[14] *IG* I^3 1062 (T7): h*όρο[ς χό]|ρας vel [ἀγο]ρᾶς Μεδ[ον]|τ[ι]δôν*, with Lambert 1993, 310 (cf. Jones 1999, 204–5). The restoration [*φράτ*]|*ρας* presupposes a technical sense of locality for a phratry unparalleled in our evidence (unless we consider the Byzantine lemma which describes a *phratrion*, but not a *phratra*, as a place; Steph. Byz. s.v. *φρατρία·* . . . *λέγεται καὶ φράτριον τόπος ἐν ᾧ οἱ τῆς αὐτῆς φρατρίας συνάγονται*, but see Lambert 1993, 194 n. 26). Similar difficulties apply to the supplement [*χό*]|*ρας*.

[15] Outside Attica, phratries owning real property include the Chian Klytidai (see Behrend 1990), if they were actually a phratry and not a tribe or a *genos*, and an unnamed Thessalian phratry hypothesized on the evidence of the cadastre *SEG* XXVI 676 ll. 2–3: [*ὁ δεῖνα* - - -]|*νος Μνασιμάχειος φρατρικὰ πέλεθρα* [*ἕ*]*ξε* etc.; cf. *BE* 1951, no. 125; Salviat and Vatin 1974, 252. Note also the notorious passage in Arist. [*Oec.*] II, 1346^{b}13–20: *Βυζάντιοι δεηθέντες χρημάτων τὰ τεμένη τὰ δημόσια ἀπέδοντο, τὰ μὲν κάρπιμα χρόνον τινά, τὰ δὲ ἄκαρπα ἀεννάως· τά τε θιασωτικὰ καὶ τὰ πατριωτικὰ ὡσαύτως* etc. (When the Byzantians were in need of funds they sold the *temene* that were administered by the polis; those under crops, for a term of years, and those uncultivated, in perpetuity. Likewise, they sold *temene* administered by thiasoi and (*temene*) *patriotika*), where the adjective *πατριωτικά* probably designates phratric landholdings. See, for instance, Van Groningen 1933, 55–6, and the translation by Wartelle 1968. Migeotte 2006*a*, 192, thinks that *πατριωτικά* refers to 'subdivisions de la cité'.

[16] It is certainly striking that not a single phratric shrine features as an object of leasing anywhere in our record (contrast, for instance, the evidence presented below concerning orgeonic sanctuaries). Regarding *IG* II^2 1241, I have made use of the text T5 as printed by Lambert 1993, 299–300, who, in turn, follows the readings by Hedrick 1984 (non vidi). The text with commentary is now reproduced by Vivliodetis 2005 [2007], 43–6, no. E2.

the odd comment on points that have been missed by previous scholars. Sakkne (*Σακκνή*), the landholding in question, was leased out by the phratry of the Dyaleis at an annual rent of 600 drachmas for a period of ten years. The location of Sakkne is not known, but the shrine of Zeus Phratrios recently discovered at Merenda is almost certainly the cultic centre of the Dyaleis;[17] Sakkne would not have been located very far away. At any rate, the leasing agents were the two phratriarchs, the paramount—presumably annual—magistrates of the Dyaleis.[18] They, or rather their successors, were also envisaged as the collectors of the rental, which was to be paid in two equal instalments in Boedromion and Elaphebolion respectively.[19] The choice of the former month is easy to interpret. It directly precedes Pyanepsion, when the phratry's expenditure could be expected to reach a peak because of the celebration of the Apatouria, and so, collection at this time would fit the financial needs of the Dyaleis quite well. There may be a logical explanation for the choice of Elaphebolion as well. Contrary to the usual practice, the lease was to come into effect in Mounichion of 300/299, and, as Lambert observed, this probably presupposes a phratry meeting other than that of Pyanepsion during the Apatouria.[20] It is tempting to postulate here a regular assembly held by the Dyaleis in Elaphebolion, the month preceding Mounichion, in which the decision was taken for the enactment of the lease to commence as soon as possible, hence in Mounichion, and for the future meetings held in the same month (Elaphebolion) to be the payment occasions for the second instalment of the rental.

[17] The results of the excavation have not been fully published yet; for a preliminary report see Sklavos 2003. The identification of the shrine was based on the late Classical priestly dedication *SEG* LIII 210: *Ξενοφῶν ἱερεὺς ἀνέθηκε παῖς Φιλοξένο | μνημεῖον αὐτοῦ κἀμὲ Φρατρίωι Διί*. Given that all the individuals named in *IG* II^2 1241 were Myrrhinousians (ll. 5–7: *ο[ἱ] φρατρίαρχοι Κα[λλ]|ικλῆς Ἀριστείδου Μυρρινούσιος κα[ὶ Δ]|ιοπείθης Διοφάντου Μυρρινούσιος*; ll. 12–13: *Διοδώρωι Κανθάρ[ο]υ Μυρρι|νουσίωι*; cf. Hignett 1952, 57; Roussel 1976, 141), and that the inscribed lease itself was discovered in Merenda (site of ancient Myrrhinous), we can deduce with certainty that the newly discovered sanctuary was the cultic centre of the Dyaleis.

[18] For their duties see Lambert 1993, 225–33.

[19] T5 (*IG* II^2 1241), ll. 25–9: *ἀποδιδόναι δὲ τῆς μ[ι]σθώσεως τὴν μ|[ὲ]ν ἡμίσειαν μηνὸς Βοηδρομιῶνος*^{v} *HHH*, | *τὴν δ' ἡμίσειαν μηνὸς Ἐλαφηβολιῶνος* [^{v} | *H*]*HH τοῖς φρατριάρχοι[ς] Δυαλέων τοῖς ἀ|[ε]ὶ φρατριαρχοῦσιν* (cf. Behrend 1970, 93).

[20] T5 (*IG* II^2 1241), ll. 29–30: *ἄ[ρ]χει δὲ τῆς μισθώσε|ως ὁ ἐπὶ Ἡγεμάχο Μουνιχιών* (the lease commences in Mounichion in the year of Hegemachos), with Lambert 1993, 305. For the Apatouria held in Pyanepsion see Parker 2005, 458–61.

So, leasing might have been an infrequent option for phratries seeking to make good use of their landed assets. Alienation constituted an alternative. Indeed, in the *Rationes Centesimarum* at least one phratry, albeit an unidentified one, is attested as disposing of part of its property. Predictably, the transaction was carried out by the phratriarch.[21] The same is not true of two other selling groups, the Oikatai and the Apheidantidai, which have been tentatively identified with phratries. In their case the selling agents are styled *epimeletai*, something that does not pose unsurpassable difficulties, since we do know of *epimeletai* in at least one other phratry context.[22] At any rate, in the one genuine phratric instance, the alienated property was an outlying estate (ἐσχατιά), and it has been reasonably argued that phratries would not have sold their core properties, namely the shrines/altars around which their cult revolved.[23]

How extensive alienation of phratric lands might have been cannot be established. It is certainly interesting that the lease of Dyaleis allowed the lessee to acquire full ownership of Sakkne upon payment of a lump sum of 5000 drachmas, an unprecedented arrangement in the history of Athenian land transactions.[24] The high assessment rate of the rental of Sakkne, 12 per cent, as well as the predilection for cash might indicate something about phratries' financial mentality towards the end of the fourth century. Note that the early third-century phratric decree honouring two individuals for their contributions

[21] Lambert 1997*a*, F15 ll. 4–6: [. . . .c.4–8. . . .]ων φρα[τρ]ία[ρχος] | [. . .c.6–7. . .]s Ἀρι̣στω[ν - - - | ἀπέδοτο] ἐσχατιά[ν - - -].

[22] Oikatai: Lambert 1997*a*, F16A ll. 15–17: *Οἰκατῶν ἐπιμελητὴς Στράτων | Μνησιφάνους Κοθωκίδης | ἀπέδοτο χωρίον* etc.; Apheidantidai: F16A ll. 19–21: *Ἀφειδαντιδῶν ἐπιμελητὴς | Λεόντιος Καλλιάδους Ἐπικηφίσιος | ἀπέδοτο χωρίον* etc., both with Lambert 1997*a*, 205. For phratric *epimeletai* see T12 (Therrikleidai) ll. 5–6: [ἑλέσθαι] | *δὲ καὶ ἐπιμελητάς*, with Walbank 1982, 50; Hedrick 1983, 300; Lambert 1993, 235, 363.

[23] Lambert 1997*a*, 228–9.

[24] T5 (*IG* II^2 1241), ll. 42–7: [ἐὰ]ν δὲ βούληται ἐν τοῖς δέκα ἔτεσιν Διόδω||[ρ]ο̣ς ἢ οἱ κληρονόμοι αὐτοῦ, καταβαλόντ̣||[ων] Δυαλεῦσιν 𐅆 δραχμάς, καὶ ἐάν τιν[α] μί|σθ̣ωσιν προσοφείλ[ω]σιν, ἀποδ[ό]σθ̣[ω]σα̣ν α||[ὐ]τοῖς οἱ φρατρίαρχοι καὶ Δυαλεῖς τὸ χ||[ωρί]ον (If Diodoros or his heirs so wish within the ten years, let them pay down five thousand drachmas to the Dyaleis, and if they are in arrears with the rent let the phratriarchs and the Dyaleis hand over the property to them, having collected the money; translation by Lambert 1993). See Köhler in *IG* II 600; Billeter 1898, 17–8 n. 3; Lambert 1993, 195–6, 306–7 (contra Behrend 1970, 92–3).

towards the reconstruction of the temple of Zeus Phratrios and Athena Phratria might evince shortage of money on the part of the phratry, suggesting that the phratry was unable to meet the building expenses by itself.[25]

It has been observed that the outlay of phratries would have entailed costs for honorific crowns, the erection of stelae, and cultic activity (i.e. sacrifices and maintenance of shrines).[26] So why does income-yielding, phratric land administration appear to be so minimal, especially in comparison to other associations? I suspect that the reason should be sought in the internal organization of phratries. Phratries appear to have incorporated, or at least included, other cultic groups such as orgeones and *gene*, which both had more patent religious features and also seem, as will be shown below, to have engaged in land transactions, especially leasing, in a more dynamic way than phratries.[27] These overlapping layers of infrastructure might have effected a fragmentation of phratric finances—a manifestation of which is detectable, for instance, in the sphere of credit—which could have affected the level of land administration as well. In other words, the (by definition) smaller, and, therefore, more compact, phratric sub-groups would have responded better to all kinds of financial exigencies than the phratries, which were, despite their territorial features, far more extensive associations.[28] To take just one example: the sacrificial calendar of the *genos* of the Salaminioi contains an entry of a pig offered to Zeus Phratrios during the

[25] T17 (ed. pr.: *SEG* III 121), for which see Hedrick 1989, 133–5; Lambert 1993, 193, 201–2, 340–1. One could also mention the list of contributors of monetary sums *IG* II^2 2345 (*SEG* XLVII 187), but its traditional interpretation as a catalogue of phratry members has now been questioned by Lambert 1999*b*.

[26] Lambert 1993, 199–201.

[27] See Lambert 1993, 59–93, who adds an *oikos*, *thiasoi*, and other unidentified groups in the list of phratric subdivisions; see also Hignett 1952, 56–7; Andrewes 1961; Humphreys 1990; Sourvinou-Inwood 1990, 317–18; Parker 1996, 316; Jameson 2000, 222. The most famous phratric example is of course the pair Demotionidai/Dekeleieis of the so-called Demotionidai decrees (Hedrick 1990, and Lambert 1993, 95–141, 285–93 are the most recent, fully annotated discussions; cf. the more succinct, but equally valuable, article by Rhodes 1997). On whichever interpretation, one of them was a phratric sub-group of the other.

[28] Territoriality of phratries: Weber 1909 [1976], 149; Sourvinou-Inwood 1990, 311 n. 56 (Archaic); Hedrick 1991; Lambert 1993, 11–12; Jones 1999, 197–8 (somewhat ambivalent). Size and number of phratries: Hignett 1952, 59–60; Flower 1985; Hedrick 1989; Lambert 1993, 18–20, 379–80; Jones 1999, 200; they all dismiss the number 12 given by Arist. [*Ath. Pol.*] fr. 2 (Chambers), *καὶ φυλαὶ ἦσαν δ΄, τῶν δὲ φυλῶν ἑκάστη μοίρας εἶχε γ΄, ἃς φρατρίας καὶ τριττύας ἐκάλουν* (cf. Rhodes 1993, 68–70).

Apatouria, the phratric festival par excellence, significantly a sacrifice explicitly stated to have been funded from rental from their own land.[29] But this case perfectly highlights the point made above: the active participation of a sub-group in phratric business would have considerably relieved the mother-phratry from some financial burdens. In any case, the validity of this claim will be tested in the following sections, which are devoted to the examination of the realty of other semi-public associations.

2. THE ATTIC GENE AND THEIR LANDED PROPERTY

i. Introductory remark

'Among the various groups [i.e. Athenian associations] . . . by far the most problematic is the genos';[30] not a far-fetched aphorism for a type of group that for years had been thought to embody all the aristocratic characteristics attributed by historians to the structure of pre-Classical Athens. The new orthodoxy, as expressed in the concurrent publications of Bourriot and Roussel, now puts it differently.[31] The French School's approach—the revisionist theory as Lambert termed it—constitutes the main modern trend and has been almost universally accepted by scholars.[32] However, Parker has recently provided a slightly altered and more convincing model of the *gene*, which, although still lined up to the aforementioned pattern, avoids some of its exaggerations and embraces some of the old, traditional aspects which had been erroneously and hastily dismissed.[33] By *gene* one should henceforth understand hereditary sacerdotal groups, that is associations defined by descent in the

[29] *Agora* XIX L4a l. 92: *Ἀπατουρίοις Διὶ Φρατρίωι ὗν ΔΔΔΔ*, with Andrewes 1961, 9–10; Parker 1996, 316; Sourvinou-Inwood 2000, 43. For the link between the sacrificial calendar of the Salaminioi and their landed assets see Section 2.ii.

[30] Jones 1999, 242.

[31] Bourriot 1976; Roussel 1976.

[32] Lambert 1999*a*, 484.

[33] Parker 1996, 56–66 and 284–327 (a fully documented checklist of all certain and spurious Attic *gene*) on whom the *genos*-theory of Lambert 1999*a* draws heavily.

male line with exclusive control of state-wide priesthoods.[34] Although nowadays the *opinio communis* is that such Attic *gene* were not the communal owners of huge fiefdoms that they were once assumed to have been during the Archaic period,[35] it does not follow that they did not own any real property. The case of the binary *genos* of the Salaminioi is illuminating and has, as such, been singled out for a thorough examination.

ii. The landed wealth of the Salaminioi: a case-study

That the Salaminioi consisted of two branches—the *Σαλαμίνιοι οἱ ἀπὸ Σουνίου* and the *Σαλαμίνιοι ἐκ τῶν ἑπτὰ φυλῶν*—and that, oddly, they are only attested epigraphically, are both well-known facts and I will spare the reader the boredom of retreading old ground. Thanks to two intact inscriptions found in the excavations of the Athenian Agora we know more about the Salaminioi's landed property than we know about the landed assets of the remaining Attic *gene* taken together.[36] And yet, despite some 'heavy-artillery' scholarship, the secrets encompassed in these texts have been anything but resolved, especially after a recent article by one of the most competent students of Attic topography who shook all received certainties concerning the properties of the *genos* under examination.[37] The first, larger stele, erected in 363/2, records the settlement of a dispute between the two branches and is accompanied by the sacrificial calendar of the *genos*.[38] Throughout the text we are given frequent glimpses of the status quo of the Salaminioi's realty. I provide a synopsis of the relevant points:

1. Upon the arbitrators' ruling it was decided that the land at the sanctuary of Herakles at Porthmos, the salt-pan, and the Agora in Koile should be divided into two equal parts, each of

[34] Jones 1999, 242–9 is rather confusing and ultimately unhelpful. On transmission of eligibility for a *genos* priesthood see now Blok and Lambert 2009, 102–4.

[35] Cf. Bourriot 1976, 727–828.

[36] The inscriptions were first published by Ferguson 1938, a marvellous study (cf. *LSCG* Suppl. no. 19). The authoritative epigraphical texts are now those published by Lambert 1997*b*, the first of which is reproduced by Rhodes and Osborne 2003 (RO 37).

[37] Lohmann and Schaefer 2000 (as it happens, it is the former who should take credit for the article).

[38] Scafuro 1997, 399 has now shown that the text was the result of reconciliation, rather than of an arbitral verdict (contra Ferguson 1938, 49 and *passim*).

which was to be assigned respectively to the Sounieis and the Heptaphyloi. Moreover, each branch had to erect boundary stones to delimit its property.[39]

2. The Salaminioi had to employ the rental from the leased landholding in order to cover expenditure for sacrifices for which the state did not provide any funds.[40]
3. The lessee of the land in question was instructed to continue cultivating it as specified by the terms of the pre-existing contract till it expired. However, until then he had to pay half the price of the rent to each branch separately.[41]
4. Each branch had to contribute money raised from the leasing of the land at the sanctuary of Herakles for the totality of the sacrifices.[42]
5. The two branches had to sacrifice in common employing the rental from the land at the Herakleion of Sounion (a provision repeated for the third time and following the itemized sacrificial calendar of the *genos*).[43]

The settlement of the Salaminioi highlights unequivocally a predominant, and yet often overlooked, aspect of religious finances, namely investment of rentals for the performance of rituals. It is obvious from the text that this scheme was not a novelty at the time of the arbitration; rather a leasing contract of strictly defined chronological scope had already been in force between an unspecified lessee and the *genos* as such.[44] The leased object is vaguely defined as the land (*γῆ*), but it might be plausibly inferred from its location next to

[39] RO 37 ll. 16–19: *τὴν δὲ γῆν τὴν ἐφ' Ἡρακλείωι τῶι ἐπὶ Πορθμ|ῶι καὶ τὴν ἀλ{λ}ὴν καὶ τὴν ἀγορὰν τὴν ἐν Κοίληι νε|ίμασθαι δίχα ἴ̣σην ἑκατέρος, καὶ ὅρος στῆσαι τῆ|s ἑαυτῶν ἑκατέρος* (cf. Parker 1996, 309).

[40] RO 37 ll. 24–7: *ὅσα δὲ ἀπὸ τῆς μισθώσεως ἔ|θυον Σαλαμίνιοι παρὰ σφῶν αὐτῶν θύειν κατὰ τὰ | πάτρια, τὸ ἥμυσυ ἑκατέρος συμβαλλομένος εἰς ἅ|παντα τὰ ἱερά* (cf. Walbank 1991, 156).

[41] RO 37 ll. 58–61: *τὴν δὲ γῆν ἐργά|ζεσθαι τὸμ μεμι[σ]θωμένον ἕως ἂν ἐξέλθηι ὁ χρόν|ος ὃν ἐμισθώσατο, ἀποδιδόντα τὴν ἡμίσειαν μίσ|θωσιν ἑκατέροις.*

[42] RO 37 ll. 83–4: . . . *ὅ τι δεῖ ἀργύριον συνβάλλεσθαι εἰς τὰ[s] | θυσίας ἁπάσας ἑκατέρους ἀπὸ τῆς μισθώσεως τῆς γῆς τῆς ἐφ' Ἡρακλείωι* (see Faraguna 1992, 346 with n. 44).

[43] RO 37 ll. 94–5: *ταῦτα θύειν κοινεῖ ἀπὸ τῆς μισθώσεως τῆς γῆς τῆ<s> ἐφ' Ἡρακλέ̣ω̣ι | Σονίο, ἀργύριον συμβαλλομένους ἑκατέρους ἐς ἅπαντ̣α τὰ ἱ̣ε̣ρ̣ά*; for the ambiguous meaning of the expression *ἐφ' Ἡρακλ|έ̣ω̣ι | Σονίο* see Lambert 1997*b*, 93.

[44] Cf. Ferguson 1938, 60–1; Behrend 1970, 90.

the shrine of Herakles at Sounion that it was a consecrated estate. Or that was at least the orthodox view, until Lohmann and Schaefer argued that we should distinguish two Herakleia, one in Sounion and another one at Porthmos, the latter placed by the German scholars in the port of Piraeus across from the island of Salamis.[45] Their topographical argument is a complicated one, but since it bears on the topic of gentilician property, it is imperative that it is dealt with in the course of the present analysis, albeit in a less detailed way than might be desirable.

Methodological reasons necessitate the prompt examination of the second inscription, an arbitration traditionally dated to 265/4, or thereabouts, on the basis of the archontic formula (but see Appendix VI for a full discussion of the chronology).[46] In the Hellenistic document the Salaminioi from Sounion and those from the Seven Tribes no longer appear as two branches of the same *genos*, but as two distinct *gene.*[47] Once more, the dispute concerns the ownership of the *genos*' real property, but this time nowhere is there any hint about the cultic activity of the Salaminioi's fourth-century predecessors. This is a land-survey full stop. As a consequence, the text is, from a topographical perspective, a real treasure. Not only is this a rare instance in which we are informed of the status quo of a given piece of land over the course of more than one hundred years, it is also an illuminating example of the arbitrariness marking the modern conventional division between the Classical and the Hellenistic periods, a chronological categorization beneath which often lies the erroneous notion of considerable change, if not discontinuity.

Instead of the land at the Herakleion at Porthmos, we now hear of the *temenos* of Herakles, divided by the two arbitrators into two distinct units: a core area which was meant to remain uncultivable,[48] and a peripheral zone, apparently of considerably larger size, which was declared the common property of both *gene.*[49] If the temenos can

45 Lohmann and Schaefer 2000, 92–5.

46 *Agora* XIX L4b ll. 1–2: *ἐπὶ Φανομάχου ἄρχ|οντος*; see also Appendix VI.

47 *Agora* XIX L4b ll. 3–5: *ἐπὶ τοῖσδε διελύσαντο τὰ γένη π|ρὸς ἄλληλα, τό τε Σουνιέων καὶ τὸ | ἀπὸ τῶν ἐξ Ἑπταφυλῶν*; see Ferguson 1938, 23; Bourriot 1976, 581–3.

48 *Agora* XIX L4b ll. 8–11: *τοῦ μὲν Ἡρακλέος τοῦ τεμέ|νους ἄνετομ μὲν εἶναι ὡς οἱ βωμοὶ κ|αὶ τὸ ἐπέκεινα τοῦ ἰκρίου ὡς αἱ ἐλ|άαι αἱ πρῶται*, with Ferguson 1938, 69. For the etymologically connected verb *ἀνιέναι* see Burkert 1996, 22–3 with n. 9.

49 *Agora* XIX L l. 11: *τὸ δ' ἄλλο τέμενος* etc.; ll. 17–18: *καὶ εἶναι κοινὸν τοῦτο τὸ | τέμενος τῶν γενῶν ἀμφοτέρων* (cf. Ferguson 1938, 70).

actually be identified with the leased landholding of the Classical document, we encounter the following paradox: now that the fission appears to have been complete the two separate *gene* are ordained to share possession of the disputed land, whereas earlier they had divided the same area between them. The problem becomes tantalizingly perplexing if we take into consideration a further assignment of properties occurring later on in the text; the Salaminioi from Sounion were to enjoy ownership of the easternmost landholdings (*χωρία*), those from the Seven Tribes of the westernmost ones, an apportionment roughly corresponding to the division of the *oikiai*.[50] But if the landholdings, obviously tillable fields, were units separate from the *temenos*, surely this would weaken the identification of the latter with the leased—and patently cultivable—land of Herakles? Ferguson and most scholars after him seem to have thought so, tentatively identifying the *χωρία* with the leased area of the first arbitration, and they are probably right.[51] For one reason, the leased land of the earlier document is actually designated as 'the land at the Herakleion' (*ἐφ' Ἡρακλείωι*; not 'in the Herakleion'), a description neatly fitting the location of the *χωρία* as abutting the *temenos* (owing to the fact that the divided houses were designated by virtue of their proximity to the *χωρία*, and, simultaneously, the easterly *οἰκία* was described as adjacent to the *temenos*). Conversely, Lohmann and Schaefer completely misunderstood the point, which, I believe, is crucial for their fallacious reconstruction of two separate Herakleia.[52] Nevertheless,

[50] *Agora* XIX L4b ll. 38–43: *τῶν δὲ χωρίων τὰ μὲ|ν πρὸς ἡλίου ἀνατολὰς εἶναι Ἀρχαιο|σαλαμινίων τῶν ἀπὸ Σουνίου ὡς οἱ ὅρ|οι κεῖνται.* v *τὰ δὲ πρὸς ἡλίου δυσμὰς ε|ἶναι Ἀρχαιοσαλαμινίων τῶν ἐξ Επτα|φυλῶν ὡς οἱ ὅροι κεῖνται* (reading with Daux 1941, 220–2, and Lambert 1997*b*, 94 *Ἀρχαιοσαλαμινίων* instead of *ἀρχαίο Σαλαμινίων*).

[51] For instance, Parker 1996, 310 contra Lohmann and Schaefer 2000, 94, who think that the *χωρία* were a separate unit ('von denen in [Inschrift nr.] 1 keine Rede ist').

[52] Lohmann and Schaefer 2000, 93–4, who observe that the land at the Herakleion at Porthmos had been divided between the two gentilician branches in the 4th cent., whereas the *temenos* mentioned in the second arbitration was to be shared in common by the two, by that time, separate *gene*; but, they carry on, since the latter was certainly situated in Sounion—for it was the Sounian branch that had constructed a threshing floor in the *temenos* and was, subsequently, ordered to build an identical one for its counterpart from the Seven Tribes (*Agora* XIX L4b ll. 18–24)—surely it cannot be identified with the *temenos* of the first inscription. The initial part of the German scholars' argument is correct, but their final conclusion is fundamentally flawed; without realizing it, they end up identifying the land at the Herakleion at

the traditional interpretation would generate a further problem: if the *temenos* is actually the shrine of Herakles, rather than a sacred cultivable estate, then what is the meaning of the provision concerning that part of the *temenos* that had to be left untouched?

This question leads us to another real riddle. The composers of the arbitration had thoughout the text dealt fair and square with the two branches up to the concluding clause when, out of the blue, a glebe designated as sacred, the ἱερὰ ἄρουρα, was assigned to the Salaminians from the Seven Tribes.[53] Ferguson simply remarked that the ἱερὰ ἄρουρα was inalienable (it could not be sold, even if income from it was to support the Salaminian cults), vaguely placing it in the area of the Herakleion.[54] One wonders whether he subconsciously tended to identify the ἱερὰ ἄρουρα with the reserved core of the Herakleion, not an intrinsically implausible theory, since only one part of the *temenos* was specifically declared the common property of the two *gene*,[55] and so we are left baffled about the ownership status of the reserved part. If so, the arbitrators would have appointed the Salaminioi from the Seven Tribes as solvent guarantors of the inviolability of the central, 'holier' zone of the Herakleion, presumably because their geographical remoteness from Sounion would have rendered them less likely perpetrators of injustice with regard to the Herakleion (since, to judge from the regulation about the threshing floors, it was the branch of the Salaminioi from Sounion which was more prone to misappropriate the sacred property). However, there is a dual, conceptual and linguistic, problem here. The term ἄρουρα (a *hapax* in Attic epigraphy) etymologically means cultivable land and, hence, it is rather unlikely that it would have been used to designate a parcel of land that had to remain untouched. ἄρουρα, however, was the standard land-unit in Ptolemaic Egypt,[56] and in the light of what is argued in Appendix VI below, its use in the Salaminian arbitration document may reflect Ptolemaic influence by virtue of the presence of Patroklos' troops in Attica during the Chremonidean War. If so, its location need not have been in Sounion at all, and, in fact, it should be looked

Porthmos with the *temenos*, whereas they were two distinct units (see also previous note).

[53] *Agora* XIX L4b ll. 41–4.

[54] Ferguson 1938, 68, 72. The Sounian location of the sacred glebe has been endorsed by Lambert 1997*a*, 235 n. 77 and Goette 2000, 72.

[55] Ferguson 1938, 70.

[56] See now Manning 2003.

for in some area lying under the effective control of the branch of the Heptaphyloi.

The only two pieces of realty whose status quo remained unaffected in both arbitrations were the salt-flat and the Agora in Koile.[57] The latter location was thought by Ferguson to refer to the urban deme Koile, which was adjacent to that of Melite, site of the Eurysakeion.[58] Over the past ten or so years, the road leading from Athens to Piraeus through the deme Koile, the Herodotean *ἡ διὰ Κοίλης ὁδός*, has been archaeologically (re)uncovered. In the middle of its route an open plateau, created by means of cuttings on the hard rock, has been investigated and is thought to be an agora of local significance. If so, it could well be the homonymous agora of the Salaminioi.[59] However, the close textual interconnection between the salt-pan and the Agora in Koile alludes to geographical proximity. In such a case, the Agora could equally well be sought near the Herakleion, since the Salaminioi sacrificed to the Hero *ἐπὶ τε̑ι ἁλε̑ι*—presumably the divine proprietor of the salt-flat—at Porthmos in the month Mounichion and that should, therefore, have been the location of the salt-pan.[60] Indeed, a spacious architectural complex, interpreted as an agora, has been thoroughly excavated in the bay of Pasalimani and has provisionally been identified as the Agora of the Salaminioi.[61] Regardless of the topographical issue, the Agora in Koile could yield income for the Salaminoi, amongst other ways, through taxation. Such a market-tax

[57] RO 37 ll. 17–18: *τὴν ἁλ{λ}ὴν καὶ τὴν ἀγορὰν τὴν ἐν Κοίληι νε|ίμασθαι δίχα ἴ̣σην ἑκατέρος*; *Agora* XIX L4b ll. 36–8: *τὴν δὲ ἁλὴν καὶ τὴν ἀγ|ορὰν τὴν ἐν Κοίλει κοινὴν εἶναι ἀμφο|τέρων τῶν γενῶν*.

[58] Ferguson 1938, 55, 59 followed by Young 1941, 163; Bourriot 1976, 580; Goette 2000, 72 n. 463; Lohmann and Schaefer 2000, 94.

[59] *Ἡ διὰ Κοίλης ὁδός*: Hdt. 6.103; cf. Judeich 1931, 180 with pl. 1; Lauter 1982 (with a thorough archaeological analysis of the agora, though he proposed no identification). For the project of fully uncovering the ancient road see Lazaride 1997, 42; *Archaeological Reports* 45 (1999), 8. See now the detailed description and analysis of this road by Dakoura-Vogiatzoglou 2010.

[60] So already Ferguson 1938, 54 ad *Agora* XIX L4a l. 85 (cf. Kearns 1989, 144; Parker 1996, 313–14); for the possible location of the salt-pan see Young 1941, 179–81, and Salliora-Oikonomakou 2004, 52 (who also attributes to the anonymous hero the dedication *IG* I[3] 1026 by Euphoros). For the sacredness of salt-producing areas as a recurring Mediterannean motif see Horden and Purcell 2000, 425–6.

[61] Salliora-Oikonomakou 1979 [1986], esp. 164, 169–71 (cf. Oliver 2001, 45–6) contra Travlos 1988, 405–6 (with tables 536–42), who not only dated the complex to the 3rd cent., but, moreover, interpreted it as the agora of the deme Sounion. Salliora-Oikonomakou 2004, 52–63, has reaffirmed her identification of the Pasalimani as the agora of the Salaminioi.

is attested in a decree of another alleged *genos*, the Mesogeioi, as well as in a Hellenistic decree from Rhamnous, where, quite importantly, the relevant tax is used for the subsidy of cultic activity.[62]

We can only speculate about the potential uses of the Salaminioi's landed assets, other than the tillable land that was stipulated to be leased out in order to generate cultic income.[63] Salt production and maybe salt trade is suggested by the existence of the salt-pan in the territory of the Salaminioi in Sounion.[64] That olive-oil was produced from the olive-trees of the *temenos* of Herakles seems a fair inference and, if not used for the cultic needs of the two *gene*, it might have been distributed in the open market via the Agora in Koile, wherever we place it.[65] Conversely, nothing implies any kind of Salaminian involvement in the mining ventures of the wider region of Laurion.[66] The threshing floors in the *temenos* of Herakles—the pre-existing one of the Salaminioi from Sounion and the new one that the former had to construct at their own expense for the exclusive use of their colleagues from the Seven Tribes—should definitely be interpreted as agricultural facilities, but it is difficult to say whether they would have served the interests of the lessee/s of the Salaminian landholdings or the Salaminioi's own needs.[67] The two houses might similarly have been used as amenities, for example as sheds for tools, though one could

[62] *IG* II^2 1245 ll. 8–9: *καὶ ἐμέρισεν τὸ ἀγοραστι|[κόν]*, with Schlaifer 1944, 26 n. 28 and Parker 1996, 306; *I.Rhamnous* 7 ll. 10–12: *πόρον δὲ ὑπάρχ[ε|ιν] τοῖς δημόταις εἰς τὴν θυσίαν τ[ὸ γε|νό]μενον αὐτοῖς ἀγοραστικόν*, with the note of Petrakos ad loc., who interprets the *ἀγοραστικόν* as a vending-licence fee. Income raised from the Agora is assumed by Ferguson 1938, 35, who, however, does not define its exact character.

[63] The assertion of Rosivach 1994, 45 that both the salt-pan and the Agora at Koile were leased out is sheer speculation. Lambert 1997*a*, 235 n. 77 is more reticent.

[64] Cf. Ferguson 1938, 35, 43. Carusi 2008, 52–5, considers the potential output of the salt-flat as limited, and thinks that the salt produced was for 'consumo domestico'.

[65] Note that two small rooms of the architectural complex in Pasalimani have been interpreted as storerooms for olive-oil (Salliora-Oikonomakou 1979 [1986], 167–8). Other agoras controlled by corporate groups include the agora of the Mesogeioi—as conjectured by a reference to a market-tax in one of their decrees, the agora of the phratry Medontidai.

[66] The dig at the agora of Pasalimani has produced evidence of metallurgical activity, which, however, dates to the Roman Imperial period: Salliora-Oikonomakou 2004, 53–5,

[67] *Agora* XIX L4b ll. 18–24: *ἄλ|ω δὲ κατασκεῦσαι Σαλαμινίους τοὺ|ς ἀπὸ Σουνίου τοῖς αὐτῶν ἀναλώμασ|ιν ἐν τῶι τεμένει τῶι κοινῶι τὸ αὐτ|ὸ μέγεθος τεῖ ἑαυτῶν, καὶ εἶναι ταύ|την τὴν ἄλω Σαλαμινίων τῶν ἐξ Ἑπτα|φυλῶν* (the reading *κατασκεῦσαι*, instead of *κατασκευάσαι*, by Lambert 1997*b*, 94).

not rule out leasing.[68] A fourth-century farmstead discovered to the north of Pasalimani was tentatively interpeted by Salliora-Oikonomakou as one of the two houses. The extensive farmstead was equipped with spaces for animals, water basins, vinification apparatus, and storage for agricultural products and honey. The Salaminioi would appear then to have possessed property that could elevate them to the status of affluent gentry, but unfortunately the excavator's identification is, by her own admission, far from certain.[69] Again, the jointly owned orchards and well of the *temenos* point towards agricultural production.[70] Here again, the temptation to identify the so-called *πηγάδι του Πασά* (Pasha's well) in the middle of the fertile Stephanatos estate with the property of the Salaminioi is great but has to be resisted.[71] Last, but not least, due attention has to be paid to the geographical designation of the site of the Herakleion; it was a *porthmos*, presumably a ferry-crossing between south-western Attica and the island of Helen (modern Makronesos), and so ferrying fees charged by the Salaminioi could be reckoned on.[72]

That some of the properties were surely income-yielding can be inferred from a further observation. Whereas land-rentals were explicitly diverted to sacrifices, we hear nothing of the defraying of such sporadic outlays as repairs of shrines. And we know from another honorific decree of the *genos* that at some point towards the end of the fourth century the Salaminioi offered golden crowns to at least two individuals, each crown costing an astonishing 1000 drachmas.[73]

[68] That there was a demand in the wider area of southern Attica for premises which could be let out to those engaged in mining is well known from Xen. *Vect.* 4.49, *ἀλλὰ πολυανθρωπίας περὶ τὰ μέταλλα ἀθροιζομένης . . . καὶ ἀπ' οἰκιῶν περὶ τἀργύρεια δημοσίων . . . πρόσοδοι ἂν πολλαὶ γίγνοιντο*, although, it has to be said, by the mid-3rd cent. the production of silver had almost come to a halt (so Konophagos 1980, 118–19, but Oliver 2001, 44–6 accepts some limited activity).

[69] Salliora-Oikonomakou 2004, 60–1.

[70] Of course, sale of water, as attested e.g. in the orgeonic record *IG* II^2 1361 ll. 9–10: *καὶ τὸ ὕδωρ ὅσου ἂμ πραθῆι ε||[ἰ̓ς τὴν] ἐπι[σ]κευὴν τοῦ ἱεροῦ [καὶ τῆ]ς οἰκίας εἰ̓ς ἄλλο δὲ μηδὲν ἀναλίσκειν*, cannot be ruled out; see also Jones 2000, 81.

[71] Salliora-Oikomakou 2004, 61.

[72] The enigmatic *ἐμβατῆρες* (*Agora* XIX L4b ll. 15–17: *ὡς οἱ ἐμβατῆρες*^{v} | *οἵ τε πρὸς τῆι θαλάττηι καὶ ὁ ἄνω κ|είμενος*) might have been maritime facilities, such as docks or quays (so Ferguson 1938, 70, but see Young 1941, 176). Needless to say, Lohmann and Schaefer, 2000, 92–3, will place the departure point for the ferry crossing in the Piraeus. For the practice of *porthmeutike* see Constantakopoulou 2002.

[73] Repairs: RO 37 ll. 4–6: *ἐὰν δέ τι δέηι ἐπισκευεάσαι τῶν ἱε|ρῶν, ἐπισκευάζεν κοινῆι συμβαλλ{λ}ομένος τὸ ἥμ|υσυ ἑκατέρος*; honorific expenditure: *IG* II^2 1232 ll. 11–13:

Although monetary contributions cannot be ruled out,[74] the vast realty managed by the Salaminioi suggests itself as a potential source of revenue for such outstanding expenditure. Indirectly, this assumption seems to be strengthened by the clause concerning the common keeping of the *γραμματεῖα* (note the plural), in all likelihood financial records of the gentilician, movable and immovable, assets.[75]

Having investigated the potential modalities of realty exploitation, we can now resume the examination of the leased landholding of the Salaminioi. Hitherto I have somewhat misleadingly stressed the importance of rentals for the calendrical sacrifices of the *genos*. This deliberate emphasis, far from being arbitrary, is borne out by the text proper in its repeated directives for the budgeting of the rental for the patrimonial sacrifices. The mathematics of the sacrificial calendar, however, tell us a different story. The envisaged investable capital was 533 drachmas (530.5 drachmas, on a different reading), but the aggregate cost of the sacrificial victims equalled merely 461 drachmas,[76] a discrepancy remedied only on the assumption that the former figure included the priestly perquisites, as Ferguson aptly observed.[77] However, this reconstruction presents some difficulties, for even allowing for the (numerically undefined) sacrifice offered to Ion in alternate years—estimated by Ferguson at 7.5 drachmas per year—the priestly emoluments appear to amount to 59 drachmas, thus leaving us short of 3 or 5.5 drachmas, depending on the exact

[ἐπαινέσ]αι αὐτοὺς καὶ στεφανῶσαι αὐτ||[ῶν ἑκάτερο]ν χρυσῶι στεφάνωι ἀπὸ Χ δραχμ||[ῶν]. Add the extra expenditure incurred for the purpose of erecting two copies of the decree in ll. 24–5: *[εἰς δὲ τὴν ἀ]ναγραφὴν τῶν σ[τ]η[λ]ῶν δ[ο]ῦ||[ναι . . .* c.5 *.. δρα]χμάς* (note that in this decree, which is chronologically placed between the two inscriptions from the Eurysakeion, there is no hint of two separate gentilician branches); cf. Ferguson 1938, 35; Parker 1996, 310.

[74] Such as those attested in an honorific decree of another *genos*, the Krokonidai; *IG* II^2 1229 ll. 4–9: *ἐπειδὴ οἱ αἱρ[εθέντες ὑπὸ τῶ]|ν γεννητῶν οἰκο[δομῆσαι τὸ ἱερ|ὸ]ν τῆς Ἑστίας ἐπε[μελήθησαν τῆς οἰ]|κοδομίας καλῶς κ[αὶ φιλοτίμως] | κα[ὶ] ἐπέδοσα[ν τὸ ἀνάλωμα παρ' ἑα]|υτῶν τὸ εἰ[ς τὴν οἰκοδομίαν*, with Parker 1996, 303–4.

[75] *Agora* XIX L4a ll. 57–8: *τὰ δὲ γραμματεῖ|α κοινὰ εἶναι ἀ[μφ]οτέρων ἅπαντα* (with Pébarthe 2006, 190 n. 128); cf. the orgeonic archives (*γραμματεῖα*) of *IG* XII (8) 19, which record credit on land security (with Finley 1952*a*, 23).

[76] *Agora* XIX L4a l.93: *κεφάλαιον οὗ δεῖ ἀναλίσκειν ἀμφοτέρος ἐς ἅπαντα τὰ ἱερὰ* 𐅅ΔΔΔỊỊỊ *vel* 𐅅ΔΔΔ⊢̣⊢̣⊢̣, with Lambert 1997*b*, 93, who also corrects Ferguson's 460.5 drachmas for the total expenditure.

[77] Ferguson 1938, 64–5, overlooked by all subsequent scholars (e.g. Parker 1996, 310 '[t]wenty-three sacrifices financed from Salaminian funds are listed . . . at a total cost of 530,5 drachmas') bar Lambert 1997*b*, 93.

figure supplemented for the capital. Some subtle adjustments might help us get round these obstacles. First of all, we should probably accept that the emoluments for the priest of Eurysakes was 12 drachmas; that is, twice the amount recorded (6 drachmas), given that the said priest also officiated in the cult of the Hero at the salt-flat. The syntax of the crucial lines makes this interpretation very plausible.[78] Then the aggregate of the expenses (461 drachmas for the annual sacrifices, 7.5 drachmas per year for the sacrifice to Ion, and 65 drachmas for priestly dues) adds up to 533.5 drachmas, which is of course half a drachma higher than the total of the invested capital. But instead of Ferguson's annual 7.5 drachmas for the sheep sacrificed to Ion, it is more reasonable to accept a slightly lower amount, since in the majority of the cases attested in the sacrificial calendar the cost of a sheep was 12 drachmas.[79] An assumed price of 7 drachmas per year for the elusive sheep due to Ion would bring us to the coveted total of 533 drachmas. Be that as it may, the inclusion of priestly emoluments in the wider set of cultic expenses met with rental from the land at Porthmos cannot be questioned and should be used as a constant reminder when analysing other instances of leasing attached to sacred activity. Control of gentilician priesthoods, the thorn in the flesh of the *genos*, affected the management of the financial resources of the controlling groups, landed assets included.[80]

Unfortunately, the size of the leased estate cannot be accurately estimated, since even its actual value is unknown to us. In any case,

[78] RO 37 ll. 34–5: *τῶι δὲ τô Εὐρυσάκος ἱερεῖ ἱερεώσυνα ΠΗ δραχμά|ς· εἰς πελανὸν ἀμφοτέρωσε Π ⊢⊢ δραχμάς*; cf. ll. 52–4: *τὸν δὲ αὐ|τὸν ἱερέα εἶναι τῶι Εὐρυσάκει καὶ τῶι ἥρωι τῶι | ἐπὶ τῆι ἁλῆι*, with Ferguson 1938, 59). The fact that the adverb *ἀμφοτέρωσε* ('for both [cults]') is attached only to the specification for the payment of 7 drachmas in lieu of *pelanos*, would appear to strengthen the interpretation put forward here. It is interesting that on this reconstruction the amount offered yearly to each official was almost identical (33 drachmas for the priest of Herakles, 32 drachmas for that of Eurysakes), even though this sum would have been realized through different disbursements.

[79] See the table in Parker 1996, 313.

[80] Disputes concerning control of priesthoods appear to have been a frequent topic of litigation in Classical Athens (Feaver 1957, 144–7; Humphreys 1985, 213), and we should not lose sight of the financial implications of such judicial battles. The whole argument can work in the opposite direction, i.e. priests were not only the recipients of perks, but they might have actively participated in the administration of the financial resources of the paying authorities (*gene*, in our case), as implied e.g. by Pl. *Leg.* 758e–759d; Arist. *Pol.* 1322^b. The process followed in the appointment of *genos* priests is now scrutinized by Blok and Lambert 2009, who strongly come down in favour of allotment.

the annual rent of the land at Porthmos ought to have been higher than the capital of 533 (or 530.5) drachmas, though probably not considerably higher. A round number like 600 drachmas per year sounds reasonable. For the sake of comparison, this is the rental collected annually by the phratry of the Dyaleis from the lessee of the *Σακκνή*, to all appearances a land of a substantial size with a multitude of crops in it. Ferguson used an estimated annual rate of 7 per cent to make his calculations, but, nowadays, it is accepted that, although no universal policy existed, 8 per cent was much commoner in Attica.[81] This would result in 6662.5 drachmas as the actual price of the land, if we estimate it on the basis of 533 drachmas (6631.25 on 530.5), or 7500 drachmas on the basis of a rounder rent of 600 drachmas. Both figures are higher than the average prices we get from literary or epigraphical sources. By virtue of Ferguson's data the size of the land at Porthmos was roughly 90 plethra, a figure which further emphasizes the affluence of the Salaminioi, who, otherwise, did not stand at the same level of prominence as more famous *gene* like the Kerykes or the Eteoboutadai.[82] To put it otherwise, if the Salaminioi were owners of a realty almost identical in size to that of a phratry—a group which, by definition, comprised many more members—then we are entitled to classify the *genos* among the prosperous associations of Classical Athens.

iii. Gentilician property: beyond the Salaminioi

As for other *gene*, the extant testimonia—even given that such evidence scarcely crosses the borderline between the highly possible and the unmistakably certain—indicate that possession of land, and more widely real property, was a frequent theme. For some *gene* we have no direct evidence, but their names may suggest landed interests.[83] Thus the Bouzygai not only have a name which implies agricultural activity (and indirectly landed assets) but are also attested as performing sacred rituals which imitated the ploughing of land in what might

[81] Ferguson 1938, 68, following Billeter 1898, 15.

[82] For the sake of comparison de Ste. Croix 1966, 112–13 has given an approximate 20,000 drachmas as the value of the estate of Phainippos, 'the largest single Athenian estate', according to his own words. The property of the Salaminioi being ⅓ the size of that of Phainippos would still have been of considerable size.

[83] Cf. Bourriot 1976, 1100–1.

have been in essence their own property.[84] Similar considerations can be made with regard to the 'pastoralist' *genos Ποιμενίδαι*.[85] And the *Γεφυραῖοι* and the *Φρεώρυχοι* both have names with topographical connotations, which it is especially tempting to connect with mine exploitation, but this is solely a guess based on a vague lexicographical entry.[86] Similar abstruse information by Stephanus Byzantius has also given rise to the theory that there was a *genos* called *Σημαχίδαι* with their own landed assets, and that the homonymous Cleisthenic deme was named after this territory.[87] Other germane literary evidence includes information about the Archaic *telesterion* of the Lykomidai at Phlya as well as their chapel/shed (maybe auxiliary premises of the *genos*?), but both are attested in very late sources and have, consequently, been contested.[88] Nevertheless, *IG* II^2 2670, a mortgage *horos*, shows them, along with the tribe Kekropis and the deme Phlya, offering a loan on security.[89] This should only be seen as a potential way on the part of the *genos* to acquire land on a debtor's default (but the multiple creditors render it a rather remote possibility), and the same applies to the case of the Glaukidai and the Epikleidai, if *gene* is what they were.[90]

We mentioned above the agora of the Mesogeioi, as attested indirectly by a market-fee extracted by one of their officials, and we

[84] See Parker 1996, 286–7; cf. Sourvinou-Inwood 1988, 143. Note that the archaizing *IG* II^2 3194 contains a double reference to the 'sacred threshing floor' (ll. 8–9: [κ]αὶ τε̂ς hιε|ρᾶς ἅλο, and 13–14: τὲν ἅλο | τὲ[ν] hιεράν), a structure that is readily reminiscent of the 'sacred ploughing' of the Bouzygai. In Chapter 2, I hesitantly argued that *IG* II^2 3194 might refer to property belonging to Athena Polias, but one cannot dismiss a possible link with the Bouzygai, an illustrious *genos* that was still very active in the Roman Imperial period, when the document in question was (re)-inscribed. In that case, Zeus Teleios rather than Athena could have been the owner of at least some of the properties enumerated in *IG* II^2 3194.

[85] Toepffer 1889, 310–11; Parker 1996, 307.

[86] Hsch. s.v. *Φρεώρυχοι· γένος Ἀθήνησιν ἢ οἱ τὰ φρέατα ὀρύσσοντες*, with Toepffer 1889, 312; Parker 1996, 317. For the *Γεφυραῖοι* see Parker 1996, 288–9.

[87] See Kearns 1989, 98 n. 93; Parker 1996, 326.

[88] Telesterion: Plut. *Them.* 1.4: τὸ γὰρ Φλυῆσιν τελεστήριον, ὅπερ ἦν Λυκομιδῶν κοινόν etc. with Toepffer 1889, 209–11 (the very existence of a shrine has been contested as well, but see *ADeltion* 41 (1987) [1992], B1, 107, where the boundary stone hόρο[ς] | ἱερο[ῦ] | Δή[μητρ]ος is said to come from Phlya); chapel: Paus. 4.1.7, ἀνέθηκε δὲ καὶ εἰς τὸ κλισίον τὸ Λυκομιδῶν etc. with Bourriot 1976, 1104–5.

[89] See Finley 1952*a*, 160 no. 146 (cf. Toepffer 1889, 223).

[90] *IG* II^2 2723: a ὅρος πεπραμένου ἐπὶ λύσει (*c.* 350); Parker 1996, 320 classifies both groups amongst the spurious *gene*, but Lambert 1993, 78–9 and 197–8 is probably right that they stand more chance of having been *gene*, rather than phratries.

can briefly point out that their main budget was of sacred character nominally belonging to 'the god', presumably Herakles; this, along with the fact that their personnel entailed annually appointed *hieromnemones* (magistrates elsewhere heavily involved in land administration), makes it very likely that the Mesogeioi did administer realty for the subsidy of their cultic activity.[91] Another *genos* usually thought to have possessed real property is that of the Kolieis;[92] a marker of unknown provenance reads: [*ὅρ*]*ος* | [*χ*]*ωρίου* | [*K*]*ωλιέω*[*ν*]. This might have been a plot of land similar to the *χωρία* mentioned in the Salaminian documents and, if so, exploitation through leasing suggests itself.[93] However, the *horos* under consideration has been linked to an entry in the *Rationes Centesimarum* which attests a group called Kolieis, and represented by at least two officials, as disposing of some property.[94] Enigmatically, and contrary to what one would have expected from a *genos*, they appear not in the stelae nos. 3 or 4, which included associations such as phratries and orgeones, but in the second stele of the series amongst demes and komai. To remedy the apparent discrepancy, Lambert suggested that the Kolieis of the *Rationes Centesimarum* might have been a relic of the Archaic *naukrariai*, a theory which would, in retrospect, weaken the identification of the Kolieis of the boundary stone with the homonymous *genos*.[95]

Another religious association featuring in the *Rationes Centesimarum*—this time, in a normal place—with a good claim to be a *genos* is the Eikadeis.[96] It is certainly remarkable that in every single

[91] Market-tax: *IG* II^2 1245 ll.8–9 (see n. 62 above); sacred budget: *IG* II^2 1247 ll. 27–31: *εἰς δὲ τ*|*ὴν ἀναγραφὴν τῆς στήλης δότω ὁ ἄρ*|*χων Ἀδείμαντος* : *Δ* : *δραχμὰς ἐκ τῆς* | *κοινῆς προσόδου τῶν τοῦ θεοῦ χρη*|*μάτων καὶ εἰς θυσίαν* : *ΔΠ* : *δραχμάς*; *hieromnemones*: *IG* II^2 1248 ll. 3–4: *καὶ τοὺς ἱερομ*[*νήμονας τοὺς ἀεὶ*] | *καθισταμένους τὸ*[*ν ἐνιαυτόν*] (but, admittedly, this document may not belong to the Mesogeioi; see Parker 1996, 306; cf., however, the *mnemones* mentioned in *IG* II^2 1247 ll. 19–20, with Schlaifer 1944, 26); for *hieromnemones* elsewhere see Chapter 3, Section 2: 'The real property of the Attic demes' pp. 143–4).

[92] Kolieis: Parker 1996, 304–5.

[93] Ed. pr.: Raubitschek 1974, who suggested a chronology in the early 4th cent., but Lambert 1997*a*, 192–3 with n. 2 doubts the tenability of this date (cf. Jones 1999, 246 n. 131).

[94] F9B ll.23–5: [. . . . . *c.9–11* . . . . .]*τερος Κωλιέων* | [. . . . . *c.9* . . . .]*οι Κωλιέων* | [. . . . . . *c.12–13* . . . .].[. . .]*ίου Φα*[*λ*- - -].

[95] Lambert 1997*a*, 223–5; cf. Parker 1996, 304–5.

[96] F13A ll. 12–16: *ἐκ Σαλαμῖνος Εἰκαδέων βουλ̣*[—]| *'Ολυμπιόδωρος Εὐμήλου Π*/ [—] | *ἀπέδοτο χωρίον ἐν Σαλα*[*μῖνι*] | *ἐν Χυτρεαῖς* | *ὠνη Δωρόθεος Θεοδώρου ἐξ Οἰ*

document pertaining to them, there is an actual or an indirect interest on behalf of the group in their real assets. Thus, a pair of unparalleled boundary stones (which were, notably, prepared by the same stonecutter) prohibited hypothecation of their land in the most categorical way.[97] And we get to learn incidentally about a plot of land belonging to the Eikadeis from a *poletai* record of 342/1–339/8, where their estate is used to mark a confiscated property. This property, which belonged to the famous politician Philokrates, lay in the deme of Hagnous and it has been suggested that the twin boundary-stones and the *poletai* record all refer to the same plot of land.[98] A decree passed by the koinon of the Eikadeis in 324/3 honours a *Πολύξενος Διοδώρου* (almost certainly an associate of the group), for denouncing some unnamed individuals, Eikadeis as well, who had given false witness in court by means of which the koinon had suffered considerable damage.[99] It has been suggested that the issue at stake was property; I dare say, real property, land. The formula used (*IG* II^2 1258 ll. 5–7: *τῶν κοινῶν τῶν | Εἰκαδέων, ἀφ' ὧν τὰ ἱερὰ τοῖς θεοῖς θ|ύουσιν Εἰκαδέες*) resembles the similar provision from the Salaminioi's early inscription in which the *genos* is ordained to subsidize sacrifices with money raised from the leasing of its land. Since we know from the two aforementioned markers and the *poletai*-record that the Eikadeis did own landholdings, it is a fair inference that the group would have mainly used land to generate cultic income.

In this sense, their appearance in the *Rationes Centesimarum* deserves further consideration. The alienated estate was located on the island of Salamis, the group bore the further designation 'from Salamis', and the agent acting on behalf of the association held the

*XX*𐅅̣[— *ἑκατ(οστή)* —], with Lambert 1997*a*, 199–200; cf. Lambert 1993, 365 and Parker 1996, 336–7 who inclines to identify the Eikadeis as a *genos*, although he does not include them in the germane list.

[97] *IG* II^2 2631 and 2632: *ὅρος χωρίου κοι|νοῦ Εἰκαδείων· | μὴ συνβάλλειν | εἰς τοῦτο τὸ χω|ρίον μηθένα | μηθέν*; a similar prohibition occurs in the arbitration of an unidentified orgeonic group (*IG* II^2 1289, with Papazarkadas 2004–9 [2010]), where the policy of protectionism aims at securing the unimpeded subsidy of the group's patrimonial sacrifices through investment of rentals (cf. Hammond 1961, 87–8; Finley 1952*a*, 98, 286 n. 48; Millett 1991, 177).

[98] *Agora* XIX P26 ll. 384–5: *Εἰκαδέων χωρί|[ον]*; l. 395 *[χωρίον?] Εἰκαδέων*; cf. Meritt 1936, 409; Parker 1996, 336 n. 18; and see the reservations of Lambert, 1997*a*, 199–200.

[99] *IG* II^2 1258 (cf. Rubinstein 2000, 81–2 and 88).

office of either a *βουλ̣[ευτής]* or a *βούλ̣[αρχος]*.[100] Lambert hesitantly suggested that there might have been a connection between the decree of the Eikadeis and the sale of the property at Salamis, but he did not pursue the point further. I think the chronological and contextual proximity between *IG* II^2 1258 and the *hekatoste*-inscriptions allows us to envisage a situation whereby the Salaminian branch of the Eikadeis decided to dispose of some of its property.[101] The opportunity lay before them, as the central government enforced, or was just simply in favour of, a programme of massive land privatization. Their action met with the strong disapproval of the koinon of Eikadeis, who condemned it both ritually and judicially.[102] This theory would help to explain why the defendants are not explicitly named in the decree of the Eikadeis. Not only does the use of the word *τινές*, 'some people', have a scornful tenor, it also avoids legalizing the dissidents' act.[103] Moreover, it binds well with the prohibitions recorded in the twin *horoi*, provisions revealing extreme sensitivity concerning the landed assets of the Eikadeis. If this is the

[100] Lambert 1997*a*, 200 and 252 opted for the first restoration taking it as an indication of an associational council. I feel uneasy about such an interpretation which lacks any good parallels whatsoever and I would fancy the supplement *βούλ̣[αρχος]* taking it as an ad hoc office. The word *βούλαρχος* is used by Aeschylus with the meaning of the 'adviser of a plan' (A. *Suppl.* 11–13: *Δαναὸς δέ, πατὴρ καὶ βούλαρχος | καὶ στασίαρχος, τάδε πεσσονομῶν | κύδιστα ἀχέων ἐπέκρανεν*; 968–70: *πέμψον δὲ πρόφρων δεῦρ' ἡμέτερον | πατέρ' εὐθαρσῆ Δαναόν, πρόνοον | καὶ βούλαρχον*; cf. Friis-Johansen and Whittle 1980, 16–17, contra Sommerstein 1977, 67, and see now Bakewell 2008, 303–4); such a term would eloquently indicate the man in charge of the initiative, while retaining some legal and political connotations. For the homonymous office outside Attica in the Classical period see Nawotka 1999, 192–3. Incidentally, the suggestion of Cargill 1995, 195 and 302 that *Εἰκαδέων* is the nominative of a personal name and that *Βούλ[αρχος]* a patronymic simply cannot pass the scrutiny of Athenian onomastics, at least not in its first leg.

[101] As pointed out above, *IG* II^2 1258 was passed in the archonship of Hegesias (324/3), and Lambert 1997*a*, 213–19 has narrowed the span of time within which stelae 3–4 of the *Rationes Centesimarum* can be placed to *c.*330–325.

[102] Oath and imprecation: *IG* II^2 1258 ll. 1–4: *ἐπειδή τι|[ν]ες ἐναντία τῶι ὅρκωι ὃν ὤμοσαν καὶ τε[ῖ] | ἀρᾶι ἣν Εἰκαδεὺς ἐπηράσατο διατελ|οῦσι* etc.; compare the curse tablet *DTA* 38 (with Wilhelm 1904, 120), tentatively related by Lambert 1997*b*, 91 to the legal disputes in the first Salaminian arbitration RO 37, esp. ll. 65–6: *τῶν δὲ ἄλλων ἐνκλημάτων ἁπάντω^{v}ν ἀφε|ῖσθαι τῶν τε ἰδί<ω>ν καὶ τῶν κοινῶν*.

[103] See the good note by Robert 1945, 37–8, with reference to the honorific decree for Dionysios (no. 11 in Robert's dossier). Unlike Dignas 2002, 101 n. 258, for whom the *τινές* of the Sinuri inscription means that 'the offenders were treated with polite discretion', I think that in both cases (Athens and Asia Minor) the pronoun suggests contempt and dismissal.

case, then we have before as a didactic example of how new branches of religious associations might come to exist through fission.

At any rate, apart from the dubious case of the Kolieis and the more likely one of the Eikadeis, some further selling units from the *Rationes Centesimarum* have been tentatively identified as *gene*, including the Chalkinidai (?), the Oikatai, and the Apheidantidai.[104] Uncertainty regarding their exact type should discourage us from using these groups as examples when discussing land administration, but, for what it is worth, their relative unimportance might, to some degree, account for the alienation of their properties, as will be argued in more detail below with regard to orgeonic groups.

Gentilician land administration was not geographically restricted to Attica, as can be seen from the case of the Pyrrhakidai, who appear as the nominal owners of an estate in a Delian document of the Hellenistic period. The property had initially been let out for 2000 drachmas—an expensive plot of land this. Some time later, a new contract was set, presumably with a new lessee who had to pay 1054.5 drachmas annually for a period of five years.[105] This sudden reduction of the rental and the resulting odd sum should be accounted for by the obligation of the new lessee to invest money in repairs (the bad preservation of the text at this point renders just possible, though plausible, this interpretation). Although both the antiquity and the ethnicity of the Pyrrhakidai have been questioned, the *genos* was

[104] Chalkinidai (?): F11B l. 7: [. . . . . . c.12–13 . . . . . . *Χ*]*ạλκινιδ*[*ῶν*?- - -], with Lambert 1997*a*, 202–3; Oikatai: F16A ll. 15–17: *Οἰκατῶν ἐπιμελητὴς Στράτων* | *Μνησιφάνους Κοθωκίδης* | *ἀπέδοτο χωρίον ἐγ Κοθωκιδῶν*; Apheidantidai: F16A ll. 19–21: *Ἀφειδαντιδῶν ἐπιμελητὴς* | *Λεόντιος Καλλιάδου Ἐπικηφί* | *ἀπέδοτο χωρίον ἐγ Κοθωκιδῶν* (for the two last groups see Toepffer 1889, 169–70, 313; Lambert 1997*a*, 205). But, as shown above, some or even all of these groups might have been phratries.

[105] *ID* 1416 B1 ll. 57–61: *τὸ χ*[*ωρίο*]*ν τὸ Πυρρακιδῶν* [*ὃ εἶχεν*] *Θεόξενος* | *Μύνδιος δραχ. Χ* [*ἐ*]*μ̣ι̣σ̣θ̣ώ̣*[*σατο*] *Π̣απύλο*[*ς*] *Λ*[*υσανίου*] *Σ̣τ̣ρ̣ατονικ̣ε̣ὺ*[*ς*] | *διὰ τὸ Θεόξενον ἐκχωρ*[*ῆσαι εἰς τοὺς*] *ὑπολοίπους* [*μ*]*ῆ*[*νας*] *δέκα καὶ* | *εἰς ἔτη τε πέντε τὰ μετ*[*ὰ ἄρχοντα Ἀνθεσ*]*τήριον ἑκάστου ἐνιαυτο*[*ῦ*] | *δραχμῶν ΧΠ⊢⊢⊢⊢ΙΙΙ*. A question that has never been satisfactorily answered concerns the exact ownership status of this estate, especially since the relevant entry occurs among other sacred properties lying under the authority of the personnel of the sanctuary of Apollo. Some scholars have argued that the estate comprised a new possession of the Delian cult following the reacquisition of the island by the Athenians (Roussel 1929, 179; Hennig 1985, 178 n. 49), but it is not inconceivable that we have here a case of joint ownership, i.e. the landholding belonged to the *genos* (so initially Roussel 1916, 158 n. 5; Parker 1996, 308), but it was later deemed more effective to have it managed by the temple authorities.

genuinely Attic and there is a good possibility that it owned land on Delos as early as the fifth century.[106]

Of much later date is the evidence for real property administered by one of the most glorious Attic *gene*, the Eteoboutadai. Two Augustan boundary stones marked what appears to have been an estate dedicated to Athena Polias, but controlled by the *genos* which held the goddess's priesthood.[107] The grandiloquent archaistic Attic script, the stoichedon style, and the antiquated term *γύης*,[108] all underpin the artificiality of the *horoi* and, hence, we are not entirely entitled to use them as evidence for gentilician land-tenure in the Classical, or even the Hellenistic, epochs.[109] In terms of social standing, the Eteoboutadai can only be matched by such *gene* as the Eumolpidai and the Kerykes. The latter had in their possession at least one house in the Eleusinian sanctuary in 329/8, where they presumably held assemblies and performed rites (compare the phratric houses discussed above).[110] Almost a century before, they had been involved in a dispute with a certain Telemachos over the construction of the shrine of the newly imported god Asklepios in a specific plot in the southern area of the Acropolis generally thought to have been situated within the so-called Pelargikon.[111] It seems more likely that their involvement emanated from their constitutional role as effective

[106] See below, Appendix V.

[107] *Agora* XIX H23 and H24. The former, which is better preserved, reads: *hóρος γύοụ Ἀθε[ναίας Πολιάδος] | προσhέκον Ἐτεọ[βουταδôν γένει] | πόδες Η* [rasura] *ἐπί* [—]. An Augustan date (instead of the ed. pr.'s '2nd century A.D.') is now favoured by Schmalz, (2007–8) [2011].

[108] For which see Faraguna 1992, 348–9, notwithstanding that he fails to mention the inscription under consideration. The same term also appears in another archaizing document from Roman Attica, *IG* II^2 3194 (l. 19: *[προσχώ]ροις γύαις*), for which see p.19, and especially n. 84 above, where I put forward a very tentative connection with another distinguished *genos*, the Bouzygai.

[109] Contra Parker 1996, 293 and Siewert 2001, 4; but nothing in our extant evidence appears to confirm this assumption.

[110] *I.Eleusis* 177 (*IG* II^2 1672), ll. 24–5: *καὶ τοῦ παρὰ τὸν Κηρύκων οἶκ|ον* (a landmark, not an edifice controlled by the issuing bodies of *I.Eleusis* 177). For its alleged archaeological remains and their interpretation see Mylonas 1961, 173–4, 234 (but Bourriot 1976, 1107–9 rightly advocated caution); another even more far-fetched suggestion for identifying the house of Kerykes with a late Geometric house has been put forward by Lauter 1985, 168 followed by Antonaccio 1995, 190–1. See now the detailed discussion by Clinton 2008, 180, 198.

[111] *SEG* XLVII 232 ll. 20–3: *Ἀ̣ρχέας· ἐπὶ το|[ύτο οἱ Κ]ήρ̣υκες ἠμφεσβ|[ήτον τô] χωρίο καὶ ἔνια | ἐπεκώλυσα̣ν ποῆσαι* (Archeas; in his archonship the Kerykes disputed the land and prevented certain actions).

administrators of the Eleusinian cult, if the disputed plot indeed lay in the Pelargikon.[112] That this was so can be seen from their jurisdiction over the Sacred Orgas as promulgated by the Athenian state in 352/1. But the Sacred Orgas was definitely no property of theirs and the same surely applies to the Pelargikon. Such activities should, therefore, be understood as of strictly administrative substance, not as proof of *genos*-type land ownership. Similarly, one reads of the Eleusinian sacred houses, of which one was the residence of the priestess of Demeter and Kore and another one of the daduch. Now, since we know that the former came from the ranks of the *genos* Philleidai and the latter from those of the *genos* Kerykes, it is tempting to trace here further evidence of gentilician realty within the Eleusinian sanctuary. However, the fact that expenditure for purification, repairs, and other works within the houses was met with money from the polis-controlled Eleusinian purse asserts the state-, rather than gentilician, ownership of those premises.[113]

iv. An overview

Let us summarize what has already been discussed. The revisionist model brought about a sort of small revolution in the way we look at the religious associations called *gene* and corrected some seriously distorting views pertinent to this subject, but, as so often happens, failed itself to eschew some exaggerations.[114] Admittedly the *gene* were not the aristocratic, massive land proprietors that the traditionalist scholarship had wanted them to be. The *gene* did own land, notwithstanding, and, sporadically, other secular facilities. As concerns the administrative policy implemented by *gene*, we are almost

[112] Aleshire 1989, 8–9; Garland 1992, 126; Clinton 1994, 28–9; Jost 1998, 302; Wickkiser 2008, 74–6 (whose novel suggestion that the Kerykes' quarrel was not with Telemachos, but with an unnamed party is not at variance with the fact that the Kerykes were the primary advocates of the Eleusinion's interests).

[113] *I.Eleusis* 177 (*IG* II^2 1672), ll. 17–18: *εἰς τὸ ἀνάλημμα τὸ κατὰ τὴν οἰκίαν τὴ<ν> Ἐλ|ευσῖνι τῆς ἱερείας*; ll. 73–4: *καὶ τ|ὴν οἰκίαν τῆς ἱερείας*; l. 189: [*κα*]*ὶ τὴν οἰκίαν τὴν ἱεράν, οὗ ἡ ἱέρεια οἰκεῖ*; l. 422: *εἰς τὰς ἱερὰς οἰκίας ταῖς ἱερείαις θυρώματα ΔIIII*; l. 434: *εἰς τὰς θύρας τῆς ἱερείας καὶ τοῦ δαιδούχου III* (cf. Garland 1984, 99, 101; and now Clinton 2008, 179–80). Philleidai and priestess of Demeter and Kore: Clinton 1974, 74; Parker 1996, 317. Kerykes and dadouch: Clinton 1974, 47–68; Garland 1984, 99–100; Parker 1996, 301.

[114] e.g. the aphorism of Bourriot 1976, 799: 'En conclusion, aucun document n'atteste l'existence d'une propriété gentilice'.

completely in the dark. Of greater importance is the fact that their landholdings seem to have been of considerable size. If this is not just a matter of coincidence attributable to the preservation of the relevant material, it probably implies a proportionately high social status for the *gennetai* and would strengthen the arguments of those scholars who persist on seeing the *gene* as a prestigious constituent part of the Athenian social structure.[115]

As for the legal status of the gentilician realty itself, things are far from clear. Part of it was patently sacred, and probably inalienable, i.e. not liable to the rules of free market, such as the *ἱερὰ ἄρουρα* of the Salaminioi, and the same should apply a priori to the actual gentilician shrines.[116] On the other hand, the Eikadeis case of the *Rationes Centesimarum* appears to imply that another part of gentilician property fell within the category of secular and could, therefore, be sold. Or rather, if we are to accept the explication put forward above, its status was by the end of the Classical period open to shifting interpretations and, therefore, challengeable; alienation and prohibition of hypothecation constitute the two opposite ends of this notional fluidity. But such changes in land-tenure patterns are surely caused by, and in their turn, generate, respective changes of religious beliefs.[117] Now, it has long been realized that the Cleisthenic reforms left untouched some aspects of Archaic religious functions, more significantly gentilician priesthoods, which were, nonetheless, redefined into a new democratic meaning.[118] One wonders what this diffusion of gentilician cultic operations within the newly instituted democracy would have meant for *genos*-economics, and more specifically, for gentilician land. If it was accompanied by an opening of previously private cults to the wider public, does this mean that

[115] Cf. Parker 1996, 56–7 with n. 3 and 59–60.

[116] Cf. Harp. s.v. *δημοτελῆ καὶ δημοτικὰ ἱερά· διέφερον ἀλλήλων καὶ τῶν ὀργεωνικῶν καὶ τῶν γενικῶν, ὡς Δείναρχος δηλοῖ ἐν τῷ κατὰ Στεφάνου*; the adjective *γενικῶν* is presumably a gloss for shrines controlled by *gene*. But the context in this lemma is obviously financial, as implied by the term *δημοτελῆ* (overview in Pirenne-Delforge 2005, 56–60), and so by *γενικῶν* one should probably understand gentilician shrines generating income.

[117] As Manville 1990, 97 splendidly put it, 'religious beliefs or political programs can determine a particular pattern of tenure within a society . . . As property becomes more or less productive, or more or less sacred, a community's desire to farm and protect it will change. Customs of ownership evolve accordingly.'

[118] Kearns 1985, 189–92, 204–7; Rhodes 1993, 258–9; Aleshire 1994*a*, 327–35; Sourvinou-Inwood 2000, 38, 41.

landed revenues sustaining the former would have come under the administration of public bodies or other tiers of the Athenian political infrastructure? Our evidence does not permit such an inference. Of course, land was a necessary condition for *gene* to subsidize their own religious functions. It is imperative to stress this, since *gene* were actively involved in polis-religion functions as well. The Salaminioi, for example, administered the public festival of *Oschophoria*, for which the polis provided some funds.[119] But all in all, the rentals administered by the *genos* concerned the patrimonial cults of the group *per se*, both their strictly ritual aspect and the emoluments provided to the respective priests.[120] Applying these observations in the case of the Eikadeis, one can reasonably surmise that alienation of their landed assets would have distorted the internal structure of the *genos* by depriving them of a long-term source of funding. Whether such a disruption would have affected their role in the religious life of the polis is contingent on their exact articulation within the framework of the polis, an issue about which we are utterly uninformed.

The interaction between the gentilician and the polis realms deserves further investigation. Nothing in the fourth-century mass leases conferred by the polis, that included realty belonging to Athena Polias, implies that the Eteoboutadai, legitimate holders of the priesthood of the goddess, were in any way involved.[121] We cannot reject, however, the possibility that they owned land conscecrated to other minor divinities, the income from which was used to cover the expenditure of their own private rites. The same point, albeit slightly modified, can be made about the venerable *gene* that served the Eleusinian cults, namely the *Eumolpidai*, *Kerykes*, *Krokonidai*, *Koironidai*, and *Eudanemoi*. By means of their participation in the governmental bodies supervising the Eleusinian sanctuary, they might have had a say on issues concerning administration of realty belonging to the Two Goddesses. This is not to say, however, that the *gene*

[119] RO 37 ll. 20–2: *ὅσα μὲν ἡ πόλις παρέχει ἐκ τô δημ|οσίο ἢ παρὰ τῶν ὠ[σ]κοφόρων ἢ παρὰ τῶν δειπνοφόρ|ων γίγνεται λαμβάνειν Σαλαμινίοις*; ll. 47–50, *ἄρχοντα δὲ κ|ληρôν ἐμ μέρει παρ᾽ ἑκατέρων ὅστις καταστήσει | τὸς ὠσκοφόρος καὶ τὰς δειπνοφόρος μετὰ τῆς ἱε|ρείας καὶ τô κήρυκος κατὰ τὰ πάτρια*. See Osborne 1994, 158–9; Parker 1996, 57–8, 310–11, 315–16.

[120] Kearns 1985, 206; Sourvinou-Inwood 2000, 43–4.

[121] See especially *Agora* XIX L6 l.3: [Ἀ]*θηνᾶς Πολιάδο*[*s*] and the properties listed in ll. 4–21 (Walbank 1983*a*, 115–16); *Agora* XIX L10B l. 40: *Ἀθηνᾶς τέλμα* etc. (cf. Walbank 1983*b*, 197; Osborne 1988, 285).

owned the real property in question; gentilician and polis-owned properties clearly stood apart. It can be reasonably inferred that by the Classical epoch no *genos* retained or administered land dedicated to any state-deity of Athens, only land consecrated to divinities or heroes who remained important exclusively within the framework of the *genos* itself. The background to this state of affairs was undeniably religious, but the principal implications were ultimately of a financial character.

3. THE REAL PROPERTY OF THE ATTIC ORGEONES

i. Leasing out orgeonic property

Any modern treatment of the Attic orgeones must inescapably start from the classificatory convention introduced almost sixty years ago by the great American scholar Ferguson, namely the division of orgeones in two classes: type A citizen orgeones—hereditary religious clubs worshipping local heroes—and type B orgeones of gods and goddesses.[122] The scheme in its broad outline has so far remained unchallenged, and its validity is not going to be questioned in the course of this discussion, unless when deemed necessary.

In the case of the Attic orgeones we are able to detect a pattern already familiar from the investigation of other types of associated landowners, namely the employment of rentals for the subsidy of cultic activity.[123] The evidence, though not impressive in terms of volume—three inscribed leasing contracts and a few other documents with passing references to leasing[124]—suffices to bring out a coherent picture of leasing in the context of orgeonic groups. To begin with, a feature worth mentioning is that in two instances no individual is attested acting as the leasing agent on behalf of any orgeonic group. On the contrary, the lessor is the group per se, a manifest

[122] Ferguson 1944 and 1949 remain the fundamental treatments of the subject. See also Pantazopoulos 1947–8 (neglected); Lambert 1993, 74–7; Parker 1996, 109–11, 337–40; Mikalson 1998, 140–55; Jones 1999, 249–67; and more recently Arnaoutoglou 2003, 31–60.

[123] Cf. Walbank 1991, 160.

[124] Most, but not all of them, summarized in Behrend 1970, 95–9.

demonstration of a perception of collectivity almost unparalleled in other types of corporate groups.[125] However, in the case of the leasing of the orchard of Hero Iatros, the orgeones, though acting collectively, seem to have been legally represented, or, we might rather say, headed, by a certain Charops of Phaleron.[126] The absence of a title for Charops is somewhat enigmatic,[127] though this formulaic construction finds a good parallel in a confiscation case from 367/6.[128]

In the case of the orgeones of Egretes the ten-year period of their lease should probably be seen as an imitation of the pattern followed by the central government. The leasing of the orchard of Hero Iatros for thirty years is idiosyncratic and unprecedented, whereas the perennial lease of the shrine of Hypodektes is neatly matched by leases in perpetuity conferred by other corporate groups.[129] Overall, the choice seems to have been left to the discretion of each separate group. It is tempting to discern here a pattern of correspondence in roughly inverse proportion between rental and lease length. In the decennial lease of the orgeones of Egretes the rental is a decent annual sum of 200 drachmas,[130] whereas the perennial lessee of the shrine of Hypodektes was expected to disburse annually only a quarter of this amount; that is 50 drachmas.[131] It is true that the lessee Thrasyboulos

[125] *IG* II² 2499, ll. 2–3: *[ο]ἱ ὀργεῶνες ἐμίσθωσαν τὸ ἱερὸν το||[ῦ] Ἐγρέτου* (the orgeones leased out the shrine of Egretes); *IG* II² 2501 l. 2: *[οἱ ὀργε]ῶνες ἐμίσθωσαν <τὸ ἱ>ερὸν τοῦ Ὑποδέκτο[υ]* (the orgeones leased out the shrine of Hypodektes).

[126] *SEG* XXIV 203 ll. 2–5: *κατὰ τ[άδ]ε ἐμίσθωσεν | Χάροψ [Φ]αληρεὺς καὶ ο|ἱ ὀργ[εῶ]νες τοῦ ἡρώιο | τὸν [κῆπ]ον* (Charops and the orgeones leased out the orchard of the hero on the following terms); ll. 21–3: *ἐὰμ μή τι | αὐτὸν πεί<θ>ει Χάροψ* ᵛ *| καὶ οἱ ὀργεῶνες* (if Charops and the orgeones do not persuade the lessee). For the identification of the anonymous hero with the Hero-Doctor see Papagiannopoulos-Palaios *apud* Pantazopoulos 1947–8, 128 (cf. Wycherley 1960, 62–3 with n. 11), but note the doubts expressed by Arnaoutoglou 2003, 112 n. 86.

[127] Behrend 1970, 96 n. 218 thought that Charops held a long-standing office, Jameson 1982, 72 that he was the very head of the organization.

[128] *Agora* XIX P5 ll. 30–1: *Αἰσχίνης Μελιτε<ὺς> καὶ κοινὸν ὀ|ργεώνων ἐνεπεσκήψαντο* etc. (see Crosby 1941, 22; Ferguson 1944, 83; Lambert 1993, 319). Add also *IG* II² 1294 ll. 1–2: *[ο]ἱ ὀργεῶνες οἱ μετ||[ὰ nomen]*, opening clause of a Hellenistic orgeonic lease(?) (an improved text to be found in Langdon 1973); cf. Ferguson 1944, 93–4.

[129] Orgeones of Egretes: *IG* II² 2499 l. 4: *εἰς δέκα ἔτη* (cf. *IG* II² 2498; *I.Rhamnous* 180); orgeones of Hero Iatros: *SEG* XXIV 203 ll. 8–9: *ἔτη τριάκον|τα* (cf. J. and L. Robert, *BE* 1950, no. 72; Wycherley 1960, 62; Schwenk 1985, 175); orgeones of Hypodektes: *IG* II² 2501 ll. 3–4: *εἰς τ[ὸν ἅπαντα χρόν|ον]*, heavily restored, but fairly secure due to repeated references to Diopeithes' descendants as legitimate lessees; see *IG* II² 2501 ll. 3; 15; 18–19).

[130] *IG* II² 2499 ll.4–5: : *HH* : *δραχμῶν τοῦ ἐ|{ε}νιαυτοῦ ἑκάστου.*

[131] *IG* II² 2501 ll.5–6: *[τὴν] μίσθωσ<ιν>* 𐅄 *δραχμὰς ἑκάστ[ου τοῦ | ἐνιαυ]τ<ο>ῦ.*

had to pay a rental of only 20 drachmas for every year of his thirty-year tenancy,[132] but the triviality of the rental must partly have been due to the fact that only part of the shrine was being let, unlike the two previous examples.

Two of the contracts under consideration contain minute details for the appropriate maintenance of the property, no doubt because in both instances the leased object was the shrine of the hero worshipped there.[133] Even the orchard leased by the orgeones of Hero Iatros seems to have been an appurtenance of the heroon.[134] The amendment at the end of this lease concerning the need to keep the sanctuary pure proves this point beyond doubt, and it is neatly matched by similar provisions in the other two documents.[135] It is noteworthy that the lessees were instructed to provide roofing for the obviously open-air premises of the leased shrines, even though they maintained the explicit right to remove and keep the building materials upon termination of the agreements.[136] It may be that similar provisions were recounted in the lost speech *Against the Orgeones* written by Isaeus for an unknown plaintiff and apparently treating a disputed piece of land.[137] Such concerns imply, in all probability, that orgeones did not usually own realty other than their cultic centres.

[132] *SEG* XXIV 203 ll. 6–9: *εἴκοσι | δραχ[μῶν] τοῦ ἐνιαυτô | ἑ̣κάστου ἔτη τριάκον|τα.*

[133] *IG* II^2 2499 and *IG* II^2 2501. The former falls also under the category of emphyteutic leases, since it contains an arboricultural provision (for similar emphyteutic clauses see *IG* I^3 84, *I.Rhamnous* 180; outside Attica the most notable example is *IG* XII (7) 62 from Arkesine, cf. Rhodes and Osborne 2003, 282–7).

[134] The leased object is actually described as the orchard of the *heroon* (*SEG* XXIV 203 ll. 4–5: *τοû ἡρώιο | τὸν [κῆπ]ον*).

[135] *SEG* XXIV 203 ll. 28–30: *χρῆ|σ<θ>αι δὲ τῶι ἱερῶι* ^{v} *κα|θ̣αρῶι* (they should keep the sanctuary clean), with Arnaoutoglou 2003, 112; *IG* II^2 2499 ll. 5–7: *χρῆ*^{vv}*σθαι τῶι ἱ|ερῶι καὶ ταῖς οἰκία<ι>ς ταῖς ἐνωικοδ|ομημέναις ὡς ἱερῶι* (they should use the shrine and the premises built in it as befits a shrine); *IG* II^2 2501 l. 4: *χρῆσθαι τῶι <τ>[εμ]ένε<ι> [καὶ τῶι τοῦ] Ὑποδέκτου ἱερῶι [ὡς ἱερῶι]* (they should use the *temenos* and the shrine of Hypodektes as befits a shrine); [*καθαρῶι*], as in *SEG* XIV 203, is conceptually and epigraphically tenable (cf. Parker 1983, 162).

[136] See the commentary of Dittenberger in *Syll.*^{3} 1097 (=*IG* II^2 2499); Osborne 1985*c*, 122–3 and 1988, 288 (cf. *Agora* XIX L15 l. 4, with Walbank's note ad loc.).

[137] Is. frs. 26–7 *apud* Harp. s.v. *ἀποφοράν· ἀντὶ τοῦ ἀπενεγκεῖν καὶ διάστημα ποιῆσαι μεταξὺ Ἰσαῖος ἐν τῷ πρὸς Ὀργεῶνας, ἐν ᾧ φησὶν οὕτως: "εἴπερ γοῦν ὥριζον ταῖς ἀποφοραῖς ταύταις τῶν ποδῶν ἀλλότριον εἶναι τὸ χωρίον"*; idem s.v. *εἰσεπόδιζον· ἀντὶ τοῦ εἰσέβαινον τοὺς πόδας τοῦ χωρίου Ἰσαῖος ἐν τῷ Πρὸς Ὀργεῶνας*; idem s.v. *παλίνσκιον· Ἰσαῖος μὲν ἐν τῷ Πρὸς Ὀργεῶνας: "μήτε παλίνσκιον γίγνεσθαι τὸ χωρίον" ἀντὶ τοῦ σύσκιον* (these entries, along with Isaeus' reputed specialization in land tenure cases, make it almost certain that the speech concerned realty, perhaps a landholding

More than in the case of other leasing bodies, it is obvious that the choice of the payment dates was made on the basis of the cultic needs of the orgeones. The case of the worshippers of Egretes has already been discussed,[138] and here it suffices to mention the lease of the shrine of Hypodektes, which stipulated payment for the first of Boedromion in anticipation of the cultic reception ceremony on the fourteenth of the same month.[139] By analogy, one can infer that Thargelion was chosen by the orgeones of Hero Iatros as the payment date of the rental exactly because their main, if not only, cultic activity took place in that month.[140] The strong link between rentals and subsidy of cultic activity can be seen more clearly in the Hellenistic document *IG* II^2 1289, where a board of arbitrators promulgated the ruling that the revenues from the landholdings of the goddess were to fund the sacrifices performed by the priest along with the orgeones according to the ancestral customs.[141] Here 'revenues' (*ἐκ τῶν π[ροσόδων]*, a fairly secure restoration) clearly refers to leasing, as it is contrasted with sale and hypothecation of property, the idea being that letting out property, instead of alienating it in a one-off deal,

leased out by orgeones to the unknown client of Isaeus; cf. Forster 1927, 456; Ferguson 1944, 84 n. 29). Note also Harp. s.v. *γεισίπους καὶ γεισιπόδισμα καὶ γεισιποδίζειν· τὸ ἐξέχον τῆς δοκοῦ, ἐφ' οὗ τὸ γεῖσόν ἐστιν γεισίπους καλεῖται καὶ γεισιπόδισμα, καὶ γεισιποδίζειν τὸ τοῦτον ποιεῖν. Ἰσαῖος ἐν τῷ Πρὸς Ὀργεῶνας; γεισίπους/γεισήπους* (cornice-support) is a vital structural element of a roof, hence my assumption that a leasing clause concerning construction of a roof may be implied here.

[138] See Chapter 3, Section 2.ii.

[139] *IG* II^2 2501 ll. 4–7: *[ἀποδιδό|ναι δὲ] αὐτοὺς τοῖς [ὀργεῶσι τὴν] μίσθωσ<ιν>* 𐅄 *δραχμὰς ἑκάστ[ου τοῦ | ἐνιαυ]τ<ο>ῦ τεῖ νουμηνίαι τοῦ [Βοηδ]ρ[ομι]ῶνος μηνός, τεῖ δὲ τετρά[δι ἐπὶ | δέκα ὅ]ταν ἱεροῖς ἀπαντ<ῶ>σιν παρέχει<ν> αὐτούς*... (and they will give to the orgeones the rental of fifty drachmas each year on the first day of the month Boedromion, and on the fourteenth day, when they meet for the sacred rites, they will provide etc.); cf. Ekroth 2002, 148–9.

[140] *SEG* XXIV 203 ll. 9–11: *ἀποδιδόναι δὲ τὴν | μίσθωσιν ἐ[ν] τῶι Θαργ|ηλιῶνι* (they should pay down the rental in Thargelion). There is no specification of a day within the month and it is possible that the first of Thargelion (*νουμηνία*) is implied here, just as in the other two orgeonic documents, for orgeones—unlike other groups such as demes—would have had very few chances to meet over a year, let alone a single month. At any rate, the vague formula *ἐ[ν] τῶι Θαργ|ηλιῶνι* probably provided a sufficient chronological indication to the interested parties.

[141] *IG* II^2 1289 ll. 4–8: *τὰ μὲν κ̲τήματ[α εἶναι τῆς] | θεο̣ῦ καὶ μηθενὶ ἐξεῖναι μὴτ' [ἀποδόσθαι] | μήτε ὑπ[ο]θεῖναι, ἀλλὰ ἐκ τῶν π[ροσόδων θύ]|ειν τὰς θυσίας τὸν ἱερέα μετ[ὰ τῶν ὀργεώ]|νων κατὰ τὰ πάτ[ρια]{ια}* (the estates will belong to the goddess and nobody will be allowed either to sell or hypothecate them, but the priest, along with the orgeones, will offer the sacrifices from the revenues according to the ancestral customs).

could secure a constant source of income for the patrimonial sacrifices to the goddess. Indeed, in a recent analysis of the text Sosin demonstrated that the arbitrators' verdict was backed by a proclamation by the goddess and the *hestiator* (?) which sanctioned the group's intention to employ rentals for the performance of the sacrifices.[142] Leasing was arguably one of the sources of revenue for covering the sacrificial expenditure mentioned in a third-century decree of the orgeones of Echelos and Heroines, which, however, reproduces regulations laid down at an earlier period.[143] If so, the administrator of the rentals would have been the magistrate under the title *hestiator* (ἑστιάτωρ).[144] Finally, it has been suggested that a very fragmentary document of the orgeones of Zeus Epakrios may record a leasing transaction; if so, the leased object might have been the shrine of the divinity worshipped there.[145]

Of course, performance of cultic activity was not the only end that rentals were intended to meet. In another orgeonic document the lease of a house was used to subsidize repairs within the house itself and the shrine of the cult (the Bendideion of the Piraeus, as most

[142] Sosin 2002, 125–8; cf. Papazarkadas 2004-9 [2010], 91–5, where I argue that Kallistratos, the incumbent involved, was not the *hestiator* but the priest (ἱερεύς) of the group.

[143] *SEG* XXI 530 ll. 12–18, esp. ll. 17–18: λογίζεσθαι (sc. τὸν ἑστιάτορα) ὅ, τι ἂν | [ἀναλ]ώσει· ἀναλίσκειν δὲ μὴ πλέον τῆς προσόδου (the *hestiator* will render account of whatever expenditure he incurs, and he should not spend more than the revenues); cf. Meritt 1942, 282–4, and Ferguson 1944, 73–9, esp. 76, where he dates the ancient decree to the mid-5th cent. To be sure, the main preoccupation of the decree is the collection of debts from members of the dual *koinon* (*SEG* XXI 530 ll. 5–8: ἀναγράψαντας τοὺς ὀφείλοντά[ς τι εἰς κοι]|νωνίαν ἐν στήλει λιθίνει στῆσαι παρὰ τ[ὸν βωμὸν] | ἐν τῶι ἱερῶι τά τε κεφάλαια καὶ τὸν τόκο[ν ὁπόσου] | ἂν ἔχει ἕκαστος; cf. Mikalson 1998, 147–8; Jones 1999, 251–4), but it is not inconceivable that the initial capital out on loan derived from rentals, just as in the case of the Plotheian decree *IG* I^3 258. Indeed τὰ ἐπιγενόμενα (l. 24 = l. 1 of the second 'ancient decree') could equally well refer to interest (so Ferguson 1944, 78) as well as to rental (Jones 1999, 252 translates simply 'the revenues'); cf. Descat 1993, 148.

[144] Cf. the decree of the orgeones of Amynon, Asklepios, and Dexion *IG* II^2 1259 (313/2), where two *histiatores* (ἱστιάτορες) are crowned because 'they had taken care of the common affairs and the sacrifices well and in a spirit of good-will' (ll. 4–5: καλῶς καὶ φιλοτίμως ἐπιμε[μέ]|ληνται τῶν [τε κ]οι[ν]ῶν κα[ὶ] τῶν θυσιῶ[ν]); their task would have entailed financial affairs.

[145] *IG* II^2 1294 with the readings of Langdon 1973; cf. Ferguson 1944, 93–4; Lambert 2000*b*, 77–8. Perhaps ll. 1–4 of this text (now *SEG* L 162) can be restored as [κατὰ τάδε ἐμίσθωσαν ο]ἱ ὀργεῶνες οἱ μετ|[ὰ name+demotic] Ἐπιγόνωι Ἐνδίο[υ | demotic τὸ ἱερὸν το]ῦ Διὸς τοῦ Ἐπα[κ|ρίου] (the orgeones headed by *so- and- so* leased out the shrine of Zeus Epakrios to Epigonos, the son of Endios, of the deme (?) on the following terms).

historians maintain).[146] Elsewhere I have argued that part of the job of Stephanos, the *epimeletes* honoured by the orgeones of Bendis in *IG* II^2 1324, might have been precisely the utilization of this rental for the repair works. That such refurbishments were considered to be a sacred affair can be clearly seen from the fact that the relevant stipulation was incorporated in a document classifiable as a *lex sacra*, since it contains numerous provisions concerning perquisites to priestesses and priests, payments to other sacred officials, sacred fines, and so on. The leasing clause of *IG* II^2 1361 is interesting for a further reason: water resources available in the building plot of the house comprised a separate item of sale, the proceeds from which were to subsidize the repair works,[147] even though the lessee was allowed to make use of the water in order to cover his own needs.[148] In this sense, *IG* II^2 1361 recalls the fifth-century lease of the Neleion, wherein the lessee was granted full use of the water flowing within a ditch of the precinct,[149] even though the mud from the dyke was to be sold separately.[150] With regard to the orgeones of Bendis and Deloptes, there is a very fragmentary late Hellenistic decree that seems to record a lease transaction, but the details are irretrievable.[151] The

[146] *IG* II^2 1361 ll. 8–11: *ὅπως δ' ἂν ἡ οἰκία καὶ | [τ]ὸ ἱερὸν ἐπισκευάζηται, τὸ ἐν[οίκιον τῆ]ς οἰ[κίας] καὶ τὸ ὕδωρ ὅσου ἂμ πραθῆι, ε|[ἰς τὴν ἐ]πισκευὴν τοῦ ἱεροῦ [καὶ τῆς] οἰκίας, εἰς ἄλλο δὲ μηδὲν ἀναλίσκειν, ἕ|[ως] ἂν [τὸ ἱερὸ]ν ἐπισκευ[ασ]θῆι κ[αὶ ἡ οἰκία]* (in order for the house and the shrine to be repaired, the rental from the house and the price from the sale of the water should be spent on the repair of the shrine and the house, but on nothing else, until the shrine and the house have been repaired). Cf. Ferguson 1944, 103 and 1949, 153; Simms 1988, 72; Jones 2000, 80.

[147] Cf. Cole 1988, 162 n. 14, citing *IG* I^3 256, esp. ll. 4–7: *τελὲν δ]ὲ ὀβολὸ[ν τ|]ὸς πίνοντας τô Ἀλυκô τô ἐνιᾳ[υ|τ]ô ἑκάστο ἐς τὰ ἱερὰ τῆσι Νύμ[φ|η]σι*; but this is not an exact parallel (contra Meyer 2004, 324–5). The formula used in the orgeonic law (*καὶ τὸ ὕδωρ ὅσου ἂμ πραθῆι*) suggests sale at an auction.

[148] *IG* II^2 1361 ll. 12–13: *ὑπολιμπάνειν δὲ ὕδωρ τῶι ἐνοικοῦντι ὡς χρῆσθ|[αι]*.

[149] *IG* I^3 84 ll. 34–7: *καὶ τês τάφρο καὶ τô ὕδατος κρατêν τô ἐγ Διὸς τὸν μισθοσά|μενον, ὁπόσον ἐντὸς ῥεῖ τô Διονυσίο καὶ τôν πυλôν ἒ<ι> ἅλαδε ἐ[χ]σελα|ύνοσιν οἱ μύσται καὶ ὁπόσον ἐντὸς τês οἰκίας τês δεμοσίας καὶ τ|ôν πυλôν αἳ ἐπὶ τὸ Ἰσθμονίκο βαλανεῖον ἐκφέροσι·*.

[150] *IG* I^3 84 ll. 20–3: *τὸν δὲ ἐονεμένον τὲν ἰλὺν ἐκκο|μίσασθαι ἐκ τês τάφρο ἐπὶ τêσδε τês βολês ἀποδόντα τὸ ἀργύριον | τôι Νελεῖ ὅσο ἐπρίατο· ὁ δὲ βασιλεὺς ἐχσαλεψάτο τὸν πριάμενον τ|ὴν ἰλύν, ἐπειδὰν ἀποδôι τὲμ μίσθοσιν*; note that the transaction is initially termed a sale but the amount paid is considered a rental, a frequent terminological ambiguity in such contracts.

[151] *Agora* XIX L16 (=*Agora* XVI 329) with the justifiable hesitation of Walbank ad loc. to accept the previous editors' interpretation of the document as a lease by the orgeones to the Athenians (so Behrend 1970, 99, and Osborne 1988, 284), which would be unprecedented (cf. Walbank 1991, 159).

mention of *Θρᾶκες* in line 4 probably indicates that the issuing body, unlike that of *IG* II² 1361, was the Thracian orgeones, or a mixed body of Thracians and Athenian citizens. The principal importance of the text therefore is that it comprises one of the last, if not the last, leasing documents before the Roman period.[152]

One final technical point needs to be addressed. In all the three fully preserved leases of orgeonic property the lessees are instructed to set up copies of the contracts, presumably at their own expense.[153] This is remarkable and two interpretations are possible here: either orgeones, in general, faced a liquidity problem with the effect that they tried to limit expenditure as much as possible,[154] or the leases were perceived as liturgies and the tenants undertook the further burden of defraying the cost of erecting inscriptions containing the leasing clauses. For reasons to be highlighted in Section 3.iii of the present chapter the latter explanation should be preferred.

ii. Sales of orgeonic property and the problem of alienation

It was noted above that the extant leases issued by orgeones might be taken to suggest that such groups usually lacked realty other than the core property necessary for the performance of their cultic activity. However, other evidence, to which we have resorted already more than once, poses a challenge to this theory. The *Rationes Centesimarum* contain one certain entry of a group of orgeones alienating their landed assets, and possibly others.[155] All these transactions appear in stelae 3 and 4, which include 'non-territorial' groups. Given the tendency of associations such as *gene* and phratries to

[152] Walbank 1991, 161; for the date (*c.*100) see Tracy 1990, 252.

[153] *SEG* XXIV 203 ll. 23–7: *στῆσ|αι δὲ στήλην Θρασύβο|υλον ἐν τῶι ἱερῶι ἀντ|ίγραφα τῶνδε τῶν συν|θηκῶν*; *IG* II² 2499 ll. 39–42: *ἀναγράψαι δὲ | τὴμ μίσθωσιν τήνδε Διόγνητον εἰς | τὴν στήλην τὴν ὑπάρχουσαν ἐν τῶι ἱ|ερῶι*; *IG* II² 2501 ll. 20–2: *ἀναγράψαι δὲ τάσδε τὰς συνθήκας τοὺς μὲν ὀργεῶνα[ς] | εἰς τὸ κοινὸν γραμματεῖον, Διοπείθην δὲ εἰς στήλην λιθίνην καὶ | στῆσαι ἐν τῶι ἱερῶι παρὰ τὸ ἄγαλμα τοῦ θεοῦ.*

[154] But most scholars have argued that orgeonic leases provide evidence of financial affluence; so Ferguson 1944, 81; Andrewes 1961; Ustinova 1996, 230 n. 15.

[155] F14, 2–8 (cult of the group unknown; see Lambert 1997*a*, 201). Lambert 1997*a*, 197, based on prosopographical indications, also raises the possibility that the group alienating an outlying estate at Phlya (F11A, 1–4) was the association of the orgeones of Zeus Epakrios.

bear collective names in clear contrast with groups of orgeones, which tend to be named after the hero or deity they cultivate,[156] it is a fair inference that where divine names are recorded in the headings of individual transactions in the *Rationes Centesimarum*, the selling groups were orgeones. Applying this criterion, one can add to the aforementioned unidentified group of orgeones those of Herakles, Hero Alkimacho[s], [Adra]stos or [Hephai]stos in Lo[usia], [Herak]les Plousios and Epianios.[157] Note that the official acting on behalf of [Herak]les Plousios descended in all likelihood from the Thracian royal house. His ancestry is reminiscent of another cult of Thracian origin, that of Bendis, which was administered by orgeones too. The similarities might indicate that the group controlling the cult of Herakles Plousios could have been enfranchised descendants of foreign orgeones.

It is worth noting that in the only indisputable case of a transaction carried out by an orgeonic group, the selling agents seem to have been designated as *epimeletai* (*ἐπιμεληταί*).[158] The same is true of the official representing the group controlling the cult of Epianios, if one endorses the theory put forward above that they were indeed orgeones.[159] Though the title *epimeletes* is ubiquitous, suspiciously flexible, and also attested in relation to other types of groups, it is significant that it occurs in financial contexts in the workings of the citizen orgeones of Bendis.[160] On the other hand, the representatives of the association alienating the property of Herakles bear the title *hieromnemones*.[161] If this is indeed a group of orgeones, the presence of *hieromnemones* should not pose a problem: a series of diverse

[156] Ferguson 1944, 61–2.

[157] Herakles: F13A, 5–9 with Lambert 1997*a*, 198–9; Hero Alkimacho[s]: F14, 9–10 with Lambert 1997*a*, 201; [Adra]stos or [Hephai]stos in Lo[usia]: F11B, 2–6 with Lambert 1997*a*, 201–2; [Herak]les Plousios: F12B, 7–13 with Lambert 1997*a*, 203–4; Epianios: F13B, 5–8 with Lambert 1997*a*, 204. With regard to the cult of Herakles, it has been known for a long time that a society of citizen orgeones operated in the (yet to be published) shrine of Herakles Pankrates (Kalogeropoulou 299–300; the iconographic analysis of the votive-reliefs has shown that the shrine flourished from the second half of the 4th to the early 3rd cent.; see Vikela 1994, 169–71, 225, 235–6).

[158] F14 A, 2–3: [*ὀ*]*ργεώ*[*νων* - - - *ἐπι*]|*μελητ*[*αί* - - -] (cf. Lewis 1973*a*, 206).

[159] F13B, 5: [. . . . .c.7–11 . . . . .] *ẸΠΙẠΝΙΟΥ ἐπιμελητής*.

[160] *IG* II² 1361 ll. 14–15, and *IG* II² 1324 with Ferguson 1949, 153 n. 63 (cf. *IG* II² 1256).

[161] F13A: *Ἡρακλέους ἱερομνήμον*[*ες*].

magistracies is attested in relation to orgeonic groups, and there is nothing inherently impossible about an office of *hieromnemones* in the framework of such an association, not to mention the fact that in deme contexts *hieromnemones* seem to have been engaged in land management.[162]

Beyond the technicalities dealt with above, the paramount question concerns the ability of orgeones to alienate part of their property.[163] This issue is related to the question of the legal status of orgeones and, by implication, that of the legal status of their real property.[164] *IG* II^2 1289, the orgeonic document mentioned above, three times makes emphatic mention of landholdings as being the personal property of the goddess worshipped by the association.[165] Though this text represents the normative response of the orgeones to the very specific problems that had previously arisen, there is no reason to doubt the sacred character of the landholdings in question. But does this principle apply to the totality of the realty of any orgeonic group, or at least to that of the citizen type? In this respect, the *Rationes Centesimarum* constitute a problem, since orgeonic groups are attested as disposing of their property for good. This would appear to indicate that some associations of orgeones did own secular, and therefore disposable, property. It is significant in this respect that the property of all groups which can be safely or only tentatively identified as orgeones in the *Rationes Centesimarum* consisted exclusively of estates (*χωρία*). Note that an estate (*χωρίον*) managed by orgeones was presumably the disputed item in the lost speech of Isaeus *Against the Orgeones*.[166] On the other hand, this terminological observation loses some force by the fact that the sacred property in *IG* II^2 1289 consisted of landholdings (*κτήματα*). And as for the orgeones of *Agora* XVI 161, although it is conceivable that they controlled property

[162] *SEG* XXVIII 103 ll. 38–9; *I.Rhamnous* 180 ll. 82–3 (see Chapter 3, Section 2.v). However, Lambert 1999*b*, 125–8 now identifies the group as a *thiasos*.

[163] Ferguson 1944, 68 thought they had full right to do so.

[164] For a more theoretical treatment of the legal dimensions of Athenian religious associations see Arnaoutoglou 1998, 70–6.

[165] *IG* II^2 1289 ll. 4–5: *τὰ μὲν κτήματ[α εἶναι τῆς] | θεοῦ*; 10–11: *[τῶν κτη*^{v}*]|μάτων τῶν ἑαυτῆς*; 13–14: *[τὰ περὶ τὰ ἑαυ]|τῆς κτήματα*.

[166] *ὀργεῶνας· Ἰσαίου λόγος ἐστὶ Πρὸς Ὀργεῶνας* (see n. 137 above).

belonging to a heroine, the crucial phrase is too vague to allow any definitive conclusions.[167]

A perhaps more fruitful exercise would be to try to investigate ways in which orgeones acquired realty in the first place. Of course orgeones might have been owners of property since time immemorial, especially if we accept that theirs was an ancient institution,[168] and indeed it has recently been argued again with great plausibility that their functions were already regulated in the Solonian legislation.[169] Their alleged ancient origin would receive further support if those linguists who think they can identify *proto-orgeones* featuring as landowners in Linear B tablets are right, but this interpretation has not been unanimously endorsed.[170] Fortunately, we know relatively more about groups created in historical times, since their act of establishment was usually accompanied by consecration of a piece of land for the foundation of their central shrine. *IG* II[2] 1283, a Hellenistic decree recording a grant to the Thracian *ethnos* of the right to acquire land in order to found a sanctuary, has featured so frequently in secondary bibliography that even a simple mention runs the risk of banality.[171] Similar rights were bestowed upon the Egyptians and the Citian merchants for the establishment of the shrines of Isis and Aphrodite respectively.[172] We do not know if these two

[167] *Agora* XVI 161 ll. 3–4: *[τῶι κοι|ν]ῶι τῶι πρὸς τοῖς Καλλιφάνους*, have been thought to refer to the locale of the devotees of the Heroines, which was 'near the property of Kalliphanes', ever since the editio princeps by Meritt 1942, 282–7, no. 55. But who was Kalliphanes? No one seems to have asked the question. Ferguson 1944, 76 n. 20, very tentatively suggested that one should read *Καλλιφανοῦς*, in reference to *Καλλιφανώ*, the presumed leader of the heroines worshipped by the orgeones in question. This makes good sense in that it attests to the sacred property of a heroine, but it still remains short of solid proof.

[168] See Ferguson 1944, 68; Andrewes 1961, 1–2; Parker 1996, 28; Ustinova 1996.

[169] Theodoridis 2002, 41–2.

[170] So Chadwick 1957, 128; cf. Ventris and Chadwick 1956, 265–6, no. 152.7, *wo-ro-ki-jo-ne-jo e-re-mo*, translated as 'the unencumbered land of the cult association' (sc. orgeones), an interpretation about which Palmer 1963, 214 expressed scepticism (later acknowledged by Chadwick 1973, 454). Lindgren 1973, 158–9 provides full bibliography on the various interpretations of the term. Bendall 2007, 73 thinks that the crucial word is a possessive adjective 'formed from a man's name, *Wroikiōn*'.

[171] *IG* II[2] 1283 ll. 4–6: *ἐπειδὴ τοῦ δήμου τῶν Ἀθηναίων δεδωκότος τοῖς Θραιξὶ μ|όνοις τῶν ἄλλων ἐθνῶν τὴν ἔγκτησιν καὶ τὴν ἵδρυσιν τοῦ | ἱεροῦ* etc.; cf. Pache 2001, 6–10.

[172] *IG* II[2] 337 esp. ll. 38–45: *δεδόχθαι τῶι δήμ|ωι δοῦναι τοῖς ἐμπόροις | τῶν Κιτιέων ἔνκτησι[ν] χ[ω]|ρίου ἐν ὧι ἱδρύσονται τὸ | ἱερὸν τῆς Ἀφροδίτης καθ|άπερ καὶ οἱ Αἰγύπτιοι τὸ | τῆς Ἴσιδος ἱερὸν ἵδρυντ|αι*; cf. Planeaux 2000–1, 170–2.

ethnic groups formed associations of orgeones, but even if they did, they would have been classified as non-citizen associations, like the Thracian orgeones of Bendis.[173] Nevertheless, once their institutions were established, they could theoretically lease out their sanctuaries, or part of them, to cover cultic expenditure, in a fashion similar to the cases examined above. Self-evidently, profitable alienation of their property could never be a realistic option, since this would not only undermine their own cultic existence, but would also go against social convention. Alienation would constitute open scorn of the political authorities, in our case Athens, which had honoured them with the enviable privilege of *enktesis*. Whereas associations of foreigners needed the permission of the Athenian state to counterbalance their legal incapacity to acquire realty, for the indigenous population things were somewhat easier. In the course of the investigation of other corporate groups' capacity to acquire property, confiscation of hypothecated realty was shown to have occurred frequently. In the case of orgeonic associations, we know of one instance in which a group brought a claim against a certain Theosebes, who had given his house as security; the amount owed to the orgeones was a paltry 24 drachmas.[174] The case, known from an intact *poletai* record dating to 367/6, poses various difficulties, not least that the house of Theosebes had been sold subject to redemption, i.e. hypothecated, to multiple creditors. As a result, the individual creditors demanded not the property itself, but the money lent to Theosebes, when the house was sold by the *poletai* following his condemnation *in absentia* for the crime of sacrilege.[175] This case, therefore, cannot be instructive other than in showing that orgeones could occasionally provide loans on security. Indeed, three late fourth-century hypothecation *horoi* from the Athenian cleruchy of Hephaistia feature groups of orgeones—in two instances the same group, i.e. the orgeones of Herakles in Kome—receiving real property as security.[176] Here the amounts at stake are

[173] Cf. Pecirca 1966, 60–1; Schwenk 1985, 143–6; Parker 1996, 337.

[174] *Agora* XIX P5 ll. 30–5: *Αἰσχίνης Μελιτε<ὺς> καὶ κοινὸν ὀ|ργεώνων ἐνεπεσκήψαντο ἐν τῆι οἰκίαι ἣν ἀπέγραψ|εν Θεόμνηστος Ἰωνίδης ἐνοφείλεσθαι ἑαυτοῖς* : | ΔΔ⊢⊢⊢⊢ *δραχμάς, πριαμένων ἡμῶν τὴν οἰκίαν ταύτ|ην παρὰ Θεοφίλου τούτο τοῦ ἀργυρίο ἐπὶ λύσει. ἔδ|οξεν ἐνοφείλεσθαι.*

[175] For the various legal and other problems concerning this case see Finley 1952*a*, 110–12; idem 1952*b*; Hallof 1990, 414; Lambert 1993, 314–19; Langdon 1994, 256–7.

[176] *IG* XII (8) 19, 21 (=Finley 1952*a*, 148–9, nos. 107–9). See now Culasso Gastaldi 2006, 519–20, no. 5; 533–5, no. 11. For the problematic dating of these *horoi* see

quite substantial (1000, 400, and a sum over 100 drachmas) and, although we cannot know whether the debtors eventually repaid the money or not, it remains a distant, albeit plausible, possibility that the orgeones would have confiscated the hypothecated properties upon debtors' default. But if this is the case, is there any reason to assume that expropriated properties would have passed to the nominal ownership of the divinities worshipped by the orgeones and not to the control of the groups themselves?

Many scholars maintain that orgeones were in effect private associations and, by implication, their assets fell within the sphere of private property.[177] I find this position highly problematic and completely incompatible with the (undoubtedly correct) interpretation of the *Rationes Centesimarum* as sales of land of public associations instigated by the central administration. In other words, the ability of the polis of Athens to recommend, induce, compel (or whatever verb one chooses) certain public or semi-public bodies to alienate part of their landed assets provides first-rate proof of the fact that orgeones, similarly to other groups like demes, *komai*, phratries, etc., had a recognized public aspect which differentiated them from actual private individuals.[178] Recently Parker, starting from a different point of view, reached a similar conclusion stating that orgeones probably 'feasted in private for the public good', despite having patent features of private structuring.[179] What is more, religion seems to have played a major part—though not an exclusive one, as the lending activities investigated above reveal—in the *modus operandi* of orgeones.[180] But given their religious orientation, surely their landed assets are much

Cargill 1995, 47–8 with the earlier bibiliography; for the groups see Ferguson 1944, 92; cf. Parker 1994, 343.

[177] Most notably Finley 1952*a*, 97.

[178] Above all we have Aristotle's blunt affirmation: *αἱ δ' ἄλλαι κοινωνίαι εἰσὶν ἢ μόριον τῶν τῆς πόλεως, οἷον ἡ τῶν φρατέρων ἢ τῶν ὀργέων, ἢ αἱ χρηματιστικαί* (Arist. *EE* 1241^{b}25).

[179] Parker 1996, 110–1 (cf. Kearns 1989, 75). I find this analysis of the role of orgeones far preferable to modernist approaches (e.g. Leiwo 1997; Arnaoutoglou 1998) which want to see orgeones as ultimately private associations aiming at strengthening solidarity between their members for the financial, social, and broader welfare of these associates (it has to be said that these new theories are not as groundbreaking as their proponents would boast they are; Pantazopoulos 1947–8 is a very early advocate of this trend). Such treatments tend to commit a methodological error by mingling together groups like citizen-orgeones with private corporations of mixed composition, such as *eranoi*, *thiasoi*, and so on.

[180] Cf. Kearns 1989, 73–4; Lambert 1993, 74–5.

more likely to have fallen under the category 'sacred' than in the case of other associations?

With this question we return to the *Rationes Centesimarum*. It was, of course, in the interest of the state to perceive the property of these groups, orgeones included, as ultimately secular. Some groups might have been content with such a scheme which provided an easy opportunity for accumulation of cash. Yet I suspect there is another, more sinister, aspect of this problem. As shown above, some of the groups tentatively identified as orgeones tended quite obscure cults. We hear nothing of Epianios, Herakles Plousios, the hero Alkimachos, and so on outside the *Rationes Centesimarum*, either prior to or after their recording. This should probably be seen as a pointer to the relative insignificance of these cults and, in this light, the *Rationes Centesimarum* might be the death-rattle of the worshipping groups concerned. In other words, from the point of view of the central government the alienation of the property of some of these groups would have had a dual purpose: the increase of the state's revenue by means of the *hekatoste* and the decisive solution to the problem of the gradual decline of the relevant associations either through their financial rejuvenation or through their final elimination.[181] Through parting with their landed assets, *de facto* dissolution was the fatal outcome for most of them.[182] My guess is that incidents like this created over-complicated situations which gave rise to disputes such as the one recorded in *IG* II^2 1289 or, as far as *gene* are concerned, the one recorded in the decree of the Eikadeis (*IG* II^2 1258). Individual orgeones would have reacted differently to the exigencies that arose. In *IG* II^2 1289 some associates, or a constitutional branch of the group, had presumably proposed, and perhaps managed, to sell part of the association's landed assets on the pretext that they belonged to the group and as such were alienable. The response was firm and unequivocal: the unhindered cultic activity of the group was warranted by the goddess's reaffirmation of her exclusive ownership of her *κτήματα*. Just as in the case of other cultic associations, the sanctity of realty controlled by orgeones was fluid and open to

[181] Contra Lambert 1997*a*, 278–80, who believes that the proceeds from the sales, minus the *hekatoste*, flowed into some secular treasury of the polis. But if his assumption is correct, that would reinforce the theory put forward here, namely that the *Rationes Centesimarum* impoverished the selling groups.

[182] For the conceptual impossibility of deliberate dissolution of such cultic groups see Poland 1909, 275 and Arnaoutoglou 1998, 71–2, contra Ferguson 1944, 84 n. 31.

varying interpretations depending on the historical developments of the time. Once challenged, it could be upturned and could jeopardize the very existence of the administrative groups.

iii. Lessees and purchasers of orgeonic property: some considerations

Unlike documents of other public and/or religious associations, those of orgeones are thoroughly cryptic concerning leasing procedures. As a result, it is difficult to figure out whether an open auction enabled outsiders to embark on land transactions with orgeones, or a more exclusive policy restricted this privilege to members of the groups proper.[183] In the absence of any evidence favouring the former theory, in the light of the tendency of other corporate groups to confer leases on individuals from their own ranks,[184] and, more importantly, given the generally more introvert behaviour of orgeonic groups, it seems wiser to assume that leasing remained in effect a strictly orgeonic business.[185]

Of the three attested lessees of orgeonic realty, Thrasyboulos of Alopeke is otherwise completely unknown. Diognetos, son of Arkesilas, of Melite (*LGPN* II, *Διόγνητος* (31) = *PAA* 327870) might have been the same as Diognetos of Melite, whose son served as councillor of the restored democracy in 304/3 (*LGPN* II, *Διόγνητος* (32) = *PAA* 327855).[186] By virtue of his patronym, and given its rarity, he was probably brother of Onetor, son of Arkesilas, of Melite (*LGPN* II, *Ὀνήτωρ* (18)), who is attested as lessee of a mine in a *poletai* record of the mid-340s.[187] If so, he was a member of a prominent family of the city deme of Melite, which performed a series of liturgies in the fourth century.[188] The last attested lessee, Diopeithes, son of Diopeithes, of Sphettos (*LGPN* II, *Διοπείθης* (53)) was even more distinguished, since he belonged to the trierarchic class.[189] He is the same individual

[183] Cf. Osborne 1988, 290.

[184] Jameson 1982, 73–4; Osborne 1985*a*, 54–6; Whitehead 1986, 157–8; Osborne 1988, 289–92; Isager and Skydsgaard 1992, 189–90; Lambert 1993, 195.

[185] So Walbank 1991, 160 and Parker 1996, 110.

[186] *Agora* XV 61 l.139: [. . . . .^c.9^ . . . .]*ης* <*Δ*>*ιογνήτο*.

[187] *Agora* XIX P26 ll. 235–6: *ὠνη* | *Ὀνήτωρ Ἀρκεσίλου Μελι: Η*𐅄.

[188] See for this family *APF* 11473.

[189] See *APF* 4328.

whom Euxenippos of the Hyperidean speech took pride in having prosecuted for the public interest.[190] If the identification is correct and the suggested chronology for *IG* II^2 2501 ('fin. s. IV a.') stands, then Diopeithes would have been an old man when he undertook the lease.[191] The perennial status of the lease, with leasing rights transferred to the heirs of Diopeithes, probably suggests a semi-liturgical motivation for the undertaking of the transaction.

With this observation we return to the question posed at the beginning of the present section. It seems hardly plausible that two quite significant figures in Athenian political life, such as Diognetos and Diopeithes, would have bothered entering in transactions of minimal financial benefit for them, unless they themselves belonged to the leasing bodies. There is, in addition, an *argumentum e silentio* which seems to verify this inference: in no extant orgeonic lease is there a provision obliging the lessees to present guarantors such as those occurring so often in similar contracts set up by corporate groups. And last, but not least, one can adduce the evidence from *IG* II^2 1289: far from being syntactically inappropriate, the expression *μηθένα ὀ[ρ]γ[εώνων τῶν κτη]|μάτων τῶν ἑαυτῆς μηδ[ὲν ἀποδίδοσθαι μη]|δὲ μισθοῦσθαι [ε]ἰς ἄ̣[λλο ἢ εἰς τὰς θυσίας]* proves that lessees of orgeonic properties were expected to be orgeones themselves.[192] All in all, although the sample is infinitesimal, the fact that two out of three (or 66.6%) lessees of orgeonic property were prominent corroborates the picture emerging from other leasing transactions, namely the active participation of pillars of the Athenian upper class in affairs concerning the well-being of the groups of which they were members.[193]

190 Hyp. 4.29: *Διοπείθη τὸν Σφήττιον, ὃς δεινότατος ἐδόκει εἶναι τῶν ἐν τῇ πόλει*; Whitehead 2000, 233–5 fails to include *IG* II^2 2501 as testimony of Diopeithes' activity (but see next note).

191 However, Traill considers the lessee (*PAA* 363700) to be the son of the liturgist Diopeithes (cf. *PAA* 363395).

192 *IG* II^2 1289 ll. 11–13, with Sosin 2002, 127–8 (*SEG* LII 132): 'No *orgeôn* shall sell any of the properties nor lease for any purpose other than for the sacrifices . . .'; see also Papazarkadas 2004–9 [2010], 94–5.

193 One could tentatively add to the above list Epigonos son of Endios of Lamptrai (=*PAA* 392145, not in *LGPN* II; the demotic was first suggested by Ferguson 1944, 93 no. 11), featuring in an orgeonic transaction (improved text of *IG* II^2 1294 in Langdon 1973, now *SEG* L 162), which may be a lease (see my restorations of the text in n. 145 above, which make Epigonos the lessee of the shrine of Zeus Epakrios). He belonged to an upper-class family treated by Davies in *APF* 4810. His inclusion in the roster of lessees of orgeonic property cannot but enhance the inferences drawn above.

As far as the prosopography of buyers of orgeonic property is concerned, the difficulties are almost colossal. On the one hand, the nature of the evidence does not allow us to conclude unequivocally which orgeonic groups disposed of their property, and on the other, the names are mostly defective. Thus Charias, son of Char- (*LGPN* II, *Χαρίας* (10)), buyer of the only undoubtable orgeonic estate, is not identifiable,[194] and neither are Deinias (*LGPN* II, *Δεινίας* (6)) and Demetrios of Alopeke (*LGPN* II, *Δημήτριος* (154)), purchasers of property sold by the group honouring Herakles Plousios.[195] Lysikrates, son of Lysimachos, of Aphidnai may or may not be affiliated to a prominent political family of the fourth century,[196] but Deinokrates, son of Menon of Acharnai (*LGPN* II, *Δεινοκράτης* (7)), buyer of an estate sold by the orgeonic (?) group worshipping [Hephai]stos or [Adra]stos in Lo[usia], probably belonged to the trierarchic class.[197] Given the deficiency of the available evidence, we should be content with observing that some wealthy Athenians did acquire land sold by public associations, orgeones included, but their motives for doing so remain elusive. Perhaps we can only guess that land transactions (both leasing and purchase) in orgeonic contexts are yet another example of what Bourdieu has so aptly denominated the 'symbolic capital'.[198]

4. OTHER TYPES OF ASSOCIATIONS AS PROPERTY ADMINISTRATORS

All the associations surveyed so far have had in common their more or less direct and organic role in the structure of the Athenian polis, a principle which, it was argued, also applies to groups of citizen orgeones. I hope to have demonstrated elsewhere that the only type of public association that has left no trace of land possession is the Cleisthenic trittys. Their pre-Cleisthenic counterparts, in contrast, probably owned and leased out landholdings to fund whatever

194 Lambert 1997*a*, 179.

195 Lambert 1997*a*, 153–4.

196 *APF* 8157; Lambert 1997*a*, 166.

197 See the detailed discussion by Lambert 1997*a*, 154.

198 Bourdieu 1990, 118; Arnaoutoglou 2003, 157.

religious activities they had not been deprived of after the democratic reforms of the late Archaic period. Thus, it seems likely now that the Epakreis of *IG* II^2 2490—previously believed to be a Cleisthenic trittys—were an archaic group administering landed property as late as the fourth century.[199] It is equally plausible that other local religious associations such as the Marathonian Tetrapolis or the League of Athena Pallenis would have been land proprietors, especially given their antiquity.[200] Evidence is tenuous but, at least with regard to the League, it was demonstrated a long time ago that Athena almost certainly owned sacred pasturage and perhaps tillable land as well. Indeed, the sacred grain mentioned by Krates *apud* Athenaeus presupposes a field consecrated to Athena Pallenis, like the Eleusinian Rharia.[201] In any case, we hear in the same context of a temple, a sacred house (*οἰκία ἱερά*), and a granary (*παρασίτιον*, identified by Athenaeus with the *ἀρχεῖον*), all in need of repairs and all lying under the supervision of the *ἱερῶν ἐπισκευασταί*. The presence of these officials indicates a date *post* 434/3, when the cult of Athena Pallenis came under the administration of the Athenian polis by virtue of Kallias' decree A. At any rate, our ignorance of the initial source of payment for the repairs quoted by Krates does not allow us to establish the exact administrative scheme followed in the case of Athena Pallenis' realty. If such property was income-producing, it could have been either under the administration of the association's magistrates or under that of the polis. Interpretative problems are similar to those regarding the cult of Apollo Zoster.[202]

[199] See Papazarkadas 2007*b*, where I argue that the management of the landholdings of the group was in the hands of the demarchs as representatives of the constituent parts of the Epakreis.

[200] Marathonian Tetrapolis: Lambert 2000*a*. League of Athena Pallenis: Schlaifer 1943*a*; Parker 1996, 330–1.

[201] Sacred pasturage: Schlaifer 1943*a*, 51–2 with his emendation (at pp. 55 n. 78; 60) on Athen. 6.235c, *τοὺς δὲ παρασίτους ἐκ τῆς βουκολίας ἐκλέγειν <βοῦν, καὶ* (*nomen loci*) *ἐκλέγειν> ἐκ τοῦ μέρους τοῦ ἑαυτῶν ἕκαστον ἑκτέα*; of course sacred pasture, such as the Tegean *temenos* of Athene Alea where sacred flocks were allowed to graze, is a prerequisite for sacred animals (cf. Jameson 1988, 104; Isager and Skydsgaard 1992, 191–8). Sacred tillable land: Schlaifer 1943*a*, 53–5 commenting upon Athen. 6.235b: *πρότερον δ' ἐκαλοῦντο παράσιτοι οἱ ἐπὶ τὴν τοῦ ἱεροῦ σίτου ἐκλογὴν αἱρούμενοι*; 6.235d: *ἐκ τούτου δῆλόν ἐστιν ὅτι ἐν ᾧ τὰς ἀπαρχὰς ἐτίθεσαν τοῦ ἱεροῦ σίτου οἱ παράσιτοι τοῦτο παρασίτιον προσηγορεύετο.*

[202] Athen. 6.235d: *εἰς τὴν ἐπισκευὴν τοῦ νεὼ καὶ τοῦ παρασιτίου καὶ τῆς οἰκίας τῆς ἱερᾶς διδόναι τὸ ἀργύριον ὁπόσου ἂν οἱ τῶν ἱερῶν ἐπισκευασταὶ μισθώσωσιν*, with Schlaifer 1943*a*, 55–7 (the foundations of the temple, '*νεώς*', have now been

We encounter difficulties of a more elaborate character in the catalogue of leases *IG* II^2 1590a. This fragmentary inscription from Salamis preserves four *agri locati*, their lessees, and their respective guarantors. By means of their names and the small amounts they generated, two of the properties in question, the *Βο<σ>φαγέα* and the *Βοειοτομία*, should probably be identified as sacred pastures. The remaining two properties, the *Συπταλία* and the *Κόλουρις*, were almost certainly located at the islet of Psyttaleia and at Salamis respectively.[203] This fact along with the inscription's findspot have by and large forced scholars to identify the issuing authority of *IG* II^2 1590a as the non-constitutional deme of Salamis.[204] If so, the administrative lessor of the properties would have been the archon of the island who, according to [Aristotle], was appointed by the central administration, just like the demarch of Piraeus. After all, this very official was in charge of most land transactions or related procedures, such as exacting taxes on illicit rentals and administering confiscated properties.[205] Still, this hypothesis does not permit unequivocal inferences concerning the status of the leased properties, that is, whether they were sacred or secular. The income they realized almost certainly flowed into a single chest, for the final line of *IG* II^2 1590a contains the aggregate sum of the preceding rentals expressed as *κεφάλαι[ον]* (capital). At any rate, the suretyship system is reminiscent of the practice followed at the central and tribal level more than that of demes. Prosopographical analysis brings out the following features: (*a*) family links between lessees and guarantors, (*b*) relative affluence of the involved parties, and (*c*) further connection to the

discovered in extensive excavations at modern Stavros (Korres 1992–8) which have brought to light many auxiliary buildings; perhaps some of them could be identified with the sacred house and the granary, but we should await full publication of the architectural remains). Schlaifer 1943*a*, 56 n. 81 aptly broached the possibility that the sacred house was being let out for cultic revenue. It is possible that some of the loans from Athena Pallenis' treasury recorded in *IG* I^3 369 ll. 71, 88 would have derived from rentals. This might explain to some degree the involvement of the *basileus*—lessor of sacred realty par excellence—in the cult, as attested by the *νόμοι βασιλικοί*.

[203] Chatzis 1930, 60; Hollis 1992, 4; Taylor 1997, 119–20.

[204] Behrend 1970, 89–90; Osborne 1988, 283; Taylor 1997, 180–2, contra Walbank 1991, 158 who assumes state ownership.

[205] Thus Taylor 1997, 158-61, on *IG* I^3 1 ll. 7–8 (*[ἐσπράτεν δὲ τὸν ἄ]|ρχο[ν]τα*), and *Agora* XIX P2d col. I ll. 8–10(*<Λ>ευκόλοφος ἐξ Σαλα[μῖνος τάδε] | ἀπέγ : Θεομένος Ξυπε̣[ταιῶνος οἰ]|κίαν ἐν Σαλαμῖνι*).

island.[206] All in all, we get roughly the same picture as with other leasing corporate groups, that is, a tendency to favour the wealthy and those with a proven interest in the affairs of the group in question.

These associations aside, there is abundant evidence about private corporate groups of religious character which flourished especially during the Hellenistic era, and it is worth investigating, albeit briefly, their possible involvement in land administration as a means of comparison with the groups examined above.[207] By and large the structure of these groups was based on voluntary contributions by their members, as clearly indicated by the telling term *ἔρανοι*, and solidarity-loans were a frequent theme in the activities of such associations.[208] It does not necessarily result from this, however, that they owned real property;[209] rather, as has already more than once been emphasized, acquisition of realty could be the side-effect of failed lending transactions. A case in point is the group amusingly called 'those who share a common cooking-pot' (*ὁμόχυτροι*), possibly an Athenian religious association, that recently emerged as creditor in a hypothecation *horos* found at Lemnos. Other non-Athenian evidence indicates that private religious associations were often endowed by their founders with revenue-bearing real property.[210] From Attica

[206] Onomastics suggests that the guarantor *Σμικυθίων Σμικύθο Ἐλευσίνιος* (l. 4) was somehow related to the guarantor *Σμικυθίων Ἰσον[ό]μ[ο]* (l. 9). At any rate, the Salaminian connection of the former is confirmed by the Hellenistic funeral stele of his descendant *Πυθοκράτης Σμικύθου Ἐλευσίνιος* (*SEG* XXI 849). According to Kirchner, the guarantor *Ναυσιγένης Να[υσικλέους | Ἀν]αγυράσιος* (ll. 6–7) was the father of the cavalryman *Ναυσικλῆς Ναυσιγένου Ἀναγυρ(άσιος)*, attested in the *hippeis*-dedication *IG* II² 1955 from Salamis. Once more, onomastics gives us ground to connect the guarantor to the lessee *Ναύμαχος* [...⁶...]*δο Περιθοίδης* (ll. 5–6; 8–9). Finally, the guarantor *Ἁγνόθεος Πειραιεύς* (l. 8) was at least well-off, to judge from the way his slaves are mentioned in a curse-tablet (Audollent 1904, no. 50).

[207] For such private associations see Parker 1996, 333–42.

[208] Millett 1991, 177–8.

[209] Contra Parker 1996, 335: 'the Dekadistai were property owners' (in relation to *IG* II² 2701); cf. Andreyev 1974, 38–9. But Arnaoutoglou 2003, 113 now adopts a position similar to the one advocated here.

[210] The most famous example is Diomedon's legacy to Herakles *LSCG* 177: *[Διομέδων ἀνέθηκ]ε τὸ τ̣έμ̣ε̣ν̣ο̣ς [τόδε] | Ἡρακλ̣ε̣ῖ Δ̣[ιομε]δ̣οντείωι, ἀνέθηκε δ̣[ὲ] | καὶ τοὺς ξενῶνας τοὺς ἐν τῶι κάπωι | καὶ τὰ οἰκημάτια* etc.; see also Poseidon's endowment at Kalauria *LSCG* 59 ll. 2–4: *[περὶ τ]|οῦ ἀργυρίου καὶ τοῦ χωρίου οὗ ἀνέθηκ̣[αν Ἀ]|γασικλῆς καὶ Νικαγόρα τῶι Ποσειδᾶνι* etc.; cf. Guarducci 1974, 245–52.

itself one particular case exemplifies the issue at stake: the society of the Amphieraistai of Rhamnous was active towards the end of the third century, especially in the period following the final liberation of Athens from Macedonian rule in 229. In a decree issued by the Amphieraistai the association appealed to its members for monetary contributions towards repairs in the shrine which was in a dire condition after a protracted period of neglect. The proclamation was followed by the honorary crowning of the Rhamnousian Onesimides 'because he had dedicated to the god the terrace walls (*αἱμασιαί*) where the cistern is and he had offered the resulting revenue to the Amphieraistai headed by Diokles of Hamaxanteia'.[211] Subsequently it was decided that the *eranistai* would 'sacrifice annually from the incoming proceeds'.[212] This document, hitherto largely ignored, is one of the very few Attic testimonia of consecration of realty by a cultic association for the investment of funds in sacrifices. In all appearances, Onesimides offered to Amphiaraos an area containing a *λάκκος* (pit, cistern, or well) under the condition that the income raised from it would underwrite an annual sacrifice to the god.[213] It used to be thought that the *lakkos* was not actually a well, rather a cistern used for the watering of cattle. It could become, for instance, profitable by being accessible to interested herdsmen upon payment of a small allowance. But of late, it has been argued that the *αἱμασιαί* were not dry-walls, but terraces, and that profit was made from the sale of the crops produced in these areas.[214] The agricultural interpretation is certainly credible, though one cannot entirely dismiss the possibility that income was generated through leasing. More interesting is the nuance emerging in the relevant clause. Terraces or simply dry-walls enclosing a cistern, the *αἱμασιαί* were consecrated to the god; the income, however, was bequeathed to the *eranistai*, who clearly had to act as the human agents securing the attribution of what was due to the god, namely the income from his own property. Although it may be precipitate to generalize merely on

[211] *I.Rhamnous* 167 ll. 16–19: *ἐπειδὴ καὶ οὗτος | ἀνατέθηκε τῶι θεῶι τὰς αἱμασιὰς ὅπου ὁ λάκκος ἐστὶν | καὶ δέδωκε τὴν πρόσοδον τοῖς Ἀμφιεραϊσταῖς τοῖς μετὰ | Διοκλέου Ἁμαξαντέως.*

[212] *I.Rhamnous* 167 ll. 19–20: *θύειν κατ' ἐνιαυτὸν ἀπὸ τῆς προ|σόδου τῆς γινομένης.*

[213] Robert 1945, 79–81; Pouilloux 1954, 97–8; Petrakos 1999, 310–12.

[214] Price and Nixon 2005, 669.

the basis of this example, it is likely that the case of the Rhamnousian Amphieraistai was not unique and that other Attic private cultic groups would have employed similar financial strategies involving consecrated landed assets.[215]

[215] For a similar, albeit tentative, interpretation see my commentary on *IG* II^2 2503 in Papazarkadas 2004–9 [2010], 95–7. Arnaoutoglou 2007 has recently offered a similar interpretation of another Rhamnousian text, i.e. *I.Rhamnous* 59, in which Apollodoros of Otryneus is honoured by the association of Sarapiastai for having donated land for the erection of a temple of Sarapis and Isis. Arnaoutoglou 2007, 333 speculates, not unreasonably, that the donated landholding would have been 'sacral and therefore inalienable', even though there is no such explicit statement in the document.

5

Public, Non-Sacred, Realty in Ancient Athens

1. THE EVIDENCE

Back in 1990, in his influential article on public property in Classical Athens, David Lewis was adamant that 'no text encourages us to think that the Athenian state ever retained, worked, or leased anything called *ge demosia* (public land)'.[1] His claim—highlighted by the prominence in Athens of sacred landed property—seems strange: the proliferation of democratic institutions in that city was of unprecedented size and one would expect this to have been consequently crystallized in a pattern of publicly owned landholdings. An effort, therefore, to test Lewis's claim becomes both compelling and essential, as does an attempt to examine the concept of 'public' with respect to land ownership from the point of view of the Athenians themselves, if such a notional nuance ever existed.

According to an entry in the *Lexicon* of the ninth-century AD Patriarch of Constantinople, Photios, the *ναύκραροι* (*naukraroi*) were the officials in charge of letting out the public lands: *ναύκραροι· τὸ παλαιὸν Ἀθήνησιν οἱ νῦν δήμαρχοι· καὶ οἱ ἐκμισθοῦντες τὰ δημόσια.* It is a commonplace that one should treat information deriving from Byzantine sources with caution, but Photios is not our only source to pinpoint a specific connection between the *naukraroi* and the administration of public lands. The second-century BC Alexandrian grammarian Ammonios makes a similar connection: *ναύκραροι δὲ οἱ εἰσπρασσόμενοι τὰ δημόσια κτήματα καὶ ναυκράρια οἱ τόποι ἐν οἷς*

[1] Lewis 1990, 251; the same inference had already been reached by Andreades 1928, 167–8.

ἀνέκειτο τὰ κτήματα (*naukraroi*: those exacting money from the public landholdings and *naukraria* the regions in which the (public) landholdings are located). Surprisingly, this *testimonium* has never been brought into the discussion concerning land tenure in Athens, an absence made all the more startling since Ammonios is considered a far more reliable authority than Photios. But for the time being it suffices to keep two things in mind: first, the peak of the *naukraroi* was the Archaic period; second, they seem to have been magistrates of local communities, not of the central administration.

Another alleged attestation of public lands is to be found in an elegy composed by Solon and transmitted to us through the Demosthenic corpus. In a poetic accusation against the contemporary ruling-class, which tended to commit all sorts of injustices, Solon laments that

> οὔθ' ἱερῶν κτεάνων οὔτέ τι δημοσίων
> φειδόμενοι κλέπτουσιν ἀφαρπαγῇι ἄλλοθεν ἄλλος.[2]

The embezzled goods are divided between sacred and public, but the crucial word κτεάνων, variously translated as 'possessions', 'holdings', or even 'property', cannot be shown to denote exclusively landed property.[3] In fact, the other sixth-century occurrence of the genitive κτεάνων (interestingly accompanied by the adjective δημοσίων), to be found in a poem of Xenophanes of Kolophon, almost certainly refers to movable public possessions, not to realty.[4] No doubt, much depends on our interpretation of that notorious Solonian crux, land tenure in the early sixth century BC. Those who believe that the 'dark Earth' liberated by Solon via the removal of *horoi* was public land will not hesitate to construe κτεάνων as landholdings.[5] We should

[2] 'They steal from one another through violent seizure, sparing neither sacred nor public property' (West 1972, 121–2 no. 4 ll. 12–13). Lewis 1990, 245 does not seem to perceive the κτέανα as landholdings, although he is not very explicit at this point; cf. Connor 1988, 165. Osborne *apud* Forsdyke 2006, 338 n. 18, rejects the interpretation of κτεάνων as land, whereas Forsdyke herself affirms it.

[3] So Ampolo 2000, 14; that public lands are implied here is—unjustifiably, in my view—accepted by Manville 1990, 111 and Link 1991, 21–2. That the passage is cited by Hall 2007, 191–2, in his discussion of Archaic land tenure, speaks volumes. Mülke 2002, 119–20 nicely explores both possibilities, without committing himself.

[4] Xenoph. 2.8, καί κεν σῖτ' εἴη δημοσίων κτεάνων, translated by Lesher 1992, 13, as 'and there would be food from the city's public stores'. But Forsdyke 2006, 338, thinks that κτεάνων refers to land.

[5] Solon, fr. 36 5–7: '. . . dark Earth, whose boundary markers fixed in many places I once removed; enslaved before, now she is free' (trans. Gerber 1999). I provisionally

certainly not overlook the δημόσιον φρέαρ ('public well') envisaged in Solonian legislation, even though that ought to have been nothing more than a narrow structure, and does not necessarily say anything about public land.[6]

Moving into the Classical period, a series of boundary stones from the Piraeus and its vicinity provide further evidence on the subject. Dated on the basis of letter-forms to the middle of the fifth century, these *horoi* designate a formidable variety of realties as *demosia*, a term conveniently, but not necessarily rightly, rendered in modern English as 'public'. Thus one reads of public lounges,[7] an anchorage,[8] a gate (or several, since five relevant boundary stones have been discovered, and it is difficult to say whether they all refer to the same construction or not),[9] as well as of trade stations, a ferryboat anchorage, streets, and a market, none of which is modified by the adjective *demosios*. Far more significant is a peculiar and rather lengthy *horos* which reads [ἀ]πὸ τε̂[σ]|δε τε̂ς [h]|οδô τὸ | πρὸς τô | λιμέν[ο]|ς πâν δ|εμόσ[ι]|όν ἐσ[τι], that is 'everything from this street towards the area of the harbour is public'.[10] It has long been recognized that the phraseology of *IG* I[3] 1109 and 1110 is reminiscent of the doctrines of Hippodamos, the famous Milesian town-planner, who first implemented some of his theories in the Piraeus. This connection has been made by virtue of two extracts from Aristotle's *Politics*. In the first, the Stagirite philosopher notes: 'Ἱππόδαμος δὲ Εὐρυφῶντος Μιλήσιος ὃς καὶ τὴν τῶν πόλεων διαίρεσιν εὗρε καὶ τὸν

accept here the interpretation of ὅροι as boundary markers (see Ober 2006), which is far from certain. 'Dark Earth' as public and/or uncultivated land: Gallant 1982; Manville 1990; Rihll 1991 (all criticized by Foxhall 1997). Forsdyke 2006, 338, accepts the existence of communal land, i.e. land 'under the control of cultic and regional associations such as *phylae, phratriai, genê*, villages and demes'; her interpretation anachronistically bundles up too many and diverse collectivities.

[6] Plut. *Solon* 23.6.

[7] *IG* I[3] 1102: λεσχέον | δεμοσίο|ν hόρος.

[8] *IG* I[3] 1103: [h]όρμο | δ[ε]μοσίο | hόρος.

[9] *IG* I[3] 1105-8: προπύλο δεμοσίο hόρος. Gill 2006, 8–9 believes they all designated the same structure. The identical *IG* I[3] 1097 from the Athenian Agora probably belongs to the same series (see next note).

[10] *IG* I[3] 1109. A duplicate (*IG* I[3] 1110), albeit less legible, of this *horos* has been found near the Acropolis. Despite an effort to disprove the assumption that the two stones bore the same text, I think there is good reason to subscribe to the traditional interpretation of the first editor of the Acropolis *horos*: somehow a stone erected initially in the area of Piraeus came to be used as building material in a house on the north slope of the Acropolis (Hill 1932).

Πειραιᾶ κατέτεμεν . . .[11] The second contains a synopsis of Hippodamos' theoretical concepts: *διῄρει* (sc. *Ἱππόδαμος*) *δ' εἰς τρία μέρη τὴν χώραν, τὴν μὲν ἱερὰν τὴν δὲ δημοσίαν τὴν δ' ἰδίαν· ὅθεν μὲν τὰ νομιζόμενα ποιήσουσι πρὸς τοὺς θεούς, ἱεράν, ἀφ' ὧν δ' οἱ προπολεμοῦντες βιώσονται, κοινήν, τὴν δὲ τῶν γεωργῶν ἰδίαν.*[12] Even though Lewis had expressed his doubt as to whether Hippodamos' operations in Piraeus could be directly linked with the boundary stones found in or around the port, the resemblance of some of the terms employed ought to have made him more keen on adopting such an approach.[13] Although the traditional view has it that Hippodamos invented gridded town-planning, archaeological evidence has shown that systems of streets designed to meet at right angles existed in colonies in Magna Graecia as early as the eighth century.[14] Aristotle's information on Hippodamos seen in its wider context, as it emerges in *Politics*, seems to imply that what Hippodamos put forward was the theoretical division of citizens into classes and land into types.[15] The keywords of this type of land allocation seem to have been the synonyms *διαίρεσις* and *νέμησις*. The former occurs in the Aristotelian excerpt, the latter in the entries *Ἱπποδάμου νέμησις* of Hesychios and Photios' *Lexica*, respectively, as well as in another *horos* from the Piraeus.[16] The Piraean boundary stones do have a distinct Hippodamian flavour.

[11] Arist. *Pol.* 1267^{b}: 'Hippodamos, son of Euryphron, a Milesian, who invented the division of the cities and cut up Piraeus' (trans. by Rackham 1944); cf. Hegyi 1976, 77; Gill 2006, 2–3.

[12] Arist. *Pol.* 1267^{b}: 'And he divided the land into three parts, one sacred, one public, and one private: sacred land to supply the customary offerings to the gods, common land to provide the warrior class with food, and private land to be owned by the farmers' (trans. by Rackham 1944).

[13] Lewis 1990, 250 contra Burns 1976, 417–18; cf. Wycherley 1964, 137–8; Garland 1987, 26–7, 181–2.

[14] Hippodamos: Burns 1976, 417; Gorman 1995, who, however, includes no discussion of the Piraean *horoi*. Town-planning in western Greece: Fischer-Hansen 1996; Hoepfner and Schwandner 1994. All these are now cited and superceded by Shipley 2005.

[15] Gorman 1995, 395.

[16] Hsch. s.v. *Ἱπποδάμου νέμησις· τὸν Πειραιᾶ Ἱππόδαμος, Εὐρυφῶντος παῖς ὁ καὶ μετεωρολόγος, διεῖλεν Ἀθηναίοις . . .* (Hippodamos' *nemesis*: Hippodamos, Euryphon's child, who was also a *meteorologos*, divided Piraeus for the Athenians); Phot. *Lexikon* s.v. *Ἱπποδάμου νέμησις ἐν Πειραιεῖ· ἦν δὲ Ἱππόδαμος †Εὐρυκόοντος† Μιλήσιος ἢ Θούριος μετεωρολόγος. οὗτος διένειμεν Ἀθηναίοις τὸν Πειραιᾶ.* Note that codices g and z of Photios' *Lexikon* transmit the pre-Euclidean Attic spelling *νέμεσις* (thus reproduced in *TLG* leading Shipley 2005, 403 n. 252 to denounce it as a

Still, it remains doubtful whether the Piraeus constituted the ground where Hippodamos fully applied his theoretical ideas. For one, the Hippodamian division of a territory into three categories of land, sacred, public, and private, should hardly be considered a novelty. Rather, it constitutes a codification of a pre-existing tenurial pattern. Far from being merely the equivalent of a modern town-planner, Hippodamos was also a political philosopher with concerns about the structure of an ideal polis. His tripartite scheme was meant to subsidize the functionings of his utopia through the allocation of different funds to different sociopolitical sectors. By the 460s–450s the political structure of Athens had been, in its general layout, consolidated, and only slight modifications were conceivable. The land tenure pattern, however, was not so firmly fixed. There must have been large areas in Attica which remained unexploited, and the situation called for a drastic solution. The Piraeus seems to have been just such an area, judging from archaeological finds which suggest that the thriving port of the fourth century remained a settlement of minor importance throughout the early Classical period, well after the reforms of Cleisthenes.[17] The coincidence of the ambitions of the Athenian political leaders with the doctrines of Hippodamos might have given rise to a new spatial organization, traces of which we happen to know from the random discovery of a few *horoi* and the scarce surviving literary sources.[18] In practice, however, the implementation of this land division in Attica could not correspond to a social classification that was extant only in the realm of political theory. No separate class of professional soldiers existed in Athens and, consequently, the demarcation of public areas in the Piraeus could not have been perceived as a source of military income.

typo). See also *IG* I^3 1113: [*ἄ*]*χρι τ*[*ἐ*|*σδε τε̂ς* | hoδô *τε̂*|*ιδε* hε M|*ονιχία*|*ς ἐστὶ νέ*|*μησις*, and *IG* I^3 1111: *ἄχρι τε̂*[*ς*] | hoδô *τε̂*|*σδε τὸ ἄ*|*στυ τε̂ι*|*δε νενέ*|*μεται*. Obviously the verb *νενέμεται* derives from the technical term *νέμησις*. See von Eickstedt 1991, 4–5; Gill 2006, 3.

17 As the numerous tables compiled by von Eickstedt 1991 show, there is very little evidence (houses, quarries, water reservoirs) dating to the 5th cent. Similarly, the dates we can retrieve for most of the quarries seem to cluster in the 4th cent.: Langdon 2000 [2004], 245–6.

18 For the lifespan of Hippodamos and the exact date of his involvement in the development of the Piraeus see Burns 1976, 414–28, who favours the 450s as the period for the Hippodamian groundwork in the port of Athens.

If they are Hippodamian, then the designated public areas in the Piraeus require another explanation. Lewis believed that they were state property specifically designated so as to discourage encroachment by greedy individuals.[19] The question was recently addressed by Matthaiou in two brief, but highly erudite, studies of a fourth-century *horos* from Paros.[20] Citing the aforementioned Attic *horoi*, as well as some other non-Attic epigraphical texts, he concluded that Greek city-states would often take pains to mark public lands not just for the sake of neat city-planning, but also in order to prevent private individuals from seizing these zones. Since many of these areas lay along circuit walls, both within and outside them, such demarcations served, in effect, a defensive purpose, a theory splendidly exemplified by the well-known cadastre from Hellenistic Skotoussa.[21] Gill has now independently reached a similar conclusion, arguing that some of the Piraeus *horoi* would have defined, and therefore protected, a militarily sensitive area behind the shipsheds of Athens' naval fleet.[22] As it happens, military preoccupations are the only linkage between Aristotle's account and the actual works undertaken in the Piraeus for the fencing-off of public areas. Yet the connection is indirect and frail and is mentioned here as a remote conjecture.

A famous passage of the Thucydidean oeuvre also seems relevant and has not hitherto entered discussion. Relating the evacuation of Attica in the first stage of the Peloponnesian War and the flow of villagers into the *astu*, Thucydides mentions the occupation of various sanctuaries, hero-shrines, as well as the *ἐρῆμα τῆς πόλεως*. The last of these could have been either previously privately- held lands that had been abandoned by 431, or simply unoccupied areas with no, or merely a vague, ownership status.[23] In the same account the

[19] Lewis 1990, 251.

[20] Matthaiou 1992-8*b*. The text in question (*SEG* XLVIII 1140: *ὅρ|ος | πό|λε|ως*) is to be found in Matthaiou and Kouragios 1992-8; cf. Matthaiou 2000.

[21] *SEG* XLIII 310, with Missailidou-Despotidou 1993, 212–13; cf. *IG* XII (3) 86: *δαμόσιον τὸ χωρίον πέντε πόδε[s] ἀπὸ το<ῦ> τείχε[os]* (the landholding as far as five feet from the wall is public).

[22] Gill 2006, 9, who attributes the scheme to Pericles' leadership in the 440s.

[23] Thuc. 2.17.1: *οἱ δὲ πολλοὶ τά τε ἐρῆμα τῆς πόλεως ᾤκησαν καὶ τὰ ἱερὰ καὶ τὰ ἡρῷα πάντα πλὴν τῆς ἀκροπόλεως καὶ τοῦ Ελευσινίου καὶ εἴ τι ἄλλο βεβαίως κληστὸν ἦν*. Gomme 1956, 62 considered these *ἐρῆμα τῆς πόλεως* as 'the uninhabited, empty, not "deserted", parts of the city'; cf. Xen. *Vect.* 2.6: *εἶτα ἐπειδὴ καὶ πολλὰ οἰκιῶν ἔρημά ἐστιν ἐντὸς τῶν τειχῶν καὶ οἰκόπεδα*, but see Kahrstedt 1934, 8.

historian narrates the occupation of the Long Walls as well as *τοῦ Πειραιῶς τὰ πολλά* ('a great part of Piraeus').[24] I suspect that these were the areas designated by the Piraean *horoi* as public. According to this line of interpretation, in the mid-fifth century the Athenians decided to proceed to a large-scale replanning of the area of Piraeus employing for this purpose the skills of the famous Milesian town-planner Hippodamos. On that occasion large stretches of land were left aside as belonging to the *demos* for future, unspecified uses, and also for defensive purposes. The initiators of the plan could not have predicted that in less than a generation these areas would accommodate the desperate villagers who sought protection in the urban centres of Athens and Piraeus. But that is how events unfolded. In the dire circumstances of the looming war there was little room for dissent, and one can assume that the squatted areas remained occupied for many years after the threat had faded away. It is hard to say whether the Athenian *demos* later tried to reverse the situation, but it seems likely that the Athenian state eventually lost part of the previously public areas.[25]

If by the mid-450s a rudimentary, albeit naive, concept of publicly owned territory had started materializing, we would expect to find more contemporary manifestations of it. To the best of my knowledge, there is only one other Thucydidean passage that could be adduced as evidence. On the eve of the first Peloponnesian raids in Attica, Pericles delivered a speech in the assembly in his capacity as general. Being the owner of extensive real property in the Thriasian plain—an obvious target for a Peloponnesian foray—he chose to take precautionary measures against any potential slanders against him that might arise from the Peloponnesians sparing his fields either because of his personal friendship (*ξενία*) to the Spartan king Archidamos or due to the ulterior motives of his rivals. He, therefore, declared his willingness to release his property to the state in the

[24] Thuc. 2.17.3: *ἀλλ' ὕστερον δὴ τά τε μακρὰ τείχη ᾤκησαν κατανειμάμενοι καὶ τοῦ Πειραιῶς τὰ πολλά* (uncommented on by both Gomme 1956 and Hornblower 1991). Again, the cadastre from Skotoussa (*SEG* XLIII 310) provides the best way to interpret the Thucydidean passage.

[25] *IG* I³ 84 (418/7), the emphyteutic lease of the *temenos* of Kodros, has been seen by scholars as the Athenian state's response to the chaotic situation that arose from the refugees' flow into the city during the Archidamian War (see Robertson 1988, 231). No similar evidence with regard to the Piraeus has survived.

event of its not being ravaged.[26] We do not know from the ensuing account whether such a situation arose and whether, subsequently, Pericles abided by his word and, therefore, we cannot retrieve the details behind such a transaction.[27] Did Pericles' pledge to render his landholdings and dwellings (*ἀγροί* and *οἰκίαι*) public (*δημόσια εἶναι*) mean that the Athenian state could acquire ownership and exploit the lands by, for instance, letting them out?[28] It is hard to say. Public houses (*δημόσιαι οἰκίαι*) are attested in Classical Attica;[29] public lands (*δημόσιοι ἀγροί*) as such are not. The phrase used by Thucydides (*δημόσια εἶναι*) evokes similar epigraphical formulas found in clauses of imposition of fines and confiscation of properties. In all likelihood, Pericles' holdings were meant to be sold at auction by the *poletai*, the revenue realized being stored in the public treasury.[30]

The defendant of the 55th Demosthenic speech stood trial for having illegally constructed a wall on a watercourse, which caused a stream to flood into his neighbour's, the plaintiff Kallikles', land.[31] He argued strongly that the wall was built in his private landholding and not in public land.[32] This is arguably the only clear-cut example of

[26] Thuc. 2.13.1: *τοὺς δὲ ἀγροὺς τοὺς ἑαυτοῦ καὶ οἰκίας ἢν ἄρα μὴ δηώσωσιν οἱ πολέμιοι ὥσπερ καὶ τὰ τῶν ἄλλων, ἀφίησιν αὐτὰ δημόσια εἶναι.*

[27] But could Isoc. *De Pace* 126: *καίτοι ὁ Περικλῆς . . . οὐκ ἐπὶ τὸν ἴδιον χρηματισμὸν ὥρμησεν, ἀλλὰ τὸν μὲν οἶκον ἐλάττω τὸν αὑτοῦ κατέλιπεν ἢ παρὰ τοῦ πατρὸς παρέλαβεν* ('And yet Pericles . . . was not bent upon his own enrichment, but left an estate which was smaller than that which he received from his father'; trans. by Norlin 1929) imply the fulfilment of Pericles' promise? It is not inconceivable, although Isocrates might simply be construing Thucydides' text here.

[28] The view of Fine 1951, 192 (Pericles granted to the state the usufruct, rather than the ownership of his property) was provisionally endorsed by Hornblower 1991, 251, but it is difficult to uphold in the light of the present discussion.

[29] *IG* I³ 84 l. 36; Xen. *Vect.* 4.49 (but see the following section of this chapter). Istros' *οἰκίαις περιειλημμένου δημοσίαις . . .* (*FGrH* 334 F16), long suspected as corrupt (Jacoby 1954*b*, 515), is of no value (see also Clinton 2005, 169).

[30] e.g. *IG* I³ 46, l. 24: [*καὶ τὰ χ*]*ρέματα δεμόσια ἔναι*; *Agora* XIX P5 ll. 8–11: *Θεόμνηστ|ος Δεισιθέο Ἰωνίδης ἀπέγραψεν Θεοσέβεος τοῦ Θε|οφίλο Ξυπεταιόνος οἰκίαν Ἀλωπεκῆσιν δημοσία|ν εἶναι* (cf. the confiscation of the Plataian territory by the Thebans in Thuc. 3.68.4, *τὴν δὲ γῆν δημοσιώσαντες* etc., with Hornblower 1991, 463–4). On these formulas see also Migeotte 2006*a*, 188.

[31] *Against Kallikles* is generally considered to be an early work of Demosthenes and must be chronologically placed in the last years of the second quarter of the 4th cent.: see Usher 1999, 186–9 (but Bers 2003, 80, is less certain: 'We cannot date *Against Callicles*').

[32] Dem. 55.12–3: *Καλλικλῆς μὲν γάρ φησιν τὴν χαράδραν ἀποικοδομήσαντα βλάπτειν ἔμ' αὐτόν· ἐγὼ δ' ἀποδείξω χωρίον ὂν τοῦτο, ἀλλ' οὐ χαράδραν. εἰ μὲν οὖν μὴ συνεχωρεῖθ' ἡμέτερον ἴδιον εἶναι, τάχ' ἂν τοῦτ' ἠδικοῦμεν, εἴ τι τῶν δημοσίων ᾠκοδομοῦμεν*; cf. Patterson 2006, 51.

public land referenced in Attic oratory. It is worth investigating what the defendant meant by speaking of public property. According to his main line of argument, the property in question contained no water channel, but was instead planted with trees, vines and fig-trees. He went on to ask rhetorically just who would have thought of growing these plants in a watercourse.[33] If public lands exploited by the state—either through being farmed by public slaves or being leased out to individuals—ever existed, his argument would have been tenuous. The implication is obvious: by referring to public lands (*τὰ δημόσια*), the defendant did not imply landholdings belonging to, and exploited by, the Athenian state by means of agriculture. He alluded instead to public land wherein 'public' denotes land belonging to no individual, but rather property designated for common use, such as land containing a watercourse. It is in the same sense that the appellant mentions 'a public road' (*τῆς ὁδοῦ τῆς δημοσίας*).[34]

Court cases of this sort may underlie a passage from Aristotle's *Ars Rhetorica*, where encroachment upon public lands is deemed a favourite theme of rhetorical deception.[35] An extract from the Old Oligarch's notorious diatribe may also have some relevance here. In his ironical allusions to the (much-detested by him) democratic Athenians' tendency for litigation, the author of the treatise *De re publica Atheniensium* reminds his readers of adjudications of cases where buildings had been allegedly erected on public ground.[36] Nevertheless, the linguistic similarity of this passage to the information provided by the Aristotelian *Athenaion Politeia* about the tasks

[33] Foxhall 1996, 46–8; Usher 1999, 186–7 with n. 64; MacDowell 2009, 63–5.

[34] Cf. *Agora* XIX P17 l. 15: *βορρᾶθεν ἡ ὁδὸς ἡ δη[μοσία]*; P26 ll. 369–70: *ὁδὸς δη|[μοσία]*. It is noteworthy that such countryside roads are still known as *δημοσιές* in colloquial Greek: see Lolos 2003, 143, whose assertion, however, that '[s]uch (public) roads were built by the state' severely stretches the evidence as far as the Classical period is concerned.

[35] Arist. *Rhet.* 1374^a: *ἐπεὶ δ' ὁμολογοῦντες πολλάκις πεπραχέναι ἢ τὸ ἐπίγραμμα οὐχ ὁμολογοῦσιν ἢ περὶ ὃ τὸ ἐπίγραμμα, οἷον λαβεῖν μὲν ἀλλ' οὐ κλέψαι . . . ἢ ἐπεργάσασθαι μὲν ἀλλ' οὐ δημοσίαν*. The last word is an emendation of the manuscripts' *δημόσια*. As Grimaldi 1988, 295 aptly observes, *δημόσια* [sc. *χωρία*] is not that improbable, but *δημοσίαν* [sc. *χώραν*] is to be preferred.

[36] Xen. [*Ath. Pol.*] 3.4: *δεῖ δὲ καὶ τόδε διαδικάζειν, εἴ τις τὴν ναῦν μὴ ἐπισκευάζει ἢ κατοικοδομεῖ τι δημόσιον* ('They also have to judge in the following cases, namely, if a man does not repair his ship, or builds something on public land': trans. by Marr and Rhodes 2008, who, at 150, emphasize the connection with the *astunomoi* (see next note). Gray 2007, 206, who translates '. . . or if anyone builds a public building', and thinks of state contractors, disregards the subtle tones of the compound *κατοικοδομεῖ*.

of the *astunomoi* makes it more likely that the reference is not to agricultural land, but to public spaces within urbanized areas of Attica, either the *astu* itself or some of the inhabited nuclei of the Attic demes.[37] In fact, a Sounian fourth-century decree concerning the foundation of a new agora on a plot provided by a demesman contains regulations about the careful designation of the donated area so that no individual could trespass upon it, as had apparently happened with the pre-existing agora.[38]

The board of *astunomoi* (ἀστυνόμοι) brings us to another literary genre, that of political theory. In Aristotle's *Politics* the board of *astunomoi* is paired with that of *agronomoi* (ἀγρονόμοι) or *hyloroi* (ὑλωροί), these being local variants of the same office. Their main task was to manage the landed property that lay in the hinterland of a given polis.[39] In fact, the earliest testimony to the officials in question can be found in Plato's *Laws*.[40] To what extent this latest of Plato's works reflects a historical reality and/or the philosophical doctrines of its author has long been a subject of dispute. Scholars are nowadays prone to believe that some material was drawn from the actual political practices followed, amongst other places, in Athens.[41] Already in 1933 Chase was able to trace instances of straightforward influence of Athenian administrative schemes on the legislation of the Platonic ideal Cretan city. As for the absence of actual Attic parallels to the board of ἀγρονόμοι, Chase conjectured that it was all due to coincidental non-preservation of epigraphical texts.[42] Given that Athens is the city-state that has produced by far the greatest amount of epigraphical testimonia, the 'accidental' factor ought to be dismissed; ἀγρονόμοι and ὑλωροί are in fact well attested in other areas

[37] Arist. [*Ath. Pol.*] 50.2: καὶ τὰς ὁδοὺς κωλύουσι (sc. ἀστυνόμοι) κατοικοδομεῖν, with Rhodes 1993, 575 (cf. Frisch 1942, 308; Faraguna 2000, 66–7 n. 6).

[38] *IG* II^2 1180 ll. 16–21: ἐπειδὴ ἡ νῦν οὖσα συν|ωικοδόμηται ἐνοικοδ|ομῆσαι δὲ μὴ ἐξε̂ναι μή|τε δημάρχωι μήτε ἄλ|λωι μηδενὶ ἐντὸς τῶν | ὅρων; in this case the responsibility of keeping out rapacious individuals would lie not with the *astunomoi*, who were only in charge of the Piraeus and Athens, but with specially assigned deme officials; cf. Stanton 1996, 350–3.

[39] Arist. *Pol.* 1321^b; 1331^b.

[40] According to the *Thesaurus Linguae Graecae* there are 17 occurrences of the term in Plato's *Laws*. Among these, only 2 are reminiscent of land administration, i.e. 760b6 and 760e2; cf. Brisson 2000, 90.

[41] Cf. Jones 1989–90.

[42] Chase 1933, esp. 187–8.

of the Greek world. That they do not feature at all in Attic documents simply means that they were never there.[43]

If the literary data are disappointingly meagre, the epigraphical ones are hardly more substantial. In a *poletai* record of 350/49, the location of a confiscated property is defined as lying north of τ[ὸ οἰκ]όπεδον τὸ δημόσιον.[44] Interestingly, this is one of the rare occurrences of the word οἰκόπεδον in an Attic context. In his classic analysis of the *Attic Stelai* Pritchett scrutinized the noun, contending that although an edifice of some sort is usually implied in the term, the meaning of a plot of land cannot be entirely dismissed.[45] The property in question, however, lay in the urban deme of Melite, which is securely located west of the Agora. It is highly improbable that agricultural land is implied here and it seems more likely that τ[ὸ οἰκ]όπεδον τὸ δημόσιον was a plot containing a confiscated, derelict house.[46] A recent robust re-examination of the term οἰκόπεδον seems to have settled the issue for good.[47] A pair of estates recorded in the *Rationes Centesimarum* did not bear any toponyms of the usual type, but rather the designation δημόσιαι. As mentioned in Chapter 3, Section 2.ix ('Epilogue'), according to Lambert these 'public' landholdings were common property, controlled, but not owned, by the deme Poros.[48] To corroborate his hypothesis Lambert cited evidence from Anaximenes' *Ars Rhetorica*: πρῶτον μὲν οὖν σκεπτέον, εἴ τι τῶν τῆς πόλεως κτημάτων ἠμελημένον ἐστὶ καὶ μήτε

[43] Examples of both bodies as well as other similar ones (differently termed), are given in Corsaro 1990 (no Attic cases). Andreades 1928, 263 was laudably careful not to connect the Platonic *agronomoi* (ἀγρονόμοι) with the actual Athenian apparatus; thus also Piérart 1974, 271–3, and 2005, 138–40. Brisson 2003, also sees the *agronomoi* as an exceptional institution comparing them to that other Platonic oddity, the νυκτερινὸς σύλλογος.

[44] *Agora* XIX P17. l. 22.

[45] Pritchett 1956, 265–7; see also Nenci 1993 and Schuler 1998, 127–30.

[46] Location of Melite: Lalonde 2006*b*. Based primarily on the findspot of many a security *horos*, Jones 2004, 36–6, has forcefully contended that tillable lands could be found inside the city-walls. I find Jones's thesis untenable: similarly to the thousands of epitaphs discovered in the Agora and its surroundings, or even on the Acropolis, these security *horoi* were almost certainly transferred into the *astu* to be used as building material.

[47] Daniel 2007.

[48] F7, ll. 9–18: ἐσχατιὰ ἐν Πόρωι̣ τὸ δ[ημόσια?] | καλούμενον *vac.* | [ὠ]ν̣η Χ̣αιρέδημος Χάρητο[ς- -] | ἕτερον χωρίον ἐν Π[όρωι τὸ δημό]|σια καλούμενον *vac.* | ὠνη Πιστίας Πιστίου Π[- -] | ἑτέρα ἐσχατιὰ ἐν Βή[σαι] | ὠνη Κλεομέδων Λέοντος Α/[- -] | ἑτέρα ἐσχατιὰ ἐν Πόρῳ[ι τὸ δη]|μόσιαι ἄλωι καλούμε[νον] (see Chapter 3, Section 2.viii–ix).

πρόσοδον ποιεῖ μήτε τοῖς θεοῖς ἐξαίρετόν ἐστι. λέγω δ' οἷον τόπους τινὰς δημοσίους ἀμελουμένους, ἐξ ὧν τοῖς ἰδιώταις ἢ πραθέντων ἢ μισθωθέντων πρόσοδος ἄν τις τῇ πόλει γίγνοιτο.[49] The parallel is good, but Demosthenes' 55th oration may be even more important due to its unmistakable Attic context. We may conclude following Lambert: the Porian *δημοσίαι* were indeed common lands—not formally owned by either the deme or the state—available to members of the local community.

The concept of commonly used lands has only recently started being understood, but it now appears that it was more widespread than previously assumed. Little attention has been paid to a double decree of the Augustan period concerning the restoration of sanctuaries in Attica.[50] Culley, the most recent editor of this document, recognized that, besides the sacred properties reclaimed by the Athenian *demos* in order to be leased out under the auspices of a series of military religious and political offcials, there existed a separate subdivision of realties that were not subject to letting, namely *τὰ ὄρη τὰ δημόσια* and *αἱ δημοτελεῖς ἐσχατιαί*.[51] Admittedly the second object of exemption from leasing is partly a restoration, but the mention of public mountains occurs twice and is unambiguous.[52] Culley also demonstrated that the most likely reason for this separate treatment of the public mountains (and, perhaps, the public outlying estates) was the open access to any interested individual for grazing or wood-fetching.[53] Apiculture should be considered too.[54] There is a

49 Anaximenes, *Ars Rhetorica* 2.33 (= Arist. [*Rh. Al.*] 1425^b. 20–4): 'Thus, one has first to consider whether any of the landholdings belonging to the city has been neglected and does not generate any income nor has it been set aside for the gods. I mean, for example, some neglected public areas from the sale or leasing of which to private individuals they city could acquire some revenue'; cf. Lewis 1973*a*, 189–90; Lambert 1997*a*, 208.

50 *SEG* XXVI 121 (*IG* II^2 1035), with Schmalz 2009, 10–11 for the date, and Schmalz 2007–8 [2011] for a thorough analysis.

51 Culley 1977, 289–90.

52 *SEG* XXVI 121 ll. 21–2: *τὰ δὲ ὄρη τὰ δημόσια καὶ τὰς δημοτελεῖ[ς|ἐσχατιάς* - - -]; l. 59, [- - - *ὄρη δ*]*ημόσια ἃ καί* etc. Whatever supplement to *δημοτελεῖ[ς]* we accept (cf. Jameson 2002, 67 n. 3), the adjective is equivalent to *δημόσιος* (cf. Parker 1996, 5–6 n. 17).

53 Culley 1977, 290; cf. the Tarantine system attested in Arist. *Pol.* 1320^b. 9–11: *καλῶς δ' ἔχει μιμεῖσθαι καὶ τὰ Ταραντίνων· ἐκεῖνοι γὰρ κοινὰ ποιοῦντες τὰ κτήματα τοῖς ἀπόροις ἐπὶ τὴν χρῆσιν εὔνουν παρασκευάζουσι τὸ πλῆθος* (contra Rackham 1944, 512 n. a).

54 Cf. Ober 1981, 76–7.

self-evident correspondence here with the observations made by Lambert about the character of the δημόσιαι recorded in the *Rationes Centesimarum*. A methodological concern must be conceded: How justified is one to apply retrospectively practices that might have been purely Roman and might, therefore, not account for the land tenure patterns of the Classical period? Nevertheless, there is such a great deal of overlap between other features of *SEG* XXVI 121 and evidence deriving from Classical Athens[55] that preoccupations of compatibility could, for once, be set aside.[56] A series of Roman rupestral *horoi* delimiting an area around the Alepovouni hill, a lower extension of Mt. Hymettos to the west, have been tentatively linked to clauses contained in *SEG* XXVI 121, especially to the contextually elliptical ὅρος τὸ πρὸς Ὑμηττῶι (line 58).[57] Langdon, who argued for the public character of the Alepovouni *horoi*, envisaged the existence of some Classical predecessors. Yet the only patently Classical examples of *horoi* found in the wider area are now seen by Langdon as denoting private property.[58]

But we might recall here two stories which highlight the peculiar status of Mt. Hymettos already in the Archaic period. The first, told by Herodotus, will take us to the dawn of Attic history. Upon completion of the wall around the Acropolis, the Pelasgian masons were rewarded by their Athenian employers with the land under Hymettos (χώρην . . . ὑπὸ τὸν Ὑμησσόν), land that was infertile (κακήν) and worthless (μηδενὸς ἀξίην). To the Athenians' surprise, the Pelasgians cultivated the land well. Demonstrating the worst kind of rapaciousness and primarily driven by a craving for land, the Athenians expelled the competent farmers and kept the area for themselves.[59] Far from trying to untangle the notorious thread of early Athenian history, I will only point out that the land in question

[55] See Chapter 2, Section 2 and 4.

[56] Cf. Andreyev 1974, 45.

[57] Langdon 1985*b*, 258–60. These are *horoi* nos. 5–8 in Langdon 1999, 484–5, 498–9 with figs. 3 and 5, where the author repeats in a more expanded form his remarks from Langdon 1985*b*.

[58] Langdon 1999, 483–4, 492–6.

[59] Hdt. 6.137: ἐπείτε γὰρ ἰδεῖν τοὺς Ἀθηναίους τὴν χώρην, τήν σφι αὐτοὶ ὑπὸ τὸν Ὑμησσὸν ἐοῦσαν ἔδοσαν οἰκῆσαι μισθὸν τοῦ τείχεος τοῦ περὶ τὴν Ἀκρόπολίν κοτε ἐληλαμένου, ταύτην ὡς ἰδεῖν τοὺς Ἀθηναίους ἐξεργασμένην εὖ, τὴν πρότερον εἶναι κακήν τε καὶ τοῦ μηδενὸς ἀξίην, λαβεῖν φθόνον τε καὶ ἵμερον τῆς γῆς, καὶ οὕτω ἐξελαύνειν αὐτοὺς οὐδεμίαν ἄλλην πρόφασιν προϊσχομένους τοὺς Ἀθηναίους, with Nenci 1998, 316–17. For a literary scrutiny of the Athenians' motives as presented

sounds suspiciously like public property. The second tale is told by both Aristotle and Diodorus, pertains to the 'tax-free district' (*χωρίον ἀτελές*) near Hymettos, and its historicity has been seriously doubted: a hard-working farmer cultivates impossibly arid land and unawares confronts the tyrant Peisistratos for his taxation measures before being granted tax exemption. The components of the tale are anecdotal, but Moreno has recently resuscitated an old theory that sees in this Peisistratean episode the beginning of an intensification of agricultural production in the area around Hymettos.[60] In any event, it is worth asking ourselves whether from Herodotus' Pelasgians to Aristotle's 'tax-free district' to the Roman *ὅρος πρὸς τῶι Ὑμηττῶι* we are not dealing with the same public property. Persistent Athenian concern—literary and epigraphical—with the area seems to suggest so.[61]

In the prospectus of the Second Athenian Confederacy from 378/7 the Athenians relinquished all their possessions, private and public alike, in the lands of those states which joined the alliance. On top of this, they provided assurances that they would refrain from acquiring real property by any means, purchase and mortgage included.[62] It is widely believed that the renounced public possessions (*δημόσια ἐγκτήματα*) were cleruchic lands, and it is hard to disagree with this interpretation.[63] However, one should not put too much stress on the evidence of Aristoteles' decree. Cleruchies were a unique Athenian

by Herodotos, see Baragwanath 2008, 136–48, who is indifferent to questions of historical authenticity.

[60] Arist. [*Ath. Pol.*] 16.4: *τοιαύτης γάρ τινος ἐξόδου τῶι Πεισιστράτωι γιγνομένης συμβῆναί φασι τὰ περὶ τὸν ἐν τῶι Ὑμηττῶι γεωργοῦντα τὸ κληθὲν ὕστερον χωρίον ἀτελές* etc. (cf. Rhodes 1993, 216); Diod. Sic. 9.37: *ὅτι ὁ αὐτὸς διαπορευόμενός ποτε διὰ τῆς χώρας κατενόησεν ἄνθρωπον κατὰ τὸν Ὕμηττον ἐργαζόμενον ἐν χωρίοις λεπτοῖς καθ' ὑπερβολὴν καὶ τραχέσι* etc. See now Moreno 2007, 53, 73–4. A model of modest intensification of agricultural production in the Archaic period is favoured by Forsdyke 2006.

[61] For insights into life at Hymettos (and other Attic mountains) in the late Imperial period, see Fowden 1988, a valuable discussion that does not, however, tackle issues of ownership.

[62] RO 22 ll. 25–31: *τοῖς δὲ ποιησ|σαμέν[οι]ς συμμαχίαν πρὸς Ἀθηναίος καὶ | τὸς συμ[μ]άχος ἀφεῖναι τὸν δῆμον τὰ ἐγκ|τήματα ὅποσ' ἂν τυγχάνηι ὄντα ἢ ἴδια ἢ [δ]||ημόσια Ἀθ[η]ναίων ἐν τῆι χ[ώραι τῶν ποιο]||μένων τὴν συμμαχίαν κ[αὶ περὶ τούτων π]||ίστιν δοῦναι Ἀ[θηναίος]*; ll. 35–41: *ἀπὸ δὲ Ν|αυσινίκο ἄρχον[τ]ος μὴ ἐξεῖναι μήτε ἰδ|ίαι μήτε δημοσ[ί]αι Ἀθηναίων μηθενὶ ἐγ|κτήσασθαι ἐν τ[α]ῖς τῶν συμμάχων χώραι|ς μήτε οἰκίαν μήτε χωρίον μήτε πριαμέ|νωι μήτε ὑποθεμ̣ένωι μήτε ἄλλωι τρόπω|ι μηθενί.*

[63] e.g. Gauthier 1973, 170–2; Cargill 1981, 146–50; Salomon 1997, 75, 169; and now Moreno 2009, 211–13.

institution, unparalleled in other city-states. The members of the new League might have been confused about, or completely unaware of, the exact legal status of lands connected to the cleruchic institution. The taxonomy *ἴδια/δημόσια* would have sufficed to remedy their insecurity and prevent any legal sophisms on the part of the Athenians. That they chose to include the term *δημόσια* in the relevant clause proves that the notion of public ownership was extant. The ineluctable inference is that at least some of the lands allotted to cleruchs were conceived of as public, that is as belonging to the Athenian polis.[64] Fittingly, the earliest Athenian decree is germane to this topic. Inter alia *IG* I³ 1 specified that the cleruchs of the island of Salamis were not allowed to let their property out to a third party.[65] This stipulation, along with provisos concerning taxation,[66] military service, etc., makes it likely that the lands in question had been granted to the cleruchs by the Athenian polis. However, the prohibition on leasing came with a caveat, which our lacunose text unfortunately does not allow us to recover. Could one, for example, rent cleruchic property as long as one lived on the island? We do not even know if the said properties had a specific designation (e.g. *κλῆροι*), nor can we establish to what extent and in what sense they were public (*δημόσια*). Taking a small chronological leap into the fifth century, we should also remember how Athens recognized services rendered to her by Aristeides 'the Just': at the instigation of Alkibiades, Aristeides' son Lysimachos received, inter alia, 200 plethra of land in Euboea, which had been relegated to the status of a cleruchy; such land was clearly the property of the Athenian polis.[67] The problem of the legal status of cleruchies, however, is an elusive one, and since cleruchies lay outside the official Attic territory, the issue has to be dealt with separately.[68]

[64] Anthropologists are not unfamiliar with the concept: see Rihll 1991, 105; cf. Todd 1993, 242 n. 10, who acknowledges the possible ad hoc character of this document.

[65] *IG* I³ 1 (with Addenda, p. 935), ll. 1–2: *τ[ὸς ἐΣ]αλαμ̣[ῖνι κλερόχ]ος | οἰκε̂ν ἐᾶ Σαλαμῖνι*; ll. 2–3: *τ̣[ὰ δ' ἐ Σαλαμῖνι] μ|ὲ μι[σθ]ôν, ἐὰ μὲ οἰκ[. . . .⁷ . . .]ο[. μισθόμενο.]*.

[66] I note that Gallo 2005*b*, 173–4 suggests that the levy in question was a produce-tax.

[67] Dem. 20.115, with Moreno 2007, 90–1, who places the donation to the middle of the 5th cent.; cf. Plut. *Arist.* 27.2, with Calabi Limentani 1964, 111.

[68] We should not disregard the implications of *SEG* XLV 1162, which attests to the duplication of Athenian institutions in cleruchic territory. Hansen 2007, 322–3, has now explicitly stated that cleruchies were '*poleis* of Athenians living abroad'.

Nevertheless, there is some limited fourth-century epigraphical evidence which seems to distort the neatness of the picture drawn above, and it is to this I will now briefly resort, if only to dismiss it. As I have already argued, the destination of the rent from the *Νέα* makes it almost certain that the area in question was sacred.[69] As for *IG* II^2 411, previously understood to be a lease of state agricultural land, Palme has forcefully argued that it was a legal contract between Athens and a metic entrepreneur, the two parties sharing alternately the produce of some unidentified mines.[70] Even Lambert in his recent dissection of the text, while denying any connection of *IG* II^2 411 to mining, has suggested that we should look 'beyond agriculture . . . and perhaps beyond any rights specifically in land'.[71] Despite its peculiarities, *IG* II^2 411 should not be seen as an obstacle to the analysis above. All the remaining Classical leases conferred by the central administration unequivocally refer to sacred lands, i.e. realty which, strictly speaking, was not public.

2. AN INTERPRETATIVE ANALYSIS

In this chapter the approach followed so far has been that of identifying public land on the basis of the occurrence of the adjective *δημόσιος*. Implementing such a purely linguistic criterion may seem naive and simplistic, but it is the best way to prevent modern biases from distorting the final picture. Time and again scholars have postulated the existence of public landholdings in Athens, without clarifying their premises, and whenever they do so, a certain methodological inconsistency underlies their endeavours.[72] To cite just one striking example, in a highly acclaimed exposition, Andreyev held the following view: 'Under the term "public land" I have grouped together land belonging to the state, to various cult institutions,

A fragmentary unpublished *horos* from Astypalaia, on display in the local Museum (personal visit, September 2005), seems to record 'public land of the Athenians'. We do not know of Astypalaia as an Athenian cleruchy from any other source. The publication of the text might change our view considerably on related issues.

69 Cf. Chapter 2, Section 2; also Papazarkadas 2009*b*, 179.
70 Palme 1987.
71 Lambert 2010.
72 e.g. Foxhall 2002, 216–17.

territorial organisations and any other associations of citizens—in other words essentially everything that is not privately held.'[73]

In recent years there has been a trend towards expounding the conflicts that led to the Solonian reforms by reference to the usurpation of public/common lands which allegedly resulted in a high proportion of villagers losing access to land and becoming impoverished.[74] This theory, characteristic of reconstructions of Archaic Athens, is built on frail evidence from Athens itself and on anthropological parallels from rural African societies.[75] Though it fits well the doctrine of common lands set aside for common exploitation by entitled individuals, it has to remain no more than a plausible suggestion.[76] To avoid such misconceptions it seems to me that a better starting point is the definition offered by the political philosopher Raymond Geuss in his treatise on the distinction of the public–private spheres: 'Public property is property thought to be owned in common by the unrestricted set of all the people in some given society—or by the state as representative of all the people.'[77] The second part of the disjunction need not occupy us here. As most scholars maintain, the concept of the state *qua* superordinate power, representing society while simultaneously standing outside it, cannot apply to the ancient Greek world.[78] As for the first part, it can be accepted only under the condition that it applies to the citizens or to those entitled by the citizenry to act on its behalf, that is, metics and/or slaves performing tasks aiming at the citizens' benefit.

Still, the endeavour turns out to be less fruitful than desired unless an agreement is reached about the exact, historically contextualized, meaning of δημόσιος. Back in 1990 Lewis was adamant that the earliest attestations of the word δημόσιος had no democratic connotations at all and that they were akin to δῆμος, perceived as *populus*.[79]

[73] Andreyev 1974, 25–6.
[74] Rihll 1991.
[75] Manville 1990, 96–112.
[76] For methodological difficulties concerning the reconstruction of Archaic tenurial patterns see Foxhall 1997, who justifiably lambasts uncritical use of social anthropology to elucidate the Graeco-Roman world.
[77] Geuss 2001, 6–7.
[78] See references collected by Anderson 2009, 5, and *passim*, who offers a nuanced account of statehood in relation to ancient Greek poleis. For the concept of the state as a superpersonal, permanent power, see the homonymous subchapter in Hansen 1998, esp. 40–2.
[79] Lewis 1990, 260–3, in the appendix entitled '*Demos* and Some of its Cognates'.

This claim was recently reinforced by Fouchard's semantic analysis of 600 occurrences of the word. He too confirmed that there are no specific constitutional nuances in the adjective δημόσιος: in Sparta, to take the most notorious example, various categories of things or institutions could be called δαμόσια, but such designations had clearly no democratic connotations. In fact δημόσιος refers to what is perceived as belonging to the polis, the political community, and as being in the interest of the polis. However, Fouchard provided the modification that δῆμος and πόλις (and consequently δημόσιος and πολιτικός) are not identical in that δῆμος/ δημόσιος emphasize the aggregate of the citizens, both on the level of administration as well as that of politics.[80]

It is against this theoretical background that land-tenure patterns in Classical Athens have to be investigated. The evidence accumulated above highlights a situation whereby the Athenian polis never owned any non-sacred, revenue-yielding arable lands, at least in the Classical period. Yet Athens did own other pieces of real property, such as the mines in the Laureotike, an invaluable source of revenue for the public reserves. Mining, a fascinating financial activity in its perplexity, could be a topic for another discussion, but for the present it is important to bear in mind that only whatever lay beneath the surface belonged to the public domain.[81] The landholdings above the mines along with their equipment belonged to private individuals, as the *poletai* records unfailingly show. It has been claimed with regard to the argentiferous subsoil, that Athens was either unwilling or unable to operate state mines, but of course she could not possibly give up on the unique mineral wealth of south-east Attica.

With the exception of the sacred quarries of Herakles at Eleusis and of Asklepios and Dionysos in Piraeus, little is known of the ownership of the other Attic quarries.[82] Parallels from other parts of the Greek

[80] Fouchard 1998.

[81] This is the *opinio communis* (e.g. Hopper 1953, 204–9; Osborne 1985*a*, 116–18; Faraguna 1992, 294–5; Kakavoyiannis 2005, 147-52; Faraguna 2006, 142–3). In that respect Athens was not exceptional: public ownership of mines has been envisaged with regard to both the Siphnian and the Thasian mines (Hdt. 3.57; 6.46–7, with Austin and Vidal-Naquet 1977, 193, 309–10). Graham Oliver has brought to my attention another type of realty whose ownership status we would like to establish, namely graveyards, and more precisely the Δημόσιον Σῆμα, the public cemetery par excellence; see now Patterson 2006, esp. 56 with n. 48.

[82] The 'passage through the quarry' (τὸ διόδιον τῆς λιθοτομίας) of the Roman Imperial decree *SEG* XXVI 121 l. 49, may refer to a landmark, but it may well refer to

world such as Corinth might suggest that some such establishments were indeed public property.[83] A strong argument in favour of this position is indirect, yet unexpectedly convincing. Amongst the dozens of epigraphical clauses instructing the *poletai* to contract the construction of marble stelae, there is not a single case of a transaction involving purchase of raw material. Very few diligent scholars have realized the implication: the marble quarries of Pentele and Hymettos were in the hands of the polis.[84] Other documents tell us a similar story. The accounts of the *epistatai* of the Parthenon, for instance, record remunerations to those who transferred the stone, those who worked the stone, but never to those who supplied the stone itself. The polis simply had no reason to purchase what she already owned. Perhaps the best hard evidence we have comes from the hundreds of quarries investigated in the area of Piraeus. In his systematic analysis of the relevant material, Langdon came out strongly in favour of the view that most of the quarries were public property. It was, moreover, Langdon who brought out another striking piece of literary evidence, without himself realizing its implications: in 409/8 a group of Syracusan captives, held in quarries at Piraeus, managed to escape by digging through the rock.[85] But could this quasi-gaol have been anything but public property? Last but not least, one should recall that *IG* II^2 244, a law regulating fortification work in 337, was probably set up next to the Piraean quarries that offered the raw material. Attic decrees and laws have been studied well enough for us to know that their places of publication—the Agora, the Acropolis, a shrine—always fell within either the public or the sacred sphere.[86] Cumulatively, the evidence just presented shows beyond a reasonable doubt that most Attic quarries were public property.

sacred property near Mt. Hymettos. Nevertheless, the divine owner still remains unknown to us.

[83] Lolos 2002.

[84] e.g. Langdon 1991, 62.

[85] Xen. *Hell.* 1.2.14: *καὶ χειμὼν ἐπῄει, ἐν ᾧ οἱ αἰχμάλωτοι Συρακόσιοι, εἱργμένοι τοῦ Πειραιῶς ἐν λιθοτομίαις, διορύξαντες τὴν πέτραν, ἀποδράντες νυκτὸς ᾤχοντο εἰς Δεκέλειαν, οἱ δ' εἰς Μέγαρα.*

[86] Location of *IG* II^2 244 (and of other inscribed laws): Richardson 2000; for its date see Conwell 2008, 134–9. Places of publication of Athenian documents: Liddel 2003.

It is often maintained that Athens possessed and probably leased out public houses, such as those mentioned in the Xenophontic *De Vectigalibus*. However, this axiom has been recently questioned by Graham's interpretation of the *δημόσιαι οἰκίαι* as brothels. His theory has many merits and tallies better with the detected absence of public farmland.[87] And is it after all a coincidence that the 'Old Oligarch' has nothing to say about state-owned hostels or similar facilities, whereas he carefully underlines the landlords' gains from their renting of tenements to visiting foreigners?[88] The policy followed in confiscation cases confirms that the Athenians were keen on realizing capital instead of settling for long-term profits. It also emphasizes their stubborn refusal to bring potentially profitable properties under the control of their polis.[89] Indeed, there is only one known case where confiscated property was bestowed as a gift on a private individual and not sold at an auction.[90] This is extraordinary. In antiquity several Greek city-states possessed a reserve of land that could be used to accommodate newly enfranchised citizens or returning political exiles whenever such a need arose. Surely these lands were of public character.[91] Nothing entitles us to believe that a similar condition applied to Athens, at least in the Classical and Hellenistic periods.[92] Honorific decrees granting citizenship to prominent

[87] *IG* I³ 84, l. 36: *ἐντὸς τε̂ς οἰκίας τε̂ς δεμοσίας* (cf. Wycherley 1960, 65); Xen. *Vect.* 4.49: *καὶ ἀπὸ οἰκιῶν περὶ τἀργύρεια δημοσίων καὶ ἀπὸ καμίνων καὶ ἀπὸ τῶν ἄλλων ἁπάντων πρόσοδοι ἂν πολλαὶ γίγνοιντο*; Gauthier 1976, 187 suggested leasing as the mode of exploitation implied by Xenophon, but see now Graham 1998, 33–7, approved by Henry 2002, 219.

[88] Xen. [*Ath. Pol.*] 1.17–18: *πρὸς δὲ τούτοις ὁ δῆμος τῶν Ἀθηναίων τάδε κερδαίνει τῶν δικῶν Ἀθήνησιν οὐσῶν τοῖς συμμάχοις. πρῶτον μὲν γὰρ ἡ ἑκατοστὴ τῇ πόλει πλείων ἡ ἐν Πειραιεῖ· ἔπειτα εἴ τῳ συνοικία ἐστι ἄμεινον πράττει* etc.

[89] Despite what Langdon 1991, 60 n. 16 has tentatively claimed regarding confiscated properties ('some land [might have been] added to the public domain'), this seems never to have been the case. Finley 1952*a*, 91 had got it right: 'Since the Athenian state had no administrative machinery with which to deal readily with land or houses it invariably sold at public auction whatever it confiscated.'

[90] Lys. 7.4: *ἦν μὲν γὰρ τοῦτο Πεισάνδρου τὸ χωρίον, δημευθέντων δὲ τῶν ὄντων ἐκείνου Ἀπολλόδωρος ὁ Μεγαρεὺς δωρειὰν παρὰ τοῦ δήμου λαβὼν τὸν μὲν ἄλλον χρόνον ἐγεώργει* etc., with Todd 2007, 515–16.

[91] Burford 1993, 16–19, 26–8; Ruzé 1998. Note in particular the extraordinary case of Kydonia, which purchased land the produce of which was granted to her *proxenoi*: *ICret.* II.x.1, esp. ll. 2–3: *τάδε ἐπρίατο ἁ πόλις τοῖς προξένοις | καρπεύειν ἆς κα ἐπιτάδειοι ὦντι.*

[92] For the Archaic period see Hdt. 6.90 (*σὺν δέ οἱ καὶ ἄλλοι ἐκ τῶν Αἰγινητέων ἕσποντο, τοῖσι Ἀθηναῖοι Σούνιον οἰκῆσαι ἔδοσαν*), but Nenci 1998, 252 notes the

foreign benefactors have clauses containing the permission to acquire realty at Athens (*ἔγκτησις*), but never direct provision of land as such.[93] Perhaps the explanation has to be sought in the relative overpopulation of Attica, which dramatically diminished, if not altogether eliminated, any such land reserve. Let us remember here that the grant of good farmland to Lysimachos was only possible because Athens had at her disposal cleruchic property outside Attica. I suspect, however, that the strikingly Athenian ideology of autochthony played its own role.[94] Very few Greek people could pride themselves on being so closely attached to their land, and to dispose of it might have struck outsiders as at least ideologically inconsistent if not blatantly hypocritical.[95]

Still, the Athenian attitude is hard to decipher. After all, despite the peculiarity of the economic infrastructure of Athens, her economy was ultimately agricultural and even to argue for this one runs the risk of retreading old ground. There is an obvious paradox in the function of the cradle of democratic institutions that Athens had undoubtedly been during the Classical period, for other city-states of limited political weight seem to have been owners of landed property that was patently public and non-sacred.[96] An elucidation of this discrepancy is, therefore, urgently needed.

In contrast to the mines with their limited geographical distribution, potentially profitable lands were scattered all around the admittedly

limited agricultural potential of Sounion and speculates that the Aiginetans who settled there would have been maritime merchants.

[93] Pecirka 1966; Niku 2007, 114–38.

[94] One should use Cohen 2000, the most recent comprehensive discussion of the Athenian autochthony, to trace the enormous earlier bibliography.

[95] In her recent discussion of *enktesis*, Niku 2007, 114–15, has also adduced scarcity of arable land and the myth of autochthony as two possible determinants of Athenian policy regarding the grant of *enktesis*.

[96] e.g. ML 13, ll. 1–3: *τεθμὸς ὅδε περὶ τâς γâς βέβαιος ἔστο κὰτ τὸν | ἀνδαιθμὸν Πλακός, Ὑλίας καὶ Λισκαρίας καὶ τôν ἀ|ποτόμον καὶ τôν δαμοσίον* (*c*.500). *Syll.*³ 964, two leases of landholdings from Keos. Both are termed *Ποιασσίων ἡ γῆ* and, thus, must be considered as public tillable lands under the administration of the city-state of Poiessa; for this notion see Hansen 1996, 169, who aptly observes 'moreover since a polis in the sense of "state" was principally a community of citizens rather than a country, the usual way of naming a polis was to use the nominative plural of the adjectival form of the name of the city as the official name of the community itself' (the use of the genitive, instead of the nominative, in *Syll.*³ 964 is due to grammatical constraints and, therefore, indifferent for my argument). Cf. also the Argive *SEG* XLI 282: *κατασταθεὶς δὲ καὶ δωτινατὴρ τâς ἱερâς καὶ δαμοσίας χώρας* (Hellenistic, but reflecting an earlier, 5th-cent., scheme according to Piérart 1997, 332–3).

expanded Attic territory. This situation was probably exacerbated by the absence of a central land cadastre, as the vast majority of scholars maintain. Perhaps Athens lacked the necessary bureaucratic machinery for administering extensive stretches of land. This role might have been much more effectively undertaken by demes. As we have already noted, although most deme-land consisted of *temene*, certain deme-properties were not of sacred character.[97] As argued elsewhere, deme boundary markers probably delimited the type of land that was unconditionally used for grazing, wood fetching, apiculture or even hunting by all members of the political microcommunities or their subordinates.

The most appropriate interpretative context is that of the political unification of Attica, the so-called *synoecism*.[98] Modern scholarship holds that the reforms of Cleisthenes modified rather than completely altered a pre-existing administrative scheme and I have already argued that the ναύκραροι of the Archaic period would have had exactly the supervision and administration of naucraric, later demotic, lands. But the *naukrariai* themselves appear to have been localities already active by the time the *synoecism* had been accomplished and, what is more, to have responded effectively to problems surrounding land administration. It is not hard to see, for instance, why there was no need for *agronomoi* (ἀγρονόμοι) in Athens: the personnel of the demes would have sufficed to carry out such tasks.[99] In the process of time common lands would have been increasingly brought under deme control. The result would have been a strange mixture of dual, albeit limited, ownership: common lands would have nominally remained the property of all Athenian citizens, but in practice they would have been enjoyed by the local residents, the demesmen. This does not mean that the polis of Athens relinquished her claims to this type of property. When, in the late Classical period, Athens decided to increase her revenues she forced her subordinate groups to alienate such surplus lands. This is not to say that the properties called δημόσια and the deme-owned lettings were identical. This latter category was perceived to be separate.[100] The conceptual distinction

[97] See Chapter 3, Section 2.
[98] Snodgrass 1982, 668–9, 676–7.
[99] Cf. Todd 1993, 248.
[100] Lewis 1990, 262. The same applies to properties belonging to other associations, such as phratries and orgeones.

between what belonged to the polis proper and what was owned by the demes is manifest in the lexicographical entries on the rites that were publicly funded (*δημοτελῆ*) as opposed to those subsidized by the demes (*δημοτικά*), and, more significantly, in contemporary literature of religious content.[101] There is also some negative evidence for the dissociation of demotic from public lands. As noted above, encroachment upon public property constituted a recognizable legal category.[102] Yet if deme lands were involved in these cases, we would have expected them to be resolved at the local level as part of the demes' internal agenda, since demes had both the necessary juridical capacity and the authorization from the central administration to bring them in their own courts.[103] It is, therefore, reasonable to conclude that public lands did not equate with demotic ones.

It seems preferable to follow Lambert's identification of a specific category of public lands that bore one or a combination of the following features: They were controlled (but not owned) by a group and used for the common benefit of its members. They were not revenue-generating. Or they were simply unused and unowned.[104] Seen in a diachronic perspective these traits could have coexisted or alternated: a strip of unproductive hilly land that had never been tilled could at some point have been used for herding flocks belonging to some kind of proto-aggregation of poor farmers, for whom the separate breeding of animals in their private landholdings was simply unfeasible. Although some property of this kind, such as the *δημόσιαι ἅλωι* at Poros, might have had an agricultural function, most public land of the type envisaged here would have been marginal and mountainous. On the whole, rendering marginal areas productive is a well-known response of moderately

[101] e.g. *Anecd. Bekk.* I.240.28–30: *δημοτελῆ καὶ δημοτικὰ ἱερὰ διαφέρει. τὰ μὲν δημοτελῆ θύματα ἡ πόλις δίδωσιν, εἰς δὲ τὰ δημοτικὰ οἱ δημόται, εἰς δὲ τὰ ὀργεωνικὰ οἱ ὀργεῶνες*; Phot. s.v. *δημοτελῆ καὶ δημοτικὰ ἱερά· διέφερον ἀλλήλων καὶ τῶν ὀργεωνικῶν καὶ τῶν γενικῶν* (cf. Mikalson 1977, 428; Whitehead 1986, 178; Parker 1996, 7 n. 22). Dem. 43.71: *ἐὰν μὴ εἰς ἱερὸν Ἀθηναίων δημόσιον ἢ δημοτικόν* etc.

[102] For instance, Demosthenes' *Against Kallikles* was delivered at a *δίκη βλάβης* (lawsuit for a damage case) in an Athenian court; cf. Todd 1993, 280–2.

[103] Deme assemblies could indeed operate as courts; see for instance, my edition (Papazarkadas 2007*a*) of *IG* II^2 1196, a text significantly addressing disputes over leased pastures.

[104] Lambert 1997*a*, 239–40; cf. Andreyev 1974, 16–17.

complex agricultural societies to an increasing demand for resources.[105] The use of the uncultivated landscape can significantly boost the overall yield of an area. It has long been estimated that of the 2,400-square-kilometre territory of Attica, some 1,000 were usable for agricultural and arboricultural activities.[106] This figure seems to represent only that part of Attica that was worked for the cultivation of cereals, olives, and vines. Even if we allow for the inhabited areas, there still remains a substantial proportion of the Attic territory (at least half of it) that was not put to straightforward agricultural exploitation of the classic type. The rather feeble evidence suggests that this mainly highland zone was conceived as public—as belonging to no private individual, corporate group, or divinity—and that, being accessible to any interested member of the political community, it could render profits that in most cases are not detectable in our sources.

To recapitulate: public realty did exist in Classical Athens, but it did not fall under the category of arable revenue-generating estates. Rather it consisted of landed zones in mainly marginal areas, used, if at all, for the common benefit of members of the political community. Some areas, such as those located along circuit walls, could also be perceived as public, but they were not financially exploited either. Lack of interest on the part of the polis, and shortage of available personnel and cadastres led to the supervision of these outlying strips of land by the local communities known as demes.[107] Nevertheless, their role was exclusively that of agencies, and demes did not have any rights of possession over the lands in question. Their own landed assets, the δημοτικὰ κτήματα, fell within a different sub-category. The polis maintained the last word over the administration of its common landholdings. The *Rationes Centesimarum* seem to reflect such a case, if one is to accept the cautious remarks made by Lambert about the proceeds from these transactions flowing into the secular funds of the

[105] Forbes 1995; Horden and Purcell 2000, 178–82.

[106] Foxhall 1992, 156.

[107] I briefly note that very similar developments have been assumed in the case of land administration in Mycenaean Greece. Probably for reasons of administrative convenience, the palace, i.e. the central administration, let the district communities known as *damoi* control *ke-ke-me-no* (communal) land, although it retained ownership and exacted profit from such landholdings: see Shelmerdine 2006, 74–5.

polis. However, the *Rationes Centesimarum* were a unique economic experiment, in fact the only recorded effort by Athens to make some profit out of her non-sacred landed resources. Paradoxically, the principle of privatization meant that the project could never again be repeated.[108]

[108] Cf. Andreyev 1974, 44–5.

6

Conspectus

Sacred realty controlled by the central authorities of Athens first emerges in the mid-fifth century. This chronology, far from being accidental or marking the foundation of such lands, roughly corresponds to the abrupt proliferation of the so-called *epigraphical habit*.[1] The antiquity of sacred real property is, therefore, hard to establish. Consequently, we must have recourse to rather tenuous evidence. It has not escaped scholarly attention, for instance, that both the terms *temene* and *basileus* have strong Mycenaean resonances. *Temene* feature prominently in Linear B tablets as land units assigned to a series of palatial functionaries, such as the *wanax* or the *lāwāgetās*.[2] On the other hand, *temene* are never attached to any *qa-si-re-u*, the Mycenaean linguistic equivalent of a *basileus*. What is more, the latter term is widely acknowledged to denote rather low-rank regional officials with no apparent religious functions.[3] In view of all this—not to say anything about the vexed problem of continuity—any Mycenaean perspective on Athenian sacred lands appears too far-fetched to be significant.[4] However, the same pair, that is, *temene* and *basileus*, also have strong Homeric resonances, and the same applies to the descriptive term *γύαι*.[5] In turn, the Homeric aspect is

[1] Cf. Hedrick 1999, 398–400.

[2] See Palaima 2006, 62; Bendall 2007, 73–4.

[3] Morpurgo Davies 1979, 96–9; Palaima 1995, 122; Carlier 1995; Palaima 2006.

[4] I note, nevertheless, that some Greek historians have started entertaining the possibility of continuation in the sector of sacred finances that interests me here; see, for instance, Davies 2001, 119: 'Historically, indeed, continuity of cult from LM IIIB is now becoming a reality, so that assignation of landed resources to deities as *temene* may have had a long past before its first attestation at *Odyssey* 8.363'.

[5] e.g. Hom. *Il.* 6.190–5; *Od.* 6.293 (with Garvie 1994, 154–5); Busolt and Swoboda 1920–6, 141; Hegyi 1976, 78; Finley 1977, 95; Raaflaub 1997, 631, 644 and *passim*. For *γύαι* see Andreades 1928, 20; Faraguna, 1992, 348–9.

reminiscent of the 'Peisistratean recension' of the Homeric epics.[6] Overall, the possible connections appear numerous and hypothetical, but in the absence of any good reason for dating the creation of Athenian *temene* in the Classical period, we should feel justified in placing them back at least as early as the Archaic epoch.[7]

Although imperial revenues tend to monopolize the discussion of fifth-century Athenian economics, domestic finances should not be overlooked. It is evident from Aristophanes' *Wasps* and from scattered epigraphical documents that sacred rentals constituted an appreciable part of such revenues, but their exact volume cannot be established. The other set of sacred realty attested for the fifth century is that of *temene* founded abroad, mainly in confiscated territories of dissident members of the Delian League. Although significant in terms of value, these properties were of limited chronological scope; they probably vanished as a result of Athens' final defeat in the Peloponnesian War.[8] Similarly, although the sacred estates of Apollo at Delos and Rheneia were under Athenian administration for most of the Classical period, they seem to have first been established in the Archaic period by the tyrant of Samos, Polykrates. At any rate, nothing indicates that the Athenians ever diverted income from these *temene* into their own coffers, and the Delian estates had their own independent history.[9]

In the first half of the fourth century the leasing system seems to have largely fallen into abeyance, to judge from the absence of any relevant evidence.[10] Otherwise, we are merely left with Isocrates' grim

[6] Cf. Janko 1992, 29–32; Van Wees 1999, 6–8. I am alluding here to possible influences on Athenian terminology resulting from the dissemination of the Homeric epics from the 6th cent. onwards.

[7] One may recall that it was at approximately that time that Athens started asserting her territorial sovereignty through both her urban and her peripheral sanctuaries (de Polignac 1995, 81–8).

[8] Polinskaya 2009, 263 seems to think that consecration was an irreversible act, but I am inclined to agree with Badian 2004, 45 who, in his discussion of Xenophon's famous dedication of an estate to Artemis, contends that such acts of consecration were not recognized by the parties damaged (i.e. previous owners of the properties concerned).

[9] Thuc. 1.13.6; 3.104.2; see Kent 1948, and now Chankowski 2008, 14–15 (on Polykrates), and *passim*.

[10] A *defixio* mentioning a γῆ hιερά (*SGD* 3) has been found in a 4th-cent. burial context in Kerameikos, though most editors will date it to the late 5th cent. on the basis of the script (cf. Peek 1941, 89–90; Jeffery 1955, 75; Guarducci 1978, 247–8). If the reference is to a sacred landholding, then this lead tablet may fall within the

picture of sacred rentals in his *Areopagitikos*, generally assumed to date to the period around the Social War.[11] By that time Athenian finances had reached an all-time low. But the Social War was also a turning point in the history of Athenian public finances. Under the prudent administration of Euboulos, the Athenians inaugurated an orchestrated effort at financial recovery. Even though one automatically tends to associate Euboulos with the Theoric Fund,[12] he and his circle appear to have implemented a much more extensive fiscal reorganization.[13] It suffices here to mention the Sacred Orgas affair and the leasing project of 343/2 onwards. The consecration of Demon's property, along with some further evidence, suggests that bringing landed property under divine protection became an increasingly common practice at the time.[14] This renewed interest in land exploitation should be seen generally as the manifestation of a concern about finances and specifically as an effort to revitalize cultic activity. The latter is a characteristic traditionally ascribed to the pious Lykourgos, but this is an oversimplification. If, as often maintained, Lykourgos had been inspired by his membership of the *genos* of Eteoboutadai, then surely Euboulos would have been similarly motivated by his archonship of the Marathonian Tetrapolis, as has been recently suggested.[15] At any rate, we can now see that Lykourgos did not start from scratch; rather, his political predecessors had already paved the way for him. His religious law for the cultic equipment of the Attic shrines presupposes a functionally adequate leasing system and this must surely be the one put into operation in 343/2. Lykourgos and his accomplices introduced a similar scheme in

category of commercial or even judicial curses (perhaps concerning a dispute over a *temenos*; for the various types of curses see Faraone 1991). Most modern interpreters have focused on the profession of the target, Lysanias the 'bellows blower' (*ἐκ τô ἀργυροκοπίο φυσετές*), but at least one scholar has understood *γὴ hιερά* to be the deity 'sacred Earth' (Gager 1992, 163–4). Eidinow 2007, 405–6 non-commitally translates 'of holy earth'. The issue ought to be revisited.

11 See Too's brief account in Mirhady and Too 2000, 182.

12 Rhodes 2007, 350, 352.

13 Cawkwell 1963, 61–7; Perlman 1967, 173–5.

14 *Agora* XIX L6 ll. 137–8: [ὃ] *Κ̣αλλικρ̣άτης καθιέρωσε|[ν....⁸....] χωρίον* (... the landholding which Kallikrates consecrated). Aeschin. 3.21: *πάλιν ὑπεύθυνον οὐκ ἐᾷ τὴν οὐσίαν καθιεροῦν, οὐδὲ ἀνάθημα ἀναθεῖναι* ... (Furthermore, [the lawgiver] does not allow the man who is subject to audit to consecrate his property, or to make a votive offering ...); cf. Finley 1968, 25, and Isager and Skydsgaard 1992, 183–4.

15 So Lambert 2000*a*, 67–9, on *SEG* L 168, face A, col. II ll. 39–40: *τάδε τὸ ἕτερον ἔτος θύεται μετὰ Εὔβουλον*ᵛ *ἄρχ[ο]|ντα Τετραπολεῦσι.*

Oropos. Equally his death did not annul all pre-existing policies. The last record in the series of sacred leases seems to date to the late fourth/early third century.[16] We now know that at the time sacred officials were still in operation, doing their best to maintain the realty of Artemis Brauronia. Such public interest in religious finances should probably be ascribed to the enthusiasm of the restored democracy of 307. It can hardly be coincidental that Lykourgos received unprecedented posthumous honours, as revealed by the famous decree of Stratokles.[17]

Produce from lands in the form of rentals appears to have subsidized the cultic activity of a series of public or semi-public groups throughout the Classical period—indeed in certain cases even in the early Hellenistic era—although the evidence comes mainly from the fourth century. Lacking the multitude of resources of the polis and/or the political strength to raise income otherwise, these associations probably relied more heavily on land for the coverage of their expenditure than did the central administration. The degree of reliance was, however, dependent upon the unique historical background of each separate group. Similarly unique were the exact administrative schemes deployed by individual groups in land management, and singling out common traits should be perceived as a modern classificatory device rather than as an actual thread connecting the groups in question. Although it was usually the paramount magistrates of those groups (the *epimeletai* of the tribes, the demarchs, the phratriarchs, and so on) who carried out leasing operations, other incumbents occasionally cooperated.

The legal and notional status of land and other immovable property controlled by such groups is more difficult to establish. Certain categories of landed property were undoubtedly sacred. They nominally belonged to divinities worshipped by the respective groups, and they were occasionally protected via legal prohibitions and imprecations. Income from such properties subsidized cultic activity, such as purchase of sacrificial animals and timber, priestly emoluments, and construction or repair of cultic buildings. There are other categories of realty, however, whose status is problematic. Demes, for instance, could confiscate property from deme-debtors and the same applied to

[16] *Agora* XIX L14; cf. Parker 1996, 268: 'many cults must still have had their traditional revenues from rented land'.

[17] Mikalson 1998, 20–5, 75–6.

groups such as phratries and orgeones which offered loans on security. It should not be taken for granted that such land, once acquired by groups, would have been consecrated. The final decision was probably left to the discretion of the associates. If the latter felt unable to administer such property effectively, they might well alienate it. Equally problematic is the case of the tribal Oropian allotments. Nothing can corroborate the hypothesis that these lands were consecrated to the tutelary heroes of the tribes, and it seems more prudent to assume that the new hilly areas were considered as the secular property of the controlling groups. Overall, one ought to be careful not to look for neat schemata by which to analyse such phenomena. Although the *raison d' être* of some of the groups in question was the performance of cultic activity, in the process of time they might have developed new strategies which went beyond the strictly sacred sector. Such novelties would have seriously challenged traditional religious norms and ideas of ownership associated with them. Evidence such as the orgeonic document *IG* II^2 1289 or the documents of the Eikadeis attest to the ongoing debate within the framework of such organizations.

Other properties were patently non-sacred. As argued in Chapters 3 and 5, local communities were probably allowed to keep landed assets in their domain in the Archaic period, when administration was centralized, and this scheme was not challenged thereafter, not even by Cleisthenes. The functions of the demes in this respect should suffice to solve a long-standing enigma of Athenian land-tenure, namely the absence of any income-yielding arable lands under the jurisdiction of the polis. Neverthless, there was one further subdivision of realty which is by definition more difficult to discern in our sources, namely common land. Marginal, mountainous, and often unproductive, such areas were of a very vague ownership status. If there is anything that we could identify as public land, it ought to be the 'uncultivated landscape'.

We can identify further palpable motifs concerning corporate land. From the level of the polis down to that of the most inconsequential associations, leasing appears to have favoured the associate members rather than outsiders, and, amongst the former, the wealthy and the famous. Analysis of the prosopographical data brings out an elaborate nexus of often mutually linked individuals, who would embark on leases not only for financial benefit, but also for reasons of social prestige, piety, in order to cement their own associations, and so on.[18] The same holds true for sale transactions. But land sales, as exemplified by the *Rationes Centesimarum*, marked, towards the end of the Classical period, a qualitative and quantitative shift in the way corporate land management was conducted. The reasons appear to have been twofold: economic and social. The consequences went far beyond what the short-sighted economic analysis of contemporary Athenians could foresee. For one thing, the *Rationes Centesimarum*, I suggested, raised for the first time in Athenian history an issue which had for centuries lain unresolved, namely the reclamation on behalf of the Athenian state of common, idle land. But this reclamation was by definition temporary; it was a necessary step before transferring these lands to private ownership. This privatization emphasized an already predominantly private sector. If the Athenian state did not suffer any major damage—for those public alienated properties were in any case non-productive—for the corporate groups this was a long-term disaster. Not only did they lose common land available for the common benefit of their members, they were also deprived of some of their revenue-bearing landed assets.

The dramatic decline of documents recording land administration in the Hellenistic period should probably be ascribed to a series of reasons, one of which is, no doubt, the radical changes just described. Demes, phratries, *gene*, and other associations become increasingly invisible as self-governed units after *c.*300. The political turmoil of the time (Macedonian occupation, democratic restoration of 307/6, the administration of Demetrios Poliorketes, the Chremonidean War, the Demetrian War), enhanced by a shift of power from traditional centres in mainland Greece to newly Hellenized parts of the world (Northern Greece, Egypt, Asia Minor), could hardly have left Athens unaffected. The desolation of the Attic countryside as is emerging in recent land surveys is the best material proof of this.[19] Religious notions were also affected. Although religious activity by no means came to a halt, it certainly underwent some qualitative transformation. Some traditional groups of public or semi-public character, such as phratries, *gene*, orgeones, trittyes, etc., fell into oblivion, and my view is that, even if this decline was not exclusively brought about by

[18] See Appendix VII, Catalogue and Chapter 3, Section 2.vi and Chapter 4, Sections 3.iii and 4.
[19] See the Epilogue to Chapter 3.

the loss of their landed assets, it was certainly accelerated by it.[20] Similar considerations apply to the central administration.[21] In about 200 our records abruptly stop: no more sacred realty or sacred rentals. Again this is just one piece of a wider puzzle. It is well into the Roman Imperial period before sacred realty controlled by the polis of Athens becomes visible again. But when it did, old concepts were fast to revive. In approximately the first century BC the Athenian assembly passed a decree whereby [*ἐψήφισται περὶ τῶν ἱερῶν*] *κ̣α̣ὶ̣ τεμενῶν ὅπως ἀποκατασταθῆι το[ῖ]ς θεοῖς καὶ τοῖς ἥρωσιν, ὧν ἐξ ἀρχῆς ὑπῆρχε*: 'it was decreed about the shrines and the *temene* that they be restored to the gods and the heroes to whom they belonged from the beginning'.[22] Throughout the centuries, the Athenians had little, if any, doubt: the *moriai*, the *temene* of Athena, the Other Gods, Demeter and Kore, Asklepios, and Amphiaraos, the landholdings of their tribal heroes and those of the divine protectors of their religious groups were sacred. The income from such properties was meant to cover expenditure for the unimpeded cultic activity that would secure political and social prosperity. Whether the lower strata of society would benefit from their participation in the lavish common feasts was a secondary, almost incidental, issue, but no one ever dared question the gods' ancient rights to receive services customarily offered to them by their mortal worshippers. The sacred lands' perpetual preservation was crucial for the affluence of Athens, and was thus a public concern. Their ownership was unquestionably divine, sanctified, and uncontested; it simply lay beyond the public sphere.

[20] Note here that the cause-and-effect interdependence between the disturbance of landownership and the decline of local groups was aptly observed by Andreyev 1974, 45. However, uncharacteristically for a scholar of a Marxist background, Andreyev put more emphasis on the demise of local associations as a factor undermining ownership patterns, whereas I believe that the process mainly worked the other way around.

[21] Note the very fragmentary *IG* II^2 736, thought by Koehler to refer to repairs of a shrine damaged during the Chremonidean War. The words *τεμένη* (l. 8) and *[μ]ισθο[ύ]μ-[ενα?]* (l. 14) might suggest an effort to employ rentals from sacred estates. If so, this would be an isolated case as regards post-300 central religious policy.

[22] *SEG* XXVI 121 = *IG* II^2 1035 (date: Habicht 1996, 84–6; Baldassarri 1998, 242–6; and now Schmalz 2009, 10–11).

APPENDIX I

The Sacred Orgas

i. The History of the Sacred Orgas

The earliest evidence of Athenian interest in the exploitation of sacred land in the fourth century stems from a decree which boasts an abundance of information and pertains to a unique situation. This is *I.Eleusis* 144, the famous document from 352/1 concerning the so-called Sacred Orgas (*ἱερὰ ὀργάς*).[1] The detailed information recorded on that stele is almost unparalleled in Attica, thus rendering *I.Eleusis* 144 a prime means of understanding Athenian administrative responses to problems concerning sacred land. On the other hand, as will be shown below, the decree under examination was passed in a period of intense international feuds and, furthermore, addressed the problem of the ambiguous ownership status of a tract of land. This peculiarity, as well as the accumulated secondary bibliography, makes a lengthy historical treatment inescapable. Far from being an undesirable necessity, such a diachronic approach allows the Sacred Orgas affair to be used as a case study.

The historical background to this *fundus sacer* is complex and has ramifications that reach back at least as far as the origins of the Peloponnesian War. Of all the alleged misdeeds of the Megarians that prompted the Athenians to pass the infamous *Megarian Decree*, the most severe was the Megarians' illicit farming of the *sacred and undefined land*.[2] The incident of

[1] *I.Eleusis* 144 (*IG* II^2 204; *Syll.*^{3} 204; *LSCG* 32; cf. Le Guen-Pollet 1991, 95–101 no. 32); see now RO 58; *SEG* LIV 115.

[2] Thuc. 1.139.2, *οἱ δὲ Ἀθηναῖοι οὔτε τἆλλα ὑπήκουον οὔτε τὸ ψήφισμα καθῄρουν, ἐπικαλοῦντες ἐπεργασίαν Μεγαρεῦσι τῆς γῆς τῆς ἱερᾶς καὶ τῆς ἀορίστου καὶ ἀνδραπόδων ὑποδοχὴν τῶν ἀφισταμένων*; cf. Thuc. 1.67.4. The story is also related by Plut. *Per.* 30.2, *ὑπῆν μὲν οὖν τις ὡς ἔοικεν αὐτῷ καὶ ἰδία πρὸς τοὺς Μεγαρεῖς ἀπέχθεια, κοινὴν δὲ καὶ φανερὰν ποιησάμενος αἰτίαν κατ᾽ αὐτῶν, ἀποτέμνεσθαι τὴν ἱερὰν ὀργάδα* (cf. Stadter 1989, 277). Shilleto 1872–80, 169 (with some hesitation); Stahl 1882–8, 342 (citing Goeller); Gomme 1945, 449; Parker 1983, 161 n. 99 think that the double definite article in Thuc. 1.139.2. suggests that 'the sacred land' (*ἡ ἱερὰ γῆ*) was different from 'the undefined land' (*ἡ ἀόριστος γῆ*); but the anonymous scholiast to Thucydides explicitly states that they were one and the same piece of land (Scholia ad Thuc. 1.139, *τῆς γῆς τῆς ἱερᾶς: τὴν γῆν λέγει τὴν μεταξὺ Μεγάρων καὶ τῆς Ἀττικῆς, ἥντινα ἀνέθεσαν ταῖς Ἐλευσινίαις θεαῖς· τὴν αὐτὴν δὲ λέγει καὶ ἀόριστον*). The date of the Megarian Decree, evidently a *terminus ante quem* for the unlawful cultivation of the sacred and undefined land (but note Pelling 2000, 105), is still the subject of fierce debate. The traditionally accepted date is 433/2–432/1 (e.g. Meiggs

the Megarian intrusion, related very succinctly by Thucydides, had for years been underrated by modern scholars, who failed to appreciate sacrilegious conduct as a sufficient justification for military action.[3] An important shift in scholarly focus was marked by the publication of de Ste. Croix's classic *The Origins of the Peloponnesian War*, a whole appendix of which was devoted to the Megarian decrees.[4] It is beyond the scope of this study to address the problem of the exact number of the decrees, their chronological sequence, or the extent to which their content can be described as provocative.[5] However, in order to grasp the importance of the fourth-century events, it is necessary to realize that the Athenians regarded the sanctity of the Sacred Orgas highly enough to treat its violation—fictional or not, that is irrelevant—as quasi-*ἀσέβεια*, the worst type of religious crime, when it suited their aims.[6]

Scholars have often maintained that the same land was ravaged by the troops of the Lacedaemonian king Kleomenes in the late sixth century.[7] According to an Athenian tradition reported by Herodotus, it was this sacrilege that caused the mental illness and, subsequently, the self-inflicted death of Kleomenes.[8] The identification of the Sacred Orgas with the late

1972, 430–1; de Ste. Croix 1972, 227 n. 2). Brunt 1993, 5–6, 16 favoured a date earlier than 433. Similarly Hornblower 1991, 111 dates the Megarian impiety to the early 430s.

3 The sole exception seems to have been Connor 1962.

4 de Ste. Croix 1972, 225–89.

5 However, the chronological order most lucidly advocated by Cawkwell 1969 and 1997, 111–14 seems to me preferable (cf. Pelling 2000, 103–11). De Ste. Croix 1972, 248–52 (followed by Salmon 1984, 424–6) would place the 'exclusion' Megarian decree after the so-called 'reasonable and courteous' decree and the subsequent one of Charinos.

6 Note the meticulous observations by de Ste. Croix 1972, 254–6 who claims that if the Athenians did not strictly treat the Megarians' offence as *ἀσέβεια*, that was because they were keen to avoid military confrontation. Moreover, Thucydides might have downplayed the significance of an incident which was primarily religious; cf. Brunt 1993, 14 (but see Parker 1983, 166 n. 129; Hornblower 1991, 111 and 2002, 108). For religion in Thucydides, see the comprehensive account by Hornblower 1992. Howe 2008, 93–5, now thinks of the Sacred Orgas as an area primarily set aside for grazing, and (contra Bowden 2005, 91) resurrects the scenario of Megarian encroachment actually precipitating the Peloponnesian War.

7 Foucart 1889, 436–7.

8 Hdt. 6.75: . . . *ἀπέθανε τρόπῳ τοιούτῳ, ὡς μὲν οἱ πολλοὶ λέγουσι Ἑλλήνων, ὅτι τὴν Πυθίην ἀνέγνωσε τὰ περὶ Δημαρήτου [γενόμενα] λέγειν, ὡς δὲ Ἀθηναῖοι μοῦνοι λέγουσι, διότι ἐς Ἐλευσῖνα ἐσβαλὼν ἔκειρε τὸ τέμενος τῶν θεῶν* (. . . and Kleomenes died in this way because, as most Greeks maintain, he persuaded the Pythia to utter the story about Demaratos, or, as the Athenians alone claim, because he invaded Eleusis and ravaged the *temenos* (shrine; precinct) of the goddesses'). Neither Nenci 1998, 240–1, nor McQueen 2000, 160, examine the possible connection to the Sacred Orgas. Bowden 2005, 90–1, hastens to assert that Herodotus was thinking of the Orgas; he certainly did not use the name *'Οργάς*.

Archaic *temenos* of the Two Goddesses is already present in Pausanias' travelogues.[9] In all likelihood, either Pausanias drew a personal, flawed inference, or by the second century of our era two different traditions, Kleomenes' foray and the disputes over the Sacred Orgas, had merged in popular narrative. To begin with, Herodotus speaks of a disaster that took place within the area of Eleusis (*ἐς Ἐλευσῖνα ἐσβαλών*). The Sacred Orgas, however, lay on the frontier between Attica and the Megarid, near, but outside, Eleusis.[10] Entries in various Lexica, as well as poetic extracts, seem to emphasize the Megarian, rather than the Attic, geographical proximity of the area.[11] Yet, it is unlikely that the *sacred and undefined land* of the Classical period would have been a *temenos* in late Archaic times.[12] The latter, ambivalent, term can equally well apply to a shrine or to a sacred estate, but always implies a fixed area with more or less clearly defined boundaries.[13] One can, therefore, surmise that the Eleusinian *temenos* of Herodotus' account, whether a sanctuary, a grove, or something similar, was a unit distinct from the Classical Sacred Orgas.

[9] Paus. 3.4.2: *ἐνταῦθα ὁ Κλεομένης ἄλλα τε ἐδῄωσε τῆς χώρας καὶ τῆς καλουμένης Ὀργάδος θεῶν τε τῶν ἐν Ἐλευσῖνι ἱερᾶς, καὶ ταύτης τεμεῖν φασιν αὐτόν* (Then Kleomenes devastated parts of the countryside, and also, they say, he cut down the so-called Orgas itself which is sacred to the goddesses of Eleusis). Pausanias is clearly expounding Herodotus when he writes that Kleomenes' suicide came about 'because, as the Athenians say, he had devastated the Orgas' (Paus. 3.4.5: *Ἀθηναῖοι δὲ ὅτι ἐδῄωσε τὴν Ὀργάδα*). Papachatzis 1976, 317, places Pausanias' Orgas in the Eleusinian plain (but see below).

[10] The topographical problem has been treated by various scholars; see mainly Kahrstedt 1932, 8–11; Van de Maele 1983; Ober 1985, 225–6; Burford 1993, 19–20; L'Homme-Wéry 1996, 131–50; McDonald 1996, 321–3.

[11] Did. col. 14.31-5, *κ(αὶ) (ἔστιν) ὁ λόγος τὰ νῦν τῶι Δη[μ]οσθένε[ι π]ερὶ τῆς Μεγαρικῆς Ὀργάδ[ος], ἧς κ(αὶ) Καλλίμαχός που μνημονεύων φησ[ί·] «Νισαίης ἀγλῖθες ἀπ' Ὀργάδος»* (And the speech of Demosthenes that we are presently concerned with is about the Megarian Orgas, which even Kallimachos has mentioned somewhere, when he says: 'Cloves of garlic from the Orgas at Nisaia'; trans. by Harding 2006, 95); Harp. s.v. *ὀργάς· Δημοσθένης ἐν τῷ Περί συντάξεως. ὀργὰς καλεῖται τὰ λοχμώδη καὶ ὀρεινὰ χωρία καὶ οὐκ ἐπεργαζόμενα, ὅθεν καὶ ἡ Μεγαρικὴ ὀργὰς προσωνομάσθη τοιαύτη τις οὖσα, περὶ ἧς ἐπολέμησαν Ἀθηναῖοι Μεγαρεῦσιν* (Orgas: Demosthenes in his speech *On Organization*. Orgas is the name of the bushy and mountainous areas that are not cultivated; hence the name of the Megarian Orgas, over which the Athenians and the Megarians fought, which was such an area); *Suda* s. v. *ὀργάς· τὰ λοχμώδη καὶ ὀρεινὰ χωρία καὶ οὐκ ἐπεργαζόμενα οὕτως καλεῖται. ὅθεν καὶ ἡ Μεγαρικὴ ὀργὰς προσωνομάσθη τοιαύτη τις οὖσα*; *EM* s.v. *ὀργάδα γῆν· παρὰ τὸ ἀργή τις εἶναι καὶ ἀνέργαστος . . . ἔστι δὲ καὶ γῆ ἐν Μεγάροις οὕτω καλουμένη ὀργάς* (Orgas land: a land that is fallow and uncultivated . . . there is even a land called Orgas at Megara).

[12] As von Prott and Ziehen 1896–1906, 88 n. 9 aptly observed 'orgadis nomen deest'.

[13] Latte 1934; I. Malkin, *OCD*[3] s.v. temenos.

The first time we hear of this particular piece of land in the fourth century is in the context of *I.Eleusis* 144. At this point the exact chronological order of the historical developments becomes uncertain. The tract in question is now named ἱερὰ ὀργάς and, by the casual way that *horoi* are mentioned in the query posed to the Delphic oracle, as well as by a vague mention of some upturned boundary stones, we can be pretty certain that it had ceased being an undefined area.[14] The initial delineation of the Orgas could have taken place any time between 432 and 353, but we cannot be more precise.[15] The 13th oration of the Demosthenic corpus contains a passing attack on the 'accursed Megarians' who had trespassed upon the Orgas. The orator narrates how the Athenians passed a decree which even allowed for military action, but which, it is implied, was never put into force.[16] The speech has traditionally been dated to 353/2.[17] Didymus, the scholiast to Demosthenes, following the Atthidographic tradition of Philochorus connects the extract to an invasion of an Athenian force under the general Ephialtes in the archonship of Apollodoros (350/49).[18] This patently contradicts Demosthenes' claim that the Athenians remained idle despite their declared and legally ratified resolution to cope with the problem. As Daverio-Rocchi has demonstrated, the discrepancy can be reconciled, if we dissociate the two events,

[14] *I.Eleusis* 144 ll. 74–5: [οἵδε ἡιρέθησαν ἐπὶ τὴν ἱερὰν] ὀργά[δ]α ἀντὶ τῶν ἐκπεπτωκό[τ|ων νέους ὅρους θεῖναι]. Of course, a lot is dependent on our comprehension of Thuc. 1.139.2 (see n. 2 above). Incidentally, Plutarch's reference to the ἱερὰ ὀργάς with regard to the area on the eve of the Peloponnesian War (Pl. *Per.* 30.2) is probably an anachronism.

[15] von Prott and Ziehen 1896–1906 would date the delineation of the Orgas after the Peloponnesian War. Kirchner in the commentary of *IG* II^2 204 merely notes that 'orgada terminatam fuisse iam ante hoc tempus ex v. 74 . . . sequitur'.

[16] [Dem.] 13.32: οἷον ἃ πρὸς τοὺς καταράτους Μεγαρέας ἐψηφίσασθε ἀποτεμνομένους τὴν ὀργάδα, ἐξιέναι, κωλύειν, μὴ ἐπιτρέπειν. Since the 19th cent. the speech has frequently been considered spurious. Nevertheless, Usher 1999, 215–17 has argued anew for its authenticity, albeit somewhat hesitantly (contra the new editor of the Demosthenic corpus M. R. Dilts, *Demosthenis Orationes*, Oxford 2002). If Usher is right, scholarly scepticism about the historicity of the recounted events should be set aside.

[17] Blass 1893, 398; Cawkwell 1963, 48 n. 9 and more recently Usher 1999, 215. However, see below for an alternative date.

[18] Did. col. 13.44–51 (=*FGrH* 328 F 155): γέγονε ταυτὶ κατ' Ἀπολλόδωρον ἄρχοντα καθάπερ ἱστορεῖ Φιλόχορος οὑτωσὶ γράφων: "Ἀθηναῖοι δ(ὲ) πρὸς Μεγαρέας διενεχθέντες ὑπὲρ τοῦ ὁρισμοῦ τῆς ἱερ(ᾶς) [Ὀ]ργάδος ἐπῆλθον εἰς Μέγαρα μετ' Ἐφιάλτου στρατηγο(ῦν)τος ἐπὶ τῆι χώραι κ(αὶ) ὡρίσαντο τὴν Ὀργάδα τ(ὴν) ἱεράν" (This happened during the archonship of Apollodoros, as is recounted by Philochoros, writing as follows: 'Because the Athenians had a dispute with the Megarians over the delimitation of the Sacred Orgas, they entered the territory of Megara with Ephialtes, the general for the homeguard, and marked out the limits of the Sacred Orgas'; trans. by Harding 2006, 91); with Gibson 2002, 132–4.

thus ascribing an interpretative error to Didymus.[19] Recently, however, Engen proposed a new dating of the speech *On the Organization*. Comparing it to the 15th Demosthenic oration *On the Freedom of the Rhodians*, which scholars unanimously consider to be genuine, Engen reached the conclusion that it was delivered after the decree *I.Eleusis* 144, but before the Athenian march against the Megarid of 350/9, and more precisely between June and November of 351.[20] A further point has to be made here. At the time of the delivery of Isocrates' speech *On the Peace*, the Athenian orator praised the Megarians for their pacifist policy.[21] If the dispute between the Athenians and the Megarians over the Orgas had already begun, Isocrates would have made a fool of himself by falsely lauding his country's foes. The speech, consequently, constitutes a *terminus post quem* for the conflict. Since *On the Peace* has of late been dated, on intertextual grounds, to between 354/3 and 353/2, the inception of the conflict can be reasonably placed somewhere between 353 and 351.[22]

On the basis of the extant evidence, various chronological reconstructions are tenable, but the traditional view which places the inception of the Attico-Megarian hostilities before *I.Eleusis* 144 seems preferable (contra Engen). The main merit of Engen's aforementioned analysis lies in his effort to place *I.Eleusis* 144 in a historical perspective, but his contextualization remains deficient because of his failure to account for some further historical parameters. In 355 Athens emerged from the so-called Social War defeated, humiliated, and drained of her financial resources.[23] Shortly afterwards, Xenophon, moved by Athens' dire economic circumstances, published his handbook entitled *Ways and Means* (*Πόροι*) in which he put forward suggestions for the rapid recovery of the city. Three points in that pamphlet intermingle with the content of *I.Eleusis* 144: the leasing of the *temene*, the restoration of the sanctuaries, and the recommendation to consult the Delphic oracle over ways to achieve prosperity for the polis in the future.[24] Although these are relatively minor points, since the kernel of Xenophon's argumentation concerns the exploitation of the silver mines, the overlap is still striking and some degree of interrelation has to be accounted for.

[19] Daverio-Rocchi 1988, 189–90.

[20] For the articulation of this intricate chronological argument see Engen 1999, 140–50.

[21] Isoc. 8.118–19; cf. Legon 1981, 265.

[22] Date of *On the Peace*: Rowe 2002, 156.

[23] Ellis 1994, 736–9; Hornblower 2002, 264–7.

[24] Xen. *Vect.* 4.19: *μισθοῦνται γοῦν καὶ τεμένη*; 6.1: *ἱερὰ δ' ἐπισκευάσομεν*; 6.2: *πέμψαντας καὶ εἰς Δωδώνην καὶ εἰς Δελφοὺς ἐπερέσθαι τοὺς θεοὺς εἰ λῷον καὶ ἄμεινον εἴη ἂν τῇ πόλει οὕτω κατασκευαζομένῃ καὶ αὐτίκα καὶ εἰς τὸν ἔπειτα χρόνον* (cf. Gauthier 1976, 220–2).

More significantly, the late 350s were the period when the so-called Third Sacred War was raging throughout Greece.[25] Strangely, one of the pretexts of that war had been the alleged cultivation of the sacred plain of Kirrha by the Phocians, themselves members of the Delphic Amphictiony, as well as their subsequent refusal to pay the fine imposed on them.[26] Scholars have long noticed the similarity between the Sacred Orgas and the plain of Kirrha, since both were consecrated to divinities and were meant to remain uncultivated.[27] However, the chronological affinity between the Megaro-Athenian conflict of the 350s and the Third Sacred War has passed unnoticed.

The uncultivability of the plain of Kirrha had constituted a favourite means of political manipulation in the history of the Delphic Amphictiony. The famous Amphictionic law of 380, known only from a copy erected in Athens, required members of the Amphictiony regularly to supervise the sacred land and, through the *hieromnamones*, impose fines upon any transgressors.[28] The Athenians themselves had apparently been bound by this obligation and, later on, in 340, their *pylagoros*, the famous orator Aeschines himself, played on this obligation in order to distract attention from Athens' own misdemeanours.[29] Given this, it is worth asking what the Athenians were up to in 352. In that year the Phocians were still in firm, albeit illegal, control of the Delphic sanctuary. For the Athenians, the Phocians' only significant loyal allies, the circumstances were favourable as far as their Delphic affinities were concerned. It may not be coincidental that the

[25] Buckler 1989, *passim*; Sanchez 2001, 173–99; Buckler 2003, 385–461.

[26] Dios. Sic. 16.23: *οἱ δὲ Φωκεῖς ἐπεργασάμενοι πολλὴν τῆς ἱερᾶς χώρας τῆς ὀνομαζομένης Κιρραίας δίκας ὑπέσχον ἐν Ἀμφικτύοσι καὶ πολλοῖς ταλάντοις κατεκρίθησαν*; Paus. 10.15.1: *ὅτε Φωκεῦσιν ἐπεργαζομένοις τοῦ θεοῦ τὴν χώραν ἐπέβαλον χρημάτων ζημίαν* (cf. Lefèvre 1998, 31–2; Sanchez 2001, 173–7; Rousset 2002*a*).

[27] Sanctity and uncultivability of Kirrha or Krisa: Aeschin. 3.108: *καὶ αὐτοῖς ἀναιρεῖ ἡ Πυθία πολεμεῖν Κιρραίοις καὶ Κραγαλίδαις πάντ' ἤματα καὶ πάσας νύκτας, καὶ τὴν χώραν αὐτῶν καὶ τὴν πόλιν ἐκπορθήσαντας καὶ αὐτοὺς ἀνδραποδισαμένους ἀναθεῖναι τῷ Ἀπόλλωνι τῷ Πυθίῳ καὶ τῇ Ἀρτέμιδι καὶ Λητοῖ καὶ Ἀθηνᾷ Προνοίᾳ ἐπὶ πάσῃ ἀεργίᾳ, καὶ ταύτην τὴν χώραν μήτ' αὐτοὺς ἐργάζεσθαι μήτ' ἄλλον ἐᾶν*; idem 3.109:... *καὶ τὴν πόλιν αὐτῶν κατέσκαψαν καὶ τὴν χώραν αὐτῶν καθιέρωσαν κατὰ τὴν μαντείαν· καὶ ἐπὶ τούτοις ὅρκον ὤμοσαν ἰσχυρόν, μήτ' αὐτοὶ τὴν ἱερὰν γῆν ἐργάσεσθαι μήτ' ἄλλῳ ἐπιτρέψειν, ἀλλὰ βοηθήσειν τῷ θεῷ καὶ τῇ γῇ τῇ ἱερᾷ* etc. (the historical context is that of the First Sacred War for which see Lefèvre 1998, 14–15 for the earlier bibliography). For this kind of sacred marginal landscape see Horden and Purcell 2000, 428, 453.

[28] *CID* I 10.15–18: [*αἴ τις τὰν γᾶν ἐπιερ*]||*γάζ*[*ο*]*ιτọ ἂν Ἀμφικτίονες ἱάρωσαν, ἐπεὶ κ̣*[*α*] *ἁ π̣ἑ̣*[*ρο*]*δ̣ọς γ̣ί̣ṇ*[*η*]*τ̣α̣ι̣, ἀ̣ποτ*[*εισάτω* - - - - - - - - - - -] | *στατῆρ̣α̣ς Αἰγιναίος κατ' τ*[*ὸ*] *πέλεθρον ἕ̣*[*κασ*]*τον· τ̣ọ̣ὶ̣ δ̣ὲ̣ ἱ̣*[*εροµνάµονες περιιόντων ἀεὶ τὰν ἱερὰν γᾶν*] | *καὶ π̣ρ̣*[*ασ*]*σόντων τὸν ἐπιεργαζόµενον*. See Bousquet's commentary on the Amphictionic Law in *CID* and the thorough treatments by Sanchez 2001, 153–63; Rousset 2002*b*, 188–92.

[29] Aeschin. 3.118–21; cf. Davies 2000, 207.

Athenians got involved in the Third Sacred War only in 352, despite obligations arising from an earlier official alliance with the Phocians.[30] If they intended to manipulate the policy advocated by the oracle, then the time was ripe.[31] Athenian manipulation of the oracle did not mean receiving the right answer; rather it meant receiving *an* answer. We should not let ourselves be misled by the Athenian-biased sources. Despite the anti-Megarian rhetoric, it seems that in 352 the real culprits were the Athenians, not their western neighbours.[32] The question posed to the Delphic oracle was articulated in a way that, in effect, ensured that the edge-lands of the Sacred Orgas would be consecrated one way or another.[33] But by predetermining the consecration of these marginal lands to their own divinities the Athenians ensured that this peripheral zone would come under their effective control. A Delphic oracle under the Phocians would certainly raise no objections to such a subtle deceit, or at least that was the impression of the Athenians.

Nevertheless, the list of the *ναοποιοὶ περὶ τὸν πόλεμον* of 353–1 shows that the Megarians were also one of the few Amphictionic people to align themselves with the Phocians.[34] Given the exigency of the situation, it is doubtful whether the Phocians could allow themselves the luxury of alienating any of their allies for the sake of a triviality.[35] For the Phocians the whole

[30] Diod. Sic. 16.27.5; cf. Ryder 2000, 47.

[31] As Philomelos' seizure of a response from Pythia (Diod. Sic. 16.27.1) demonstrates, the Phocians could become unscrupulously cynical; cf. Parke and Wormell 1956, 224; Fontenrose 1978, 250–1.

[32] A similar approach is taken by Scafuro 2003, who detects Athenian 'political arrogance and pretence', believing that *IG* II^2 204 would have escalated tension between the two parties.

[33] *I.Eleusis* 144 ll. 23–30: *γρά[ψαι δὲ τὸ]ν γραμματέα τῆς βουλῆς εἰς δύο κα||[ττ]ιτέρω ἴσω καὶ [ὁμοίω, εἰς μὲν] τὸν ἕτερον· εἰ λῶιον καὶ ἄμει||[νό]ν ἐστι τῶι δήμ[ωι τῶι Ἀθηναίων μισ]θοῦν τὸμ βασιλέα τὰ νῦ||[ν ἐ]νειργασμ[έ]να [τῆς ἱερᾶς ὀργάδος τὰ ἐκ]τὸς τῶν ὅρων εἰς οἰ||[κ]ọδομίạ[ν] τοῦ πρọ[στώιου καὶ ἐπισκευὴν τοῦ ἱ]ẹροῦ̣ τοῖν θεο|ῖν εἰς δὲ τὸν ἕτερον κ[α]ττίτ[ερον· εἰ λῶιον καὶ ἄμει]νόν ἐστι | τῶι δήμωι τῶν Ἀθηναίων τὰ ν[ῦν ἐκτὸς τῶ]ν ὅ[ρων ἐ]νειργ[α]σμέν|α τῆς ἱερᾶς ὀργάδος ἐᾶν ἄνετα [τοῖν θ]εοῖν* (The secretary of the council is to write upon two pieces of tin which are equal and alike, on one, 'If it is preferable and better for the Athenian people that the *basileus* should rent out the parts of the Sacred Orgas currently being cultivated outside the boundaries, for the building of a colonnade and the equipping of the sanctuary of the Two Goddesses'; and on the other, 'If it is preferable and better for the Athenian people that the parts of the Sacred Orgas currently being cultivated outside the boundaries be left to the Two Goddesses untilled'; trans. by Rhodes and Osborne 2003). But I follow Parker 1983, 161, and RO 58 in reading [*ἐκτός*], rather than the old [*ἐντός*] which is now favoured anew by Clinton.

[34] *CID* II 31.33–70. As Davies 1998, 4 aptly observes, 'the "naopoioi in the war" ... were politically acceptable to the Phokians in the worst years of the Third Sacred War'; cf. Giuliani 2001, 220. For the financial office of the *ναοποιοί* see Lefèvre 1998, 263–6.

[35] Cf. Rhodes and Osborne 2003, 281.

issue must have constituted an unnecessary nuisance that they would have been keen to dispose of at the least political cost. On the whole, the turbulent international situation—and by this I mainly refer to the rapid emergence of Philip II in the political arena of mainland Greece[36]—must also account for the delay in the settlement of the Megaro-Athenian conflict, at least as much as the military equilibrium between the two main protagonists. The Delphic answer was unprecedentedly delayed, in all likelihood because of Megarian opposition. Since the military intervention of the Athenians in the Megarid must have preceded the compromise between the two sides, the final demarcation of the area, a result of the Delphic answer itself, should have occurred at least in 350/49, if not later. This is one of the few fortunate occasions where the literary sources supplement the lacuna left by the epigraphical ones. Didymus, once more citing the Atthidographers Androtion and Philochorus, tells us that Apollo chose the second option, that is, that the *eschatiai* around the Orgas had to remain uncultivated.[37] At first sight the Delphic verdict seems to have been unfavourable to the Athenians, since they were prevented from making a profit out of the *eschatiai.* Yet, these *eschatiai* were to be consecrated to the Goddesses (note *καθιέρωσαν*). The Athenians could always return to the oracle with a renewed request for permission to cultivate these sacred edge-lands. The Orgas does not feature again in any Classical sources.[38] A document from Roman Athens, however, implies that the Sacred Orgas could still be considered by the Athenian polis as an area under its protection, a fact that has escaped scholarly attention so far.[39] Despite the elliptical phraseology, it is obvious that the *eschatiai* were still considered sacred, marked by boundary stones, protected against any potential transgressors, and most importantly, income raised through their

[36] For Philip II in that period see Ryder 2000.

[37] Did. col. 13.54–6, *κ(αὶ) τὰς ἐσχατίας τὰς περὶ τὴν Ὀργάδα καθιέρωσαν τοῦ θεοῦ χρήσαντος λῶιον κ(αὶ) ἄμεινον ἀνεῖσι κ(αὶ) μὴ ἐργαζομ(έν)οισι* (And they also consecrated the edge-lands around the Orgas, after the sanctuary had replied that it was more profitable and better for them if they left the edge-lands untilled and did not work them); Did. col. 14.44–7: *κ(αὶ) τὰς ἐσχατίας ὅσαι ἦσαν πρὸς τῆι Ὀργάδι καθιέρωσαν, διαμαντευσάμ(εν)οι κ(αὶ) ἀνελόντος τοῦ θεοῦ λῶιον κ(αὶ) ἄμεινον (εἶναι) μὴ ἐργαζομένοις* (And they consecrated the edge-lands, as many as were beside the Orgas, after they had consulted the oracle and after the god had replied that it was more profitable and better for them not to work them). Daverio-Rocchi 1988, 191, is a misinterpretation of the extract.

[38] The Orgas is not recorded e.g. in the Eleusinian Accounts *IG* II^2 1672 of 328/7, unless it underlies the *μισθώματα* of ll. 242–7, for which see Chapter 2, Section 3.

[39] *IG* II^2 1035, re-edited with improvements by Culley 1975 (=*SEG* XXVI 121), esp. ll. 20–12: *τὰ δὲ ὄρη καὶ τὰς δημοτελεῖ[ς ἐσχατιὰς - - - Δή]μητρος καὶ Κόρης [. . . .]ωσ [. . . ^{6} . . .]εισ[. . .]πασιν· εἰ δ̣[έ τι]ν̣ες ὑ̣π̣ερβάντες τοὺς ἱεροὺς ὅρους ἐπειργάσαν|[το τὴν ἱερὰν γῆν - - -]ν[..]τον[..]ναιτηι̣α̣[. . .]σθ̣[.]ον [εἰς τ]ὴν ἐπισκευὴν̣ τοῦ [ἐν Ἐλ]ε̣υσῖνι ἱεροῦ* etc. Maybe, instead of *τὴν ἱερὰν γῆν* (the sacred land), one should restore *τὴν ἱερὰν ὀργάδα* (the Sacred Orgas).

exploitation was to be used for the repair of the Eleusinion. The degree of overlap between the actual situation of the mid-fourth century and that of the Roman Imperial period is so striking that continuity must be assumed. In other words, unless the Augustan epigraphical text reflects an innovation, the Athenians must have at some point rendered the Sacred Orgas cash-generating, and our ignorance of the event results from non-preservation of the pertinent data.[40]

II. The Administration of the Sacred Orgas

Keeping this succession of events in mind, one can proceed with the examination of the administrative scheme employed by the Athenians with regard to the Sacred Orgas. At first glance the issue is treated as part of the agenda of internal affairs of Athens.[41] The delimitation of the disputed area was assigned to an elected board of fifteen men, five members of the Boule and ten from the citizenry. Nevertheless, it has largely passed unnoticed that the convention of the elected committee had to take place in the City Eleusinion.[42] This means that more was at stake than merely a spatial organization, though the latter was obviously meant to be the end of the whole procedure, and, in fact, the Orgas was eventually defined with circularly arranged *horoi.*[43] That the delegates had to work on the basis of a map seems rather unlikely, though not impossible.[44] The oath sworn implies that at least two parties were involved as litigants. If the restoration *μήτε χάριτος ἕνεκα μήτ' ἕ[χθρας ψηφιεῖσθαι]* is sound, then we can posit some sort of interstate

[40] Chronological preciseness is unattainable especially since the very date of *IG* II^2 1035 (*SEG* XXVI 121) is unknown. Culley 1975 would place it in the Augustan period, but Baldassarri 1998, 242–6, preferred an earlier date within the 1st cent. BC, but after the sack of Athens by Sulla in 86. Schmalz 2009, 10–11, no. 2, has now returned to a date in the reign of Augustus. Evidently the date of *IG* II^2 1035 constitutes the *terminus ante quem* for the cultivation of the Sacred Orgas.

[41] Daverio-Rocchi 1987, 102 speaks of 'terra sacra poliade'.

[42] *I.Eleusis* 144 ll. 7–8; for the City Eleusinion see Miles 1998, *passim*, esp. 64–6.

[43] Did. col. 13.54: *καὶ στήλαις ὡρίσθη κύκλωι λιθίναις Φιλοκράτους εἰπόντος* (and it was delimited in a circle with stone stelae, upon a proposal by Philokrates).

[44] Our ignorance of ancient Greek maps is notorious, and perhaps something of the sort might have been in use, as Dilke 1985, 88 seems to imply. Nevertheless, it seems to me that the elected committee of *I.Eleusis* 144 could hardly have claimed expertise on land survey matters. Their task was more of a judicial, political type. Scafuro 2003, 134–5, cautiously broaches both possibilities (on-site tours vs. commissioners working from Athens) without favouring either.

conflict.[45] On the basis of the extant evidence the Megarians are the obvious candidates to make up one of the parties in this suit, though admittedly their ethnic is not preserved anywhere on the stone.[46] But even if, at that stage, the Megarians had not become embroiled in the Orgas episode, can we seriously surmise that the Athenians would not have expected them to become so, given the common, bitter experiences of the past? Furthermore, the very decision of Athens to seek a response from Delphi strengthens the assumption that the problem was not exclusively one of internal politics, for in the past the Athenians had taken pains to consult the Pythian oracle only over religious matters of interstate significance.[47] Nevertheless, there is scope to speculate that the implied transgressors might have been private individuals, even ones of Athenian origin, especially since private rapacity often targeted borderlands suitable for grazing.[48]

The task of the delimitation had to be supervised by the *basileus*, the *hierophantes*, the *daduch*, the *gene* of Kerykes and Eumolpidai as well as any interested Athenian.[49] This extended supervisory board highlights two different aspects of the problem: the sacred character of the disputed area, especially its Eleusinian affiliations, and the wider public concern of the polis. The two *gene* of Kerykes and Eumolpidai had traditionally enjoyed a privileged and almost exclusive role in the administration of the Eleusinian cult.[50] The *daduch* and the *hierophant* came from their ranks respectively.[51] Philochorus and Androtion *apud* Didymus recount that the Megarians eventually conceded that the delimitation of the Sacred Orgas be undertaken by these very Eleusinian magistrates.[52] This compromise underlines their

[45] The aphorism of de Ste. Croix 1972, 388 n. 1, '[i]ndeed, there is nothing to connect the dispute about the eschatiai with Megara: the inscription (IG II^2 204=SIG^3 204) . . . speaks of that dispute as if it were something that concerned Athens alone', seems rather stressed.

[46] In line 4, however, of *I.Eleusis* 144 it might be tempting to see the succession of letters *EΩN* as the ending of the ethnic [*Μεγαρ*]*έων* (but I note that Clinton's new reading of a slanting stroke before epsilon renders my suggestion above untenable).

[47] ML 52, ll. 64–7 (oracle uncertain); ML 73 (offering of the first-fruits); Thuc. 3.104.1 (usually assumed to refer to Delphi, but see Hornblower 1991, 525–6); Thuc. 5.32.1. Parker 1985, 325 n. 95, suspects Athenian consideration of the Megarian factor with regard to the inquiry.

[48] Burford 1993, 19–20, 23. The most famous case of private rapacity targeting sacred landholdings is that recorded in the bronze *Tabulae Heracleenses* (*IG* XIV 645), for which see Uguzzoni and Ghinatti 1968.

[49] *I.Eleusis* 144 ll. 12–14 (cf. Garland 1984, 76).

[50] For the Eumolpidai and the Kerykes see Parker 1996, 293–7 and 300–2 respectively.

[51] *Daduch*: Clinton 1974, 47–68; *hierophant*: ibid. 10–47.

[52] Did. col. 13.51–3: *ὁρισταὶ δ' (ἐ)γένοντο συγχωρησάντων Μεγαρέων Λακρατείδης ὁ ἱ[ε]ροφάντης κ(αὶ) ὁ δαιδοῦχος Ἱεροκ[λ]είδ̣ης* (with the Megarians' agreement the men who marked out the boundaries were Lakrateides the hierophant and

theoretically impartial agency. Despite their Athenian origin, the *daduch* and the *hierophant* were expected to act in the interest of the sanctuary, not of their polis. One can argue that the Megarian concession was the result of military pressure from the Athenians, but we should not lose sight of the fact that on at least two occasions—the recall of Alcibiades and the mock initiation of Demetrios the Besieger in the Eleusinian Mysteries—the two *gene* or their representatives acted in compliance with religious norms and regardless of what was advantageous for Athens.[53] It is hard to say whether the *daduch* and the *hierophant* had permanent authority over the Sacred Orgas or whether their involvement in the events of the 350s was only an ad hoc undertaking. Both had a conspicuous role in the performance of various rites concerning the Eleusinian cult, but no independent attestation of any possible link between the Orgas and the cult as such exists.

As for the two *gene*, it is even more difficult to see how they could have effectively supervised the delimitation of the Orgas. In conjunction with the clause that allowed for the participation of any interested citizen, the two *gene* could simply be summoned with the aim of strengthening the public control of the procedure, simultaneously providing the aura of some religious authority.[54] Nevertheless, it is worth noting that none of the other *gene* that had direct or indirect connections with the Eleusinian cults, namely the Eudanemoi, the Krokonidai, and the Koironidai, were delegated by the Athenians to participate in the delimitation of the sacred land.[55] Perhaps it is not irrelevant that the Kerykes and the Eumolpidai provided from their ranks, apart from the *daduch* and the *hierophant*, some other officials who were in charge of performing rites concerning the cult and who would have

Hierokleides the daduch'; idem col. 14.37–43: *Ὡρ̣ί̣σαντο δ(ὲ) κ(αὶ) Ἀθην[αῖο]ι πρὸς Μεγαρέας τὴν Ὀργάδα διὰ τ[οῖ]ν θεοῖν ὅπως βούλοιντο· συνεχώρησαν γ(ὰρ) οἱ Μεγαρεῖς ὁριστὰς γενέσθαι τὸν ἱεροφάντ(ην) Λακρατείδην κ(αὶ) τὸν δαιδοῦχον Ἱεροκλείδην* (But the Athenians, too, marked the boundaries of the Orgas in the direction of the Megarians on account of the Two Goddesses, in whatever way they wanted. For the Megarians agreed that the boundary commissioners would be the hierophant, Lakrateides, and the daduch, Hierokleides); trans. by Harding 2006, slightly modified.

[53] 'Face-saving compromise': Clinton 1974, 18; refusal to ratify the return of Alcibiades: Thuc. 8.53.2; daduch's opposition to Demetrios' impious initiation: Plut. *Dem*. 26 with Mikalson 1998, 89; cf. Garland 1984, 77.

[54] Cf. Parker 2005, 91. In this sense, a good parallel can be found in *Agora* XVI 56 ll. 29–31, which, although it legislated the establishment of the board of the *ἐπιμεληταὶ τῶν μυστηρίων* (two of whom came from the ranks of the Kerykes and the Eumolpidai respectively), also recognized the jurisdiction of the two *gene* as such to the same effect, i.e. the supervision of the Mysteries.

[55] For these *gene* see Parker 1996, 293, 302–4.

been expected to provide their religious expertise.[56] We now know from an inscription dating to 20/19 that the priesthood of Zeus Horios and Athena Horia—protectors of boundary stones—belonged to the *genos* of Kerykes.[57] Interestingly, the inception of the procedure for the delimitation of the Orgas, obviously meant to last more than a day, was set on the sixteenth day of the month Poseideon.[58] According to the famous Erchian sacrificial calendar, on that particular day the demesmen of Erchia sacrificed a pig to Zeus Horios,[59] a chronological coincidence that has been considered more than merely a happenstance;[60] it seems even less so, if we combine it with the observation above about the priesthood of Zeus Horios. Finally, the well-known tale of the assassination of Anthemokritos may have some relevance here. He was the Athenian herald (*κήρυξ*) sent to the Megarians to settle a dispute, but the Megarians allegedly murdered him thus arousing immediate Athenian fury.[61] The dispatch of Anthemokritos seems to have taken place in the context of the dispute between the Athenians and the Megarians over the Orgas in the 430s.[62] Interestingly, in the Demosthenic *Letter to Philip* it is stated that one of the bans imposed on the Megarians for their killing of Anthemokritos was their exclusion from the Eleusinian Mysteries.[63] Moreover, Anthemokritos' monument was known to be located outside the Dipylon on the Sacred Way which led from Athens to Eleusis.[64] Given the strong Eleusinian affiliations, there is a possibility that Anthemokritos was not only a publicly appointed messanger, but also a member of the *genos* Kerykes and that his murder was considered an insult towards the Eleusinian Goddesses whom Anthemokritos, by virtue of his *genos*, served.[65] If so, the

[56] For instance, the altar-priest was selected from the Kerykes (Clinton 1974, 85–6), and it was members of the Eumolpidae that performed *exegesis* (ibid. 89–93).

[57] *SEG* XXX 93 l. 16; cf. Roussel 1934, 824–5; Zeus Horios: Pl. *Leg.* 842e.

[58] *I.Eleusis* 144 ll. 10–12.

[59] *SEG* XXI 541, col. E, ll. 22–30.

[60] Mikalson 1975, 92 citing Burkert observing that 'it seems to be no coincidence that the meetings to settle the boundary dispute began on the day of a sacrifice to Zeus Horios'.

[61] Plut. *Per.* 30.2, *ἐπεὶ δ' ὁ πεμφθεὶς κῆρυξ Ἀνθεμόκριτος αἰτίᾳ τῶν Μεγαρέων ἀποθανεῖν ἔδοξε, γράφει ψήφισμα κατ' αὐτῶν Χαρῖνος, ἄσπονδον μὲν εἶναι καὶ ἀκήρυκτον ἔχθραν.*

[62] Connor's 1962 and 1970 ingenious attempt to place Antemokritos' mission in the events surrounding the dispute of the 350s has not met with scholarly acceptance.

[63] [Dem.] 12.4, *Μεγαρέων γοῦν Ἀνθεμόκριτον ἀνελόντων εἰς τοῦτο ἐλήλυθεν ὁ δῆμος ὥστε μυστηρίων μὲν εἶργον αὐτούς* etc.

[64] Paus. 1.36.3 with Papachatzis 1974, 461–2; Harp. s.v. *Ἀνθεμόκριτος*; *Suda* s.v. *Ἀνθεμόκριτος* (cf. Travlos 1971, 180).

[65] Cawkwell reached a similar conclusion from a different starting point when he identified Anthemokritos as a *spondophoros* (Bearer of the Truce), and therefore a member of the Kerykes (but see Parker 1996, 301 n. 48; *Agora* XVI no. 48). This would

involvement of at least the Kerykes in the supervision of the Sacred Orgas in the fourth century is anticipated by a practice already found in the 430s.

There are two different ways of looking at the nomination of the *archon basileus*. He was the paramount Athenian official in religious matters, but he also had a specific connection with the Eleusinian cult as is attested from other sources.[66] Towards the end of the fifth century the assembly had empowered him with a similar task, namely the delimitation of the sacred area called Pelargikon.[67] But the decree itself provides a more specific explanation of the *basileus*' involvement. The answer sought by the Athenians from the Delphic oracle concerned whether or not the *basileus* could lease out the edge-lands of the Orgas. Leasing out sacred property seems to have been a regular obligation of the *basileus*.[68] His role, far from being purely symbolical, had very tangible, economic ramifications.

With this we come to a second, and perhaps more substantial, point of the decree. Through a graphically elaborate process, the Athenians inquired of Pythian Apollo whether they could go ahead with the leasing of these marginal parts of the Orgas that had already been farmed by some unspecified individuals.[69] The question was articulated in such a way as to leave no uncertainty about the sanctity of the *ἐσχατιαί* of the Orgas. If it became revenue-yielding, the income realized was to return to the nominal owners of the Orgas, the Eleusinian Goddesses, and that was to be achieved by using the money for the construction of the porch of the Telesterion and for such other repairs in the sanctuary as were deemed appropriate.[70] This observation allows us to highlight the practical facet of the Sacred Orgas affair. Now, at approximately the same time the Athenians passed a law concerning the reorganization of the Eleusinian Mysteries,[71] which allows for the possibility that the Orgas case was part of a wider programme regarding the cultic centre of Eleusis. Indeed, the quadrennial board of the *epistatai* of the Eleusinian cult of 356/5–352/3 had already published an architectural con-

mean, nevertheless, that Anthemokritos was not specifically concerned with the Orgas.

66 Lys. 6.4; Arist. [*Ath. Pol.*] 57.1, with Rhodes 1993, 636–7; Carlier 1984, 329–37; Clinton 2008, 141 (see above, Chapter 2, Section 3).

67 ML 73, ll. 54–5: *τὸν δὲ βασ[ι]λέα hορίσαι τὰ hιερὰ τὰ ἐν τ[ô]||ι Πελαργικôι*; cf. Foucart 1889, 441.

68 See Chapter 2, Section 5.

69 *I.Eleusis* 144 ll. 24–30, but with the restoration suggested by Parker 1983, 161 n. 99: [*τῆς ἱερᾶς ὀργάδος τὰ ἐκ*]*τὸς τῶν ὅρων*, not [*ἐν*]*τός* as previous editors (cf. Harding 1994, 126–7) and now anew Clinton in the Eleusinian corpus. See also Amandry 1950, 151–3; Fontenrose 1978, 251; Gauthier 1998, 70.

70 Hintzen-Bohlen 1997, 18–21.

71 Clinton 1980; see now *I.Eleusis* 138.

tract concerning the construction of the porch in question.[72] So, it seems that in 352/1, when the Athenians broached the possibility of employing income from the *eschatiai* of the Sacred Orgas for their building project in Eleusis, it was the architectural programme that constituted their main incentive for raising the question and not the other way around. Yet again, it appears that the Sacred Orgas episode did not come out of the blue, rather it was an affair first moved by the Athenians, and not by their western neighbours.[73]

Yet further hints are offered by *I.Eleusis* 144 itself. First, an antecedent decree concerning the sanctuaries of Athens (or more broadly sacred affairs, τὰ ἱερά), proposed by a certain Philokrates, is vaguely mentioned, although, it must be said, the reading is heavily restored.[74] This Philokrates might have been the famous demagogue who concluded the homonymous peace pact of 346,[75] but the name is common and, in the absence of other attributes, the identification should remain hypothetical. He is almost certainly, however, the individual attested by the Atthidographers as proposing the decree for the delimitation of the Orgas with which the Megarians complied.[76] Secondly, and most importantly, the preoccupation with the Orgas is placed in a wider context of concern for all Athenian shrines, or rather τεμένη, sacred estates.[77] This point is of particular interest, since the law quoted names a series of Athenian magistrates as responsible parties not only in the care of the Orgas, but of all Attic *temene*.[78] The nomination of some of these officials

[72] *IG* II^2 1666 (now *I.Eleusis* 143), esp. B ll. 53–4: [τοῦ π]ροστώιου τοῦ Ἐλευσῖνι ἀνακαθηράμενον etc.; cf. Kirchner's commentary ad loc., and now Clinton 2008, 135–8.

[73] Bowden 2005, 91–2, has recently offered a different reconstruction, hypothesizing, inter alia, that the Athenians had experienced a bad crop which they attributed to their own impious cultivation of the *eschatiai*. The consultation of the Delphic oracle was, in this scenario, an attempt at appeasing the god. This whole story is not particularly convincing.

[74] *I.Eleusis* 144, ll. 54–5: [νῦν δὲ ἀν]αγράψα[ι] τόδε τὸ ψήφισμα κα̣ὶ̣ τὸ πρότερον τὸ | Φι[λ]ο[κ]ράτου[υς τὸ περὶ τῶν] ἱ[ερῶν].

[75] *LGPN* II s.v. Φιλοκράτης (76), according to the identification proposed by Dittenberger in *Syll.*^{3} 204, and recently reaffirmed by Clinton 2008, 142.

[76] *FGrH* 328 F155, καὶ ἀφώρισαν κύκλωι στήλαις κατὰ ψήφισμα Φιλοκράτους.

[77] *I.Eleusis* 144 ll. 16–18: [ἐπι]μελεῖσθαι [δ]ὲ τῆς ἱερᾶς ὀργάδος καὶ τῶν ἄλλω|[ν ἱερῶν τεμεν]ῶν τῶν Ἀθήνησιν ἀπὸ τῆσδε τῆς ἡμέρας εἰς τὸν | [ἀεὶ χρόνον οὕ]ς τε ὁ νόμος κελεύει περὶ ἑκάστου αὐτῶν etc. (From this day onwards those specifically so commanded by the law are to look after the Sacred Orgas and all the other sacred *temene* at Athens; trans. by Rhodes and Osborne 2003, slightly modified). The restoration [ἱερῶν τεμεν]ῶν, instead of Ziehen's [ἱερῶν ἁπάντ]ων, goes back to Philios and has been recently resurrected by both Lambert 2005 (cf. *SEG* LIV 115), and Clinton 2008, 141.

[78] Whitehead 1986, 127–8 n. 39 suggests that *IG* II^2 1362, an edict of the priest of Apollo Erithaseos, was a local enforcement of the law cited in *I.Eleusis* 144 ll. 16–23. This is certainly wrong. In ll. 16–23 of *I.Eleusis* 144 the citation is that of a law (νόμος), whereas *IG* II^2 1362 mentions a decree (ψήφισμα). And whereas *I.Eleusis* 144

is anything but surprising. The demarchs were in charge of letting out *temene* controlled by their demes, whereas the Areopagos had authority over the administration of the *moriai*, the sacred olive-trees of Athena.[79] Similar powers over religious matters have been acknowledged in the case of the Athenian Boule.[80] The presence of military officers, however, such as the *general ἐπὶ τὴν χώραν* and the *περιπόλαρχοι*, is baffling, to say the least.

The former office is first securely attested in this decree.[81] It is hardly a coincidence that the next chronological attestation is that of Ephialtes, general *ἐπὶ τὴν χώραν* in 350/49 and leader of the force that invaded the Megarid in order to settle unilaterally the Sacred Orgas affair.[82] The legal justification of his intrusion into the Orgas almost certainly lies in the law quoted in *IG* II^2 204. The *περιπόλαρχοι* were officers under the command of the aforementioned general and, in their turn, commanders of the *περίπολοι*, patrols consisting, at least after *c.*334, of ephebes.[83] The famous Attic ephebic oath, which contained a clause about the protection of sacred interests (RO 88, ll. 8–9, *ἀμυνῶ δὲ καὶ ὑπὲρ ἱερῶν καὶ ὁσ|ίων*) and which evoked the boundary stones of the fatherland as witnesses (ibid. ll. 16–20, *ἴστορες . . . ὅροι τῆς πατρίδος* etc.) might have some relevance here.[84] After the reformation of the ephebic institution, Eleusis and the frontier between Attica and the Megarid was one of the posts assigned to the *περίπολοι*. Therefore, the involvement of military officers in the administration of the Attic sanctuaries as envisaged in the law evoked in *I.Eleusis* 144 must have been strictly military, one of protection of the peripheral sanctuaries and in particular their landed property either through defence or, if need arose, through

is, indeed, a decree, it should not be identified with the law quoted in ll. 16–23. The two texts were not identical.

[79] Demarchs: see Chapter 3, Section 2.ii; *Areopagos*: Wallace 1985, 106–7; De Bruyn 1995, 113–16; now Clinton 2008, 141.

[80] Rhodes 1972, 127–34.

[81] Rhodes 1993, 678–9; cf. Hamel 1998, 15–16; Rhodes and Osborne 2003, 278. According to Petrakos, *I.Rhamnous* 1 ll. 2–4 reads: *[ἐπειδὴ Φιλοκλῆς] καὶ Διόδω̣[ρ]ος χιλίαρχοι κ̣[α|τασταθέντες ὑπ]ὸ Διομ̣[ήδ]ου [το]ῦ σ̣τρα[τη|γοῦ ἐπὶ τὴν χώραν] ἐπὶ Ἐλ̣[πίνο]υ̣ ἄρ[χ]οντο[ς]* (i.e. 356/6). Nevertheless, Brun and Couvenhes 2006, have rejected this reconstruction of the archontic formula, and have strongly argued that the decree belongs to the Hellenistic period. Therefore the attestation of a general *ἐπὶ τὴν χώραν* in *I.Rhamnous* 1 (heavily restored, it has to be said) is impertinent to our discussion.

[82] *FGrH* 328 F155.

[83] On *περίπολοι* and *περιπόλαρχοι*: Pélékidis 1962, 35–47; Rhodes 1993, 508; Taylor 1997, 236–7 n. 66. For the date of the reorganized ephebic institution see Reinmuth 1971, 2, 123–4, contra Lewis 1973*b*, whose view has almost without exception prevailed.

[84] Siewert 1977, 109; Rhodes and Osborne 2003, 445.

attack, as the story of Ephialtes' raid clearly demonstrates.[85] Overall, this marginally religious role of military magistrates is unprecedented in Athens. Only much later, in the Roman period, does a general, ὁ ἐπὶ τοὺς ὁπλείτας στρατηγός (hoplite general), assume a conspicuous role in the actual administration of sacred properties.[86]

In any case, what remains beyond doubt is the increasing Athenian activity in the sphere of sacred property from the mid-fourth century onwards. The law cited in lines 16–23 of *I.Eleusis* 144 may have constituted the basic legal framework for this boost in the realm of sacred land. Although one is tempted to identify this law with the νόμος τῶν τεμενῶν from 418/7,[87] the mention of the στρατηγὸς ἐπὶ τὴν χώραν renders this identification implausible. The law was relatively new, since it obviously postdated the creation of the aforementioned military office, which in turn should postdate the archontic year 357/6.[88] But if the law was indeed passed sometime within the second half of the 350s, the most suitable context would be the financial programme fostered by Diophantos of Sphettos or Euboulos of Probalinthos and his associates after the end of the Social War.[89] This interest was to culminate in the second half of the century with a huge increase in the publication of relevant epigraphical documents, such as those recording an extensive programme of leases of sacred land starting from 343/2.[90] If these leases were indeed instigated by Euboulos and his circle then the Orgas affair could be perceived as a preliminary model case.[91]

[85] For other ways by which developments in the 330s, including the ephebic reform, affected land-tenure patterns in Athens, see Chapter 3, Section 1.ii.

[86] *SEG* XXVI 121 ll. 14–15; cf. Sarikakis 1951, 18–20, 71; Geagan 1967, 29–30 (see also Chapter 2).

[87] *IG* I^3 84 l. 25, with Behrend 1970, 59–60; Walbank 1991, 154–5.

[88] RO nos. 48 and 52 both show that in 357/6 specific postings for generals had not been created yet (cf. Rhodes 1993, 678). As argued above (n. 81), *I.Rhamnous* 1 does not bear on the problem of the στρατηγός ἐπὶ τὴν χώραν in the mid-4th cent.

[89] See the still paramount article of Cawkwell 1963, esp. 48–9, for the main Athenian financiers of the late 350s; also Leppin 1995, 558–9.

[90] See Chapter 2.

[91] It is hardly a coincidence that with the exception of *IG* II^2 1590a, leases of sacred property on Salamis which belong to approximately the same time as *IG* II^2 204, but which, however, might have been issued by a local body (Taylor 1997, 181–2; see Chapter 4, Section 4 above), no other 4th-cent. inscriptions concerning sacred realty administered by the polis of Athens pre-date 350.

APPENDIX II

Moriai: Sacred Arboriculture in Classical Athens

i. Athena's Olives: Administration, Politics, and Economics

> *Τὴν γοῦν Ἀττικὴν ἐκ τοῦ ἐπὶ πλεῖστον διὰ τὸ λεπτόγεων ἀστασίαστον οὖσαν ἄνθρωποι ᾤκουν οἱ αὐτοί.*
>
> Certainly Attica, where the soil is poor and thin, enjoyed for the longest time freedom from civil strife and so was occupied by the same inhabitants.[1]

This is how Thucydides describes, in his distinctively succinct style, the infertility of the Attic earth in the preface to his *History*. Yet it was the same meagre soil that forced the Athenians to cultivate that holiest of fruits, the olive. Oleoculture must have been an important element of the Athenian economy from an early period, for Solon is famously said by Plutarch to have prohibited the export of all agricultural products except for olive oil.[2] Even more revealing of Athenian attitudes is the depiction of olive leaves on Athena's helmet on the obverse, and of a small olive twig on the reverse, of the Athenian silver coinage.[3] Last but not least, a certain category of olive-trees, the *moriai*, was singled out as so sacred that a specific administrative scheme had to be deployed for its management. In fact, among the various types of sacred real property the *moriai* constitute such an unusual case that a

[1] Thuc. 1.1.5 with Hornblower 1991, 12.

[2] Plut. *Vit. Sol.* 24.1–2: *τῶν δὲ γινομένων διάθεσιν πρὸς ξένους ἐλαίου μόνον ἔδωκεν, ἄλλα δ' ἐξάγειν ἐκώλυσε, καὶ κατὰ τῶν ἐξαγόντων ἀρὰς τὸν ἄρχοντα ποιεῖσθαι προσέταξεν, ἢ τίνειν αὐτὸν ἑκατὸν δραχμὰς εἰς τὸ δημόσιον· καὶ πρῶτος ἄξων ἐστὶν ὁ τοῦτον περιέχων τὸν νόμον* (He allowed the sale of products to foreigners only in the case of olive oil, and prohibited their export, and he ordered the archon to lay curses against those who exported them, or else pay a fine of a hundred drachmas to the public treasury. The first axon is that which contains this law; trans. by Dillon and Garland 1994, 82); cf. Descat 1993. For the Mediterranean perspective see Horden and Purcell 2000, 211. The claim by Moreno 2007, 334, that the ban was enforced by the *σιτοφύλακες* (grain-guardians) fails the evidential test.

[3] The olive leaves on the brow of Athena's helmet are thought to have been introduced on Athenian coinage after 480, if not later (after 475): Starr 1970, 8–12; Wartenberg 1995, 6. The olive twig, however, is usually associated with the Group L owl tetradrachms (post-510 according to Kroll 1981, 24–30). For these and related problems of early Athenian coinage, see now Flament 2007, 34–54.

separate treatment seems indispensable.[4] As it happens, we possess an array of precious scraps of information bearing on the issue, although not enough to avoid some speculation, and, of course, the wish that more evidence had survived.

The myth about the contest between Poseidon and Athena for the patronage of Athens is well known. The name of the illustrious city-state leaves no doubt about the outcome of the struggle, and the event was sculpted on the west pediment of arguably the most sumptuous edifice of antiquity, the Parthenon.[5] Athena's gift to her protégés was the olive she planted on the sacred rock of the Acropolis. From this primordial olive twelve new trees were transplanted in the sanctuary of the hero Akademos and comprised a sacred grove. These trees, we are told by our ancient sources, were called *moriai.*[6] The etymology remains obscure, but the most compelling explanation is the connection of the word *moria* with the stem **μερ*, which bears the meaning 'to be part of': the *moriai* were part of Athena's property.[7] Regardless of the soundness of this etymology, the fact remains that the sacred olives

[4] For brief separate discussions of the *moriai* see Latte 1935; Isager and Skydsgaard 1992, 203–5; *Der Neue Pauly* 10 (1990), s.v. *μορία.*

[5] Parker 1987*b*, 198–200; Palagia 1998, 40–59.

[6] Ar. *Nu.* 1005: *ἀλλ' εἰς Ἀκαδημείαν κατιὼν ὑπὸ ταῖς μορίαις ἀποθρέξει* (but you will go down to the Akademeia and you will start a race under the *moriai*); Paus. 1.30.2: *ἐν Ἀκαδημίᾳ δέ ἐστι Προμηθέως βωμός . . . καὶ ἔνδον Ἀθηνᾶς, τὸν δὲ Ἡρακλέους ἐποίησαν. καὶ φυτὸν ἐλαίας, δεύτερον τοῦτο λεγόμενον φανῆναι* (In the Akademia there is an altar to Prometheus . . . and one to Athena, and within they have built one to Herakles. There is also an olive-tree, said to be the second that appeared), with Papachatzes 1974, 394–5; Phot. s.v. *μορίαι ἐλαῖαι· ἱεραὶ τῆς Ἀθηνᾶς, ἐξ ὧν τὸ ἔπαθλον ἐδίδοτο τοῖς νικῶσι τὰ Παναθήναια· ἦσαν δὲ πρῶται ιβ´ τὸν ἀριθμὸν αἱ μεταφυτευθεῖσαι ἐκ τῆς ἀκροπόλεως εἰς τὴν Ἀκαδημίαν* (*moriai* olives; the sacred olives of Athena from which the prizes used to be given to the Panathenaic victors. There were at first 12 olives which were transplanted from the Acropolis into the Akademeia); thus *Suda* s.v. *μορίαι.* It seems likely that the planting of the twelve trees in the Akademeia was the initiative of Kimon, who was the first to create a grove in the shrine, according to Plutarch, although the latter does not explicitly mention *moriai*; Plut. *Vit. Cim.* 13.7: *πρῶτος δὲ ταῖς λεγομέναις ἐλευθερίοις καὶ γλαφυραῖς διατριβαῖς, αἳ μικρὸν ὕστερον ὑπερφυῶς ἠγαπήθησαν, ἐκαλλώπισε τὸ ἄστυ, τὴν μὲν ἀγορὰν πλατάνοις καταφυτεύσας, τὴν δ' Ἀκαδήμειαν ἐξ ἀνύδρου καὶ αὐχμηρᾶς κατάρρυτον ἀποδείξας ἄλσος, ἠσκημένον ὑπ' αὐτοῦ δρόμοις καθαροῖς καὶ συσκίοις περιπάτοις* (he was the first to beautify the city with the so-called liberal and elegant resorts, which were so excessively popular a little later, by planting the Agora with plane trees and by coverting the Academy from a waterless and arid spot into a well-watered grove, which he provided with clean running-tracks and shady walks; trans. by Perrin 1914).

[7] Frisk 1970 s.v. *μορίαι*; Isager and Skydsgaard 1992, 203–4. The alternative etymological interpretations offered by Photios (s.v. *μορίαι ἐλαῖαι· ἤτοι ἀπὸ τοῦ μόρου καὶ τοῦ φόνου τοῦ Ἁλιρροθίου ὀνομασθεῖσαι οὕτως ἢ ὅτι ἐνέμοντο καὶ ἐμερίζοντο τὸ ἔλαιον τὸ ἐξ αὐτῶν Ἀθηναῖοι ἅπαντες*: *moriai* olives; they were thus called either from the death and the murder of Halirrothios or because all the Athenians enjoyed and shared the oil from them) are hardly convincing.

were considered as considerably more important than common plants and that accordingly the Athenians adopted an overprotective stance towards them. An aetiological myth was promptly invented, and has been transmitted to us by Herodotus: the legendary olive-tree was burnt by the Persians, when they occupied the Acropolis in 480, but sprouted new growth the very next day. From that day onwards the Athenians considered it their task to protect at all costs the scions of the sacred gift of their patron goddess.[8] The myth, of course, reflects the longevity of olives as well as their ability to regenerate even after having been burnt: *oliva in totum ambusta revixit.*[9] In any case, the sacred olive in question might have been blossoming on the Acropolis already in the late seventh century: Epimenides, we are told, requested a branch from the tree as his reward for the purification of the city. Late literary evidence aside, the archaeological record is hard to dismiss. Few if any would now doubt that the incised tree of the so-called olive-tree pediment from around the mid-sixth century actually represents Athena's gift.[10]

As far as the relevant ancient sources are concerned, by far the most important testimonium is to be found in the Aristotelian *Athenian Constitution*. Writing about the allotted officials of Athens, the author of the *Ath. Pol.* comes to the theme of the *athlothetai* (*Commissioners of the prizes*), who were in charge of the Great Panathenaia:

> *κληροῦσι δὲ καὶ ἀθλοθέτας δέκα ἄνδρας, ἕνα τῆς φυλῆς ἑκάστης. οὗτοι δὲ δοκιμασθέντες ἄρχουσι τέτταρα ἔτη, καὶ διοικοῦσι τήν τε πομπὴν τῶν Παναθηναίων καὶ τὸν ἀγῶνα τῆς μουσικῆς καὶ τὸν γυμνικὸν ἀγῶνα καὶ τὴν ἱπποδρομίαν, καὶ τὸν πέπλον ποιοῦνται, καὶ τοὺς ἀμφορεῖς ποιοῦνται μετὰ τῆς βουλῆς, καὶ τὸ ἔλαιον τοῖς ἀθληταῖς ἀποδιδόασι. συλλέγεται δὲ τὸ ἔλαιον ἀπὸ τῶν μοριῶν· εἰσπράττει δὲ τοὺς τὰ χωρία κεκτημένους ἐν οἷς αἱ μορίαι εἰσὶν ὁ ἄρχων, τρί' ἡμικοτύλια ἀπὸ τοῦ στελέχους ἑκάστου. πρότερον δ' ἐπώλει τὸν καρπὸν ἡ*

[8] Hdt. 8.55: *ταύτην ὦν τὴν ἐλαίην ἅμα τῷ ἄλλῳ ἱρῷ κατέλαβε ἐμπρησθῆναι ὑπὸ τῶν βαρβάρων· δευτέρῃ δὲ ἡμέρῃ ἀπὸ τῆς ἐμπρήσιος Ἀθηναίων οἱ θύειν ὑπὸ βασιλέος κελευόμενοι ὡς ἀνέβησαν ἐς τὸ ἱρόν, ὥρων βλαστὸν ἐκ τοῦ στελέχεος ὅσον τε πηχυαῖον ἀναδεδραμηκότα* (Now it was so, that the olive-tree was burnt with the rest of the shrine by the foreigners; but on the day after its burning, when the Athenians bidden by the King to sacrifice went up to the shrine, they saw a shoot of about a cubit's length sprung from the trunk; trans. by Godley 1925), with Vannicelli 2003, 257–9; cf. Sourvinou-Inwood 1990, 306.

[9] Plin. *HN* 17.241 (an olive tree, even after being completely incinerated, rejuvenates). The miraculous aspect of Herodotus' story was therefore not the regrowth of the olive (thus Harrison 2000, 69), but its celerity.

[10] Plut. *Vit. Sol.* 12.12: *Ἐπιμενίδης μὲν οὖν μάλιστα θαυμασθεὶς, καὶ χρήματα διδόντων πολλὰ καὶ τιμὰς μεγάλας τῶν Ἀθηναίων, οὐδὲν ἢ θαλλὸν ἀπὸ τῆς ἱερᾶς ἐλαίας αἰτησάμενος καὶ λαβὼν ἀπῆλθεν* (Well then, Epimenides was vastly admired by the Athenians who offered him much money and large honours; but he asked for nothing more than a branch of the sacred olive-tree, with which he returned home; trans. by Perrin 1914). Olive-tree pediment: Kiilerich 1989, esp. 10–21; Ridgway 1993, 290–1; Hurwit 1999, 113–14 (dates proposed for the pediment range from 580 down to 540).

πόλις· καὶ εἴ τις ἐξορύξειεν ἐλαίαν μορίαν ἢ κατάξειεν, ἔκρινεν ἡ ἐξ Ἀρείου πάγου βουλή, καὶ εἴ [τ]ου καταγνοίη, θανάτῳ τοῦτον ἐζημίουν. ἐξ οὗ δὲ τὸ ἔλαιον ὁ τὸ χωρίον κεκτημένος ἀποτίνει, ὁ μὲν νόμος ἔστιν, ἡ δὲ κρίσις καταλέλυται. τὸ δὲ ἔλα[ιον] ἐκ τοῦ κτήματος, οὐκ ἀπὸ τῶν στελεχῶν ἐστι τῇ πόλει. συλλέξας οὖν ὁ ἄρχων τὸ ἐφ' ἑαυ[τοῦ] γιγνόμενον, τοῖς ταμίαις παρ[αδί]δωσιν εἰς ἀκρόπολιν, καὶ οὐκ ἔστιν ἀναβῆναι πρότερον εἰς [Ἄρε]ιον πάγον, πρὶν ἂν ἅπαν παραδῷ τοῖς ταμίαις. οἱ δὲ ταμίαι τὸν μὲν ἄλλον χρόνον τηροῦσιν ἐν ἀκροπόλει, τοῖς δὲ Παναθηναίοις ἀπομετροῦσι τοῖς ἀθλοθέταις, οἱ δ' ἀθλοθέται τοῖς νικῶσι τῶν ἀγωνιστῶν. ἔστι γὰρ ἆθλα τοῖς μὲν τὴν μουσικὴν νικῶσιν ἀργύριον καὶ χρυσᾶ, τοῖς δὲ τὴν εὐανδρίαν ἀσπίδες, τοῖς δὲ τὸν γυμνικὸν ἀγῶνα καὶ τὴν ἱπποδρομίαν ἔλαιον.

Ten men are appointed by lot as athlothetai, one from each tribe. After being scrutinized they hold office for four years: they administer the Panathenaic procession, and the musical contests, the athletic contests and the horse race; they are responsible for the making of the robe (*peplos*), and together with the council for the making of the amphorae, and they present the olive oil to the athletes. The oil is collected from the sacred olive-trees (*moriai*). The (eponymous) archon exacts it from the owners of the land on which *moriai* grow, one and a half *kotylai* from each tree. Formerly the city let out the contract for collecting the crop, and if anyone dug up or cut down a *moria* he was tried by the council of the Areiopagos and, if convicted, sentenced to death. Nowadays, however, the oil is levied from the owners of the land, and the law remains but trials are no longer held: the state now obtains the oil simply from the property, not specifically from the sacred olive-trees. The (eponymous) archon collects the oil produced in his year of office, and hands it over to the treasurers (of Athena) on the Acropolis: he is not allowed to take his place in the council of the Areiopagos, until he has handed all the oil to the treasurers. The treasurers keep the oil on the Acropolis for the meantime, and then at the Panathenaia they measure it out to the *athlothetai*, and the *athlothetai* give it to the victorious contestants. The prizes are money and gold for the winners of the musical contests, shields for the winners of the *euandria*, and olive oil for the athletic contests and the horse race.[11]

It is clear from this extract that at some unspecified point sacred olive oil was being collected through a tax-farming system, but by the time of the *Athenaion Politeia* another scheme was in operation. Now, Aristotle's account partly corresponds to, and partly contradicts, what we know from another ancient writer: Lysias' seventh speech, entitled *Areopagitikos: Defence in the Matter of the Sekos*, addressed a charge brought by a certain Nikomachos against an anonymous Athenian for having uprooted a σηκός (*sekos*). *Sekos* is a difficult word, and already in post-Classical antiquity

[11] Arist. [*Ath. Pol.*] 60.1–3; translation by Rhodes 1984.

commentators were struggling to understand whether it designated the stump of a sacred olive or a fence surrounding a *moria*.[12] Be that as it may, the alleged offence took place in 397/6, even though the case came to court at a slightly later, unspecified date.[13] In fact, as the defendant claimed in the course of his speech, he had initially been indicted for clearing an olive-tree from his land, but, as the initial charge could not be sustained, a new one was brought against him, namely that he had removed a *sekos*. Needless to say, the defendant categorically denied that a single private olive-tree, let alone a *moria*, had ever existed in his plot.[14] Primarily by virtue of the literary evidence above, several reconstructions of the administration of *moriai* have been put forward, with varying degrees of success. Here a full critical synthesis of these various suggestions will be attempted.

Although groves of sacred olive-trees, such as the one in the Akademeia, certainly existed, it would appear that the usual pattern was that of isolated *moriai* on private estates.[15] Of late, it has been suggested that already before the late sixth century the large estates of the landed gentry abounded with

[12] Harp. s.v. *σηκός* (cf. Gernet and Bizos 1959, 107; Todd 2000, 79 with n. 5). There seems to be little, if any, value in Phot. *Bibliotheka*, 489a14, *ὁ σηκὸς δὲ νῦν εἶδός ἐστιν ἱερᾶς ἐλαίας* ('in this context the word *sekos* is used of a type of sacred olive'), probably a guess. In this I follow a suggestion by Wilson 1994, 250 n. 3, even though both he and Todd 2007, 478, ultimately favour the interpretation of *νῦν* as 'now', detecting echoes of Hellenistic exegesis.

[13] The date of the speech is given as 'considerably later than 397' by Lamb 1930, 145; as 396 by Tzoumeleas, 159; as *c*.396–395 by Carey 1989, 114, who is cautiously followed by Todd 2007, 480–1; Gernet and Bizos 1959, 110 simply note that 397/6 is the *terminus post quem*.

[14] Lys. 7.5: *ἡγοῦμαι τοίνυν, ὦ βουλή, ἐμὸν ἔργον ἀποδεῖξαι ὡς, ἐπειδὴ τὸ χωρίον ἐκτησάμην, οὔτ' ἐλαία οὔτε σηκὸς ἐνῆν ἐν αὐτῷ* (In my view, therefore, members of the council, my task is to show that, when I acquired the land, there was neither an olive-tree nor a *sekos* upon it); 7.10: *ὃς δύο ἔτη ἐγεώργησεν, οὔτε ἰδίαν ἐλαίαν οὔτε μορίαν οὔτε σηκὸν παραλαβών* (he farmed it for two years, and did not take over any private olive-tree, or *moria*, or *sekos*); trans. here and throughout by Todd 2007.

[15] Note Lys. 7.24, where the defendant claims, certainly with rhetorical exaggeration, that there were a lot of *moriai* in his other landholdings, and Arist. [*Ath. Pol.*] 60.2 (cf. Foxhall 2007, 118–19). Surely something similar underlies the notoriously obscure passage of Arist. [*Oec.*] II, 1346[b]: *Βυζάντιοι δὲ δεηθέντες χρημάτων τὰ τεμένη τὰ δημόσια ἀπέδοντο, τὰ μὲν κάρπιμα χρόνον τινά, τὰ δὲ ἄκαρπα ἀεννάως·τά τε θιασωτικὰ καὶ τὰ πατριωτικὰ ὡσαύτως· καὶ ὅσα ἐν χωρίοις ἰδιωτικοῖς ἦν* (When the Byzantians were in need of money they sold the *temene* that were administered by the city; those under crops, for a term of years, and those uncultivated, in perpetuity. Likewise they sold *temene* administered by *thiasoi* and *temene* administered by phratries, especially those located on private estates), where state-controlled landholdings feature as enclaves in private properties; cf. Lambert 1997*a*, 279, and see Chapter 4, n. 15 above. As late as the 1960s in villages of Lakonia one could find in the middle of landholdings isolated trees that belonged to owners other than those of the encapsulating lands (account of A. P. Matthaiou, an eyewitness).

moriai, an interesting theory that is hard to prove.[16] What lies beyond doubt is that the haphazard distribution of *moriai* across Attica gave rise to a complicated situation, which called for an elaborate response on behalf of the Athenian state. At the beginning of the fourth century the surveillance of the *moriai* lay with the Areiopagos, the venerable court which occupied itself with religious matters.[17] A board of assessors (*ἐπιγνώμονες*) was sent once a year to inspect the sacred olive-trees, but a monthly inspection carried out by members of the Areiopagos seems to have been in operation too, though we are unaware of the exact nature of both procedures.[18] It is worth noting that these committees had the power to impose fines on farmers mishandling *moriai*, or more probably on farmers tilling land too close to the trees, without necessarily bringing the culprits to the court.[19] The absence of the

[16] See Tiverios 2000*b*, 520–2, who interprets Attic graffiti on Archaic SOS amphorae as belonging to Athenian olive cultivators; more recently Tiverios 2007, 8–9. Harding 1994, 149 will speculatively connect olive-oil production to the twelve trittyes and push the whole institution back to the Bronze Age.

[17] Apart from the evidence discussed below, the jurisdiction of the Areiopagos is clear from the transmitted title of Lysias' speech and, of course, from Aristotle's unambiguous statement *ἔκρινεν ἡ ἐξ Ἀρείου Πάγου βουλή*, presumably the same as the *βουλή* of the Lysianic speech (cf. Foxhall 2007, 118).

[18] Lys. 7.25: *αὐτοὺς τοίνυν ὑμᾶς τούτων μάρτυρας παρέξομαι, ἐπιμελουμένους μὲν ἑκάστου μηνός, ἐπιγνώμονας δὲ πέμποντας καθ' ἕκαστον ἐνιαυτόν* (so I shall provide you yourselves as witnesses, since you supervise every month and you send out inspectors every year), with Wallace 1985, 122 (Albini 1955, 46 is wrong to conflate the two boards); Harp. s.v. *ἐπιγνώμονας*, with Rhodes 1993, 673 (cf. the *epignomones* of the Klytidai—interestingly, supervising transactions related to wood-felling—in *SEG* XXII 508 ll. A42–5, B43–7, with Fantasia 1977, 52; Behrend 1990, 241). The official title of those councillors of the Areiopagos carrying out the monthly inspection was probably *ἐπιμεληταί*, as implied by Lys. 7.29: *τοῦτον δ' ὃς γεωργῶν ἐγγὺς τυγχάνει οὔτ' ἐπιμελητὴς ᾑρημένος* (this man who, as it happens, is neither farming near me nor has he been elected as a supervisor); cf. Todd 2007, 531. To judge from the participle *ᾑρημένος*, the superintendents were elected, rather than chosen by lot. At any rate, Lys. 7.7: *ἐπίστασθε δέ, ὦ βουλή, ὅσοι μάλιστα τῶν τοιούτων ἐπιμέλεσθε* (and you know, members of the Council, especially those of you who have supervised such things), shows that not all members of the Areiopagos participated in the inspection.

[19] This is certainly the implication of Lys. 7.25–6: *ὧν οὐδεὶς πώποτ' ἐζημίωσέ μ' ὡς ἐργαζόμενον τὰ περὶ τὰς μορίας χωρία. καίτοι οὐ δήπου τὰς μὲν μικρὰς ζημίας οὕτω περὶ πολλοῦ ποιοῦμαι* (none of these has ever penalized me for working the ground around the *moriai*. Now surely, when I pay so much regard to those small penalties . . .), and 7.29: *δεινὸν δέ μοι δοκεῖ εἶναι ὑμᾶς μέν, οἷς ὑπὸ τῆς πόλεως τὸν ἅπαντα χρόνον προστέτακται τῶν μορίων ἐλαιῶν ἐπιμελεῖσθαι, μήθ' ὡς ἐπεργαζόμενον πώποτε ζημιῶσαί* <*με*> . . . (and I feel it is extraordinary that you, who have been charged with the supervision of the sacred olive-trees in perpetuity by the city, have never either penalized me for encroaching on one of the them . . .); cf. Rhodes 1993, 673; Horster 2006, 168. Here *ζημίαι* must be the technical term designating summary fines imposed by officials for minor offences (thus Gernet and Bizos 1959, 116; Todd 2007, 531). This and the speaker's reference to the tilling of ground around the *moriai* are reminiscent of

eponymous archon from the procedure is noticeable, and perhaps not coincidental. By this time, the penalty for those breaking the relevant law must no longer have been death, but rather exile and confiscation of the convict's property, as repeatedly implied in the speech.[20] However, the existence of *moriai* on one's land did not modify one's rights over it. The owner could pretty well farm his land by himself or lease it out to an interested individual for as long as he wished, his only obligation being the protection and cultivation of Athena's own trees.[21] At approximately the same time a major legal and procedural alteration seems to have taken place. This inference is drawn not only from the combined study of the two passages in question, but also from archaeological observations. An explicatory digression is necessary at this point.

Aristotle's account underpins a very strong connection between the fruit of the *moriai* and the most glorious Athenian festival, the Great Panathenaia, a link that can be traced archaeologically.[22] Of course, organic materials such as olive oil are not for the most part preserved, but the same is not true of their containers. These are the so-called Panathenaic Amphorae, ceramic vessels that due to various circumstances have survived in large numbers and constitute one of the best studied types of fine Greek pottery.[23] This shape of ware first appears in the middle of the sixth century with the establishment of

the Solonian law that prohibited farmers from planting trees too close to neighbouring plots: Plut. *Vit. Sol.* 23.7: *ὥρισε δὲ καὶ φυτειῶν μέτρα μάλ' ἐμπείρως, τοὺς μὲν ἄλλο τι φυτεύοντας ἐν ἀγρῷ πέντε πόδας ἀπέχειν τοῦ γείτονος κελεύσας, τοὺς δὲ συκῆν ἢ ἐλαίαν ἐννέα* (he also showed great experience in the limits which he set to the planting of trees; no one could set out a tree in a field within five feet of his neighbour's field, or, in case it was a fig-tree or an olive-tree, within nine; trans. by Perrin 1914), with Foxhall 2007, 116.

[20] In Lys. 7.3, 25, 41, the two things at stake are the speaker's fatherland (*πατρίς*) and property (*οὐσία*). See Rhodes 1993, 673; Todd 2000, 77–8. Clearly the *de facto* abandonment of the death penalty mentioned by Aristotle had already taken place before 397/6. Horster 2006, however, suspects inadvertent distortion of the truth on behalf of Aristotle.

[21] Thus the property in question of the seventh Lysianic speech changed hands seven times within a period of fifteen years! For a scholastic tabulation of the relevant transactions see Carey 1989, 125.

[22] See also n. 6 above, and Lucian, *Anach.* 9: *ΑΝΑΧΑΡΣΙΣ: Τὰ δὲ ἆθλα τίνα ὑμῖν ταῦτά ἐστιν; ΣΟΛΩΝ: Ὀλυμπίασι μὲν στέφανος ἐκ κοτίνου... παρ' ἡμῖν δὲ τοῖς Παναθηναίοις τὸ ἔλαιον τὸ ἐκ τῆς μορίας* (Anacharsis: What sort of prizes do you have? Solon: For the Olympics the prize is a crown from a young olive branch, whereas for our Panathenaia the prize is the oil from the *moriai*).

[23] The most up-to-date discussion is now Bentz 1998; see also Tiverios 2007. Eschbach 2007 and especially Themelis 2007 have provocatively suggested that the Panathenaic amphorae should be dissociated from the games. Despite some seemingly believable arguments, this new revisionist position violates the semantics of Panathenaic amphorae, including the existence of archontic inscriptions for which see below. For a critical (and persuasive) response see Johnston 2007.

the Panathenaia by the archon Hippokleides, an event which is today unanimously dated to 566/5.[24] But what is really unique is the persistence of the shape and its decoration for more than five hundred years, down to the first century before our era, a persistence that went as far as the preservation of the old-fashioned black-figure decoration long after it had been rendered oudated by the new red-figure technique. As for the iconography, it consisted of a front panel with an Athena of the warrior-type framed by two columns and a reverse one with the depiction of the athletic event at which the winning contestant had excelled. The conservatism of the Panathenaic amphorae does not mean that they did not undergo any changes over the course of time. On the contrary, the turn of the fifth century marked major innovations. The first novelty was artistic: instead of roosters, the potters started depicting statues on the two columns framing Athena. The second change was the appearance of the name of the eponymous archon next to the trademark dipinti that read *τῶν Ἀθήνηθεν ἄθλων* (from the prizes of Athens).[25] This latter feature has been justifiably connected to the introduction of the administrative scheme described by Aristotle. That is, the old procedure whereby the city leased out to individuals the right to collect olive oil from the *moriai* was replaced by a new one in which the responsibility lay with the eponymous archon of each year.[26] The first fully preserved example is that of Pytheas, eponymous archon of 380/79, but most scholars accept that the name of Philokles, archon of 392/1, can be restored with plausibility in a certain fragmentary vase-inscription and thus the chronology of the new law can be placed somewhere between 396/5 and 393/2.[27]

But why should the administrative procedures have undergone such a drastic modification? At first glance, the Lysianic speech seems to provide a satisfactory answer. The devastation of Attica in the course of the

[24] Parker 1996, 89, and now Neils 2007.

[25] Statues on columns: Bentz 1998, 53–4; archontic inscriptions: Bentz 1998, 57–9, who at 57 n. 310 justifiably reproaches scholars for taking the genitive *ἄθλων* to mean 'from the contests' and not 'from the prizes'. Tiverios 1974, 142–4 n. 4 claims that Panathenaic amphorae not bearing archon-inscriptions should not be considered as prizes offered to the winners of the Panathenaic contests.

[26] That a tax-farming system operated before the change discussed here is almost unanimously recognized from Arist. [*Ath. Pol.*] 60.2 (cf. Todd 2007, 483). Commenting on Lys. 7.2., Foxhall 2007, 119, simply translates 'those who bought the fruit of the sacred olives'. Todd 2007, 513, suggests that *τοὺς ἐωνημένους τοὺς καρποὺς τῶν μοριῶν* 'is a shorthand for a system of tax-farming, in which the *polis* sells to the highest bidder the right to collect in this case the olives'. In view of terms used in the Athenian grain-tax law *SEG* XLVIII 96 (*πωλεῖν, πριάμενος/οι*; cf. Stroud 1998, 28–30, 51–2), Todd is almost certainly right.

[27] Valavanis 1987, 479; Bentz 1998, 24, 57–9. Evidently the upper chronological limit is provided by the seventh Lysianic speech. Shear 2003, 96–7 has challenged some of these dates, but good epigraphic work by Tracy seems to offer new corroboration (see n. 32 below).

Peloponnesian War had presumably reduced oil production down to the point that olive-oil needs for the Great Panathenaia and the other public religious feasts could not be met. Furthermore, in the atmosphere of lawlessness that accompanied the harsh regime of the Thirty, the whole economic infrastructure of Athens was so severely disrupted that reorganization soon became a necessity.[28] Others disagree. If this had been the case, why should a considerable span of time have lapsed before measures were eventually taken? Besides, there is a new consensus among scholars that the ravaging of Attica by the Peloponnesians was less dramatic than previously assumed. Hanson, in his double capacity as ancient historian and agriculturalist, has cogently pointed out that olive-trees in particular are very difficult to uproot or burn and that the effort demanded for a large-scale devastation of this kind is so enormous that it renders such plans unappealing to any potential perpetrators.[29] Thus, for the revisionists, the reorganization was of political importance, a proof of the Athenians' willingness to reassert their power by glorifying anew their most majestic festival, the Panathenaia, something in which they had excelled during the fifth century.[30]

These scholars draw attention to the partly preserved inscription *IG* II^2 2311 (*Syll.*^{3} 1055), a list of prizes awarded to the victors of the Panathenaic contests.[31] On epigraphical grounds the list has traditionally been dated to the first quarter of the fourth century—a chronology tallying well with the procedural alteration described above—but Tracy has now fixed the *floruit* of the letter-cutter in question between 409/8 and 386/5.[32] The decision to inscribe the list on stone, rather than on some perishable material, has justifiably been seen as indicative of a major change in the form of the games; hence its connection to the new system for the collection of the oil from the *moriai.* Here it is worth recalling that *IG* II^2 2311 may not be the earliest list of Panathenaic prizes after all. A long-neglected fifth-century document, *IG* I^3 1386, has more than once been associated with the Panathenaic Games.[33] The inscription records prizes for victors of athletic contests, with Lewis thinking of amphoras of oil but doubting the connection to the Panathenaia mainly because the amphoras in question seem to be half those recorded in *IG* II^2 2311.[34] But Johnston, who has saved *IG* I^3 1386 from

[28] See Lys. 7.6–7, with Carey 1989, 122–4; Rhodes 1993, 674; Todd 2007, 517–21.

[29] Hanson 1998, *passim*, esp. 157–61; 236–7. Eder 1995 and Davies 1995 equally dismiss the notion of a large-scale crisis in early 4th-cent. Athens.

[30] Valavanis 1987, 479–80.

[31] Shear 2003 now provides the authoritative text (= *SEG* LIII 192, to which I will be referring throughout).

[32] Tracy 2003*b*.

[33] First, it seems, by Raubitschek 1939, 158.

[34] See Lewis, *IG* I^3 1386 ad loc.

oblivion, has reaffirmed the Panathenaic origin of the list.[35] If so, *IG* II^2 2311 becomes all the more important, because it arguably shows a very conscious attempt on the part of Athens to strengthen the prestige of her paramount festival by doubling the prizes offered. All things considered, is there anything that could have triggered Athenian imperialistic aspirations and, by implication, the new statute concerning the *moriai*? The battle of Knidos lends itself to this idea. After the shock of their defeat in 404 by the Lacedaemonians, the Athenians showed a remarkable ability for expeditious recovery. Still, it was only after the naval battle of Knidos in 394, when the Persian fleet under the command of the self-exiled Athenian Konon crushed the Peloponnesians, that Athens re-emerged in the front line of Greek affairs, claiming for herself a protagonist's role.[36] It is in the light of this success, I submit, that one must understand Athenian decisiveness in the use of the Panathenaia as a vehicle for the pursuit of a renewed expansionist policy. A date after the battle of Knidos seems perfectly plausible. Since the battle occured in August 394, almost simultaneously with the Great Panathenaia of that year, a new law could have been passed and put into effect starting from the following Panathenaia, that of 391/0.

If the significance assigned to the reorganization of the Panathenaia seems exaggerated, some statistics might suffice to strengthen this claim. *SEG* LIII 192 (i.e. *IG* II^2 2311) shows that there were three age classes of Panathenaic competitors, namely boys, beardless youths, and men. It also slightly modifies Aristotle's account by demonstrating that both those taking first and second victories in the gymnastic and the equestrian events were awarded jars of olive oil. Victorious men were naturally offered a higher prize than their younger counterparts in the same competition, but differentiation also existed among winners of different sports in the same age category. As for the ratio of prizes conferred on victors and runners-up of individual contests respectively, this is, by and large, 5 to 1, though the proportional pattern is not strictly followed throughout. This observation, coupled with more than a century of meticulous study, has established that the total number of jars needed for the Great Panathenaia should have been somewhere between 1200 and 2150 vessels. Shear's maximal figure of 2100 can be considered a satisfactory starting-point for calculations.[37] Still, a quantitative analysis based on the aforementioned estimate can be rather elusive for two reasons. First, there is the fact that amphorae for any forthcoming Great Panathenaia

[35] Johnston 2007, 103–4.

[36] Seager 1967; Mossé 1973, 32–4; Strauss 1986, 125–9; Hornblower 2002, 223–4, 227.

[37] For the lowest figure of 1200 jars see Tiverios 1974, 147–9 n. 29; Johnston 1987, 125–9 has suggested 1423 amphorae per Panathenaia, whereas Bentz 1998, 17, 1567 jars. Shear 2003, 102–3 has convincingly demonstrated that more than 2000 vessels were needed for each quadrennial celebration.

were made during the three years that preceded the festival, the tendency being for the majority of them to be made two years ahead. The reasons for this have been postulated in terms of practicality: the officials in charge would not take the risk of collecting olive oil just a year ahead of the games, when a bad crop could result in an insufficient supply, nor did they like the idea of collecting the fruit three years in advance, thus running the risk that the juice would go rancid.[38] Reasonable though this may seem, I suspect that biennial cropping of olive-trees could also have had its importance. Alternate-year bearing of the olive is a well-known phenomenon that even modern advanced agricultural research has failed to explain adequately. Biennial cropping is quite often followed by what botanists call *synchronization*. In comprehensible terms this means that over considerable areas or regions 'on' and 'off' fruiting years of thousands of olive-trees coincide. Therefore, a picture can be envisaged in which most Attic olive groves had their 'on' years two years ahead of the Great Panathenaia.[39] A second obstacle in any quantitative analysis is that not all Panathenaic jars were of the same size. At first sight this is perplexing, but parallels from Venetian Crete should help us dispel any difficulties. Thus the standard capacity unit for olive oil in sixteenth-century Crete shows a remarkable fluctuation over time.[40] Clearly, what mattered was not long-term stability of the capacity, but uniformity within the same year or within the same short period. Indeed, statistical analysis of the Panathenaic amphorae would show that the trend is for the capacity of the jars to decrease in the course of time. The smallest ones come from the late 320s, both before and after the destructive Lamian War. Such a decrease probably reflects a deterioration of Athenian finances and/or a reduction in oil production, the two factors standing in a mutual, dialectical relationship.[41] Yet it seems that jars pertaining to individual Panathenaia were roughly of the same size with only a couple of tantalizing exceptions. Independently, Johnston recently revisited the capacity problem, noted that most 'Classical Panathenaics lie within the 35–39 l. range', and concluded, no doubt soundly, that such limited differentation in size was tolerated by those involved in the whole procedure.[42]

[38] Gardiner 1912, 192; Vos 1981, 43 contra Rhodes 1993, 674; cf. Amouretti 1986, 195. Note that olive-harvesting for oil takes place from November to February: too late for the Great Panathenaia of any archontic year, too early for the forthcoming Panathenaia.

[39] Forbes 1992; Shear 2003, 96–7, though realizing the significance of biennial cropping, dismisses the lack of evidence for oil collected on Panathenaic years as coincidental; but our sample is big enough to render the accidental factor unlikely.

[40] Hatzaki 2003, 86; Polymerou-Kamelake 2003, 210–11.

[41] Cf. Bentz 1998, 40. The actual equivalent of a *metretes* was 38.88 litres according to Neils 1992, 39; 39.395 litres according to Shear 2003, 102.

[42] Johnston 2007, 102.

With these things established, one can proceed with the estimation of the average volume of Panathenaic amphorae. A relatively well-documented Panathenaic cycle is that of 358/7 with an average capacity of 38.34 litres per jar, which is slightly smaller than an Attic *metretes*.[43] This would mean that at least 80,514 litres of olive oil were awarded to the winners of the games, if we accept *c*.2100 amphorae per Panathenaic contest. Since Aristotle explicitly states that the archon collected one and a half *kotylai* from each trunk, that is *c*.405 c.c., it is not hard to estimate how many trees the prize oil could have come from. The result is an extraordinary 198,800 trees. This was not the aggregate of olive-trees cultivated in Attica, but was obviously higher than the total number of the *moriai*, since Aristotle clearly says that by his time oil was not exclusively collected from the sacred trees.[44] Now, the size of Attica has long been estimated at about 2400 km^2, out of which some 840 km^2 were available for agricultural and arboricultural activities.[45] Is, then, the number of 198,800 trees arrived at above a realistic one, given the cultivable extent of Attica? It appears so. The estimated density of tree-planting in Roman Tripolitania is 30–40 trees per hectare.[46] On the basis of the median of 35 trees per hectare, 198,800 trees would correspond to 5680 hectares (*c*.64980 plethra), that is almost 56.8 km^2, or 6.76 per cent of the Attic cultivable soil. Foxhall, however, believes that the planting density in Classical Athens was much closer to that of modern Methana (*c*.100 trees per ha.).[47] If so, we should be thinking in terms of 1980 hectares, or 19.8 km^2 of Attic soil (*c*. 2.35 percent of the cultivable land) contributing to the production of Panathenaic oil. Looking at the issue from a different perspective, we might recall another of Foxhall's recent estimations: the yearly oil consumption per wealthy Athenian household was between 200 and 330 kg.[48] On a 1 litre = 0.96 kg ratio, the 80,514 litres of Panathenaic oil would have weighed some 77,293 kg. So much oil would have covered the yearly needs of 235 to 386 wealthy Athenian families (or, self-evidently, the yearly needs

[43] Tiverios 1974, 149 n. 31.

[44] The scepticism expressed by Todd 2007, 483 n. 26, is unwarranted. Arist. [*Ath. Pol.*] 60.2, unequivocally states that the olive oil was not extracted from individual trees, but from the whole property. The interpretation of this passage by Rhodes 1993, 674 is crystal-clear and should leave no open questions.

[45] Foxhall 1992, 156, thinks that some 1000 km^2 were cultivated in Attica; Garnsey 1985, 65, based on Jardé 1925, 48–52, reaches 28.75% of Attica as cultivable land, that is 690 km^2 (but this probably does not include forested areas); cf. Sallares 1991, 309–13. I have benefited substantially from the numbers that Moreno 2007, 3–15 has meticulously collected and I accept here 35%, or 840 km^2, as the extent of Attica's cultivable land.

[46] Mattingly 1985, 32; Forbes 1992, 93.

[47] The concentration of 156 trees per hectare accepted by Moreno 2007, 65 for Euonymon seems implausibly high.

[48] Foxhall 2007, 85–95.

of many more families of low economic standing). Obviously the figures are estimations, but they can at least provide a rough idea of the arboricultural background of the sacred-oil system.

These statistics give rise to a further question. Why would the Athenian state have provided such lavish prizes, and, more importantly, why would it have wasted some of its more precious agricultural assets? The Athenians certainly had a huge appreciation for their olive oil production and applied strict regulations to its trade. A scholion on Pindar's tenth Nemean hymn informs us that no one, other than the Panathenaic victors, was allowed to export olive oil out of Attica.[49] This position has often been taken at face value, but archaeological evidence modifies the assertion. Panathenaic amphorae have been discovered all over the ancient Greek world, though, as expected, the majority have been found in Attica. They were deposited as votives in sanctuaries, put in tombs to accompany the dead, but were also used in domestic contexts.[50] Some certainly belonged to athletes who had taken their prize, or part of it, back home after the end of the games. The vast quantity of amphorae found in shrines are usually seen as the tangible manifestation of the victorious athletes' gratitude to propitious divinities.[51] In this light, it may not be surprising that most of them have been found on the Athenian Acropolis.[52] However, we are told a different story in cases where a number of Panathenaic amphorae, with depictions of contests as diverse as the pankration and horse-racing, are found together. Such archaeological contexts certainly suggest commercial activity, especially since Panathenaic amphorae sometimes bear 'trademarks'.[53] It seems almost impossible that the winner of the full-grown horse race, for instance, would have been able to move his prize of 140 vessels a considerable distance, let alone to consume it by himself.[54] And it is highly unlikely that a merchant in Cyrenaica would have been involved in the trade of exclusively Panathenaic jars. The most plausible hypothesis is that Panathenaic amphorae full of olive

[49] Scholia in Pind. *Nem.* 10. 64a: *οὔκ ἔστι δὲ ἐξαγωγὴ ἐλαίου ἐξ Ἀθηνῶν εἰ μὴ τοῖς νικῶσι*; Böckh 1886, II 54 thought that the law stipulated the exemption of the victors from taxes imposed upon their olive oil, but his interpretation is flimsy.

[50] Bentz 1998, 95–116.

[51] Tiverios 2000*a*, 28–9.

[52] Bentz 1998, 111; Tiverios 2000*a*, 25; Kotsidou 2001, 56. However, Aristotle's statement that the sacred olive oil was stored by the treasurers on the Acropolis could certainly account for the great numbers of Panathenaic amphorae from the sacred rock. Moreover, in Attica itself there were some other divinities who were recipients of the prestigious vessels. One found in the Eleusinian sanctuary, for example, bore a dedicatory inscription to the local hero Dolichos (this is the interpretation of the amphora Bentz 1998, no. 4.327, favoured by Tiverios 2000*a*, 29 n. 86).

[53] Tiverios 1974, 150–1; Valavanis 1986, 456; Bentz 1998, 107–8.

[54] *IG* II^2 2311 ll. 67–8 (=*SEG* LIII 192 ll. 116–17): *ἵππων ζεύγει ἀδηφάγωι | ΗΔΔΔΔ ἀμφορῆς ἐλαίο.*

oil were purchased in Attica by tradesmen who approached the victors offering them cash in order to acquire the precious commodity.[55] Now, this scenario certainly does not comply with the law which purportedly allowed only the victors to export olive oil. But the law ought not to be completely fictional. What, in fact, it might have promulgated was that only Panathenaic olive oil could be exported. Even this interpretation, however, appears to contradict the Solonian law on the ban on exports of all Attic agricultural products with the exception of olive oil.[56] The legal mismatch has passed largely unnoticed. One could assume the revocation of the Solonian law and its substitution with the one attested by the scholiast on Pindar, but this presupposes that the former really dates back to the early sixth century. Though some scholars are keen to believe its Solonian origin by virtue of it having been inscribed on an *axon*, others think that the reference to the public treasury (τὸ δημόσιον) makes it more likely that the text is a fourth-century invention.[57] This in turn would make the two laws, the 'Solonian' and the 'Panathenaic', contemporary, although a different chronological set for each law within the fourth century cannot be ruled out. In fact, it is not inconceivable that the two passages are extracts from one and the same legal text. In any case, even if we accept the authenticity of the Solonian law in question, as I am inclined to, we should seriously doubt that the law was still in use in the Classical period. The exportation of olive oil cannot have been as widespread a phenomenon as students of Classical Athens uncritically assume.

As demonstrated above, the quantities of olive oil offered every four years as prizes for the Great Panathenaia were substantial. To my mind this observation points in a hitherto unnoticed direction: beyond their political significance, the Great Panathenaia were part of a carefully orchestrated plan for the state-controlled supply of Attic olive oil in international markets.[58] Admittedly, fewer than half of the preserved Panathenaic amphorae have

[55] Valavanis 1991, 17–18; Tiverios 2000*b*, 525. Vos 1981, 41 (cf. Mommsen 1898, 79 n. 1) has suggested that any olive oil surplus was sold by the state, but this is not supported by our sources.

[56] Plut. *Vit. Sol.* 24.1–2; see n. 2 above.

[57] Samons 2000, 57 argues that the existence of a public treasury (τὸ δημόσιον) before the reforms of Cleisthenes should be doubted, though not entirely dismissed. The authenticity of the law is, however, accepted by Descat 1993, Kroll 1998, 225–6, and now Gagarin 2006, 267–8. As for the so-called Solonian laws, scholars tend nowadays to believe that the majority of them are 4th-cent. documents in the guise of Solonian statutes. However, Scafuro 2006, and Blok 2006, are recent studies that put more trust in the genuine Solonian origin of some of these laws.

[58] The co-operation of the Boule (the Council of the 500, not the Areiopagos) with the *athlothetai* for the supervision of the construction of Panathenaic vessels (Arist. [*Ath. Pol.*] 60.2) is indicative of the significance attached to the whole scheme by the Athenians.

been found outside Attica and, given the periodicity of the games, Panathenaic olive oil could not have contributed enormously to the trade balance of Athens. Yet the fact that most of the preserved Panathenaic amphorae outside Attica are to be found in areas which comprised important exporters of grain to Athens can hardly be coincidental.[59] The short-term benefit to the Athenian state in the shape of tax imposed on the exported cargoes of olive oil would have been modest. In the long term, however, Athens would have lured merchants into the Athenian market; and of course merchants, more often than not, arrived with the longed-for grain. This hypothesis finds some corroboration from other evidence. When the Athenians decided in 346 to bestow exuberant honours on the Bosporan rulers Spartokos and Pairisades for their role in the grain supply of Athens, they did so by commissioning the *athlothetai* to fulfil this in the Great Panathenaia—not just the games of 346, but *every* Great Panathenaia. By undertaking to oversee this unusually regular award together with the traditional preparation of the Panathenaic amphorae, the *athlothetai* might have been carrying out two duties less incompatible with each other than the casual observer may initially think.[60] Moreover, archaeologists have long noticed that the Panathenaic amphorae stylistically draw their origin from the so-called SOS amphorae—vessels used for transportation of olive oil in the seventh and early sixth centuries—either directly or indirectly via the 'à la brosse' amphorae.[61] But the SOS amphorae (or their immediate successors, the 'à la brosse' ones) disappear at approximately the same time when Panathenaic ones make their appearance, the implication being that the latter took over their predecessors' function.[62] And last but not least, there is here a very

[59] e.g. North Africa and the Black Sea states (see Valavanis 1986, 457; Bentz 1998, 111–19; Kotsidu 2001). The early 2nd-cent. honorific inscription *IG* II^2 903 perfectly illustrates the interconnection between grain import and olive oil export between mainland Greece and the grain-producing areas of Pontos; cf. Gauthier 1982, esp. 289–90, who provides an improved text and insightful observations, and Horden and Purcell 2000, 211–12.

[60] RO 64 (*IG* II^2 212), ll. 20–42. The comment by Rhodes and Osborne 2003, 323 ('The award of crowns regularly, rather than on a single occasion, was an unusual and expensive honour, for rulers whose continuing support for Athens was highly valued . . . ') says it all. The particular aspect of exchange of commodities, grain for oil, explored here is noted by Gauthier 1985, 156 (see also n. 59 above). Not unreasonably, Hagemajer Allen 2003, 235–7, sees *IG* II^2 212 as 'a commercial and political treaty' disguised into 'an honorary grant' of multiple benefactions.

[61] Johnston and Jones 1978, 132–4, 140–1; Valavanis 1986, 454; Docter 1991 (see the caution advocated by Descart 1993, 159–60, and Garlan 2000, 89–90). By publishing the inscribed fragment (in Attic script) of an SOS amphora from the Thermaic Gulf, Tiverios 2000*b*, 519-23, has conveyed further good evidence for the interpretation of these vessels as containers of Athenian olive-oil.

[62] See the discussion by Tiverios 2000*b*, the synopsis in Tiverios 2007, 2, and the good remarks by Johnston 2007, 101–2. Note also that one of the earliest issues of

strong case for constructing an *argumentum e silentio*. Hard as one might search, it is impossible to find for the Classical period any archaeological evidence of Attic oil exports other than that of the Panathenaic amphorae.[63]

One further point needs clarification: after the introduction of the new legislation that allowed the exploitation of all olive-trees indiscriminately for the collection of Panathenaic oil, one might expect the latter to have lost its symbolic value; it would no longer have been the sacred product of the goddess Athena herself. Todd provisionally branded this process *desacralisation*, before, rightly, dismissing it.[64] An apt remark made by Bentz in his most recent treatment of the issue could remedy this puzzle. The one and a half *kotylai* of olive oil that had to be collected from each root roughly corresponds to a tenth of the estimated fruit of olives: it was a *dekate*, a tithe.[65] Though not explicitly stated by Aristotle, it seems possible that the olive oil collected for the Panathenaia was a sacred tax in kind, a 10 per cent imposed on Attic oleoculture on behalf of Athena. This hypothesis can be reinforced by comparison with independent sources. In the 24th Demosthenic oration there are two references to tithes of the Goddess (*τὰ ἱερά, τὰς δεκάτας τῆς Θεοῦ καὶ τὰς πεντηκοστὰς τῶν ἄλλων Θεῶν*), though no context is provided as to their provenance.[66] The Demosthenic corpus preserves another law which contains clauses for the protection of private olive-trees:

> *Ἐάν τις ἐλάαν Ἀθήνησιν ἐξορύττῃ, ἐὰν μὴ εἰς ἱερὸν Ἀθηναίων δημόσιον ἢ δημοτικόν, ἢ ἑαυτῷ χρῆσθαι μέχρι δυοῖν ἐλάαιν τοῦ ἐνιαυτοῦ ἑκάστου, ἢ ἐπὶ ἀποθανόντα δέῃ χρήσασθαι, ὀφείλειν ἑκατὸν δραχμὰς τῷ δημοσίῳ τῆς ἐλάας ἑκάστης, τὸ δὲ ἐπιδέκατον τούτου τῆς θεοῦ εἶναι. ὀφειλέτω δὲ καὶ τῷ ἰδιώτῃ τῷ ἐπεξιόντι ἑκατὸν δραχμὰς καθ' ἑκάστην ἐλάαν. τὰς δὲ δίκας εἶναι περὶ τούτων πρὸς τοὺς ἄρχοντας, ὧν ἕκαστοι δικασταί εἰσι. πρυτανεῖα δὲ τιθέτω ὁ διώκων τοῦ αὑτοῦ μέρους. ὅτου δ' ἂν καταγνωσθῇ, ἐγγραφόντων οἱ ἄρχοντες, πρὸς οὓς ἂν ᾖ ἡ*

Athenian 'Wappenmünzen' has on the obverse the design of an amphora, thought to be of the Panathenaic type (Kraay 1968, 2). The date of this issue roughly coincides with the inception of the Panathenaia *and* with the introduction of the Panathenaic amphorae (thus Cahn 2001). Incidentally, Flament 2007, 14–17 associates the earliest 'Wappenmünzen' with the rule of Peisistratos, who is often credited with the inception of the Great Panathenaia.

63 Observed already by Tiverios 2000*b*, 525 in relation to the second half of the 6th cent.; cf. the important brief note by Lawall 2005, 203. This observation may have implications for the viability of the model of olives as a cash-crop recently advocated by Moreno 2007, esp. 64–76.

64 Todd 2007, 484–5.

65 Thus Bentz 1998, 117 n. 619. The point is now taken up by Foxhall 2007, 118.

66 Dem. 24.120; cf. 24.130: . . . *ὥστε διὰ τούτους ἢ τῶν δεκατῶν τῶν τῆς θεοῦ ἀμελῆσαι.*

δίκη, τοῖς πράκτορσιν, ὃ τῷ δημοσίῳ γίγνεται· <ὃ δὲ τῇ θεῷ γίγνεται>, τοῖς ταμίαις τῶν τῆς θεοῦ. ἐὰν δὲ μὴ ἐγγράφωσιν, αὐτοὶ ὀφειλόντων.[67]

This law dates to the fourth century, a period when the procedure described by Aristotle was already in force. If my interpretation is correct, the 10 per cent fine owed to the goddess by the violators of the law constituted Athena's compensation for the loss of her 10 per cent share in the oil-production. No surprise then that her treasurers were enjoined to recover the fine. It is worth noting that only the needs of public cults could permit the breach of the relevant restriction in the felling of olive-trees.[68]

Another document which has surprisingly never been brought into discussion in connection with the *moriai* is the famous First-Fruits decree. Regardless of its exact date, it contains a rider proposed by Lampon—presumably the well-known seer—on the drafting of a regulation about the *aparche* of olive oil. It is Lampon himself who is authorized to present the draft to the Council in the ninth prytany; subsequently the Council is ordered to submit the draft to the assembly.[69] Due to the elliptical diction not much of substance can be said about the rider. It follows a decree which sets up regulations for the delivery of the first-fruits of grain to the officials of the Eleusinion in honour of Demeter and Kore. Olives, however, were not under the protection of the divine Eleusinian duo; the privilege belonged to Athena.[70] And in all probability, it was her officials, the treasurers, who would be assigned tasks similar to those undertaken by the *hieropoioi* in the main decree. More than a century ago, and in a different context, Mommsen made the very apt comparison between the *Ῥάριον πεδίον*—a sacred field at Eleusis that belonged to the two Goddesses and where their sacred crops were cultivated—and the *μορίαι*, the sacred trees of Athena.[71] Yet time and again scholars have overlooked this point and have been misled into taking

[67] Dem. 43.71. The speech is dated by Gernet 1957, 94 to *c.*370/65; however, his claim (ibid. 120) that the law may be Solonian does not seem sustainable. Thompson 1976, 63 and Usher 1999, 267 n. 79 suggest *c.*345 as the date of the speech. For the template of the law see Carey 1998, 99–100.

[68] Cf. Wilhelm 1951, 1–3; although his emendation *ἐὰν μὴ εἰς ἔργον Ἀθηναίων δημόσιον* is not necessary, his adducing of *LSCG* 150A (protection of the cypress-trees in a Koan *temenos*) is illuminating. See also Kränzlein 1963, 56–7.

[69] *IG* I[3] 78 (ML 73), ll. 59–61: *περὶ δὲ τô ἐλαίο ἀπαρχêς χσυγγράφ|σας Λάμπον ἐπιδειχσάτο τêι βολêι ἐπὶ τês ἐνάτες πρυτανείας· | hε δὲ βολὲ ἐς τὸν δêμον ἐχσενενκέτο ἐπάναγκες* (traditionally dated to 422, but Cavanaugh 1996, 92–92 suggested a date *c.*435, and some scholars, e.g. Rhodes 2008, 505, are now nodding favourably).

[70] This point was raised very early by Foucart 1880, 252, but ever since it has received no attention. Cole 1995, 314–15 and 324 n. 130 has brought out a similar connection between the first-fruits from the *καρποὶ ξύλινοι* and Dionysos as attested in *SEG* XLI 1003 B53–5 (Teos).

[71] Mommsen 1898, 7; thus more recently (unaware of Mommsen's remark) Siewert 2001, 3.

the *aparche* of olive oil in the amendment to refer to the Eleusinian cult. Not only is this not self-evident, but, I believe, it is wrong. If anything connects the second rider to the main decree it is the similarity of the addressed problem, the administration of an *aparche.* As the first rider, with its provision for the intercalation of a second Hekatombaion, shows, there is no a priori reason to try and look for an internal correlation between Lampon's second rider and the decree itself. It is true that no mention of *moriai* is made in the amendment. Since the inscription belongs to the fifth century one might have expected some reference of a more explicit nature. I do not, however, regard this omission as particularly serious: the crux of the extract is the administration of the ἔλαιον, the olive oil, not of the olive-trees. Unless one day the decree on the first-fruits of olive oil comes to light we cannot retrieve the content of the draft that Lampon would have submitted to the Boule. Given our present state of knowledge about the rider, it is plausible, albeit not certain, that Lampon's missing decree would have contained the old regulations concerning the farming of the right to collect olive oil from the *moriai*, as described by Aristotle.

Be that as it may, the last Panathenaic amphora bearing an archontic inscription dates to 312/11, and on this basis it has been inferred that a further change in the administration of the festival was introduced by Demetrios of Phaleron. First the treasurer of the military fund and, after the 140s, the *agonothetes* of the Panathenaia appear to have taken over the role previously held by the eponymous archon.[72] Yet the cause of these changes and the way they might have affected the administration of the *moriai* is unclear and goes beyond the scope of this study.[73]

ii. The Sanctity of the *moriai*

One more theoretical question is still in need of an answer: should one attribute any specific sacredness to the *moriai* or was their religious aspect a superficial one? We can start our investigation with a unique vase scene attributed to the Dinos Painter. An amphora found in the Geroulanos estate at Trachones (site of the deme Euonymon) has on its front the depiction of the collection of olive oil from a *moria*. A bearded man called Alkimos appears to pour the oil from one amphora to another (perhaps a Panathenaic jar). Alkimos is helped by a younger man who wears similar clothes. The two men have been interpreted as farmers in whose lands *moriai* thrived. Interestingly the whole scene takes place under the watchful eye of none other

[72] Shear 2003, 97–8.
[73] See now Barringer 2003; Williams 2007, esp. 150–1.

than Athena herself. One could hardly expect a more eloquent iconographical confirmation of the divine ownership of the *moriai*: they lay under the protection of Athena.[74] From Sophocles' *Oedipus Coloneus* we know that not only Athena, but also Zeus, with the telling epithet Morios, held the sacred trees under divine protection.[75] As it happens, in this capacity Zeus was considered significant enough to be included as the recipient of a triple sacrifice in the official sacrificial calendar of Athens from the late fifth century.[76] Moreover, the defendant of the *Ἀρεοπαγίτικος: περὶ τοῦ σηκοῦ ἀπολογία* delivered his speech before the Areiopagos precisely because that was the court that adjudicated on certain religious cases.[77] When the same man rhetorically raised the point of his competence to cut down and encroach upon *moriai* lying in his other estates, he employed the verb *ἐπεργάζεσθαι*, a technical term long perceived by scholars to denote trespassing upon sacred land.[78]

Thus, from the Athenians' point of view the *moriai* certainly fell within the category of sacred realty. It is, however, surprising to discover that even their enemies took a similar stance. Fragments from the work of both Androtion and Philochorus, the two most prominent Atthidographers, concur on the point that when the Lacedaemonians invaded Attica during the first stage of the Peloponnesian War, they spared the sacred olive-trees out of fear of Athena's vengeance.[79] Another less eminent Atthidographer, Istros,

[74] *ARV*^{2} 1154/38 bis; cf. Fink 1963; Steinhauer 1998, 39; Neils 2001, 126–7; Themelis 2007, 21–3, who rightly describes the vase as a family heirloom. For Trachones/Euonymon see now the ultimate, albeit highly challenging, account by Moreno 2007, 37–76.

[75] Soph. *OC* 704–6, *ὁ δ' αἰὲν ὁρῶν κύκλος | λεύσσει νιν Μορίου Διὸς | χἀ γλαυκῶπις Ἀθάνα* (for [the olive] is looked upon by the ever-seeing eye of Zeus Morios and by grey-eyed Athena; trans. by Lloyd-Jones 1994) with Kamerbeek 1984, 108–9, and Guidorizzi *et al.* 2008, 290–1. Zeus' altar was probably located in the Akademeia: cf. Travlos 1971, 42.

[76] *SEG* LII 48, face A, fr. 12, ll. 8–9: *Δ<ιὶ> Μορίω<ι> τρ[ίττοιαν] | βόạρχοṿ*, with Lambert 2002*c*, 385.

[77] Harrison 1971, 38; Wallace 1985, 106–12; Todd 1993, 306–7; De Bruyn 1995, 113–16, who argues that the procedure followed in cases involving damaged *moriai* was that of *eisangelia*; cf. the same court's concern with the administration of the *Sacred Orgas* (Appendix I).

[78] Lys. 7.24, 29 (cf. Lattermann 1909), and n. 19 above. *ἐπεργάζεσθαι* in the context of sacred land: Aeschin. 3.113; *IG* II^2 1126.15; cf. the noun *ἐπεργασία* in Thuc. 1.139. Perhaps we should consider anew Scheibe's emendation of *ἐργαζόμενον* into *ἐπεργαζόμενον* in Lys. 7.25 (but Carey in the latest OCT edition of Lysias has retained *ἐργαζόμενον*).

[79] The fragments have been transmitted to us in the scholia to Sopohocles' *Oedipus Coloneus* l. 699: *ἐγχέων φόβημα δαΐων*. Androtion (*FGrH* 324 F39): 'For when the Lacedaemonians invaded Attica with (?)x10000 Peloponnesians and Boeotians under the leadership of Archidamos, son of Zeuxidamos, king of the Lacedaemonians, they kept their hands off the so-called *moriai* out of fear for Athena (. . . *ἀπέσχοντο τῶν*

provides a more explicit account: curses were imposed upon anyone who felled the *moriai*.

> *ὁ δ' Ἴστρος καὶ τὸν ἀριθμὸν αὐτῶν δεδήλωκεν γράφων οὕτως * * * εἶναι δὲ κλάδον † ἀπὸ τῆς ἐν Ἀκαδημείαι ἐλαίας ἀπὸ τῆς ἐν ἀκροπόλει φυτευθῆναί φασιν. ἐπάρατον † δ'ἐποιήσαντας τοὺς ἐμβαλόντας† αὐτὰς ἐκκόψειε φίλος ἢ πολέμιος, δι' ὃ Λακεδαιμόνιοι τὴν λοιπὴν γῆν δηιοῦντες τῆς μὲν Τετραπόλεως ἀπέσχοντο διὰ τοὺς Ἡρακλείδας, τῶν δὲ μορίων διὰ τὰς ἀράς.*[80]
>
> And Istros defined their number writing thus * * * there is a branch † from the olive-tree in Akademeia which, they say, was planted from the olive on the Acropolis. † making accursed those who invaded (?), † should anyone, either friend or foe, cut them down; that is why when the Lacedaiemonians were ravaging all the rest of the countryside they stayed away from the Tetrapolis because of the Heraklidai, and away from the *moriai* because of the curses.

Those imprecations involved both friendly *and* hostile perpetrators and hence there is no reason to assume that they were an Athenian defensive device against their invading foes, but rather a generally applied religious prohibition. A gloss found in the *Etymologicum Genuinum* is relevant:

> *μορία: ἡ ἐλαία. οἱ μὲν πᾶσαν ἐλαίαν οὕτω καλοῦσιν, οἱ δὲ τὰς ἱερὰς τῇ θεῷ . . . τινές δέ φασι διὰ τὸν ἐπὶ Ἁλιρροθίῳ μῦθον, ὃς ἑαυτὸν ἀνεῖλεν πελέκει <ἐκκόπτων τὰς ἐλαίας, οἱ δὲ ὅτι Ἄρης αὐτὸν ἀνεῖλεν> βιασάμενον αὐτοῦ τὴν θυγατέραν Ἀλκίππην. ἀπὸ οὖν τοῦ περὶ αὐτοῦ μόρου, ὅτι ἀνῃρέθη κόπτων τὰς ἐλαίας, μορία ἐκλήθη. Σέλευκος.*
>
> moria: the olive. Some call thus every single olive-tree, others those consecrated to the goddess . . . some say [that the moriai are thus called] because of the myth concerning Halirrothios, who killed himself with an axe while cutting down the olives, others say that Ares killed him because he had raped his daughter Alkippe.

λεγομένων μορίων Ἀθηνᾶν δείσαντες)', with Harding 1994, 69, 148–50; Philochorus (*FGrH* 328 F125): 'Various scholars including Philochoros recount that the Lacedaemonians kept their hands off the *moriai* (. . . *ὅτι ἀπέσχοντο τῶν μορίων*)'. It is tempting to see a certain juxtaposition between Archidamos' pious disposition and Kleomenes' hubris in felling the trees of the Eleusinian grove (Hdt. 6.75.3), for which cf. Appendix I.

[80] *FGrH* 334 F30, with Jacoby 1954, 644–5. It is worth noting that the offering to Zeus Morios mentioned above (n. 76) occurs in a set of sacrifices that can be localized in the area of the Marathonian Tetrapolis (Lambert 2002*c*, 385) and we may hypothesize a certain connection between this and the lemma of Istros. A late 5th-cent. amphora from the Athenian Agora (*Agora* XXX, 138–9 no. 22) has a scene which has been connected to the *moriai*. Interestingly, one of the figures is labelled *Κοπρεύς*, a secondary Attic hero related to the reception of the Heraklidai in Attica (cf. Corbett 1949, 306–8; Wilkins 1993, 56). Note also the Heraklean connection envisaged in *IG* I^3 255.

> Thus it was after his death (moros), since he had died cutting down the olives, that the tree was named moria. Seleukos.[81]

Seleukos' etymology cannot stand up to linguistic scrutiny, but the tale might have been the mythological crystallization of the imprecations discussed above: death was the destiny of anyone who dared decimate the sacred olive-trees, heroes included. The story does not end here. The *Parium Chronicum* and almost all Atthidographers connect Halirrothios' murder by Ares and the latter's subsequent trial on a hill in Athens with the naming of the hill as Areios Pagos.[82] Here again, what we witness is probably the rationalistic retrospection of the Areiopagos' involvement in trials concerning the felling of *moriai*, although the actual sequence of events is hardly retrievable.

In his account of the enmity between the Athenians and the Aeginetans, Herodotus tells one of those fabulous stories he is so fond of: in olden times Epidauria was totally barren and, in their despair, its inhabitants asked for the help of the Delphic oracle. Pythia advised them to set up statues of Damia and Auxesia, eloquent personifications of regenerating powers, and, moreover, to make these statues of olive-wood. Subsequently, the Epidaurians asked for the assistance of the Athenians considering the Attic olive-trees to be of supreme holiness (*ἱρωτάτας δὴ κείνας νομίζοντες εἶναι*). The Athenians agreed to supply them with olive wood asking in return that the Epidaurians offer annual sacrifices to Athena Polias and to Erechtheus. The oracle proved to be working.[83] What followed need not occupy us here. The crucial thing is that the sacredness of Attic olive-trees was a condition accepted by the parties involved. And yet Herodotus fails to mention *moriai*. Given his acclaimed religious interests, this is surprising and leaves us bewildered as to whether *moriai* were the source of the timber at issue at all. But then Herodotus refrains from mentioning *moriai*, even when he recounts the miraculous blooming of the incinerated olive-tree on the Acropolis. Furthermore, the fact that it is Athena Polias and Erechtheus—*alter ego* of Poseidon—who feature as the recipients of sacrifices from the Epidaurians would suggest an underlying connection between the timber used and the

[81] *EM* 590.42–50 with Reitzenstein 1897, 165; cf. *Suda* I. 1248 and Schol. in Ar. *Nu.* 1005d–h, where the death of Halirrothios is related to the contest between Athena and Halirrothios' father Poseidon.

[82] *IG* XII (5) 444, ll. 5–6: *ἀφ' οὗ δίκη Ἀθήνησι[ν ἐγέ]νετο Ἄρει καὶ Ποσειδῶνι ὑπὲρ Ἁλιρροθίου τοῦ Ποσειδῶνος, καὶ ὁ τόπος ἐκλήθη | Ἄρειος Πάγος, ἔτη* XHH𐅄ΔXHH𐅃*III* (From the time when the lawsuit between Ares and Poseidon was held in Athens over Halirrothios, the son of Poseidon, and the place was named Areiopagos, 1268 years). The relevant sources have been conveniently collected, translated, and analysed by Harding 2008, 33–5, 205–7.

[83] Hdt. 5.82, with Figueira 1991, 117; Nenci 1994, 277–9; Horster 2006, 182.

moriai via the contest myth.[84] Whatever the truth, the tale is an important proof of the notional sacredness of the Attic olive-trees. Similarly, and maybe even more importantly, the ancient holy image of Athena Polias was made of olive-wood.[85] Both stories, then, perfectly illustrate another dimension of the sacredness attributed to the olive trees: it was an immortal property, inherent and transferable in a way similar, but antithetic, to the way that miasma can be transferred from a polluted agent to whomever he comes in contact with.[86] Retrospectively one realizes how the ἔλαιον from the *moriai* would have kept the sacredness of the producing trees.

If the Herodotean passage abounds with ambiguity, independent epigraphical evidence points to the existence of sacred olive-trees that cannot be classified as *moriai*. In a late fourth-century sacred calendar of unknown provenance, we encounter the phrase τῶν ἱερῶν ἐλαῶν;[87] these do not appear to have been *moriai*, but rather olive trees planted in a *temenos* belonging to Herakles and rendered sacred by virtue of their location. We remain baffled concerning the olive trees in the Euboean *temene* leased out by the Athenians in the 420s, though an epigraphical restoration would make them sacred too.[88] Finally, no sacredness is immediately evident in the case of the olive trees in another Herakleion, that of the Salaminioi,[89] or of the two hundred olive trees that were to be planted in the *temenos* of Neleus in the emphyteutic lease *IG* I³ 84 (418/7). Overall, such evidence urges us to identify two different categories of sacred trees: on the one hand *moriai*, distinguishable sacred olives with no or very limited geographic concentration, and, on the other hand, flora consecrated to divinities as part of a wider frame of sacred real property.[90]

84 Poseidon-Erechtheus: see Gourmelen 2004, *passim*, and esp. 294; 342.

85 Schol. in Dem. 13.

86 Cf. the explanation put forward by Bentz 1998, 62 in relation to Panathenaic amphorae dedicated to Athena Polias: the sanctity of the olive oil rendered the vessels suitable for cultic use (endorsed by Kotsidu 2001, 56). A similar point could be made with regard to the well-known *IG* I³ 1454 (now scrutinized by Ma 2009), in which an Eteokarpathian family is being honoured for having provided a cypress tree for the temple of Athena Polias. The cypress came from the sanctuary of Apollo at Karpathos. Meiggs 1982, 200–1, offers a utilitarian interpretation of the inscription, but the sacred origin of the cypress in question tallies perfectly with the two passages quoted above.

87 *IG* II² 1211B l. 4: [ἐκ τ]ῶ̣ν ἱερῶν ἐλ<α>ῶν (with Papazarkadas 2007*a*, 170–1).

88 L. 6 of *IG* I³ 418 reads: [. . . .]*I* ἐλαῖαι, φσιλὲ ΔΔ etc. Since the text is stoichedon, [ἱερα]ὶ ἐλαῖαι is a possibility, if the letter in the fifth stoichos is indeed an *iota* and not a numerical figure.

89 *Agora* XIX L4b ll. 8–11: τοῦ μὲν Ἡρακλέον τοῦ τεμέ|νους ἄνετομ μὲν εἶναι ὡς οἱ βωμοὶ κ|αὶ τὸ ἐπέκεινα τοῦ ἰκρίου ὡς αἱ ἐλ|άαι αἱ πρῶται.

90 The sacred olive tree in Plut. *Vit. Thes.* 18.1 might have been such a case, although the use of the definite article might allude to *the* sacred olive on the Acropolis: 'When the lot was cast, Theseus took those upon whom it fell from the prytaneion and went to the Delphinion, where he dedicated to Apollo on their behalf

The preceding discussion has various implications. In particular, the extracts of Atthidographic lore would prove the defendant of the seventh Lysianic speech a liar, in that his insistence on the destruction of *moriai* by the Peloponnesians contradicts the picture we have drawn above. Secondly, they confirm the often adduced and yet rarely proven doctrine that sacred property was considered inalienable. Still, it seems at least enigmatic how the invaders would have been able to distinguish the sacred olive trees from the profane ones.[91] Surely some must have been enclosed with a wooden fence such as that implied by the title of the Lysianic speech, in which case the issue at stake would have been an entrenched area containing a *moria*, not solely a tree.[92] By way of comparison, we might recall here the sacred fig in the Eleusinion, which seems to have been surrounded by a specifically designed structure.[93] The possibility of delimitation has now been forcefully explored by Foxhall, who pronounces: 'Marked off as they were, [the *moriai*] would have been immediately identifiable to both local farmers and invading armies'.[94] That elsewhere olive trees themselves could be and were perceived as landmarks can now be seen beyond doubt in a recently published Parian deed of sale.[95] Two further suggestions, not incongruous with the one just investigated, could be put forward: (*a*) the *moriai* were distinguishable because of their age;[96] (*b*) the *moriai* were distinguishable because of their subspecies, or probably cultivar.[97] I raise these possibilities only to plead agnosticism.

his suppliant's badge. This was a bough from the sacred olive-tree (*τῆς ἱερᾶς ἐλαίας*), wreathed with white wool.' The distinction between *moriai* and other sacred olive-trees advocated by Horster 2006, 183 is based on an erroneous reading of the sources. Outside Attica, I note the case of the olive trees of a Syracusan *temenos* that were uprooted, apparently with no qualms, by Syracusans defending their beleagured city against the Athenian invaders (Thuc. 6.99.3: *τάς τε ἐλάας ἐκκόπτοντες τοῦ τεμένους*, with Hornblower 2008, 529, who notes Thucydides' silence about the impious act).

[91] A question that baffled Mommsen 1898, 78 n. 7, and in modern times Harding 1994, 149.

[92] Todd 2000, 79 with n. 5. Phot., *Bibliotheka* 489a14, identifies a *sekos* with a *moria*, but this is almost certainly an educated, albeit erroneous, guess.

[93] *IG* I^3 386 ll. 163–4: ⊢ ⊢ *ἐφ' ἱερᾶι συκε͂ι κέραμον | σκευάσαντι*, where money is disbursed for the repair of the roofing of this alleged building.

[94] Foxhall 2007, 120–1.

[95] *SEG* LIV 794 ll. 8–10: *μῆκος δὲ ἀπὸ τοῦ ὅρου εὐθε[- - - | ἕως] τῆς ἐλαίας τῆς ἐπὶ τῆς ὁδοῦ τῆς δευτέρας : ἀ|[πὸ τοῦ] ὅρου τοῦ παρὰ τὴν ἐλαίαν.*

[96] Cf. Foxhall 2007, 118. Note that a lost Aristophanic play comically branded the sacred olive on the Acropolis *πάγκυφος* (Pollux, *Onomast*. 6.163 and Hesych. s.v. *ἀστὴ ἐλαία ἡ ἐν ἀκροπόλει ἡ καλουμένη πάγκυφος διὰ χθαμαλότητα*), no doubt because it had been reduced to a pitiful aged bush.

[97] Cf. Mommsen 1898, 78 with n. 4; *EM* s.v. *μορίαν: οἱ μὲν πᾶσαν ἐλαίαν οὕτω καλοῦσιν· οἱ δὲ τὰς ἱερὰς τῷ θεῷ ὅτι δημοσίαν μοῖραν ἐκ τῶν καρπῶν ἐλάμβανον·*

Paradoxically, whereas the visibility of the *moriai* can prove a frustratingly elusive topic, their very existence and especially their proliferation might be susceptible to good interpretative attempts. The functional explanation might be the easiest: from the Acropolis to the Akademeia, and from there to the Attic hinterland, the dissemination of the olive might have followed a centrifugal pattern formulated by the polis. The aims might have been practical—increase of agricultural output—but the means might have been religious: consecration of the fruit-bearing tree. But the dissemination need not have been state-sponsored. Still in mainland Greece: thousands were the olive trees donated to monasteries or church establishments throughout the Byzantine and Ottoman period. A society that was wont to dedicate an assortment of objects, garments, precious jewellery, would not have shied away from dedicating trees.

In conclusion, it seems that, since exogenous circumstances did not allow the Athenians to stay attached to ancient religious traditions by relying on their dying *moriai*, a formula was found which did not disturb the sacred prerequisites in the course of their administrative tactics. Agrarian societies demonstrate a remarkable ability to accomplish a balance between their practical needs and their embedded religious beliefs, and the Athenians constitute an excellent example of this.[98] Despite the evidence adduced, scholars have often favoured the designation of *moriai* as state-property.[99] This is a biased misreading of Greek religion within the framework of the polis. As with the *temene*, the revenue-bearing estates, the administration of the sacred olive trees was in the hands of human agents, citizens appointed by, and accountable to, the *polis*. The nominal ownership, however, belonged to the Goddess, as most ancient writers repeatedly emphasize. More precisely, it related to Athena in her capacity as Polias, the official divine protectress of the city. In effect, we may conclude, her *moriai* along with their fences (*σηκοί*) were nothing but tiny *temene* like those attested as belonging to Athena in inscribed leases.[100] Over and over again it has been illustrated how the political community of Athens perceived and articulated itself in a nexus of myths and rituals comprising ideas like the autochthony

Ζήνων ὁ Μύνδιος, ὅτι τὸ βρῦον τῶν ἐλαίων ἐκάλουν μόρον· ἔνθεν αἱ ἀνθοῦσαι ἐλαῖαι μορίαι ἐλέγοντο, seems to imply a differentiation by subspecies.

[98] Cf. Manville 1990, 97.

[99] Thus Fernández-Galiano 1953, 139: 'Los olivos públicos (*μορίαι ἐλᾶαι*)'; Albini 1955, 46: 'olivi sacri (*μορίαι*) appartenenti allo Stato'; Vos 1981, 41: 'The moriai were the property of the State'; Rihll 1991, 107: 'All [moriai] were public property'. Todd 1993, 307–8 n. 20, 'The fruit of these moriai (sacred olives) belonged to the state', is more carefully phrased.

[100] Similar conclusion drawn by Foxhall 2007, 120: 'The *moriai*, therefore, appeared symbolically as "mini-temene" (sacred precincts) in the fields of Attica, separated from the secular world by a physical boundary.'

or the exclusive grant of agricultural knowledge by the Gods.[101] It is in this light that *moriai* should be dealt with, as a means by which one can capture some glimpses of Athenian history, from religious taboos to personal legal skirmishes, to imperialistic aspirations and economic ventures.

[101] e.g. Detienne 1973.

APPENDIX III

IG II^2 1593 Revisited

IG II^2 1593 constitutes, by any account, a most peculiar financial document. After Walbank's and Lambert's recent articles, we can safely assume that, from an epigraphical point of view, the text is a closed issue.[1] Intepretatively, however, it remains a riddle. For convenience, the format of the inscription should be briefly recalled. Names of purchasers and guarantors alternate throughout the surface of the stone. No prices or property descriptions are recorded, and in fact no other textual information can be derived from the document proper. The absence of any prices has justifiably made scholars believe that equal quantities or equally priced items of the same type underlie this list. The question, however, remains: what sort of items are really meant? The first editor of the text had suggested landholdings, and the same position was maintained by Walbank. This interpretation can quickly be dismissed. As noted, the absence of any numerical figures indicates that the items sold all fetched the same price. In terms of real property, this could only mean that all the alleged landholdings were of roughly equal size or, even more implausibly, that they were assessed at the same price regardless of their size. But there is no parallel for such a pattern, nor is there one for guarantors being provided in case of sales of realty.[2]

Walbank, however, improved his thesis, when he broached the possibility of concession of public contracts underlying this document, and it is strange that, despite these apt observations, which are roughly on the right lines, he chose the inappropriate title 'Sales of Property in Attica' for his article.[3] By public works one presumably has to understand building activity of some kind. Indeed, both Walbank and Lambert entertained the idea that 'quarried stone for a public monument' is being sold here.[4] The interpretation that the document records construction contracts fails, however, in that the relevant procedure was considered to be a lease, and the subsequent terminology was

[1] Walbank 1995 (*SEG* XLVIII 155); Lambert 2001, 57–8 n. 29; Lambert 2002*b*, 123–4 (*SEG* LII 142).

[2] Here I refer to actual sales, as we understand them today. The *Rationes Centesimarum* show a considerable variety of prices and, to a lesser extent, property types (Lambert 1997*a*, 225–33), whereas nowhere is there to be found any reference to sureties being demanded from the purchasers of the properties in question.

[3] Walbank 1995, 72.

[4] Walbank 1995, 72; Lambert 2002*b*, 124.

phrased around the word *μισθός* and its cognates, whereas *IG* II^2 1593 unmistakingly contains the word *ὠνητής* (purchaser), either complete or in some abbreviated form.[5] Nonetheless, two particular cases merit further investigation. Two Eleusinian decrees from 332/1 (*SEG* XXVIII 103) refer to the concession of quarry rights both as a lease and a sale. Similarly, in 324/3 the demesmen of the Piraeus leased out the rights from theatre tickets to four individuals who undertook some repairs. Whereas the procedure is called *μίσθωσις*, the contractors are termed *πριάμενοι* or *ὠνηταί*.[6] These operations need not trouble us further. In the first case there was only one lessee/purchaser and an open auction, whereas in the document from the Piraeus the contributions of the individual *πριάμενοι* were unequal and such a scheme cannot be shown to correspond to *IG* II^2 1593 in any way.[7]

The only other transactions designated as *ὠναί* (sales) by the Athenians included sales of mines and taxes.[8] Theoretically, most of these *ὠναί* were conferred at a more or less open auction to the highest bidder. Consequently, the prices realized would fluctuate and such a pattern would not conform to our inscription in which, as stated above, the purchasers seem to have bought equally priced items. Nevertheless, sales—i.e. leases—of mines deserve a further look. It has long been observed that the prices of the mines recorded in the *poletai* records demonstrate a suspicious uniformity, with amounts of 20 and 150 drachmas being overrepresented.[9] This regularity evidently

[5] For instance, in the famous law for the repair of the fortification walls of Athens and the Piraeus of 307/6, the phraseology consistently suggests leasing: *IG* II^2 1463 ll. 8–9: *ὃ ἂν [μ]ισθώσητ[α|ι μέρος]*; l. 29: *[ἀναγράψ]α[ι τό τε ὄνομ]ạ τοῦ μεμισθωμέν[ου] καὶ τὸ ἀργύριον*; l. 119: *κατὰ τάδε μεμίσθωται τὰ ἔρ[γα]*. Similarly in *IG* II^2 1678, where each contractor had to provide one suitable guarantor for every 1000 drachmas of the contract price, the contractor was called *μισθωτής*, not *ὠνητής*. See also *I.Oropos* 290 and 292, both documents from periods of Athenian administration of Oropos, where the construction contracts are described as leases, not sales (cf. Osborne 1985*a*, 101–7). For *μίσθωσις* as *Werkvertrag* see Thür 1984; Thür 2000, 273–4; see also the useful comments by Martini 1997, 42–5.

[6] *Agora* XIX L13; cf. Stroud 1974*b*, 296.

[7] *Agora* XIX L13, ll. 29–31; two of the *ὠνηταί* paid 1100 drachmas each, and the other two 600 and 500 drachmas respectively. For the confusion in phraseology see Coumanoudis and Gofas 1978, 304 and Behrend 1970, 86–8. It would be worth bringing into the discussion the neglected passage Dem. 53.21 (*ὁπότε γὰρ οἱ ἄνθρωποι οὗτοι ἢ ὀπώραν πρίαιντο ἢ θέρος μισθοῖντο ἐκθερίσαι ἢ ἄλλο τι τῶν περὶ γεωργίαν ἔργων ἀναιροῖντο, Ἀρεθούσιος ἦν ὁ ὠνούμενος καὶ μισθούμενος ὑπὲρ αὐτῶν*), but since it pertains to private transactions, its assessment lies, for the time being, beyond my scope of interest.

[8] Arist. [*Ath. Pol.*] 47.2, with Rhodes 1993, 552–5; Stroud 1998, 28.

[9] Hopper 1953, 231–9; Aperghis 1997–8; Shipton 1998. This is not the place to enter the discussion whether the recorded sums represent payments made per prytany, yearly, or on a one-off basis.

excludes competitive bidding.[10] The closest link seems that between fixed amounts of 150 drachmas and *ἐργάσιμα*, mines which, according to a recent interpretation, had only just been found to contain ore, but which still presented to the *πριάμενοι* a great deal of risk.[11] Could, then, sales of *ἐργάσιμα* possibly be associated with *IG* II² 1593? After all, the prosopographical data emanating from this document demonstrate a high pool of upper-class Athenians, and mine-leasing has been shown to have attracted the interest of a disproportionally high percentage of the wealthiest strata of Athenian society.[12] This tentative connection must be ruled out. There is no reason why *ἐργάσιμα* should have been written down separately from other mines and, in fact, the *poletai* records show that all types of mines were sold *en masse.*[13] The existence of these records would make the separate registration of *ἐργάσιμα* a pointless exercise. Another objection to such an interpretation is that the mines were readily recognizable entities, bearing distinctive, usually theophoric, names, whereas the units recorded in *IG* II² 1593 seem to be of a more uniform and impersonal character.[14] Finally, as has been aptly observed by Faraguna, our extant evidence of mine concessions shows that no guarantors were required from the successful bidders.[15]

Having rejected all other possibilities, I think that the key to the interpretation of *IG* II² 1593 lies in a clause to be found in the recently published *Grain-Tax Law*. This *nomos*, dated to 374/3, stipulates the sale, i.e. the farming out, of the *δωδεκάτη* (twelfth or 8⅓%) of the grain produced on the islands of Lemnos, Imbros, and Skyros.[16] The tax was assessed in kind, not cash, and was assessed in predefined portions, *μερίδες*. Each portion (*μερίς*) consisted of 100 *medimnoi* of wheat and 400 *medimnoi* of barley.[17] Each bidder had to provide two solvent guarantors per portion who were to

[10] Hall of 1990; Langdon 1994, 259; cf. Lambert 1997*a*, 266 n. 193 who is justifiably hesitant.

[11] Aperghis 1997–8, 7, 13 (but see Kakavoyiannis 2005, 199–200, for the *ἐργάσιμα* as promptly productive mines); Faraguna 2006, 147 for a critical response.

[12] Shipton 2000, 31–7.

[13] See the documents published by Langdon in *Agora* XIX.

[14] Names of mines: Crosby 1950, 193; Kakavoyiannis 1977 [1982], 184–8. A list of *horoi* designating several mines in the wider area of Laurion has been compiled by Kakavoyiannis 2005, 40–67.

[15] Faraguna 2006, 146.

[16] Ed. pr.: Stroud 1998 (*SEG* XLVIII 96 = RO 25). A decade later, the secondary bibliography has already increased considerably. Two scholars have even suggested that the object of sale is not a tax at all, but the right to transport it to Athens: see Jacab 2007; Hansen 2009. I follow here the interpretation of the ed. pr. which has been accepted, with some modifications, by the majority of scholars. Stroud 2010 offers a convenient account of the *status quaestionis*.

[17] *SEG* XLVIII 96 ll. 8–10: *ἡ δὲ μερὶς ἐκ̣[ά]||στη ἔσται πεντακόσιοι μέδιμνοι, πυρ[ῶ]||ν μὲν ἑκατόν, κριθῶν δὲ τετρακόσιοι.*

be approved by the Boule.[18] No provision prohibiting potential tax farmers (*πριάμενοι*; note the term *ὠνητής* of our text) from bidding for more than one portion was laid down.[19] In his exemplary publication of Agyrrhios' law, Stroud argued that apart from the payment of a 20-drachma lump sum for *ἐπώνια* (sales tax) and *κηρύκεια* (auctioneer's fee) per portion, the bidders did not have to pay any further money, unlike farmers of normal cash-value taxes.[20] *IG* II^2 1593 neatly fits such a backdrop. Only a statute like the one introduced by Agyrrhios could produce a record in which all sold items were of equal value, a guarantor was required for each sold item and more than one item could be bought by interested individuals. Thus, in *IG* II^2 1593 some buyers, such as the liturgists Xenokles of Sphettos and his brother Androkles, bid successfully for three shares, Aristomachos of Halai and [-]machos of Oe for at least two, whereas the rest merely for one, though, if the entire text had been preserved, we might have found more multiple purchasers.

Once it has been established that some kind of tax-farming is implied in *IG* II^2 1593, we can pursue our investigation further. It is now recognized that *IG* II^2 1593 can be chronologically placed in the era of the Lykourgan administration.[21] The fact that only one surety had to be furnished for each purchased item indicates that our list cannot be connected to the Law of Agyrrhios, which might anyway have become obsolete or replaced by another statute by the 330s–320s. The Athenian taxation system remains a notoriously slippery and unexplored theme of Athenian finances.[22] Very hesitatingly, I would point to the 2 per cent tax mentioned in the Law on

[18] *SEG* XLVIII 96 ll. 29–31: *ἐγγυητ<ὰ>ς καταστήσ[ε]||ι ὁ πριάμενος δύο κατὰ τὴν μερίδα ἀξι[ό]||χρεως, οὓς ἂν ἡ βουλὴ δοκιμάσηι.*

[19] A similar concept seems to underlie the accounts of Nemesis of Rhamnous from the mid-5th cent. (*IG* I^3 248 = ML 53 = *I.Rhamnous* 182); thus, in the year in which Demophanes was demarch, the temple funds were divided into 48 loans of 300 drachmas and 185 ones of 200 drachmas respectively. Finley 1952*a*, 285 n. 43 protested that this would result in an unacceptably high number of private debtors (48+185=233), but Pouilloux 1954, 149 rightly observed that certain individuals could borrow, i.e. they were entitled to do so, more than one loan, just as in Agyrrhios' law and *IG* II^2 1593; cf. Millett 1991, 175–6.

[20] Stroud 1998, 61, 64, 110. Incidentally, the 20 drachmas *ἐπώνεια* and *κηρύκεια* fee is reminiscent of the aforementioned 20 drachmas sum which so often occurs in the sales of mines and which has often perplexed scholars. Although I do not intend to elaborate on this point, I suspect a certain connection. For other taxes conferred at auctions see Langdon 1994, 260; Stroud 1998, 27–30.

[21] Tracy 1995, 107, ascribes *IG* II^2 1593 to the 'Cutter of *IG* II^2 354', whose activity spans the period from 337 to 324; cf. Lambert 2001, 59.

[22] See the apt remarks by Stroud 1998, 27–8 with n. 47, especially his statement that 'the time is ripe to harvest the rich evidence on taxation that has accumulated in Attic inscriptions published since the days of Boeckh and Andreades'. Stroud's remarks have generated some positive response: see e.g. Gallo 2005*b*.

the Lesser Panathenaia as an example of a tax that might have given rise to the catalogue of names under consideration, that is if that *pentekoste* was a tax in kind, which is far from certain.[23] There were, of course, numerous other duties during the Lykourgan era, and on the basis of the extant evidence even the most tentative connection between *IG* II^2 1593 and any particular tax is doomed to failure.

The prosopography proves of little help to any effort to test the validity of the claim made above. The few individuals who can be safely identified were prominent members of Athenian society, with Xenokles standing out as a close associate of Lykourgos. This does not mean that these upper-class Athenians put common interest above personal wealth; they could well have been involved in more profitable activities, like tax-farming. This receives some corroboration if we identify Androkles of Sphettos with the homonymous speaker of the 35th pseudo-Demosthenic oration.[24] On that occasion Androkles was involved in a complicated trial against three metics to whom he, along with some other individuals, had lent money so that they could export wine to Pontus and import a cargo from there to Athens. If the identification is sound, Androkles might have had an inside knowledge of the complexities of trade and could presumably have been involved in the collection of a tax in kind, such as grain. Admittedly, this hypothesis is built upon too many assumptions and should be treated with great caution. On the other hand, Lambert's remark on the participation of the Athenian elite in the financial rejuvenation of Athens during the Lykourgan administration should not be lightly dismissed as unrelated. Agyrrhios' Law, for instance, explicitly stated that the aim of the new legislation was to secure the existence of 'grain for the people in the public domain'.[25] Tax-farmers, who by means of their activities helped the Athenian polis meet this target, could always boast that they offered their country invaluable service.

There is one last obstacle to the interpretation of *IG* II^2 1593 as a list of tax-buyers and their guarantors. According to the author of the *Athenaion Politeia*, names of collectors of annual taxes along with the fetched prices were written on whitened boards which were, thereafter, delivered to the Boule. Commenting upon this passage Rhodes reaffirmed that 'the poletai

[23] For instance, Robert 1960, 197–9, thought that the *πεντηκοστὴ ἐν τῆι Νέαι* was a cash tax collected at the port(s) of Oropos (but Robert's interpretation has now been contested by Gallo 2005*b*, 179–80).

[24] Traill accepts the identification as possible (*PAA* nos. 128290 and 128295 contra *LGPN* II s.v. *Ἀνδροκλῆς* with two separate entries, i.e. nos. 56 and 58), and Lambert 2001, 57–9 (cf. idem 2002*b*, 123–4) now brings more evidence in support of this connection.

[25] *SEG* XLVIII 96 ll. 5–6: *ὅπως ἂν τῶι δήμωι σῖ[το]|ς ἦι ἐν τῶι κοινῶι*; cf. Stroud 1998, 25–6.

did not publish permanent records of tax contracts'.[26] This should not be deemed a hindrance to my analysis though. As noted elsewhere, Aristotle's account of the *temene* would have us believe that leases were not inscribed on stone and yet we have numerous lapidary records of such transactions. Why the *poletai*, or some other board of magistrates, should have issued permanent records of taxes on just one occasion, I do not know. In an excellent article on Athenian accounts Davies claimed that there exist no records of tax-collection from Classical Athens.[27] If the interpretation offered here is sound, *IG* II^2 1593 can now fill some small part of this gap.

[26] Arist. [*Ath. Pol.*] 47.2: *καὶ τὰ τέλη τὰ εἰς ἐνιαυτ[ὸ]ν πεπραμένα, ἀναγράψαντες εἰς λελευκωμένα γραμματεῖα τόν τε πριάμενον καὶ [ὅσου] ἂν πρίηται, τῇ βουλῇ παραδιδόασιν*, with Rhodes 1993, 555.

[27] Davies 1994, 210.

APPENDIX IV

The Theodoreion of the Prasieis

The name of the landholding leased out by the Prasians in *IG* II^2 2497, *Θεοδώρει[ον]* (Theodoreion), has drawn no scholarly attention. Unlike deme properties such as the Aixonian *Φελλεύς* or the Piraean *Σχοινοῦς* and *Ἁλμυρίς* which derive their names from certain topogographical features, the *Θεοδώρει[ον]* stands in another category. At first glance, it appears to bear a generic theophoric name ('gift from/to the god'),[1] like the ones attested for silver mines in the *poletai* records (e.g. *Ἀπολλωνιακόν*, *Ἀρτεμισιακόν*, *Ἀφροδισιακόν*, etc.).[2] However, all these *nomina* evoke specific deities and even the name *Ἡρωικόν* must refer to some specific (local?) hero,[3] rather than to *a hero*. This interpretation of the *Θεοδώρει[ον]* must, therefore, be rejected. This leaves us with only one possibility: the Prasian landholding must have drawn its *nomen* from a personal name.[4] Now *Θεόδωρος* is, indeed, a good Attic name and, even more significantly, a good Prasian name. I shall return to the prosopography below. First the inevitable question has to be posed: how could a private property have come under the control of a deme? There are two possible ways: (*a*) confiscation, and (*b*) donation. As seen in the section on deme property (Chapter 3, Section 2), forfeiture of private property was theoretically possible for all sorts of reasons, and in practice it did occur from time to time, although we do not know how frequently. As for donation, perhaps the best-known example is the grant of a piece of land by Leukios of Sounion to his demesmen for the construction of a new deme agora.[5] Which interpretation should be preferred here? Common sense says that, for ideological reasons, the

[1] For theophoric toponyms in general see Loewe 1980, 7–16; cf. Parker 2000, 56–7.

[2] See Kakavoyannis 1977 [1982], 187; Themelis 1992–8, 81–2. Aperghis 1997–8, 9–10, is probably wrong to connect the mine called *Λευκίππειον* with a personal name, but right to suggest so for the mines *Θεόγνειον* and *Θεοδόσειον*. Likewise, Kakavoyiannis 2005, 59–62, derives the name of the mine *Εὐτέλειον* (*SEG* LIV 244) from the personal name *Εὐτέλης*, and attributes the mine called *Καλλαίσχ*<*ρ*>*ειον* (*SEG* LIV 246) to the Siphnian entrepreneur *Κάλλαισχρος*.

[3] Perhaps the eponymous hero of the local deme? Cf., in this sense, the mine called *Ἀρχηγέτειον* (*Agora* XIX P5 l. 72), presumably named after the Hero Archegetes of Besa.

[4] For similarly formed property names see, for instance, *Agora* XIX P5 ll. 61: *ἐπ[ὶ] Λαυρείωι Θεογνίδειον*; 63–4: *ἐν Νάπει Πυρρίει | ον*. See also n. 2 above.

[5] *IG* II^2 1180 (cf. Stanton 1996, 350–2).

name of an estate previously held by a private individual and subsequently confiscated by a public association should change. However, common sense is not always a reliable guide: Athens' ex-Royal Garden, for example, was renamed the National Garden by the Greek Republic after the abolition of the monarchy, but, even nowadays, there are plenty of people who keep calling it by its previous name. These are no uncompromising monarchists trying to make some political statement, just common people who find it difficult to eradicate old habits. But for the purposes of our discussion one has to keep in mind that, regardless of the result, the official authority did attempt to alter the old name.

I return to the prosopography now. The second volume of the *Lexicon of Greek Personal Names* has 309 entries under the name *Θεόδωρος*, two of which belong definitely, and one possibly, to Prasians.[6] The first was Secretary of the Boule at some point in the second half of the fifth century and, though nothing else is known about him, his office indicates that he was a man of prominence.[7] The second acts as guarantor for the lease of a sacred property undertaken by an Automenes, son of Andromenes in 343/2. The father of this *Θεόδωρος* is called *Κίρων* and features, amongst generally prominent Athenians, in a curse tablet. Now, the lessee of the *Θεοδώρει[ον]* is called *Κιρρίας*, a Prasian too and a member of a very prominent family,[8] and given the apparent etymological interconnection between the names *Κίρων* and *Κιρρίας* and especially the extreme rarity of Attic names deriving from the root *Κιρ(ρ)*-, there are grounds for believing that all these Prasians, *Κίρων*, *Θεόδωρος*, and *Κιρρίας* belonged to the same family.[9] If so and if the *Θεοδώρει[ον]* was indeed named after the Prasian *Θεόδωρος*, we have here an interesting instance wherein the lessee rents from the deme a landholding previously belonging to his family. Fascinatingly, this is not entirely unprecedented in Attica. One, and possibly two, of the properties sold by the deme Poros (?) in the *Rationes Centesimarum*, bore the name *Χαρινίδαι* and were sold to two individuals called *[Χαιρ]ών<υ>μος* and *Χαιρέδημος* respectively, who were possibly brothers, to judge from the common patronym *Χάρης*.[10]

6 *LGPN* II s.v. *Θεόδωρος* nos. 223–5.

7 *LGPN* II s.v. no. 223, known from *IG* I^3 31 l. 1: *[Θ]εόδορος Πρασιεὺς ἐγραμμάτευε*, probably from the late 430s to early 420s (see Jameson 2000–3, 27–8). Prominence of the Secretaries of the Boule: Arist. [*Ath. Pol.*] 54.3, with Rhodes 1972, 134, and 1993, 599–603; now confirmed by statistical analysis: Taylor 2007, 337–9.

8 *APF* no. 12132 (with the stemma of the family).

9 Cf. Walbank 1983*a*, 125. Bechtel 1897, 98–9, was the first to suggest the possible etymological connection between the two names, even if only to dismiss it (though not wholeheartedly); cf., however, Frisk 1960, s.v. *κίρα* and *κιρρός*, and Chantraine 1999, s.v. *κιρρός* and *κίρων*, both of whom accept the possibility of geminate *rhos* connecting all these words. Beekes 2010, s.vv. *κιρρός* and *κίρων* appears agnostic.

10 *Rationes Centesimarum* F7A. 3–8: *[ἕτερ]ọ[ν] χ̣[ωρί]ọν ἐν Πọ́[ρωι τὸ | Χαρι]νị́δ [αι?] κα<λ>ούμε[νον | ὠνη Χαιρ]ών<υ?>μος Χάρητος [- - -] | ἕτερον χωρίον ἐν*

The etymological link between the name of the sold properties and those of the buyers did not escape the sharp eye of Lambert, even though he refrained from risking any speculations.[11] Two interpretations are at hand here, with regard to both the *Θεοδώρει[ον]* and the *Χαρινίδαι*. If the landholdings had been confiscated, then we may envisage an attempt on the part of members of the families of the initial owners to resume control of their patrimonial properties. If, on the other hand, the landholdings had been donated, then we encounter the paradox whereby the donators or their descendants tried to maintain some control over their ex-properties. Dignas has now splendidly demonstrated that Hellenistic Caria and particularly the area of Mylasa saw the massive phenomenon whereby private landholders transferred their estates to the local deities and, subsequently, rented them from the temple authorities. According to her interpretation, the scheme was instigated by Mylasa in order to meet the need for sufficient income for cultic expenditure in a way that would be economically acceptable to private individuals as well.[12] Although nothing implies that the *Θεοδώρει[ον]* was a sacred estate, Dignas's main line of argument might apply, with some modification, to the Prasian estate. It has long been observed that renting deme property was, to some extent, a kind of semi-liturgy. In this light, it makes perfect sense to interpret the leasing of the *Θεοδώρει[ον]* by Kirrias as a service of the renter to his deme, all the more so since Kirrias came from a distinguished Athenian family with a record of liturgical contributions.

Πόρ̣[ωι | τὸ] Χ̲α̣ρ̲ι̲ν̲ίδαι καλούμεν[ον | ὠ]ν̲η̲ Χ̲α̲ι̲ρ̲έ̲δημος Χάρητος [- - -] (cf. Lambert 1997*a*, 177–8).

[11] Lambert 1997*a*, 206.

[12] Dignas 2000, and 2002, 95–106.

APPENDIX V

The *Genos* of the Pyrrhakidai

The *Πυρρακίδαι* (Pyrrhakidai) are attested relatively early, towards the end of the fifth century. Two religious monuments from Delos bear the inscriptions *Τριτοπάτωρ Πυρρακιδῶν Αἰγιλιῶν* (Tritopator of the Pyrrhakidai of the Aigilieis) and *Νύμφαι Πυρρακιδῶν* (Nymphs of the Pyrrhakidai) respectively.[1] On the basis of the lettering, the first editor dated both texts to *c.*400 and, as Parker has pointed out, this would dissuade us from classifying the *genos* among the Attic ones because Delos acquired her independence, with a little help from Sparta, in approximately 403.[2] But the lettering criterion is not compelling, as nothing excludes the possibility that the monuments were erected at the very end of the period of Athenian control of the island within the fifth century. By contrast, the demotic *Αἰγιλιῶν* is decisive. Humphreys *apud* Parker raised the possibility of the demotic being a later amendment of the second century, when the Pyrrhakidai are securely attested to be one of the Athenian *gene* that sent Pythaists to the Delphic oracle.[3] In the same century the *genos* had still close connections with the island of Apollo, as attested by a landholding named after them.[4] Nothing should prompt, however, such far-fetched assumptions.

Πύρρακος (Pyrrhakos), the eponymous hero of the *genos*, is known to us from an entry in the *Lexicon* of Hesychius.[5] Nonetheless, scholars have not hitherto examined Attic prosopography, a venture which could prove fruitful. The name *Πύρρακος* is attested in Attica only three times, all in the Classical period.[6] An *Ἀχ[αρνεύς]* or *Ἀχ[ερδούσιος]* occurs in a naval catalogue of the late fifth century.[7] Another *Πύρρακος* was the father of *Εὐκολίων Ἀναγυράσιος*, councillor in 367/6.[8] The former, therefore, must have flourished towards the end of the fifth/beginning of the fourth century. Finally, and more interestingly, a *Πύρρακος Αἰγιλιεύς* was owner of a property at

[1] *I.Délos* 66, and *I.Délos* 67.

[2] Date of the inscribed monuments: Roussel 1929, 174; cf. Parker 1996, 308. Liberation of Delos: RO 3.

[3] Parker 1996, 308; *FD* III (2) 7; 8; 13; 10.

[4] *χωρίον Πυρρακιδῶν*: *I.Délos* 1416B ll. 57–63 (see also Chapter 4, Section 2.iii).

[5] Hesych. s.v. *Πύρρακος· ἥρως κατ' Ἐρυσίχθονα γεγονώς*.

[6] See *LGPN* II s.v. *Πύρρακος*.

[7] *IG* I^3 1032 l. 176, where *Πυρράκος*, instead of *Πύρρακος*, has been printed, an extremely rare case of misaccentuation in the corpus.

[8] *Agora* XV 14 l. 18.

Sounion in the same year.[9] But this combination of name and demotic can hardly be a coincidence given the rarity of the name; rather it confirms the special ties between the *genos* and the small Attic deme, as well as the genuineness of the Attic origin of the *genos*. Note also the demotic of the second *Πύρρακος*; according to the latest scholarly view, *Αἰγιλία* (Aigilia) must be placed at Thorai, very close to modern Vari, the securely identified site of the ancient deme *Ἀναγυροῦς*.[10]

Some time ago, Lambert argued that the Pyrrhakidai might have been a phratry and the *Αἰγιλιεῖς* (Aigilieis) of the Delian inscription a sub-group of the phratry, similarly to the way in which the *Δεκελειεῖς* of the so-called Demotionidai decree were a sub-group of the phratry of the *Δημοτιωνίδαι*.[11] But this is based on his own interpretation of the decree, which is unprovable. Besides, there is no reason to dismiss the identification of the Pyrrhakidai of the Delphic Pythais documents as a *genos*. They are registered among other known *gene*,[12] while Attic associations of a different status stand on their own. It seems more prudent to accept a special relation of the Pyrrhakidai with the deme Aigilia in the fashion of the Salaminioi from Sounion. Whether the *Πυρρακίδαι Αἰγιλιῶν* were a branch of a wider *genos* cannot be ascertained or rejected, for we have seen elsewhere how the separate branches of the Salaminioi failed to appear in the honorific decree *IG* II^2 1234.[13]

A last remark may strengthen my argument. A *Πύρρακος* is attested in a fragmentary inscription from Delos of 410/9, actually an account of the Athenian Amphiktyones who seem to have collected from this individual a rather trivial sum of 25+ drachmas.[14] It is not certain whether this *Πύρρακος* was an Athenian or a Delian, a debtor or a lessee.[15] There is a good possibility, however, that he was an Athenian, maybe a member of the *genos* in question, perhaps acting on its behalf. This would concur with the strong Delian affiliations of the *genos*, affiliations which outlived the turbulent political history of the sacred island, at least down to the mid-second century.

[9] *Agora* XIX P5 l. 80.

[10] Traill 1986, 144–8.

[11] Lambert 1993, 218, 368; idem 1997*b*, 104.

[12] See in particular Karila-Cohen 2005, 80–1.

[13] The branch theory was first put forward by Bourriot 1976, 1168.

[14] *IG* I^3 1460 l. 46: [. . . ^{7} . . . *π*]*ạρὰ Πυρράκο ΔΔΠ̣*. The text can also be found in Chankowski 2008, 403–4, no. 5, who in her 'Prosopographical Index' includes Pyrrhakos amongst the Delians and hesitantly considers him to be a 'débiteur'.

[15] Note, however, that he has been included in *LGPN* I, not in the Attic volume.

APPENDIX VI

The Split of the Salaminioi and the Eponymous Archon Phanomachos

The archon Phanomachos, whose name occurs in the preamble of the Hellenistic arbitration of the Salaminioi, has been considered, ever since the editio princeps, as the eponymous archon of Athens, rather than the archon of the *genos*, and probably for good reason.[1] Otherwise unattested, Phanomachos had long floated throughout the third century,[2] before being placed in the year 265/4 of the notorious Athenian archontic list for lack of better candidates, a date ostensibly strengthened by the lettering criterion.[3] Now, under any other circumstances the date might have passed uncontested. However, 265/4 was not a random year; it fell well within the Chremonidean War, or, on another view, it marked its outbreak.[4] Of course, for the advocates of the latter view Phanomachos could not belong to 265/4, since this slot is reserved for the archon Peithidemos, but, on the other hand, they have never bothered probing into the issue of dating Phanomachos. Recently, however, Osborne, *faute de mieux*, reassigned Phanomachos to the year 263/2.[5] This replacement might appear to have certain merits, even though ones probably not fully realized by its proponent, but, unfortunately, things are far from clear.

I must clearly state my case in advance. From a historical perspective, to place Phanomachos in 265/4, 263/2, or any other year during the Chremonidean War presents major difficulties, for how likely is it that the two *gene* would have embarked on an arbitration concerning their landed assets, while the war was still raging? In his excellent recent monograph Oliver

[1] Ferguson 1938, 69; Lambert 1997*b*, 99, and 1999*b*, 119.

[2] See e.g. Meritt 1981, 89.

[3] 265/4: Osborne 1989, 229–30; accepted hesitantly by Walbank in *Agora* XIX L4b; see also Lambert 1997*b*, 89 n. 3. Lettering: Tracy 1988, 305 and now idem 2003*a*, 86.

[4] The chronology of the Chremonidean War constitutes one of the most vexed questions of Athenian chronology. 268/7 (archon Peithidemos) is the date favoured for its inception by Heinen 1972, 213; Bouraselis 1982, 158; Osborne 1989, 216; Steinhauer 1995, 140–1; Habicht 1997, 142–5; Tracy 2003*a*, 15 with n. 2. The placement of Peithidemos in 265/4, advocated by Meritt (e.g. Meritt 1981), is still favoured, albeit hesitatingly, by Woodhead in *Agora* XVI, pp. 275–6; Dreyer 1999, 374 and *passim*. For a recent conspectus see O'Neil 2008, 68–71. Note, however, that Byrne 2006–7, 175–9, has now dated Peithidemos to 269/8.

[5] Osborne 2000, 519–20 n. 42.

convicingly showed that the Attic countryside was particularly affected during the conflict.[6] The *opinio communis* is that Sounion, unlike Rhamnous, was constantly under Macedonian occupation from 287 down to 229.[7] The disputed property lay in the area of Sounion, within the grip of Macedonian troops garrisoned there. The decree recording the arbitration was found in the Agora and was certainly set up in the Eurysakeion. The findspot along with the inscription's content presupposes open access to Sounion and is incongruent with a war situation. Now, it is generally assumed that the Chremonidean War seriously interrupted the effort of cultic rejuvenation that started after Athens' independence of 287/6.[8] What is more, there is internal evidence in our arbitration that the structure of the Salaminioi had been severely affected by the political situation; the Salaminioi of Sounion and the Salaminioi from the Seven Tribes are portrayed as distinct *gene*, rather than as two branches of the same association. This has been implicitly understood to be the inevitable result of a gradual separation between the two Classical branches. But if the geographical distance had not prevented the two branches from cooperating over a long period—and it is reasonably assumed that the Salaminioi had already been a bicellular organization by the time of the Cleisthenic reforms—one should seek a more palpable reason to explain the eventual split. In my view, the cause is none other than the political exigencies of the early Hellenistic period. The idea is not new; it was first expressed by Ferguson in his masterly editio princeps, but, surprisingly, it has received no attention whatsoever.[9] For a large part of the third century Sounion was under Macedonian domination, but then again so was Athens.[10] It was probably only during the Chremonidean War that the two branches would have been *de facto* hindered from jointly performing their ancient rites. Surely, such a split would have affected their whole structure and regular operation. We could envisage a situation whereby the Sounian branch kept performing the gentilician rites in the Herakleion of Porthmos, whereas the Seven Tribes branch would use the Eurysakeion. Such a situation might have continued for as long as the Chremonidean War lasted. By the

[6] Oliver 2007, 127–31 ('The territory of Attica was at the heart of the conflict').

[7] Lauter 1988, 32–3; Lohmann 1993, 250; Habicht 1997, 130; Goette 2000, 55; Habicht 2003, 52–3; Goette 2003, 160 (who asserts Macedonian occupation of Sounion only for the duration of the Chremonidean War); Oliver 2007, 148; O'Neil 2008, 74.

[8] See especially Mikalson 1998, 105–36; cf. Mari 2003, 90–1. It is often maintained that Piraeus, its cultic nexus included, was hit particularly hard by Macedonian domination (Taylor 1997, 230–1, offers a synopsis though she eventually downplays the effects of Macedonian control); Sounion might have been affected in a similar fashion.

[9] Ferguson 1938, 74.

[10] But as Goette 2003, 160 has shown, and Oliver 2007, 120 accepts, Sounion was in Athenian hands at least in 298/7.

end of the War the split would have been crystallized and the two branches would have counted as separate *gene*. This reconstruction opens various possibilities: first, that Sounion was firmly in Athenian hands when the arbitration was inscribed, an unlikely scenario. Second, that the archon Phanomachos was not actually the eponymous archon of Athens, but rather the main magistrate of the *genos*. Third, and in my opinion more likely, that the eponymous archon Phanomachos has been misplaced in 265/4. A cursory look at the archontic list would suffice to demonstrate that such a placement is only tenable somewhere in the late 260s or in the 250s.

To recapitulate. For contextual reasons, it seems highly unlikely that the dispute between the two *gene* was resolved during the Chremonidean War. The settlement must have happened at a time when communication between the urban centre of Athens and Sounion was open, but I concede my inability to fix this point chronologically on any firm grounds. The lettering would allow any year between 286/5 and *c.*239.[11] For reasons I highlighted above, the end of the Chremonidean War should probably be a *terminus post*, rather than *ante*, *quem*.[12] At any rate, it seems prudent to remove the archon Phanomachos from the 265/4 (or 263/2) slot which has been assigned to him by those scholars who place the Chremonidean War between 268/7 and 263/2. The onus of finding a new location lies with them.[13]

[11] Thus Tracy 1988, 304 and, mainly, idem 2003*a*, 80–98, esp. 86, where he assigns the Hellenistic arbitration to the Cutter of Agora I 3238 and 4169, providing a vague date of *c.*240 for archon Phanomachos (cf. idem 2003*a*, 168).

[12] Only for the sake of bringing the arbitration in line with my interpretation of it as regulating distress caused by the Chremonidean War, I would favour, extremely hesitantly, the year 261/0, which has been left unassigned by Tracy 2003*a*, 167, but not by Osborne 2000, 515 (archon Arrheneides).

[13] Osborne 2009, has now produced an updated list of 3rd-cent. archons, in which Phanomachos has been assigned a new slot in 242/1 BC. In view of my analysis above (of which Osborne, for obvious reasons of accessibility, could not have been aware), this relocation is an improvement, although it is still based on the principle of 'vacancies' (see in particular Osborne 2009, 97) rather than on any historical considerations. It goes without saying that my suspicions have been confirmed, albeit in an indirect way.

APPENDIX VII

Catalogue of Lessees and Guarantors of Polis-controlled *Temene*

General remarks

In the most recent study devoted to the investigation of the financial facet of leases of 'public land' (*sic*), Shipton made the rather astonishing claim that the vast majority of entrepreneurs involved in land transactions—either directly, through renting, or by implication, by providing sureties—consisted of nonentities.[1] Her deductions appear all the more important for two reasons: firstly, because they oppose the previously held opinion that the liturgical class was heavily involved in such operations,[2] and, secondly, because they contrast with the pattern emanating from Shipton's own analysis of mine leases whereby wealthy Athenians were indeed wholeheartedly devoted to mine exploitation. Shipton's attempt at quantification certainly had great potential, and yet it largely failed due to certain flawed preconceptions. In her chapter 'Lenders in the Horoi', she demonstrated commendable caution by enlarging her 'Index of Prominence' to allow for the frequent absence of patronyms in the hypothecation *horoi*.[3] But what is inherently problematic in the formulaic texts of the lending *horoi* is equally, albeit incidentally, an obstacle with regard to the series of leases of sacred lands. In other words, the condition of most of the relevant stelae is so fragmentary that quite often we lack the name, the patronym, the demotic (or residence in the case of metics), or some combination thereof, of the lessee/guarantor of a given transaction. Shipton, however, chose to treat individuals lacking full prosopographical attributes as if they were fully documented, with the self-evident—and deceptive—result that they were all awarded 'nonentities stars', that is F status in accordance with the author's jargon. To take just one example at random: what possible information could we gain from the name of the lessee Ἡρακλείδης (no. 29), since it lacks other attributes? Conversely, only individuals such as Ξενοκράτης Γνιφωνίδου Μαραθώνιο[ς] (no. 61), who is otherwise unattested, can be securely classified as nonentities. As if this was not enough, Shipton classified as upstarts

[1] Shipton 2000, 39–49.

[2] Osborne 1985*a*, 54–6; 1988; Foxhall 1992, 157.

[3] Shipton 2000, 20: 'The horoi records very rarely give patronyms and so identification is much less certain . . .'.

lessees and guarantors who did meet the very criteria posed by her that would have allowed them to avoid the doom of F-status. The result was one where statistical analysis distorted the actual picture and thus an excellent opportunity was lost.

Thus, given that our statistical sample is at best paltry, a quantitative analysis can only be useful if accompanied by a reassessment of the prosopographical data which will take account of various qualifying sociopolitical factors. A rudimentary prosopographical analysis of those involved in leases conferred by the central polis-authorities has already been attempted by Walbank. Working before the appearance of the *Lexicon of Greek Personal Names* and the *Persons of Ancient Athens*, he raised a series of prosopographical points, some of which can be easily dismissed as sheer speculation.[4] I have not commented upon such observations, but the interested reader should consult Walbank's articles. But some other of his remarks have a sound basis and should not have been passed over so lightly by Shipton. I have merely commented below upon some of the identifications brought forward by Walbank by adding some further suggestions and by rejecting those that seem feeble on the basis of our evidence. Also included in the following catalogue are the four lessees attested in the Eleusinian records *I. Eleusis* 177 (*IG* II^2 1672). The prosopographical tabulation has been formed on the blueprint of Lambert's similar catalogue of people attested in *Rationes Centesimarum*.[5] I have endorsed the Index of Prominence introduced by Shipton with the following modifications: (i) in classes C and D I have included lessees/guarantors whose ascendants/descendants too were active in one or more areas of activity apart from land leasing; (ii) I have included neither in the database nor in the statistical analysis individuals whose names are too defective to allow even the most speculative restorations; (iii) letters followed by question marks designate attributions which are possible, but not certain. Thus the index of prominence is built on the following principles:

Class A: liturgists.

Class B: ascendants/descendants of liturgists.

Class C: personal or family involvement in several areas of activity apart from leasing.

Class D: personal or family involvement in one area of activity apart from leasing.

Class E: several personal or family activities in leasing only.

Class F: one activity in leasing only.

[4] For example, identifying a priori individuals of few attributes with the most famous homonymous Athenians or metics often builds a circular argument.

[5] Lambert 1997*a*, 149–82.

1. *Αἰσχίνη[ς . . . .⁷ . . .]νίδου Πειραιεύς*. *Agora* XIX L9, ll. 79–80.
LGPN II, *Αἰσχίνης* (68) = *PAA* 115012.
Lessee of an orchard. [*Αἰσχρω*ᵛ]*νίδου* has been suggested as the patronym (Walbank 1983*b*, 190 with n. 63), but this is far from certain. Restorations which do not assume the existence of a vacant space at the end of line 79 include [*Εὐτελιω*]*νίδου*, [*Ἀνθεμιω*]*νίδου*, [*Αἰσιμιω*]*νίδου*, [*Ἀριστιω*]*νίδου*; none of them is attested for Piraeus. Probably a vacant space did exist after all, but the possible restorations are so numerous that the patronym is best left unrestored and the lessee unidentified.[6] F.

2. *Αἰσχύλος Ἱππίσκου Παιονίδης*. *I.Eleusis* 177, l. 376.
LGPN II, *Αἰσχύλος* (36) = *PAA* 116205.
Lessee of an Eleusinian landholding (cf. Kirchner in the commentary of *IG* II² 1672; Davies in *APF*, pp. 7–8), not an *ἐπιμελητὴς τῶν μυστηρίων*. Well-known trierarch and choregos, member of a prominent Athenian family treated in *APF* 450. A.

3. [. . . . .⁹ . . . .]ς *Ἀλεξίου ἐξ Ο*[*ἴ*(*ου*)]. *Agora* XIX L6, ll. 148–9.
Father: *LGPN* II, *Ἀλεξίας* (5) = *PAA* 120225.
Lessee of a *temenos* belonging to Zeus Olympios. The patronym is very rare (6 entries in *LGPN* II), and this in conjunction with the demotic makes it almost certain that the elusive lessee was a member of a well-known trierarchic family treated in *APF*. In fact, one may even restore the etymologically akin [*Ἀλέξανδρο*]ς, since it fits the lacuna perfectly. If so, the lessee would be the Alexandros mentioned by Hypereides in his speech *In Defence of Euxenippos* 12, as a prosecutor (cf. Whitehead 2000, 193–5). At any rate, the lessee should be awarded B status.

4. *Ἀντίμ*[*α*]*χο*[*ς*]. *Agora* XIX L6, l. 166.
LGPN II, *Ἀντίμαχος* (16); (not in *PAA*?)
Lessee of a property belonging to Artemis Brauronia. The name is too common to allow identification. F.

5. *Ἀπήμων Ἀδε*[. . . . . . ¹⁵ . . . .] *ἰσοτ*(*ελὴς*): *ἐμ Πειραιεῖ ο*[*ἰκῶν*]. *Agora* XIX L6, ll. 133–4.
LGPN II, *Ἀπήμων* (8) = *PAA* 140585.
Lessee of a property. A metic of isotelic status. The restoration of the patronym would be either *Ἀδε*[*ιμάντου*] or, less likely, *Ἀδε*[*ίστου*]. Otherwise unknown. F.

6. [*Ἀ*]*ρισταγόρας Ἀριστοδήμ*[*ου . . . .⁷ . . .*] *ἐν Κυδαθηναίωι οἰκῶν*. *Agora* XIX L6, ll. 6–7.
LGPN II, *Ἀρισταγόρας* (22) = *PAA* 163340.

[6] I only note that an *Αἰσχίνης* (no further qualifications) is recorded in the 4th-cent. epitaph *IG* II² 11352 from a family grave found at Piraeus.

Lessee of a house in Kydathenaion. Otherwise unknown. The only prominent foreign resident in Attica who could be chronologically connected is the famous actor and politician Aristodemos of Metapontion who often mediated for the Athenians in their negotiations with Philip (*FRA* 3711 = Stephanis 1988, no. 332). On this assumption our Aristagoras might have been Aristodemos' son. F?

7. *Ἀρ̣[ίστιππος] Ἡγησίππου ἐκ Κερ̣(αμέων)*. *Agora* XIX L9, ll. 82–3.
Father: *LGPN* II, *Ἡγήσιππος* (8) = *PAA* 166085.
Lessee of a swamp near Mounichia. The patronym is not rare, but not very common either (21 entries in *LGPN* II). Thus, *Ἡγήσιππος* can almost certainly be identified with the homonymous individual of the same deme, whose son Hegemon is attested as the ex-owner of a liberated slave (*IG* II^2 1567, ll. 15–16: *Λῦσις : ἐμ Πει : οἰκ : ἀποφυγὼν | Ἡγήμονα Ἡγησίππου : ἐκ Κερ : φιά : στα : H*). Note that Piraeus as the residence of the manumitted slave certainly reflects the locality of his master's activities, which in turn ties in well with the same family's engagement in leasing in the area of Piraeus. Since *Agora* XIX L9 dates to *c.*338–326 and the Attic Manumissions seem to postdate 330 (Lewis 1959*a*, 236–7), there is no way of establishing their exact chronological interconnection, so it suffices to keep in mind the Piraean interests of this family. At all events, it is very likely that the family descended from *Ἡγησίστρατος Ἡγησίλεω ἐκ Κερ(αμέων)*, who features in the *diadikasia*-document *SEG* XXXII 171 (cf. Walbank 1983*b*, 190). The family appears to belong to the upper echelons of Athenian society (*APF*, p. 210). Class B.

8. *Ἀριστίων Ἀρ[- - -]*. *Agora* XIX L6, ll. 107–8.
LGPN II, *Ἀριστίων* (15) = *PAA* 166420.
Guarantor of a lease undertaken by Theodotos. Identification is unattainable. F.

9. *Ἀριστόδημος Ἀριστοκλέους Οἰ[ν]αῖ(ος)*. *Agora* XIX L6, ll. 120–1; L9, ll. 40–1, 45–6.
LGPN II, *Ἀριστόδημος* (52) = *PAA* 169050.
Renter of 3 properties, the first of which is in Mesokomai. He is the individual who features by far the most frequently in our documents, and the only one who almost certainly appears in two different sets of leases. His father was Superintendent of the Docks, an office which *Ἀριστόδημος* himself held at a later age (*IG* II^2 1623, l. 5). D.

10. *Ἀριστοκλ[είδης] Λυσανίου Προβαλί(σιος)*. *Agora* XIX L9, ll. 52–3.
LGPN II, *Ἀριστοκλείδης* (13) = *PAA* 169840.
Lessee. His identification with the father of the councillors of *c.*330 *Λυσανίας* and *Κλεομήδης* (*Agora* XV 47, ll. 38–9) seems very possible (thus now Traill in *PAA* 169835). In general the renter's family seems to have been active at various levels of the administration. On the basis of the patronym Wallbank 1983*b*, 188 plausibly suggested that the renter's brother was *Ἀντικράτης*

Λυσανίου Προβαλίσιος, *thesmothetes* in 329/8 (*IG* II^2 2836) and *hieropoios* in the only attested dedication of the Marathonian Tetrapolis (*IG* II^2 2933). It is noteworthy that in the latter inscription the archon of the religious association of the Tetrapolis was also called *Λυσανίας*. We know that the cultic centre of the Marathonian Tetrapolis was indeed a Dionysion (Parker 1996, 332–1; Lambert 2000*a*, 69 on the unpublished *SEG* XLVIII 129). Divine epithets with the prefix *Λυσι-* are often attributed to Apollo, who in the context of the Tetrapolis is very closely associated with Dionysus (Lambert 2000*a*, 53–4 on *SEG* L 168; Lambert 2000*b*, 72). I therefore suggest that the agglomeration of *Λυσι-* names attested for people connected directly or indirectly to the Marathonian Tetrapolis is reminiscent of the centrality of the cults of Apollo and Dionysos to this particular cultic group. C.

11. [*Ἀριστοκλῆς*?] *Ἀριστοκλέους Ἁμα̣(ξαντεύς)*. *Agora* XIX L9, l. 26.
Father: *LGPN* II, *Ἀριστοκλῆς* (41) = *PAA* 170155.
Guarantor. Hamaxanteia was a small-size deme (bouleutic quota 2), so the restoration of the name suggested by Walbank 1983*b*, 186 is very likely to be correct. In this view our guarantor was son of a Treasurer of the Sacred Monies in 398/7 and perhaps himself a trierarch (cf. *APF*, p. 55). B.

12. *Ἀριστομένης Εὐπο*[- - -]. *Agora* XIX L9, l. 81.
LGPN II, *Ἀριστομένης* (8) = *PAA* 173120.
Guarantor for a lease of an orchard. The patronym has been tentatively restored as *Εὐπό*[*λιδος*], but *Εὐπο*[*λέμου*] is equally possible (cf. Walbank 1983*b*, 190). Unidentified. F.

13. *Ἀρρε̣*[*νείδης*] *Χαρικλέους Παιανι(εύς)*. *Agora* XIX L10 ll. 42–3.
LGPN II, *Ἀρρενείδης* (4) = *PAA* 204050.
Lessee of a swamp. General, trierarch, entrepreneur, and member of the long-lived propertied family treated in *APF* 2254. Note that in *I.Eleusis* 177, l. 258 he is contracted with the haulage of earth to the Eleusinian shrine. A.

14. *Ἀρ̣*[*χέδη*]*μος Ἀρχεδήμο*[*υ*] *Αὐρί(δης)*. *Agora* XIX L6, ll. 10–11.
LGPN II, *Ἀρχέδημος* (18) = *PAA* 209065.
Guarantor for the lease of a house in Kydathenaion. Member of a liturgical family (*APF* 2321). B.

15. [. . .]*ιτο̣*[*ς*] [*Α*]*ὐτολ̣ύ̣κ̣ου Π*[-]. *Agora* XIX L6, l. 83.
Father: *LGPN* II, *Αὐτόλυκος* (9) = *PAA* 239840.
Guarantor. Unidentified. F.

16. *Αὐτομένης Ἀνδρο*[*μ*]*ένους Ε̣*[ ]. *Agora* XIX L6, ll. 11–12.
LGPN II, *Αὐτομένης* (7) = *PAA* 241060.
Lessee of a house in Kydathenaion. Both name and patronym are fairly unusual, but identification is impossible. F.

17. *Γνίφω*[*ν*]. *Agora* XIX L14, l. 4.
LGPN II, *Γνίφων* (4) = *PAA* 279800.

Lessee of a *temenos*? As acknowledged by Walbank 1984, 365, the name could well be *Γνιφω[νίδης]*. Both names, though rare, are attested in the late fourth century (cf. no. 18). F.

18. *Γνίφων Προκλέο[υς]*. *Agora* XIX L10, l. 44.
LGPN II, *Γνίφων* (3) = *PAA* 279820.
Guarantor for the lease of a swamp. Son of *Προκλῆς Γνίφωνος* (the demotic is uncertain; cf. Walbank 1983*b*, 199), whose name is inscribed under a relief of three cavalrymen (*IG* II^2 12523). The inscription is not sepulchral, but either a dedication by Prokles or part of a decree passed in his honour, and it has reasonably been inferred that Prokles was either a phylarch or a hipparch and hence a member of the census class of *hippeis* (Lawton 1995, 157 no. B186 with the earlier bibliography). D.

19. [....⁷...]*ạτος Δημέου Χολαρ(γεύς)*. *Agora* XIX L6, ll. 76–7.
Father: *LGPN* II, *Δημέας* (27) = *PAA* 306913.
Guarantor in a lease of a property. His father is possibly the same as Demeas whose sepulchral stele has been found in Piraeus (*IG* II^2 7772, *Δημέα[ς] | Δημοκλέου[ς] | Χολαργεύ[ς]*). F.

20. *Διονυσόδωρ[ος]*. *Agora* XIX L6, ll. 41–2.
LGPN II, *Διονυσόδωρος* (3) = *PAA* 360500.
Guarantor of the lease of a *temenos* at Thria. The name is too common to allow identification. F.

21. [*Διο*]*ṿυσόδω[ρος]*. *Agora* XIX L6, ll. 47–8.
LGPN II, *Διονυσόδωρος* (4) = *PAA* 360505.
Lessee. Unidentified. F.

22. [- - -] *Διονυσοδώρ[ου]*. *Agora* XIX L14, l. 5.
LGPN II, *Διονυσόδωρος* (7) = *PAA* 360430.
Patronym of a guarantor (?). Unidentified. F.

23. *Ἐργόφιλος Φίλω[νος ....⁸....]υλῆσι οἰκ(ῶν)*. *Agora* XIX L6, ll. 75–6.
LGPN II, *Ἐργόφιλος* (13) = *PAA* 401178.
Metic, lessee of a house consecrated to Zeus Olympios. Place of residence could be either [*Ἀγρ*]*υλῆσι* or [*Ἀγκ*]*υλῆσι*. Note that both places are located around Ardettos, therefore close to the shrine of Zeus Olympios, whose house Ergophilos rents; it is likely that Ergophilos is looking for an abode. On the basis of the restoration [*Ἀγρ*]*υλῆσι* Walbank 1983*a*, 128 tentatively identified enfranchised descendants of our metic, such as *LGPN* II, *Φίλων* (59) and (60), but this is by no means certain. In fact, even the patronym could be restored differently, e.g. *Φιλω[νίδου]* (thus Traill in *PAA* 401178 on unspecified authority), *Φιλω[τάδου]*, *Φιλώ[του]*, etc. Amongst non-Athenian residents in Attica the name *Ἐργόφιλος* occurs only once, borne by a slave serving as an oarsman in the late fifth century (*IG* I^3 1032, l. 450; cf. *FRA* 7601). In fact, the name with its obvious labour connotations might well

belong to a descendant of a liberated slave (for *Ἐργόφιλος* as a typical *Sklavenwunschname*, see Fragiadakis 1986, 47–50). F.

24. *Ἑστιαῖος Λυ*[- - -]. *Agora* XIX L14, l. 3.
LGPN II, *Ἑστιαῖος* (3) = *PAA* 423530.
Guarantor of a sacred estate (?). Unidentified. F.

25. [- - -]*μαχος Εὐθί*[*ου*?]. *Agora* XIX L14, l. 17.
Father: *LGPN* II, *Εὐθίας* (4) = *PAA* 431570.
Lessee? If the patronym is rightly restored, then one is tempted to supplement [*Φυρό*]*μαχος Εὐθί*[*ου Κολωνῆθεν*] on the basis of the grave-inscription *IG* II^2 6522, *Εὐθίας* | *Φυρομάχου* | *Κολωνῆθεν*. However, the patronym *Εὐθί*[*ου*] is not certain. *Εὐθί*[*ππου*] is also a possibility, in which case one should opt for [*Εὐθύ*]*μαχος Εὐθί*[*ππου Ξυπεταιών*], proposer of the decree *Agora* XV 78 in 273/2. D?

26. *Εὐθίας Φαι*[- - -]. *Agora* XIX L9, ll. 24–5.
LGPN II, *Εὐθίας* (3) = *PAA* 431575.
Renter of a property. Unidentified. F.

27. *Εὐθυκράτης Δρακοντίδου Ἀφιδναῖος*. *I.Eleusis* 177, l. 373.
LGPN II, *Εὐθυκράτης* (16) = *PAA* 433150.
Lessee of an Eleusinian estate (not an *ἐπιμελητὴς τῶν μυστηρίων* as erroneously maintained by Develin 1989, 390; Lambert 1997*a*, 158; Traill in *PAA* 433150; cf. no. 2 above). Councillor in 337/6 (*IG* II^2 242, and now in Themos 2000–3=*SEG* LI 77) and, again, in 328/7, when he was honoured along with two other individuals for his exceptional contribution to a dedication offered by a group of councillors to Amphiaraos. He was descendant of Drakontides, one of the infamous Thirty Tyrants (son or great-grandson, according to Lambert 1997*a*, 158, but he could have been a grandson as well), so almost certainly of ultra-conservative, oligarchical, and hence wealthy background. A descendant (perhaps his son; cf. *PAA* 433155), Drakontides, son of Euthykrates, was proxenos of the Boeotian *koinon* in the early second century (*I.Oropos* 188). Our lessee is now thought to be one of the purchasers attested in the *Rationes Centesimarum* (Lambert 1997*a*, 158) This will be a striking case of a prominent individual heavily involved in landed investments, leasing and purchasing alike. It is noteworthy that the combination of the names *Εὐθυκράτης* and *Δρακοντίδης* occurs also in the prominent *genos* of the Eteoboutadai. C.

28. *Εὔ̣μη*[*λος*]? [. . . .^{8}. . . .*ο*]*υ̣ Εὐ̣ω*(*νυμεύς*). *Agora* XIX L6, ll. 88–9.
Not in *LGPN* II. *PAA* 439310.
Lessee of a property. The other possible restorations for the name are *Εὐ̣μή*[*δης*], *Εὐ̣μη*[*λιάδης*], *Εὐ̣μη*[*λίδης*], and *Εὐ̣μή*[*νιος*] (all rare), but only *Εὔ̣μη*[*λος*] is attested in Euonymon so that the proposed supplement seems very likely. *Εὔμηλος Ἐμπεδίωνος Εὐωνυμεύς*, Secretary of the Boule in 234/3 (*IG* II^2 788; cf. Tracy 2003*a*, 168), and his son, *Ἐμπεδίων Εὐμήλου*

Εὐωνυμεύς, proposer of *IG* II² 839, decree concerning the finances of the Hero-Doctor, would have been prominent descendants. Note also that *Ἀντίδωρος Εὐμήλου Εὐωνυμεύς*, another possible descendant, served as ephebe in *c.*235 BC (*SEG* LII 146), at a time when ephebic status was contingent on high socioeconomic status. D?

29. *Ἡρακλείδη[ς]*. *Agora* XIX L14, l. 6.
LGPN II, *Ἡρακλείδης* (11) = *PAA* 484795.
Lessee. Unidentifiable. F.

30. *Θεόδοτος Ἀπολλοδώρου [Ο]ἰ̣ν̣αῖ(ος)*. *Agora* XIX L6, ll. 106–7.
LGPN II, *Θεόδοτος* (70) = *PAA* 505525.
Lessee of a *temenos*. Probably older brother of the ephebe *Πυθόδωρος Ἀπολλοδώρου Οἰναῖος* (Walbank 1983*a*, 130); if so, the family was at least not poor. F.

31. *Θεόδωρος Κίρων[ος Πρ]ασι(εύς)*. *Agora* XIX L6, ll. 13–14.
LGPN II, *Θεόδωρος* (224) = *PAA* 507360.
Guarantor for a lease of a house in Kydathenaion. *Θεόδωρος Πρασιεύς*, a possible distant ancestor, features as Secretary of the Boule in *IG* I³ 31 (cf. Develin 1989, 110), at a time when the post was filled by election and was held by men of distinction (Arist. [*Ath. Pol.*] 54.3, with Rhodes 1993, 601–3; cf. Taylor 2007, 337–9). Onomastics makes it very likely that these individuals belonged to the well-known Prasian trierarchic family of Poseidippos, son of Kirrias (cf. Walbank 1983*a*, 125, and Appendix IV: The *Θεοδώρειον* of the Prasieis). If the identification is correct, this will be the only case whereby members of the same family were involved in land-leasing conducted at both the polis and the deme level. B.

32. [- - -]*χ̣είτων Θεοπόμπου Α*[- - -] . *Agora* XIX L14, l. 9.
Father: *LGPN* II, *Θεόπομπος* (26) = *PAA* 509640.
Guarantor? The common second element of the name and the multitude of Athenian demes starting with an *alpha* make identification impossible. F.

33. *Ἱππεὺς Κηφισοδ[ώρου Κυδα(θηναιεύς)]*. *Agora* XIX L6, ll. 144–5.
LGPN II, *Ἱππεύς* (3) = *PAA* 537800.
Guarantor for the lease of a swamp. Apart from the telling aristocratic connotations of his rare name, Hippeus was councillor in 336/5 (*Agora* XV 42, l. 155). His son was honoured with citizenship by the Ephesians in the late fourth century (*SEG* XXXIII 932, l. 11). The family was prominent and its stemma has been reconstructed by Habicht 1987, 84. C.

34. [*Ἱππόστρα*]*τος Ἐτεα*[*ρχίδου Παλλη(νεύς)*]? *Agora* XIX L11, ll. 2–3.
New identification: not in *LGPN* II, *PAA* 423980.
Probably guarantor of a property. There are very few Attic names which would fit the sequence of letters preserved from the patronym (*Ἐτεα*[*γόρας*], *Ἐτέα*[*νδρος*], *Ἐτεα*[*ρχίδης*], *Ἐτέα*[*ρχος*]; all extremely rare), but the only

satisfactory restoration is [Ἱππόστρα]τος Ἐτεα[ρχίδου]. He was proposer of the decree *IG* II^2 228. D?

35. *Καλλιάδης Αἰ*[- - -]. *Agora* XIX L14, l. 7.
LGPN II, *Καλλιάδης* (12) = *PAA* 552990.
Guarantor. The name is common (72 entries in *LGPN* II, and 2 further entries in the Addenda) and in the absence of any further attributes identification is impossible. F.

36. *Κ*[α]λλικράτης *Κ*[α]λλι[κρατίδου Στειρι(εύς)]. *I.Eleusis* 177, l. 373.
LGPN II, *Κ*[α]λλικράτης (93) = *PAA* 556925.
Lessee of an Eleusinian estate (not an ἐπιμελητὴς τῶν μυστηρίων, as has been repeatedly maintained, e.g. by Develin 1989, 390; Aleshire 1991, 134 no. 4; Traill in *PAA* 556925; cf. nos. 2 and 27 above). His son *Καλλικρατίδης* (*II*) *Καλλικράτους* (*I*) *Στειριεύς* served as ἐπιστάτης of Artemis Brauronia (*IG* II^2 1524, l. 127), as ἀναγραφεύς *c.*330 (*IG* II^2 415, l. 23; for this annual democratic office see Ferguson 1898, 40–1; Dow 1963, 39–40; Rhodes 1972, 138: the honorific inscription implies that this magistracy was more important than usually assumed), and was one of ten dedicators in *IG* II^2 2825, no doubt state-officials, to judge from the tribal order in which their names were recorded. For other members of this prominent family whose activity continues well into the Roman period, see Aleshire 1991, 134–7 with table VI. C.

37. *Κελεύων Ναυσιστράτου Πειρα*[ιεύς]. *Agora* XIX L9, ll. 76–7.
LGPN II, *Κελεύων* (1) = *PAA* 566200.
Guarantor for a lease of an orchard, almost certainly acting in the interest of his son *Ν*[αυσί^{vv}]στρατος *Κελεύοντος* [*Πειραιε*(ύς)] (Walbank 1983*b*, 190). The name is a *hapax* in Attic prosopography. E.

38. *Κη*[φισόδω]ρος *Σμικύθου Κυδαθη*(ναιεύς). *Agora* XIX L6, ll. 14-15.
LGPN II, *Κηφισόδωρος* (85) = *PAA* 568535.
Lessee of a house in Kydathenaion. Nephew of the guarantor Hippeus (no. 33), he belonged to an active Athenian family (cf. Habicht 1987) and in 325/4 held the office of the Treasurer of Dockyards (*IG* II^2 1631, ll. 350ff. with Develin 1989, 402). C.

39. *Κηφισοφῶν Κεφαλίωνος Ἀφιδνα*(ῖος). *Agora* XIX L6, ll. 99–100.
LGPN II, *Κηφισοφῶν* (22) = *PAA* 569180.
Lessee of a house at Kollytos belonging to Artemis Agrotera. This is definitely the most high-profile individual of the whole series. He functioned as general, lawgiver, and, more importantly, ἐπὶ τὸ θεωρικόν in 343/2 (for full discussion see *APF* 8410). No scholar has noticed that his tenure of the most significant financial office in fourth-century Athens coincides with the inception of the series of leases under examination. Various interpretations are possible. It may be that Kephisophon wished to function as an inspirational model for his fellow-citizens, thus inciting them to activities that would boost the state-revenue. Or, to take a gloomy view, he might well be

accused of corruption, in that he took advantage of his position in order to pursue his own profit. What cannot be disputed is that Kephisophon is almost emblematic of a class of prominent Athenians engaging in various activities of public life. A.

40. [. . . .⁷. . .]ς *Κλεαινέτου Ἐρχι(εύς)*. *Agora* XIX L6, ll. 96–7.
Father: *LGPN* II, *Κλεαίνετος* (9) = *PAA* 574375.
Guarantor for the lease of a landholding belonging to Artemis Agrotera. Otherwise unidentifiable, he might be the father of the lessee *Λυσ[ίμ]ạ[χος?] [?Λυσ]ικλέους Ἐρχι(εύς)* for whom he acted as a guarantor; they share the same deme affiliation and the restoration *[Λυσικλῆ]ς* (or, less likely, *[Σωσικλῆ]ς*) fits the space available perfectly. F.

41. *Κλεότιμ[ος] [Ἀτηνεύς]*? *Agora* XIX L6, l. 128.
LGPN II, *Κλεότιμος* (1) = *PAA* 577975.
Lessee. This common-looking name is in fact so rare (only 3 entries in *LGPN* II) that identification of our lessee with the only other fourth-century *Κλεότιμος*, a member of a liturgical family, is almost certain. Incidentally, the alternative restoration, i.e. *Κλεοτιμ[ίδης]*, does not affect my argument at all, since the only known *Κλεοτιμίδης* from Classical Athens was a member of the same upper-class family (similar conclusions reached by Davies in *APF*, p. 318). B.

42. *Κριτόδημος Ạ[- - -]*. *Agora* XIX L6, ll. 37–8.
LGPN II, *Κριτόδημος* (3) = *PAA* 585515.
Guarantor of the lease of a *temenos* in Thria. Unexpectedly, the name is fairly uncommon (16 attestations in *LGPN* II, of which only 6 fall within the fourth century). It is tempting to restore *Κριτόδημος Ἀ̣[ριστομάχου Ἀλ(ωπεκῆθεν)]*, which would make the lessee a member of a liturgical family (cf. *APF* 1969), but the identification should remain provisional. B?

43. *Λάχη[ς . . . .]δου Ῥαμνο(ύσιος)*. *Agora* XIX L6, ll. 17–18.
LGPN II, *Λάχης* (44) = *PAA* 602370.
Lessee of a house in Kydathenaion. He features in a catalogue *generis incerti* (*IG* II^2 2400, l. 10), and is now attested as councillor of the cleruchic Boule of Samos (*IG* XII (6) 262, l. 297, with Hallof and Habicht 1995, 282; cf. *I.Oropos*, index s.v. *Λάχης*). C.

44. *Λεοντεὺς Ἀντικλείδου Κ[υδαντ(ίδης)?]*. *Agora* XIX L6, ll. 15–16.
LGPN II, *Λεοντεύς* (9) = *PAA* 603090.
Guarantor for the lease of a house at Kydathenaion. In the fourth century the patronym is attested in four different demes whose names start with a *kappa*, namely Kephisia, Kettos, Kydantidai, and Kydathenaion. However, the not so common name *Λεοντεύς* (20 entries in *LGPN*, only 6 in the fourth century) appears only in Kydantidai (twice), and Traill in *PAA*, probably correctly, identifies Kydantidai as the deme of our guarantor. The latter was probably relative (cousin?) of *Λεοντεὺς Ἀντιφάνους Κυδαντίδης*, proposer of

the well-known double decree of the demes Kydantidai and Ionidai, and of *Λεοντεὺς Μενεστράτου Κυδαντίδης*, *kolokrates* of the tiny Attic deme honoured in the same document (*SEG* XXXIX 148). The family obviously dominated the micropolitics of their deme, but in view of our guarantor they also got involved in more central transactions. Note that Traill also believes that *Λεοντε[ύς]*, proposer of the decree *IG* II^2 1267, of the religious dining-club *Δαιταλεῖς*, is either our man or a close relative. D.

45. *Λυκέας Λυ̣[- - -] [Ῥαμνούσιος?]*. *Agora* XIX L6, l. 20.
LGPN II, *Λυκέας* (4) = *PAA* 610150.
Lessee of a house (?) in Kydathenaion. The name *Λυκέας* is firmly attested only in Rhamnous (see *LGPN* II, *Λυκέας*; cf. Choremi, Papazarkadas, and Petropoulou 2000–3, 87), hence the proposed restoration for the demotic. If the identification is sound, then our lessee belonged to a prominent Rhamnousian family. D.

46. [. . . ^{9} . . . .]*ης Λυσίου Ἀμαξ(αντεύς)*. *Agora* XIX L6, ll. 81–2.
Father: *LGPN* II, *Λυσίας* (54) = *PAA* 613910.
Lessee of a house belonging to Zeus Olympios. Unidentifiable. F.

47. [. . . ^{10} . . .] *Λυσιδή[μου] Κεφαλ(ῆθεν)*. *Agora* XIX L6, ll. 67–8.
Father: *LGPN* II, *Λυσίδημος* (6) = *PAA* 614330.
Gurarantor for the lease of a *temenos* in Hermos. The patronym, though rare, does not allow any sound identification. The elusive guarantor may be related to other known individuals of the same deme with names containing the lexical element *λυσι-*, such as *Λυσίθεος*, *Λυσικλῆς*, *Λυσικράτης*, and so on. F.

48. *Λυσιθείδης Λυσιμ̣[άχου] Οἰναῖος*. *Agora* XIX L9, ll. 54–5.
LGPN II, *Λυσιθείδης* (11) = *PAA* 614420.
Epigraphically, the restoration of the patronym is the only one tenable and has to be considered certain. The descendant *[Λ]υσίμαχος Οἰναῖος* must have been well-off, to judge from his contribution of 200 drachmas, the highest allowed *ἐπίδοσις*, to the stratiotic fund of 248/7 (*SEG* XXXII 118, with Oliver 2007, 200–4), and it may not be very precarious to envisage retrospective prosperity for the family. The onomastics of the family stress a persistence of the prefix *Λυσι**. It may be of some importance, therefore, that a name of the same derivation occurs in the family of the renter, for whom our *Λυσιθείδης* acted as guarantor, even though the former came from another deme (see no. 10 above); perhaps inter-family ties should be considered. D.

49. *Λυσ[ίμ]α̣[χος?] [?Λυσ]ικλέους Ἐρχι(εύς)*. *Agora* XIX L6, ll. 94–5.
LGPN II, *Λυσίμαχος* (55) = *PAA* 616395.
Lessee of a landholding belonging to Artemis Agrotera. Despite the entry in *LGPN* II the restoration of the name is not certain; *Λυσ[ιφ]ά̣[νης]* and *Λυσ[ιχ]ά̣[ρης]* are also possible. Fortunately, all 3 restorations leave a

three-letter space for the missing beginning of the patronym. Of the 15 possible restorations for the father's name, only 4 occur in Erchia, namely *Ἀμφικλῆς*, *Ἀρχικλῆς*, *Λυσικλῆς*, and *Σωσικλῆς*. But of those, *Ἀμφικλῆς* and *Ἀρχικλῆς* are only attested in the third century, and *Σωσικλῆς* in the first century AD, so that none of them provides any likely identification. *Λυσικλῆς* appears more tempting, especially in the light of its first composite which would be shared with the name of the lessee, on whatever restoration of the latter. Significantly, *Λυσικλῆς* of Erchia was the son of Isocrates' adoptive son Aphareus (*APF* 9433). However, the generation successions do not work perfectly and, unless we accept some family link on the matrilineal side, our individual should probably be dissociated from the pedigree of Isocrates. F?

50. *Μẹ[ι]δ[ί]ας* [.]υδ[- - -]. *Agora* XIX L11, l. 7.
LGPN II, *Μειδίας* (6) = *PAA* 637205.
Guarantor. Unidentifiable. F.

51. *Μειδύλος Μειδυλίδου Ἀζηνιεύς*. *Agora* XIX L6, ll. 103–4.
LGPN II, *Μειδύλος* (2) = *PAA* 637480.
Lessee of a *temenos* belonging to Zeus at Kynosarges. Otherwise unknown, but *Μειδύλος*, councillor in 281/0, is a certain descendant, given that the name is very rare (3 entries in *LGPN* II), and the deme small (bouleutic quota 2; see Traill 1975, 68). A less likely connection can be made with *[Μειδω]ν[ί]δης Ἁγṿ[ο]δ̣ήμου Ἀζηνιεύς*, buyer of a landholding for 4000 drachmas in the *Rationes Centesimarum* (cf. Lambert 1997*a*, 167–8). D.

52. *Μοίριππος Μοιραγ[έ]νους [Κυδαθ]η(ναιεύς)*. *Agora* XIX L6, ll. 8-9.
LGPN II, *Μοίριππος* (2) = *PAA* 658425.
Guarantor for the lease of a house in Kydathenaion. The name is a *hapax* (see *LGPN* II Addenda, s.v.). Although assigned F-status by Shipton, on the basis of *IG* II^2 1524 Moirippos was the son of the *epistates* of the Brauronion in 350/49 (Walbank 1983*a*, 125; unjustifiably, not endorsed in *LGPN* II). D.

53. *[Μο]σ̣χίων Εὐφαμίδο[υ]*. *Agora* XIX L6, ll. 36–7.
LGPN II, *Μοσχίων* (6) = *PAA* 659260.
Lessee of a *temenos* at Thria. The patronym is a *hapax* in Attic prosopography, unless we allow for *Εὐφαμίδας*, which appears in a *kalos*-inscription on a black-figure alabastron (*ABV*, p. 666). Otherwise, *Εὐφαμίδης* is only known as that of an 'operarius' at Aigina (see *IG* IV^2.2 1007, where Hallof considers the name Hellenistic precisely because of the Ionic termination), whereas *Εὐφαμίδας*, let alone *Εὔφαμος*, is known from other places of the non-Ionic world (see *LGPN* I, III.A, III.B, IV, s.vv. *Εὐφαμίδας*, *Εὔφαμος*). One wonders whether we have here an enfranchised Athenian of Doric origin, or even one of the very few foreign lessees. F.

54. [- - -] *[Μ]ύος Φαλ[(ηρεύς)]*. *Agora* XIX L11, ll. 9–10.
Father: *LGPN* II, *Μῦς* (3) = *PAA* 663440.

Lessee of a property in the area of Phaleron. The rare patronym has allowed identification of the lessee's father with the homonymous contractor in *IG* II^2 1673.6. D.

55. *Ναυ<σ>[ία]ς Νικοστράτο[υ Ἀτηνεύς?]*. *Agora* XIX L6, l. 125.
LGPN II, *Ναυσίας* (2) = *PAA* 701485.
Lessee of a *gyes* (?). The name, if read correctly, is fairly unusual, with 13 entries in *LGPN* II. Strangely, the small Atene is the deme with the highest percentage of attestations (2 certain cases and 1 possible). One of these individuals was *Νικόστρατος*, son of *Ναυσίας*, a fact that leaves few if any doubts about the demotic of our individual. The Nikostratos in question was recognized as benefactor of Oropos and was honoured accordingly. His father Nausias was *thesmothetes* in 216/5. The epitaph of Nikostratos has been found in Phyle. Strangely, this family from the southernmost tip of Attica appears to have been active near the north border of their polis. Interestingly, the property rented by Nausias was probably located in the Marathonian Tetrapolis or thereabout.[7] Last but not least, a Nausias from Atene held the prestigious office of Secretary of the Assembly and the Council in *c.*378/7 (Develin 1989, 229; cf. *PAA* nos. 701495, 701500). No doubt, the family was important. C.

56. *Ν̣[αυσί^{vv}]στρατος Κελεύοντος [Πειραιε(ύς)]*. *Agora* XIX L9, ll. 74–5.
LGPN II, *Ναυσίστρατος* (21) = *PAA* 702440.
Lessee of an orchard. His name is restored on the basis of the lessee's patronym (see no. 37). Traill in *PAA* suggests identification of this individual with the homonymous contractor (*ἐργώνης*) known from the building-accounts of Epidauros (*IG* IV^2.1 103). D.

57. *Νικόδη[μος] [. . .^{5}]κράτους Μυρρινούσι[ος]*. *Agora* XIX L9, ll. 67–8.
LGPN II, *Νικόδημος* (46) = *PAA* 714355.
Guarantor for a lease of an orchard. There are numerous ways to restore the patronym and, since it seems that letter spaces were occasionally left uninscribed at the end of lines, it is tempting to supplement *Νικόδη[μος] [Νικο^v]|κράτους*. But even on this reading, our man cannot be identified with *[Νικό]δημος Νικοκρ[άτους]*, president of the *epistatai* in the decree *IG* II^2 490, since the latter's demotic consisted of 8 letters only. Walbank 1983*b*, 189, followed by Vivliodetis 2005 [2007], 214, has suggested identification of Nikodemos' father with *Φειδικράτης Δημοσθένους Μυρρινούσιος* of the grave stele *IG* II^2 6906, but one might also consider identification with *Καλλικράτης* of the epitaph *IG* II^2 6895. F.

58. *Νικόστρατος Ν[- - - Ἀτη(νεύς)]*. *Agora* XIX L6, l. 126.
LGPN II, *Νικόστρατος* (16/17) = *PAA* 718000.

[7] See Walbank 1983*a*, 120–1.

Guarantor, almost certainly stepping in for his own son. For the demotic and the family, see no. 55 above. It is tempting to restore the patronym as *Ν*[*αυσίου*], in which case the guarantor could have been the son of Nausias, Secretary of the Boule in *c.*378/7. C.

59. *Νικόφημος Φορ̣*[. . . . . .^{12}. . . . . .] [*'Ραμ*]*ν̣*[*ο*(*ύσιος*)?]. *Agora* XIX L9, ll. 87–8.
LGPN II, *Νικόφημος* (4) = *PAA* 719120.
Lessee of a garden. In line 89 the dotted *nu* ought to belong to the demotic of the lessee. Since there is a tendency on the stone for word and syllable division across lines, this *nu* should actually be the fourth letter of the demotic. Two possibilities arise then: [*Εὐω*]*ν̣*[*υ*] or [*'Ραμ*]*ν̣*[*ο*]. The name *Νικόφημος*, though rare, is attested in both demes, but, amongst the possible restorations for the patronym, *Φορ̣*[*μίωνος*] is the only one attested in any of the demes, namely in Rhamnous. *Νικόφημος Φορ̣*[*μίωνος*^{vvvvvv}] [*'Ραμ*]*ν̣* [*ο*(*ύσιος*)] should therefore be considered as a very remote possibility, but no more. F.

60. [- - -]*ς Νίκωνος Ἀχαρ*[*ν*(*εύς*)]. *Agora* XIX L6, ll. 113–14.
Father: *LGPN* II, *Νίκων* (32) = *PAA* 720175.
Guarantor for the lease of an unknown property. The patronym is common (170 entries in *LGPN* II), but it is worth noting that amongst Acharnians it is attested for a prytanis of 360/59 (*Agora* XV 17. 57) and for a deceased man (*SEG* XXI 839) who may be the same as the prytanis and perhaps a member of a liturgical family (see *APF* 9480). B?

61. *Ξενοκράτης Γνιφωνίδου Μαραθώνιο*[*ς*]. *Agora* XIX L9, ll. 47–8.
LGPN II, *Ξενοκράτης* (29) = *PAA* 732895.
Guarantor. Unidentified. F.

62. [- - -] *ς Ξενοκρίτο*[*υ*] *Ἀφ*[*ιδ*(*ναῖος*)]. *Agora* XIX L6, l. 164.
Father: *LGPN* II, *Ξενόκριτος* (4) = *PAA* 733075.
Guarantor. Neither the man nor the father can be identified, but their family can be traced down to the second century (*IG* II^2 5769). What is more, a descendant was priest of Asklepios in the mid-third century (*IG* II^2 1534 with Aleshire 1991, 164–5). F.

63. *Ξεν*[. . . . . . ^{16} . . . . . .] *Προβ*(*αλίσιος*). *Agora* XIX L6, ll. 116-17.
Not in *LGPN* II.
Lessee of a property. Walbank 1983*a*, 131 tentatively restored *Ξεν*[*οπείθης Ξενοφῶντος*] *Προβ*(*αλίσιος*), identifying him with *Ξενοπείθης*, father of a councillor of 304/3, but the supplement is one letter too long. He is, however, almost certainly related to his guarantor [*Ξενοφῶν*?] *Ξενοφῶντος Προβ*(*αλίσιος*) (no. 64), but we had better concede that we cannot work out either the onomastics or the exact connection. F.

64. [*Ξενοφῶν*?] *Ξενοφῶντος Προβ*(*αλίσιος*). *Agora* XIX L6, ll. 117–18, 121–2.

PAA 734405 (not in *LGPN* II); father: *LGPN* II, *Ξενοφῶν* (43) = 734404. Guarantor of two leases. The restored name, though epigraphically tenable, is by no means certain. Since he comes from the same deme as the first lessee for whom he puts in security (no. 63 above), and since their names share the same first element, they are probably related (cf. Walbank 1983*a*, 131). F.

65. *Ὀλυμπιό[δωρος] Δ̣ιογείτονος Ἀχ[αρνεύς]*. *Agora* XIX L9, ll. 84–5.
LGPN II, *Ὀλυμπιόδωρος* (23) = *PAA* 743030.
Although printed with a question mark in *Agora* XIX L9, the restoration of the name is certain. The demotic can either be *Ἀχ[αρνεύς]* or *Ἀχ[ερδούσιος]*, but taken independently the name and the patronym only occur in the deme of Acharnai, so that *Ἀχ[αρνεύς]* looks almost certain. In that case, *Ὀλυμπιόδωρος* would have been the son of the Treasurer of Athena, Diogeiton (*IG* II[2] 1388, l. 5; 1391, l. 8; 1392, l. 5), as already acknowledged—albeit hesitantly—by Walbank 1983*b*, 190–1. This Diogeiton was also Superintendent of the Dockyards in 377/6 (*IG* II[2] 1604, l. 2, with Develin 1989, 237). He was considered impartial enough to be appointed as common arbitrator in a lawsuit concerning the infamous Neaira ([Dem]. 59.45; 47). At any rate, given pseudo-Aristotle's information that the Treasurers of Athena were chosen by sortition amongst members of the *pentakosiomedimnoi* even in the 320s (Arist. [*Ath. Pol.*] 8.1; 47.1, with Rhodes 1993, 550–1; cf. Davies 1981, 36–7), Olympiodoros certainly belonged to a well-off family (see now Taylor 2007, 334–5, who also accepts that Treasurers came from the ranks of the wealthy). B.

66. *Παυσίστρατος Λυσιμάχου Πειρ(αιεύς)*. *Agora* XIX L6, ll. 101–2.
LGPN II, *Παυσίστρατος* (3) = *PAA* 770350.
One of the two guarantors acting on behalf of the grand Kephisophon. The name is very rare, but this individual is otherwise unattested. Note, however, that his co-guarantor Philophron appears as a mine lessee, so that our Pausistratos may well be the homonymous lessee in *Agora XIX* P24. At any rate, by virtue of his patronym he is probably related to *Λυσίμαχος* who along with his brother was honoured by the citizen orgeones of Dexion in *IG* II[2] 1252. D.

67. [. . .[5]]*βουλος Πεισικλέου[ς]*. *Agora* XIX L9, ll. 65–6.
Father = *LGPN* II, *Πεισικλῆς* (1) = *PAA* 771540.
Lessee of a garden. The patronym is very rare (4 entries in *LGPN* II, one of whom is our individual), and in the fourth century it only occurs in the deme Anaphlystos. Unidentified. F.

68. *Πολέμ[ων Δι]οκλέους Φλυε̣(ύς)*. *Agora* XIX L6, ll. 9–10.
LGPN II, *Πολέμων* (24) = *PAA* 776770.
Lessee of a house in Kydathenaion. His father was a prominent opponent of Isaeus' clients and, although Davies was reluctant to include him in the liturgical class (cf. *APF* 8443), he must have been well-off. A possible, albeit

remote, descendant *Σώπατρος Πολέμωνος Φλυεύς*, was a member of the Boule *c.*30 (*SEG* XXVIII 95), at a time when membership in the Council was more or less dependent upon social prominence. D.

69. [. . . [10] . . .]*της Πολυκλέους* [*Προβαλίσιος*?]. *Agora* XIX L9, ll. 42–3.
Father: *LGPN* II, *Πολυκλῆς* (7) = *PAA* 779035.
Guarantor of a lease. Only names ending in -*κράτης* give restorations long enough to fill the estimated lacuna before the preserved letters of the guarantor's name, so that [. . . .[7] . . . *κρά*]*της Πολυκλέους* seems a fair supplement. As for the long demotic, given that all the individuals named in ll. 40–55 appear to have come from the Marathonian Tetrapolis, it ought to have been *Μαραθώνιος*, *Προβαλίσιος*, or *Τρικορύνθιος* (*Οἰναῖος* is too short), of which only *Προβαλίσιος* meets the epigraphical requirement of 11 letters; in any case the name *Πολυκλῆς* is not attested at Trikorynthos at all, and is only attested for Marathon in the Roman Imperial period. A *Πολυκλῆς Προβαλίσιος* was councillor in 336/5 (*Agora* XV 42. 164), and a possible relative (son?), *Πουλυτίων Πολυκλέους*, was councillor the year after (*Agora* XV 43. 64–5). If my suggestion for the demotic of the elusive lessee is correct, the latter may be related to the councillor and/or his alleged son. D?

70. *Πυθόδωρος Φιλοκλέους Ἐπι*(*κηφίσιος*). *Agora* XIX L6, ll. 78–81.
LGPN II, *Πυθόδωρος* (51) = *PAA* 794550.
Father of a lessee of a house belonging to Zeus Olympios, acting also as guarantor for his own son; almost certainly the same man as the homonymous proposer of the deme decree *IG* II^2 1205. D.

71. *Σιλανὸς Σωσίππ*[*ου*]. *Agora* XIX L6, ll. 108–9.
LGPN II, *Σιλανός* (1) = *PAA* 819950.
Guarantor of the lease of a *temenos*. Although the name is rare, the patronym is more common and in the absence of the demotic no identification can be made. F.

72. *Στέφαν*[*ος*] [. . . .[7] . . .]*δου Παια*(*νιεύς*). *Agora* XIX L6, ll. 139-40.
LGPN II, *Στέφανος* (63) = *PAA* 834535.
Guarantor acting on behalf of a metic lessee. Unidentifiable. F.

73. *Σ̣ώ̣ϊ̣το*[*ς*] [. . . [6] . . .]*ενίδο*[*υ*] *Παιανιεύς*. *Agora* XIX L6, ll. 91–2.
LGPN II, *Σώϊτος* (1) = *PAA* 855070.
Lessee of a landholding and a house belonging to Artemis Agrotera. As Traill in *PAA* duly notes, the only attested Attic name fitting the missing letters of the patronym is [*Αὐτοσθ*]*ενίδο*[*υ*], but this is an extremely rare name occurring only in the deme Xypete. F.

74. *Σωνδρίδης Σ̣*[*ωστρ*]*άτου Ἐροιά*(*δης*). *Agora* XIX L9, ll. 58–9.
LGPN II, *Σωνδρίδης* (2) = *PAA* 857565.
Lessee of a *gues*. In all appearances, the father of Nausistrate, dedicatrix of *IG* II^2 4026. The inscribed dedication, a marble base of large dimensions, was

obviously expensive and, though Kron 1996, 160–6 has justifiably advocated caution in automatic assignment of costly dedications by female offerands to upper-class families, the dedication in conjunction with the transaction in question probably shows that the family of Sondrides was affluent. D.

75. *Σωσίδημος Γλαύκω[νος]*. *Agora* XIX L9, l. 72.
LGPN II, *Σωσίδημος* (5) = *PAA* 861325.
Guarantor for the lease of an orchard. Otherwise unidentified, he might be a relative of *Γλαύκων Σωσικράτου Χολλείδης*, attested as a member of an honouring committee in *I.Rhamnous* 19. However, on this assumption, the abbreviated demotic would have been *Χολ*, which would have provided scope for confusion with the deme *Χολαργός*. It has to be noted that whereas *Γλαύκων* is a fairly common name (51 entries in *LGPN* II), *Σωσίδημος* is only attested 10 times. Paradoxically, the three demes in which *Σωσίδημος* occurs (Acharnai, Alopeke, Xypete) have also produced instances of *Γλαύκων*. All things considered, identification appears impossible. F.

76. [*Τελεσίας*] [*Τελ*]*έστου Π̣ροβ(αλίσιος)*. *Agora* XIX L6, ll. 112–13.
PAA 879305; father: *LGPN* II, *Τελέστης* (16) = *PAA* 879870.
Lessee of a property. The combination of the rather uncommon patronym with the demotic makes the restoration of the name of the lessee certain. Syntrierarch treated in *APF* 13519. A.

77. *Τιμόθεος Τιμοκράτου̣*[*ς* . . . [5]]. *Agora* XIX L9, l. 71.
LGPN II, *Τιμόθεος* (7) = *PAA* 886045.
Lessee of an orchard near Mounichia. Although both name and patronym are banal (110 and 130 entries in *LGPN* II, respectively), the combination does not occur in any deme. Unidentified. F.

78. *Τιμοκλῆς Τιμοκράτο*[*υς*]. *Agora* XIX L6, ll. 143–4.
LGPN II, *Τιμοκλῆς* (5) = *PAA* 887080.
Lessee of a swamp. The names are so common that any effort to connect the patronym with those in the preceding and the following entries of this catalogue (nos. 77, 79) is hazardous. F.

79. [. . . . [8] . . . .]*τος Τιμοκράτ*[*ους*]. *Agora* XIX L6, ll. 40–1.
Father: *LGPN* II, *Τιμοκράτης* (12) = *PAA* 887895.
Lessee of a property. Identification of the lessee's father with the father of the lessee *Τιμοκλῆς* (no. 78), though tempting, ought to be resisted. F.

80. *Ὑπερείδης Γλαυκίππου Κολλυ(τεύς)*. *I.Eleusis* 177, l. 382.
LGPN II, *Ὑπερείδης* (3) = *PAA* 902110.
Lessee of the Eleusinian Rharia. The eminent Athenian orator and politician. Member of a liturgical family (*APF* 13912). There is indirect evidence that Hypereides' renting of the *Ῥαρία* could have had speculative ramifications and should not be seen as a liturgical manifestation of piety. An anecdote concerning his life has it that Hypereides was owner of private property at

Eleusis, which he was wont to use as a resort for his erotic encounters with the prostitute Phila ([Plut.] *Mor.* 849d). Since Hypereides was registered in the city-deme of Kollytos, there is a slight chance that the private property attested in [Plutarch] was his base for the supervision of his investments in the *Ῥαρία* (the connection is now noted by Clinton 2008, 226). A.

81. *Φίλαγρος Λε*[. . . ⁹ . . . .]. *Agora* XIX L6, ll. 135–6.
LGPN II, *Φίλαγρος* (3) = *PAA* 922020.
Guarantor of a lease undertaken by a metic. The name is of average frequency (32 entries in *LGPN* II), but on the basis of the remains of the patronym it is tempting to restore *Φίλαγρος Λέ*[*οντος Ἁλαι*(*εύς*)] (thus already Walbank 1983*a*, 132; the suggested supplement is likely because the 9 missing letters demand a fairly short name for the patronym). If so, the guarantor was a member of the liturgical family treated in *APF* 14208 bis. B?

82. *Φιλιά̣*[*δης*]. *Agora* XIX L6, l. 168.
LGPN II, *Φιλιάδης* (3) = *PAA* 927185.
One of two guarantors for the lease of a property belonging to Artemis Brauronia. The name is accompanied by a question mark in *Agora* XIX and in *LGPN* II, no doubt because *Φιλία̣*[*ς*] is epigraphically acceptable, although it is a *hapax* in Attic prosopography. *Φιλιά̣*[*δης*], however, is rare too (5 further entries in *LGPN* II). F.

83. *Φιλοκράτης Φιλοκράτ̣*[*ους Ἀχα*(*ρνεύς*)?]. *Agora* XIX L9, l. 60.
LGPN II, *Φιλοκράτης* (18) = *PAA* 937675.
Guarantor for the lease of a *gues*. The demotic is not certain and hence this individual is not included amongst the Acharnians in *LGPN* II. If he is, however, to be identified with the Acharnian individuals (as per Traill), he should be promoted to class B.

84. *Φιλόφρων Φιλοκλέους Πειραι*(*εύς*). *Agora* XIX L6, ll. 100–1.
LGPN II, *Φιλόφρων* (7) = *PAA* 952050.
One of two guarantors acting on behalf of Kephisophon. This 'F class' individual, according to Shipton, turns out to be an energetic Athenian with a presence even outside the borders of Attica. The name is rare enough to make identification with *Φιλόφρων Πειραιεύς* of the mine leases *Agora* XIX P9 and P26 almost certain. His epitaph has been found in Imbros (*IG* XII (8) 110, with Cargill 1995, no. 1342). Together with *Κηφισοφῶν Κεφαλίωνος Ἀφιδνα*(*ῖος*) (no. 39), the two compose a dynamic duo which seems to encompass everything characteristic of the most advanced section of Athenian society: active participation in politics, multifaceted economic activities, distinguished social profile. C.

85. *Φίλων Φίλτωνος ἐκ Κοί*(*λης*). *Agora* XIX L6, ll. 104–5.
LGPN II, *Φίλων* (122) = *PAA* 955475.

Guarantor for the leasing of a *temenos*. His homonymous grandfather is mentioned by Isocrates as having been a member of an Athenian embassy (Isoc. 18.22), so he must have been of some standing (Briant 1968, has demonstrated that Athenian ambassadors effectively constituted a specialized, almost 'semi-professionnel' institution; Xen. [*Ath. Pol.*] 1.18, with Marr and Rhodes 2008, 93, assumes that ambassadors, along with generals and trierarchs, came from the upper class). *Φίλων ἐκ Κοί(λης)*, a possible descendant, was stationed in the fortress of Eleusis in the mid-third century (*IG* II^2 1958). D.

86. *Φορμί[ων] [....⁷...] [Φα]λη(ρεύς) vel [Παλ]λη(νεύς)*. *Agora* XIX L6, ll. 69–70.
LGPN II, *Φορμίων* (24) = *PAA* 963115.
Lessee of an orchard (or more than one?) near Ilissos. The less common *Φορμί[δης]* and *Φορμί[σιος]* are also possible, though they would demand an extremely short patronym. Unidentifiable. F.

87. *Φόρυσκος [...⁶...ἐν Ἀ]λ̣ω(πεκῆι) : οἰ(κῶν)*. *Agora* XIX L6, ll. 138–9.
LGPN II, *Φόρυσκος* (10) = *PAA* 963420.
Lessee of an estate. Metic. Lewis *apud* Walbank 1983*a*, 132–3 suggested that *Φορυσκίδης Ἀριστομένου Ἀλωπεκῆθεν* might have been an enfranchised descendant. However, a cursory look at the *LGPN* volumes would suffice to demonstrate that *Φόρυσκος* is a good Athenian name already in the fourth century, whereas outside Attica it is extremely uncommon (not attested in *LGPN* IIIA or IV, 1 entry in *LGPN* I, 1 entry in *LGPN* IIIB, both in the early Hellenistic period). In view of this, it seems more possible that the name passed from Athens into the family of our metic, rather than the other way around. But if so, then the connection of Phoryskos to Attica must have been at least one generation old, a fact that has to be taken into consideration when exploring the topic of metics as lessees. F.

88. *Χαιρέστ[ρατος] [....⁸....] Σφήτ(τιος)*. *Agora* XIX L6, ll. 129–30.
LGPN II, *Χαιρέστρατος* (52) = *PAA* 975225.
Guarantor. Unidentified. F.

89. *[Χαριναύτης? Χα]ιρίωνος Φαλη(ρεύς)*. *Agora* XIX L6, ll. 64–5.
LGPN II, *Χαριναύτης* (5) = *PAA* 983860.
Guarantor. The name has been restored on the basis of the patronym. A Chairion (*LGPN* II s.v. *Χαιρίων* (19)) was Secretary of the Boule in 361/0 (*IG* II^2 116, l. 6). A likely relative (brother?) of our guarantor is [- - -]*νοκλῆς Χαιρίωνος Φαληρεύς*, councillor in the democratic Boule of 304/3 (*Agora* XV 59. 7; 61. 245). D.

90. *[Χαριάδης Χ]αιροκλέους Λευκο[νο(ιεύς)]*. *Agora* XIX L6, ll. 18-19.
PAA 980360. Father: *LGPN* II, *Χαιροκλῆς* (5).
Guarantor for a lease of a house in Kydathenaion. The patronym is so rare (5 entries in *LGPN* II, only 2 in the fourth century; Walbank 1983*a*, 126 is

wrong to state that it is a common name) that the restoration of the guarantor's name on the basis of *Χαριάδης [Χ]αιροκλέος* of Leukonoion, councillor in 370/69 (*Agora* XV 13, ll. 35–6) is almost unquestionable. Obviously, the guarantor would have been of advanced age at the time of his surety (see no. 91). D.

91. [- - -]ς *Χαριάδ[ο Λευκονο?]*. *Agora* XIX L6, ll. 33–4.
Father: *LGPN* II, *Χαριάδης* (18) = *PAA* 980365.
Lessee of a property. Numerous restorations are possible, so identification ought to remain tentative, though the editors of *LGPN* II have hesitantly accepted the identification of this *Χαριάδης* with the alleged guarantor no. 90. E.

92. [. . . ⁹ . . . . Χ]*αρίου Παια(νιεύς)*. *Agora* XIX L9, l. 29.
Father: *LGPN* II, *Χαρίας* (64) = *PAA* 981505.
Renter of a property. Possibly a descendant of *Χαρίας Παιανιεύς*, candidate for ostracism in *c.*417–5 (Brenne 2001, 128–9). He may be related to the guarantor *Χαιρ̣[. . . ⁵] [Χαρίου] Παιανιε(ύς)* (*Agora* XIX L9, ll. 36–7). D?

93. [³.]*έ̣ξανδρος Χαριδήμο̣[υ] Πρ̣[οβαλίσι]ος* (or *Πρ̣[οσπάλτι]ος*). *Agora* XIX L9, ll. 30–1; 35–6.
Father: *LGPN* II, *Χαρίδημος* (55) = *PAA* 982560.
Guarantor and lessee. The only possible restorations for the defective name are *[Ἀλ]έ̣ξανδρος* and *[Δ]έ̣ξανδρος*. The 3 missing letters printed in L9 are not a problem, since elsewhere in our record the chiseller has left uninscribed letter-spaces (e.g. l. 27: *[τ]ούτω* ᵛ *τῶ γύα*; l. 29: *[Χ]αρίου* ᵛ *Παια:*). Thus, *[Ἀλ]έ̣ξανδρος*, being one letter longer, is only marginally preferable, though neither it nor *[Δ]έ̣ξανδρος* were common in the Classical era (*Ἀλέξανδρος* became very popular in the Hellenistic period, no doubt because of Alexander the Great, but this is not the case here). In fact, it is not even certain whether the same individual acted as guarantor and lessee in two different transactions, but the patronym suggests that in the second case the lessee would have been the brother of the guarantor. Otherwise unidentifiable. E.

94. *Χαρίδη[μος]*. *Agora* XIX L14, l. 13.
LGPN II, *Χαρίδημος* (12) = *PAA* 981840.
Lessee of a *temenos*? The rare *Χαριδη[μίδης]* is a remote possibility. Unidentifiable. F.

95. *Χα[ρικλῆς?]* [..]*ά̣θωνος Λακ̣(ιάδης)*. *Agora* XIX L6, l. 93.
Father: cf. *LGPN* II, *Γνάθων* (10) = *PAA* 279245.
Guarantor. The patronym *[Γν]ά̣θωνος* is not self-evident; the more common *[Ἀγ]ά̣θωνος* is also a possibility, but neither is attested for the deme Lakiadai. However, both names leave 6 missing letters to be supplemented in the name of the guarantor. Of the twenty (20) different options starting with *Χα-* only *Χαρικλῆς* is attested in Lakiadai (councillor in 303/2 in *Agora* XV 62; his

patronym, which starts with a *sigma*, does not allow identification with our guarantor, though they could have been cousins). D?

96. [- - -]τọς *Χαρίσọ[υ]*. *Agora* XIX L6, ll. 149–50.
Father: *LGPN* II, *Χάρισος* (1) = *PAA* 985430.
Guarantor. The patronym is extremely rare (on top of our individual 3 more entries in *LGPN* II). Of his son's name only the ending -τọς is preserved. One could possibly restore [*Θεόδο*]τọς *Χαρίσọ[υ Σφήτ]*, on the basis of *Χάρισος Θεοδότου Σφήττιος*, councillor and proposer of the honorific decree *IG* II^2 489 in 303/2. On this supplement, our guarantor would have been the father of the proposer, but identification should remain uncertain. D?

CLASS A: 5 (5.21%)

CLASS B: 11 (11.47%)

CLASS C: 9 (9.37%)

CLASS D: 23 (23.96%)

CLASS E: 3 (3.12%)

CLASS F: 45 (46.87%)

Citizen Lessees and Guarantors

Of those engaging in land-leasing at the polis level 5 were liturgists and 11 were certainly or very likely members of liturgical families (5.21+11.47 =16.68%).[8] 9 appear to have been actively engaged in various fields of public life, even if they did not demonstrably belong to the upper echelons of Athenian society (9.37%). Moreover, 23 individuals were very possibly active in public life or belonged to families which were active (23.96%). It is noteworthy that upper-class Athenians involved directly or indirectly in land-leasing constitute a percentage very close to that of their peers attested at the level of mine-leasing.[9] What is more, the statistical analysis offered here is deliberately minimalistic and thus distorting. Most of those classified in class F lack various attributes and it is almost certain that otherwise some of them would have been identifiable, in which case the respective percentages of those grouped in the other classes would have risen considerably.[10] All in all, the real wonder is not that there are few lessees and guarantors

[8] Class A: nos. 2, 13, 39, 74, 78. Class B: nos. 3, 7, 11, 14, 18, 31, 41, 42, 58, 63, 79, 81.

[9] Mine-leasing: 18.87%; cf. Shipton 2000, 30–7.

[10] See the commendable notes of Rosivach 1994, 126–7, who in his polite criticism of Walbank's treatment of the same set of data, duly observed that the 'assumption that anyone who cannot be identified as either rich . . . or famous must be poor is a very hazardous one'.

from the upper strata of Athenian society, but that there are too many,[11] as already noted by Rosivach in a rather overlooked study.[12]

Yet the cold logic of mathematics fails to bring out some subtler aspects of the issue in question, aspects which can be more efficiently investigated by looking at what I would tentatively label 'mini-patterns'. Such are, for instance, geographical considerations, professional interests, family ties, political aspects, and religious concerns. Direct access to the leased properties would have been a factor to consider before any lessee decided to bid for a given property. This appears to have been the case with two of the lessees who rented houses located at Kydathenaion, namely Kephisodoros of Kydathenaion and the metic Aristagoras whose registered abode lay in the same deme. Similar considerations apply to the orchards at Mounichia leased by the Peiraieis Nausistratos and Aischines as well as to a seaside property at Phaleron rented by the son of Mys of Phaleron. I have already argued that the leasing of a swamp in Mounichia by Aristippos (?) of the deme Kerameis reflects his family's financial engagements in the area of the port. Last, but not least, one can mention the case of Hypereides, the lessee of the Rharia, who was also owner of private property in the wider area of the Thriasian plain. However, all things considered, geographical propinquity does not seem to have been as predominant a pattern as one would have thought.

But the cases of Hypereides and Aristippos (?), especially that of the latter, clearly demonstrate that geographical proximity is not some abstract concept, but has to be construed in terms of accessibility. This is nowhere clearer than in the case of Arrheneides (no. 13). Not surprisingly, his trierarchic status has blurred a very interesing aspect of his leasing activity: Arrheneides had leased a swamp that was consecrated to Athena. Osborne, evaluating this and other instances of wealthy Athenians leasing sacred properties, hazarded an interpretation: 'Their motives may well not have been purely financial: holding these lands conceivably brought a certain social advantage'. This may well be true, but Arrheneides' leasing of the marsh was almost certainly motivated by financial interest. We have already seen that the other less-

[11] This applies to a limited chronological period: that of the 340s–320s. There is hardly any prosopographical evidence from the 5th cent. with the possible exception of *Παναίτι[ος]*, lessee of sacred land at Hestiaia in *IG* I^3 418 l. 6, identified by Raubitschek 1943 with the well-known *Παναίτιος* of the *Attic Stelai* (who, in turn, has been identified with the *Παναίτιος* of Ar. *Eq.* 243, member of the cavalry class; cf. Sommerstein 1997, 155–6). The rarity of the name along with the chronological range makes identification highly likely (see now Moreno 2007, 90); if so, Panaitios' prominence portends the 4th-cent. pattern. And let me briefly mention here that Lambert 2001, 59–60, after hesitantly interpreting the Lykourgan *SEG* XLV 206 as a lease record, has suggested identification of the man in l. 9, 'lessee, guarantor, property owner *vel sim.*', with *Χίονις Δημοστράτου Παιανιεύς*, member of a propertied family.

[12] Rosivach 1994, 126–7.

than-glaring professional activity for which Arrheneides is known is his contract with the Eleusinian administrators. For a mere 12 drachmas and 3 obols, Arrheneides undertook to transport Skiran earth to Eleusis. It is inconceivable that Arrheneides himself would have cared to enter a one-off transaction for such a small profit. Surely this was just a small part of his overall business. We can now see what was there for Arrheneides in his bidding for Athena's swamp: marshes, swamps, *et similia* are prime sources of high-quality earth, and, more importantly, of clay. Arrheneides, the lessee, could easily have extracted the clay from Athena's swamp and sold it for a profit to the Eleusinian authorities. All the better, then, that he could prove himself a pious individual to two major deities, while advancing his own interest.

Another mini-pattern discernible in our leases concerns family-based behaviour.[13] The family factor is of course indisputable in cases where fathers appear to have stepped in as guarantors on behalf of their sons and vice versa, as, for instance, in the case of Keleuon and Nausistratos of Piraeus or the elusive lessee of a house near the Dionysion and his father Pythodoros of Epikephisia. The same can be said about the leasing undertaken by Nausias, son of Nikostratos, a transaction supported by his father.[14] No surprise here, since the pattern is detectable at the deme-level as well.[15] But family bonds seem to permeate leasing transactions in a far more elaborate way that defies our understanding. Thus Kephisodoros of Kydathenaion features as renter of a house at Kydathenaion, whereas his uncle Hippeus was the surety for the lease of a swamp which is by no means connected to the transaction of his nephew. Maybe such a case merely demonstrates purely entrepreneurial interests on the part of the individuals involved and we should not try to detect any specific significance in the family aspect. But what about the son of Charias of Paiania who rented a property for which Alexandros(?), son of Charidemos, of Probalinthos (or Prospalta) stood as guarantor and who (or his brother) in return was the surety of a property rented by a relative, possibly a brother, of this Alexandros?[16] In the end, it has to be conceded that the fragmentary condition of our data may be distorting the final picture, especially since family links outside the strict patrilineal line are difficult to trace.[17]

[13] Cf. Andreyev 1974, 43.

[14] Walbank 1983*d*, 224–5.

[15] e.g. *IG* II^2 2496 (renter: *Εὐκράτης Ἐξηκίου Ἀφιδναῖος*; guarantor: *Ἐξηκίας Ἀφιδναῖος*).

[16] See no. 93 with Walbank 1983*d*, 225 n. 114.

[17] Particularly with regard to onomastics deriving from the maternal line (Pomeroy 1997, 72–5) and/or as a result of adoption (Habicht 1994, 127; cf. Rubinstein 1993, *passim*); see also Osborne 1985*a*, 127–53 for the intricate realities of kinship links.

It has often been thought that religious motives might have instigated certain lessees. One suspects that this might be the explanation behind the mini-pattern emerging in the cluster of names in *Agora* XIX L9 ll. 38–55, where, apart from the dubious case of the son of Polykles (but see no. 69), all the remaining lessees and guarantors originate from demes of the Marathonian Tetrapolis. The prosopographical analysis shows that, despite coming from different, albeit adjacent, demes, those individuals might have been linked through family and religious affiliations (see no. 10). Indeed, it is not inconceivable that links built within the framework of associations such as phratries, *gene*, thiasoi, and *similia* might account for some of the lessee-guarantor pairs emerging in our records in a way that cannot be traced. From a slightly different perspective, it is noticeable that some of the individuals in our database are connected, directly or indirectly, through close relatives, to religious offices.[18] Again, one can counter-argue that such positions were essentially political in nature; with this observation we can proceed to our final mini-pattern.

Political aims should also be taken into consideration. As shown in the prosopographical appendix, one of the most prominent lessees in our database is the Aphidnian Kephisophon. Now, it has largely passed unnoticed that in 343/2, the date of our leases, Kephisophon took over the administration of the theoric fund (*IG* II^2 223C ll. 6–7). Far from being a happenstance, this chronological coincidence could be viewed from two different angles. On the one hand, Kephisophon's tenure of the office would have enabled him to outbid any potential rivals in the case of competitive bidding. On the other hand, by engaging in a transaction de facto profitable for the Athenian coffers Kephisophon would have provided an eloquent example worthy of emulation. No doubt, the leasing of the Rharia would have constituted a useful tool of religious propaganda for the politically ambitious Hypereides too. Kallikrates of Steiria was lessee of an Eleusinian estate in 331/0, and interestingly his son Kallikratides was ἀναγραφεύς at approximately the same time, that is, he held an office de facto connected to the leasing procedure in Athens. For two individuals there is evidence that they or their families were quite prominent in the micropolitics of their demes.[19]

It is true that land leases in comparison to mine operations attracted a slightly less conspicuous agglomeration of individuals. This is easily explicable, since mining provided a bigger profit margin. This is not to say, however, that lessees and guarantors attested in our records consisted mainly of nonentities. On the contrary, a lot of them belonged to the upper and middle strata of Athenian society. Overall, the theory that the leasing scheme in Athens should, to some extent, be seen as a measure of social policy

[18] e.g nos. 10, 11, 65.
[19] Nos. 44, 70.

whereby the Athenian polis enabled the landless citizens to acquire agricultural property should be discounted.[20] Not only is concrete evidence of such poverty-relief measures lacking, the contemporary programme of land privatization known as *Rationes Centesimarum* points in the opposite direction.[21] The theory which would see the Athenian polis deliberately diminishing its income in order to assist impoverished citizens has no place in the Euboulean and Lykourgan programmes of increasing Athenian revenue. Far from being one man's job, the religious rejuvenation of Athens, which is so often connected to the Eteoboutad Lykourgos, had the energetic material support of some of the most prosperous segments of Athenian society, as prosopographical analysis demonstrates.

Metics as Lessees of Sacred Lands

A trait of the leases of sacred lands that has struck scholars as inexplicable is the tiny proportion of metics attested as lessees; only four metics feature in our sources.[22] And, despite what has been frivolously reiterated as a truism,[23] the prosopographical analysis shows that all four of them are otherwise completely unknown. What is more, there is some evidence, albeit tenuous, which allows us to believe that one of the metic lessees was the descendant of a slave.[24] Elsewhere I argued that, prior to the legislative change that gave rise to the bulk leases of 343/2 onwards, metics had probably been barred from renting sacred property. It is worth asking, therefore, why, even after the bestowal of this right, they were not heavily involved in land-leasing. This abstention is hardly reconcilable with the fact that legal prohibitions on acquisition of land by foreigners would have presumably made leases an attractive prospect to metics. To put it otherwise, since no realty placed as security was required in order to bid for a lease, metics could easily participate in auctions where *temene* were put up for sale.[25] Various explanations could be put forward. The circumstances under which the average metic would have decided to settle in Attica must be accounted for. The vast majority of the free foreign residents in Attica were mostly engaged in

[20] Cf. Andreyev 1974, 44 (hesitantly); Walbank 1983*d*, 225; Shipton 2000; Shipton 2001, 143. The existence of any systematic 'sozialstaatliche Politik' in Classical Athens is dismissed as anachronistic by Engels 2000, 117–19.

[21] Lambert 1997*a*, 280–91.

[22] Nos. 5, 6, 23, 87; cf. Todd 1993, 249 (Cohen 2000, 127 is entirely mistaken in claiming that 'religious and social associations . . . often leased local property to . . . metics').

[23] Walbank 1983*a*, 128, 132–3; 1983*d*, 224 n. 113; more emphatically Osborne 1988, 289.

[24] See no. 23 (Ἐργόφιλος). But the point may be totally irrelevant: as Cohen 1998 has recently reminded us, some slaves were extremely wealthy.

[25] Osborne 1988, 289 with n. 28.

professions other than agriculture.[26] The scope of land-leasing was, however, predominantly agricultural. It results from this that even when opportunity arose, inexperience might have discouraged metics from engaging in the agricultural sector of the economy. On the other hand, the fact that two of the four metics in our records are attested as having rented houses fits well with their easily understood concern to obtain domiciles. In fact, one of them, Ergophilos, almost certainly rented a house near his registered place of residence. But this remark brings us back to a slightly altered form of the principal question, namely why more metics do not appear to have sought to acquire residences through leasing.

Osborne's contention that social convention and the religious connotations of leasing property nominally belonging to Athenian divinities should be seen as the reason for metics' underrepresentation in land leases has some strength, but demands further analysis, since it says as much about metics as it does about the leasing agents. Surely, it is tenable that for an Athenian to render service to a cult by providing income through renting could be an incentive strong enough to force him to outbid even over-ambitious foreigners.[27] On the other hand, the final decision about whom any given lease would be assigned to lay with the Athenian governmental instruments. More precisely, the whole procedure lay under the auspices of the Boule. This council was the ultimate authority to decide whether to ratify a certain lease or not and, although its role is often overlooked as a mere formality, there might have been cases where it would have annulled certain transactions as void.[28] Recently, it has been strongly argued that, despite metics being theoretically allowed to make full use of the Athenian judiciary machinery, they more often than not found themselves in a social environment of animosity and inefficiency.[29] Though this claim was made with regard to lawsuits, it is not difficult to see how a similar principle could apply to the realm of economy. Each metic was required by law to have the protection of a προστάτης (*prostates*), but the exact bond between the two parties remains debatable. It seems a fair guess that in a public auction where a metic would bid for a *temenos*, he would need the presence of his *prostates*, and, equally plausible, that the latter would serve as the metic's guarantor. Only a few metics would have been able to break through the ideological barriers. In this light, the fact that one of the four metics was an *isoteles*—he had been given

[26] Whitehead 1977, 70–1; Davies 1981, 50–1; Németh 2001, 336 (Jones 1960, 91 points out the metics named γεωργοί, 'farmers', in RO 4, but some might, in fact, have been slaves; cf. Jameson 1977, 134–5; Rhodes and Osborne 2003, 27).

[27] Whitehead 1986, 157–8.

[28] Shipton 2000, 48.

[29] Patterson 2000, *passim*, building on the doctrines of Whitehead 1977; contra Walbank 1983*d*, 218–19 n. 81, who thinks that Athens 'made no attempt to stop metics from renting such properties'.

various rights normally restricted to citizens—might be taken to demonstrate that only a few chosen ones would be acceptable as foreign lessees.[30] The equally noticeable absence of metics from mines leases probably corroborates this hypothesis.[31]

[30] Cf. Andreyev 1974, 43.
[31] Shipton 2000, 45–6.

Bibliography

Albini, U. (1955), *Lisia, I Discorsi* (Florence).

Aleshire, S. B. (1989), *The Athenian Asklepeion: The People, their Dedications, and the Inventories* (Amsterdam).

——(1991), *Asklepios at Athens: Epigraphic and Prosopographic Essays on the Athenian Healing Cults* (Amsterdam).

——(1994*a*), 'The Demos and the Priests: The Selection of Sacred Officials at Athens from Cleisthenes to Augustus', in R. Osborne and S. Hornblower (eds.), *Ritual, Finance, Politics: Athenian Democratic Accounts Presented to David Lewis* (Oxford), 325–37.

——(1994*b*), 'Towards a Definition of "State Cult" for Ancient Athens', in R. Hägg (ed.), *Ancient Greek Cult Practice from the Epigraphical Evidence. Proceedings of the Second International Seminar on Ancient Greek Cult, organized by the Swedish Institute at Athens, 22–24 November 1991* (Stockholm), 9–16.

——(1999), 'The Identification of Archaizing Inscriptions from Roman Attica', in *XI Congresso Internazionale di Epigrafia Greca e Latina. Roma, 18–24 settembre 1997, Atti II* (Rome), 153–61.

Alipheri, S. (2009), 'The Eleusinian Decrees *REG* 91 (1978) 289–306 Reconsidered', in A. A. Themos and N. Papazarkadas (eds.), *Ἀττικὰ ἐπιγραφικά. Μελέτες πρὸς τιμὴν τοῦ Christian Habicht* (Athens), 183–92.

Amandry, P. (1950), *La mantique apollinienne a Delphes: essai sur la fonctionnement de l'oracle* (Paris).

——(1977), 'Trépieds d'Athènes, II. Thargélies', *BCH* 101, 165–202.

Ameling, P. (1989), 'Das neue attische Dekret für Oropos: ein Datierungsvorschlag', *ZPE* 77, 95–6.

Amouretti, M.-C. (1986), *Le pain et l'huile dans la Grèce ancienne* (Paris).

Ampolo, C. (1982), 'Le cave di pietra dell'Attica: problemi giuridici ed economici', *Opus* 1, 251–60.

——(1992), 'The Economics of the Sanctuaries in Southern Italy and Sicily', in T. Linders and B. Alroth (eds.), *Economics of Cult in the Ancient Greek World. Proceedings of the Uppsala Symposium 1990*, Boreas 21 (Uppsala), 25–8.

——(2000), 'I Terreni Sacri nel Mondo Greco in Età Arcaica e Classica', in E. Lo Cascio and D. W. Rathbone (eds.), *Production and Public Powers in Classical Antiquity*, *PCPhS* suppl. 26, 14–19.

Anderson, C. A., and Dix, T. K. (1997), 'Politics and State Religion in the Delian League: Athena and Apollo in the Eteocarpathain Decree', *ZPE* 117, 129–32.

ANDERSON, G. (2003), *The Athenian Experiment: Building an Imagined Political Community in Ancient Attica, 508–490 B.C.* (Ann Arbor).

——(2009), 'The Personality of the Greek State', *JHS* 129, 1–22.

ANDREADES, A. M. (1928), *Ἱστορία τῆς Ἑλληνικῆς Δημοσίας Οἰκονομίας* (Athens).

ANDREWES, A. (1961), 'Philochoros on Phratries', *JHS* 81, 1–15.

ANDREYEV, V. N. (1974), 'Some Aspects of Agrarian Conditions in Attica in the Fifth to Third Centuries B.C.', *Eirene* 12, 5–46.

ANTONACCIO, C. M. (1995), *An Archaeology of Ancestors: Tomb Cult and Hero Cult in Early Greece* (London).

APERGHIS, G. G. (1997–8), 'A Reassessment of the Laurion Mining-Lease Records', *BICS* 42, 1–20.

APOSTOLAKES, K. E. (2003), *[Λυσίου] Ὑπὲρ Πολυστράτου. Ἑρμηνευτικὸ Ὑπόμνημα* (Athens).

ARANGIO-RUIZ, V. (1936), 'Epigrafia giuridica greca e romana', *SDH* 2, 429–520.

ARNAOUTOGLOU, I. N. (1998), 'Between Koinon and Idion: Legal and Social Dimensions of Religious Associations in Ancient Athens', in P. Cartledge, P. Millett, and S. von Reden (eds.), *Kosmos: Essays in Order, Conflict and Community in Classical Athens* (Cambridge), 68–83.

——(2003), *Thusias heneka kai sunousias: Private Religious Associations in Hellenistic Athens* (Athens).

——(2007), 'Group and Individuals in *IRhamnous* 59 (*SEG* 49.161)', in J.-C. Couvenhes and S. Milanezi (eds.), *Individus, groupes et politique à Athènes de Solon à Mithridate* (Tours), 315–37.

AUDOLLENT, A. (1904), *Defixionum Tabellae*, Paris.

AULT, B. A. (1999), '*Koprones* and Oil Presses at Halieis: Interactions of Town and Country and the Integration of Domestic and Regional Economies', *Hesperia* 68, 549–73.

AUSTIN, M. M., and VIDAL-NAQUET, P. (1977), *Economic and Social History of Ancient Greece: An Introduction* (London).

BADIAN, E. (2004), 'Xenophon the Athenian', in C. Tuplin (ed.), *Xenophon and his World. Papers from a Conference Held in Liverpool in July 1999*, *Historia* Einzelschr. 172 (Stuttgart), 33–53.

BAKEWELL, G. (2008), 'Aeschylus' *Supplices* 11–12: Danaus as πεσσονομῶν', *CQ* 58, 303–7.

BALDASSARRI, P. (1998), *ΣΕΒΑΣΤΩΙ ΣΩΤΗΡΙ: Edilizia monumentale ad Atene durante il Saeculum Augustum* (Rome).

BARAGWANATH, E. (2008), *Motivation and Narrative in Herodotus* (Oxford).

BARRINGER, J. M. (2003), 'Panathenaic Games and Panathenaic Amphorae under Macedonian Rule', in O. Palagia and S. V. Tracy (eds.), *The Macedonians in Athens 322–229 B.C.* (Oxford), 243–56.

Barron, J. P. (1964), 'Religious Propaganda of the Delian League', *JHS* 84, 35–48.

——(1983), 'The Fifth-Century *Horoi* of Aigina', *JHS* 103, 1–12.

Baynham, E. (2003), 'Antipater and Athens', in O. Palagia and S. V. Tracy (eds.), *The Macedonians in Athens 322–229 B.C.* (Oxford), 23–9.

Bechtel, F. (1897), 'Griechische Personennamen aus den Supplementa Inscr. Att. vol. alterius (=IG. II^{1} 5)', *Beiträge zur Kunde der indogermanischen Sprache* 23, 94–9.

Beekes, R. (2010), *Etymological Dictionary of Greek*, 2 vols. (Leiden and Boston).

Behrend, D. (1970), *Attische Pachturkunden: Ein Beitrag zur Beschreibung der μίσθωσις nach der griechischen Inschriften* (Munich).

——(1990), 'Die Pachturkunden der Klytiden', in G. Nenci and G. Thür (eds.), *Symposion 1988. Vorträge zur griechischen und hellenistischen Rechtsgeschichte* (Cologne and Vienna), 231–50.

Bendall, L. M. (2007), *Economies of Religion in the Mycenaean World: Resources Dedicated to Religion in the Mycenaean Palace Economy* (Oxford).

Bentz, M. (1998), *Panathenäische Preisamphoren: Eine athenische Vasengattung und ihre Funktion vom 6.–4. Jahrhundert v. Chr.* (Basel).

Bers, V. (2003), *Demosthenes, Speeches 50–59* (Austin).

Bertelli, L. (1993), 'La "costituzione di Atene" era una democrazia?', in L. R. Cresci and L. Piccirilli (eds.), *L' 'Athenaion Politeia' di Aristotele* (Genoa), 53–98.

Billeter, G. (1898), *Geschichte des Zinsfusses im griechisch-römischen Altertum bis auf Justinian* (Leipzig).

Billigmeier, J. C., and Dusing, M. S. (1981), 'The Origin and Function of the Naukraroi at Athens: An Etymological and Historical Explanation', *TAPA* 111, 11–6.

Biraschi, A. M. (2004), 'A proposito di affitti di proprietà sacre in Attica', *PP* 339, 429–35.

Blamire, A. (2001), 'Athenian Finance, 454–404 B.C.', *Hesperia* 70, 99–126.

Blass, F. (1893), *Die attische Beredsamkeit*, 2nd edn., III.1 (Leipzig).

Blok, J. H. (2006), 'Solon's Funerary Laws: Questions of Authenticity and Function', in J. H. Blok and A. P. M. H. Lardinois (eds.), *Solon of Athens: New Historical and Philological Approaches* (Boston and Leiden), 197–247.

——(2010), 'Deme Accounts and the Meaning of *hosios* Money in Fifth-Century Athens', *Mnemosyne* 63, 61–93.

——and Lambert, S. D. (2009), 'The Appointment of Priests in Attic *Gene*', *ZPE* 169, 95–121.

Böckh, A. (1886), *Die Staatshaushaltung der Athener*, 3rd edn. (Berlin).

Boegehold, A. L. (1972), 'The Establishment of a Central Archive at Athens', *AJA* 76, 23–30.

——(1990), 'Andocides and the Decree of Patrokleides', *Historia* 39, 149–62.

Bouraselis, K. (1982), *Das hellenistische Makedonien und die Ägais* (Munich).

Bourdieu, P. (1990), *The Logic of Practice*, translated by R. Nice (Stanford).

Bourriot, F. (1976), *Recherches sur la nature du génos: Étude d'histoire social athénienne-périodes archaique at classique* (Lille).

Bowden, H. (2005), *Classical Athens and the Delphic Oracle: Divination and Democracy* (Cambridge).

Brenne, S. (2001), *Ostrakismos und Prominenz in Athen: Attische Bürger des 5. Jhs. v. Chr. auf den Ostraka, Tyche* suppl. 3 (Vienna).

Briant, P. (1968), 'La boulè et l'élection des ambassadeurs à Athènes au IVe siècle', *REA* 70, 7–31.

Brisson, L. (2000), 'Lcs Magistratures non judiciaires dans les Lois', *CCG* 11, 85–101.

——(2003), 'Les *agronómoi* dans les *Lois* de Platon et leur possible lien avec *nukterinòs súllogos*', in S. Scolnicov and L. Brisson (eds.), *Plato's* Laws: *From Theory into Practice. Proceedings of the VI Symposium Platonicum* (Sankt Augustin), 221–6.

Brock, R., and Heath, M. (1995), 'Two Passages in pseudo-Xenophon', *CQ* 45, 564–6.

Bruce, I. A. F. (1968), 'Plataea and the Fifth-Century Boeotian Confederacy', *Phoenix* 22, 190–9.

Bruit Zaidman, L., and Schmitt-Pantel, P. (1992), *Religion in the Ancient Greek City* (Cambridge).

Brumfield, A. C. (1981), *The Attic Festivals of Demeter and their Relation to the Agricultural Year* (Salem).

Brun, P. (1983), *Eisphora, syntaxis, stratiotika: Recherches sur les finances militaires d'Athènes au IVe siècle av. J.-C.* (Paris).

——(2000), *L' orateur Démade: Essai d'histoire et d'historiographie* (Bordeaux).

——and Couvenhes, J.-C. (2006), 'Des chiliarques à Athènes au milieu du IVe siècle?', *ZPE* 157, 107–15.

Brunet, M. (2002), 'Les biens fonciers et immobiliers d'Apollon', in C. Prêtre (ed.), *Nouveau choix d'inscriptions de Délos: Lois, comptes et inventaires* (Athens), 250–5.

——, Rougemont, G., and Rousset, D. (1998), 'Les Contrats agraires dans la Grèce antique', *Histoires et Sociétés Rurales* 9, 211–45.

Brunt, P. A. (1966), 'Athenian Settlements Abroad in the Fifth Century B.C.', in *Ancient Society and Institutions. Studies presented to Victor Ehrenberg on his 75th birthday* (Oxford), 71–92.

——(1993), 'The Megarian Decree (with a *Postscript*)', in *Studies in Greek History and Thought* (Oxford), 1–16.

Buck, C. D., and Petersen, W. (1944), *A Reverse Index of Greek Nouns and Adjectives* (Chicago).

Buckler, J. (1989), *Philip II and the Sacred War*, *Mnemosyne* suppl. 109 (Leiden).

——(2003), *Aegean Greece in the Fourth Century BC* (Leiden).

Bugh, G. R. (1988), *The Horsemen of Athens* (Princeton).

——(1998), 'Cavalry Inscriptions from the Athenian Agora', *Hesperia* 67, 81–90.

Burford, A. (1993), *Land and Labor in the Greek World* (Baltimore).

Burke, E. M. (1985), 'Lycourgan Finances', *GRBS* 26, 251–64.

——(1992), 'The Economy of Athens in the Classical Era: Some Adjustments to the Primitivist Model', *TAPA* 122, 199–226.

Burkert, W. (1985), *Greek Religion* (Oxford).

——(1996), 'Greek Temple-Builders: Who, Where and Why?', in R. Hägg (ed.), *The Role of Religion in the Early Greek Polis. Proceedings of the Third International Seminar on Ancient Greek Cult* (Stockholm), 21–9.

Burns, A. (1976), 'Hippodamus and the Planned City', *Historia* 25, 414–28.

Bury, R. G. (1926), *Plato, Laws* (Cambridge, Mass., and London).

Busolt, G., and Swoboda, H. (1920–6), *Griechische Staatskunde* I–II, 3rd edn. (Munich).

Byrne, S. G. (2006–7), 'Four Athenian Archons of the Third Century BC', *MeditArch* 19/20, 169–79.

Cahn, H. A. (2001), 'Amphoren auf frühen attischen Münzen', in M. Bentz and N. Eschbach (eds.), *Panathenaïka. Symposion zu den Panathenäischen Preisamphoren, Rauischholzhausen 25.11.–29.11.1998* (Mainz), 145–6.

Calabi Limentani, I. (1964), *Plutarchi Vita Aristidis* (Florence).

Camp, J. McK. (1984), 'Water and the Pelargikon', in *Studies Presented to Sterling Dow on his Eightieth Birthday* (Durham, NC), 37–41.

——(2007), 'Excavations in the Athenian Agora: 2002–2007', *Hesperia* 76, 627–63.

Carey, C. (1989), *Lysias, Selected Speeches* (Cambridge).

——(1998), 'The Shape of Athenian Laws', *CQ* 48, 93–109.

Cargill, J. (1981), *The Second Athenian League: Empire or Free Alliance?* (Berkeley).

——(1995), *Athenian Settlements of the Fourth Century B.C.*, *Mnemosyne* suppl. 145 (Leiden).

Carlier, P. (1984), *La Royalté en Grèce avant Alexandre* (Strasbourg).

——(1995), '*QA-SI-RE-U* et *QA-SI-RE-WI-JA*', in R. Laffineur and W.-D. Niemeier (eds.), *Politeia: Society and State in the Aegean Bronze Age* (Liège and Austin), 355–64.

Carusi, C. (2006), 'Alcune considerazioni sulle *syngraphai* ateniesi del V e del IV secolo a.C.', *ASAtene* 84, 11–36.

——(2008), *Il sale nel mondo greco (VI a.C.–III d.C.): Luoghi di produzione, circolazione commerciale, regimi di sfruttamento nel contesto del Mediterraneo antico* (Bari).

CAVAIGNAC, E. (1908), *Études sur l'histoire financière d'Athènes au Ve siècle: Le trésor sacré d'Éleusis jusqu'en 404* (Paris).

CAVANAUGH, M. B. (1996), *Eleusis and Athens: Documents in Finance, Religion and Politics in the Fifth Century B.C.* (Atlanta).

CAWKWELL, G. L. (1963), 'Eubulus', *JHS* 83, 47–67.

——(1969), 'Anthemocritus and the Megarians and the Decree of Charinus', *REG* 82, 327–35.

——(1997), *Thucydides and the Peloponnesian War* (London).

CHADWICK, J. (1957), 'Potnia', *Minos* 5, 117–29.

——(1973), *Documents in Mycenaean Greek*, 2nd edn. (Cambridge).

CHAMBERS, M., GALLUCI, R., and SPANOS, P. (1990), 'Athens' Alliance with Egesta in the Year of Antiphon', *ZPE* 83, 33–63.

CHANDEZON, C. (2003), *L'Élevage en Grèce, fin V^e–fin Ier siècle a.C. : l'apport des sources épigraphiques* (Pessac).

CHANIOTIS, A. (1988), 'Habgierige Götter, habgierige Städte—Heiligtumbesitz und Gebietsanspruch in den kretischen Staatsverträgen', *Ktema* 13, 21–39.

——(1994), 'Review of *The Athenian Agora. Volume XIX*', *Gnomon* 66, 695–8.

CHANKOWSKI, V. (2001), 'Athènes, Délos et les Cyclades à l'époque classique: un réseau économique?', *REA* 103, 83–102.

——(2005), 'Techniques financières, influences, performances dans les activités bancaires des sanctuaires grecs', *Topoi* 12–13, 69–93.

——(2008), *Athènes et Délos à l'époque classique: Recherches sur l'administration du sanctuaire d'Apollon délien*, BEFAR 331 (Paris).

CHANTRAINE, P. (1999), *Dictionnaire étymologique de la langue grecque*, augmented edn. (Paris).

CHASE, A. H. (1933), 'The Influence of Athenian Institutions upon the Laws of Plato', *HSCP* 44, 131–92.

CHATZIS, A. C. (1930), '*Ἐπιγραφὴ ἐκ Σαλαμῖνος*', *AEphemeris* 1930, 59–60.

CHOREMI, E., PAPAZARKADAS, N., and PETROPOULOU, T. (2000–3), '*Κατάλογος Ἀθηναίων δημοτῶν*', *Horos* 14–16, 83–8.

CHRIST, M. R. (2007), 'The Evolution of the *Eisphora* in Classical Athens', *CQ* 57, 53–69.

CLINTON, K. (1974), *The Sacred Officials of the Eleusinian Mysteries*, TAPS NS 64 (Philadelphia).

——(1979), '*IG* I^2 5, the Eleusinia, and the Eleusinians', *AJP* 100, 1–12.

——(1980), 'A Law in the City Eleusinion concerning the Mysteries', *Hesperia* 49, 258–88.

Clinton, K. (1984), 'Eleusinian Treasures in the Late Fifth and Early Fourth Centuries', in *Studies Presented to Sterling Dow on his Eightieth Birthday* (Durham, NC), 51–60.

——(1994), 'The Epidauria and the Arrival of Asclepius in Athens', in R. Hägg (ed.), *Ancient Greek Cult Practice from the Epigraphical Evidence. Proceedings of the Second International Seminar on Ancient Greek Cult, organized by the Swedish Institute at Athens* (Stockholm), 17–34.

——(2005), 'Pigs in Greek Rituals', in R. Hägg and B. Alroth (eds.), *Greek Sacrificial Ritual, Olympian and Chthonian. Proceedings of the Sixth International Seminar on Ancient Greek Cult, organized by the Department of Classical Archaeology and Ancient History, Göteborg University, 25–27 April 1997* (Stockholm), 167–79.

——(2008), *Eleusis. The Inscriptions on Stone: Documents of the Sanctuary of the Two Goddesses and Public Documents of the Deme*, vol. II: *Commentary* (Athens).

Cohen, D. (1990), 'Late Sources and the "Reconstruction" of Greek Legal Institutions', in G. Nenci and G. Thür (eds.), *Symposion 1988. Vorträge zur griechischen und hellenistischen Rechtsgeschichte* (Cologne and Vienna), 282–93.

Cohen, E. E. (1992), *Athenian Economy & Society: A Banking Perspective* (Princeton).

——(1998), 'The Wealthy Slaves of Athens: Legal Rights, Economic Obligations', in H. Jones (ed.), *Le Monde antique et les droits d'homme. Actes de la 50e Session de la Société internationale Fernand De Visscher pour l'histoire des droits de l'antiquité. Bruxelles, 16–19 septembre 1996* (Brussels), 105–29.

——(2000), *The Athenian Nation* (Princeton).

Cole, S. G. (1988), 'The Uses of Water in Greek Sanctuaries', in R. Hägg, N. Marinatos, and G. C. Nordquist, *Early Greek Cult Practice. Proceedings of the Fifth International Symposium at the Swedish Institute at Athens* (Stockholm), 161–5.

——(1995), 'Civic Cult and Civic Identity', in M. H. Hansen (ed.), *Sources for the Ancient Greek City-State* (Copenhagen), 292–325.

Connor, W. R. (1962), 'Charinus' Megarian Decree', *AJP* 83, 225–46.

Connor, W. R. (1970), 'Charinus' Megarean Decree Again', *REG* 83, 305–8.

——(1988), '"Sacred" and "Secular": *Ἱερὰ καὶ ὅσια* and the Classical Athenian Concept of the State', *AS* 19, 161–88.

——(1991), 'The Other 399: Religion and the Trial of Socrates', in M. A. Flower and M. Toher (eds.), *Georgica: Greek Studies in Honour of George Cawkwell* (London), 49–56.

Constantakopoulou, C. (2002), 'Connectivity in the Aegean: The Practice of *Porthmeutice* and its Importance for Small-Scale Interaction', *JMS* 12, 223–6.

——(2007), *The Dance of the Islands: Insularity, Networks, the Athenian Empire and the Aegean World* (Oxford).

Conwell, D. H. (1993), 'Topography and Toponyms between Athens and Piraeus', *JAT* 3, 49–62.

——(2008), *Connecting a City to the Sea: The History of the Athenian Long Walls* (Boston and Leiden).

Cook, B. F. (1987), *Greek Inscriptions* (London).

Corbett, P. E. (1949), 'Attic Pottery of the Later Fifth Century from the Athenian Agora', *Hesperia* 18, 298–351.

Corsaro, M. (1990), 'Qualche osservazione sulle procedure di recupero delle terre pubbliche nelle città greche', in G. Nenci and G. Thür (eds.), *Symposion 1988. Vorträge zur griechischen und hellenistischen Rechtsgeschichte* (Cologne and Vienna), 213–29.

Cosmopoulos, M. B. (1995), 'L'ancienne histoire d'Oropos', in J. M. Fossey (ed.), *Boeotia Antiqua*, V. *Studies on Boiotian Topography, Cults and Terracotas* (Amsterdam), 3–34.

——(2001), *The Rural History of Ancient Greek City-States: The Oropos Survey Project* (Oxford).

Coumanoudis, S., and Gofas, D. (1978), 'Deux décrets inédits d'Éleusis', *REG* 91, 289–306.

Couvenhes, J.-C. (1999), 'La réponse athénienne à la violence territoriale aux IVe et IIIe siècles av. J.-C.', *CCG* 10, 189–207.

Crosby, M. (1941), 'Greek Inscriptions', *Hesperia* 10, 14–27.

——(1950), 'The Leases of the Laureion Mines', *Hesperia* 19, 189–312.

Csapo, E. (2007), 'The Men Who Built the Theatres: *Theatropolai*, *Theatronai*, and *Arkhitektones*', in P. Wilson (ed.), *The Greek Theatre and Festivals: Documentary Studies* (Oxford), 87–115.

Culasso Gastaldi, E. (2006), 'Lemnos: i cippi di garanzia', *ASAtene* 84, 509–50.

Culley, G. R. (1975), 'The Restoration of Sanctuaries in Attica: *IG* II^{2} 1035', *Hesperia* 44, 207–23.

——(1977), 'The Restoration of Sanctuaries in Attica, II', *Hesperia* 46, 282–98.

Dakoura-Vogiatzoglou, O. (2010), '*Η "διὰ Κοίλης" οδός*', in M. Korres (ed.), *Αττικής Οδοί. Αρχαίοι δρόμοι της Αττικής* (Athens), 220–35.

Dalmeyda, G. (1930), *Andocide, Discours* (Paris).

Daniel, R. (2007), '*Οἰκόπεδα* in Xenophon, Diodorus Siculus and elsewhere', *ZPE* 159, 61–9.

Daux, G. (1941), 'Notes épigraphiques et philologiques', *REG* 54, 218–27.

——(1963), 'La Grande Démarchie: un nouveau calendrier sacrificiel d'Attique (Erchia)', *BCH* 87, 603–34.

——(1983), 'Le calendrier de Thorikos au musée J. Paul Getty', *AC* 52, 150–74.

Daverio-Rocchi, G. (1987), 'La *ΙΕΡΑ ΟΡΓΑΣ* e la frontiera Attico-Megarica', in *Studi di antichità in memoria di Clementina Gatti* (Milan).
——(1988), *Frontiera e Confini nella Grecia Antica* (Milan).
Davies, J. K. (1981), *Wealth and the Power of Wealth in Classical Athens* (New York).
——(1994), 'Accounts and Accountability in Classical Athens', in R. Osborne and S. Hornblower (eds.), *Ritual, Finance, Politics: Athenian Democratic Accounts Presented to David Lewis* (Oxford), 201–12.
——(1995), 'The Fourth Century Crisis: What Crisis?', in W. Eder (ed.), *Die Athenische Demokratie im 4. Jahrhundert v. Chr.* (Stuttgart), 29–39.
——(1998), 'Finance, Administration and *Realpolitik*: The Case of Fourth-Century Delphi', in M. Austin, J. Harries, and C. Smith (eds.), *Modus Operandi. Essays in Honour of Geoffrey Rickman* (London), 1–14.
——(2000), 'Athenaeus' Use of Public Documents', in D. Braund and J. Wilkins (eds.), *Athenaeus and his World: Reading Greek Culture in the Roman Empire* (Exeter), 203–17.
——(2001), 'Temples, Credit, and the Circulation of Money', in A. Meadows and K. Shipton (eds.), *Money and its Uses in the Ancient Greek World* (Oxford), 117–28.
——(2007), 'Classical Greece: Production', in W. Scheidel, I. Morris, and R. Saller (eds.), *The Cambridge Economic History of the Greco-Roman World* (Cambridge), 333–61.
De Bruyn, O. (1995), *La compétence de l'Aréopage en matière de procès publics: des origines de la polis athénienne à la conquête romaine de la Grèce, Historia* Einzelschr. 90 (Stuttgart).
Delorme, J. (1960), *Gymnasion: Étude sur les monuments consacrés à l'éducation en Grèce* (Paris).
De Marcellus, H. V. (1994), *The Origins and Nature of the Attic Ephebeia to 200 B.C.* D.Phil., (Oxford).
De Sanctis, G. (1926), 'Oropo', *Rivista di Filologia* 54, 222–3.
Descat, R. (1993), 'La loi de Solon sur l'interdiction d'exporter les produits attiques', in A. Bresson and P. Rouillard (eds.), *L'Emporion* (Paris), 145–61.
De Souza, P. (1999), *Piracy in the Graeco-Roman World* (Cambridge).
Detienne, M. (1973), 'L'olivier: un mythe politico-religieux', in M. Finley (ed.), *Problèmes de la terre en Grèce ancienne* (Paris), 293–306.
Deubner, L. (1932), *Attische Feste* (Berlin).
Develin, R. (1989), *Athenian Officials. 684–321 B.C.* (Cambridge).
Dignas, B. (2000), 'The Leases of Sacred Property at Mylasa: An Alimentary Scheme for the Gods', *Kernos* 13, 117–26.
——(2002), *Economy of the Sacred in Hellenistic and Roman Asia Minor* (Oxford).
Dilke, O. A. W. (1985), *Greek and Roman Maps* (London).

Dillery, J. (1993), 'Xenophon's *Poroi* and Athenian Imperialism', *Historia* 42, 1–11.

——(2002), 'Ephebes in the Stadium (not the Theatre): *Ath. Pol.* 42.2 and *IG* II^2 351', *CQ* 52, 462–70.

Dillon, M. (1997), 'The Ecology of the Greek Sanctuary', *ZPE* 118, 113–27.

——and Garland, L. (1994), *Ancient Greece: Social and Historical Documents from Archaic Times to the Death of Socrates (c. 800–399 BC)* (London and New York).

Dindorf, G. (1849), *Demosthenes, Volumen VI. Annotationes Interpretum ad XX.-XXVI* (Oxford).

Dinsmoor Jr., W. B. (1982), 'Anchoring Two Floating Temples', *Hesperia* 51, 410–52.

Docter, R. F. (1991), 'Athena vs Dionysos. Reconsidering the Contents of SOS Amphorae', *BABesch* 66, 45–9.

Dow, S. (1937), 'The Egyptian Cults in Athens', *HTR* 30, 184–232.

——(1938), '*Inscriptiones Graecae, Voluminis II et III Editio Minor*', *AJP* 59, 357–60.

——(1960), 'The Athenian Calendar of Sacrifices: The Chronology of Nikomakhos' Second Term', *Historia* 9, 271–93.

——(1963), 'The Athenian Anagrapheis', *HSCP* 67, 38–54.

——(1965), 'The Greater Demarkhia of Erkhia', *BCH* 89, 180–213.

——(1968), 'Six Athenian Sacrificial Calendars', *BCH* 92, 170–86.

——(1976), 'Companionable Associates in the Athenian Governement', in L. Bonfante and H. von Heinze (eds.), *In Memoriam Otto J. Brendel: Essays in Archaeology and the Humanities* (Mainz), 69–84.

Dreher, M. (1995), *Hegemon und Symmachoi. Untersuchungen zum Zweiten Athenischen Seebund* (Berlin).

——(1999), *Untersuchungen zur Geschichte des spätklassischen Athen (322–ca. 230 v. Chr.), Historia* Einzelschr. 137 (Stuttgart).

Eder, W. (1995), 'Die Athenische Demokratie im 4. Jahrhundert v. Chr. Krise oder Vollendung?', in W. Eder (ed.), *Die Athenische Demokratie im 4. Jahrhundert v. Chr.* (Stuttgart), 11–28.

Edwards, M. J. (1999), *Lysias, Five Speeches (Speeches 1, 12, 19, 22, 30)* (Bristol).

Eickstedt, K.-V. von (1991), *Beiträge zur Topographie des antiken Piräus* (Athens).

——(2001), *Τὸ Ἀσκληπιεῖον τοῦ Πειραιῶς* (Athens).

Eidinow, E. (2007), *Oracles, Curses, and Risk among the Ancient Greeks* (Oxford).

Ekroth, G. (2002), *The Sacrificial Rituals of Greek Hero-Cults in the Archaic to the Early Hellenistic Periods, Kernos* suppl. 12 (Liège).

Eliot, C. W. J. (1962), *The Coastal Demes of Attica: A Study of the Policy of Kleisthenes, Phoenix* suppl. 5 (Toronto).

ELLIS, J. R. (1994), 'Macedon and North-West Greece', in D. M. Lewis, J. Boardman, S. Hornblower, M. Ostwald (eds.), *The Cambridge Ancient History*, vol. VI: *The Fourth Century B.C.*, 2nd edn. (Cambridge), 723–59.

ENGELS, J. (1989), *Studien zur politischen Biographie des Hypereides: Athen in der Epoche der lykurgischen Reformen und des makedonischen Universalreiches* (Munich).

——(2000), 'Das athenische Getreidesteuer-Gesetz des Agyrrhios und angebliche "sozialstaatliche" Ziele in den Massnahmen zur Getreideversorgung spätklassischer und hellenistischer Poleis', *ZPE* 132, 97–124.

ENGEN, D. (1999), '*IG* II^2 204 & *On Organization* (Dem.? 13): The Dispute over the Sacred *Orgas* of Eleusis and the Chronology of Philip II of Macedon', in R. Mellor and L. Tritle (eds.), *Text & Tradition: Studies in Greek History & Historiography in Honor of Mortimer Chambers* (Claremont, Calif.), 135–52.

ESCHBACH, N. (2007), 'Panathenaic Prize Amphorae from the Kerameikos: Some New Aspects and Results', in O. Palagia and A. Choremi-Spetsieri (eds.), *The Panathenaic Games* (Oxford), 91–100.

FANTASIA, U. (1977), 'Documenti d'affitto delle terre dei Klytidai (Chio, IV sec. a.C.)', *ASNP* ser. III, 7, 27–55.

FARAGUNA, M. (1992), *Atene nell'età di Alessandro: Problemi politici, economici, finanziari* (Rome).

——(1997), 'Registrazioni catastali nel mondo Greco: il caso di Atene', *Atheneum* 85, 1–33.

——(1998), 'Un nuovo studio sulle "Rationes Centesimarum"', *Dike* 1, 171–80.

——(2000), 'A proposito degli archivi nel mondo greco: terra e registrazioni fondiarie', *Chiron* 30, 65–115.

——(2006), 'La città di Atene e l'amministrazione delle miniere del Laurion', in H.-A. Rupprecht (ed.), *Symposion 2003: Vorträge zur griechischen und hellenistischen Rechtsgeschichte (Rauischholzhausen, 30. September - 3. Oktober 2003)* (Vienna), 141–60.

FARAONE, C. A. (1991), 'The Agonistic Context of Early Greek Binding Spells', in C. A. Faraone and D. Obbink (eds.), *Magika Hiera: Ancient Greek Magic and Religion* (Oxford), 3–32.

FEAVER, D. D. (1957), 'Historical Development in the Priesthoods of Athens', *YCS* 15, 123–58.

FERGUSON, W. S. (1898), *The Athenian Secretaries* (Ithaca, NY).

——(1901), 'The Delian Amphictyony', *CR* 15, 38–40.

——(1911), *Hellenistic Athens* (London).

——(1932), *The Treasurers of Athena* (Harvard).

——(1936), 'The Athenian Law Code and the Old Attic Trittyes', in *Classical Studies presented to Edward Capps* (Princeton), 144–58.

——(1938), 'The Salaminioi of Heptaphylai and Sounion', *Hesperia* 7, 1–74.

——(1944), 'The Attic Orgeones', *HTR* 37, 61–140.

——(1949), 'Orgeonika', in *Commemorative Studies in Honor of Theodore Leslie Shear*, *Hesperia* suppl. 8 (Baltimore), 130–63.

Fernández-Galiano, M. (1953), *Lysias, Discursos* (Barcelona).

Ferrucci, S. (2005), 'La richezza nascosta: Osservazioni su ἀφανής e φανερὰ οὐσία', *MedAnt* 8, 145–69.

Figueira, T. J. (1991), *Athens and Aigina in the Age of Imperial Colonization* (Baltimore).

Fine, J. V. A. (1951), *Horoi*, *Hesperia* suppl. 9 (Baltimore).

Fink, J. (1963), 'Lieferanten der Athena', *Gymnasium* 70, 133–6.

Finley, M. I. (1952*a*), *Land and Credit in Ancient Athens, 500–200 B.C: The Horos-Inscriptions* (New Brunswick).

——(1952*b*), 'Multiple Charges on Real Property in Athenian Law: New Evidence from an Agora Inscription', in *Studi in Onore de Vincenzo Arangio-Ruiz nel XLV Anno del suo Insegnamento*, vol. III (Naples), 473–91.

——(1968), 'The Alienability of Land in Ancient Greece: A Point of View', *Eirene* 7, 25–32.

——(1975), 'The Ancestral Constitution', in *The Use and Abuse of History* (London), 34–59.

——(1977), *The World of Odysseus*, 2nd edn. (London).

Fischer-Hansen, T. (1996), 'The Earliest Town-Planning of the Western Greek Colonies, with special regard to Sicily', in M. H. Hansen (ed.), *Introduction to an Inventory of Poleis* (Copenhagen), 317–65.

Fisher, N. (2001), *Aeschines, Against Timarchos: Introduction, Translation, and Commentary* (Oxford).

Flament, C. (2006), 'Autour d'*IG* I^3 375: Étude des finances athéniennes au sortir de la première révolution oligarchique', *ZPE* 158, 165–72.

——(2007), *Le monnayage en argent d'Athènes: de l'époque archaïque à l'époque hellénistique (c. 550 – c. 40 av. J.-C.)* (Louvain-la-Neuve).

Flower, M. A. (1985), '*IG* II^2 2344 and the Size of Phratries in Classical Athens', *CQ* ns 35, 232–5.

Fontenrose, J. (1978), *The Delphic Oracle: Its Responses and Operations* (Berkeley).

Forbes, H. (1992), 'The Ethnoarchaeological Approach to Ancient Greek Agriculture: Olive Cultivation as a Case Study', in B. Wells (ed.), *Agriculture in Ancient Greece. Proceedings of the 7th International Symposium at the Swedish Institute at Athens, 16–17 May 1990* (Stockholm), 86–101.

——(1995), 'The Uses of the Uncultivated Landscape', in G. Shipley and J. Salmon (eds.), *Human Landscapes in Classical Antiquity* (London and New York), 68–97.

Fornara, C. W. (1983), *Translated Documents of Greece and Rome: Archaic Times to the End of the Peloponnesian War* (Cambridge).

Fornara, C. W. (2003), 'Thuc. 2.13.3: 600 T. of Tribute', in G. W. Bakewell and J. P. Sickinger (eds.), *Gestures: Essays in Ancient History, Literature, and Philosophy presented to Alan L. Boegehold* (Oxford), 251–7.

Forsdyke, S. (2006), 'Land, Labor and Economy in Solonian Athens: Breaking the Impasse between Archaeology and History', in J. H. Blok and A. P. M. H. Lardinois (eds.), *Solon of Athens: New Historical and Philological Approaches* (Boston and Leiden), 334–50.

Forster, E. S. (1927), *Isaeus* (London).

Fowden, G. (1988), 'City and Mountain in Late Roman Attica', *JHS* 108, 48–59.

Fossey, J. M. (1988), *Topography and Population of Ancient Boiotia*, vols. I–II, (Chicago).

Foucart, P. (1880), 'Inscription d'Éleusis du Vme siècle', *BCH* 4, 225–56.

——(1884), 'Note sur les comptes d'Éleusis sous l'archontat de Képhisophon. OL. 112,4 (329/8)', *BCH* 8, 194–216.

——(1889), 'Décret Athénien de l'année 352 trouvé à Éleusis', *BCH* 13, 433–67.

Fouchard, P. (1998), '*Dèmosios et Dèmos*: sur l'état grec', *Ktema* 23, 59–69.

Fowden, G. (1988), 'City and Mountain in Late Roman Attica', *JHS* 108, 48–59.

Foxhall, L. (1992), 'The Control of Attic Landscape', in B. Wells (ed.), *Agriculture in Ancient Greece. Proceedings of the 7th International Symposium at the Swedish Institute at Athens, 16–17 May 1990* (Stockholm), 155–9.

——(1996), 'Feeling the Earth Move: Cultivation Techniques on Steep Slopes in Classical Antiquity', in G. Shipley and J. Salmon (eds.), *Human Landscapes in Classical Antiquity* (London), 44–67.

——(1997), 'A View from the Top: Evaluating the Solonian Property Classes', in L. G. Mitchell and P. J. Rhodes (eds.), *The Development of the Polis in Archaic Greece* (London and New York 1997), 113–36.

——(2002), 'Access to Resources in Classical Greece', in P. Cartledge, E. E. Cohen, and L. Foxhall (eds.), *Money, Labour and Land: Approaches to the Economies of Ancient Greece* (London and New York), 209–20.

——(2007), *Olive Cultivation in Ancient Greece: Seeking the Ancient Economy* (Oxford).

Fragiadakis, C. (1986), *Die attischen Sklavennamen von den spätarchaischen Epoche bis in die römische Kaiserzeit: Eine historische und soziologische Untersuchung* (Mannheim).

Friis Johansen, H., and Whittle, E. W. (1980), *Aeschylus. The Suppliants*, vol. II. *Commentary: Lines 1–629* (Copenhagen).

Frisch, H. (1942), *The Constitution of Athens: A Philological–Historical Analysis of pseudo-Xenofon's Treatise de re publica Atheniensium* (Copenhagen).

FRISK, H (1960), *Griechisches etymologisches Wörterbuch*, vol. I (Heidelberg).

——(1970), *Griechisches etymologisches Wörterbuch*, vol. II (Heidelberg).

FRÖHLICH, P. (1999), 'Les Magistrates de la guerre', in F. Prost (ed.), *Armées et sociétés de la Grèce classique: Aspects sociaux et politiques de la guerre aux Ve et IVe s. av. J.-C.* (Paris), 108–36.

FROST, F. J. (1994), 'The Rural Demes of Attica', in W. D. E. Coulson *et al.* (eds.), *The Archaeology of Athens and Attica under the Democracy* (Oxford), 173–4.

GABRIELSEN, V. (1986), '*Φανερὰ* and *ἀφανὴς οὐσία* in Classical Athens', *C&M* 37, 99–114.

——(1987), 'The *Diadikasia*-Documents', *C&M* 38, 39–51.

GAGARIN, M. (2006), 'Legal Procedure in Solon's Laws', in J. H. Blok and A. P. M. H. Lardinois (eds.), *Solon of Athens: New Historical and Philological Approaches* (Boston and Leiden), 261–75.

GAGER, J. G. (1992), *Curse Tablets and Binding Spells from the Ancient World* (Oxford).

GALLANT, T. W. (1982), 'Agricultural Systems, Land Tenure, and the Reforms of Solon', *BSA* 77, 111–24.

GALLO, L. (2005*a*), 'Samo e Atene', in L. Breglia and M. Luppi (eds.), *Da Elea a Samo: Filosofi e politici di fronte all'impero ateniese* (Naples), 247–58.

GALLO, L. (2005*b*), 'La tassazione della terra nelle *poleis* greche: alcune considerazioni sul caso di Atene', *MedAnt* 8, 171–81.

GARDINER, E. N. (1912), 'Panathenaic Amphorae', *JHS* 32, 179–93.

GARLAN, Y. (2000), *Amphores et timbres amphoriques grecs: Entre érudition et idéologie* (Paris).

GARLAND, R. (1984), 'Religious Authority in Archaic and Classical Athens', *BSA* 79, 75–123.

——(1987), *The Piraeus: From the Fifth to the First Century B.C.* (New York).

——(1992), *Introducing New Gods: The Politics of Athenian Religion* (New York).

GARNSEY, P. (1985), 'Grain for Athens', in P. A. Cartledge and F. D. Harvey (eds.), *Crux. Essays Presented to G. E. M. de Ste Croix on his 75th Birthday* (Devon), 62–75.

——(1988), *Famine and Food Supply in the Graeco-Roman World* (Cambridge).

GARVIE, A. F. (1994), *Homer, Odyssey. Books VI–VIII* (Cambridge).

GAUTHIER, P. (1966), 'Les clérouques de Lesbos et la colonisation athénienne au Ve siècle', *REG* 79, 64–88.

——(1973), 'A propos des clérouquies athéniennes de Ve siècle', in M. I. Finley (ed.), *Problèmes de la terre en Grèce ancienne* (Paris), 163–78.

——(1976), *Un commentaire historique des Poroi de Xénophon* (Paris).

——(1982), 'Les villes athéniennes et un décret pour un commerant (*IG*, II2, 903)', *REG* 95, 275–90.

Gauthier, P. (1985), *Les cités grecques et leurs bienfaiteurs (IVe–Ier siècle avant J.-C.): Contribution à l'histoire des institutions*, *BCH* suppl. 12 (Paris).

——(1998), 'La date de l'élection des magistrats Athéniens et l'oracle de Delphes', *CRAI*, 63–75.

Gawlinski, L. (2007), 'The Athenian Calendar of Sacrifices: A New Fragment from the Athenian Agora', *Hesperia* 76, 37–55.

Geagan, D. J. (1967), *The Athenian Constitution after Sulla*, *Hesperia* suppl. 12 (Princeton).

Gerber, D. E. (1999), *Greek Elegiac Poetry: From the Seventh to the Fifth Centuries B.C.* (Cambridge, Mass.).

Gernet, L. (1957), *Démosthène, Plaidoyers civils* II (Paris).

Gernet, L. (1960), *Démosthène, Plaidoyers civils* IV (Paris).

Gernet, L., and Bizos, M. (1959), *Lysias, Discours*, vol. I: *I–XV*, 4th edn. (Paris).

Geuss, R. (2001), *Public Goods, Private Goods* (Princeton).

Gibson, C. A. (2002), *Interpreting a Classic: Demosthenes and his Ancient Commentators* (Berkeley).

Giglioni, G. B. (1970), *Xenophontis De Vectigalibus* (Florence).

Gill, D. W. J. (2006), 'Hippodamus and the Piraeus', *Historia* 55, 1–15.

Giovannini, A. (1990), 'Le Parthénon, le Trésor d' Athéna et le Tribut des Alliés', *Historia* 39, 129–48.

Giuliani, A. (2001), *La città e l'oracolo: I rapporti tra Atene e Delfi in età arcaica e classica* (Milan).

Godley, A. D. (1925), *Herodotus, Books VIII–X* (Cambridge, Mass., and London).

Goette, H. R. (1992–8), '*Ο δήμος της Παλλήνης. Επιγραφές από την περιοχή του ναού της Ἀθηνᾶς Παλληνίδος*', *Horos* 10–12, 105–18.

——(1994), 'Neue attische Felsinschriften', *Klio* 76, 120–34.

——(2000), *'Ο ἀξιόλογος δῆμος Σούνιον, Landeskundliche Studien in Südost-Attika* (Rhaden).

——(2003), 'Cape Sounion and the Macedonian Occupation', in O. Palagia and S. V. Tracy (eds.), *The Macedonians in Athens 322–229 B.C. Proceedings of an International Conference held at the University of Athens, May 24–26, 2001* (Oxford), 152–61.

Gomme, A. W. (1945), *A Historical Commentary on Thucydides*, vol. I (Oxford).

——(1956), *A Historical Commentary on Thucydides*, vol. II (Oxford).

——, Sandbach, F. H. (1973), *Menander. A Commentary* (Oxford).

——, Andrewes, A., and Dover, K. J. (1981), *A Historical Commentary on Thucydides*, vol. V (Oxford).

Gorman, V. B. (1995), 'Aristotle's Hippodamos (Politics 2.1267b 22–30)', *Historia* 44, 384–95.

Gourmelen, L. (2004), *Kékrops, le Roi-Serpent: Imaginaire athénien, représentations de l'humain et de l'animalité en Grèce ancienne* (Paris).

Graham, A. J. (1998), 'The Woman at the Window: Observations on the "stele from the harbour" of Thasos', *JHS* 118, 22–40.

Gray, V. J. (2007), *Xenophon on Government* (Cambridge).

Grimaldi, W. M. A. (1988), *Aristotle, Rhetoric II: A Commentary* (New York).

Gschnitzer, F. (1958), *Abhängige Orte im griechischen Altertum* (Munich).

Guarducci, M. (1937), *L'istituzione della fratria nella Grecia antica e nelle colonie greche di Italia. Parte Prima* (Rome).

——(1974), *Epigrafia Greca,* III: *Epigrafi di carattere privato* (Rome).

——(1978), *Epigrafia Greca,* IV: *Epigrafi sacre pagane e cristiane* (Rome).

Guidorizzi, G., Avezzù, G., and Cerri, G. (2008), *Sofocle, Edipo a Colono* (Milan).

Guiolias, M. A. (1989), *Η κτηνοτροφία στην αρχαία Αττική* (Athens).

Guiraud, P. (1893), *La Propriété foncière en Grèce jusqu' à la conquête romaine* (Paris).

Guizzi, F. (1997), 'Conquista, occupazione del suolo e titoli che danno diritto alla proprietà: l'esempio di una controversia interstatale cretese', *Athenaeum* 85, 35–52.

Habicht, C. (1987), 'Eine Familie aus Kydathen', *ZPE* 69, 83–4.

——(1994), 'Namensgleiche Athener in verschiedenen Demen', *ZPE* 103, 117–27.

——(1996), 'Salamis in der Zeit nach Sulla', *ZPE* 111, 79–87.

——(1997), *Athens from Alexander to Antony* (Harvard).

——(2003), 'Athens after the Chremonidean War: Some Second Thoughts', in O. Palagia and S. V. Tracy (eds.), *The Macedonians in Athens 322–229 B.C.* (Oxford), 52–5.

Hagemajer Allen, K. (2003), 'Intercultural Exchanges in Fourth-Century Attic Decrees', *ClAnt* 22, 199–246.

Hall, J. M. (2007), *A History of the Archaic Greek World* (Oxford).

Hallof, K. (1990), 'Der Verkauf konfiszierten Vermögens von der Poleten in Athen', *Klio* 72, 402–26.

——and Habicht, C. (1995), 'Buleuten und Beamte der athenischen Klerruchie in Samos', *MDAI (A)* 110, 273–304.

Hamel, D. (1998), *Athenian Generals: Military Authority in the Classical Period, Mnemosyne* suppl. 182 (Leiden).

Hamilton, R. (1992), *Choes and Anthesteria* (Ann Arbor).

Hammond, N. G. L. (1961), 'Land Tenure in Athens and Solon's *Seisachteia*', *JHS* 81, 76–98.

Hansen, M. H. (1976), *Apagoge, Endeixis and Ephegesis against Kakourgoi, Atimoi and Pheugontes: A Study in the Athenian Administration of Justice in the Fourth Century B.C.* (Odense).

Hansen, M. H. (1980–1), 'Seven Hundred *Archai* in Classical Athens', *GRBS* 21, 151–73.
——(1985), 'Athenian *Nomothesia*', *GRBS* 26, 345–71.
——(1990), 'Asty, Mesogeios and Paralia: In defence of Arist. ATH. POL. 21.4', *CM* 41, 51–4.
——(1995*a*), '*Kome:* A Study in how the Greeks Designated and Classified Settlements which were not *Poleis*', in M. H. Hansen and K. Raafalaub (eds.), *Studies in the Ancient Greek Polis, Historia* Einzelschr. 95 (Stuttgart), 45–81.
——(1995*b*), *The Trial of Socrates—from the Athenian Point of View* (Copenhagen).
——(1996), 'City-Ethnics as Evidence for Polis Identity', in M. H. Hansen and K. Raaflaub (eds.), *More Studies in the Ancient Greek Polis, Historia* Einzelschr. 108 (Stuttgart), 169–96.
——(1998), *Polis and City-State: An Ancient Concept and its Modern Equivalent* (Copenhagen).
——(1999), *The Athenian Democracy in the Age of Demosthenes: Structure, Principles and Ideology*, repr. (Norman).
——(2007), 'A Comment on the Review Article of the Publications of the Copenhagen Polis Centre in *AWE* 5', *AWE* 6, 321–7.
——(2009), 'A Note on Agyrrhios' Grain-Tax Law of 374/3 BC', in L. Mitchell and L. Rubinstein (eds.), *Greek History and Epigraphy: Essays in Honour of P. J. Rhodes* (Swansea), 145–54.
Hansen, O. (1989), 'On the site of Nea', *Eranos* 87, 70–2.
Hanson, V. D. (1998), *Warfare and Agriculture in Classical Greece*, 2nd edn. (Berkeley).
Harding, P. (1994), *Androtion and the Atthis* (Oxford).
——(2006), *Didymos on Demosthenes* (Oxford).
——(2008), *The Story of Athens: The Fragments of the Local Chronicles of Attika* (London and New York).
Harris, D. (1995), *The Treasures of the Parthenon and Erechtheion* (Oxford).
Harris, E. M. (1993), '*Apotimema*: Athenian Terminology for Real Security in Leases and Dowry Agreements', *CQ* 43, 73–95.
Harrison, A. R. W. (1968), *The Law of Athens: Family and Property* (Oxford).
——(1971), *The Law of Athens: Procedure* (Oxford).
Harrison, T. (2000), *Divinity and History: The Religion of Herodotus* (Oxford).
Hatzaki, A. (2003), '*Η ελαιουργία στην περιοχή της Ιεράπετρας κατά τη Βενετοκρατία* (16ος αι.), in A. Polymerou-Kamelake, P. Kamelakes, L. Karapidake (eds.), *Η ελιά και το λάδι από την αρχαιότητα έως σήμερα. Πρακτικά διεθνούς συνεδρίου. Αθήνα, 1–2 Οκτωβρίου 1999* (Athens), 81–94.

HAUSSOULLIER, B. (1884), *La vie municipale en Attique: essai sur l'organisation des dèmes au quatrième siècle* (Paris).

HEDRICK, C. W. (1983), 'Old and New on the Attic Phratry of the Therrikleidai', *Hesperia* 52, 299–302.

——(1984), *The Attic Phratry*, Ph.D. Dissertation (University of Pennsylvania).

——(1988), 'The Temple and Cult of Apollo Patroos in Athens', *AJA* 92, 185–210.

——(1989), 'The Phratry from Paiania', *CQ* 39, 126–35.

——(1990), *The Decrees of the Demotionidai* (Atlanta).

——(1991), 'Phratry Shrines of Attica and Athens', *Hesperia* 60, 241–68.

——(1999), 'Democracy and the Athenian Epigraphical Habit', *Hesperia* 68, 387–439.

HEGYI, D. (1976), '*Τεμένη ἱερὰ καὶ τεμένη δημόσια*', *Oikumene* 1, 77–87.

HEINEN, H. (1972), *Untersuchungen zur hellenistischen Geschichte des 3. Jahrh. v. Chr.*, *Historia* Einzelschr. 20 (Wiesbaden).

HELLMANN, M.-C. (1992), *Recherches sur le vocabulaire grecque d'après les inscriptions de Délos*, BEFAR 278 (Paris).

HELLY, B. (1970), 'A Larisa: Bouleversements et remise en ordre de sanctuaires', *Mnemosyne* 23, 250–96.

HENNIG, D. (1985), 'Die "heiligen Häuser" von Delos', *Chiron* 15, 165–86.

HENRY, A. S. (2001), 'The Sigma Stigma', *ZPE* 137, 93–105.

——(2002), 'Hookers and Lookers: Prostitution and Soliciting in Late Archaic Thasos', *BSA* 97, 217–21.

HIGNETT, C. (1952), *A History of the Athenian Constitution to the End of the Fifth Century B.C.* (Oxford).

HILL, D. K. (1932), 'Boundary Stones from the Piraeus', *AJA* 36, 254–9.

HINTZEN-BOHLEN, B. (1997), *Die Kulturpolitik des Eubulos und des Lykurg: Die Denkmäler- und Bauprojekte Athen zwischen 355 und 322 v. Chr.* (Berlin).

HODKINSON, S. (1988), 'Animal Husbandry in the Greek Polis', in C. R. Whittaker (ed.), *Pastoral Economies in Classical Antiquity*, *CPS* suppl. 14, 35–74.

HOEPFNER, W., and SCHWANDNER, E.-L. (1994), *Haus und Stadt im Klassischen Griechenland* (Munich).

HOLLIS, A. S. (1992), 'Attica in Hellenistic Poetry', *ZPE* 93, 1–15.

HOPPER, R. J. (1953), 'The Attic Silver Mines in the Fourth Century B.C.', *BSA* 48, 200–54.

——(1961), '"Plain", "Shore" and "Hill" in Early Athens', *BSA* 56, 189–219.

HORDEN, P., and PURCELL, N. (2000), *The Corrupting Sea: A Study of Mediterranean History* (Oxford).

HORNBLOWER, S. (1991), *A Commentary on Thucydides*, vol. I: *Books I–III* (Oxford).

Hornblower, S. (1992), 'The Religious Dimension to the Peloponnesian War, or, what Thucydides does not tell us', *HSCP* 94, 169–97.

——(1996), *A Commentary on Thucydides*, vol. II: *Books IV–V. 24* (Oxford).

——(2002), *The Greek World, 479–323 BC*, 3rd edn. (London).

——(2008), *A Commentary on Thucydides*, vol. III: *Books 5.25–8.109* (Oxford).

Horster, M. (2004), *Landbesitz griechischer Heiligtümer in archaischer und klassischer Zeit* (Berlin and New York).

——(2006), 'Die Olivenbäume der Athena und die Todesstrafe', in H.-A. Rupprecht (ed.), *Symposion 2003. Vorträge zur griechischen und hellenistischen Rechtsgeschichte (Rauischholzhausen, 30. September - 3. Oktober 2003)* (Vienna), 167–85.

Howe, T. (2008), *Pastoral Politics: Animals, Agriculture, and Society in Ancient Greece* (Claremont).

Humphreys, S. C. (1985), 'Lycurgus of Butadae: An Athenian Aristocrat', in J. W. Eadie and J. Ober, *The Craft of the Ancient Historian. Essays in Honor of Chester G. Starr* (Lanham), 199–252.

——(1990), 'Phrateres in Alopeke, and the Salaminioi', *ZPE* 83, 243–8.

——(2004), *The Strangeness of Gods: Historical Perspectives on the Interpretation of Athenian Religion* (Oxford).

——(2008), 'Attika and Kleisthenes', in A. P. Matthaiou and I. Polinskaya (eds.), *Μικρὸς Ἱερομνήμων. Μελέτες εἰς μνήμην Michael H. Jameson* (Athens), 13–24,

Hunter, V. J. (2006), 'Pittalacus and Eucles: Slaves in the Public Service of Athens', *Mouseion* 6, 1–13.

Hurwit, J. M. (1999), *The Athenian Acropolis: History, Mythology, and Archaeology from the Neolithic Era to the Present* (Cambridge).

Irwin, E. (2005), *Solon and Early Greek Poetry: The Politics of Exhortation* (Oxford).

Isager, S. (1983), *Forpagtning af jord og bygninger i Athen* (Copenhagen).

——(1992), 'Sacred and Profane Ownership of Land', in B. Wells (ed.), *Agriculture in Ancient Greece. Proceedings of the 7th International Symposium at the Swedish Institute at Athens, 16–17 May 1990* (Stockholm), 119–22.

Isager, S. (2005), 'Review of M. Horster, *Landbesitz griechischer Heiligtümer in archaischer und klassischer Zeit*, Berlin, 2004', *BMCR* 2005.07.02.

——and Skydsgaard, J. E. (1992), *Ancient Greek Agriculture* (London and New York).

Jacab, É. (2007), 'SEG XLVIII 96: Steuergesetz oder Frachtvertrag?', in E. Cantarella (ed.), *Symposion 2005. Vorträge zur griechischen und hellenistischen Rechtsgeschichte (Salerno, 14.–18. September 2005)* (Vienna), 105–21.

Jacoby F. (1954*a*), *Die Fragmente der griechischen Historiker. Dritter Teil. Geschichte von Staedten und Voelkern (Horographie und Ethnographie) b (Supplement). A Commentary on the Ancient Historians of Athens*, vol. I: *Text* (Leiden).

Jacoby F. (1954*b*), *Die Fragmente der griechischen Historiker. Dritter Teil. Geschichte von Staedten und Voelkern (Horographie und Ethnographie) b (Supplement). A Commentary on the Ancient Historians of Athens*, vol. II: *Notes—Addenda—Corrigenda—Index* (Leiden).

Jacquemin, A. (1979), '*ΒΟΡΕΑΣ Ο ΘΟΥΡΙΟΣ*', *BCH* 103, 189–93.

Jameson, M. H. (1977), 'Agriculture and Slavery in Classical Athens', *CJ* 73, 122–45.

——(1980), 'Apollo Lykeios in Athens', *Archaiognosia* 1, 213–36.

——(1982), 'The Leasing of Land in Rhamnous', in *Studies in Attic Epigraphy, History and Topography presented to Eugene Vanderpool, Hesperia* suppl. 19 (Princeton), 66–74.

——(1988), 'Sacrifice and Animal Husbandry in Classical Greece', in C. R. Whittaker (ed.), *Pastoral Economies in Classical Antiquity* (Cambridge), 87–119.

——(1999), 'The Spectacular and the Obscure in Athenian Religion', in S. Goldhill and R. Osborne (eds.), *Performance Culture and Athenian Democracy* (Cambridge), 321–40.

——(2000), 'An Altar for Herakles', in P. Flensted-Jensen, T. H. Nielsen, and L. Rubinstein (eds.), *Polis & Politics: Studies in Ancient Greek History* (Copenhagen), 217–27.

——(2000–3), 'Athens and Phaselis, *IG* I^3 10 (EM 6918)', *Horos* 14–16, 23–9.

——(2002), 'Attic *Eschatia*', in K. Ascani, V. Gabrielsen, K. Kvist, and A. Holm Rasmussen (eds.), *Ancient History Matters. Studies Presented to Jens Eric Skydsgaard on his Seventieth Birthday* (Rome), 63–8.

Janko, R. (1992), *The Iliad, a commentary*, vol. iv: *Books 13–16* (Cambridge).

Jardé, A. (1925), *Les céréales dans l'antiquité grecque* (Paris).

Jeffery, L. H. (1955), 'Further Comments on Archaic Greek Inscriptions', *BSA* 50, 67–84.

Johnston, A. W. (1987), '*IG* II^2 2311 and the Number of Panathenaic Amphorae', *BSA* 82, 125–9.

——(2007), 'Panathenaic Amphorae, Again', *ZPE* 161 (2007), 101–4.

——and Jones, R. E. (1978), 'The "SOS" Amphora', *BSA* 73, 103–41.

Jones, A. H. M. (1960), *Athenian Democracy* (Oxford).

Jones, N. F. (1987), *Public Organization in Ancient Greece: A Documentary Study* (Philadelphia).

——(1989–90), 'The Organization of the Kretan City in Plato's *Laws*', *CW* 83, 473–92.

——(1995), 'The Athenian Phylai as Associations: Disposition, Function and Purpose', *Hesperia* 64, 503–42.

JONES, N. F. (1999), *The Associations of Classical Athens: The Response to Democracy* (New York).

——(2000), 'Epigraphic Evidence for Farmstead Residence in Attica', *ZPE* 133, 75–90.

——(2004), *Rural Athens under the Democracy* (Philadelphia).

JONES, W. H. S. (1918), *Pausanias, Description of Greece* (Cambridge, Mass., and London).

JORDAN, D. R., and ROTROFF, S. I. (1999), 'A Curse in a Chytridion: A Contribution to the Study of Athenian Pyres', *Hesperia* 68, 147–54.

JOST, M. (1998), 'Sanctuaires publics et sanctuaires privés', *Ktema* 23, 301–6.

JUDEICH, W. (1931), *Topographie von Athen*, 2nd edn. (Munich).

KAHRSTEDT, U. (1932), 'Die Landgrenzen Athens', *MDAI (A)* 32, 8–28.

——(1934), *Staatsgebiet und Staatsangehörige in Athen* (Stuttgart).

KAKAVOYIANNIS, E. (1977) [1982], '*Σουνιακά-Λαυρεωτικά*', *ADeltion* 32 A′, 182–217.

——(2005), *Μέταλλα Εργάσιμα και Συγκεχωρημένα. Η οργάνωση της εκμετάλλευσης του ορυκτού πλούτου της Λαυρεωτικής από την Αθηναϊκή Δημοκρατία* (Athens).

KALLET, L. (1998), 'Accounting for Culture in Fifth-Century Athens', in D. Boedeker and K. A. Raaflaub (eds.), *Democracy, Empire, and the Arts in Fifth-Century Athens* (Harvard), 43–58.

KALLET-MARX, L. (1989), 'Did Tribute Fund the Parthenon?', *CA* 8, 252–66.

——(1993), *Money, Expense, and Naval Power in Thucydides' History 1–5.24* (Berkeley).

KALLINKA, E. (1913), *Die pseudoxenophontische ΑΘΗΝΑΙωΝ ΠΟΛΙΤΕΙΑ* (Leipzig and Berlin).

KALOGEROPOULOU, A. G. (1987), '*Ἀπὸ τὸ ἱερὸ τοῦ Παγκράτους στὴν Ἀθήνα*', in *Πρακτικὰ τοῦ Η′ Διεθνοῦς Συνεδρίου Ἑλληνικῆς καὶ Λατινικῆς Ἐπιγραφικῆς*, vol. II (Athens), 298–304.

KAMERBEEK, J. C. (1984), *The Plays of Sophocles. Commentaries,* Part VII: *The Oedipus Coloneus* (Leiden).

KAPPARIS, K. A. (1998), 'Assessors of Magistrates (Paredroi) in Classical Athens', *Historia* 47, 383–93.

KARILA-COHEN, K. (2005), 'Les Pythaïstes athéniens et leurs familles: l'apport de la prosopographie à la connaissance de la religion à Athènes au IIe siècle avant notre ère', in M.-F. Baslez and F. Prévot (eds.), *Prosopographie et histoire religieuse. Actes du colloque tenu en l'Université Paris XII-Val de Marne les 27 & 28 octobre 2000* (Paris), 69–83.

KAROUZOS, C. (1923) [1925], '*Ἀπὸ τὸ Ἡράκλειον τοῦ Κυνοσάργους*', *ADeltion* 8, 85–102.

KEARNS, E. (1985), 'Change and Continuity in Religious Structures after Cleisthenes', in P. A. Cartledge and F. D. Harvey (eds.), *Crux. Essays presented to G.E.M. de Ste. Croix on his 75th birthday* (Devon), 189–207.

——(1989), *The Heroes of Attica* (London).

Kennelly, J. J. (2003), 'Kallias A (*IG* I3 52A) and Thucydides 2.13.3', in G. W. Bakewell and J. P. Sickinger (eds.), *Gestures: Essays in Ancient History, Literature, and Philosophy presented to Alan L. Boegehold* (Oxford), 284–6.

Kent, J. H. (1948), 'The Temple Estates of Delos, Rheneia and Mykonos', *Hesperia* 17, 243–338.

Keramopoullos, A. D. (1934–5), '*Τὸ Πελαργικόν, τὸ Ἀσκληπιεῖον, αἱ ὁδοὶ αἱ ἄγουσαι πρὸς τὰ Προπύλαια*', *AEphemeris*, 85–116.

Kern, O. (1914), "*Ραρία, 'Ράριον*', *RE* 2nd ser. 1A, 251–2.

Kiilerich, B. (1989), 'The Olive-Tree Pediment and the Daughters of Kekrops', AAAH 7, 1–21.

Kindt, J. (2009), 'Polis Religions—A Critical Appreciation', *Kernos* 22, 9–34.

Kirchner, J., and Dow, S. (1937), 'Inschriften vom attischen Lande', *MDAI (A)* 62, 1–12.

Klaffenbach, G. (1926), 'Samische Inschriften', *MDAI (A)* 51, 26–40.

Knoepfler, D. (1985), 'Oropos—colonie d'Erétrie', *Histoire et Archéologie: les Dossiers* 94 (Mai 1985), 50–8.

——(1986), 'Un document attique à reconsidérer: Le décret de Pandios sur l'Amphiaraion d'Oropos', *Chiron* 16, 71–98.

——(1993), 'Adolf Wilhelm et la *pentétèris* des Amphiaraia d'Oropos', in M. Piérart (ed.), *Aristote et Athènes* (Paris), 279–302.

——(1997), 'Le territoire d'Erétrie et l'organisation politique de la cité', in M. H. Hansen (ed.), *The Polis as an Urban Centre and as a Political Community* (Copenhagen), 352–449.

——(2001), *Décrets érétriens de proxénie et de citoyenneté, Eretria. Fouilles et recherches XI* (Lausanne).

Koliopoulos, J., and Veremis, T. (2002), *Greece: The Modern Sequel, from 1831 to the Present* (New York).

Konophagos, K. E. (1980), *Τὸ ἀρχαῖο Λαύριον καὶ ἡ ἑλληνικὴ τεχνικὴ παραγωγῆς τοῦ ἀργύρου* (Athens).

Korres, M. (1992–8), '*Από τον Σταυρό στην αρχαία Αγορά*', *Horos* 10–12, 83–104.

Kotsidu, H. (2001), 'Zur Verbreitung der Preisamphoren', in M. Bentz and N. Eschbach (eds.), *Panathenaïka. Symposion zu den Panathenäischen Preisamphoren, Rauischholzhausen 25.11.–29.11.1998* (Mainz), 55–61.

Koumanoudes, S. (1872), '*Ἀττικῆς ἐπιγραφαὶ ἀνέκδοτοι*', *Athenaion* 1, 14–6.

Koumanoudes, S. N. (1970), '*Χορηγικαὶ ἐπιγραφαὶ Θαργηλίων*', *ADeltion* 25 A′, 143–9.

——and Matthaiou, A. P. (1987), '*Κατάλογος Ἀθηναίων διαιτητῶν*', *Horos* 5, 15–24.

Kourouniotes, K. (1927–8), 'Τὸ ἱερὸν τοῦ Ἀπόλλωνος τοῦ Ζωστῆρος', *ADeltion* 11, 9–53.

——(1932), Ἐλευσινιακά (Athens).

Kraay, C. M. (1968), *Coins of Ancient Athens* (Newcastle).

Kralli, I. (2006), 'Aspects of Athenian Military Command under the Antigonids (262–229 B.C.). Continuity or Change?', *Athenaeum* 94, 543–61.

Kränzlein, A. (1963), *Eigentum und Besitz im griechischen Recht des fünften und vierten Jahrhunderts v. Chr.* (Berlin).

Krasilnikoff, J. A. (2000), 'On the Gardens and Marginal Lands of Classical Attica', in S. Isager and I. Nielsen (eds.), *Proceedings of the Danish Institute at Athens III*, 177–93.

——(2008), 'Attic φελλεύς: Some Observations on Marginal Lands and Rural Strategies in the Classical Period', *ZPE* 167, 37–49.

Kroll, J. H. (1981), 'From Wappenmünzen to Gorgoneia to Owls', *ANSMN* 26, 1–32.

——(1998), 'Silver in Solon's Laws', in R. Ashton and S. Hurter (eds.), *Studies in Greek Numismatics in Memory of Martin Jessop Price* (London), 225–32.

Kron, U. (1976), *Die zehn attischen Phylenheroen: Geschichte, Mythos, Kult und Darstellungen* (Berlin).

——(1996), 'Priesthoods, Dedications and Euergetism: What Part did Religion Play in the Political and Social Status of Greek Women?', in P. Hellström and B. Alroth (eds.), *Religion and Power in the Ancient Greek World. Proceedings of the Uppsala Symposium 1993* (Uppsala), 139–82.

Kuhn, G. (1985), 'Untersuchungen zur Funktion der Säulenhalle III', *JDAI* 100, 200–26.

Kyparissis, N., and Peek, W. (1941), 'Attische Urkunden', *MDAI (A)* 66, 218–39.

Lalonde G. V. (1999), 'Agora I 6656: A Fragment of *IG* I^3, 243', *Horos* 13, 9–16.

——(2006*a*), *Horos Dios: An Athenian Shrine and Cult of Zeus* (Leiden and Boston).

——(2006*b*), 'IG I^3 1055 B and the Boundary of Melite and Kollytos', *Hesperia* 75, 83–119.

Lamb, W. (1930), *Lysias* (London).

Lambert, S. D. (1993), *The Phratries of Attica* (Ann Arbor).

——(1996), 'Notes on Two Attic Horoi', *ZPE* 110, 77–83.

——(1997*a*), *Rationes Centesimarum: Sales of Public Land in Lykourgan Athens* (Amsterdam).

——(1997*b*), 'The Attic Genos Salaminioi and the Island of Salamis', *ZPE* 119, 85–106.

——(1999*a*), 'The Attic Genos', *CQ* 49, 484–9.

——(1999*b*), '*IG* II^2 2345, Thiasoi of Herakles and the Salaminioi Again', *ZPE* 125, 93–130.
——(2000*a*), 'The Sacrificial Calendar of the Marathonian Tetrapolis: A Revised Text', *ZPE* 130, 43–70.
——(2000*b*), 'Two Notes on Attic *Leges Sacrae*', *ZPE* 130, 71–80.
——(2001), 'Ten Notes on Attic Inscriptions', *ZPE* 135, 51–62.
——(2002*a*), 'Parerga III: The Genesia, Basile and Epops Again', *ZPE* 139, 75–82.
——(2002*b*), 'Afterwords', *ZPE* 141, 122–4.
——(2002*c*), 'The Sacrificial Calendar of Athens', *BSA* 97, 353–99.
——(2004), 'A House of the Piraeans?', *ZPE* 146, 91–2.
——(2005), 'Athenian State Laws and Decrees, 352/1–322/1: II Religious Regulations', *ZPE* 154, 125–59.
——(2010), 'Athens, Sokles and the Exploitation of an Attic Resource (*IG* II^2 411', in N. Sekunda (ed.), *Ergasteria: Works Presented to John Ellis Jones on his 80th Birthday*, Gdańsk, 115–125.
LANGDON, M. K. (1973), 'Two Epigraphical Notes', *AJA* 77, 195–6.
——(1985*a*), 'The Territorial Basis of the Attic Demes', *SO* 60, 5–15.
——(1985*b*), 'Hymettiana I', *Hesperia* 54, 257–70.
——(1987), 'An Attic Decree concerning Oropos', *Hesperia* 56, 47–58.
——(1991), 'Poletai Records', in *Agora* XIX, 55–69.
——(1994), 'Public Auctions in Ancient Athens', in R. Osborne and S. Hornblower (eds.), *Ritual, Finance, Politics: Athenian Democratic Accounts Presented to David Lewis* (Oxford), 253–65.
——(1999), 'Hymettiana III: The Boundary Markers of Alepovouni', *Hesperia* 68, 481–508.
LANGDON, M. K. (2000) [2004], 'The Quarries of Peiraieus', *ADeltion* 55A, 235–50.
——(2005), 'A New Greek Abecedarium', *Kadmos* 44, 175–82.
LARSEN, J. A. O. (1968), *Greek Federal States: Their Institutions and History* (Oxford).
LATTE, K. (1934), '*Τέμενος*', *RE* 2nd ser. 9, 435–7.
——(1935), '*Μορία*', *RE* 16, 302–3.
LATTERMANN, H. (1909), '*Ἐπεργάζεσθαι* und Verwandtes', *MDAI (A)* 34, 363–8.
LATTIMORE, S. (1998), *Thucydides, The Peloponnesian War*, trans. with introd., notes, and glossary (Indianapolis and Cambridge).
LAUTER, H. (1982), 'Zum Strassenbild in Alt-Athen', *AW* 13.4, 44–52.
——(1985), *Der Kultplatz auf dem Turkovuni*, Attische Forschungen I (Berlin).
—— (1988), 'Das Teichos von Sunion', *Marburger Winckelmann-Programm* 1988, 11–33.

Lawall, M. L. (2005), 'Amphoras and Hellenistic Economies: Addressing the (Over)emphasis on Stamped Amphora Handles', in Z. H. Archibald, J. K. Davies, and V. Gabrielsen (eds.), *Making, Moving and Managing: The New World of Ancient Economies, 323–31 BC* (Oxford), 188–232.

Lawson F. H., and Rudden, B. (2002), *The Law of Property*, 3rd edn. (Oxford).

Lawton, C. L. (1995), *Attic Document Reliefs: Art and Politics in Ancient Athens* (Oxford).

Lazaride, K. (1997), '*Εργασίες ενοποίησης αρχαιολογικών χώρων*', *ADeltion* 52 Β΄1, 39–43.

Lefèvre, F. (1998), *L'Amphictionie Pyléo-Delphique: histoire et institutions* (Paris).

Legon, R. P. (1981), *Megara: The Political History of a Greek City-State to 336 B.C.* (Ithaca and London).

Le Guen-Pollet, B. (1991), *La vie religieuse dans le monde grec du Ve au IIIe siècle avant notre ère* (Mirail).

Lehner, H. (1890), *Über die athenischen Schatzverzeichnisse des vierten Jahrhunderts* (Strassburg).

Leiwo, M. (1997), 'Religion or other Reasons? Private Associations in Athens', in *Early Hellenistic Athens: Symptoms of a Change* (Helsinki), 104–17.

Leppin, H. (1995), 'Zur Entwicklung der Verwaltung öffentlicher Gelder im Athen des 4. Jahrhunderts v. Chr', in W. Eder (ed.), *Die athenische Demokratie im 4. Jahrhundert v. Chr. Vollendung oder Verfall einer Verfassungsform?* (Stuttgart), 557–71.

Lesher, J. H. (1992), *Xenophanes of Colophon: Fragments. A Text and a Translation with a Commentary, Phoenix* suppl. 30.

Lévêque, P., and Vidal-Naquet, P. (1996), *Cleisthenes the Athenian*, translated and edited by D. A. Curtis (Atlantic Highlands).

Lewis, D. M. (1959*a*), 'Attic Manumissions', *Hesperia* 28, 208–38.

——(1959*b*), 'Law on the Lesser Panathenaia', *Hesperia* 28, 239–47.

——(1960), 'Apollo Delios', *BSA* 55, 190–4.

——(1963), 'Cleisthenes and Attica', *Historia* 12, 22–40.

——(1966), 'After the Profanation of the Mysteries', in *Ancient Society and Institutions. Studies presented to Victor Ehrenberg on his 75th birthday* (Oxford), 177–91.

——(1968), 'Dedications of Phialai at Athens', *Hesperia* 37, 368–80.

——(1973*a*), 'The Athenian Rationes Centesimarum', in M. I. Finley (ed.), *Problèmes de la terre en Grèce ancienne* (Paris), 187–212.

——(1973*b*), 'Attic Ephebic Inscriptions', *CR* 87, 254–6.

——(1979), 'An Inventory in the Agora', *ZPE* 36, 131–4.

——(1983), 'Review of Peter Siewert: *Die Trittyen Attikas und die Heeresreform des Kleisthenes*', *Gnomon* 55, 431–6.

——(1986), 'Temple Inventories in Ancient Greece', in M. Vickers (ed.), *Pots and Pans* (Oxford), 71–81.

——(1990), 'Public Property in the City', in O. Murray and S. Price (eds.), *The Greek City from Homer to Alexander* (Oxford), 245–63.

——(1997), 'On the Financial Offices of Eubulus and Lycurgus', in P. J. Rhodes (ed.), *Selected Papers in Greek and Near Eastern History* (Cambridge), 212–29.

L'Homme-Wéry, L. M. (1996), *La perspective éleusinienne dans la politique de Solon* (Liège).

Liddel, P. (2003), 'The Places of Publications of Athenian State Decrees from the 5th Century BC to the 3rd Century AD', *ZPE* 143, 79–93.

——(2007), *Civic Obligation and Individual Liberty in Ancient Athens* (Oxford).

Linders, T. (1975), *The Treasurers of the Other Gods in Athens and their Functions* (Meisenheim am Glan).

——(1992), 'Sacred Finances: Some Observations', in T. Linders and B. Alroth (eds.), *Economics of Cult in the Ancient Greek World. Proceedings of the Uppsala Symposium 1990, Boreas 21* (Uppsala), 9–13.

Lindgren, M. (1973), *The People of Pylos: Prosopographical and Methodological Studies in the Pylos Archive* (Uppsala).

Link, S. (1991), *Landverteilung und sozialer Frieden in archaischen Griechenland, Historia* Einzelschr. 69 (Stuttgart).

Lipsius, J. H. (1905–15), *Das attische Recht und Rechtsverfahren*, vols. I–III (Leipzig).

Lloyd-Jones, H. (1994), *Sophocles* II (Cambridge, Mass., and London).

Loewe, B. (1980), *Ancient Greek Theophoric Toponyms. Griechische theophore Ortsnamen*, reprint (Chicago).

Lohmann, H. (1993), *ATENE. Ἀτήνη. Forschungen zu Siedlungs-und Wirtschaftsstruktur des klassischen Attika* (Cologne).

——(1994), 'Flur-und Demengrenzen im klassischen Attika', in E. Olshausen and H. Sonnabend (eds.), *Stuttgarter Kolloquium zur historischen Geographe des Altertums 4, 1990* (Amsterdam), 251–90.

——(1995), 'Die Chora Athens im 4. Jahrhundert v. Chr.: Festungswesen, Bergbau und Siedlungen', in W. Eder (ed.), *Die Athenische Demokratie im 4. Jahrhundert v. Chr. Vollendung oder Verfall einer Verfassungsform?* (Stuttgart), 515–48.

——and Schaefer, H. (2000), 'Wo lag das Herakleion der Salaminioi?', *ZPE* 133, 91–101.

Lolling, H. G. (1879), 'Inschriften aus Nordgriechenland', *MDAI (A)* 4, 193–227.

Lolos, Y. A. (2002), 'A Public Column Drum from a Corinthian Quarry', *Hesperia* 71, 201–7.

Lolos, Y. A. (2003) [2005], 'Greek Roads: A Commentary on the Ancient Terms', *Glotta* 79, 137–74.

Loomis, W. T. (1998), *Wages, Welfare Costs and Inflation in Classical Athens* (Ann Arbor).

Lougovaya-Ast, J. (2006), 'Myrrhine, the First Priestess of Athena Nike', *Phoenix* 60, 211–25.

Lupu, E. (2003), 'Sacrifice at the Amphiareion and a Fragmentary Sacred Law from Oropos', *Hesperia* 72, 321–40.

——(2005), *Greek Sacred Law: A Collection of New Documents* (Leiden and Boston).

Ma, J. (2009), 'Empire, Statuses and Realities', in J. Ma, N. Papazarkadas, R. Parker (eds.), *Interpreting the Athenian Empire* (London), 125–48.

McDonald, J. (1996), 'Athens and the *Hiera Orgas*', in M. Dillon (ed.), *Religion in the Ancient World: New Themes and Approaches* (Amsterdam), 321–32.

MacDowell, D. M. (1962), *Andocides, On the Mysteries* (Oxford).

——(1978), *The Law in Classical Athens* (Ithaca).

——(1990), *Demosthenes, Against Meidias* (Oxford).

——(2009), *Demosthenes the Orator* (Oxford).

McInerney, J. (2006), 'On the Border: Sacred Land and the Margins of the Community', in R. M. Rosen and I. Sluiter (eds.), *City, Countryside, and the Spatial Organization of Value in Classical Antiquity*, *Mnemosyne* suppl. 134, 33–59.

McQueen, E. I. (2000), *Herodotus, Book VI* (London).

Maffi, A. (1982), '*Τὰ ἱερὰ καὶ τὰ ὅσια*. Contributo allo studio della terminologia giuridico-sacrale greca', in A. Modrzejewski and D. Liebs (eds.), *Symposion 1977* (Cologne), 33–53.

Maidment, K. J. (1941), *Minor Attic Orators*, I: *Antiphon, Andocides* (Cambridge, Mass., and London).

Maier, F. G. (1959), *Griechische Mauerbauinschriften*, 2 vols. (Heidelberg).

Makres, A. K. (2004), 'The Rediscovery of *IG* I^{3} 253–4', in A. P. Matthaiou and G. E. Malouchou (eds.), *Ἀττικαὶ Ἐπιγραφαί: Πρακτικὰ Συμποσίου εἰς μνήμην Adolf Wilhelm (1864–1950)* (Athens), 123–40.

Malkin, I. (1984), 'What were the Sacred Precincts of Brea? (IG I^{3} no. 46)', *Chiron* 14, 43–8.

Manning, J. G. (2003), *Land and Power in Ptolemaic Egypt: The Structure of Land Tenure* (Cambridge).

Manville P. B. (1990), *The Origins of Citizenship in Ancient Athens* (Princeton).

Marchant, E. C., and Bowersock, G. W. (1968), *Xenophon*, VII: *Scripta Minora* (Cambridge, Mass., and London).

Mari, M. (2003), 'Macedonians and pro-Macedonians in Early Hellenistic Athens: Reflections on ἀσέβεια', in O. Palagia and S. V. Tracy (eds.), *The*

Macedonians in Athens, 322–229 B.C. Proceedings of an International Conference held at the University of Athens, May 24–26, 2001 (Oxford), 82–92.

MARR, J. L., and RHODES, P. J. (2008), *The 'Old Oligarch': The Constitution of the Athenians attributed to Xenophon* (Oxford).

MARTINA, A. (2000), *Menandro, Epitrepontes*, II 2. *Commento* (Rome).

MARTINI, R. (1997), 'Lavori pubblici e appalto nella Grecia antica', in *I rapporti contrattuali con la pubblica amministrazione nell'esperienza storico-giuridica (Atti del congresso internazionale della Società Italiana di Storia del Diritto, Torino 1994)*, (Naples), 35–53.

MATHIEU, G. (1942), *Isocrate, Discours*, III (Paris).

MATTHAIOU, A. P. (1989), '*Ψήφισμα Κυδαντιδῶν καὶ Ἰωνιδῶν*', *Horos* 7, 7–16.

——(1990–1*a*), '*Χορηγικὴ ἐπιγραφὴ Θαργηλίων*', *Horos* 8–9, 53–8.

——(1990–1*b*), '*Ἡρακλέως. Κωλακρέται*', *Horos* 8–9, 183–9.

——(1992–8*a*), '*Αἰξωνικά*', *Horos* 10–12, 133–69.

——(1992–8*b*), '*Ὀλίγα περὶ τοῦ παριακοῦ ὅρου πόλεως*', *Horos* 10–12, 441–7.

——(2000), '*Ὅρος πόλεως*', in D. Schilardi and D. Katsonopoulou (eds.), *Paria Lithos: Parian Quarries, marble and workshops of sculpture* (Athens), 113–15.

——(2000–3), '*Πρασιέων μίσθωσις*', *Horos* 14–16, 71–6.

——(2003), '*Ἀπόλλων Δήλιος ἐν Ἀθήναις*', in D. Jordan and J. Traill (eds.), *Lettered Attica: A Day of Attic Epigraphy* (Toronto), 85–93.

——(2004), '*Περὶ τῆς IG* I³ 11', in A. P. Matthaiou and G. E. Malouchou (eds.), *Ἀττικαὶ Επιγραφαί: Πρακτικὰ Συμποσίου εἰς μνήμην Adolf Wilhelm (1864–1950)*, (Athens), 99–122.

——(2007), '*Το θέατρον και το Λύκειον*', in E. Semantone-Mpournia, A. A. Laimou, L. G. Mendone, N. Kourou (eds.), *Ἀμύμονα ἔργα: τιμητικός τόμος για τον καθηγητή Βασίλη Κ. Λαμπρινουδάκη* (Athens), 501–8.

——(2008), '*Νέο θραῦσμα της ἐπιγραφῆς IG* II² 1195', in A. P. Matthaiou and I. Polinskaya (eds.), *Μικρὸς Ἱερομνήμων. Μελέτες εἰς μνήμην Michael H. Jameson* (Athens), 87–102.

——(2009), 'Attic Public Inscriptions of the Fifth Century BC in Ionic Script', in L. Mitchell and L. Rubinstein (eds.), *Greek History and Epigraphy: Essays in Honour of P. J. Rhodes* (Swansea), 201–12.

——and KOURAGIOS, G. (1992–8), '*Ἐπιγραφὲς Πάρου*', *Horos* 10–12, 438–40.

MATTINGLY, D. J. (1985), 'Olive Oil Production in Roman Tripolitania', in D. J. Buck and D. J. Mattingly (eds.), *Town and Country in Roman Tripolitania. Papers in honour of Olwen Hackett* (Oxford), 27–46.

MATTINGLY, H. B. (1961), 'Athens and Euboea', *JHS* 81, 124–32.

——(1968), 'Athenian Finance in the Peloponnesian War', *BCH* 92, 450–85.

——(2002), 'The Athenian Decree for Chalcis (*IG* I³ 40)', *CQ* 52, 377–9.

Mazarakis-Ainian, A. (1998), 'The Kythnos Survey Project: A Preliminary Report', in L. G. Mendoni and A. Mazarakis-Ainian (eds.), *Kea-Kythnos: History and Archaeology. Proceedings of an International Symposium* (Athens), 363–435.

Meiggs, R. (1972), *The Athenian Empire* (Oxford).

——(1982), *Trees and Timber in the Ancient Mediterranean World* (Oxford).

Meritt, B. D. (1936), 'Greek Inscriptions', *Hesperia* 5, 355–441.

——(1939), 'Greek Inscriptions', *Hesperia* 8, 49–82.

——(1942), 'Greek Inscriptions', *Hesperia* 11, 275–303.

——(1945), 'Attic Inscriptions of the Fifth Century', *Hesperia* 14, 61–133.

——(1968), 'Greek Inscriptions', *Hesperia* 37, 266–98.

——(1974), 'The Choiseul Marble: The Text of 406 B.C.', in *Mélanges helléniques offerts à Georges Daux* (Paris), 255–67.

——(1981), 'Mid-Third Century Athenian Archons', *Hesperia* 50, 78–99.

Meyer, E. A. (1993), 'Epitaphs and Citizenship in Classical Athens', *JHS* 113, 99–121.

Meyer, G. (2004), 'Le prix de l'eau et le tarif du sanctuaire des Nymphes: *IG*, I^3, 256', *REG* 117, 321–5.

Migeotte L. (1984), *L' emprunt public dans les cités grecques* (Paris).

——(1998), 'Finances sacrées et finances publiques dans les cités grecques', in J. F. G. Castro (ed.), *Actas del IX Congreso Español de Estudios Clásicos* (Madrid), 181–5.

——(2006*a*), '*Téménè dèmosia*', in P. Brillet-Dubois and É. Parmentier (eds.) *Φιλολογία. Mélanges offerts à Michel Casevitz* (Lyon), 187–95.

——(2006*b*), 'Les gestions des biens sacrés dans les cités grecques', in H.-A. Rupprecht (ed.), *Symposion 2003. Vorträge zur griechischen und hellenistischen Rechtsgeschichte (Rauischholzhausen, 30. September - 3. Oktober 2003)* (Vienna), 233–46.

Mikalson, J. D. (1975), *The Sacred and the Civil Calendar of the Athenian Year* (Princeton).

——(1977), 'Religion in the Attic Demes', *AJP* 98, 424–35.

——(1983), *Athenian Popular Religion* (Chapel Hill).

——(1998), *Religion in Hellenistic Athens* (Berkeley).

Miles, M. M. (1998), *The Athenian Agora*, vol. XXXI: *The City Eleusinion* (Princeton).

Miller, S. G. (1995), 'Old Metroon and Old Bouleuterion in the Classical Agora of Athens', in M. H. Hansen and K. Raaflaub (eds.), *Studies in the Ancient Greek Polis* (Stuttgart), 133–56.

Millett, P. (1991), *Lending and Borrowing in Ancient Athens* (Cambridge).

Mirhady, D. C., and Too, Y. L. (2000), *Isocrates* I (Austin).

Missailidou-Despotidou, V. (1993), 'A Hellenistic Inscription from Skotoussa (Thessaly) and the Fortifications of the City', *BSA* 88, 187–217.

——(2001), 'Μία νέα ἐπιγραφὴ ἀπὸ τὴν Ἄφυτο', in Α' Πανελλήνιο Συνέδριο Ἐπιγραφικῆς (Thessalonike), 79–90.

MITCHEL, F. W. (1970), *Lykourgan Athens: 338–322* (Cincinatti).

——(1975), 'The So-Called Earliest Ephebic Inscription', *ZPE* 19, 233–43.

MITSOPOULOU, C. (2005), 'Βρυόκαστρο Κύθνου: κεραμεική, λύχνοι καὶ εἰδώλια ἀπὸ τὴν ἀρχαία πόλη καὶ τὸ ἱερὸ τῆς Ἀκρόπολης. Πρῶτα στοιχεῖα ἀπὸ τὴν ἐπιφανειακὴ ἔρευνα', in *Ἐπετηρὶς Ἑταιρείας Κυκλαδικῶν Σπουδῶν* 18 (2002–2003), 293–358.

MITSOS, M. T. (1965), ''Εκ τοῦ Ἐπιγραφικοῦ Μουσείου', *AEphemeris* 1965, 131–8.

MÖBIUS, H. (1924), 'Neue Inschriften aus Attika und Argos', *MDAI (A)* 49, 1–16.

MOMMSEN, A. (1898), *Feste der Stadt Athen im Altertum* (Leipzig).

MORENO, A. (2003), 'Athenian Bread-Baskets: The Grain Tax Law of 374/3 B.C. Reinterpreted', *ZPE* 145, 97–106.

——(2007), *Feeding the Democracy: The Athenian Grain Supply in the Fifth and Fourth Centuries BC* (Oxford).

——(2009), ' "The Attic Neighbour": The Cleruchy in the Athenian Empire', in J. Ma, N. Papazarkadas, and R. Parker (eds.), *Interpreting the Athenian Empire* (London), 211–21.

MORISON, W. S. (2000), 'An Honorary Deme Decree and the Administration of a Palaistra in Kephisia', *ZPE* 131, 93–8.

——(2003), 'Property Records for Athenian Cleruchs or Colonists', *ZPE* 145, 109–13.

MORPURGO DAVIES, A. (1979), 'Terminology of Power and Terminology of Work in Greek and Linear B', in E. Risch and H. Mühlestein (eds.), *Colloquium Mycenaeum* (Neuchâtel), 87–108.

MOSSÉ, C. (1973), *Athens in Decline 404–86 B.C.* (London).

MÜLKE, C. (2002), *Solons politische Elegien und Iamben* (Leipzig).

MURRAY, A. T. (1939), *Demosthenes*, V: *Private Orations* (Cambridge, Mass., and London).

MUSSCHE, H. (1998), *Thorikos. A Mining Town in Ancient Attica* (Ghent).

MYLONAS, G. E. (1961), *Eleusis and the Eleusinian Mysteries* (Princeton).

NAWOTKA, K. (1999), *Boule and Demos in Miletus and its Pontic Colonies from Classical Age until Third Century A.D.* (Wrocław).

NEILS, J. (1992), 'Panathenaic Amphoras: Their Meaning, Makers, and Markets', in J. Neils (ed.), *Goddess and Polis: The Panathenaic Festival in Ancient Athens* (Princeton), 29–51.

——(2001), 'Panathenaics in the West', in M. Bentz and N. Eschbach (eds.), *Panathenaïka. Symposion zu den Panathenäischen Preisamphoren, Rauischholzhausen 25.11.–29.11.1998* (Mainz), 125–30.

Neils, J. (2007), 'Replicating Tradition: The First Celebrations of the Greater Panathenaia', in O. Palagia and A. Choremi-Spetsieri (eds.), *The Panathenaic Games* (Oxford), 41–51.

Nemes, Z. (1980), 'The Public Property of Demes in Attica', *ACD* 16, 3–8.

——(1987), 'On the EM 7748/IG II2 1206', *ACD* 23, 19–25.

——(1991), 'On the EM 7722 (IG II2 1211)', *ACD* 27, 15–21.

Németh, G. (2001), 'Metics in Athens', *Acta Ant. Hung.* 41, 331–48.

Nenci, G. (1993), '*ΟΙΚΟΠΕΔΟΝ* e *ΓΗΠΕΔΟΝ*. Contributo al lessico urbanistico greco', in M.-M. Mactoux and E. Geny (eds.), *Mélanges Pierre Lévêque 7* (Paris), 273–86.

——(1994), *Erodoto, Le Storie*, vol. V: *Libro V* (Milan).

——(1998), *Erodoto, Le Storie*, vol. VI: *Libro VI* (Milan).

Niku, M. (2007), *The Official Status of the Foreign Residents in Athens, 322–120 B.C.* (Helsinki).

Norlin, G. (1929), *Isocrates* II (Cambridge, Mass., and London).

Ober, J. (1981), 'Rock-Cut Inscriptions from Mt. Hymettos', *Hesperia* 50 (1981), 68–77.

——(1985), *Fortress Attica: Defence of the Athenian Land Frontier 404–322 B.C.*, *Mnemosyne* suppl. 84 (Leiden).

——(1995), 'Greek Horoi: Artifactual Texts and the Contingency of Meaning', in D. B. Small (ed.), *Methods in the Mediterranean: Historical and Archaeological Views on Texts and Archaeology* (Leiden), 91–123.

——(2006), 'Solon and the *Horoi*: Facts on the Ground in Archaic Athens', in J. H. Blok and A. P. M. H. Lardinois (eds.), *Solon of Athens: New Historical and Philological Approaches* (Boston and Leiden), 441–56.

——(2008), *Democracy and Knowledge: Innovation and Learning in Classical Athens* (Princeton).

Oikonomides, A. (1958), *Ὑπερείδου λόγοι* (Athens).

Oliver, G. J. (2001), 'The Politics of Coinage: Athens and Antigonus Gonatas', in A. Meadows and K. Shipton (eds.), *Money and its Uses in the Ancient Greek World* (Oxford), 35–52.

——(2007), *War, Food, and Politics in Early Hellenistic Athens* (Oxford).

Oliver, J. H. (1967), 'Philosophers and Procurators, Relatives of the Aemilius Juncus of *Vita Commodi* 4, 11', *Hesperia* 36, 42–56.

Olson, S. D. (1996), 'Politics and Poetry in Aristophanes' *Wasps*', *TAPA* 126, 129–50.

——(2002), *Aristophanes, Acharnians* (Oxford).

O'Neil, J. L. (2008), 'A Re-examination of the Chremonidean War', in P. McKechnie and P. Guillaume (eds.), *Ptolemy II Philadelphus and his World*, *Mnemosyne* suppl. 300, 65–89.

Orlandos, A. K., and Travlos I. N. (1986), *Λεξικόν αρχαίων αρχιτεκτονικών όρων* (Athens).

Osborne, M. J. (1989), 'The Chronology of Athens in the Mid Third Century BC', *ZPE* 78, 209–42.

——(1999), 'Voyaging through Strange Seas of Thought—The Study of Athenian Inscriptions', *PAAth* 74, 67–80.

——(2000), 'Philinos and the Athenian Archons of the 250s BC', in P. Flensted-Jensen, T. H. Nielsen, and L. Rubinstein (eds.), *Polis & Politics: Studies in Ancient Greek History* (Copenhagen), 507–20.

——(2009), 'The Archons of Athens 300/299–228/7', *ZPE* 171, 83–99.

Osborne, R. (1985*a*), *Demos: The Discovery of Classical Attica* (Cambridge).

——(1985*b*), 'Law in Action in Classical Athens', *JHS* 105, 40–58.

——(1985*c*), 'Buildings and Residence on the Land in Classical and Hellenistic Greece: The Contribution of Epigraphy', *BSA* 80, 119–28.

——(1987), *Classical Landscape with Figures: The Ancient Greek City and its Countryside* (London).

——(1988), 'Social and Economic Implications of the Leasing of Land and Property in Classical and Hellenistic Greece', *Chiron* 18, 279–323.

——(1990), 'The *Demos* and its Divisions in Classical Athens', in O. Murray and S. Price (eds.), *The Greek City from Homer to Alexander* (Oxford), 265–93.

——(1991), 'Land Use and Settlement in Hellenistic Keos: The Epigraphic Evidence', in J. F. Cherry, J. L. Davis, and E. Mantzourani (eds.), *Landscape Archaeology as Long-Term History: Northern Keos in the Cycladic Islands from Earliest Settlement until Modern Times* (Los Angeles), 319–25.

——(1994), 'Archaeology, the Salaminioi, and the Politics of Sacred Space in Archaic Attica', in S. E. Alcock and R. Osborne (eds.), *Placing the Gods: Sanctuaries and Sacred Space in Ancient Greece* (Oxford), 143–60.

Ostwald, M. (1986), *From Popular Sovereignty to the Sovereignty of Law. Law, Society and Politics in Fifth-Century Athens* (Berkeley).

——(1988), 'The Reform of the Athenian State by Cleisthenes', in J. Boardman, N. G. L. Hammond, D. M. Lewis, M. Ostwald (eds.), *The Cambridge Ancient History*, vol. IV: *Persia, Greece and the Western Mediterranean, c. 525 to 479 B.C.*, 2nd edn. (Cambridge), 303–46.

Pache, C. O. (2001), 'Barbarian Bond: Thracian Bendis among the Athenians', in S. R. Asirvatham, C. O. Pache, and J. Watrous (eds.), *Between Magic and Religion: Interdisciplinary Studies in Ancient Mediterranean Religion and Society* (Lanham), 3–11.

Paga, J. (2010), 'Deme Theaters in Attica and the Trittys System', *Hesperia* 79, 351–84.

Palagia, O. (1998), *The Pediments of the Parthenon*, 2nd unrevised edn. (Leiden).

Palaima, T. G. (1995), 'The Nature of the Mycenaean *Wanax*: Non-Indo-European Origins and Priestly Functions', in P. Rehak (ed.), *The Role of the Ruler in the Prehistoric Aegean*, *Aegaeum* 11, 119–39.

Palaima, T. G. (2006), '*Wanaks* and Related Power Terms in Mycenaean and Later Greek', in S. Deger-Jalkotzy and I. S. Lemos (eds.), *Ancient Greece: From the Mycenaean Palaces to the Age of Homer* (Edinburgh), 53–71.

Palme, B. (1987), 'Ein attischer Prospektorenvertrag? *IG* II^2 411', *Tyche* 2, 113–39.

Palmer, L. R. (1963), *The Interpretation of Mycenaean Greek Texts* (Oxford).

Pantazopoulos, N. I. (1947–8), '*Ὀργεῶνες. Παρατηρήσεις εἰς τὰ νεώτερα ἐπιγραφικὰ εὑρήματα καὶ τὰς πηγὰς καθόλου τοῦ Ἀττικοῦ σωματειακοῦ δικαίου*', *Polemon* 3, 97–128.

Papachatzis, N. (1974), *Παυσανίου Ἑλλάδος Περιήγησις: Ἀττικά* (Athens).

——(1976), *Παυσανίου Ἑλλάδος Περιήγησις: Κορινθιακὰ καὶ Λακωνικά* (Athens).

Papagiannopoulos-Palaios, A. A. (1929), '*Ἀττικαὶ Ἐπιγραφαί*', *Polemon* 1, 227–48.

Papazarkadas, N. (2004), 'Notes on Inscriptions from Attica and Oropos', *ZPE* 149, 69–70.

——(2007*a*), 'Four Deme Documents Revisited', *ZPE* 159, 155–77.

——(2007*b*), '*IG* II^2 2490, the Epakreis and the pre-Cleisthenic trittyes', *CQ* 57, 22–32.

——(2009*a*), 'Epigraphy and the Athenian Empire: Re-shuffling the Chronological Cards', in J. Ma, N. Papazarkadas, and R. Parker (eds.), Interpreting the Athenian Empire (London), 67–88.

——(2009*b*), 'The Decree of Aigeis and Aiantis (Agora I 6793) Revisited', in A. A. Themos and N. Papazarkadas (eds.), *Ἀττικὰ ἐπιγραφικά. Μελέτες πρὸς τιμὴν τοῦ Christian Habicht* (Athens), 165–81.

——(2004–9) [2010], '*Ἀττικὰ ἐπιγραφικὰ σημειώματα*', *Horos* 17–21, 91–108.

Pappadakis, N. (1937), '*Ἱερὸς νόμος Βενδιδείων*', *AEphemeris*, 808–23.

Parke, H. W. (1967), *The Oracles of Zeus: Dodona—Olympia—Ammon* (Oxford).

——and Wormell, D. E. W. (1956), *The Delphic Oracle*, Vol. I: *The History* (Oxford).

Parker, R. (1983), *Miasma: Pollution and Purification in Early Greek Religion* (Oxford).

——(1985), 'Greek States and Greek Oracles', in P. A. Cartledge and F. D. Harvey (eds.), *Crux. Essays presented to G.E.M. de Ste. Croix on his 75th Birthday* (Exeter), 298–326.

——(1987*a*), 'Festivals of the Attic demes', in T. Linders and G. Nordquist (eds.), *Gifts to the Gods. Proceedings of the Uppsala Symposium 1985*, (Boreas: Acta Universitatis Uppsaliensis 15) (Uppsala), 137–47.

——(1987*b*), 'Myths of Early Athens', in J. Bremmer (ed.), *Interpretations of Greek Mythology* (London), 187–214.

——(1993), 'Two Guesses about Attic Cult', *Tria Lustra*, 25–7.

——(1994), 'Athenian Religion Abroad', in R. Osborne and S. Hornblower (eds.), *Ritual, Finance, Politics: Athenian Democratic Accounts Presented to David Lewis* (Oxford), 339–46.

——(1996), *Athenian Religion: A History* (Oxford).

——(2000), 'Theophoric Names and the History of Greek Religion', in S. Hornblower and E. Matthews (eds.), *Greek Personal Names: Their Value as Evidence* (Oxford), 53–79.

——(2005), *Polytheism and Society at Athens* (Oxford).

——and Obbink, D. (2000), 'Aus der Arbeit der "Inscriptiones Graecae" VI: Sales of Priesthoods on Cos I', *Chiron* 30, 415–49.

Partsch, J. (1909), *Griechisches Bürgerschaftsrecht*, I: *Das Recht des altgriechischen Gemeindestaats* (Leipzig and Berlin).

Patterson, C. (2000), 'The Hospitality of Athenian Justice: The Metic in Court', in V. Hunter and J. Edmondson (eds.), *Law and Social Status in Cleassical Athens* (Oxford), 93–112.

——(2006), 'Citizen Cemeteries in Classical Athens?', *CQ* 56, 48–56.

Pébarthe, C. (2006), *Cité, démocratie et écriture: histoire de l'alphabétisation d'Athènes à l'époque classique* (Paris).

Pecirka, J. (1966), *The Formula for the Grant of Enktesis in Attic Inscriptions* (Prague).

Peek, W. (1941), *Kerameikos: Ergebnisse der Ausgrabungen*, III: *Inschriften, Ostraka, Fluchtafeln* (Berlin).

Pélékidis, C. (1962), *Histoire de l'éphébie Attique des origines à 31 avant Jésus-Christ* (Paris).

Pelling, C. (2000), *Literary Texts and the Greek Historian* (London).

Perlman, S. (1967), 'Political Leadership in Athens in the Fourth Century B.C.', *PP* 22, 161–76.

Perrin, B. (1914), *Plutarch's Lives* (Cambridge, Mass., and London).

Petrakos, B. (1968), *Ὁ Ὠρωπὸς καὶ τὸ ἱερὸν τοῦ Ἀμφιαράου* (Athens).

——(1996), *Marathon* (Athens).

——(1999), *Ὁ δῆμος τοῦ Ραμνοῦντος, I: Τοπογραφία* (Athens).

Picard, O. (1979), *Chalcis et la confédération eubéenne: Étude de numismatique et d'histoire (IVe – Ier siècle)*, BEFAR 234 (Paris).

Pickard-Cambridge, A. (1968), *The Dramatic Festivals of Athens*, 2nd edn. rev. by J. Gould and D. M. Lewis (Oxford).

Piérart, M. (1974), *Platon et la cité grecque: Théorie et réalité dans la Constitution des 'Lois'* (Bruxelles).

——(1997), 'L'attitude d'Argos à l'égard des autres cités d'Argolide', in M. H. Hansen (ed.), *The Polis as an Urban Centre and as a Political Community* (Copenhagen), 321–51.

——(2005), 'L'utopie magnète: Réflexions sur les *Lois* de Platon', in M. H. Hansen (ed.), *The Imaginary Polis* (Copenhagen), 124–51.

Pirenne-Delforge, V. (2005), 'La cité, les dèmotelè hiera et les prêtres', in V. Dasen and M. Piérart (eds.), *Ἰδίᾳ καὶ δημοσίᾳ: Les cadres 'privés' et 'publics' de la religion grecque antique, Kernos* suppl. 15 (Liège), 55–68.

Planeux, C. (2000–1), 'The Date of Bendis' Entry into Attica', *CJ* 96, 165–92.

Platonos-Yiota, M. (2004), *ΑΧΑΡΝΑΙ. Ιστορική και τοπογραφική επισκόπηση των αρχαίων Αχαρνών, των γειτονικών δήμων και των οχυρώσεων της Πάρνηθας* (Acharnai).

Poland, F. (1909), *Geschichte des griechischen Vereinswesens* (Leipzig).

Polignac, F. de (1995), *Cults, Territory, and the Origins of the Greek City-State*, trans. J. Lloyd (Chicago).

Polinskaya, I. (2009), 'Fifth-Century Horoi on Aigina: A Reevaluation', *Hesperia* 78, 231–67.

Pollitt, J. J. (1961), 'Fragment of a Sacred Calendar and Other Inscriptions from the Attic Deme of Teithras', *Hesperia* 30, 293–8.

Polymerou-Kamelake, A. (2003), '*Μέτρηση ελαίου, ελαιών και ελαιώνων*', in A. Polymerou-Kamelake, P. Kamelakes, L. Karapidake (eds.), *Η ελιά και το λάδι από την αρχαιότητα έως σήμερα. Πρακτικά διεθνούς συνεδρίου. Αθήνα, 1–2 Οκτωβρίου 1999* (Athens), 179–229.

Pomeroy, S. B. (1997), *Families in Classical and Hellenistic Greece: Representations and Realities* (Oxford).

Pouilloux, J. (1954), *La forteresse de Rhamnonte: Étude de topographie et d'histoire* (Paris).

Pounder, R. L. (1984), 'The Origin of *θεοί* as Inscription-Heading', in *Studies Presented to Sterling Dow on his Eightieth Birthday* (Duke, NC), 243–50.

Premerstein, A. von (1910), 'Phratern-verbände auf einem attischen Hypothekenstein', *MDAI (A)* 35, 103–17.

Price, S. (1999), *Religions of the Ancient Greeks* (Cambridge).

——and Nixon, L. (2005), 'Ancient Greek Agricultural Terraces: Evidence from Texts and Archaeological Survey', *AJA* 109, 665–94.

Pritchett, W. K. (1956), 'The Attic Stelai, part II', *Hesperia* 25, 178–317.

——(1996), *Greek Archives, Cults and Topography* (Amsterdam).

Pritchett, W. K., and Meritt B. D. (1940), *The Chronology of Hellenistic Athens* (Cambridge, Mass).

Prott, H. T. A. von, and Ziehen, L. (1896–1906), *Leges Graecorum Sacrae e Titulis Collectae*, 2 vols. (Leipzig).

Purvis, A. (2003), *Singular Dedications: Founders and Innovators of Private Cults in Classical Greece* (London).

Quinn, G. M. (1971), *The Sacrificial Calendar of the Marathonian Tetrapolis* (Ph.D. Dissertation, University of Harvard).

Raaflaub, K. (1997), 'Homeric Society', in I. Morris and B. Powell (eds.), *A New Companion to Homer* (Leiden), 624–48.

Rackham, H. (1944), *Aristotle, Politics* (Cambridge, Mass., and London).

RAUBITSCHEK, A. E. (1939), 'Leagros', *Hesperia* 8, 155–64.

——(1943), 'Greek Inscriptions', *Hesperia* 12, 12–88.

——(1974), 'Kolieis', in *ΦΟΡΟΣ. Tribute to Benjamin Dean Meritt* (New York), 137–8.

REGER, G. (1994), *Regionalism and Change in the Economy of Independent Delos* (Berkeley).

REINMUTH, O. W. (1971), *The Ephebic Inscriptions of the Fourth Century B.C.*, *Mnemosyne* suppl. 14 (Leiden).

REITZENSTEIN, R. (1897), *Geschichte der Griechischen Etymologika* (Leipzig).

RHODES, P. J. (1972), *The Athenian Boule* (Oxford).

——(1982), 'Problems in Athenian *Eisphora* and Liturgies', *AJAH* 7, 1–19.

——(1984), *Aristotle: The Athenian Constitution* (Harmondsworth and New York).

——(1991), 'The Athenian Code of Laws, 410–399 B.C.', *JHS* 111, 87–100.

——(1993), *A Commentary on the Aristotelian Athenaion Politeia*, 2nd edn. with addenda (Oxford).

——(1997), 'Deceleans and Demotionidai again', *CQ* 47, 109–20.

——(2001*a*), 'Public Documents in the Greek States: Archives and Inscriptions, part I', *G&R* 48, 33–44.

——(2001*b*), 'Public Documents in the Greek States: Archives and Inscriptions, part II', *G&R* 48, 136–53.

——(2007), 'διοίκησις', *Chiron* 37, 349–362.

——(2008), 'After the Three-Bar *Sigma* Controversy: The History of Athenian Imperialism Reassessed', *CQ* 58, 501–6.

——with LEWIS, D. M. (1997), *The Decrees of the Greek States* (Oxford).

——and OSBORNE, R. (2003), *Greek Historical Inscriptions, 404–323 BC* (Oxford).

RICHARDSON, M. B. (2000), 'The Location of Inscribed Laws in Fourth-Century Athens: *IG* II^2 244, on Rebuilding the Walls of Peiraieus (337/6 BC)', in P. Flensted-Jensen, T. H. Nielsen, and L. Rubinstein (eds.), *Polis & Politics: Studies in Ancient Greek History* (Copenhagen), 601–75.

RICHARDSON, R. B. (1895), 'A Sacrificial Calendar of the Marathonian Tetrapolis', *AJA* 10, 209–26.

RIDGWAY, B. S. (1993), *The Archaic style in Greek sculpture*, 2nd edn. (Chicago).

RIHLL, T. E. (1991), '*ΕΚΤΗΜΟΡΟΙ*: Partners in Crime?', *JHS* 11, 101–27.

ROBERT, L. (1945), *Le sanctuaire de Sinuri près de Mylasa: Les inscriptions grecques* (Paris).

——(1960), 'Sur une loi d'Athènes relative aux Petites Panathénées', *Hellenica* 11–12, 189–203.

ROBERTSON, N. (1988), 'Melanthus, Codrus, Neleus, Caucon: Ritual Myth as Athenian History', *GRBS* 29, 201–61.

Robertson, N. (1990), 'The Laws of Athens, 410–399 BC: The Evidence for Review and Publication', *JHS* 43, 43–75.

——(2005), 'Athenian Shrines of Aphrodite, and the Early Development of the City', in E. Greco (ed.), *Teseo e Romolo. Le origini di Atene e Roma a confronto. Atti del Convegno Internazionale di Studi. Scuola Archeologica Italiana di Atene. Atene, 30 giugno - 1 luglio 2003* (Athens), 43–112.

Roebuck, D. (2001), *Ancient Greek Arbitration* (Oxford).

Roesch, P. (1965), *Thespies et la confédération Béotienne* (Paris).

Rosivach, V. J. (1991), '*IG* 2^2 334 and the Panathenaic Hekatomb', *PP* 46, 430–42.

——(1993), 'The Rationes Centesimarum (IG 2^2 1594–1603+)', *Eirene* 28, 49–61.

——(1994), *The System of Public Sacrifice in Fourth-Century Athens* (Atlanta).

Rotroff, S. (1978), 'An Anonymous Hero in the Athenian Agora', *Hesperia* 47, 196–209.

Roussel, D. (1976), *Tribu et cité: Études sur les groupes sociaux dans les cités grecques aux époques archaique et classique* (Paris).

Roussel, P. (1916), *Délos colonie Athénienne* (Paris).

——(1929), 'Deux familles athéniennes a Délos', *BCH* 53, 166–84.

——(1934), 'Un nouveau document concernant le *génos* des *ΚΗΡΥΚΕΣ*', in *Mélanges Bidez* (Brussels), 819–34.

Rousset, D. (2002*a*), 'Terres sacrées, terres publicques et terres privées à Delphes', *CRAI*, 215–41.

——(2002*b*), *Le territoire de Delphes et la terre d'Apollon* (Athens).

Rowe, G. O. (2002), 'Two Responses by Isocrates to Demosthenes', *Historia* 51, 149–62.

Rubel, A. (2000), *Stadt in Angst: Religion und Politik in Athen während des Peloponnesischen Krieges* (Darmstadt).

Rubinstein, L. (1993), *Adoption in IV. Century Athens* (Copenhagen).

——(2000), *Litigation and Cooperation: Supporting Speakers in the Courts of Classical Athens, Historia* Einzelschr. 147 (Stuttgart).

Ruschenbusch, E. (1966), *ΣΟΛΩΝΟΣ ΝΟΜΟΙ*: *Die Fragmente des solonischen Gesetzeswerkes mit einer Text-und Überlieferungsgeschichte* (Wiesbaden).

Russell, D. A. (1995), 'Plutarch, *Alcibiades* 1–16', in B. Scardigli (ed.), *Essays on Plutarch's Lives* (Oxford), 191–207.

Ruzé, F. (1998), 'La cité, les particuliers et les terres: installations ou retours de citoyens en Grèce archaïque', *Ktema* 23, 181–9.

Ryder, T. T. B. (2000), 'Demosthenes and Philip II', in I. Worthington (ed.), *Demosthenes. Statesman and Orator* (London and New York), 45–89.

Ste. Croix, G. E. M. de (1953), 'Demosthenes' *τίμημα* and the Athenian *εἰσφορά* in the fourth century B.C.', *C&M* 14, 30–70.

——(1966), 'The Estate of Phaenippus (Ps.-Dem. xlii), in *Ancient Society and Institutions. Studies Presented to Victor Ehrenberg on his 75th Birthday* (Oxford), 109–14.

——(1972), *The Origins of the Peloponnesian War* (Oxford).

Sakellariou, M. B. (1999), '*Η Ἀθηναϊκὴ Δημοκρατία* (Herakleion).

Sallares, R. (1991), *The Ecology of the Ancient Greek World* (London).

Salliora-Oikonomakou, M. (1979) [1986], '*Αρχαία Αγορά στο Λιμάνι Πασά Λαυρίου*', *ADeltion* 34 *Meletes I*, 161–73.

——(2001) [2003], "*Ἐπιγραφὲς ἀπὸ τὴν Λαυρεωτική*', *AEphemeris*, 159–66.

——(2004), *Ο αρχαίος δήμος του Σουνίου. Ιστορική και τοπογραφική επισκόπηση* (Koropi).

Salmon, J. B. (1984), *Wealthy Corinth: A History of the City to 338 BC* (Oxford).

Salomon, N. (1997), *Le cleruchie di Atene: Caratteri e funzione* (Pisa).

Salviat, F., and Vatin, C. (1971), *Inscriptions de Grèce centrale* (Paris).

——(1974), 'Le Cadastre de Larissa', *BCH* 98, 247–62.

Samons II, L. J. (1993), 'Athenian Finance and the Treasury of Athena', *Historia* 42, 129–38.

——(2000), *Empire of the Owl: Athenian Imperial Finance, Historia* Einzelschr. 142 (Stuttgart).

Sanchez, P. (2001), *L'Amphictionie des Pyles et de Delphes: recherches sur son rôle historique, des origines au IIe siècle de notre ère, Historia* Einzelschr. 148 (Stuttgart).

Sandys, J. E. (1893), *Aristotle's Constitution of Athens* (London).

Sarikakis, T. C. (1951), *The Hoplite General in Athens* (Princeton).

Sartre, M. (1979), 'Aspects économiques et aspects religieux de la frontière dans les cités grecques', *Ktema* 4, 213–24.

Saunders, T. J. (1972), *Notes on the Laws of Plato, BICS* suppl. 28 (London).

Scafuro, A. C. (1997), *The Forensic Stage: Settling Disputes in Graeco-Roman New Comedy* (Cambridge).

——(2003), 'IG II^2 204: Boundary Setting and Legal Process in Classical Athens', in G. Thür and F. J. Fernández Neito (eds.), *Symposion 1999. Vorträge zur griechischen und hellenistischen Rechtgeschichte* (Cologne), 123–43.

——(2006), 'Identifying Solonian Laws', in J. H. Blok and A. P. M. H. Lardinois (eds.), *Solon of Athens: New Historical and Philological Approaches* (Boston and Leiden), 175–96.

——(2009), 'The Crowning of Amphiaraos', in L. Mitchell and L. Rubinstein (eds.), *Greek History and Epigraphy: Essays in Honour of P. J. Rhodes* (Swansea), 59–86.

Schiller, A. K. (1996), *Political Territoriality of the Classical Athenians, 508–338 BC* (Ph.D. Dissertation, University of Wisconsin-Madison).

Schlaifer, R. (1940), 'Notes on Athenian Public Cults', *HSCP* 51, 233–60.

SCHLAIFER, R. (1943*a*), 'The Cult of Athena Pallenis', *HSCP* 54, 35–67.
——(1943*b*), 'Demon of Paeania, Priest of Asclepius', *CP* 38, 39–43.
——(1944), 'The Attic Association of the *Μεσόγειοι*', *CP* 39, 22–7.
SCHMALZ, G. C. R. (2009), *Augustan and Julio-Claudian Athens: A New Epigraphy and Prosopography*, *Mnemosyne* suppl. 302 (Leiden and Boston).
——(2007–8) [2011], 'Inscribing a Ritualized Past: The Attic Restoration Decree *IG* II^2 1035 and Cultural Memory in Augustan Athens', *Eulimene*, 8–9, 9–46.
SCHULER, C. (1998), *Ländliche Siedlungen und Gemeinden im hellenistischen und römischen Kleinasien* (Munich).
SCHWENK, C. J. (1985), *Athens in the Age of Alexander. The Dated Laws & Decrees of the Lykourgan Era. 338–322 B.C.* (Chicago).
SCULLION, S. (2005), ' "Pilgrimage" and Greek Religion: Sacred and Secular in the Pagan *Polis*', in J. Elsner and I. Rutherford (eds.), *Pilgrimage in Graeco-Roman and Early Christian Antiquity: Seeing the Gods* (Oxford), 111–30.
SEAGER R. (1967), 'Thrasybulus, Conon and Athenian Imperialism, 396–386 B.C.', *JHS* 87, 95–115.
SEGRE, M. (1993), *Iscrizioni di Cos* (Rome).
SHEAR, J. L. (2003), 'Prizes from Athens: The List of Panathenaic Prizes and the Sacred Oil', *ZPE* 142, 87–108.
SHEAR, T. L. Jr. (1995), 'Bouleuterion, Metroon and the Archives at Athens', in M. H. Hansen and K. Raaflaub (eds.), *Studies in the Ancient Greek Polis* (Stuttgart), 157–90.
SHELMERDINE, C. W. (2006), 'Mycenaean Palatial Administration', in S. Deger-Jalkotzy and I. S. Lemos (eds.), *Ancient Greece: From the Mycenaean Palaces to the Age of Homer* (Edinburgh), 73–86.
SHERWIN-WHITE, S. M. (1978), *Ancient Cos: An Historical Study from the Dorian Settlement to the Imperial Period*, Hypomnemata 51 (Göttingen).
SHILLETO, R. (1872–80), *Thucydidis I et II* (Cambridge).
SHIPLEY, G. (1987), *A History of Samos: 800–188 B.C.* (Oxford).
——(2005), 'Little Boxes on the Hillside: Greek Town Planning, Hippodamos, and Polis Ideology', in M. H. Hansen (ed.), *The Imaginary Polis* (Copenhagen), 335–403.
SHIPTON, K. M. W. (1998), 'The Prices of the Athenian Silver Mines', *ZPE* 120, 57–63.
——(2000), *Leasing and Lending: The Cash Economy in Fourth-Century BC Athens*, *BICS* suppl. 74, (London).
——(2001), 'Money and the Élite in Classical Athens', in A. Meadows and K. Shipton (eds.), *Money and its Uses in the Ancient Greek World* (Oxford), 129–44.

Sickinger, J. (1999), *Public Records and Archives in Classical Athens* (Chapel Hill).

Siewert, P. (1977), 'The Ephebic Oath in Fifth-Century Athens', *JHS* 97, 102–11.

——(1982), *Die Trittyen Attikas und die Heeresreform des Kleisthenes* (Munich).

——(2001), 'Zum historischen Hintergrund der frühen Panathenäen und Preisamphoren', in M. Bentz and N. Eschbach (eds.), *Panathenaïka. Symposion zu den Panathenäischen Preisamphoren, Rauischholzhausen 25.11.–29.11.1998* (Mainz), 3–5.

Simms, R. M. (1975), 'The Eleusinian in the Sixth to Fourth Centuries B.C.', *GRBS* 16, 269–79.

——(1998), 'The Phrearrhian *Lex Sacra*: An Interpretation', *Hesperia* 67, 91–107.

Simms, R. R. (1988), 'The Cult of the Thracian Goddess Bendis in Athens and Attica', *AW* 18, 59–76.

Sinn, U. (2005), 'Theatron', in *ThesCRA IV: Cult Places: Representations of Cult Places* (Los Angeles), 112–20.

Sklavos, M. (2003), 'The Sanctuary of Zeus Phratrios', in O. Kakavoyianni (ed.), *Archaeological Investigations at Merenda, Marcopoulo, at the New Race-Course and Olympic Equestrian Centre* (Athens), 49.

Skydsgaard, J. E. (2000), 'The Meaning of *Polis* in Thucydides 2.16.2. A Note', in P. Flensted-Jensen, T. H. Nielsen, and L. Rubinstein (eds.), *Polis & Politics. Studies in Ancient Greek History* (Copenhagen), 229–30.

Smarczyk, B. (1990), *Untersuchungen zur Religionspolitik und politischen Propaganda Athens im Delisch-Attischen Seebund* (Munich).

Smyth, H. W. (1956), *Greek Grammar*, rev. edn. by G. M. Messing (Harvard).

Snodgrass, A. M. (1982), 'Central Greece and Thessaly', in J. Boardman, I. E. S. Edwards, N. G. L. Hammond, E. Sollberger (eds.), *The Cambridge Ancient History*, vol. III, Part I: *The Prehistory of the Balkans; and the Middle East and the Aegean World, Tenth to Eighth Centuries B.C.*, 2nd edn. (Cambridge), 657–95.

Sommerstein, A. H. (1977), 'Notes on Aeschylus' *Suppliants*', *BICS* 24, 67–82.

——(1996), *The Comedies of Aristophanes: Wasps*, reprinted with corrections (Warminster).

——(1997), *The Comedies of Aristophanes: Knights*, reprinted with corrections (Warminster).

Sosin, J. D. (2002), 'Two Attic Endowments', *ZPE* 138, 123–8.

——(2004), 'An Endowed Peace', *MH* 61, 2–8.

Sourvinou-Inwood, C. (1988), *Studies in Girls' Transitions: Aspects of the Arkteia and Age Representation in Attic Iconography* (Athens).

Sourvinou-Inwood, C. (1990), 'What is *Polis* Religion?', in O. Murray and S. Price (eds.), *The Greek City from Homer to Alexander* (Oxford), 295–322.

——(2000), 'Further Aspects of *Polis* Religion', in R. Buxton (ed.), *Oxford Readings in Greek Religion* (Oxford), 38–55 [reprinted from *Annali dell'Istituto Universitario Orientale di Napoli, Sezione di Archeologia e Storia Antica*, 10 (1988), 259–74].

Spence, I. G. (1993), *The Cavalry of Classical Greece* (Oxford).

Stadter, P. A. (1989), *A Commentary on Plutarch's Pericles* (London).

Stafford, E. J. (1997), 'THEMIS: Religion and Order in the Archaic *polis*', in L. G. Mitchell and P. J. Rhodes (eds.), *The Development of the Polis in Archaic Greece* (London), 158–67.

Stahl, J. M. (1882–8), *Thucydidis libri octo. Explanavit E. F. Poppo. Ed. altera et tertia, quas auxit et emendavit J. M. S.* (Leipzig).

——(1891), 'Über athenische Amnestiebechlüsse', *RhM* 46, 250–86.

Stanton, G. R. (1994*a*), 'The Rural Demes and Athenian Politics', in W. D. E. Coulson *et al.* (eds.), *The Archaeology of Athens and Attica under the Democracy* (Oxford), 217–24.

——(1994*b*), 'The Trittyes of Kleisthenes', *Chiron* 24, 161–207.

——(1996), 'Some Inscriptions in Attic Demes', *BSA* 91, 341–64.

Starr, C. G. (1970), *Athenian Coinage, 480–449 B.C.* (Oxford).

Steinhauer, G. (1992), '*Δύο δημοτικὰ ψηφίσματα τῶν Ἀχαρνέων*', *AEphemeris* 131, 179–93.

——(1994), '*Παρατηρήσεις στην οικιστική μορφή των αττικών δήμων*', in W. D. E. Coulson *et al.* (eds.), *The Archaeology of Athens and Attica under the Democracy* (Oxford), 175–89.

——(1995), '*Ἡ χρονολόγηση τοῦ 3ου αἰ. π.Χ. καὶ ὁ κατάλογος τῶν Ἀθηναίων ἀρχόντων*', *Mentor* 36, 134–49.

——(1998), *Τα μνημεία και το αρχαιολογικό μουσείο του Πειραιά* (Athens).

——(2001*a*), 'From the Prehistory of the Mesogaia: Two Neolithic Settlements', in *Mesogaia: History and Culture of Mesogeia in Attica* (Athens), 29–34.

——(2001*b*), 'The Classical Mesogaia (5th–4th century BC)', in *Mesogaia: History and Culture of Mesogeia in Attica* (Athens), 80–139.

——(2009), 'A propos du décret de Rhamnonte en l'honneur d'Épichares', in A. A. Themos and N. Papazarkadas (eds.), *Ἀττικὰ ἐπιγραφικά. Μελέτες πρὸς τιμὴν τοῦ Christian Habicht* (Athens).

Stengel, P. (1893), '*Ἀπαρχαί*', *RE* 1, 2666–8.

——(1920), *Die Griechischen Kultusaltertümer*, 3rd edn. (Munich).

Stephanis, I. E. (1988), *Διονυσιακοὶ τεχνῖται. Συμβολὲς στην προσωπογραφία τοῦ θεάτρου καὶ τῆς μουσικῆς τῶν ἀρχαίων Ἑλλήνων* (Herakleion).

Strauss, B. S. (1986), *Athens after the Peloponnesian War: Class, Faction and Policy, 403–386 BC* (London and Sydney).

Stroud, R. S. (1968), *Drakon's Law on Homicide* (Berkeley and Los Angeles).
——(1971), 'Inscriptions from the North Slope of the Acropolis, I', *Hesperia* 40, 146–204.
——(1974*a*), 'An Athenian Law on Silver Coinage', *Hesperia* 43, 157–88.
——(1974*b*), 'Three Attic Decrees', *CSCA* 7, 279–98.
——(1998), *The Athenian Grain-Tax Law of 374/3 B.C.*, *Hesperia* suppl. 29 (Princeton).
——(2002), 'Review of *Peisistratos and the Tyranny: A Reappraisal of the Evidence* (ed. by Heleen Sancisi-Weerdenburg)', *Mnemosyne* 55, 120–3.
——(2010), 'Introduction', in A. Magnetto, D. Erdas, and C. Carusi (eds.), *Nuove ricerche sulla legge granaria ateniese del 374/3 a.c.* (Pisa), 11–25.
Taylor, C. (2007), 'From the Whole Citizen Body? The Sociology of Election and Lot in the Athenian Democracy', *Hesperia* 76, 323–45.
Taylor, M. C. (1997), *Salamis and the Salaminioi: The History of an Unofficial Athenian Demos* (Amsterdam).
Themelis, P. (1992–8), '*Ἀνάθημα Εὐδώτηι*', *Horos* 10–12, 77–82.
——(2002), 'Contribution to the Topography of the Sanctuary at Brauron', in B. Gentili and F. Perusino (eds.), *Le orse di Brauron: Un rituale di iniziazione femminile nel santuario di Artemide* (Milan), 103–16.
——(2007), 'Panathenaic Prizes and Dedications', in O. Palagia and A. Choremi-Spetsieri (eds.), *The Panathenaic Games* (Oxford), 21–32.
Themos, A. A. (2000–3), '*IG* II^2 243 + MA 18096', *Horos* 14–16, 51–4.
Theodoridis, C. (2002), 'Eine unbeachtete Buchangabe zum Bruchstück des Philochoros über die attischen Orgeonen', *ZPE* 138, 40–2.
——(2003), 'Weitere Bemerkungen zum Onomastikon des Julius Pollux', *ZPE* 143, 71–8.
Thomas, R. (1989), *Oral Tradition and Written Record in Classical Athens* (Cambridge).
Thompson, H. A. (1937), 'Buildings on the West Side of the Agora', *Hesperia* 6, 1–226.
Thompson, H. A., and Wycherley, R. E. (1972), *The Athenian Agora*, vol. XIV: *The Agora of Athens* (Princeton).
Thompson, W. E. (1969), 'Kleisthenes and Aigeis', *Mnemosyne* 22, 137–52.
——(1970), 'A Rubric in the Propylaia Accounts', *CQ* 20, 39–40.
——(1971), 'The Deme in Kleisthenes' Reforms', *SO* 46, 72–9.
——(1976), *De Hagniae Hereditate: An Athenian Inheritance Case*, *Mnemosyne* suppl. 44 (Leiden).
Thomsen, R. (1964), *Eisphora: A Study of Direct Taxation in Ancient Athens* (Copenhagen).
Threatte, L. (1980), *The Grammar of Attic Inscriptions*, vol. I: *Phonology* (Berlin).

Threatte, L. (1996), *The Grammar of Attic Inscriptions*, vol. II: *Morphology* (Berlin).

Threpsiades, J. (1939), 'Decree in Honor of Euthydemos of Eleusis', *Hesperia* 8, 177–80.

Thür, G. (1984), 'Bemerkungen zum altgriechischen Werkvertrag (die Bauvergabeordnung aus Tegea, IG V/2, 6A)', in *Studi in Onore de Arnaldo Biscardi* (Milan), 471–514.

——(2000), 'Misthosis', *Der Neue Pauly* 8, 271–5.

Tillyard H. J. W. (1904–5), 'Boundary and Mortgage Stones from Attica', *BSA* 11, 63–71.

Tiverios, M. (1974) [1977], '*Παναθηναϊκά*', *ADeltion* 29, 142–53.

——(2000*a*), *Μακεδόνες και Παναθήναια: Παναθηναϊκοί αμφορείς από τον βορειοελλαδικό χώρο* (Athens).

——(2000*b*), '*Αθηναϊκό λάδι στον μυχό του Θερμαϊκού κόλπου κατά τον 6ο αι. π.Χ.*' in P. Adam-Veleni (ed.), *Μύρτος. Μνήμη Ιουλίας Βοκοτοπούλου* (Thessalonike), 519–27.

——(2007), 'Panathenaic Amphoras', in O. Palagia and A. Choremi-Spetsieri (eds.), *The Panathenaic Games* (Oxford), 1–19.

Tod, M. (1948), *A Selection of Greek Historical Inscriptions*, vol. II (Oxford).

Todd, S. C. (1993), *The Shape of Athenian Law* (Oxford).

——(1996), 'Lysias against Nikomakhos', in L. Foxhall and A. Lewis (eds.), *Greek Law in its Political Setting: Justification not Justice* (Oxford), 101–31.

——(2000), *Lysias* (Austin).

——(2007), *A Commentary on Lysias, Speeches 1–11* (Oxford).

Toepffer, J. (1889), *Attische Genealogie* (Berlin).

Tracy, S. V. (1988), 'Two Attic Letter Cutters of the Third Century: 286/5–235/4 B.C.', *Hesperia* 57, 303–22.

——(1990), *Attic Letter-Cutters of 229 to 86 B.C.* (Berkeley and Los Angeles).

——(1994), '*IG* II^2 1195 and Agathe Tyche in Attica', *Hesperia* 63, 241–4.

——(1995), *Athenian Democracy in Transition: Attic Letter-Cutters of 340 to 290 B.C.* (Berkeley and Los Angeles).

——(2003*a*), *Athens and Macedon: Attic Letter-Cutters of 300 to 229 B.C.* (Berkeley).

——(2003*b*), 'A Major Athenian Letter-Cutter of the Late 5th and Early 4th Centuries B.C.: The Cutter of *IG* II^2 17 (*Dates: 409–8–386/5*), in G. W. Bakewell and J. P. Sickinger (eds.), *Gestures: Essays in Ancient History, Literature, and Philosophy presented to Alan L. Boegehold* (Oxford), 351–63.

Traill, J. S. (1975), *The Political Organization of Attica: A Study of the Demes, Trittyes, and Phylai, and their Representation in the Athenian Council*, *Hesperia* suppl. 14 (Princeton).

——(1978), 'Diakris, the Inland Trittys of Leontis', *Hesperia* 47, 89–109.

——(1982), 'An Interpretation of Six Rock-Cut Inscriptions in the Attic Demes of Lamptrai', in *Studies in Attic Epigraphy, History and Topography Presented to Eugene Vanderpool, Hesperia* suppl. 19 (Princeton), 162–71.

——(1986), *Demos and Trittys: Epigraphical and Topographical Studies in the Organization of Attica* (Toronto).

Travlos, J. (1939–41), '*Ἡ παλαιοχριστιανικὴ βασιλικὴ τοῦ Ἀσκληπιείου τῶν Ἀθηνῶν*', *AEphemeris*, 35–68.

——(1971), *Pictorial Dictionary of Ancient Athens* (London).

——(1988), *Bildlexikon zur Topographie des antiken Attika* (Athens).

Tréheux J. (1944–5), 'Études d'Épigraphie Délienne', *BCH* 68–69, 271–95.

——(1949), 'Les Dernières Années de Délos sous le protectorat des Amphictions', in *Mélanges d'archéologie et d'histoire offerts à Charles Picard* (Paris), 1008–32.

Trevett, J. (1994), 'Demosthenes' Speech *On Organization* (Dem. 13)', *GRBS* 35, 179–93.

Trigger, B. G. (2003), *Understanding Early Civilizations: A Comparative Study* (Cambridge).

Tsakos, K. (1977) [1982], '*Ἐπιγραφὲς Σάμου*', *ADeltion* 32 A', 74–9.

Tsophopoulou-Gkine, E. (1980), '*Παλαιοχριστιανικὴ βασιλικὴ στὴ θέση "Μυγδαλέζα" Ἀττικῆς*', *AEphemeris*, 85–96.

Tzoumeleas, S. (n.d.), *Λυσίας: Λόγοι. Α'* (Athens).

Uguzzoni, A., and Ghinatti, F. (1968), *Le Tavole Greche di Eraclea* (Rome).

Usher, S. (1999), *Greek Oratory: Tradition and Originality* (Oxford).

Ussher, R. G. (1973), *Aristophanes, Ecclesiazusae* (Oxford).

Ustinova, Y. (1996), 'Orgeones in Phratries: A Mechanism of Social Integration in Attica', *Kernos* 6, 227–42.

——(2005), '*Lege et Consuetudine*: Voluntary Cult Associations in the Greek Law', in V. Dasen and M. Piérart (eds.), *Ἰδίᾳ καὶ δημοσίᾳ: Les cadres 'privés' et 'publics' de la religion grecque antique, Kernos* suppl. 15 (Liège), 177–90.

Valavanis, P. (1986), 'Les amphores Panathénaïques et le commerce athénien de l'huile', in J.-Y. Empereur and Y. Garlan (eds.), *Recherches sur les amphores grecques, BCH* suppl. 13, 453–60.

——(1987), 'Säulen, Hähne, Niken und Archonten auf panathenäischen Preisamphoren', *AA* 92, 467–80.

——(1991), *Παναθηναϊκοί αμφορείς από την Ερέτρια: συμβολή στην αττική αγγειογραφία του 4ου π.Χ. αιώνα* (Athens).

——(2002), 'Thoughts on the Public Archive in the Hellenistic Metroon of the Athenian Agora', *MDAI (A)* 117, 221–55.

Vallendas, P. G., and Pantazopoulos N. I. (1948) [1950], '*Συμβολὴ εἰς τὰ περὶ μισθώσεως κατὰ τὸ ἀρχαῖον ἑλληνικὸν δίκαιον* (*Ἐπιγραφὴ μισθώσεως τοῦ 4ου π. Χ. αἰῶνος*)', *PrAkAth* 13, 5–23.

Van de Maele, S. (1983), 'L'Orgas eleusinienne: étude topographique', in *Mélanges Édouard Delebecque* (Aix-en-Provence), 419–33.

Vanderpool, E. (1969) [1971], 'A Palaistra in Kephisia', *ADeltion* 24 A' *Meletai*, 6–7.

Vanderpool, E., McCredie, J. R., and Steiberg, A. (1962), 'Koroni: A Ptolemaic camp on the East Coast of Attica', *Hesperia* 31, 26–61.

Vannicelli, P. (2003), *Erodoto: Le storie, Libro VIII: La vittoria di Temistocle* (Milan).

Van Groningen, B. A. (1933), *Aristote, Le second livre de l'Économique* (Leiden).

Vannier, F. (1993), 'Remarques financières à Athènes, au lendemain de la guerre des alliés', in M-M Mactoux and E. Geny (eds.), *Mélanges Pierre Lévêque 7* (Paris), 339–44.

Van Wees, H. J. (1999), 'Introduction: Homer and Early Greece', in I. J. F. de Jong (ed.), *Homer: Critical Assessments* (London), 1–32.

Vartsos, I. A. (1972), *Ἀθηναϊκαὶ κληρουχίαι* (Athens).

Ventris, M., and Chadwick, J. (1956), *Documents in Mycenaean Greek* (Cambridge).

Verbanck-Piérard, A. (1998), 'Héros attiques au jour le jour: les calendriers des dèmes', in V. Pirenne-Delforge (ed.), *Les panthéons des cités des origines à la* Périégèse *de Pausanias* (Liège), 109–27.

Vikela, E. (1994), *Die Weihreliefs aus dem Athener Pankrates-Heiligtum am Ilissos: Religionsgeschichtliche Bedeutung und Typologie* (Berlin).

Vince, J. H. (1935), *Demosthenes*, III (Cambridge, Mass., and London).

Vivliodetis, E. P. (2005) [2007], *Ὁ δῆμος τοῦ Μυρρινοῦντος: ἡ ὀργάνωση καὶ ἡ ἱστορία του*, *AEphemeris* 155 (Athens).

Vlassopoulos, K. (2007), *Unthinking the Greek Polis: Ancient Greek History beyond Eurocentrism* (Cambridge).

Vos, M. F. (1981), 'Some Notes on Panathenaic Amphorae', *Oudheidkundige Mededelingen* 31, 33–46.

Wace, A. J. B. (1905–6), 'Laconia, II: Excavations at Sparta, 1906. §8. The stamped tiles', *BSA* 12, 344–50.

——(1906–7), 'Laconia, I: Excavations at Sparta, 1907. §3. The stamped tiles', *BSA* 13, 17–43.

Walbank, F. W. (1957), *A Historical Commentary on Polybius*, vol. I: *Commentary on Books I–VI* (Oxford).

Walbank, M. B. (1974), 'Criteria for the Dating of Fifth-Century Attic Inscriptions', in D. W. Bradeen and M. F. McGregor (eds.), *ΦΟΡΟΣ. Tribute to Benjamin Dean Meritt* (New York), 161–9.

——(1982), 'Greek Inscriptions from the Athenian Agora: Fifth to Third Centuries B.C.', *Hesperia* 51, 41–56.

——(1983*a*), 'Leases of Sacred Properties in Attica, Part I', *Hesperia* 52, 100–35.

——(1983*b*), 'Leases of Sacred Properties in Attica, Part II', *Hesperia* 52, 177–99.
——(1983*c*), 'Leases of Sacred Properties in Attica, Part III', *Hesperia* 52, 200–6.
——(1983*d*), 'Leases of Sacred Properties in Attica, Part IV', *Hesperia* 52, 207–31.
——(1984), 'Leases of Sacred Properties in Attica, Part V', *Hesperia* 53, 361–8.
——(1985), 'Leases of Sacred Properties in Attica, Part V: A Correction', *Hesperia* 54, 140.
——(1990), 'The Property of Aiantis and Aigeis', *ZPE* 84, 94–9.
——(1991), 'Leases of Public Lands', in *Agora* XIX, 149–69.
——(1994), 'A Lex Sacra of the State and the Deme of Kollytos', *Hesperia* 63, 233–9.
——(1995), 'Sales of Property in Attica: New Readings in *IG* II^2,1593', *ZPE* 107, 69–72.
——(1997), 'Two Notes on Leases of Sacred Property in Attica', *ZPE* 116, 39–40.
WALLACE, R. W. (1985), *The Areopagos Council, to 307 B.C.* (Baltimore).
——(1986), 'The Date of Isokrates' *Areopagitikos*', *HSCP* 90, 77–84.
WALLINGA, H. T. (2000), 'The Athenian Naukraroi', in H. Sancisi-Weerdenburg (ed.), *Peisistratos and the Tyranny: A Reappraisal of the Evidence* (Amsterdam), 131–46.
WALTERS, K. R. (1976), 'The "Ancestral Constitution" and Fourth-Century Historiography in Athens', *AJAH* 1, 129–44.
WARTELLE, A. (1968), *Aristote. Économique* (Paris).
WARTENBERG, U. (1995), *After Marathon: War, Society and Money in Fifth-Century Greece* (London).
WEBER, M. (1909) [1976], *The Agrarian Sociology of Ancient Civilizations*, trans. R. I. Frank (London).
WEST, M. L. (1972), *Iambi et Elegi Graeci*, II (Oxford).
WHITEHEAD, D. (1977), *The Ideology of the Athenian Metic* (Cambridge).
——(1982), 'Notes on Athenian Demarchs', *ZPE* 47, 37–42.
——(1983), 'Competitive Outlay and Community Profit: *philotimia* in Democratic Athens', *C&M* 34, 55–74.
——(1986), *The Demes of Attica, 508/7 – ca. 250 B.C.* (Princeton).
——(1993), 'The *κωλοκράται* of Kydantidai and Ionidai', *ZPE* 95, 159–62.
——(2000), *Hypereides, The Forensic Speeches* (Oxford).
WHITEHEAD, D. (2001), 'Athenian Demes as *Poleis* (Thuc. 2.16.2)', *CQ* 51, 604–7.
WICKKISER, B. L. (2008), *Asklepios, Medicine, and the Politics of Healing in Fifth-Century Greece* (Baltimore).

Wilamowitz-Moellendorf, U. v. (1929), *Griechische Tragödien, 2: Die Orestie* (Berlin).

Wilhelm, A. (1904), 'Über die Zeit einiger attischer Fluchtafeln', *JÖAI* 7, 105–26.

Wilhelm, A. (1909*a*), *Beiträge zur griechischen Inschriftenkunde mit einem Anhange über die öffentliche Aufzeichnung von Urkunden* (Vienna).

——(1909*b*), 'Inschriften aus Erythrai und Chios', *JÖAI* 12, 126–50.

——(1935), 'Attische Pachturkunden', *APF* 11, 189–217.

——(1942), 'Attische Urkunden V', *SAAW* 200.5, 1–192.

——(1951), 'Griechische Inschriften rechtlichen Inhalts', *PAAth* 17, 1–107.

Wilkins, J. (1993), *Euripides, Heraclidae* (Oxford).

Williams, A. (2008), 'The Law Concerning the Little Panathenaia and the Leasing of the Nea *κατὰ δικληρίαν*', *ZPE* 167, 33–6.

Williams, D. (2007), 'The Panathenaic Stadium from the Hellenistic to the Roman Period: Panathenaic Prize-Amphorae and the Biel Throne', in O. Palagia and A. Choremi-Spetsieri (eds.), *The Panathenaic Games* (Oxford), 147–58.

Wilson, N. G. (1994), *Photius, The Bibliotheca* (London).

——(1997), *Aelian, Historical Miscellany* (Cambridge, Mass., and London).

Wilson, P. (2000), *The Athenian Institution of the Khoregia: The Chorus, the City and the Stage* (Cambridge).

——(2007), 'Choruses for Sale in Thorikos? A Speculative Note on SEG 34, 107', *ZPE* 161, 125–32.

Windekens, A. J. van (1986), *Dictionnaire étymologique complémentaire de la langue grecque: Nouvelles contributions à l'interprétation historique et comparée du vocabulaire* (Leuven).

Woodward, A. M. (1940), 'Two Attic Treasure-Records', in *Athenian Studies Presented to William Scott Ferguson, HSCP* suppl. 1 (Cambridge, Mass.), 377–407.

Wycherley, R. E. (1960), 'Nelelon', *BSA* 55, 60–6.

——(1964), 'Hippodamus and Rhodes', *Historia* 13, 135–9.

Young, J. H. (1941), 'Studies in South Attica: The Salaminioi at Porthmos', *Hesperia* 10, 163–91.

Zacharia, K. (2003), *Converging Truths: Euripides' Ion and the Athenian Quest for Self-Definition, Mnemosyne* suppl. 242 (Leiden).

Zelnick-Abramovitz, R. (2004), 'Settlers and Dispossessed in the Athenian Empire', *Mnemosyne* 57, 325–45.

Index of Sources

B. INSCRIPTIONS

Subject Index

Greek words are arranged alphabetically as if transliterated into English. Aspirated words can be found under *H*. For Greek words beginning with *kappa* please look under both *C* and *K*.

The manufacturer's authorised representative in the EU for product safety is Oxford University Press España S.A. of el Parque Empresarial San Fernando de Henares, Avenida de Castilla, 2 – 28830 Madrid (www.oup.es/en or product.safety@oup.com). OUP España S.A. also acts as importer into Spain of products made by the manufacturer.

www.ingramcontent.com/pod-product-compliance
Lightning Source LLC
Chambersburg PA
CBHW051251200926
51612CB00001B/1
9780199694006